P9-DMX-998

More praise for THE TEENAGE LIBERATION HANDBOOK:

"Bursting with clever strategies, valuable resources and wise guidance on how to design an interest-driven self-education. It was the sole inspiration for our family to take on an endeavor we thought was out of the question."
—Griff Wigley in *The Millennium Whole Earth Catalog*

"Every teenager, schooled or not—and every parent of a teenager—should get a chance to read *The Teenage Liberation Handbook*. It is a real eye-opener to many of life's possibilities, as well as a celebration of the personal freedoms homeschoolers enjoy . . . Llewellyn's dream, it seems, is to set every teenager free to think and explore for herself, to make her world what she wants it to be . . . Even as an adult she's affected my life and encouraged me to new heights. She understands well what it's like to be a teenager, and she has anticipated every question and every argument that teenagers are likely to bring up . . . Give copies to kids having problems, anxious parents, everyone you can think of. Do your part to liberate teenagers everywhere!"
—Pam Gingold in the *Northern California Homeschool Association Newsletter*

"The *TLH* is more than a book. It's a map . . . well written and entertaining. Shall I beg you to read it? If I must . . . *Please? Please read this book . . . it'll help! It's not like other books, this one is only looking out for your best interests* . . . Sometimes funny, sometimes sad, but always thought provoking, the *TLH* is for anyone who wakes up with pains in their stomach at the thought of another day of rote memorization and pointless busywork."
—Michael Condon in *In 2 Print*.

"Uh-oh. State schools keep turning out partially literate drones, despite twenty years of varying levels of panic in the mainstream media . . . I have found the single essential book for those who value learning but not school and want to slap society to its senses. *The Teenage Liberation Handbook* is a complete tool kit for aspiring human beings. . . This review cannot convey to you the loopy daring and wonder of Grace Llewellyn's prose, the sheer megatonnage of shock value in her suppositions . . . Get this book. Order many copies and infiltrate them into school libraries, leave them at bus stops and in plain view of the neighbor's kids and in the Education Department of your local university . . . I'd lend you my copy, but there is a fair queue of people waiting for it."
—Brien Bartels in *LUNO* (*Learning Unlimited Network of Oregon*)

"This book could foment revolution . . . I have only good things to say about [it]. Brilliant and wise, it's brimming with insight, information and humor . . . *The Teenage Liberation Handbook* should be required reading (for those who believe in required reading) or simply pleasure reading for anyone who's ever wondered what they're doing in school."
—Kirsten Chevalier in *Merlyn's Pen*

"Inspiring and very practical . . . Llewellyn helps her readers think about what they *can* do by giving them examples of what actual teenagers *have* done, so her book is grounded in concrete experience. She answers all of the common questions about learning outside of school and helps teenagers see that they can take control of their lives and make adolescence, instead of the stereotypical period of boredom, alienation, and rebellion that we are accustomed to, a time of interesting discoveries, real learning, and meaningful work."
    —Susannah Sheffer, editor of *Growing Without Schooling* magazine,
        author of *Writing Because We Love To: Homeschoolers at Work*,
            and *A Sense of Self: Homeschooled Adolescent Girls*

"What a wonderful book! I sat down with it intending to glance through it now and give it more attention later—only to find myself unable to put it down. Everything is there—not only do you have many wise and on-target things to say to the teenagers you wrote the book for, but you've succeeded in putting together a great sourcebook for homeschoolers as well as the best book on *education* that I've come across in a long, long time . . . How good it would be if every teacher, every school administrator, and, of course, schoolchild, who knows that there must be a better way, had a copy of this book."
    —David Colfax, author of *Homeschooling for Excellence*
    and *Hard Times in Paradise*, father of three homeschooled Harvard graduates

"This book will inspire formal school students to leave school and take control of their time; will embolden homeschoolers to be courageously creative about their educations; and will encourage parents to trust their children's choices. Gives gentle guidance for those who are uncertain about how to make autodidactism a glorious reality. Packed with unschooling philosophy and a wealth of resources."
    —Clonlara Home Based Education Program

"[Llewellyn's] enthusiasm for learning, her great faith in kids, and the wonderful educational possibilities she presents will make her book tantalizing reading for teens who can't make it in school but have the discipline and the passion to learn on their own."
    —American Library Association *Booklist*

"Every autodidact should get down on their knees in gratitude to Grace Llewellyn for her commitment to education in the true sense of the word. Every house that has a teenager should also have a copy of *The Teenage Liberation Handbook* . . . important and magical."
    —Kendall Hailey, author of *The Day I Became an Autodidact*

"An irreverent and thought-provoking guide . . . very thorough and highly entertaining."
—*Home Education Magazine*

"Packed with information for young people who want more than schools can offer . . . an invaluable and unique resource . . . Llewellyn presents a credible and appealing case for becoming self-taught . . . This is a fascinating, frightening, and exhilarating book that is sure to prove controversial among parents and teachers. At the very least it will open eyes and minds. At the most it might open whole new worlds of possibilities for its young readers."
—*Voice of Youth Advocates* Magazine *(VOYA)*

"This is the classic book that changed all of our lives. If you don't get what we're doing, it's because you haven't read this book."
—The Self-Education Foundation

"No homeschooling teenager should be without this book, which will get you excited about learning, even if you're long past your teens."
—Mary Griffith in *The Homeschooling Handbook*

"This is a very dangerous book. It contradicts all the conventional wisdom about dropouts and the importance of a formal education. It is funny and inspiring. Do not, under any circumstances, share this book with a bright, frustrated high-schooler being ground into mind fudge by the school system. This writer cannot be responsible for the happiness and sense of personal responsibility that might [result]."
—Pat Wagner in *Bloomsbury Review*

"Heartily recommended to every flavor of human being, not just teenagers.... Sooner or later you're going to realize that you've been cheated out of a real life by missing a real education—when that time comes Grace Llewellyn's *Handbook* will save you a thousand hours of frustration, false starts and missed opportunities. Anyone who follows this clear blueprint is certain to meet the future with courage, enthusiasm, resourcefulness and the abundant love of life that the author has. She demonstrates brilliantly that school and education are two very different things, defining the latter precisely and with such a wonderful zest the reader is left dazzled with his own rich possibilities. Get this book now so it will be on hand for the great emergency when you wake up."
—John Taylor Gatto, New York State Teacher of the Year, 1991,
New York City Teacher of the Year, 1989-1991,
author of *Dumbing Us Down: The Hidden Curriculum of Compulsory Schooling*

Dear Grace Llewellyn...

"I am (almost) unable to summon words to express my thanks and admiration for what you've done . . . I may not be the person you intended your book for. I am 28, graduated from Berkeley and have one master's degree and have almost completed another. But whilst I was in a metaphysical bookstore, I saw your book and bought it by virtue of the title alone. It struck a deep chord. I desperately needed your book . . . While reading your book, I cried. There is so much joy for life in your book, such a passion for learning . . . While reading your book, I decided to unschool myself. I needed to detox, to get some real pleasure out of learning again! . . . You have changed my life." —M.M., Sunnyvale, California

"I've just finished reading *The Teenage Liberation Handbook* and I really can't find words to tell you how helpful it was to me. You've just dredged all my fears and hassles out, looked at them, and waved them goodbye. *Thank you*!!! . . . What the . . . *Handbook* did was to give me back that faith [in my kids] and make me look at them again. And I saw that to take their freedom, inventiveness, curiosity, energy, and joy and bury them in a classroom would be a terrible waste of vital life . . . Thank you for giving me back that confidence. Thanks for your enthusiasm and trust and love in these kids." —T.S., Ireland

"The book was tremendous. As mother of a teenager I appreciated your respect for the energy and passion of the teenage years."—B.M., Perry, Kansas

"Thank you a million times for writing *The Teenage Liberation Handbook*. It is absolutely *the* best . . . I'm telling everyone about it! . . . Life is so exciting! And you've helped in a *big* way!"—A.D., Parkers Prairie, Minnesota

"I originally bought *The Teenage Liberation Handbook* to prepare and encourage myself for my two sons' coming teen years . . . After reading your book I came away with a lot more than I had expected. I felt like a teenager again while reading it . . . At one point I almost cried when I realized that my low self esteem is quite possibly attributed to the hours and hours of time spent sitting at school with absolutely no attention being paid to *me* . . . It's time to get on with life!"—G.M., Santa Cruz, California

"My heart is so full! So full of excitement, terror, doubt, and possibilities . . . I'm a nineteen-year-old college freshman . . . who's just come to the realization that I'm one of the (too) many teenagers in the world who've sat through thirteen years of school squashing our dreams. I never even imagined there was a not only plausible alternative, but an IDEAL alternative . . . but this isn't a letter of regret or sorrow, it's a letter of hope."—J.T., Madison, Ohio

"I have been unschooled all my life, but your book made me want to go to school so I could quit! . . . It holds a place of honor on my book shelf. Thank you so much!"—M.O., Conway, Arkansas

"Thank you for your *Teenage Liberation Handbook*. I purchased it last weekend and read it at one sitting. The name and description had intrigued me . . . I am a . . . credentialed . . . home school instructor working for a County Office of Education Home School Program . . . I am recommending to all my families that they read your book, as it has profoundly affected me at an age and point in my life where I certainly didn't expect it! . . . I want to try to express to you the support, excitement, freedom and regrets for missed opportunities that I feel from reading your book . . . What I really want to thank you for is my own liberation. After reading your book, I have felt the renewed excitement and energy of learning again for myself, my way, without having to make excuses, apologize for it or wrap it up in an acceptable facade—acts that have wasted too much of my energy. I have visited schools in about thirty countries, looking for ideas, methods, trends and patterns that connect learning and growing with life and the community in hopes of being able to help my students do the same. Your book was the quickest (and cheapest) of those journeys I have yet made."—R.F.D., Newcastle, California

"I am a 31-year-old music teacher . . . getting my graduate degree. Last night, instead of completing some inane assignments, I read your book . . . It was a timely book to read. I wonder why I have been so dense my whole life."—R.D., Parker, Colorado

"I'm seventeen years of age. This is my second year in homeschooling and I love it. I'm finding creative ways to learn by experimenting with different sorts of books and materials. Your book was excellent. Once I picked it up I couldn't put it down! It was wonderful, in my opinion, how you emphasized 'freedom' (one of my favorite words). The way you put other teenagers' letters and statements in the book was neat . . . The way you described what it would be like to leave school was exactly how it was for me. In the morning, now I can wake up happy instead of frustrated and depressed all the time. It feels almost like being four again, living in the now instead of the tomorrow . . . You're a great author!"—C.J., Goldendale, Washington

"Your book is helping many people. All of the books you recommended are wonderful. Reading your book took any doubts I had about letting go of my old ways. Everyone I meet who is teenaged or interested in leaving school I tell about your book."—J.C., sixteen, Mountaindale, Oregon

"A few weeks ago, my parents bought me your book. It is hard to describe the difference in my life. I no longer feel alone, or as though I am running from captivity, hiding out so bounty hunters won't find me. I feel free and, yes, blessed: my imagination has flowered, I am physically, mentally, and spiritually stronger."—A.E.G., sixteen, Bellevue, Idaho

"Thank you for being courageous enough and dedicated enough to put together such a wonderful book . . . I really wish I had been unschooled—I'm envious of those who have been . . . I'm 22 and graduated from UC Santa Cruz last year with a degree in English and American literature . . . Thanks so much for writing such an important, groundbreaking book. Like yourself, I wish that it was available to me when I was in school. Do these unschoolers know how lucky they are???"—D.L., Santa Cruz, California

"Let me start out by saying how much I enjoyed reading your *Teenage Liberation Handbook!* To say that it was a breath of fresh air is a drastic understatement...it nearly knocked me off my feet (and my career path—I'm a teacher)! I couldn't put it down until I had completely savored every last boat-rocking word. While it made it difficult for me to muster up the motivation to get back in the classroom this year, your book gave me an inspiring perspective that I'm certain will influence the way I look at education from now on." —J.S., Seattle, Washington.

"Reading *The Teenage Liberation Handbook* gave our fourteen-year-old daughter the last dose of courage she needed to walk out of Waluga Junior High School...one morning last May, vowing never to return! It also forced her father and me to open our hearts and minds to *hear* her, to become her advocates, and fight for her freedom . . . Each day, the freedom and difference in our lives without school is an incredible gift. I have watched [our daughter] heal from the social assaults she was exposed to on a daily basis, becoming strong, healthy, happy, and an even more thoughtful and delightful person in every way than she was before."—K.L., Portland, Oregon

"Your *Teenage Liberation Handbook* really gave me the courage to allow my son, and then my daughter, to leave high school. It is no exaggeration to say that it changed my life, which, as the mother of four young people who were miserable in school and desperate for a new perspective, is no small thing. I am also untangling my own—mostly boring—mostly useless education in the sixties and becoming an outspoken proponent of self-education. What an exciting new adventure you helped launch here in my family!" —M.P., California.

"My son Adam, and I, recently discovered your two books and 'devoured' them quickly. What a wonderful vision you have for children, particularly those in their teens. Your words are soothing, encouraging and inspiring and have played a large part in Adam's decision to resume homeschooling at the age of fifteen. His younger sisters are at home and we are having a marvelous time together. As for myself, I have rediscovered my own conviction that people can be responsible for their own learning at any age." —C.W., Portland, Oregon

The Teenage Liberation Handbook

Revised Edition

Edited by Grace Llewellyn:

Real Lives: Eleven Teenagers Who Don't Go to School Tell Their Own Stories, Eleven Year Anniversary Edition with updates by all the writers (Lowry House, 2005)

Freedom Challenge: African American Homeschoolers (Lowry House, 1996)

By Grace Llewellyn and Amy Silver:

Guerrilla Learning: How to Give Your Kids a Real Education With or Without School (Wiley, 2001)

The Teenage Liberation Handbook

how to quit school and
get a real life and education

Revised Edition

Grace Llewellyn

LOWRY HOUSE PUBLISHERS
Eugene, Oregon

LOWRY HOUSE PUBLISHERS
Post Office Box 1014
Eugene, Oregon 97440
(541) 686-2315
www.LowryHousePublishers.com

THE TEENAGE LIBERATION HANDBOOK:
HOW TO QUIT SCHOOL AND GET A REAL LIFE AND EDUCATION
(*Second edition*)
Copyright © 1991, 1998 by Grace Llewellyn.

Grateful acknowledgment is made for permission to use the following material:

All material from *Growing Without Schooling* magazine reprinted with permission from *Growing Without Schooling* © 1998 Holt Associates Inc.

Excerpts from DOVE By Robin Lee Graham and Derek L.T. Gill. Copyright © 1972 by Robin Lee Graham and Derek L.T. Gill. Reprinted by permission of HarperCollins Publishers.

Excerpt from UPI story on Paul Lutus reprinted by permission of United Press International.

Kim Kopel's work (in Chapter 42 of this book) copyright © 1991 Kim Kopel. Used by the kind permission of the author.

Most interior illustrations are from the Dover Pictorial Archive series.

All rights reserved. No part of this book may be reproduced or transmitted in any manner whatsoever, including photocopying, except in the case of graffiti on bathroom walls and brief quotations embodied in critical articles and reviews. For information, contact the publisher.

Printed in the United States of America

Publisher's Cataloging-in-Publication data

Llewellyn, Grace
  The teenage liberation handbook : how to quit school and get a real life and education/ by Grace Llewellyn. —2nd ed.

  p.   ; cm.

  Included bibliographical references (p.   ) and index.
  ISBN 0-9629591-7-0

    1. Self-culture. 2. Home schooling--United States. 3. Education (Secondary)--United States. 4. High Schools--United States--Controversial works.
I. Title.

LC32   371.3'944 [20]

10 9 8 7

COVER DESIGN BY TILKE ELKINS AND NICHOLAS WALKER
WWW.ALLROUNDMAGAZINE.COM

For Heather.

For Shira, John M. and John R., Ross, Shawni, Matt, Aaron G.,
Andy, Brian, Jeff, Demian, Rick, Noah, Kris, Amy, David, Chris, Karen, Morgen,
Aaron R., Aaron Z., Susan, Marc, Melissa, Young, Amanda, Beanie,
Josh, Kartik, Jason G., Jason V., Yu, Laura, Becky, Lesley, Clara, and Emile.
No strings.

And for the dream of the wild horses.

Thanks

THIS BOOK HAS been nurtured and built by many people. To adequately acknowledge them, I'd need at least a hundred pages. What follows, therefore, is inadequate.

In writing this book, I stood on the shoulders of a giant. John Holt's visionary, compassionate books on education and unschooling opened my eyes and clarified my beliefs. He died in 1985, two years before I even heard of him. Nevertheless, like most people whose lives are changed by his books, I think of him as a personal friend. Without his work this book wouldn't have been possible. I wouldn't have thought of it, let alone written it. Many of my ideas throughout this book are built directly on his.

Next, I am extremely grateful to the homeschooling community—the thousands of people who have taken John's ideas and turned them into reality. Without their examples, my book would be flat, hypothetical, and utopian. They give the rest of us a beginning sense of what's possible without schools.

More than a hundred teenagers filled out my lengthy questionnaire on unschooling, some in great detail. I am especially grateful to Anne Brosnan, Joshua Smith, and Kim Kopel, who took time to write me long, informative, and entertaining letters.

During her driving trip around the country, never-schooled Anita Giesy stopped in Oregon and fascinated me for days with descriptions of unschoolers nationwide and stories from inside the early homeschooling movement.

Parents who wrote me especially insightful letters include Jj Fallick, Gwen A. Meehan, Bonnie Sellstrom, Michaele Maurer, Bea Rector, Penny Barker, Theresa Lui, and David R. Graham.

I am grateful, also, to the many families who invited me to their homes. Of these, I am most grateful to the wonderful family whose invitation I accepted—the Raymonds of Port Townsend, Washington: Kath, Dan, Seth, Vallie, and Lydia Grace.

The generous people at Holt Associates gave me permission to use material from *Growing Without Schooling* magazine, and it is this material which helps me to show, again and again, what a range of activities is possible for a person unrestricted by school.

I thank the college admissions officers and professors who shared their opinions and advice, and the people from various organizations who patiently answered my questions and sent information.

And in a general sense, all of us who support homeschooling or unschooling are indebted to the families who spent (and continue to spend) years of their lives working for fair homeschooling laws.

However. I don't want my thanks to incriminate these helpful people. Many whom I quote share my faith in teenagers and wholeheartedly support unschooling in the same sense I do. Others might be less completely in agreement with me. For instance, just because a college admissions officer expresses enthusiasm about unschooled applicants doesn't mean he endorses my entire philosophy, and it doesn't mean he's not equally enthusiastic about schooled applicants. A few of the unschoolers and homeschoolers whom I quote will undoubtedly think I am out of hand when I insist that you do not necessarily need to learn higher math or even read a lot to have a worthwhile life. Several homeschooling parents who have helped me might think I underestimate the parents' role in a teenager's education. And in a general sense, this book does have more than its share of sassy rebellious moments. The sass and rebellion is all mine, except where you detect it within somebody else's directly quoted words. I was born with these unfortunate qualities; just ask my mother. To sum up, the opinions of this book, except where otherwise stated, belong to me.

Also: I want to make it abundantly clear that this book is not a personal attack on schoolteachers. There would be little point in that, since I was a teacher myself and continue to hold the same ideals that sent me into teaching in the first place. Anyway, I want to publicly thank my teachers who dealt in excellence despite the complex set of difficulties all schoolteachers face. Foremost among these is Jerry Vevig, choir director extraordinaire, who blessed me and hundreds of other teenagers with the opportunity to work incredibly hard and sound exquisite. Others who especially inspired or encouraged me include Mrs. Darnell, Mrs. Welch, Mrs. Anderson, Mr. Jenkins, Mr. Ah Fong, Mr. Smith, and Mr. Coughlin. (I can't bring myself to write their first names. I don't even *know* most of their first names.)

The teachers and administrators with whom I worked at the Colorado Springs School were not only brilliant, but also generous and wise. I was especially inspired by Bruce Hamilton, Ava Heinrichsdorff, Tom Howes, Karen Huff, Pat Musick, Gary Oakley, Hela Trost, and Charlie Tye. It is very much in spite of these people, rather than because of them, that I wrote this book.

Finally, I am grateful to friends and family who have supported my work in various ways. Many pointed out resources that I included in this book. Others, like my teaching colleague Gary Oakley, encouraged me and/or talked at length with me, helping me clarify ideas.

I am immensely indebted to people who carefully read the manuscript or parts of it, helping me identify and fix many weaknesses: Heiko Koester, Clement Cheung, Kris Shapiro, Dick Ruth, and the trusty Llewellyn pack: Ned, Richard, Heather.

For support both personal and intellectual, I thank Richard, Heather D., Colleen, Heather, Kelly, Heiko, and especially Ned. I thank my housemate Caroline Diston, who kept me sane and happy by bringing me warm dinners and hot tea and coaxing me away from my computer to go dancing—any joyous overtones you detect in these pages have a lot to do with living around her. And from my heart, I thank my parents, whose love, trust, and support has buttressed so much of my life.

And thanks again.

As I complete this revised edition, I remain deeply grateful to everyone mentioned above.

Huge thanks to the hundreds of people who wrote me letters after reading the original edition—sharing the stories of their lives, sending money and encouragement and handpainted cards and gifts, and continuing to teach me about unschooling.

I am grateful to the parents, teenagers, and others who wrote to me about homeschooling beyond the U.S., including: Kyoko Aizawa, Janine Banks, Debbie Bennett, Jan Brownlie, Sarah Cashmore, Lantien Chu, Konomi Shinohara Corbin, Kate Durham, Elizabeth Edwards, Colleen Erzinger, Sophie Haesen, Carolyn Hamilton, Katherine Hebert, Marie Heitzmann, Ywonne and Gunnar Jarl, Debra Kempt, Karen Maxwell, Roland Meighan, Valerie Bonham Moon, Pat Montgomery, Bippan Norberg, Maureen Normoyle, Robert Ozmak, Lyndon Pugh, Monica Reid, Candis Ritsey, Aleta Shepler, Sally Sherman, Brenda J. Smith, Levina Snow, Eleanor Sparks, Denise Sutherland, Lomi Szil, Candace Thayer-Coe, Margy Walter, Kim Wark, and Jill Whitmore.

Thanks to all of the Not Back to School Campers and staffers of 1996 and 1997, whose exemplary, joyful lives gave my work a jump start and re-awakened my own sense of adventure and purpose.

My dear friend and assistant Janet Taylor provided invaluable, energetic help in preparing this revised edition, and brightened many days.

Susannah Sheffer, editor of *Growing Without Schooling*, has been a constant source of inspiration and enlightenment. I thank her for her vision, her clear and persevering intellect, and her unwavering and patient friendship.

My brother Ned Llewellyn made many 45-mile trips to my house during moments of computer crisis; I don't know how I'd manage without him.

And most especially I thank my true love Skip: autodidact, dinner cook, best friend, and soulmate.

I recognize June by the flowers, now. I used to know it by review tests, and restlessness.
                    —Lisa Asher, unschooled teenager,
                        in *Growing Without Schooling* magazine

What is life? It is the flash of a firefly in the night. It is the breath of a buffalo in the winter time. It is the little shadow which runs across the grass and loses itself in the sunset.
—Crowfoot, Blackfoot warrior and spokesman

Contents

Part Four—Touching the World: Finding Good Work

Part Five—The Lives of Unschoolers

Appendices

first,
a nice little story

*What a distressing contrast there is between the radiant intelligence
of the child and the feeble mentality of the average adult.*

—Sigmund Freud

ON A SOFT green planet, a smiling baby was born in an orchard resplendent with every kind of fruit in the universe. The baby's parents called her Tanika, and Tanika spent her days roaming the warm wet ground on hands and knees. Spotting a clump of gulberries off in the distance, she'd crawl after it and crush the sweet fruit in her mouth, red juice staining her brown chin and neck. A muavo would fall fatly from the high crown of the muavo tree, and she'd savor its golden tang. Each day revealed new wonders—bushapples, creamy labanas, the nutty crunch of the brown shrombart. The orchard's fruit sparkled in the dew and sun like thousands of living moist jewels against the green fragrance of cushioning leaves.

As her eyes grew stronger Tanika lifted her gaze. The opulent branches above her hung heavy with fruits she'd never dreamed of, globular and glistening. Tanika's mother and father wandered the orchard too, sometimes, and she watched them reach out easily and take a shining cluster here, a single green satinplum there. She'd watch them eat and imagine being tall enough to roam and reach so freely as they.

Sometimes one of them would bend down and give Tanika one of those fruits from up there in the moving leaves. Fresh from the branches, it intoxicated her, and her desire to know and taste all the fruits of the orchard so consumed her that she began to long for the day she could reach that far.

Her longing strengthened her appetite, and the fruit strengthened her legs, and one day Tanika crawled to the base of a mysterious bush at the edge of the stream that watered the orchard. She leaned carefully forward and braced her arms as she positioned her feet. Unsteadily she rose and groped for the shrub's pale fruit. Tugging knocked her off balance and she sat down hard in an overripe muavo, but she barely noticed the fruit squishing under her thighs: in her hands she grasped a fruit thin-skinned and silver, fresh and new. She pressed it to her nose and face before she let her teeth puncture it.

No sooner had she tossed the smooth pit into the stream, than she heard a rustling behind her. A jolly bespectacled face grinned down at her.

"Well, well, well! You're a mighty lucky little girl! I've come to teach you to get the fruit down from the tall trees!"

Tanika's happiness unfurled like a sail. She could hardly believe her good luck. Not only had she just picked and eaten her first bush fruit, but here was a man she didn't even know offering to show her how to reach the prism of treats high above her head. Tanika was so overcome with joy that she immediately rose to her feet again, and plucked another of the small moonish fruits.

The jolly stranger slapped the fruit from Tanika's wrist. Stunned, she fell again and watched her prize roll into the stream. "Oh dear," said the man, "You've already picked up some bad habits. That may make things difficult." The slapping hand now took Tanika's and pulled her up. Holding on this way, Tanika stumbled along behind the stranger.

She wanted to ask questions, like, "Why didn't you just show me how to pick those berries hanging above the bush where I was?" But she kept her mouth shut. If she was going off to pick the high fruit, she guessed it didn't matter where, or that she'd sacrificed her one beautiful moonfruit. Maybe they were going to a special tree melting with juicing fruits, branches bent almost to the ground, low enough for her outstretched fingers. Yes! That must be it. Excitement renewed, she moved her legs faster. The stranger grinned and squeezed her hand.

Soon Tanika saw the biggest, greyest thing she'd ever laid eyes on. In quiet fascination she tripped along as they stepped off the spongy humus of the orchard floor onto a smooth sidewalk. "Here we are!" beamed the guide. They entered the building, full of odd smells and noises. They passed through a pair of heavy black doors, and the man pushed Tanika into a loud, complicated room full of talking children and several adults. She looked at the children, some sitting on the floor, some crawling about or walking. All of them had trays or plates in front of them heaping with odd mushy lumps of various colors. Also, some of the children were busy coloring simple pictures of fruits, and some wore pins and tags on their shirts displaying little plastic pears and mistbulbs. Baffled, Tanika tried to figure out what the children were doing in such a dark, fruitless place, what the lumpy stuff was, and above all, why her guide had stopped here on their way to the bountiful tree.

But before she had time to think, two things happened. First, one of the kids took something metal and used it to scoop a lump of dull pinkish stuff into his mouth. Tanika opened her mouth in panic to warn the kid. Maybe there was something wrong with him; he was much bigger than she was, old enough to know better. But just as she began to yell, a new hand, slick, pulled her up again. "OK, Tanika," said the cheery woman that went with the hand, "This is the cafeteria. We're looking forward to helping you grow, and we're certain we can help you learn to pick tree fruit, as long as you do your part."

Tanika felt confused. She didn't see what this place could have to do with picking gulberries, and at the moment she was particularly hungry for more of that shining moonfruit. But she had no time to think. The slick-hand woman put Tanika on a cold chair at a table. "Here," she said, and nudged a box of crayons and a black outline of a plum at her. "Today you will color this, and it will help you get ready for eating tomorrow." Tanika started to feel foolish. She'd never guessed that learning to pick fruit would be so complicated. She colored the plum with all the colors in the box, trying in vain to make it round and enticing like the fruits of the orchard.

The rest of the day passed in a daze. Tanika was made to color more of the pictures, and to her disgust most of the children ate the formless mush on the plates in front of them. Some of the fat and greasy children asked for more and stuffed themselves. Whenever this happened, the adults ran in and put gold stars all over the kid's arms and face. Many things happened—children fought, napped, sat quietly fidgeting with the stuff. Finally, the jolly man took Tanika's hand and led her out of the dark building. As her bare feet met the orchard grass, she caught the scent of ripe labana. She asked the stranger if he would get one for her, but he merely laughed.

Tanika was far too confused to put any of her questions into words. By the time they arrived at the tree where Tanika slept with her parents, the evening light had turned the leaves to bronze, and she was exhausted. Too tired to look for fruit, she fell asleep and dreamed fitfully.

In the morning her mind was clear. She still wanted to reach the high fruit, but she did not want to go back to the noisy smelly dark cafeteria. She could already reach the bushfruit; maybe in time she'd grasp the high fruit too.

But when the spectacled person arrived, he told her that she'd never reach the trees without many years in the cafeteria. He explained it—"You can't reach them now, can you?" and "Your parents can reach them. That's because they went to the cafeteria. I can reach them, because I went to the cafeteria." Tanika had no time to think this through, because he'd pulled her to her feet again and they were off. She hadn't had time to find breakfast, and her stomach rumbled painfully.

Tanika went in the room and sat down politely. "Please," she asked one of the adults, "Can you help me pick tree fruits today? That's why I'm here, and also today I didn't have time for breakfast."

The tall lady laughed. "Well, well, well! Aren't we cute! *Tree* fruit! Before you're ready for tree fruit, you have to prepare!" She disappeared behind a curtain and returned carrying a tray with a scoop of greenish stuff. Tanika jerked back. She looked around wildly for an escape route. Out of the corner of her eye she saw a boy watching with soft dark quiet eyes. The lady grabbed her hand.

"Don't be afraid, Tanika," she laughed. "How will you ever work up to eating tree fruit if you can't handle plate fruit?" She put the tray on the table, and took the metal thing, spooning up a piece of the stuff and holding it in front of the small girl. Tanika pushed the spoon away violently. Then she put her head down on the table and cried.

The lady's voice changed. "So you're going to be a tough one, Tanika? Just remember, you're only hurting yourself when you refuse to eat. If you want to succeed, you'd better do as we ask." She walked away.

When Tanika stopped crying, her stomach was desperately empty. She sat up and looked at the tray. She was afraid of the stuff. She bent down to smell it and caught a faint, stale whiff of limbergreen berry. The smell, even distorted, was a familiar friend. She picked up the spoon and ate her first bite of cafeteria food.

Tanika was relieved. Although the goop was slimy, far too sweet, and mostly tasteless, it wasn't as bad as it looked. And it did seem to be made from limbergreen berries. She ate it all, and felt a little better. The lady came back. "Very good," she smiled. She stuck a green star on the back of Tanika's hand. "We'll do some more exercises and then later on you can try something new to eat."

Hours later, Tanika had been the apple in "Velcro the Stem on the Apple," and had drawn a muavo tree and listened to an older student explain what fruits contained vitamins P, Q, and Z. Apparently she had done all these things right, because the lady came back and put more green and gold stars on her hands and cheeks. Some of the children looked at her angrily, though, so perhaps she'd done something wrong.

At this point a man rang a little bell. Immediately all the children sat down at the tables and folded their hands neatly. A girl grabbed Tanika's hand and shoved her onto a chair. Then six children walked into the room carrying stacks of trays. They put one in front of each child, and Tanika saw that each tray contained five purple and blue wafers. "Yum!" said the girl next to Tanika, "Violetberry cakes!" Tanika jumped. She'd seen her parents eat violetberries, and also seen the accompanying ecstasy on their faces. She easily pictured the graceful coniferous trees on which they grew.

She picked up a wafer. It was warm, but not with the gentle warmth of the sun. She put it in her mouth. Dry, sandy... she chewed obediently but sadly. This was it? Disappointment sank her stomach and she put the cake down, mentally crossing violetberries off her wishlist forever.

In the end Tanika was made to eat the violetberry cake—all five hunks of it— before the spectacled man would lead her out the door. Her stomach throbbed all the way home. That night she crawled into her mother's arms and sobbed. Her mother rocked her, then whispered something to Tanika's father. He disappeared, and returned a minute later with an armload of tiny, glowing violetberries.

"It's time," said her mother sweetly, "For your first fresh violetberries."

Her father dangled them teasingly above her lips, but Tanika only cried harder. The berries' fragrance, though delicate and sweet, clashed with her distended heavy stomach. She was far too full, and it was violetberries' fault. Both parents teased and offered, but they finally gave up. Her mother laid Tanika down to rest alone, and the two adults stood whispering while the moon rose, worry in their voices.

At the cafeteria the next day the adults met Tanika with an unpleasant stare. "You're making things difficult for yourself," scolded the woman with slick hands, "Your parents have reported that your attitude at home is not meeting standards for girls your age. You need to eat *much* more thoroughly." A girl brought a plate crowded with dried out, wrinkly little fruits. Tanika ate them, tough and tasteless. Her stomach hurt again. After they dissected a preserved bushapple, she ate another tray full of canned gulberry. Then she went back home and slept.

Days passed, and months. Tanika ate obediently and earned lots of stars. There was a picture of a bright green tree painted on one of the walls, and when the whole roomful of children ate their food quickly, the adults had them play a game. They taped three or four cut-out paper fruits to the tree, and then the kids were made to take turns jumping or reaching to try to take them. Whoever reached a fruit got to keep it, and also was called a winner and plastered with dozens of gold stars.

One day when the spectacled man walked her home he told her the cafeteria would be closed for two days for cleaning. He handed her a little white carton and said, "Be sure to eat all of this while I'm gone, and I'll pick you up in two days."

As he waddled away, a strange inspiration seized Tanika's brain. She touched her swollen belly and flung the carton away. Out of it tumbled cakes, red mush, hard little biscuits smelling flatly of labanas.

When she woke the next morning her stomach rumbled and she got up to look for breakfast. Leaving the clearing, she accidentally kicked a biscuit. Out of habit, she picked it up and almost put it in her mouth, then caught herself and aimed instead for a bush full of gulberries. Furtively she snatched a handful and crushed them to her lips. Sweet and wild, they made her want to sing.

Tanika's father saw her then, and called excitedly to her mother. Both of them ran to their child and squeezed her. "Look what you've learned at the cafeteria!" cried her mother. "My baby is growing up!"

"Be sure to eat all your homefood," said her father, "So you won't be behind when you go back." Then his tone of voice changed. "What's that?" he said. He sprinted off and grabbed up the white carton. Tanika watched in horror as he searched the orchard floor. A few minutes later he returned with everything—biscuits, cake, mush.

Tanika ate it all.

The cafeteria opened again and Tanika went back. Every day she ate faster, and gradually stopped resisting, even in her own mind. One day she reached the highest paper fruit on the painted tree. All the adults patted her head and she could barely see her brown skin under all the gold stars. She started walking to the cafeteria every day by herself. The adults started giving her food for the evenings, and usually she'd eat it like they said. One day, walking home, she flung her hands to the sky and they touched, accidentally, a muavo hanging down from its branch. Tanika jumped back. "I can pick it," she said slowly, "It worked." She thought for a minute. The cooks had said it would happen, someday, if she ate what they gave her and jumped as high as she could during the tree game.

Tanika gracefully severed the muavo from its stem, examined it, and tossed it neatly into a shadow.

She wasn't hungry. ☀

the note to parents

Respect the child. Be not too much his parent. Trespass not on his solitude.
—Ralph Waldo Emerson

AGAINST THE ADVICE of lots of people, I didn't write this book for you. I wrote it for teenagers. I wrote it for teenagers because I wished that when I was a teenager someone had written it for me. I wrote it for teenagers because my memory and experience insist that teenagers are as fully human as adults. I wrote it for teenagers because I found an appalling dearth of respectful, serious nonfiction for them. In short, I wrote it for teenagers because they are the experts on their own lives.

No, I have not forgotten your child's "place." I know that if you want to, you can probably prevent him from leaving school. I have written this book anyway, in the hope that after careful thought, you will see fit to honor the choice he makes.

Yes, if your son or daughter leaves school, it will change your life. If the experiences of pioneering homeschoolers can predict your future, you will see family relationships deepen; a teenager without eight hours of school and homework has time to make friends with her parents. You will see family relationships heal, uncomplicated by displaced anger about school. You will feel less harshly evaluated according to teenage fashion magazine standards. Depending on your own background and schooling, you may undergo a period of depression, anger, and bitterness. *You* went to school, after all, and in contrast to your children's unexpected freedom you may feel overwhelmed by a sense of loss—all the things you could have done with that time, all the choices you never thought you had, all the labels that stuck when schoolpeople put them on you. This funk, if you get it, will eventually give way to a new sense of freedom—at least mine did. You can't change the past, but you can change the present. You can peel the labels off, you can start making real choices, you have the rest of your life to *live*.

Homeschooling parents of teenagers are rarely *teachers*, in the school sense of the word, and this book never suggests that you forsake your own career or interests in order to learn calculus (etc.) fast enough to "teach" it. Healthy kids can teach themselves what they need to know, through books, various people, thinking, and other means. (A freshly unschooled person may at *first* be a lousy learner; like cigarettes, school-style passivity can be a slow habit to kick.)

Nevertheless, you will probably find yourself more involved than before with your son's or daughter's education. If you have helped with or supervised your children's homework, or stayed in close touch with their teachers, homeschooling need not drain your energy any more than that. Your role will change, however. No longer is it your job to nag or lecture; instead, you answer questions and help find people or resources to answer the questions that you can't answer. Instead, when your daughter starts sketching castles, you introduce her to the architect you know or tell her about the lecture on medieval life that you saw advertised in the paper.

If an unschooled teenager doesn't need *teaching* from you, what does he need from you? *Parenthood*, of course, and all the love and stability therein.

Also, help with logistics, as implied in the castle example above. Few people can immediately take complete responsibility for their educations after being forcefully spoonfed for years. Please be willing to make some phone calls to set up meetings or lessons, to tell your kid about events or resources he might not otherwise know about, to draw a map to the planetarium or explain how to use the university library. Also, you will need to accompany your son or daughter through your state's homeschooling legal requirements. Fortunately, every state has support groups to help you make sense of this process.

Also, trust. When you tell your daughter about that upcoming lecture on medieval life, make it clear that you are simply passing along information, not giving an *assignment*. If you don't believe in her, it won't work. If you give up on her, snoop, push, or frequently anxiously inquire into the status of her algebraic knowledge, you will destroy any chance you had for a healthy family relationship, *and* you will send her right back to school, where there is so much less to lose.

Part of trusting means respecting your teenager's need for transition time. As Chapter 12 points out, new unschoolers often need time to work through a flood of feelings about school and life, *before* they can start attending to things "intellectual" or "academic." Ride out the storm with your child. Offer your support, your ideas, your arms. Don't rush him.

Do I expect you to swallow all this? Not now; not by reading this short note. Later, *yes*. I expect you to change your mind in favor of unschooling by 1) reading John Holt's books, *Freedom and Beyond, Instead of Education, Teach Your Own,* and *Escape From Childhood,* 2) reading literature by parents who have homeschooled their teenagers—especially Micki and David Colfax's *Homeschooling for Excellence,* Cafi Cohen's *And What About College?,* and Nancy Wallace's *Child's Work,* and 3) getting to know homeschoolers near you (like people, they come in all varieties; don't give up if you're put off at first), 4) reading *Growing Without Schooling* magazine, 5) reviewing your own adolescence and your present life, and 6) humbly observing your teenaged child, allowing for the possibility that he might be a *person...* like you.

As for the rest of this book, you are a welcome guest. From time to time, you will find the words of other parents and adults, some of which may reassure you. Depending on your perspective, you may detect an overall tone of intoxicating hope or dangerous insubordination. Mostly, you will find piles of information you do not need: stuff that is common knowledge to adults but not so familiar to teenagers who have spent most of their lives secluded from the world and its array of wonders.

Finally, on a different note: if you are already disillusioned by your child's "education," or even sympathetic to the cause of unschooling, and if you live with a

Stuck or Depressed teenager, I hope this book can be your ally in offering her or him some vision for healthy, self-directed change.

Best wishes. ☀

hello!

about this book

DID YOUR GUIDANCE counselor ever tell you to consider quitting school? That you have other choices, quite beyond lifelong hamburger flipping or inner-city crack dealing? That legally you can find a way out of school, that once you're out you'll learn and grow better, faster, and more naturally than you ever did in school, that there are zillions of alternatives, that you can quit school and still go to A Good College and even have a Real Life in the Suburbs if you so desire? Just in case your counselor never told you these things, I'm going to. That's what this book is for.

What it's not

This is not a book about the kind of "homeschooling" in which you stay home all day and hang a chalkboard in the family room and write essays designed by your father and work geometry problems assigned by your mother.

There are some good things to say about that kind of homeschooling, especially for young children who haven't yet acquired basic reading, writing, and math computation skills. There are also some bad things to say about it. In this book I will say little about it.

Most people who do fantastic unschoolish things with their time *call* themselves homeschoolers, because it keeps them out of trouble and it doesn't freak out the neighbors. Anne Brosnan put it well in a letter to *Growing Without Schooling* magazine:

> When an adult comes up and asks, "Why aren't you in school?" you're supposed to soften it by saying, "My mom (or dad) teaches me at home." If you say, "I don't even *go* to school. So far, I've taught myself everything I want to know," they think you've run away from school or are a lunatic. Whereas the other way, they think your parent's a teacher and you get private lessons.
> The usual adult person in America thinks it's terribly hard to teach yourself something, and if you want to learn something, you've got to find somebody to teach it to you. This leads to the idea that kids are dumb unless taught or unless they go to school.[1]

If you quit school, you too will probably wish to call yourself a homeschooler, at least when you talk to the school board. But that doesn't require bringing the

---

[1] From *Growing Without Schooling* #73.

ugliness of school into your home, or transforming your parents into teachers. Nor, for that matter, does it require that you stay home. The idea is to catch *more* of the world, not less. To avoid these kinds of connotations, I usually use the term *unschooling*. But be aware that many people who talk about *homeschooling* mean the same thing I do when I say *unschooling*.

This is not a book specifically about Christian homeschooling, although most Christians will find it as useful as anyone else. I point this out because many people associate homeschooling with fundamentalist Christianity and Fear of Darwin. Many homeschoolers *are* fundamentalist Christians, which has some heavy impact on what they do instead of *school* school. Many others, however, are agnostics, mellow Christians, Jews, pagans, Rastafarians, atheists, and Buddhists. Help yourself to any religious belief you like, but in these pages I won't suggest that you read your Bible instead of a biology book.

What it *is*
This book is a wild card, a shot in the dark, a hopeful prayer.

This book wants you to quit school and do what you love. Yes, I know, that's the weirdest thing you ever heard. Hoping to make this idea feel possible to you, I tell about teenagers who are already living happy lives without school, and I offer lots of ideas and strategies to help you get a real life and convince your adults to cooperate.

"*Excuse me?*" you interrupt, "*Quit school? Right. And throw away my future and pump gas all my life and get Addicted to Drugs and be totally lost in today's world. Right.*"

If you said that, please feel free to march straight to the nearest schoolperson and receive a bushel of gold stars, extra credit points, and proud smiles. You've learned exactly what they taught you. After you get tired of sticking stars to your locker, do please come back and read further.

This book is built on the belief that life is wonderful and schools are stifling. It is built on an impassioned belief in freedom. And it is built on the belief that schools do the opposite of what they say they do. They prevent learning and they destroy one's love of learning.

Of course, there are hundreds of other books with similar premises. Some of these books go on to suggest that if certain changes were made, or brighter teachers were hired, schools would be good places. Other books say compulsory schools are *fundamentally* bad places and society, or at least individual people, should abandon them. This book agrees with that, but it doesn't stop there.

This is a *practical* book—a book for individual teenagers, a real-life handbook meant to be used and acted on. I have no hope that the school system will change enough to make schools healthy places, until it makes school blatantly optional. But I have plenty of faith that *people*—you, your friends—can intelligently take greater control over their own lives. So this book bypasses the rigid, uncreative red tape of that System and instead speaks directly to you.

If school didn't make people so stupid, this could be a very short handbook. But unfortunately, most of the teenagers I've known and worked with—like the teenager I was—are more clueless than preschool children when it comes to knowing how to ask and answer important questions. So, much of this book is about access—how to do this, find that out, what your choices are and how to take advantage of them.

Whom it's for

As the title gently implies, this is a book for *teenagers*, though their parents and little brothers are welcome too. If you are nine and want to use this book to get free, more power to you. If you are eleven and think of yourself as a teenager, that's fine with me too.

Is this book for *all* teenagers? Here are five answers.

If you are like me, this book is definitely for you. When I was in school, people asked me if I liked it. Sometimes I said yes. Sometimes I said no. I didn't think about it much, because I figured it didn't matter. Whether I liked it or not, I knew (or thought I knew) there were no other options. I believed in school in an abstract sense—education, learning, great writers and poets and thinkers and all that. My grades were good. I hated homework—and rarely did any—but I felt constantly guilty, rather than proud, about this. I wasn't offended by the disrespect my peers and I lived with, because I'd never imagined that it was *possible* for adults to treat me differently.

Usually, I thought I'd be fine if only I was a senior instead of an eighth grader, or if only I went to some artsy boarding school instead of boring Capital High School. I liked about half of my teachers, but felt no enthusiasm for their classes. I craved Friday afternoons and June. Except for choir, my life in school was dreary and uninspired, but I had nothing else to compare it to. I'd never heard of homeschooling, let alone unschooling, and dropping out was not on my List of Possibilities in Life. I wonder now, sometimes with bitterness, how things might have been different if I had heard then of the possibilities beyond school. The first wave of the unschooling movement caught some people about my age, and I envy them.

Very definitely, this book is *not* just for people who are labeled gifted. I make this point because in these pages you will run into a lot of examples of unschooled teenagers who do rather impressive things with their time. I don't want you to be intimidated by them, only inspired. They don't live brilliantly because they are more intelligent than you; they live brilliantly because they have the time and encouragement they need. Many of them did very badly in school before their parents set them free.

This book is for you whether you live in the U.S.A., Wales, Peru, South Africa, or anywhere else on Planet Earth. I wrote the first edition with only the U.S. in mind, and most of these pages still reflect my experience as a U.S. citizen. But, as Chapter 11 points out, unschooling is a growing trend in many far corners of the globe, and you can be part of it.

If you have already considered leaving school—as a "dropout" or anything else, of course this book is for you. If you have been feeling guilty or inadequate because of your "failure" in school, perhaps I can knock some optimistic sense into you. Perhaps I can get you to think of yourself as *rising* out instead of *dropping* out.[1] The way we think of ourselves makes all the difference.

If you truly enjoy school and all of its paraphernalia more than anything else you

---

[1] I got this terminology from Herb Hough's letter in *Growing Without Schooling* magazine #79.

can possibly imagine doing, I suppose I'm not writing for you, because I don't understand you. I'm not sure you exist, but if you do, we live in different universes. I used to think everyone was strong willed and independently inclined. Now I'm not sure. Sometimes I think perhaps school really does completely destroy that fierce, free spirit in some people. Other times my mother half convinces me that some people are naturally docile and passive. Maybe I have something to learn about docility. Or maybe I have a healthy aversion to something dead in people that should be alive.

However, I invite you to have a look at this book anyway. Even if it doesn't change the way you think about school, or convince you to stop going, it might make you aware of some useful opportunities and resources—things you can do with your life in *addition* to school. After you finish your homework, naturally.

Of course, some places we call school are less schoolish than others. I feel pretty strongly that even the most alternative school, *as long as it is compulsory*, is not a healthy place to be. But I'd be an idiot to say every single school is bad for every single person. If you go to a humane school, and love it, even in May, and have a gut feeling that it's a good and healthy place, stay there. I hope I never tell anyone to ignore their gut feelings. I always listen to mine, and usually act on them. Of course, you have to make sure you're not confusing fear and deeply imbedded guilt with your true feelings.

Why I wrote it

Just in case you are dying to know.

When I went to college, I knew from the start that I wanted to be an English teacher. I had always loved to read and write, but I had rarely enjoyed any of the work I had done in my English classes. In my naïveté, I blamed this on my teachers. Several of them were obviously very intelligent, interesting, and creative people, but their classes were nevertheless dull, and I thought this was their fault. I knew I would be a different kind of teacher.

My own classes would be dynamic, entertaining, and always engaging. I would love the stimulation of being around "learning" all my life, and my students would shower me with continual gratitude for rescuing them from the brain-death of their previous existence.

Student teaching took some of the sparkle out of that arrogance, but I chalked up my victims' lack of complete enthusiasm to my inexperience and lack of adequate time to prepare. (Somehow, I assumed that later I'd have more time to prepare.) Yes, a few of them said I was the best teacher they'd ever had. Most of them just turned in most of their homework on time and looked at me funny when I rhapsodized about writing. I did not find a real teaching position for the autumn after college graduation, and I ended up substitute teaching in the public schools of Oakland and Berkeley, California.

Subbing put me in the position to see the ugliest aspects of school, and my life-long tendency to rebel against or at least make fun of authority surfaced and grew. In between sending students to the office for calling me a "white bitch" or for pinching me or for loudly interrupting too many times, I'd sit and despairingly ponder the meaninglessness of these huge inner-city schools. I still felt that with determination, I could make a difference. However, I began to realize that working with the kinds of administrators I most often encountered could only be an uphill battle. Furthermore, for many of these students it was probably too late—schools had so crushed their "love of learning" that I could hardly hope to inspire all of them to write or think or discover wonderful things.

After that school year, I took a break to travel in Peru and then spent three months substituting in the homogeneous, well-behaved schools that I grew up in in Boise, Idaho. I still felt that I wanted to teach kids to read and write but I began to yearn to escape the rigidity and dullness of public schools. I began contemplating starting my own tiny, inexpensive, independent school. I imagined a group of about ten students who spent their time taking field trips and hanging out in someone's basement making movies or writing novels. While I was brainstorming and researching the logistics of setting up something like this, I first stumbled across the writing of John Holt. By that time I'd heard of homeschooling but dismissed it, as most people seem to, as the activity of a bunch of scaredy-cat fanatics afraid their kids would find out about evolution and condoms if they went to school. John Holt's writings threw a bright new light on the subject, and on the whole concepts of school and learning.

Essentially, he argued that learning is a *natural* process that happens to anyone who is busy doing something real for its own sake, and that school destroys and confuses this process. Although most of his ideas had never occurred to me, they immediately made so much sense that I felt as though I'd thought of them myself. His books were eloquent yet simple, by far the wisest words I had ever found about education. I realized that although a tiny school like the one I'd envisioned might be a good alternative for students, I wasn't equipped to start it—I didn't have any real expertise, and I didn't know anything worth teaching besides how to embroider, go backpacking, bake bread, dance a little, play the piano, and maybe write. I realized how few skills I had, and that the few skills I *did* have hadn't come from school. I knew about a lot of things from reading and keeping my ears open, but few of the books that had shaped my mind had been assigned or recommended in school. I felt freshly angry about having given up ballet (instead of school) in junior high, and about having pushed that biggest love of mine, dancing, into a mostly-neglected cupboard. Mainly, I felt flooded by a sense of loss and bitterness—all that time I'd *wasted* sitting and staring out windows when I could have been out traveling, learning, growing, *living*.

I determined to start living my life, then and there. I packed up and migrated to Taos, New Mexico, where I slept on the mesa in a house made of bottles and wind, and feasted every morning on sky and space and sage-scent. (At the same time, I supported my little sister's decision to quit high school.) I spent as much time as I could dancing.

I continued to read John Holt, but I eventually decided to teach anyway. After all, school was going to exist whether I wanted it to or not, and I figured I might as well jump in and make it the best experience I could. Anyway, I didn't know *how* to do anything that I wanted to do more. I still felt that public school was a horrendous institution, but I daydreamed about finding a private school that was humane and lively.

I found a position teaching seventh and eighth grade English at a small independent school in Colorado. I was thrilled. It believed firmly in experiential education—learning by *doing*—and my colleagues and the administrators were wonderful people: flexible, enthusiastic, imaginative, intelligent, funny, and warm. With only nineteen students, I'd have the chance to know each of them well. It seemed so different from public school that I looked forward to it with great excitement.

The year did go smoothly in most regards. However, I began to feel that this small school was not essentially healthier than ordinary public schools for most of its students. Naturally, they received more individual attention than they would have in public school, but some of them experienced an uglier flip side of that individual attention: we teachers seemed to see or otherwise find out nearly everything about students' lives, and then to hound students endlessly about things that were none of our business—missing homework assignments, social conflicts, messy notebooks. Even when we were not inclined to pry or push, students had little privacy, no way to escape our eyes.

Furthermore, this small, "caring," "creative" school was fundamentally the same as any ordinary public school, because *it controlled students' lives*. It continually dictated to them how to use their time. So what if they were role playing the lives of the early colonists instead of just reading the dry words of their American history textbook? These cute "experiential" activities we teachers took pride in had the same effect any schoolwork does. They stole kids' time and energy, so that John-the-math-genius-and-artist had no time to build his geometric sculptures, so that Andy couldn't pursue his fascination with well-made knives and guns, so that Kris and Chris and Rick and Young didn't have enough time to read, so that Shira—a brilliant actress and talented musician—was threatened with having to drop out of her outstanding chorale group if she missed any homework assignments.

In some ways, in fact, it seemed *more* harmful than public school. Homework was excessive, leaving students little freedom even at home. Lots of parents expected the school to help turn their offspring into lawyers and Successful Executives, and the school catered to this image enough that it put tremendous pressure on kids.

But despite all this, I decided to stay with teaching, and I brainstormed ways to make my classroom as healthy as possible. I wanted to give my students as much freedom within the realm of language arts as I could, so I devised an independent study program complete with an innovative "All A's" grading system borrowed from Richard E. Koop of Gulf Middle School in Florida. The assistant headmaster, a courageous, warm woman, gave me her blessing, saying that since I obviously had the kids' needs and growth foremost in my mind, she'd support my experiment.

I began my second year of teaching with high hopes that soon plummeted. Four or five people who loved to write (enough to do so in their spare time and vacations) thrived in the program. It gave them official time to do what they wanted to do anyway—write novels or collections of short stories or long long essays—rather than drain their energy with arbitrary assignments of arbitrary lengths fit into arbitrary schedules. But most of my students saw it as just another way to make them do something they really didn't want or need to do, at least not every day. So much for freedom.

After I had felt dismal for a while because my curriculum hadn't dramatically changed the nature of school, we went on a week-long field trip to Washington, D.C. Conflict was inevitable; the teachers who designed the trip naturally wanted to take as much advantage as possible of all the things to see and do in the area, so our schedule was hectic and demanding. At one point, the students were scolded for slouching and whispering during a dull evening lecture after a particularly exhausting day. As students exploded in their own defense, and one of my favorite students said sincerely that he wanted to go home, my mind reeled. It was perfectly fair, I thought, to expect people to behave wonderfully in any situation they chose freely to be part of. If I went to a movie and talked all through it, I'd deserve to get kicked out. If I didn't feel like sitting quietly, I shouldn't go in the first place. But our students hadn't been given any choice as to whether they wanted to sit through a lecture, or even whether they went to Washington, or, for that matter, whether they sat in English and science every day.

That night I lay in bed agitating till 4:00 A.M. Although I hadn't upbraided our students on that particular evening, I had certainly done so countless other times, for similar and sometimes less justifiable reasons.

I called Holt's writings up in my mind and admitted to myself that he was right—school was a bad place, a *controlling* place, and I wasn't going to change anything by being there. I could see that some of my students were fed up with school, but I knew they had no clue as to other possibilities. And so the seeds of this book sprouted in my brain. Also, in the back of my head I knew I could not continue to teach, but at first I refused to look this knowledge in the face. The prospect of life without my "career" was frightening and uncertain. However, I started looking at the world with a fresher, more honest perspective. While bustling along the sidewalk and scolding students for dawdling, I thought longingly how I would enjoy spending a leisurely week in D.C. with a few of my students, talking with the homeless who camped across from the White House, roaming the Smithsonian for days, taking time out for skateboarding and sky staring.

Back in Colorado, my convictions strengthened daily. I noticed an Emerson quote on the "Civil War" bulletin board, and I shivered: "If you put a chain around the neck of a slave," it said, "the other end fastens itself around your own." The final catalyst came the Friday I read Thoreau with my classes. Nearly everything he said seemed to pertain to the whole school issue, but one fragment in particular of "On the Duty of Civil Disobedience" lodged itself in my brain. After explaining that he would not pay his taxes as long as they supported such evils as slavery, Thoreau had written:

> If any tax gatherer, or any other public officer, asks me, as one has done, "But what shall I do?" my answer is, "If you really wish to do anything, resign your office." When the subject has refused allegiance, and the officer has resigned his office, then the revolution is accomplished.

That was that. Forced to face my own responsibility, I resolved first to quit teaching, and then to write this book. John Holt and a few others had written a stack of excellent books on unschooling, but I felt that teenagers needed their *own* book, one to tell them they weren't wrong to hate school, and to make them aware of alternatives.

The rest of the teaching year was horribly difficult and odd. In the classroom I vacillated between the easy going, honest human being I wanted to be, and the businesslike teacher I knew I had to be if my class was to function. One day I'd sit laughing with my students, talking about a story one of them had written, ignoring their gum (against school rules) or "off-task" behavior. The next day I'd hand out detentions for "swearing," tardies, and of course any rude, sarcastic, or otherwise "inappropriate" statements. In my confused inconsistency, I imagine I was a more frightening authority figure than a military-style teacher would have been; sometimes it seemed that no sooner had students let down their guard and begun to relate to me as a real person, than I would snap nervously back into teacher mode and bitch at them for "disrupting."

I could not tell my students about my raging opinions with a clean professional conscience, but I couldn't *not* tell them with a clean moral conscience. A friend sent me a button that said "Free the Kids," and I wore it. Some days I was afraid that by writing I'd lose all my friends and even the trust of my students themselves. I finally told two students what I was up to, and of course had some guilty professional twangs about doing so. But I desperately hoped that I would finish, and that my book would find its way into my students' hands, in time for them to decide whether they wanted it to make a difference in their lives. June came; I hugged my students and colleagues goodbye amidst plenty of tears; I moved to Oregon and set up camp with my computer. Then, with a shiver and a grin, I hunkered down to write these pages for you.

How to use it

Notice that it's divided into six parts. The first tells why you should consider leaving school. The second tells how to get ready to do it. The third and fourth suggest ideas for how to do it once you're doing it. The fifth describes people who have already lived without school. The appendices are crammed full of addresses and publishers and Web sites, as well as my own "afterword" and other stuff. I put it all in the best order I could, but you can read it diagonally if you like.

Don't forget to share this book with your friends, or suggest that they find themselves a copy.

I recommend dozens of books, as well as other resources. Some of the books are out of print, but still available in libraries and used bookstores. I have put a great deal of energy and thought into the recommendations and I often hear from readers that my suggestions are very helpful. But please don't feel that you *need* a book to start a project (like making a zine, or starting a book group, or studying the ants in your kitchen). If you can't easily find the books I suggest, you'll generally do fine with others on the same subject. And obviously, this handbook, revised in 1998, can't tell about anything published afterward, nor do I know about everything that's already available, or have room here to list all the discoveries I've made since the first (1991) edition. (My mail-order book catalog, Genius Tribe, is a repository for my ongoing book recommendations.)

When I give prices for books or other items, they are 1997 or 1998 prices, in U.S. dollars. Like beanstalks, they will go up. If you order something without first checking with a supplier, ask them to bill you for any extra.

Most of the organizations mentioned in this book will send you free information if you ask for it. (Their addresses, phone numbers, and Web site URL's are listed in Appendix E.) Keep in mind that it costs them money to send stuff. Especially if it's a do-gooder organization, think about saving trees and money by checking their Web sites first. Or, if you've got extra cash, send a dollar along with your information request.

There is a lot of information in your hands. Don't feel obligated to follow up on all of it, or most of it. Don't let it overwhelm you. Don't feel you should read everything I recommend. Let it guide you to a few important things and let the rest go. The silences and spaces in your "education" are as necessary and beautiful as your activity.

On the other hand, this book does not tell everything that's possible. Don't be limited by my suggestions, just use them as beginning points. Someday I may revise this book again or write a different one, so I welcome your recommendations for resources, or news of your own activities, or any other responses.

One more thing. All of us rise or sink to other people's expectations of us. Our society seems not to believe in teenagers enough to expect much of them. This book may shock you, therefore, when it tells how to plan a trip around the world, or when it suggests you start a business or become seriously involved in some academic field you love. But you're no imbecile—I'm certain because at fifteen *I* wasn't an imbecile. I didn't *know* much, but if the right information and some freedom had come my way, I could have soared. I hope that this book can provide some of that "right information" for you, and that it also helps you find the freedom you need.

When I mention ages of particular teenagers, I mean their ages at the time that they wrote to me or to *Growing Without Schooling* magazine (hereafter referred to as *GWS*). Some of the sixteen-year-olds are now twenty-six.

Enjoy your flight... and tell me where you land. ❀

Part 1

Making the Decision

sweet land of liberty

 The most potent weapon in the hands of the oppressor is the mind of the oppressed.
—Steven Biko

Hოw strange and self-defeating that a supposedly free country should train its young for life in totalitarianism.

"No, David, wait until after class to use the bathroom."

"Unfortunately, your daughter would rather entertain the class than participate appropriately."

"Good morning, class. Please open your textbooks to page thirty. Thank you. John, you need to open your book to page thirty."

"Carter, if I have to ask you again to sit down, you'll be taking a trip to the office."

"Miguel, you are not in math. Please put it away. Remember, fifteen percent of your grade in my class comes from participation and attitude."

"Ladies! Gentlemen! Let's keep the noise down in the halls."

"I'd love to hear what you have to say, Monty, but you need to raise your hand first."

"Tonight you need to finish the exercises on page 193 and read the next section."

"Marisa, I need a written explanation as to why you didn't turn in your homework today."

"Laura, put away the book. If I catch you again it's a zero for the day, and that's not something you can afford."

What do you think of when you hear the word *freedom*? The end of slavery? The end of the Berlin wall? A prisoner tunneling his way out of solitary confinement in Chile with a spoon? An old woman escaping her broken body in death? Gorillas dancing in the jungle instead of sulking behind bars? When I hear the word *freedom*, I remember the sweetest sunlight pouring over my teenaged cheeks on the first sleeping-in mornings of summer vacations.

Do you go to school? Yes? Then...

You are not free.

The most overwhelming reality of school is CONTROL. School controls the way you spend your time (what is life made of if not time?), how you behave, what you read, and to a large extent what you think. In school you can't control your own life. Outside of school you can, at least to the extent that your parents trust you to. "Comparing me to those who are conventionally schooled," writes twelve-year-old unschooler Colin Roch, "Is like comparing the freedoms of a wild stallion to those of cattle in a feedlot."[1]

The ultimate goal of this book is for you to start associating the concept of freedom with *you*, and to start wondering why you and your friends don't have much of it, and for you to move out of the busy-prison into the meadows of life. There are lots of good reasons to quit school, but to my idealistic American mind, the pursuit of freedom encompasses most of them and outshines the others.

If you look at the history of "freedom," you notice that the most frightening thing about people who are not free is that they learn to take their bondage for granted, and to believe that this bondage is "normal" and natural. They may not like it, but few question it or imagine anything different. There was a time when many black slaves took a sort of pride—or talked as if they took pride—in how well-behaved and hard-working they were. There was a time when most women believed—or talked as if they believed—that they should obey and submit to their husbands. In fact, people within an oppressed group often internalize their oppression so much that they are crueler, and more judgmental, to their peers than the oppressors themselves are. In China, men made deformed female feet into sexual fetishes, but *women* tied the cords on their own daughters' feet.

Obviously, black and female people eventually caught sight of a greater vision for themselves, and change blazed through their minds, through laws, through public attitudes. All is not yet well, but the United States is now far kinder to people of color and mammary glands than it was a hundred years ago. What's more, these people are kinder to *themselves*. They dream bigger dreams, and flesh out grander lives, than picking cotton for the master or fixing a martini for the husband.

Right now, a lot of you are helping history to repeat itself; you don't believe you *should* be free. Of course you *want* to be free—in various ways, not just free of school. However, society gives you so many condescending, false, and harmful messages about yourselves that most of you wouldn't trust yourselves with freedom. It's all complicated by the fact that the people who infringe most dangerously and inescapably on your freedom are those who say they are helping you, those who are convinced you need their help: teachers, school counselors, perhaps your parents.

Why *should* you have freedom?
Why should anyone? To become human, to live fully. Insofar as you live what someone else dictates, you hardly live. Choice is a fundamental essence of life, and in the fullest life, each choice is deliberate and savored.

Another reason you should be free is obvious. You should learn to live responsibly and joyfully in a free country.

Recently, schoolpeople talk a lot about "experiential education." Educators have wisely realized that the best way to teach anything includes not only reading about a subject, but also practicing it. For example, my colleague Gary Oakley taught science by having students rehabilitate a polluted pond. Naturally, learning

---

[1] From *GWS* #78.

this way sinks in deeper than merely reading, hearing lectures, and discussing. It means participating—*being* a scientist or musician rather than watching from the outside.

What the educators apparently haven't realized yet is that experiential education is a double-edged sword. If you do something to learn it, then *what you do, you learn.* All the time you are in school, you learn through experience how to live in a dictatorship. In school you shut your notebook when the bell rings. You do not speak unless granted permission. You are guilty until proven innocent, and who will prove you innocent? You are told what to do, think, and say for six hours each day. If your teacher says sit up and pay attention, you had better stiffen your spine and try to get Bobby or Sally or the idea of Spring or the play you're writing off of your mind. The most constant and thorough thing students in school experience—and learn—is the antithesis of democracy.

When I was in sixth grade, I had the good fortune to learn that democracy in the "real world" is not a crime, at the same time that I learned (not for the first time) that democracy in schools *is* a crime. Two of my friends and I were disgusted by the state of our school lunches. After finding mold on the rolls one day and being generally fed up with the cardboard taste of things, we decided to take action. Stephanie and Stacey started a petition. Its purpose was a bit misspelled and unclear, but at the top it said something that meant, "Sign below if you are tired of revolting lunches, and put a check by your name if your roll was moldy on Tuesday." People signed the petition during lunch; we had three pages or so of sloppy signatures on wrinkly notebook paper.

Apparently some teachers got wind of what we were up to, and Miss Petersen (fake name) told Stephanie to give her the petition. After Miss Petersen looked at it through stern eyeglasses, she said she'd have to turn it over to the principal. Stephanie and I panicked. We held a secret meeting that afternoon in the hills and looked at each other with sick scared faces. We tried to convince ourselves that young criminals got off easily.

The next day Miss Petersen was moving a piano down the hall. Our brave friend Kelly walked by in his line on the way in from lunch. He saw the petition sitting on the piano, and he snatched it up. Miss Petersen didn't see him. He returned the petition to me. Go, team.

Stephanie and Stacey were summoned to the principal. He demanded to have the petition back, but since they didn't yet know about the Recovery, they said earnestly that Miss Petersen had it. He lectured them for their disrespect of authority, and said there was nothing wrong with the lunches, and that he didn't want to *ever* hear anything about petitions again, was that clear?

I took out my sky blue stationery with the mushrooms on it and wrote a letter to the governor. I apologized for not typing and for the wrinkliness and bad spelling of the petition. Then I explained why it was important that our lunches improve. I didn't say anything about the trouble we were in at school; I didn't want him to know how bad we were. I looked up his address in the phone book, guessed on the zip code, and sent it off. I was afraid he would report me to the principal, but I was ready to sacrifice myself for the cause.

The week after school was out, my father brought the mail in with a strange face. "Grace," he said, "Are you personally acquainted with Cecil Andrus?"

I tore the letter open. The governor said not to worry about my handwriting, that he would have responded sooner had I mailed the letter to his office instead of his house, and that he sympathized with my plight. He told me that school lunches weren't in his control, but he gave me the address of the people who could make a difference. Best—and most surprising—of all, he congratulated me on my "good citizenship" and encouraged me to keep on speaking up when something wasn't right in the world. During the next six years, the memory of that experience often helped me keep my hope and sanity while my friends and I were silenced, subtly and blatantly, again and again, by "authority."

Ah yes...

Authority.

Regardless of what the law or your teachers have to say about this, you are as human as anyone over the age of eighteen or twenty-one. Yet, "minors" are one of the most oppressed groups of people in the U.S., and certainly the most discriminated against legally.

It starts at home. Essentially, your parents can require you to do almost anything and forbid you to do almost anything. Fortunately, most parents try not to abuse this power. Yet, from a legal standpoint, the reason schools have so much tyrannical power over you is that they act *in loco parentis*—in place of the parent. As legal parental substitutes, they can search your locker or purse, tell you to be quiet, read your mail (notes), sometimes hit or "spank" you, speak rudely to you, and commit other atrocities—things I hope your parents would not do with a clean conscience, and things no sensible adult would do to another adult, for fear of losing a job or ending a friendship.

Many teenagers, of course, do clash with their parents to some extent. But most parents like and love their children enough to listen to their side, grant more freedom as they grow, back off when they realize they're overbearing, and generally be reasonable. The schools may do this with *some* "rebellious" students, but not usually, and not after a second or third "offense." Schools are too big, and the adults in them too overworked, to see "rebels" as people—instead, they'll get a permanent-ink "bad person" label and unreasonable treatment. Even in a small private school, authority is often unyielding and unfairly judgmental.

When I was substitute teaching in Oakland, California, one day they told me I could have a month-long job teaching choir and piano while the regular teacher had a baby. As it happened, I did have a fairly substantial musical background and could have handled at least that aspect of the job just fine. But the administrators showed no interest in my musical knowledge—all they wanted was someone who could maintain order for a month. When the principal introduced me to the choir class, one of the students raised his hand and asked, "Since she's not a music teacher, what are we supposed to do if she's not any good?"

The principal launched into a tirade about how it doesn't matter what you think of her teaching, you'll do exactly what she says and I don't want to hear about any problems from any of you; the state board of education decided she was good enough to be certified and that's all you need to know. Etc.

One of the worst things about this sort of arbitrary authority is it makes us lose our trust in natural authority—people who know what they're doing and could share a lot of wisdom with us. When they make you obey the cruel and unreasonable teacher, they steal your desire to learn from the kind and reasonable teacher. When they tell you to be sure to pick up after yourselves in the cafeteria, they steal your own natural sense of courtesy.

Many times, I have heard teachers resort defiantly to the proclamation that "The bottom line is, they need to do what we tell them because they're the kids and we're the adults." This concept that teenagers should obey simply because of their age no longer makes any sense to me. I can't figure out what it is based on, except adults' own egos. In this regard, school often seems like a circus arena full of authority-craving adults. Like trained animals, you are there to make them look good, to help them believe they are better than you.

But maybe you're not yet convinced. The sudden proclamation that you deserve to be free sounds too glib, too easy. Let's turn the question upside down:

Are there any good reasons you *shouldn't* have freedom?

Since schools supposedly exist to help you learn, the only legitimate answer they could offer is that you have to sacrifice freedom for the sake of learning. If learning and freedom were incompatible, having to choose would be tragic. But learning is *not* dependent upon school or upon slavery. If this doesn't strike you as obvious, I hope it will by the time you're finished reading Chapter 2.

A wise friend of mine, who grew up in Germany under Hitler and later did time in American prison camps, startled me with a different reason you shouldn't have freedom. First, he agreed that schools are the antithesis of freedom. Then he said, but how can you really appreciate the freedom that comes with adulthood in a democracy, if you never know what it's like to live without it? I thought a lot about what he said, but I ended up deciding that a twelve-year experiential lesson in bondage doesn't make freedom seem *precious*; it makes it seem *impossible*. It also misrepresents the nature of learning. After school, too many people continue to slap chains on themselves. Before school, few people are so self-hating. Maybe after we abolish compulsory schooling we can set up voluntary month-long camps where people sit at desks and obey, just so they realize how lucky they are not to live their lives that way, just so they promise themselves to always live in celebration of their freedom.

Maybe you believe you aren't ready for freedom?

On some level, no one ever is; it's not a matter of age. People of all ages make mistakes with their freedom—becoming involved with destructive friends, choosing college majors they're not deeply interested in, buying houses with rotten foundations, clearcutting forests, breaking good marriages for dumb reasons. People cause tremendous pain and disaster, and you will never be so wise or perfect that you don't do stupid things. Sure, teenagers make mistakes. So do adults, and it seems to me adults have a harder time admitting and fixing theirs. While you are young, perhaps you are more likely to break your arm falling off a horse, but you are less likely to cause an oil spill or start a useless war. The only alternative to making mistakes is for someone to make all your decisions for you, in which case you will make their mistakes instead of your own. Obviously, that's not a life of integrity. Might as well start living, rather than merely obeying, before the age of eighteen.

Part of my work in writing this book involved contacting all the unschooled teenagers I could find. I asked them, each, as part of a questionnaire, what they considered the greatest advantages of unschooling. Almost unanimously, they agreed: *freedom!* Here are some typical comments:

"You can spend your time and energy doing things you like."

"I don't have to raise my hand to speak."

"Not being forced to do certain uninteresting subjects. Not sitting around for six hours doing something I don't like."

"Having time to do what I want."

"[In school] you had to have *permission* to go to the bathroom!"

"I feel sorry for the kids who have to go to 'prison' for six to eight hours a day. I felt like we were the victims of a mass production enterprise."

"We are able to do so many things (go to the zoo, ride bikes, etc. etc.) while other kids are just sitting in classes and desks being bored." (One reason this unschooler's sane parents kept her out of school was they "didn't like the idea of kids staying inside on sunny days.")

"Time, Time, Time. I have my life back for my own use. I am no longer having to wait and wait and wait for everyone else. I can concentrate on what I want to learn. I can work on my computer as long as I like. Or if I want to spend a lot of time diagramming sentences one day and no time again for two days, it's all right. Also we can travel and in general control our own lives! It is great!"

"I'm *free!*"

John Taylor Gatto, the 1991 New York State Teacher of the Year, puts it thus: "It is absurd and anti-life to move from cell to cell to the sound of a gong for every day of your natural youth in an institution that allows you no privacy and even follows you to the sanctuary of your home demanding that you do its 'homework.'"[1]

And in *GWS* #65, Lisa Asher writes about a day spent visiting her old high school:

> Despite the freedom that I have now, I feel limited by my past. I spent a total of 86 months in public schools, attending for at least part of every grade but seventh. There are still two years before I would graduate, but I don't plan to go back. I am angry with society for the time they made me waste. I wish I could have the time back again, and learn the way I feel I should have.
>
> Near the end of the day, the hallways empty as the kids leave early to go to the beach. They have to come back tomorrow, and I don't. I don't have to get up at five to catch a bus at quarter to seven. I don't have to stay up 'til one studying for a test on something I don't care about, don't need, and am going to forget the minute the bell rings. I will not have to struggle with locks that the school is allowed to open anyway, fight my way through throngs of kids who once spent hours learning how to walk quietly in line, eat a sixty-cent lunch not fit to feed to pets, let alone growing teenagers and children. I won't be fighting for space in a tiny mirror mounted on a graffiti-plastered wall in the girls' room, where the door has been taken off the hinges to expose any tell-tale cigarettes. I won't be sleeping through classes where I am supposed to be learning math, doodling through

---

[1] John Taylor Gatto, *Dumbing Us Down.*

classes where I am supposed to be learning history, or daydreaming through classes where I am supposed to be learning French.

I'll be sitting at home reading a book. Since I am not in school, perhaps I will learn something. ☀

2

school
is not for
learning

We are shut up in schools and college recitation rooms for ten or fifteen years, and come out at last with a bellyful of words and do not know a thing.
> —Ralph Waldo Emerson

My schooling not only failed to teach me what it professed to be teaching, but prevented me from being educated to an extent which infuriates me when I think of all I might have learned at home by myself.
> —George Bernard Shaw

Schools and schooling are increasingly irrelevant to the great enterprises of the planet. No one believes anymore that scientists are trained in science classes or politicians in civics classes or poets in English classes. The truth is that schools don't really teach anything except how to obey orders.
> —John Taylor Gatto

Men are born ignorant, not stupid; they are made stupid by education.
> —Bertrand Russell

I very strongly believe that no homeschooler, or anyone else for that matter, has a prejudice against learning something, until someone makes them learn it.
> —unschooler Anne Brosnan

An average second grader is a person slightly smarter than an average third grader, because they've had a year less of school.   —an eighth grade student

THE CONSENSUS IS overwhelming. After dozens of nearly identical, predictable conversations with friends and acquaintances, I'm no longer certain this chapter is necessary.

"Do you think you learned a lot in school?" I'd ask.

"Oh no, of course not," came the typical reply, "I mean, I memorized a lot of facts for tests, but I don't remember any of it except a few things I was really interested in."

The unschooled teenagers who responded to my questionnaire offered similar comments. "The one thing I didn't do in school," wrote Jason Lescalleet, fourteen, "was learn."

Becky Cauthen, fourteen, remembers school: "I had to sit and wait for others to complete their work."

Patrick Meehan, fourteen, said, "Many teachers seem to dislike students who ask questions."

Benjamin Israel Billings, sixteen, said, "I have never had a liking for regimented things and school is so strict that I found more pressure to get good grades (cheating, copying and lucky guessing) than to learn my subjects."

Indeed, many of these teenagers had quit school because of "lack of learning" or intellectual boredom.

Once out of school, things improved. I asked unschooled teens how they would rate their "academic" knowledge and skills in comparison to that of their schooled peers. Most of them felt like Kevin Sellstrom, fourteen, who said, "Far superior. More knowledgeable in most subjects including common sense."

Many teenagers angrily complained that school had wasted their time. Without it, they said, "you learn more in less time." Jason Lescalleet says that out of school "I get to learn instead of sitting with my head down."

This common sense we all seem to share—people don't need school to learn—is proved in a more academic and official way by the work of Dr. Brian Ray's *Home School Researcher*. Ray and other researchers have shown that homeschoolers' academic test scores are consistently higher than school students'.[1]

Why don't people learn in school?

The most basic and overwhelming reason shoots us right back into the last chapter. Our brains and spirits are the freest things in the universe. Our bodies can live in chains, but our intellects cannot. It's that simple. The mind *will* be free, or it will be dead. It can be numbed, quieted, and restrained so that it memorizes names of Portuguese explorers and plods through grades one to twelve. If it is fiercely alive and teamed up with a forgiving spirit, it may find a way to be free even in school, and stay awake that way. But these strategies are defenses, not full-fledged learning. Albert Einstein, as compassionate and insightful as he was brilliant, said:

> It is, in fact, nothing short of a miracle that the modern methods of instruction have not yet entirely strangled the holy curiosity of inquiry; for this delicate little plant, aside from stimulation, stands mainly in need of freedom; without this it goes to wrack and ruin without fail. It is a very grave mistake to think that the enjoyment of seeing and searching can be promoted by means of coercion and a sense of duty.

There are other reasons school prevents learning too—fear of "bad" grades, lack of faith in one's abilities (usually due to previous unpleasant experiences with grades—including A minuses), an occasional uninformed teacher, illogical or inherently dull teaching methods and books, lack of individual attention, oxygen-starved classrooms.

These problems are the ones the educators can see. They exhaust themselves seeking solutions—hiring the brightest teachers they can get, searching the ends of the earth for easier ways to learn spelling, providing counseling services, buying textbooks with technicolor photographs, working hard on "anticipatory sets" (the

---

[1] Information from National Home Education Research Institute; especially see their 1986 publication *A comparison of home schooling and conventional schooling: With a focus on learner outcomes.*

beginning part of lessons which are supposed to "grab students' attention"). Most of these educators—especially when they are teachers rather than superintendents of school boards—do some good. If lots of people continue to go to school, I hope that the idealistic educators continue their efforts. These efforts make school more pleasant, the same way that clean sheets and warm blankets make a prison more pleasant than do bare scratchy mattresses with thin covers.

Their efforts cannot, however, make you free. Even if they encourage you to write research papers on topics that interest you, even if they reduce the amount of homework they assign, they cannot encourage you to joyfully follow your own intellectual mysteries, except in your spare time after your homework. To do so would be to completely undermine the basic structure of the schools.

Because they can never make you free, schools can never allow you to learn fully.

Love of learning

If you had always been free to learn, you would follow your natural tendency to find out as fully as possible about the things that interest you, cars or stars. We are all born with what they call "love of learning," but it dives off into an elusive void when we go to school.

After all, school does not help you focus on what you love, because it insists that you devote equal time to six or so "subjects." While interviewing an unschooled actress for *GWS* #73, editor Susannah Sheffer made an astute observation: "It's funny that people think kids should be well-rounded but don't seem to have the same expectations of adults. Adults seem to realize you can't do everything." In *Walden*, Thoreau laments, "Our lives are frittered away by detail," and admonishes, "Simplicity, simplicity, simplicity! I say, let your affairs be as two or three, and not a hundred or a thousand."

Of course, quitting school doesn't guarantee that you are going to learn more in *every* subject than you did in school. If you hate math in school, and decide to continue studying it outside of school, it's possible that you won't enjoy it any more or learn it much better, although being able to work without ridicule at your own speed will help. You *will* see a dramatically wonderful change in the way you learn about the things that interest you. What's more, you will find out that you are interested in things that haven't yet caught your attention, and that you can love at least some of the things which repulsed you in school.

Beyond the love and pursuit of something specific, there's another quality you might also call love of learning. It's simple curiosity, which kills more tired assumptions than cats. Some people move around with their ears and eyes perked open like raccoons, ready to find out something new and like it. Do everything you can to cultivate this characteristic; it will enliven your life immeasurably.

However, curiosity is another stubborn quality that thrives on freedom; therefore, school squishes it. Curiosity is an active habit—it needs the freedom to explore and move around and get your hands into lots of pots. It needs the freedom to watch TV with the remote control and flip through the channels at will. It needs the freedom to thumb through *Science News* and stop only where you want to. It needs the freedom to browse through your library's whole shelf of poetry. It needs the freedom to visit a museum solo, spending an hour with the birds of prey exhibit and walking right past the collection of seventeenth century embroideries, or vice versa.

Curiosity puts itself on hold when it isn't allowed to move at its own pace. I am thinking of the week-long field trip our middle school took to Washington, D.C., and of how my own curiosity took a nap during most of our "guided tours," even at the "fun" places like Williamsburg and Jamestown, and how I raced around excitedly when we had an unleashed day at the Smithsonian.

On the up side, the ironic truth is that everyone loves to learn—or at least did as a baby, and can get to be that way again. As John Holt points out, "Children do not need to be made to learn about the world, or shown how. They want to, and they know how." In fact, it could all add up to a great opening line the night you decide to break the news to your parents: "Mom, Dad, I'd really like to quit school because I'd rather learn."

Report Cards vs. Freedom

Schools do have a few K-Mart quality substitutes for freedom. They know that if you dry up people's love for learning, you will certainly dry up their learning itself, unless you come through with a handy replacement: Pressure. Threats. Bribes. Tests. A's, B's, C's, D's, and F's. Yes, indeed, school does have one way to make you learn that you might *not* easily duplicate in a free life. Without an exam on Friday, maybe you wouldn't learn how to solve differential equations. Without a twenty-five dollar prize from Mommy, maybe you wouldn't memorize the periodic table in order to get an A in chemistry. Maybe the pressure of grades and all the expectant hoopla surrounding them *do* help you to learn more.

Temporarily.

The day after the test, or the week after school's out, will you even take time to kiss your fact collection goodbye as it floats off on the breeze? In the long run, pressure is an ineffective substitute for curiosity and freedom to pursue those things you love, because people only remember and think about things they use or care about.

A lot of teachers believe learning depends on grades, because they are only used to seeing education take place in the forced environment of school. Physicist Frank Oppenheimer had a clearer head, putting massive energy into non-school learning environments (for example, he started the Exploratorium, an innovative museum in San Francisco). About learning without grades, he said, "People built fires to keep warm long before Galileo invented the thermometer."[1]

Furthermore, the emphasis schools put on grades *prevents* healthy learning, even if it coaxes you into quickie learning.

Report Cards vs. Learning

Bad grades start a vicious circle. They make you feel like a failure. A sense of failure cripples you and *prevents* you from succeeding. Therefore, you continue to get bad grades and continue to be stifled. Of course, bad grades are relative—in many families B's are bad grades, especially if the First Born Son did better or Uncle Harold went to Yale. Feeling like a failure is a self-fulfilling prophecy, which is why

---

[1] Hilde S. Hein, *The Exploratorium: The Museum as Laboratory.*

most high-school dropouts make statistics that the schoolpeople love to quote. Think about it. Would you continue to enjoy (and improve at) skateboarding or hiking if someone scrutinized your every move, reported to your parents, and acted as if you'd never succeed in life if you didn't finesse your double kick flip before Friday, or add ten pounds to your backpack and reach the pass by noon?

Obviously, we all need both privacy and respect to enjoy (learn) any activity. By privacy, I don't mean solitude. I mean freedom from people poking their noses into your business or "progress."

People assume that grades tell how intelligent you are, but of course they don't. They mostly reflect how well you cooperated by doing what your teachers said. They also reflect whether your teachers like you. Grades don't mean you can't read, write, or think. They don't show whether you can find out how to do something you believe in and then follow through and do it. They don't show the most fundamental aspect of intelligence—whether you learn from your experiences and "mistakes." They don't show whether you live with courage, compassion, curiosity, or common sense. Even in an objective scientific sense, grades and test scores are not accurate measurements of your intelligence. (A very interesting book on the subject of intelligence measurement is *The Mismeasure of Man*, by Stephen Jay Gould.)

The world and its complex terrible wonderful webs of civilization are far bigger and older than our nineteenth-century factory-style compulsory schooling system. There is room for all kinds of people—those who love books, and those who'd rather build things and take them apart all day, not just for an hour in woodshop or autoshop. There's room for those who would rather wander dreaming on a glacier, and perhaps awaken the rest of us with some truthful words in the tradition of Thoreau, Ed Abbey, Annie Dillard. There's room for those who want to make lasagna and French bread and apple pie all day. None of these callings are better or worse than others. None mean failure as a human being, but they may likely cause "failure" in a dull system that you never asked to be a part of in the first place.

Furthermore, bad grades and other consequences of not doing your "work" punish you for what you *do* do (making friends, reading extracurricular novels) as much as for what you don't do. Tell me why, if you want to spend two days following badger tracks, you should be penalized for your choice with "zeroes" in five or six gradebooks and a truancy to boot.

Good grades are often equally dangerous. They encourage you to forsake everything worthwhile that you might love, just to keep getting them. When schoolpeople give you good grades, you give them your unquestioning loyalty in return. It makes me think of the Algonkian Indians who gave Manhattan Island to the Dutch in exchange for six dollars' worth of trinkets. We are not talking here about fair bargains; we are talking about manipulation and colossal rip-off.

Good grades, moreover, are addictive. You start to depend on them for your sense of self-worth, and then it becomes nearly impossible to do anything that will jeopardize them. When you have good grades, you have something to lose, and so you stop taking risks. The best things in life come from taking risks. My little sister, who is more intelligent than I am, always got bad grades. She also has an easier time being honest and direct with people than I do. I think these two bits of data are closely connected. The system never gave her any gold stars, so she didn't feel obligated to give it any soft false silent agreement in return. (On the other hand, she ended up with plenty of unnecessary failure-complex to work through.)

Finally, grades confuse the meaning of education. Patrick Meehan, fourteen-year-old unschooler, wrote me, "Giving grades puts the wrong focus on learning. It points a student toward competition and learning for the wrong reasons: to make grades rather than to become educated."

More ways that schools prevent people from learning

 Schools require passivity. When I taught language arts and history, I learned far more about them than I ever had in school and—in some ways—even in college. That's because teaching is an active role: seeking out and selecting readings, designing assignments, evaluating others' work. Sitting and doing those assignments and receiving those grades is the bottom of the learning ladder.

Schools cram you too full too fast. I don't mean they challenge you. I mean they throw too much busywork in your face. Being in school is like being incredibly hungry and sitting at Burger King eating too much, too fast to be satisfied, and then puking it up. Good learning, like good eating, is not only mental and physical, but also spiritual. Generally, you can satisfy the craving only in calm. If you don't have sufficient time or peace to digest knowledge, it only gives you a headache.

Schoolpeople care more about appearances than about learning. Just before a field trip, an administrator I worked with talked to students about "expectations." "We just want you to look nice," she said, "that's the most important thing." I don't think she heard herself, or quite meant to say that, but I couldn't forget it—as it says in the Bible, the mouth speaks what the heart is full of. In my own classroom, I forever harped on the way students sat. It didn't matter how well they could concentrate curled up on the couch; I was petrified that another adult would walk in and decide I was Incompetent. So most days students sat with their feet flat on the floor, stiff-spined, uncomfortable and trying to learn anyway.

School isn't challenging enough if you're academically inclined. It's not merely that school is too easy; you are not necessarily a straight-A student and in fact may feel overwhelmed by piles of homework. But so much of it is busywork with no connection to the molten cores of physics, mythology, philosophy. It also doesn't help that most of your fellow students would rather *not* be reading Milton.

Schools present learning backwards, emphasizing answers instead of questions. Answers are dead ends, even when they're "correct." Questions open the galaxies. "It is better to know some of the questions than all of the answers," said James Thurber. In *Organic Gardening*, October 1982, Robert Rodale wrote:

> I've been out of school for over thirty years, yet no matter how I manage to arrange my life, I still keep learning. In fact, I seem to learn faster the further in time I get from my school experience . . .
>
> When you are in school, you are asked the questions, and are expected to be able to find the answers. Presumably, when you are sufficiently filled up with correct answers, you are educated, and then released.
>
> I now believe, though, that real learning occurs when you become able to ask important questions. Then you are on the doorstep of wisdom, because by asking

important questions you project your mind into the exploration of new territory. In my experience, very few people have learned how important is the asking of good questions, and even fewer have made a habit of asking them. Even in my own case, I had to wait until I'd almost totally forgotten the experience of schooling to be able to switch my mind into the asking as well as the answering mode.

School asks you to get stressed out attaining mediocrity in six or so subjects rather than be amazing at one or two you love. Some schools and educators *believe* in cultivating students' uniquenesses, but without major structural changes, they can't. As long as focusing on algebra means you get a C in psychology, or as long as you get lectured for falling asleep in history on mornings after late gymnastics meets, you are being pushed away from excellence toward anxious shoddiness.

Schools are overly obsessed with and manipulative of the learning process. Take lesson plans, for instance. A proper lesson plan is supposed to include an "anticipatory set" (attention getter), a purpose statement, a diagnostic check (a few questions to see how many people already know how to organize a five-paragraph essay, or whatever), "input" (lecture, filmstrip, etc.), monitoring ("Johnny, now that I've explained how to organize a five-paragraph essay, please remind the class what your first paragraph should accomplish"), modeling (reading the class a five-paragrapher that got an A), guided practice (everyone begins essaying while you stroll around and answer questions), and independent practice (they finish the essay that night instead of watching the sparrows on the windowsill).

This kind of planning reflects some sense and logic, I admit. But two danger signals zap my little brain. First, all this strategy is just a mild substitute for Pressure. It's not necessary to manipulate someone if they already want to do or learn what you want them to do or learn. In other words, all this scientific strategy is only necessary because education professors know how unpleasant it is to sit in school all day. The will to freedom rears its stubborn head again. Therefore, they try to mix your head around a little to make it work.

Second, messing with your mind this way is harmful and foolish the same way that it is harmful and foolish to try to "manage" nature. After centuries of idiocy, people are finally learning to respect the complexity and self-regulation of nature. No longer does America assume that we can help deer by killing off all the wolves, or help forests by putting out all of their fires. We are beginning to acquire a bit of necessary humility, beginning to see that when we interfere, we usually ruin.

We need to develop a similar respect for the natural processes of human minds. The most difficult thing most people ever learn to do is talk. Yet, everyone learns it on their own, without a teacher or a briber or a threatener or props or games. In families where adults read to children and read in front of children, leave all kinds of books around for children to look at, and answer their children's questions about reading, people learn to read with the same pleasure and confidence that accompanies their acquisition of speech. In general, people learn and grow as long as they are not prevented from doing so.

School won't answer the door when real chances to learn come knocking. There's nothing wrong with planning and setting goals—they help us to accomplish big things like writing books or pulling off a bike trip across Turkey. But life is unexpected. Sometimes it offers us something more glorious than what we'd planned, and we lose if we're not ready to let go of our agenda. Christians call it surrendering to the will of God. Eastern mystics call it letting go of ego, floating in the flow. Whatever you call it, school has little room for it.

For example: in Washington, D.C., our self-imposed schedule demanded that we visit the Capitol for a predetermined length of time and then proceed directly to the next attraction. This schedule left no time for what might happen on the way into the Capitol. What did happen was that on the steps, five students and two teachers stopped to talk to a Vietnam vet fasting for U.S. reconciliation with Vietnam. He'd swallowed nothing but juice for seventy days. We listened to him with awe. At one point he asked, "Do you know what constitutional amendment guarantees me the right to sit here and talk about this?" Young, who always had the answers to all the questions, said, "The first!"

"Very good," pronounced another teacher, who at that moment had arrived on the scene. We all jumped. What did "very good" have to do with anything? She continued: "And which amendment prohibited slavery?" "The thirteenth," answered Young. "Exactly! And with that, let's be on our way," suggested our chaperone brightly. The rest of us looked at each other in vague incredulity; the disruption of learning was more awkwardly obvious than usual. Then we trudged up the steps behind her.

(By the way, this event also makes a perfect example of the way teachers and administrators are not allowed to be themselves in school, being required instead to fulfill ridiculous authoritarian roles. The woman who disrupted our fascination was as curious and human as any of the rest of us, but at the moment she felt a particularly strong responsibility to keep us on schedule. Later she told me she wished she could have encouraged a longer conversation.

I understood her position exactly, thinking of all the times I'd told students to come away from the window and sit at their tables, knowing whatever they saw or dreamed out the window was more important than writing a short story they didn't want to write.)

In general, school screens us off from reality—no matter how we define reality. Is reality in books, in the intellect? School censors more than it reveals. Does reality lurk in raw adventure? In religion? In culture? In friendship and community? In work? School just gets in the way.

Not only does your actual time in school block out learning, but it also prevents you from learning outside of school. It drains your time and energy. After you write your descriptive essay and review your Spanish verbs and it's time for bed, how are you supposed to think or write the poem you were imagining in history? How are you supposed to find energy to want to go outside and look at the newly sprung buds on the cottonwood tree?

School wouldn't be nearly so oppressive if it didn't demand center stage in your life. More times than I can count, I've heard adults tell teenagers, with appalling arrogance, that if they don't start getting their homework in on time, they'll have to quit drama, or chorale, or hockey, or their job, or sleeping over at friends' houses, or whatever it is that they love. Imagine a concert pianist getting ready for a performance. As she throws on her coat, her husband blocks the doorway. "Oh, honey," he says, "I'm afraid I can't let you go. You haven't prepared next week's menus, and you've left the music room in a mess. Until you get your priorities straight, you'll just have to stay at home."

Finally, schools play a nasty trick on all of us. They make "learning" so unpleasant and frightening that they scare many people away from countless pleasures: evenings browsing in libraries, taking an edible plants walk at the nature center, maybe even working trigonometry problems for the hard beauty and challenge of it. Luckily (and ironically), many things we learn from are not *called* "learning experiences" by schools, so we don't attach that schoolish learning stigma to everything. But by calling school "learning," schools make learning sound like an excruciatingly boring way to waste a nice afternoon. That's low.

Well, perhaps you I hear you say, *Indeed I do not learn much in school, but I do learn a little. If I quit, I won't learn anything.*

Forgive my rudeness, but that's upside-down-thinking. As John Holt said, if it's the medicine that makes you sick, more medicine will just make you sicker. And if you quit taking it, you'll get well.

You wouldn't suggest that you can't learn without school, if school hadn't torn your faith in yourself in the first place. Before you went to school, you taught yourself to speak. After you leave school, you will teach yourself how to live on your own and how to find out answers to questions that interest you. Even now, you learn on your own, every time you do *anything* of your own free will—kicking a soccer ball, falling in love, playing on computers, riding horses, reading books, thinking, disobeying rules.

In school, too, you already teach yourself; you just do it in the company of people who take the credit for your progress. I talk a lot with my brother Ned about education. He got marvelous grades in high school, won a city-wide contest sponsored by Hewlett-Packard, and went on to graduate from Caltech with a degree in electrical engineering. He learned in school, he says, because of the reading he did and the questions he thought about. Teachers had little to do with it. If the laboratory equipment and other resources in high school had been high quality, it could have helped immensely—but it wasn't, so it couldn't. He was in school, but in school he taught himself. And he learned more at home, on his own—building a computer, taking things apart, messing around.

Yes, when your teacher talks he shares his knowledge, which may be high quality fascinating knowledge or low quality dull knowledge. But your teacher cannot bridge the gap between what you know and what you want to know. For his words to "educate" you, you must welcome them, think about them, find somewhere in your mind to organize them, and remember them. Your learning is your job, not your teachers' job. And all you need to start with is desire. You *don't* need a schoolteacher to get knowledge—you can get it from looking at the world, from watching films, from conversations, from reading, from asking questions, from experience. As John Holt says in *GWS* #40, "The most important thing any teacher has to learn, not to be learned in any school of education I ever heard of, can be expressed in seven words: *Learning is not the product of teaching.* Learning is the product of the activity of learners."

In fact, in today's information-laden world, anyone who has acquired basic skills in reading, writing, asking questions (researching) and math computation can learn nearly anything they want to, on their own. Books, libraries, generous and knowledgeable people, the Internet, and other resources make this possible. Young or old, anyone can in fact become an expert in a field they love, if they are not restrained and occupied by the petty nonsense of school or meaningless work. Part of learning is often contacting and receiving help from others, but learning does not require a boss, a rigid schedule, a schoolroom, or most of the other things schools provide. Nor does it require a whip. Until school destroys the joy and naturalness of learning, young children revel wide-eyed in the intricacies of their world, learning to talk without teachers, asking questions, growing. In her book *Wishcraft*, Barbara Sher says:

> All the people we call "geniuses" are men and women who somehow escaped having to put that curious, wondering child in themselves to sleep. Instead, they devoted their lives to equipping that child with the tools and skills it needed to do its playing on an adult level. Albert Einstein was playing, you know. He was able to make great discoveries precisely because he kept alive the originality and delight of a small child exploring its universe for the first time.

Well, but what about all the things school has to make me learn?

What about them? The good things schools have are equipment, your friends, and teachers. The bad things they have are schedules, grades, compulsory attendance, authority, dull textbooks, busywork, sterile atmospheres, too much homework, your enemies, and teachers. You do not need to go to school to have teachers (or helpers, tutors, mentors) or equipment. If you want school teachers and equipment without school, maybe you can swing it. See Chapter 19.

But what about all the mysterious techniques and scientific approaches they use to make me learn? Don't teachers know a lot more than I do about learning?

Hell no. Most teachers know about classroom management—how to threaten, manipulate, or cajole a class into quietly doing its work. Many can explain things clearly. Some even overflow with true enthusiasm for their subject, so that a few students are infected with a love of that same subject. All this, however, is a sorry substitute for the recognition that you have a mind of your own and are capable of using it. Teachers would be infinitely more helpful if they knew a lot and cheerfully answered questions, dispensed wisdom, and pointed out resources—but only when you asked them to.

As for all those mysterious techniques, relax. Nothing happens in school that can't happen elsewhere, and in fact most of what happens there is nothing but a shadow of real world learning. After all, nothing complicated takes place in school. In order to "learn," you are made to read, write and receive criticism on written work, do other exercises and have them corrected, listen to a teacher talk, discuss ideas or information with teachers or with classmates under teacher supervision, conduct laboratory experiments, receive individual attention, and "do" things, fashionably called "experiential education." Almost all of these school things you can do on your own. Substitute "wise adult" for "teacher," and you don't need school for *any* of them. Let's have a quick, demystifying, analytical look at these schoolish methods, one by one.

Reading

Which has more books, a school or a library?

Which has better books, a school or a library?

Where are you made to read deadly textbooks?

a) the library, b) school, c) while exploring a bog

Where can you read at your own pace, for your own pleasure, without being tested and tricked and otherwise disrupted?

a) the library, b) school, c) a bog, d) a and c

Enough said.

Writing

Perhaps you've always bought your pens and pencils from a machine at school. I'm here today to tell you that they can also be found at the corner drugstore. Paper too. Yes, it's true. And what more do you need to write without school?

In school, you write five-paragraph persuasive essays (although who ever heard of a five-paragraph persuasive essay showing its face in *Harper's* or *The Atlantic?*) and short stories and essay test answers and poems and whatever else your teachers demand of you. Out of school, you can do all of the above and whatever else you demand of yourself.

Don't you need a writing teacher to write? Well, no, probably not. If you read frequently and you have something to say, most of the logistics will take care of themselves. If you *don't* have something to say, you don't need to write. (I'm not being sarcastic. Why chatter on paper just to chatter on paper?) The reason many teenagers struggle violently with writing is that like most people, they are not burning with desire to communicate something particular in writing on a weekly basis.

Even if they are burning with that desire from time to time, they know that their five-paragraph essay is destined for their teacher's and maybe classmates' eyes only. When you're communicating with just twenty people, it often makes more sense to simply talk.

Sure, you may be confused about grammatical rules or mechanics. Books and occasional people can clear it all up for you. You don't need six years of "English" to make sense on paper.

On the other hand, if you are a serious future novelist or journalist, you might want to enroll in a writing workshop or course—but you will find the quality and seriousness you need in a college or independent course, not in school.

Doing exercises and having them corrected

Many courses—especially math—consist mainly of working problems and having them checked. Sometimes—especially in math—working these problems is truly necessary for absorbing course material. In others, exercises are busywork—assigned arbitrarily so you don't feel you're "getting away" without doing anything.

When exercises seem valuable to you, take heart. Doing algebra problems in bed at ten A.M. produces exactly the same effect as doing them at ten A.M. in a classroom. Decent math textbooks (which is to say, Saxon books and a few others) are clearly written. Most have answers in the back. When they don't, you can usually find a separate answer key.

Listening to Your Teacher Talk

When you have a knowledgeable and/or wise and/or funny teacher, listening to her weave stories and lectures can be delightful. Assuming, that is, that she feels "allowed" by other schoolpeople to be herself and say what she truly knows and thinks. Unfortunately, this is seldom so, since most important schoolpeople always worry about offending any of the parents who might re-elect them, and therefore strive to keep their teachers as mousy and un-opinionated as possible.

This is one of the fundamental badnesses of schools (and politics): almost everyone lives in fear of their superiors because their superiors live in fear of their constituents (voters, i.e. parents). Therefore, all the interesting ideas get censored:

Your teacher can't say, "Wait a minute. What's fueling this so-called war on drugs?" because Johnny's mother will call the principal outraged in her assumption that a teacher (of all people) is "encouraging drug use," and the principal will worry that the superintendent will hear about it, and ask the teacher to please not talk about drugs in a deviant way. Your teacher probably can't say, at least not with force and conviction, that the United States is far from perfect or that the government still cheats Native Americans, or that children have no rights in this country or that Thoreau, Martin Luther King Jr., Ghandi, and many other heroes all believed in and acted on one's duty to peacefully break unjust laws. Ridiculous as it seems, schoolpeople would rather keep your head and mouth empty and uncontroversial than risk their jobs by giving teachers free rein. "No one is fired for hiding the truth from children," writes John Holt, "But many are fired for telling the truth." Jessica Vitkus puts her finger on a lot of it when she describes one of her days as a substitute teacher:

> We're talking about the upcoming marriage of Romeo and Juliet. And this girl who keeps pulling fuzz balls off her sweater points out that it's kind of gross that a fourteen-year-old girl would be getting married. "Had you even kissed a boy when you were fourteen?" she asks me. Obviously, part of me would really love to take off my shoes and sit on the floor and tell the class how my first kiss (I was in eighth grade) was nothing like Juliet's and that I don't think people fall in love at first sight. Those are some of the things I think about when I read. But they're the kind of thoughts I save for my friends. And in the classroom, I can't act like a friend because it's hard (and not too effective) to tell a friend to be quiet or that she may not go to her locker. Harsh as it may sound, teachers and students are not equals, and I have to maintain a certain distance. This also means that I can't one hundred percent act like myself—which to me is the hardest thing about teaching. I smile at the girl to let her know that I heard her question, but I don't answer it. She gets the hint.[1]

When your teacher is *not* so knowledgeable, wise, funny—or confident that she can keep both her job and her honesty—listening to her lecture lag along is worse than watching *A Nightmare on Elm Street* for the ninth time.

And if you are especially on top of things, I bet you have figured out by now that people lecture in other places besides Your High School History Room.

If you like, go listen to one or ninety talks outside of school. There are lectures at local colleges and universities, libraries, museums, etc., and courses to be audited at colleges and universities. (Most college professors are *expected* to be controversial or at least original.)

However, a hunch tells me that although most people are moved by an occasional dynamic or profound speaker, few want to spend lots of hours every day on their butts soaking in someone else's words. It's not only too passive for most of

---

[1] Jessica Vitkus, "Hello, I'm Your Substitute Teacher," *Sassy* magazine, March 1991, p. 37.

us—more passive than reading—but also too slow.

Class discussion

Exploring ideas with people interested in similar subjects is undoubtedly one of life's finest wines, as well as a stimulating way to "learn," and thus please all the adults who need you to do that in ways they understand. Especially when you want to clarify, resolve, or broaden your opinions, you must talk. Many of the best books, institutions, organizations, etc., began in, or fed on, talk. For example, J.R.R. Tolkien and C.S. Lewis met regularly to talk about their work in a small writers' group they called The Inklings.

Unfortunately, the difference between most "classroom discussions" and real, honest talk is equivalent to the difference between stale Wonder Bread and the rich warmth, sweetness, and complexity of homemade cinnamon rolls.

Imagine instead: you and your friends in front of a fire, feet on the sofa, planning how to get CFC-produced polystyrene foam banned in your city. Inventing an ideal society. Improvising haiku on the spot. Debating why Hamlet did what he did. Deciding what kind of research to carry out with your shared science lab. Considering the pros and cons of gun control. Why settle for a dismal school version of the real thing?

Experience

Like many cumbersome terms that issue from schoolpeople's jaws, "experiential education" is an inflated, fancy term referring to a simple concept: learning by doing. School examples are learning government by experimenting with student governments and courts, or learning about literature partly by giving readings of students' own sonnets. The school where I taught deservedly attracts many students because of its experiential emphasis, consisting mainly of purposeful travel. Obviously, learning Spanish by staying with a family in Madrid beats learning Spanish by merely drilling in a classroom. Learning architectural design by sketching adobe buildings throughout the southwest beats learning architectural design by merely reading textbooks.

The Educators are on to something here. They figured out that life and the world are exciting, so they would try to squeeze a little more of it in between desks, chairs, walls, schedules, limited resources and transportation, and standardized tests. Lucky for you, if you quit school, you are automatically swimming in that whole big world that you call living and they call "experiential education."

By the way. An absurdity in the concept of experiential education is that "doing" has to be organized in some particular scientific-schoolish way in order for "learning" to take place. Worse, teaching this way implies that the experience would be unimportant if it were not engineered to generate "education" also. As you and I know, there would be little meaning in building and programming a computer solely to learn about electronics or math. Rather, knowledge about these subjects would happen naturally as a by-product of all the fun you were having if you just happened to want to build and program a computer. But the Educators haven't yet got their priorities straight. They hang on to an awful habit of thinking that school is reality and the universe only exists to make school "more educational." Instead, of course, the big wet world is reality and school should serve only to help us live better lives in that reality, not to block it off.

Individual attention

If you attend a small school, or have enrolled in small classes, you may also be lucky enough to receive frequent individual attention from teachers. Everyone has a different learning style, and many people prefer to learn directly from people rather than from books. "When I want to learn something," says my friend Lesly, "I don't like to go read a book; I want someone to show me how to do it." Private conversations, whether they focus on your next screenplay, on why you messed up on half the equations on yesterday's algebra, or on how to sew a straighter seam, can be truly helpful.

One of the things that kept me going when I taught school was my class schedule, in which I met daily with most of my 26 students to discuss their writing. Though these conferences rarely strayed from the "point," they also enabled me to know each student well, making the whole thing a lot more human and a lot more fun. In fact, individual instruction is probably the only valuable instruction most of us get in school.

If you attend a typical public school, as I did, your teachers can only fantasize about having personal contact with all of their students. But if you're accustomed to it and you like it, you will like a full-blown relationship with a mentor better. And if there are particular teachers you especially like, you can likely continue those relationships, either in an informal way or perhaps by hiring them as weekly tutors. Anyway, when adults aren't giving you grades, it's much easier to learn from them and enjoy their company without guilt or anxiety.

End of analysis. School did not invent these activities and does not own them; they can be found outside of school in much fresher, juicier form. Schools have no monopoly on learning, or even on "school" methods of learning.

In the end, the secret to learning is so simple: forget about it. Think only about whatever you love. Follow it, do it, dream about it. One day, you will glance up at your collection of Japanese literature, or trip over the solar oven you built, and it will hit you: learning was there all the time, happening by itself. ❀

3

what
school *is* for

Almost all education has a political motive: it aims at strengthening some group, national or religious or even social, in the competition with other groups. It is this motive, in the main, which determines the subjects taught, the knowledge offered and the knowledge withheld, and also decides what mental habits the pupils are expected to acquire. Hardly anything is done to foster the inward growth of mind and spirit; in fact, those who have had the most education are very often atrophied in their mental and spiritual life.

—Bertrand Russell

IF SCHOOLS GET in the way of learning, why do we have them? Why did anyone ever think they would work?

Compulsory schooling in the U.S. started because of some lofty, beautiful hopes for democracy, unfortunately mixed up with a lethal dose of arrogance and tainted with a few other impurities. Thomas Jefferson, John Adams, and other early American leaders argued that in a democracy, people needed to have knowledge and wisdom in order to make decent decisions together. Also, they hoped America could be a country where "everyone" (meaning all the white boys who hadn't immigrated too recently) had an equal chance to succeed. Thus, they all needed a chance to learn and read and grow as children, rather than be packed off to factories for hard labor, rather than be shut off from the world of books and ideas.

People hadn't always thought this way; in most of the old kingdoms of Europe, no one particularly wanted Johnny to learn to read, because Johnny's purpose in life was to herd cows and do what the king said. In England, compulsory school for poor people had started in the fifteenth century, but not in support of democracy. Instead, the idea was to train the destitute for jobs so that rich people wouldn't have to support them with tax money.[1]

In other words, the ideals that led to American public education were idealistic and revolutionary ones. How wonderful if the people who held them could have been democratic enough to trust others to make the most of an opportunity.

If so, we might have had one bonanza extravaganza of an educational system,

---

[1] See Lawrence A. Cremin, *American Education: The National Experience 1783-1876*, Harry G. Good, *A History of American Education,* and Lawrence Kotin and William F. Aikman, *Legal Foundations of Compulsory School Attendance.*

one in which children were legally guaranteed their basic material needs—shelter and food—until a certain age—sixteen, eighteen, twenty-two, whatever—and allowed to freely explore the physical and cultural worlds. Libraries and books could have been accessible to all. Tutors and academic specialists could have been paid by the government to answer people's questions, to teach them more intensely when a student wanted that. Apprenticeships could have been available, as well as open laboratories staffed by scientists ready to let young people assist in their research. Children and teenagers could have roamed around sticking their hands into frog ponds, bread dough, and art supplies. They could have invented gadgets, cataloged fossils, and written poetry at will.

Instead, the people who thought up American education believed in no one but themselves. They did not trust children to learn, and they did not trust the "lower classes" to want their children to learn. I doubt any kind of intellectual freedom even occurred to them. They believed that in order to have education, it would have to be forced. Thus came compulsory schooling. They modeled the American system on the German one, which never pretended and was not intended to create a democracy.

Another reason we have schools even though they prevent learning is that schools are intended not *only* for learning. They have other purposes too, somewhat less charming.

Although compulsory schooling was begun partly in hopes of educating people worthy of democracy, other goals also imbedded themselves in the educational system. One was *the goal of creating obedient factory workers who did not waste time by talking to each other or daydreaming.* Historian Lawrence A. Cremin writes, "There was one educational problem that proved ubiquitous wherever factories did appear, and that was the problem of nurturing and maintaining industrial discipline." Cremin goes on to explain that before the industrial revolution, people had scheduled their lives in harmony with the seasons, holidays, and their own preferences. But factories

> required a shift from agricultural time to the much more precise categories of industrial time, with its sharply delineated and periodized work day. Moreover, along with this shift in timing and rhythm, the factory demanded concomitant shifts in habits of attention and behavior, under which workers could no longer act according to whim or preference but were required instead to adjust to the needs of the productive process and the other workers involved in it . . . The schools taught [factory behavior], not only through textbook preachments, but also through the very character of their organization—the grouping, periodizing, and objective impersonality were not unlike those of the factory. [1]

This industrial indoctrination continues full force in schools today, turning out people who conveniently obey authority, don't think too much, and work hard for little reward. (Yet, as we hurtle into the information age, it makes even less sense for people to spend twelve years training for factory-work. As visionary "free school" innovator Dan Greenberg points out,

> In the post-industrial society there is essentially no place for human beings who are not able to function independently. There is no room for people trained to be cogs in a machine. Such people have been displaced permanently from the economic system. The economic demands of post-industrial America are something that you hear from personnel

---
[1] *Lawrence A. Cremin, American Education: The National Experience 1783-1876, pp. 350-1.*

directors in every industry and company today, small or large. The demands are for creative people with initiative, self-starters, people who know how to take responsibility, exercise judgement, make decisions for themselves. [1])

Another early goal of American education was religious; in fact, the first compulsory education act came in 1642 in Massachusetts, one of the strictest puritan colonies. According to the puritans, "that old deluder Satan" kept "men from the knowledge of the Scriptures." Though we no longer officially learn to read in order to read the Bible, schools preserve some rather smelly leftovers from this influence. The puritan assumption that everyone would emerge from school with the same religious beliefs evolved into the secular idea that school should produce people who all think alike in a general sense.

(The middle colonies and Southern colonies, which were not focused around religion, did not have compulsory education until centuries later. They were a much more diverse group of people and had no desire to lose that diversity.[2])

When schools started educating everyone—girls and Native Americans and new immigrants as well as white boys—they took on another, related purpose. For all of its idealism about democracy, America wasn't ready to treat people respectfully or equally. *Schools took on the task of stamping out "minority" and other differing cultures.* "The Indian schools were like jails and run along military lines, with roll calls four times a day," says Sioux medicine man Lame Deer in *Lame Deer, Seeker of Visions*. He goes on to lament:

> The schools are better now than they were in my time. They look good from the outside—modern and expensive. The teachers understand the kids a little better, use more psychology and less stick. But in these fine new buildings Indian children still commit suicide, because they are lonely among all that noise and activity. I know of a ten-year-old who hanged herself . . . When we enter the school we at least know that we are Indians. We come out half red and half white, not knowing what we are.[3]

Schools also exist to provide babysitting: preventing teenagers from competing in the job market or running loose in the streets. Like other school purposes, this goal stands smack in the way of learning; it translates mainly into an unforgivable waste of time. If we could scrap it, school could surely teach everything more efficiently, not "reviewing" year after year, and you'd finish in half the time. When adults go to workshops, there is usually little of the educational hanky-panky and muddle and time wasting you get in school. Unschooler Jessica Franz, twelve, wrote me, "I feel that I am about at the same level as the kids at my grade although I do 'school' only occasionally as opposed to six or seven hours a day." Her comment is echoed by the experiences of thousands of other unschoolers who spend little formal time on academics but know much more, and get better scores on standardized tests than the average schooled student.

Contrast school's use of time with the way people study for the GED. The GED (General Equivalency Diploma) actually tests a higher level of knowledge than what

---

[1] Dan Greenberg, "School for a Post-Industrial Society," in *Friends of Summerhill Trust Journal*, Issue 11.

[2] See Lawrence Kotin and William F. Aikman, *Legal Foundations of Compulsory School Attendance.*

[3] John (Fire) Lame Deer and Richard Erdoes, *Lame Deer, Seeker of Visions.*

school teaches; supposedly one third of high school *graduates* would fail it. Nevertheless, when high school dropouts want to take it, they are typically coached for 16 to 24 hours over a period of four to six weeks. Books that prepare people to take the GED suggest around thirty home-study sessions, each about one to three hours. That's all they need, *not* four years sitting at a desk with someone else's bubble gum stuck underneath.

I am reminded of a conversation my colleagues and I had with a parent when I was teaching. We had suggested that this man's son skip the eighth grade and go directly into the ninth, since he was extremely bright, competent, socially adept, and "responsible" in doing his schoolwork. At first, the father had some qualms. He was worried that his son would miss some of the "building blocks" of courses such as math, science, and foreign language. No, said the teachers, Jasper (fake name) would miss nothing important by skipping a grade.

That information was good for Jasper, since he was allowed to skip eighth grade and save himself a year of "nothing important." But the implications of that conversation are horrendous. Year after year, you attend school for many reasons. You may think the most important reason is learning, but in reality you are receiving "nothing important" in exchange for your twelve years of drudgery. Sure, schools teach some potentially helpful skills and information. But the amount of good stuff is insignificant next to the piles of inanity, and furthermore, the meat of most year-long courses could be covered in a good two or three day session.

Schools didn't *begin* in order *to provide millions of jobs for teachers, administrators, maintenance people, and office workers,* but since they provide those jobs now, that is one of their main purposes. It is probably the one that will kick hardest if lots of young people get hip and quit. Yes, it would be tragic for all those people to be out of work. But why must you provide their livelihood with the skin of your souls? The government pays them to do dirty-work; it might as well pay them to do good work—help in libraries and museums, provide teaching and tutoring to people of all ages who ask for it, read to blind and elderly people. In the meantime, it shouldn't be your burden.

Why do we stand for it? Why do most people believe unquestioningly in compulsory education?

Because they are mystified, shamed, and intimidated into believing in it, that's why.

Schoolpeople talk in specialized, complicated language, as if learning were a specialized, complicated process. "Mastery learning," they say, "Criterion-referenced testing, multicultural education, prosocial behavior, expository teaching, and stanine scores. So there." They pretend—and believe—that what they do is all very tricky and difficult.

Teachers take themselves very seriously when they do things like design courses and lesson plans. They try to sound very scientific when speaking to students and talking about students. (Remember, I know because I was a teacher. I didn't just see it, I did it. It's a tremendously addicting power trip.)

Indeed, all their complicated undertakings *are* probably necessary to induce *forced* learning. They are also necessary in order to make schoolpeople themselves feel important. But none of it should intimidate you. Most of what teachers actually know about teaching has to do with classroom management (a.k.a. "discipline"). In other words, most of what they know is stuff that obviously wouldn't matter if you were learning what you want to learn.

Ben Gipson, a college student who plans to teach high school psychology, life management, and reading skills, and who was a student delegate to an NEA (teachers' union) convention, wrote an essay which was printed in the December 1990 *NEA Today*. Gipson wrote arguing that it is best to major in education rather than in the field one hopes to teach: "Not only is a child's thinking different from an adult's, but a five-year-old's is different from a seven-year-old's. If you haven't studied Piaget, Kohlberg, and Erikson, you won't really know that."

Oh, you won't? Well, no, not if you bury your nose in books and never think about your own childhood or talk with kids.

But schools push you beyond intimidation; they *shame* you into believing you need them. By giving out grades, they cancel people's faith in their perfectly good brains. Once you accept a report card's verdict that you're not so bright, you're hardly in a position to say you don't need school. If they happen to decide you *are* intelligent, you have the opposite problem—your ego is addicted. You "succeed" in school, so why risk leaving it for a world where you might not get straight A's?

It boils down to something called "blaming the victim": school blames you instead of itself for your intellectual influenza. After first grade, you forget about your heaping supply of natural curiosity. When they tell you the reason you don't do your schoolwork well enough is that you have no drive, curiosity, or love of learning, you start believing them. By the time they tell you that if you can't make it *with* school, you certainly can't make it *without* school, you're really lost.

Obviously, schools need you to believe that you couldn't learn without them. Once they convince you of this, through intimidation and shame, it's over; you submit without much argument to twelve years of it. You become susceptible to the illogical kind of line one of my colleagues fed his students when they didn't finish their math: "OK, don't turn in your homework. Grow up and be a junkie."

The good part is that once you recognize their game for what it is, you can think about it clearly and start trusting yourself again.

So, dear reader, here we are at the end of another chapter. I invite you to sit down with your feet up and reflect upon your values and goals. Do they mesh with school? Are you tickled pink to have your mind programmed into Obedient Worker mode? To cash in your cultural heritage for Mainstream American Suburbia-think? To be babysat 35 hours every week?

Yes? Good girl. Good boy. Just put your feet back down, sit a little straighter, please, and do not look to the left or right.

No? Uh-oh. Welcome. Read on. ☀

schoolteachers— the People vs. the Profession

I am always ready to learn, but I do not always like being taught.

—Winston Churchill

THIS BOOK HAS no intention of lessening your appreciation for the people who teach school. Yet, my commentary in this chapter is both sweet and sour. On one hand, I want to acknowledge the wonderful qualities teachers have, and to explain a few difficult and ironic aspects of their profession. In general, it is not teachers' faults that School Is Bad—although if they all quit there would be no more school. On the other hand, I want to point out some less healthy aspects of common teacher personalities, to help you understand some of the guilt you may feel at school, and to help you give yourself permission to leave.

Most teachers are generous, intelligent, beautiful people. Some are very talented or knowledgeable in their fields and would make great mentors or tutors outside the constraints of school. Many have given up chances to make lots of money because they believe in teaching even though it pays poorly. Especially if they are men, they sometimes endure years of being hassled by their families—"Why don't you find a *real* career?" In any grip-on-reality contest, your average schoolteacher would win four times as many trophies as your average Gillette or Exxon executive.

Most teachers and other people in schools believe they are doing the Right Thing. They are not preventing democracy, freedom, and education on purpose. When they do purposely prevent freedom, they think it is in your best interest, so that you'll be ready to work hard and "succeed" in your afterlife. Respect their good intentions.

A few teachers are amazing enough to conquer. In their classes, something strong and beautiful happens, despite all the unpleasant forces of the opposition. The classic example is Elliot Wigginton, who started an oral history program in Georgia. His students write the famous *Foxfire* books and magazines. These books enlighten the whole world both about the richness of Appalachian culture and the capabilities of teenage journalists.

Jerry Vevig, my own high school choir director, is not so famous but was also an extraordinary teacher before he got promoted. Whenever I entered his room—for 6:30 A.M. practice, jazz choir, or concert choir—I forgot I was a high school student and instead became a serious artist in likeminded company. He wasn't always nice, and usually made us sing fifteen minutes into our lunch break, but he treated us like musicians, not kiddies, and he knew his stuff. I especially remember once when our jazz choir performed for a huge business Christmas banquet at The Red Lion—one of our twenty performances that month. The adult audience ignored us while we set up microphones. But when Carl rolled the first lush chords over the piano, all the talking hushed, and when Ronelle sang the first ripe note of the opening solo, a man dropped his fork. We were for real. Mr. V. brought out our best, and we loved him for it. I don't want to deny that some teachers can make wonderful things happen in school. I just know that the odds are way against them.

Also, just because someone teaches doesn't mean they're mentally "in league" with the school system. Many teachers start teaching in the first place because they think school is a bad place and they hope to make it better.

Unfortunately, most of these teachers either end up quitting or else compromising their ideals—the system is so much bigger and stronger than they are. Still, a lot of teachers have a few years of passionate vision in them. Don't assume, because schools squash you, that teachers *want* to squash you. For most teachers, as well as students, the world will be a more chocolate place when school is not compulsory and full of administrative backwash.

Which brings me to a different point. Not all teachers want to run your lives, but they have no choice. They *must* "manage" you. It is their *job* to give you F's if you don't do "your" work, to report your absences, to make you be quiet, to assign homework, to enforce school rules they don't personally believe in, such as You Have to Wear Socks With Tennis Shoes, and No Leaning Back in Your Chair. No teacher could keep a job if she said, "It doesn't matter whether you do the homework tonight. If you'd prefer to spend more time doing something else, please do. You won't get a zero, and I won't be disappointed in you." Teachers' job descriptions leave no way for them to treat you with the respect they would show their friends.

I can illustrate my point in a backwards way by telling you about a day I just couldn't do the job. I was substitute teaching physics. One of the people in the class, a fourteen-year-old-boy, was a good friend of mine. Because he was there, I came in the door as myself, not Miss Llewellyn. The class zoomed way out of control. Airplanes flew into the chalkboard; everyone talked while I gave the assignment; two boys in dark glasses put their feet on their desks, leaned back, crossed their arms, and grinned. Any other day, I would have snapped into the role they'd created for me. I was good at it. "Ladies and *gent*lemen," ran my usual substitute talk, "*Where* is your self-respect. Mr. Washington and Mr. Garcia, please remove the glasses. If any of you would care to visit the office, you can let me know by sending another airplane in this direction. Any questions?"

But with Otto's perceptive eyes on me, I couldn't bring myself to say the words. In his presence, they seemed suddenly so petty and artificial. They had nothing to do with Grace Llewellyn. I did a lousy job that day because Otto brought a flash of a deeper reality. What that says about the days I *could* do my job is unpleasant indeed.

Something that surprised me when I started teaching was that my fellow teachers were terrific people. Almost all of them. That hurt my brain a little. I remembered having a lot of mean, stupid teachers in school—was I wrong? Or had the teaching profession changed radically in five years?

The truth didn't strike until I substitute taught for a few months in my own former junior high and high school, rubbing my adult shoulders with the very same people who used to grade my tests and ask me not to read novels during their brilliant lectures. All of *them* were terrific people too—in my adult company. From the glimpses I caught of them in their classes, and the student conversations I overheard in the halls, some were apparently still mean and stupid in their classrooms.

I started wondering how many teenagers thought *I* was mean and stupid when I stood in front of a classroom. And over the next few years, I came to believe firmly: the majority of teachers are amazing, intelligent, generous and talented *people*. But the role they are forced to play in school keeps them from showing you these beautiful sides of themselves. Their talent and energy is drained instead by their constant task of telling people what to do.

Not everything about teachers is terrific, of course. Like a lot of other kinds of people, they have their weak points as well as their good qualities. And some of the things for which we praise teachers most loudly are the ways they cause the most harm.

For instance, many teachers seem to have an inborn desire to run other people's lives (also known as "help people"). Even if it were tolerable that others should run our lives, teachers are rarely any good at doing so, being as fully human as their students.

It makes sense that controlling sorts of people would gravitate toward teaching. It's a great profession for people who wish they were a king or God. Me, for example. When I was six or so I used to love to play school. I was the teacher. I called it Pee-Wee. My brothers, the students, were usually unenthusiastic but I was older and I could bribe or force them into it. I choreographed dances and made them learn, pinching them when they lost the beat. In general, I didn't feel my own life was enough territory—I wanted to design theirs too (just like my teachers got to design *my* life, I might add). It is this controlling and designing quality that disturbs me again and again in teachers—including myself—and in administrators. The most dangerous people in life are often those who want most to help you, whether or not you want their "help." "She's the sort of woman who lives for others," wrote C.S. Lewis, "You can tell the others by their hunted expression."

Teaching also turns you into an automatic Authority Figure. It is ideal work for anyone who likes to feel superior. No one questions much where your authority comes from, or how much is deserved.

Moreover, being a teacher is a perfect way to get attention and praise for being selfless and generous. Do you know anyone who loves to suffer nobly, as long as someone's watching and feeling sorry for them? A lot of teachers do. They thrive not on money, but on the brownie points they get for staying up all night to grade quizzes, for bringing their advisees Halloween candy, for earning abominable salaries, for driving across town in a blizzard to rent *The Story of English* on video, for explaining fractions thirty times to Suki on Friday afternoon, for neglecting their own favorite sports in order to coach basketball. Unfortunately, people who are good at suffering and working hard in public are also good at giving other people guilt trips.

One of the most dedicated, popular, and brilliant teachers I've known worked hard to arrange a weekend outdoor-film festival for his boarding school students. It was optional, and few went. The teacher was sad and disappointed in students for showing so little enthusiasm. I wondered how he would feel if his boss expressed disappointment in *him* if he missed a free U2 concert. Another teacher responded to his frustration with wisdom: "We have to provide a wide array of activities for them," she said, "But not be so personally invested in them that we get hurt when they'd rather do something else."

What do we need instead of people who love to sacrifice themselves for others? We need people who do what they most love, and do it well, and let others hang around or join in unforced, and share their knowledge instead of hoarding it. This behavior requires *true* generosity, because it allows other people to be equals, not helpless victims.

Another unfortunate aspect of teacher personalities is a limited perspective. Most have not worked at other kinds of jobs, beyond summers at a cash register. Like you, they have spent all their lives in school. This leaves them almost incapable of imagining their students' potential futures. They can't help but communicate to you their narrow sense of the possibilities in life.

Finally, there is nothing wrong with teaching, only with teaching in the conditions of compulsory school. Lots of people do learn certain things best by being taught or shown. So don't limit yourself by assuming that a teacher in school is the same as a teacher out of school. A teacher out of school—in a martial arts studio, a book discussion group, or a community education French class—can be himself and teach from his heart. Also, since you are not required to undergo his teaching, you will stay only if his method works for you.

When choice, freedom, and individuality are introduced into a teaching situation, it can be great for everyone involved. That's why I love my new work giving dance lessons. The old issues of guilt simply don't come up. If people want to learn middle eastern dance and swirl sequined veils, and if they like my teaching and my dancing, they pay me to teach them. If they stop liking it, they quit, or perhaps look for a different teacher. I don't stress out or take it personally—everyone learns differently. No one takes my ex-students to court for truancy or gives them an F. Those of us who stay in class are empowered by our common goal and our common success. ☀

5

The Power and Magic
of Adolescence
vs.
The Insufferable
Tedium of School

Youth is the time to go flashing from one end of the world to the other both in mind and body; to try the manners of different nations; to hear the chimes at midnight; to see sunrise in town and country; to be converted at a revival; to circumnavigate the metaphysics, write halting verses, run a mile to see a fire, and wait all day long in the theatre to applaud 'Hernani.'
—Robert Louis Stevenson, *Crabbed Age and Youth*

IF YOU EVER read any anthropology, one of the first things you notice is that primal cultures simmer up all of their mystery and magic and power and ask their teenagers to drink deeply.

A sixteen-year-old Dakota boy fasts until an empowering vision overtakes him. A newly-menstruating Apache girl becomes the goddess White Painted Woman in an intense, joyful theatrical ritual which lasts four days. All over the planet, traditional cultures provide various ritual experiences to adolescents, bringing them into contact with the deepest parts of themselves and their heritage.

There is danger and pain, as well as beauty and exultation, in some of these traditional ways of initiating people into adulthood. I don't want to make any shallow statement that we've got it all wrong because we don't ask pubescent boys to endure three days of biting wasps.

But I would like you to reflect for a minute on the contrast between the way *our* society initiates its young and the vivid undertakings of the primal world.

What do you get instead of vision? You get school—and all of the blind passivity and grey monotone it trains into you.

For an institution to ask you, during some of your most magical years, to sit still and be good and read quietly for six or more hours each day is barely even thinkable, let alone tolerable. How do you feel when the sun comes out in March and makes the most golden day imaginable, but you have to stay in and clean your room?

In case you've lost touch with your burgeoning beauty, let me remind you that that's exactly what's going on, for at least six years of your teenaged schooling. Adolescence is a time of dreaming, adventure, risk, sweet wildness, and intensity. It's the time for you to "find yourself," or at least go looking. The sun is rising on your life. Your body is breaking out of its cocoon and ready to try wings. But you have to stay in—for *such* a long time—and keep your pencils sharpened. School is bad for your spirit, except the pep club kind.

It's no accident, I'm sure. The way our society is set up now, something's got to prevent visionary experience. Otherwise, ninety percent of the American monoculture would shatter. People who are fully and permanently awakened to the wildness and beauty in and around them make lousy wage-slaves. On the other hand, people who are *not* distracted by a wellspring of spiritual and sexual yearnings can assemble clock radios or automobiles very quickly, or focus their intellects on monthly sales charts.

More importantly, unawakened people are less likely to question the things in our society which are horrifically dull and ridiculous. The point of seeking any kind of visionary experience is to *see*. When vision comes to you, eternity is its black velvet backdrop. Everything else comes out on the stage to sing and dance. Some of it fits in with the grandeur of that backdrop, and some of it only clashes, looking ugly and cheap. You end up wanting to adjust your life so that it's full of stuff that fits in with eternity, and not crammed with things that don't matter.

Therefore, one reason many primal cultures can confidently guide their young toward visionary experiences is that they're not worried. They don't have to worry that the visions will show anything horrible about the society itself. If there *is* something going wrong with the cultural state of affairs, they want to know, so they can fix it.

In this culture the opposite is true. When you have a messy house, you don't offer a magnifying glass to your guests. You probably don't even open the curtains and let the light in.

If we did teenaged visions, democracy would get a boost, but the powers of Mass Production and Rat Racing Consumerism would take a dive. We would see that far too much of what we accept as "reality" is a blasphemy against true reality. Since our consumptive culture is out of balance with the rest of the universe, it would look mighty bad under the inspection of visionary young people. Get it? The Powers That Be do not invite their young to seek visions, because those visions would force a Big Change.

No force of dullness and ignorance is strong enough, however, to stop you from seeking. Eternity, God, Goddess, whatever you call it—is too strong. It will get in, though it has to battle school and other strongholds of society. Writers and artists bring us some inklings, though when school introduces us to them, it nearly destroys their potency.

The Big Mystery creeps in through all your fascinations with the unknown—music with heavy pulses and strange lyrics, sexual fantasies and experiences, the occult, drugs (including alcohol). Obviously, some of these things can be taken to unhealthy excess. Drug abuse is a disease. Drug *use*, however, is often the sign of someone's intense spiritual quest. Hallucinogens can be an easy, though risky, way to tap into visionary experience. There are other ways, healthier though more difficult—through trance and fasting, for instance.

Unfortunately, most adults refuse to acknowledge the powerful impulse behind any of these activities, labeling them as "bad," as if that would make them go away. Why? Their own visionary tendencies got cancelled out by society at sweet sixteen.

Misery, as they say, loves company. It is *incredibly* painful for an emotional cripple to be around someone who is emotionally free. And so most adults would rather pretend desperately to visionary teenagers that the world is nothing more than green lawns, white socks, and recently sanitized carpets.

Visionary tendencies come in dark and light, or a combination thereof.

Some teenagers want dark experiences. They walk in cemeteries at night. They write stories about suicide; they obsess on black clothing and Pink Floyd lyrics. None of it means they are "bad" or twisted. When they are finished playing with the dark, they will understand the light much better. If they are ignored or ridiculed, maybe they will do something drastic, but their search is usually only an earnest attempt to understand the depths.

Others gravitate toward the light—daytime psychedelic colors, long solitary hikes. They determine to become a dancer or artist instead of something "realistic." If their family is sedately Catholic, maybe they go to the Assembly of God and speak in tongues. If their family goes to the Assembly of God, maybe they climb a hill and offer flowers to Apollo.

Schools—and many parents—lie a lot at this point, telling you you're out of touch with reality. The truth is, you're out of touch with the expectations and patterns of an *un*real, man-made industrial society. You are *in* touch with the reality that counts. Look at the Milky Way some night and think about it. You'll know. In *Lame Deer, Seeker of Visions*, a Sioux medicine man talks about the reality of "the white world" versus the deeper reality of artists and Indians:

> Artists are the Indians of the white world. They are called dreamers who live in the clouds, improvident people who can't hold onto their money, people who don't want to face "reality." They say the same things about Indians. How the hell do these frog-skin[1] people know what reality is? The world in which you paint a picture in your mind, a picture which shows things different from what your eyes see, that is the world from which I get my visions. I tell you this is the real world, not the Green Frog Skin World. That's only a bad dream, a streamlined, smog-filled nightmare.
>
> Because we refuse to step out of our reality into this frog-skin illusion, we are called dumb, lazy, improvident, immature, other-worldly. It makes me happy to be called "other-worldly," and it should make you so. It's a good thing our reality is different from theirs.[2]

Furthermore...

Schools—and this society they represent—go beyond blocking your visionary tendencies. They further cripple you by making fun of you, as if you were not quite human, the new niggers. Why? Probably because every hierarchical society seems to need niggers to put down, and women and African-Americans won't take it anymore. When someone puts *you* down, you want to put somebody else down.

Dr. Seuss, reliable social commentator, wrote a story called "King Looie Katz." King Looie Katz makes Fooie Katz carry his long proud royal tail around. So Fooie Katz sticks his own nose in the air and makes another cat haul *his* tail. Pretty soon all the cats in Katzenstein are walking around carrying the tail of the cat in front of them... except the very last little cat, who doesn't have anyone to carry his.

---

[1] "Frog-skins" are dollar bills.

[2] John (Fire) Lame Deer and Richard Erdoes, *Lame Deer, Seeker of Visions*.

That little cat, who is a bit like you, takes action. He yells "I Quit!" and slams down the tail in his paws. Everybody else follows suit. The story concludes:

And since that day in Katzen-stein,
All cats have been more grown-up.
They're all more demo-catic
Because each cat holds his own up.[1]

Another reason adults make fun of you is that they're jealous. Teenagers are beautiful and fresh; the perfume of a flower is concentrated in the bud. Yes, many teenagers are awkward, pimpled, or strangely tall and thin. Far more adults, however, are awkward (having forgotten how to use their bodies), sallow-skinned (too much sitting in air-conditioned offices) and predictably heavy (not enough skateboarding).

A healthy adult society would acknowledge the beauty of youth, make up some good poems about it, and then not think about it too much. There are certainly more productive activities in life than fixating on the rosy cheeks you'll never have again. But since we do not have a healthy adult society, we get all bent out of shape over it, create a cult of young-beautiful-people-in-magazines, and punish real live teenagers by telling them they are ugly.

Just in case you do realize that you are beautiful, we make sure that you can't appreciate it, by telling you that you are confused and overly emotional during these traumatic years and for pete's sake don't go and make any decisions for yourself, and don't let loose and have any free wild experiences with life. Dogs in mangers, we turn the power of adolescence into a weak disease. Teachers sit in the teachers' lounge and laugh about you behind your backs.

Isn't he cute, they say. Poor Kristy, with no idea of how she sticks out in that magenta skirt. This, from people who are overweight, in ruts, out of touch with their dreams, insecure, and otherwise at least as imperfect as the subjects of their conversation. Thank god I'm not that age any more, says Mrs. Wallace, leaning her double chin over her desk. We read tacky cute articles in *Family Circle* called "How to Survive the Terrible Teens: An Owner's Guide." The owner being the parent, of course. *School*, yes, is something to survive, but being a teenager is something that flies.

We force you to act younger than you are, legally withholding your ability to control your own life. The *World Book* encyclopedia says, "Most teenagers mature psychologically at the rate set by their society. As a result, psychological adolescence normally lasts at least as long as the period of legal dependence." Certainly, there is no *biological* limitation to teenage independence. In other times and places, teenagers have commonly married, raised children, held jobs, operated businesses, and occasionally ruled countries.

It seems you're talking about more than just schools here. Aren't you getting off the point a bit?

Yes, school is not the only bad guy in the war against whole adolescence. But it *is* our culture's deathly substitute for powerful growing experiences. It *is* the way we take your time so you don't explore your own inklings of truth. It *is* where you learn to be passive instead of active. Quitting school won't guarantee you a healthy, passionate adolescence, but at least it will remove the biggest obstacle against that flowering. ☀

---

[1] "King Looie Katz," in Dr. Seuss (Theodor Geisel), *I Can Lick Thirty Tigers Today, and other stories.*

6

and
a few other
Miscellaneous
Abominations

School days, I believe, are the unhappiest in the whole span of human existence. They are full of dull, unintelligible tasks, new and unpleasant ordinances, brutal violations of common sense and common decency. —H.L. Mencken

ASIDE FROM THE previously described Big Reasons to quit school, there are dozens of random miscellaneous ones, also important, like

School puts you into intense, forced contact with people who are only your own age. It discourages you from making friends with other people. If you don't like being shut up with your peers all day, that doesn't mean you're socially maladjusted. Why should you prefer the company of hundreds of people your own age to a healthy mix of more diverse people? Adults have been around longer than teenagers. Therefore, they have experiences and perspectives that teenagers lack.

When adults aren't your schoolteachers (and therefore have no control over you), most will treat you like real people. Outside of school, if you're busy doing something, most adults won't think of you as a "kid"—at least not for long. You will learn from them, and they will learn from you. Also, you can have friends younger than yourself.

School socializes you into narrow roles. Girls wear makeup. Boys play football. Girls giggle. Boys stammer and grunt. All teenagers are incapable of serious thought—unless they're nerds or at least "different."

School destroys self-esteem. Teenager Jenny Smith writes:

How is it that going to school can often stomp out our self-worth, especially in girls? Our dreams and aspirations are literally knocked out of us. I feel school turns out students who aren't in touch with their dreams, their values, or their spirit. They don't learn to think for themselves; they are led along by the television and by the school. We're told when we can go to the bathroom (I peed my pants in first grade thanks to this!), when we can talk to our friends, when we can eat (as if we don't know when we're hungry), what version of history we shall read, if we are "smart" or if we are "dumb." Overall, this leaves people feeling angry at the lack of control in their lives and they don't trust themselves anymore.

According to *Educator's Newsletter*, eighty percent of us have high self-esteem in first grade; by twelfth grade only five percent of us still feel good about ourselves. As the *Luno* newsletter comments, those statistics raise "the possibility that school is the biggest mental health problem we've ever known."[1]

School labels people, putting them into limiting categories. Schools have lots of people. When we have to deal with large quantities, sorting things into categories helps us to make sense of them. Most people tend to use this survival mechanism in school, so everyone ends up with hundreds of conveniently labeled acquaintances. According to the unspoken rules of most schools, you are one thing or another. You are an artsy fartsy drama freak *or* a cheerleader-type, not both. Your school life is autoshop class *or* college prep, not both. It's not easy to cross these boundaries, so many people never try. Out of school, you can forget them.

School teaches frenzy. When adults get turned loose after college, lots of them go to bookstores and buy self-help books. These books help them unlearn the lessons of school. Slow down, they say. Concentrate only on the important things. Don't give yourself guilt trips for not Doing Everything. Live your life the way *you* want to live it. If you quit school now, maybe you can reclaim this childhood wisdom before you sprout wrinkles, and save thirty dollars or so in self-help books.

School is toxic! As Doris J. Rapp, M.D., points out in her book *Is This Your Child's World?*, school environments are filled with chemical and other substances that cause chronic headaches, violent mood swings, learning disabilities, and allergies.

If you go to school, you almost have to be a jerk to other people, to yourself, or to both. When other people are jerks, life loses a bit of its sheen. When *you* are a jerk, life loses a lot of its sheen. Yet school sometimes gives you no choice.

A simple example is my day in May at the natural history museum, a school field trip. The tour guide and the teachers told the students to sit quietly and listen to the tour guide. The tour guide stood in front of the exhibits, blocking them. She rambled dully, as tour guides are prone to do. The exhibits, on the other hand, were stunning and infinitely more "educational" than any dry-rot lecture or textbook.

The students had two choices. They could show the expected "respect" to the tour guide and sit quietly, bored as bureaucrats, disrespecting themselves. Or they could show "disrespect" and disobedience to the guide and stand up, walk around, and look and learn. Andy did. Andy got scolded. I hate remembering.

Schools create meaningless, burdensome problems for you to solve. School claims to be a system which is accountable to the larger world around it. In other words, what you learn in school is supposed to help you make sense of the rest of the world. In good moments, you do learn useful information. But much of your time in school is spent simply learning how to get along in *school*. Schoolpeople impose elaborate homework policies, consequences, and language—"You're earning an F. That's a problem. How are you going to solve it?" They call things like grades and homework your "responsibility," without giving you the slightest choice in accepting that responsibility.

---

[1] From *Educator's Newsletter*, 1987, as reported in *Luno* 11:5.

Schoolpeople justify their actions by saying they're teaching you to be responsible and "follow through" later in school and later in life. But all of this is so different from "real life" that it's ridiculous. In "real life," you *choose* what to take responsibility for. Under circumstances of freedom, following through is a completely different game from the one you play in school.

Schools give you an incurable guilt trip. When I taught school, we watched a videotape about getting good grades. You *should* get good grades, the speaker kept saying. If you are capable of an A, he said, but you only get a C, that ought to be unacceptable to you. Maybe, he added, not quite joking, you ought to make yourself sleep on the floor that night.

In a parent-teacher conference, a wealthy, "successful" father complained about Jill's (fake name) C's and B's. "I wouldn't care if she couldn't do the work," he said, "I'm just angry that she doesn't. Why does she throw her talent away?" As if C's and B's meant that one was doing nothing with one's life. It all boils down to a guilt trip if you spend your energy on what you care about, and pats on the head if you forget who you are and do what you're told.

Schools blame victims. In other words, they inflict all manner of nasty experiences and expectations on you, and then tell you it's your fault for not liking it. They blame *you* for *their* problems. An advice column in *Scholastic Choices*, March 1990, ran this letter:

> I'm thirteen and I want to quit school. I think it's boring. Besides, my teachers are all
> mean. I think I could get a job on a farm and make a living that way. What should I do?

Easy enough to answer—"Quit school, of course. It *is* boring. Teachers *are* mean, though it's part of their job to be that way. Work on a farm if you *want*, but as a thirteen-year-old you shouldn't have to worry about earning a living." The king of the advice column, however, had different ideas:

> The way you write and express yourself tells me that you are smart, though unhappy, and
> are blaming your dissatisfaction on things outside of yourself. [In other words, you should
> be blaming your dissatisfaction on yourself.] You don't feel bored because school is
> boring or teachers are mean. You don't feel secure or comfortable with yourself. If you
> can't settle these feelings in a year or so, counselors can help you learn to understand your
> feelings more clearly.

No comment.

There's more to life. You yearn. I grow furious and heartbroken when I think on this one too long. You know: life is *not* the color of linoleum halls or the drab hum of industrial lighting or the slow ticking of the clock. Look at the stars. Look hard at the faces of people throwing frisbees in a park, singing in church, passing the potatoes, planting tomatoes, fixing a kitchen table or the engine in an old pickup. Look at a baby or a piece of handcarved furniture or a three-hundred-year-old tree or a pebble or a worm or the sweater your grandmother knitted for you. Perhaps school's greatest danger is that it may convince you life is nothing more than an institutionalized rat race.

School, of course, is not the only big gray institution our country relies on to suck the spirit out of its people. Hospitals, big office buildings, and numerous governmental interferences pull the same trick. But school is the first such institution most of us endure, and it wears down our resistance to the later ones. It makes them seem normal; it makes us feel greedy or idealistic or stupidly poetic when we hear our hearts telling us, "It shouldn't be like this! I'm better than this! I was made for more wonderful things."

School conditions you to live for the future, rather than to live in the present. In *GWS* #39, Marti Holmes, mother of a sixteen-year-old, wrote, "Homeschooling has not closed any doors that I can see, and has provided rich, full years of living (rather than 'preparing for life')." Contrary to the teachings of school, you are not in dress rehearsal. More than anything else, this book is about living—*now,* as well as twenty years from now. Quit school before it convinces you life is nothing but a waiting game, an *ugly* waiting game. "We are always getting ready to live, but never living," wrote Emerson. Don't let the schoolpeople write that on your tombstone. ❖

but
Miss Llewellyn...

PANIC STRIKES YOUR hungry heart. You cry out:

I want to be free... But I also want to go to college and get a good job! My friends are all in school, and what would I do without football?

Yeah, there are a lot of buts. They all have answers. Let's look. One at a time.

But I want to go to college and get a good job!

Fine. Neither depend on graduating from high school. For college, see Chapter 31. As far as jobs go, yes, there is plenty of prejudice against "drop-outs," and if you refer to yourself as one, forget it. If, on the other hand, you call yourself a homeschooler or explain exactly what you did instead of school, and why, intelligent employers will smile approvingly. (One academic study of adults who had been homeschooled found that *none* of them were unemployed or on welfare; the majority were self-employed or had professional careers; all were satisfied with their work.)[1]

However... be prepared to change your thoughts about what you want out of life. School shapes so much of your mind that when you leave it, you may no longer feel certain that you want college—or you may feel *more* certain. You may grow different ideas as to what kind of work you want to do, and your definition of a "good job" may change. Furthermore, by quitting school and beginning to make independent choices, you run the risk of turning into a person who sculpts creative, fulfilling ways to earn money without reporting to a boss.

Does school actually prepare you for the world of work? If you plan to scrub floors or assemble plastic toys all your life, then yes, school will break your spirit ahead of time so you don't fight when you get nothing wonderful out of adulthood. For that matter, school will condition you to accept *any* kind of work you don't love, whether as an M.D. or a secretary.

School, however, does not prepare you to identify your own dreams and make them come true.

---

[1] Dr. J. Gary Knowles, "Now we are adults: Attitudes, beliefs, and status of adults who were home-educated as children."

But I have to learn school subjects—math, history, literature, etc. —because they will make me into a Proper Citizen!

Yes, investigating all these subjects will probably make you a better citizen.

Going to school all day and Obeying Authority as if you lived in a dictatorship will make you a worse one.

What's a patriot to do? Quit school and learn all that juicy stuff and do your best to prevent bad stories (histories) from repeating themselves. Read widely and thoughtfully. The more you do, the less all of us will need to worry about our future. Education, as they call it, should make you a more intelligent voter, and more importantly a good *leader* in any situation—serving on a city planning committee, nudging your aunt Marcia to recycle her beer cans. Certainly, the more informed and thoughtful a group of citizens are, the wiser decisions they ought to make as a group.

True, people who don't go to school might end up knowing different types of things from schoolteenagers, depending on their interests. This, too, is a sign of good citizenship. A community is made more intelligent if its people bring many different perspectives and a wide expanse of knowledge. If you wind up knowing more about Jacques Rousseau than Martin Luther King, or Hopi farming practices instead of the structure of DNA, or motorcycle engines instead of computers, your citizenship will be as intact as the Jones's. *More* intact, actually, because you'll like what you know, and you'll keep it in mind whenever you think about anything.

Furthermore, I don't know about ingraining it in your brain that any sort of learning is your *responsibility.* Your life and time belong to you and the universe, and to the government only to the extent that the government is in harmony with the universe. Anyway, lots of heavily "educated" people are rotten citizens. So read to feed your hungry head, not to fulfill some pinched sense of duty.

But my school has a good choir!
I live to play football!
And what about me? I want to be Miss Drill Team U.S.A.!

This one's tough. Some schools do offer outstanding performing and sports opportunities that are difficult to find elsewhere. My own melodious memory of singing with and playing piano for two outstanding choirs in high school almost compensates for the lackluster hours I spent enduring everything else. Almost, but not quite. If you truly love your opportunity to belong to a school team or performing group, consider two things:

First, you *can* leave school and continue to participate in these activities—either at school itself or elsewhere. Chapters 26 and 27 expound on this topic. Chapter 19 contains specific information about participating in school just as much as you want to—i.e. marching band and photography but no math, English, or anything else.

Second, if you can't replace the activity, or participate in it without being enrolled in school full-time, is it terrific enough that it makes up for the drudgery of the rest of school? If you want to play professional football, maybe so. Everyone makes trade-offs; millions of adults live somewhere without liking it because it offers them work they do like. But if you'd have as much fun playing hockey with an independent league as playing school football, get clear. Cash in your shoulder pads for freedom.

But in school I learn lots of facts!

It's much easier, and far more delectable, to get them from an encyclopedia,

Harper's "Index," or Trivial Pursuit answer cards.

But I'm learning disabled!

If indeed you are, unschooling should help magnificently. Much more than in school, you'll be able to make plans and choose resources that support your best ways of learning. At least one study has concluded that learning disabled homeschoolers experience more "academic engaged time" and greater "academic gains" than their schooled counterparts.[1]

It is also useful and empowering for some people to question the label "learning disabled." Some scholars, as well as some homeschoolers and common sense thinkers, suspect that learning disabilities are largely a myth, that instead: there are many ways to learn, each person is naturally inclined toward particular ways of learning and less inclined toward others, and some of these ways coincide with conventional school-style activities, while others do not. I recommend the booklet *Everyone is Able: Exploding the Myth of Learning Disabilities,* edited by Susannah Sheffer, and Thomas Armstrong's books *In Their Own Way: Discovering and Encouraging Your Child's Personal Learning Style* and *Seven Kinds of Smart: Identifying and Developing Your Many Intelligences.*

In general, it seems that *in* school, "learning disabled" can be a helpful label for many students (if it doesn't wreck their self-esteem), since it helps them get individual instruction and helps explain why they have difficulty *despite* their working hard and being bright people. Out of school, the label often simply becomes irrelevant.

But what if all I want to do instead of school is watch TV all day?

Well. Don't misunderstand me. I would turn heartsick and give up if this book led to a cult of TV parasites who soaped instead of schooled, and I personally would rather be stuck going to junior high all day than force-fed channel zero for six hours.

However, I don't worry. If you think what you want most is to soak in sit-coms all day, probably all you really need and want is the mandatory vacation described in Chapter 12. After a week or so of TV, you'll feel restless and ready to move on. If you don't yet have any ideas, you'll be ready to find some. Furthermore, I'm convinced that addiction to TV is a by-product of schooling. School doesn't encourage you to take action. Once you get used to sitting passively all day, it's hard to be a Person with Initiative. But school doesn't really kill your brain; it only sends it into deep freeze. After it thaws, you'll want more than TV.

But what if I don't get along with my parents and don't want them to be my teachers?

or

But what if my parents both work and can't stay home to homeschool me?

If unschooling or homeschooling depended on parents to be teachers, I'd never write a book about it. Lots of teenagers get along with their parents (especially teenagers who don't go to school) but lots don't. And no matter how well you get along with your parents, that doesn't mean you'd like them to direct your education. I would have *hated* for my parents to be my "teachers" in the school sense. The

---

[1] From a 1994 study by Dr. Steven Duvall, information available from National Home Education Research Institute.

conflicts and power struggles we already had could only have intensified.

On the other hand, I would have loved to be an "unschooler," in charge of my own education. If my parents and I had known about unschooling and tried it, I think they would have been wise and trusting enough to let me explore independently. Likely, our relationship would have improved since I would have felt better about my own life. But I would have fiercely resisted any well-meant parental attempts to control my learning.

So, once and for all, let's get this straight: I am not talking about turning your parents into your main teachers, *unless that is specifically what you and they want to do.* Your teachers can be yourself, books, basketball courts, adults you talk to or write letters to, your friends, museums, plants, and rivers.

I know of many teenage unschoolers, by the way, whose parents both work away from home. Not only that, but in *GWS* there are occasional letters from parents with *younger* children who stay home without adults during the days—and like it, and don't die. More importantly, the majority of teenaged homeschoolers who wrote me said that their parents played a minor role in their educations. They answer questions when asked, talk a lot, and sometimes share their expertise *when the teenager is interested.* In other families, the parents really do get involved, learning right along with their children, but that happens more often at younger ages. Both the parents and teenagers who contacted me seemed to share an understanding that a teenager is old enough to direct his own education and activities.

To be sure, there are families where the parent takes over the role of teacher and principal—sometimes in a very authoritarian way. The idea repels *me*, but if you like it that's your business.

But I love outsmarting authority!

I sympathize; there's great satisfaction in beating someone at their own game. If you're a fighter and a rebel, however, there are worthier causes than school. Outsmart the big businesses who destroy rainforests and ozone. Outsmart the lying politicians. Get out in the world where we need you.

And understand this: petty though school is, it has more power to break your spirit than these bigger forces do. That's because its *business* is breaking you. The more you rebel, the more they'll tell you you're a failure with F's and suspensions on your Permanent Record. When they do, no matter how tough you are, you'll have a hard time believing in yourself. Out in the real world, the opposite comes true. No matter how hard you work against a wrongdoing corporation or government, they can never flunk you. Instead, the madder you make them, the more successful you know you are.

Understand this, too: the ultimate way of outsmarting school is to leave it and start learning.

(Of course, quitting school doesn't necessarily mean you're anti-authority. Lots of very authority-respecting Christians do it. It just means you're anti-*abuse* of authority, and perhaps anti-*fake* authority.)

But I'm lazy! If no one makes me learn, I won't.

How do you know you're lazy when you've never had the chance to choose what to work at?

If you call yourself lazy, your biggest job in unschooling will be remembering, glimmer by glimmer, how much you loved to learn before school took that love away. Frogs, wheels, words, blocks, dogs—when you were a little kid, the world dazzled you. Also, you will need to allow yourself to admire ("learn") the things that still sparkle in your kaleidoscope, whatever they are.

And laziness shouldn't be confused with zen-like tranquility—"lazy" travelers who hang out in a little Peruvian village for a week will soak up the life and ambience of Peru far more than the typical tourist who in one week sucks in Macchu Picchu, three market towns, four museums, two ancient ruins, and one horseback ride along the Urubamba river. People who find ways to get out of the "rat race" or the obscene commercialism attending Christmas improve the quality of their lives by deliberately avoiding frantic, mindless activity. The same goes for learning: watching the sky for two hours will do more for anyone's cortex than a harried afternoon of longitude worksheets.

But my friends are in school!

Ah yes. The big one. So get your friends to quit with you. See your school friends on evenings or weekends when they're finished with their homework. Make new friends through your interests. (Jeff Richardson, fourteen, comments, "You don't need to go to school to have a lot of friends. I meet a lot of friends through skateboarding. Even if you don't know a skater that's going down the street you say 'Hey dude! Come here!' You automatically have something in common. I've met a couple of homeschooling skaters before too.") Read Chapter 14, which exists solely to coach you along in the social department.

Anyway, stop and think about it. We are social creatures, yes—but not *institutional* creatures.

How much communication do you usually have with your friends on school? Except at lunch and potty breaks, you are rarely supposed to talk with them. If you have friends in some of your classes, you see them—but I'm not sure this is the way to build trust, compassion, generosity, and other qualities integral to healthy friendship. In some courses you compete for A's with the other students. Your discussion is overseen and censored by a teacher. Working together is called cheating. What really gets cheated is your ability to help each other climb.

And remember: your enemies are in school too. Adults control and humiliate teenagers, and teenagers even things out for themselves by controlling and humiliating each other. Few people emerge from school's obsessive popularity and conformity contest without scars.

But it's so scary to think about suddenly quitting school forever!

So quit school temporarily. Take a year off to do what you love, and at the end of that time you can either decide to keep doing what you love, or go back to doing what you don't love. The worst possible scenario is that you would pick up at the grade level where you left off, like foreign exchange students usually do when they return home. In many cases, homeschoolers who return to school enroll in a higher grade level than their peers, since they learn a lot while their brains are out on parole.

But there's nothing better to do!

One of my favorite and usually most profound students gave this sloppy slogan as the reason he'd stay in school even if he didn't have to. He explained a bit by saying that he was too young to have a job and anyway all his friends were there, so he could neither work nor socialize. Indeed, without a meaningful alternative and good company, school might seem the least of several evils.

Yes, this society is hostile and unwelcoming to teenagers, and laws do prevent teenagers from working for money in certain situations. However, with a small carton of creativity and confidence, you'll dream up an infinite number of enjoyable and enlightening alternatives. That's what parts Two, Three, and Four of this book are for.

But it's easy to go to school—I don't have to think for myself!

To you, I have nothing to say. Stay right there at your graffiti-adorned desk. When you turn eighteen, proceed directly into the army. Be all that you can be, according to somebody else.

Miss Llewellyn, you're not being nice.

Sorry. You're right. By the way, you can call me Grace.

Who would consciously stay in school just to avoid thinking for themselves? No one, probably. And if everything we did was based on conscious, rational choice, life would be simple indeed.

But we are not such rational creatures. Until we face them, fears from our subconscious can ruin our lives. If you don't tingle at the thought of quitting school, please look inside. Think hard about whether you're afraid of independence. It's natural to be scared of facing the drums in your own dancing shoes; if you think for yourself, you have no one but yourself to blame for your successes and failures.

Adults, too, hide from the chance to direct their own lives and minds—which is why a lot of them stay in "safe" jobs they detest all their lives, idly fantasizing about the career risk they will take when the kids are grown, or the adventures they will seek once they retire.

Yes, when we live in dreams, we can imagine our "futures" in tissue-wrapped perfection. When we get out of dreams into the present, we find no such perfection. Instead, we find life. It's scary stuff. But it's *real.* Acknowledge your fear, but don't give into it. Dance bravely and brightly. Learn to be a human bean and not instant mashed potatoes. ☀

8

class dismissed

The universe is full of magical things, patiently waiting for our wits to grow sharper.
—Eden Phillpotts

TANIKA HAS BEEN in the cafeteria a long time now. She is heavy; she feels clogged; her cheeks are greasy; but she understands that these conditions are part of life.

She helps to serve the trays of food now. Sometimes she is asked to assist in convincing a reluctant new pupil to eat. She is especially good at this since she can testify how she felt the same way once, but now realizes how wrong she was. She enjoys telling how she has learned to take control of her eating habits.

Tanika takes considerable pride in her achievements. Last year, for instance, she won a prize during testing week for eating a pint of processed moonfruit strips in less than a minute. It is true that she threw the prize—a jar of gulberry puree wrapped in pink paper—into the stream, but no one else knows and Tanika never thinks about it.

"You are a fantastic eater!" the spectacled man said to her just last week.

At home she barely notices the trees and their fruit. She has so many more pressing, more important things on her mind—planning the welcoming picnic for children who have moved to the orchard from other parts of the planet, inventing a creative new way to serve gulberries, eating her homework.

Today she is coaching an annoying little girl who has so far refused to eat. However, Tanika knows she didn't have time for breakfast, and so she patiently lifts a spoonful of limbergreen berry pudding to the child's face.

But the little girl does not open her mouth. Instead, she pushes the spoon away violently, so that its contents splat on the floor. Then she puts her head down on the table and cries as if everything, *everything* is lost.

Suddenly, something unfurls deep inside of Tanika. Life comes fast sometimes. She looks up. She notices that there are no windows in the cafeteria. Out of the corner of her eye she catches a boy watching with soft dark quiet eyes. She turns her head and watches him back. He stands, and she sees that he is lean, as if he has not eaten all of his food. He asks her something with those eyes. She trembles in limbo.

Tanika swallows. A strange inspiration has seized her brain. Touching her swollen belly, she grabs the small girl's hand and walks quickly toward the door. The boy is at her side in an instant and swings the baby to his hip. In the blurred background, a cook lifts a confused, suspicious mouth. They race through the dark hallways. They push the heavy black doors open and burst out onto the spongy humus. They escape their shoes. It has just rained; the sky is dark and translucent but streams of sunlight catch the glittering leaves and soak into their hair.

Tanika runs forward, slipping her brown body out of its cafeteria smock. She gracefully severs a muavo from its stem, and, kneeling, gives it to the little girl. The little girl sucks at it like a monkey in paradise.

The boy laughs. He leaps like a gazelle and captures a cluster of mazina berries. He hands them to Tanika. She smiles and hands them back. She had a big lunch, and she isn't hungry. But there is tomorrow, and a whole orchard resplendent with every kind of fruit in the universe. ☀

Part 2

The First Steps

9

your first unassignments

I DID IT. I decided not to go to school anymore. NOW WHAT???

First, celebrate your audacity with deep chocolate ice cream.

Second, consult your parents. You might get this over with after dinner tonight, or you might acclimate them slowly to the idea. See Chapter 10.

Third, decide what legal or official steps to take, if any. Read Chapter 11. Contact a local support group and ask for advice. If it turns out you live in an area where homeschoolers are tortured by school districts, perhaps you should continue to attend school until you've enrolled in an umbrella school or filed the necessary paperwork. In other areas, all you'll need to do is get your parents to write a letter announcing your actions. In most states and in many countries, the bothersome requirements are few, and should produce only one short annoying headache. Of course, if you're legally old enough (sixteen in most parts of the U.S.), you can just plain quit. If any of this is overwhelming and you want to just get *on* with it, or if you or your parents want the sense of security that comes with earning a diploma, sign up with the Clonlara Home Based Education Program[1] or another good umbrella organization and let them deal with your red tape.

After you've settled with parents and legalities, you're free. Now the real fun begins. The first big thing you need is a vacation, but that needs a whole chapter to itself, so I'll first suggest some smaller things you may wish to do in the beginning of your unschooling career:

Subscribe to Growing Without Schooling *magazine.* You will immediately have access to unschooling/homeschooling friends all over the country. The magazine is full of fascinating letters from parents, teenagers, and younger children. Also, *GWS* publishes a directory of many of its subscribers, which you can use to contact others. Teenager Sylvia Stralberg commented in *GWS* #80:

> *GWS* has been a source of great comfort to me in the past few months. As I read about other kids who are homeschooling and benefiting from it, I no longer feel guilty about my decision to leave school. I rather feel proud of myself and excited about what the future will bring.

---

[1] More information on Clonlara in Chapter 11 and Appendix D.

Join a local homeschool organization, such as the one that helps you out when you need legal advice. If your group needs help, consider volunteering. Meet other homeschooled/unschooled teenagers through this group. Choose your group carefully—they vary widely. Some lack vision.

Hook up with other unschoolers on the Internet. A wonderful starting place is Reanna Alder's Web site, which has a lot of great stuff, including a directory of other teenage unschoolers and links to their Web sites. Or try Jon Shemitz's site, "Jon's Homeschool Resource Page," as a jumping-off place.

See if your city has a resource center for homeschoolers or suchlike. Every few months I hear of another small program in which a few adults (often former teachers) organize classes, study groups, and other opportunities. For some teenagers, these programs provide a helpful transition between school and completely self-directed learning. They're useful for people who want more adult guidance than their parents can give (or who don't want guidance from their parents) but who still want the freedom of unschooling. And the good ones are operated by people who share your unschooling point of view and who want to support you in taking charge of your own education—unlike teachers in many alternative schools. (Unfortunately, many alternative school teachers *don't* believe in deep freedom for young people—they simply feel that their political viewpoints and teaching methodologies are better than those of public schools. Praiseworthy exceptions are the Sudbury Schools, which refer to themselves as "The Unschooling Schools.")

I often hear about these resource centers because their directors order numerous copies of this handbook for their clients, and often they refer to people such as John Holt, John Gatto and myself as their influences. One organization that sounds great is Pathfinder Learning Center, operated by former teachers Josh Hornick and Ken Danford, in Amherst, Massachusetts. PLC is open to homeschoolers and other self-directed learners; members pay a reasonable fee in exchange for numerous opportunities. Josh and Ken offer short term classes in math and other subjects, and host various get-togethers and field trips. They also provide tutoring, help families meet state and local requirements, provide college counseling, arrange internships and mentor relationships, and much more.

When you start to wish your friends had more time to spend with you, become a pernicious influence in their lives. Phone them up after dinner to remind them to do their homework. Get them a copy of this book. Propose that they help you start a science co-op or a bakery. During school hours, of course.

Think about your space. You don't necessarily need any new or fancy equipment, but you do need a place where you feel comfortable, happy, and organized. Likely, you already have a desk or homework corner in your room. Take the time now to make it wonderful. Hang posters. Find a place to keep notebooks, library books, and other paraphernalia. Make sure you have a cozy chair by a window where you can sit and read or write. Consider potential laboratory space, workshop space, studio space, a corner for a museum or collection. Sacrifice a few dollars to an office supply store, for a desktop organizer, file folders, whatever.

What will you call yourself?

Think about the words you will use to talk about yourself. Some of the potential vocabulary includes "self-taught," "self-directed learner," "self-schooler," "autodidact," "doing independent study," "tutored at home," "dropped out," "dropped in," "homeschooled," "home educated," "unschooled," "lifeschooled," "not going to school, just living my life..." Each term has different implications and connotations, as you will discover when you start talking to other people about your new life.

One of my students noticed my ears perk up when she said she had a friend who didn't go to school. However, when she explained that her friend "went to school at home," writing reports and reading books prescribed and overseen by her mother, my ears plunked down again.

"I am not really interested in that sort of homeschooling, but in unschooling," I told her.

She stared incredulously. "*Un*schooling?" she sneered, "There's a name for that. It's called dropping out."

On *that* term—"dropping out"—John Holt wrote, "It is interesting to note that even the people who hate school most, get the least from it, see it most clearly as a profoundly stupefying and alienating experience, still use this word to describe leaving this unreal and useless situation. I urge them to stop using this phrase, and point out that it is 28 or so years since I was last in an educational institution, and I have not been out of the world; one does not disappear into outer space when one steps out the door of a school building. Indeed, it might make more sense to speak of dropping *in*." [1] And Herb Hough wrote in *GWS* #79, "Self-learning upwardly mobile students . . . do not drop out of school—they rise out."

A mother wrote me about neighbors who snooped into her family's unschooling: "People were often nosy, insensitive. [The kids] learned to deal with it by saying that they were tutored. People shut right up! Rich people aren't harassed?!!"

Ben and Theressa Billings, sixteen and thirteen, felt slighted by the term "unschooling." Theressa wrote me, "I don't like it when you call homeschooling 'unschooling' because we do schoolwork just like all our peers."

A mother and father told me that although they thought of themselves as *un*schoolers, they had good friends who taught school, and therefore called themselves *home*schoolers to lessen any defensiveness.

As I said in the introduction, I don't care for the term "homeschooling"—it makes me imagine people who keep an overhead projector in the living room. But there's nothing inherently wrong with the term "school;" in the beginning it was a Greek word—"scole"—that meant *leisure*. Learning in Greece (for boys, anyway) was so pleasant—spending free time strolling along and talking with philosophers— that the word for leisure came to have educational connotations.

Advice
Finally, listen to the teenagers who wrote me with suggestions for new unschoolers:

"Relax! . . . Don't think you aren't learning enough if you aren't sitting for seven hours in a desk."

"If school is your problem, start by taking a six week vacation."

"Get rid of any guilt feelings—unschool yourselves psychologically first— expand, the sky is the limit."

---

[1] John Holt, "Notes for a Talk to Students," *GWS* #74

"Enjoy what you are doing now and you will truly 'learn'!"

"Do things you are interested in. Explore your interests. Try to use yourself as a guide."

"Sometimes when kids start homeschooling they're a little overcome by their freedom and spend it mostly watching television . . . I just say that an unschooling life has got to grow on you, and...when you get out of school take advantage of your freedom and do the things you wanted to when you were in school and thought you didn't have time. (Hopefully that's not watching television!)"

"Try to find the things you like to do the most and then pursue them and forget about academic subjects for awhile."

"Don't get locked in the house—no matter how much you love your parents, you need to get out or the days will get longer."

and finally...

"Party on!" ☀

10

the perhaps delicate parental issue

MOST UNSCHOOLED PEOPLE have, in the past, been out of school because of their *parents'* beliefs. This is where the book in your hands tries to dream something new—that *you*, because of *your* initiative and *your* yearning, march in front of your own parade.

Lovely, you say, *but that means I have to convince my parents that unschooling is a good thing for me and for them.*

Yes.

Fortunately, with a little care and planning, you will probably be able to help them see the light. Ideally, it will go well enough that your parents support and encourage you without too much entangling themselves in your hair, and become so inspired by you that their own lives become richer and braver.

First, though, let's confront some fears *you* might have about unschooling and parents.

Your fears

What if I don't get along with my parents? Won't unschooling just make it worse?

I have some comfort to offer you. Unschooling generally seems to make parents into allies and friends rather than disciplinarians and authority figures. At least, dozens of unschooling parents and teenagers have told me so. Kacey Reynolds, sixteen, gave a typical comment: "I must have missed something in Junior High, because there was a turning point somewhere where my peers have stopped loving and started hating their parents. I'm glad I missed it."

Joel Maurer, thirteen: "My mom likes me better than when I was in school."

Tabitha Mountjoy, fourteen: "My parents and I have a really good relationship with each other. I think that being home educated helps and I love having them around."

A mother: "Most of our friends with teenagers seem to either not know their kids very well, or else to not like them very much. They seem to think of the teenage years as something to endure, or survive. I'm very thankful to both know and like [my son]."

Another parent wrote in *GWS #26,*

Have other parents noticed a very easy adolescence with unschooled kids? I think that my fifteen-year-old son's early acquaintance with responsibility for his own actions has made it unnecessary for him to rebel and fight for independence. He is willing to accept my judgment at times because it is offered as one adult to another and not as a restriction on a kid who doesn't know anything.

A Canadian father told me that homeschooling "has greatly improved family dynamics since we have less time pressures and those we have are of our choosing. Both kids are really happy . . . come to think of it my wife and I are not too glum ourselves!"

Judy Garvey wrote in *GWS #70,* "Homeschooling is so much easier than having to deal with children who have been in school all day."

Many unschoolers told me that once they left school, all kinds of family arguments and hostilities just disappeared. It makes sense; no more quarrels about grades or homework, no more need to take revenge on parents for what happens at school.

If you still have doubts, think of activities you would enjoy away from home—volunteering, apprenticing, babysitting while you read or do math.

My parents have always hounded me about my schoolwork. I'm afraid if I quit school they'll be even worse, since they won't have any teachers to help "control" me.

Make sure when you discuss unschooling with them that they understand your need for independence. Make a point of talking with them often about your activities. Show them what you accomplish, or keep a daily log that they are welcome to read. If you admit your concerns as well as your joys, they will see that you are in touch with reality, and won't need to preach constantly. Ask their advice when you can—they will feel valued and it will encourage them to give up their controlling role in favor of a softer advisory one. *You* set the tone.

The Gentle Art of Persuasion

You know your parents. I don't. What causes giggling in one family might cause slamming doors in another. Perhaps your relationship with your parents is warm and trusting enough that you can simply bring your ideas up casually at the dinner table with confidence that they'll understand and support your decision to quit school. On the other hand, maybe you hide this book under your mattress and know they'll say *no* before you finish your first sentence. Most likely, you fit somewhere between these two extremes, and you should find at least some ideas in this chapter that enable you to convince your parents and then live happily with them for some more years.

Unless you know that your parents will agree easily, I suggest a bit of structure, planning, and method. There are lots of ways you could organize this. You might start by asking them to attend a homeschoolers' meeting with you, or by leaving books on homeschooling laying around the house in conspicuous places. What follows is a detailed explanation of *one* way to do it. It is rather formal, because formal procedures get most adults to sit up and pay attention.

1. Before you talk to them, know what you're talking about.
Do some background investigation so that you can discuss homeschooling and

unschooling with some confidence and expertise. I recommend a) reading a sample issue of *GWS* magazine, b) skimming through *Homeschooling for Excellence*, by David and Micki Colfax, c) reading at least a few chapters of a John Holt book—preferably *Teach Your Own, Instead of Education,* or *Freedom and Beyond,* d) contacting a local homeschooling support group and asking them briefly for their suggestions as to legal and logistical procedures, e) acquainting yourself with an actual unschooled teenager, preferably a fairly independent one.

2. Write a proposal.

Even if you're not sure exactly what you want to do once you're free, your parents can't help but be favorably impressed by a thoughtfully written plan of action. Also, writing it will challenge you to think about some important questions, which will both prepare you to talk with your parents and also clear your vision as to what it is you hope to do with your new life. In your proposal, include some or all of the following:

- *Your reasons for wanting to leave school.* Tell stories from your own school experiences, without exaggerating. If you don't think your perspective is enough, quote other people too. John Holt always works. You might want to reread Chapters 1 through 7 of this book.

- *What you would like to do instead.* Don't commit to anything too specific, because your mind will surely open and change after you're accustomed to freedom. However, do give a fairly specific possible plan of action, so your parents know you've really thought about it. For example, you might say something like:

  I recognize that when I'm out of school, I might find new interests or goals, and that might lead me to change my activities. But since I am very interested right now in dance, this is what I'd like to start focusing on. My ideas are to

  ♦keep taking ballet lessons
  ♦start taking African jazz dance lessons
  ♦begin volunteering at the Center for the Performing Arts in exchange for free passes to dance performances
  ♦read the following books: Doris Humphrey, *The Art of Making Dances*; Joan Brady, *The Unmaking of a Dancer;* Isadora Duncan, *My Life;* Walter Terry, *How to Look at Dance*
  ♦practice at home at least one hour daily
  ♦audition for the next musical sponsored by the Little Theater
  ♦work out an apprenticeship or internship at my dance studio, preferably as a teacher of pre-ballet classes
  ♦Learn more about my muscles, skeleton, and ligaments by coloring Wynn Kapit's *Anatomy Coloring Book.*

- *Your academic plans.* You might handle this in two ways: you could say that you *want* to keep studying all of the major academic subjects—math, science, literature, social sciences, perhaps foreign language—because you want to go to college, or whatever. Explain how you might study each of these. Or, you could say that you would prefer to discontinue the formal study of some or all of these subjects, in order to have more time for focusing on your interests. Sweeten this by saying that you are willing to compromise, if you are. Also, point out ways in which your interests encompass academic subjects. If your plan is to ride horseback through the ghost towns of Idaho, remind them that you will be doing history, geography, and P.E. all day long. If you write a newsletter article or a zine about it afterward, you are doing English. If you take photos or make sketches, that's art. If you plan how far to ride each day and how long it will take, that's math, though basic. If you ask questions and read up on the lay of the land you pass through, that's geology. If you cook your meals on a campstove, that's home economics. The bigger you live, the more "academics" get automatically kneaded into your days.

- *How you see your parents' roles in your new life and education.* This will be especially important, since most people think of homeschoolers as being taught by their parents. If you want to work independently, say so. If you want their help in finding resources or in making decisions, say so. If you think you may need a lot of help from them, say so. Obviously, you need to be considerate of their own needs and lives. If they are busy people, suggest alternate ways of getting the help you need—from other adults, former teachers, tutors, books, relatives. You may want your parents to be heavily involved or barely involved in your education. Your parents themselves may be excited and flattered at your including them, or they may feel burdened and frightened. If both your parents work outside your home, assure them that other unschooled teens do just fine that way. If they don't like the thought of your being home alone all day, point out your plans for apprenticeships, volunteering, or other away-from-home activities. Likely, this won't be an issue—after all, teenagers are the nation's babysitters. Dori Griffin describes her working relationship with her mom in *GWS* #115:

  > I'm not simply floating around doing whatever strikes my fancy. My mom isn't uninvolved in my education. True, she doesn't outright teach me when it comes to school. But we work together. I keep her up-to-date on what I'm doing. We discuss my ideas, and her ideas. I tell her what I'm planning on doing in the near future . . . If Mom and I talk about some projects I want to do, and it takes me a month to finish those projects to my satisfaction, then it's a month before we really discuss anything else. If an idea only takes a few days for me to complete, then I might confer with her again after a short amount of time . . . Usually, I'll do a project first and then think about its educational value later. Sometimes Mom points out to me that what I've been working on counts as "school."

- *A statement that you will need a vacation at the beginning of your unschooling career to recover from school.* If your parents are difficult to convince, you don't want to shock them by sleeping through the first two weeks of unschooling. If you plan to take a purging break (and I hope you do—see Chapter 12), let them know from the outset.

- *A tentative outline of the legal or official steps you will need to take together.* Depending on what state you live in, you may need to think these procedures through carefully later, but for your parents' introduction, you can be somewhat general. Use the advice given to you by local unschoolers.

- *A projection of how much money you think unschooling might cost, and how much it might save.* List equipment, books, lessons, courses, etc. you think you'll need or want with cost estimates for each item—and a list of the school-related expenses (lots of clothes? cafeteria lunches?) that will decrease. If you want to give your parents a broader sense of costs and savings, you might want to add in other factors, like money you might earn in a job or business without cutting into "academic" time, etc.

- *A bibliography.* It need not be fancy, but do include a short list of books or articles you think might be helpful for them to read. For suggestions, see Appendix A at the end of this book.

3. Role play.

Imagine all the questions and arguments your particular parents might come up with, and decide how you can most honestly and thoughtfully respond to them. Also, imagine all the secret fears they might have that could prevent them from supporting you. The more you understand about your parents' values and lives, the better.

To get you started, here are some of the obvious questions some parents I know might bring up, along with ideas for possible responses:

- *You've never done very well in school, even with all those teachers to prod you along. How am I supposed to believe you could quit school and actually learn anything on your own?*

If you've ever been interested in anything—in school or out—and gone after it in an independent way, remind them. If you've had an interest but not developed it due to lack of time, point out that more time will help you to follow through. Explain that in order to learn, you must have the freedom to explore things that interest you. Ask them if *they* are any good at learning things on command. Ask them to think about the ways they learn—now, not in their ancient pasts.

Acknowledge that unschooling would require them to trust you to learn and grow independently, and that at first this might be very difficult for them. If you wish, tell them you could unschool on a trial basis. You might want to share other parents' experiences:

Bea Rector wrote from Arizona while her twelve-year-old daughter Aurelia was performing in Yellowstone with a singing and dancing troupe called Kids Alive. "Trust kids to want to learn," she says, "They don't need to be forced. If given a good example and encouraged to follow their own interests, they'll work for the knowledge needed to be 'successful' adults."

A formerly frustrated Brooklyn parent wrote in *GWS* #32:

> [My daughter] wouldn't let me tutor her and she wouldn't do all the educational things I had planned, like go to museums and stuff. She hung around in her bathrobe and drew pictures all day. For nearly three years. Summers, too.
> Well, you should see her art work today. Fantastic!

Gwen A. Meehan wrote me a year after she'd taken her son Pat, then thirteen, out of school:

> Pat had asked me after fourth grade to please, please let him stay home and learn. My reaction was the same as most people's: (1) I didn't dream that it was, in fact, a legal option, (2) I couldn't imagine his not having daily, active social interaction with the other students, and (3), selfishly, "there goes any time I might have for my own projects." I'm not even mentioning the sheer terror at the idea of being his official "TEACHER." Parenting is responsibility enough. (Turns out I was only spooking myself all the way around! It has been a piece of cake!) . . .
> I should have listened then. If I had, we could have avoided so much pain and so much lost self-esteem. I don't know if I'll ever see again the relaxed, happy, confident, healthy young person who went so happily into kindergarten."

- *I'm not qualified to teach you,* or *I don't have time to teach you.*

Point out that you're not asking them to be your teachers (unless you are), that you can pursue your interests on your own and in the company of people with similar interests. Remind them that you know how to read, make friends, use phones and computers, write letters, and look up books at the library. Ask them if they always need teachers when they become interested in a subject. If you currently ask them for help with homework, and expect to continue to ask for a similar amount of help, acknowledge this. Tell them that one researcher conducted a study of homeschoolers and their parents, and concluded that the less direct instruction the parents gave, the more the kids achieved academically.[1] Tell them that most unschooling parents do not *teach* their children, but rather allow them to learn on their own. Here are some testimonies on that subject:

"[My parents] used to be very involved but this year I have mainly been doing my own work with just a little help and *lots* of encouragement from them." — Tabitha Mountjoy, fourteen.

"We're available whenever she needs us or is searching for answers. We suggest, support, make things available but trust her to search for herself what *she's* interested in." —Linda J. Savelo, mother of thirteen-year-old unschooled Andrea.

Maria Holt wrote in *GWS* #35 after ten years of homeschooling her sons:

> The most important thing I want to impress upon people about our family school is this: WE NEVER TAUGHT ANYTHING. My husband refused to allow it. The closest I came to "teaching" our four sons was during the evening reading-aloud session. We've waded, mulled, or stormed through the *Old Testament, War and Peace*, and *Moby Dick*, among many, many other classics. It was never required to come and listen, and one of our sons gave it up, preferring to read to himself. We provided for and supported the boys—never taught them. Their studies grew out of their own interests. They used all the local libraries and we sent for books from the state library. At one time, they spent months just fixing up an old fishing boat. We never really know *what* they were learning! My husband says we won't know the success or failure of our home schooling for a very long time, if *ever*. We always said they'd "graduate" from the home school when the direction of their lives was outward from home. And that is what has happened.

> [Maria tells about the two who decided to go to college, and then continues.] The youngest . . . worked during his last two years at home at a local restaurant to earn money for flying lessons. (He had taught himself to read through a stamp collection and magazines about flying. He is a good historian. His specialty is the American Civil War, which, for him, developed from the stamp collection.) Now, at eighteen, he has been hired as a flight instructor at a respected flying school at Bradley Field in Hartford, Connecticut.

On a similar note, Ruth McCutchen writes in *GWS* #52:

> The most frequent response that I get nowadays to the statement that my children are homeschooled is, "Really? How wonderful! I admire you, but I could *never* do that! I just don't have what it takes, etc. etc." When I tell them that *I* don't do it, the *children* do and explain a bit what I mean, I'm met with incredulity . . .

> Now that Deborah, Rebekah and Abigail are seventeen, fifteen, and twelve, I find more and more that they really are doing it on their own. They long ago reached the point of asking me more questions that I *don't* know than ones that I *do*.

---

[1] A study by Richard Medlin, reported in *Natural Life* magazine, according to AERO newsletter.

Ruth goes on to describe her girls' interests, including geography, math, anatomy, quilting, clarinet, writing pen pals, Bible prophecy, ancient history, physics, Latin, drawing, maps, and current international events.

Jade Crown, fourteen, whose mother is a single parent, says:

> When people ask me if my parents teach me at home I tell them that my mom works full-time and my dad lives on the other side of the country. My mom doesn't have extra time to tutor me in algebra because she works and cleans and cooks dinner every day (almost). One of the main reasons my mom was opposed to unschooling at first was because she was scared to leave me alone so much of the time. She often said, "In a two-parent family, I might consider it. But it's not a choice for you right now." I have proved her wrong. I have gained a lot of independence from unschooling alone, but I've also gotten better at finding the help I need. I have built a social structure outside of school (Good god! That too?) and found teachers and mentors to help me with the things I can't learn, or have no desire to learn by myself. I've also hooked up with other unschooling teenagers and built relationships with their parents. When I'm inspired to do something, I do it, and my mom is usually thrilled to hear about what I'm learning and who I meet. She once said to me that unschooling was the best decision she ever made as a parent. That made me feel really close to her. It's certainly one of the best decisions I ever made. She's become a big advocate (I never expected that) and we are both proud of each other.

In the *Oregon Home Education Network Newsletter*, longtime homeschooling parent Vivienne Edwards says, "Many parents get worried that they will not be able to teach high school. All you can do is help your children find environments where they can learn. This could be an apprenticeship, tutor, job, correspondence course, travel, neighbor, college, pen-pal, library, local business, volunteer job, museum, sport, vacation, ethnic neighborhood, church, family project—the list is endless, but all of these are valuable learning opportunities."

David and Micki Colfax, in *Homeschooling for Excellence*, write: "In homeschooling, the children typically teach themselves, with the parents appropriately relegated to the job of suggesting courses of study and being available to answer questions—an uncomplicated process."

And in her book *And the Children Played*, Patricia Joudry writes, "Some people think that if you're going to educate your children at home, you have to be constantly at the ready with blackboard and pointer. Not a bit: you have to do something much harder than that. Mind your own business."

- *I can believe you'll do fine in chemistry and history because you've always liked them, but what about learning Spanish?*

You could either promise to do Spanish first every day, in order to relieve their anxiety, or you could try to help them understand that you don't need to learn Spanish now, that if and when you want it, you can learn it. You may decide to compromise at first, by structuring your academics quite a bit, but chances are, your parents will mellow in time. Ideally, they will be able to share the perspective of Rachel Diener, who writes about her thirteen-year-old son:

> His education is entirely self-directed—that is, he chooses what he wants to learn and how and when he wants to learn it. As a result, if compared with his peers, he is far ahead in some areas (computer knowledge, electronics, vocabulary) and behind in some others (math computation, handwriting skills). He and I are both satisfied with this. I think if he is allowed to focus on his strengths and pursue them to the limit rather than plodding along

trying to remediate his weaknesses, he will be a happier and more successful person.

Far more important than the fears your parents will express are the fears they won't express. Your job is to guess what these fears might be, think them through, and then bring them up during your meeting without directly accusing your parents of thinking this way. Here are some things your parents might feel but not be able to say:

- *I had to go to school and suffer. It would be too painful to see you go free when it's too late for me.*

Realize that if your parents agree with your feelings about school, that might force them to admit to themselves that a lot of their own schooling was a waste of time. Recognize that they are likely to feel a rush of despair and sense of loss over this, and that they may avoid these feelings by denying that there's anything wrong with school—yours or theirs. As homeschooling father and psychotherapist Ken Lipman-Stern says in *Growing Without Schooling* Magazine #113,

> I ran a men's group for three years. It was a therapy and support group—and I've seen that the toughness of some men is really a wall or a defense system. The man who says, "My child should have to go through the same tough experiences that I did, because those bad experiences build character," is, I think, holding onto the exterior wall of toughness without examining the pain he felt at going through experiences that were unwanted and harmful.

The solution is grand and beautiful, though perhaps difficult. Unschooling is a statement of faith in human nature. By living your life as proof that you can learn and grow without an institution's control, you show them that they can do the same. If they had childhood interests which they've squelched, it's not too late to reclaim them. In a report by the Washington Homeschool Research Project, one parent comments, "I have my master's degree, so I am well schooled, but I didn't have the zest or energy to learn new things. Homeschooling has awakened in me a desire to discover and learn that I had never had (though I had always been a good student)." If your parents hate their jobs, they can find ways to replace them with work they love. In *GWS* #113 Joe Kelly, publisher of *New Moon* magazine, says:

> For me, there's a way in which my daughters' liberty from school and its constraints taught me how to be free, too, and gave me the permission to take risks I hadn't taken before. Starting *New Moon* was a big risk for us. Both Nancy (my wife) and I worked in management positions at established organizations, and were finally making decent salaries after years of living in poverty. Somehow, despite this, we took the risk of following a dream. Although it wasn't conscious at the time, I'm not sure we would have taken that risk if we hadn't been unschooling for several years. By experiencing how unschooling worked for the girls, it was possible for us to say, "We can do that too. Like the girls, we can follow our own interests and passions where they take us. We can stay home and enjoy each other's company and do something worthwhile together." And that's what we did! Just one more way unschooling has radically changed our lives.

Don't preach or be condescending to your parents, of course, but do find ways to support their interests. If your mom says she always wished she had time to plant a flower garden, bring her library books full of flower gardens, or offer to help with planting and weeding.

- *I'm afraid you want to be so independent that you won't need me. That makes me feel insecure.*

Don't force your parents to say this. Just point out that you value and need their support, that you can't succeed without their blessing, that unschooling helps to destroy barriers in other families and likely will in yours too. Assure them that you'll let them know what you're doing. Tell them you'll need their advice and help in certain areas. Make them feel important. They are.

- *I'm afraid of what my friends, boss, or colleagues will think.*

Don't force your parents to bring this one up either; they won't want to sound mundane or insecure when you are discussing the lofty principles of trust, freedom, and learning. And obviously, you mustn't say you know they want you to stay in so they can avoid shame and embarrassment. That's an accusation, and then they have to defend themselves against you instead of supporting you. (Anyway, you *don't* know this, any more than they know the inside of *your* brain.) Instead, take away their fear without ever mentioning it.

Tell your parents about some of the people who have been "successful" without school. (Chapter 40 is a good start.) You could agree to use terminology that your parents find comfortable—perhaps "doing independent study" rather than something brash like "unschooling" or, god forbid, "dropping out." If you are college bound, tell your parents they can say so to anyone who asks.

Once you are an actual unschooler, keep making it easy for them by being articulate, presentable, funny, intelligent, interesting, and expert—that is, as much as you can be these things without compromising yourself. In general, give them every opportunity to be proud of you and the unschooling movement.

4. Schedule a meeting.

In choosing a time, ask yourself: when are your parents in the best mood? When are you most refreshed and articulate? When are they most likely to trust you? (Just after they see your report card? Just before they see your report card? After you scrub the toilet? After you read *Paradise Lost* even though your English teacher never mentioned it?) It's probably best at this point not to tell them exactly what you'll be discussing. Don't sound too mysterious or choked up, though, or they'll do nightmares on your behalf until the meeting. Just say, "Could we set a time this week to sit down and talk? There's something I'd like to discuss with you."

5. Hold the meeting:

In everything you say, give your parents the benefit of the doubt. Believe that they want the best for you, and that therefore they'll probably cooperate as soon as they truly understand what you want. *Don't* put them on the defensive by assuming that they're going to fight.

Introduce the subject, not by saying that you are asking them if you can deschool yourself, but by saying you are interested in the subject of homeschooling and would like to share some of your ideas with them. Tell them you don't want any sort of answer from them during the meeting, but that they are free to ask questions and bring up any points for discussion. Throughout the meeting, continue to focus on presenting information rather than asking permission.

Give them each a copy of your proposal, keeping a copy for yourself also, and then read through it together, stopping for discussion whenever someone wants to ask a question or make a comment. If you decided not to write a proposal, then you should have at least thought through the same issues so you can discuss them intelligently.

Have paper and pencil ready. If they ask you something you don't have an answer for, don't panic or try to fake it. Instead, write the question down and tell them you'll think about it and get back to them. Obviously, you strengthen your case by following through.

Bring evidence of your interests to remind them that you are not just a student, but a person. This evidence could be photographs, books you've enjoyed, ski poles, rocks, vintage clothing, scrapbooks.

Capitalize on your talents. If you are an actor or storyteller, present scenes from a typical day at school. If you are a writer, write a poem or story that expresses your plight.

If you don't have any talents, capitalize on that. Everyone has talents, of course, but if yours are hidden or underdeveloped, point out that unschooling will allow you to discover and build them. Talk about the ways you want your life to change when you are out of school.

Have books on hand for them to look at, such as those recommended in Appendix A. Choose a passage to read aloud during your meeting. Help them realize that in letting you out of school they have intelligent company and moral support.

If you've already met unschoolers through local support groups, consider inviting a parent and/or unschooled teenager to the meeting. (Make sure your parents know ahead of time that you'll have guests.) You might wish, instead, to invite these people to your second meeting, by which time your parents are likely to have lots of questions.

Encourage them to ask questions. Do not be glib or patronizing. Essentially, in asking to unschool, you are asking your parents to honor your uniqueness and to take you seriously. Return the favor.

Conclude the meeting by asking them to think about your ideas, and by scheduling another meeting about a week later.

6. Hold your second meeting.

Ask them for their response to your ideas. If they say yes, great. If they say maybe, work through their hesitations until you get to yes. What if worse comes to worst and they say no?

Grieve and moan on your best friend's shoulders. Throw darts. Do whatever you do in the face of disaster.

When you're ready to deal with it, here are some strategies for round two:

Beyond no

Ask your parents why they said no. See if you can strike a compromise. Ask them if there's anything you can do that would get them to say yes.

Suggest a trial run. You could start unschooling in the middle of August, so they have a couple weeks to see how you manage. Also, that would allow you to recover from the previous school year. You could agree that if they're not satisfied with your way of educating yourself, that you go to school. A drawback to this sort of timing is that you may feel cheated out of your normal summer vacation, and thus not as exhilarated as you would if you quit in, say, October. Also, the whole idea of being watched and evaluated runs contrary to the idea of pursuing interests because you *want* to. Still, you could probably psyche yourself into it and make it work.

Continue to read up on the subject of unschooling and education in general, and keep giving your parents articles and library books. On *your* birthday, give them a subscription to *GWS.* Read aloud to them or make tapes they can listen to in the car. *GWS* is full of stories of one parent convincing the other parent to unschool after enough exposure to *GWS* and John Holt.

Ask them to attend a local homeschoolers' meeting, fair, or convention with you. Find one that supports unschooling, or at least has a broad perspective rather than simply advocating "school-at-home." Worthwhile conferences are often listed in the calendar in *GWS.* Some good speakers who travel a lot and speak frequently are Susannah Sheffer, John Taylor Gatto, Pat Farenga, David and Micki Colfax, Mark and Helen Hegener, and Cafi Cohen.

Become pen-pals with one of the teens listed in GWS, *or with someone you meet through an unschooling email discussion list.* Keep your parents posted on your friendship.

Help them feel *what you feel.* Ask them to attend school with you for a day, and to take notes and do the homework just as if they were students. Or, without sounding threatening, ask them to think about how they want to be treated when *they* are powerless. For example, when they are old do they want you to take their choices seriously, or would they like you to abandon them to a "nursing home" or other institution?

Befriend as many unschoolers and their families as possible. When you meet some your parents might like, invite them to dinner. Be sure they know what they might be getting into.

When you have a choice of topics for research papers or essays, write on unschooling. Show your parents your work.

See if any of your parents' friends or relatives can understand your side. If they can, ask them to intervene on your behalf.

Ask them again to think hard about their own ways of learning and their own past, and whether they think school was truly good for them, and how much they learned in it.

Watch Dead Poets' Society *with them.* At heart, it's a movie about unschooling; at heart, unschooling is all about "seizing the day."

If you can, survive spiritually by focusing more on your life outside of school and not worrying too much about your grades. I know, from the mail I receive, that many parents do say no—sometimes just for a few months, sometimes until birthday #18. Sometimes people quit without their parents' permission, and the guilt trips their families punish them with can make unschooling miserable. So, if your parents do say no, your best choice might be to accept that decision and then consciously take control of your education as much as you can while still going to school. Or, your best choice might be to stand up firmly and assertively for your right and your need to leave school. It depends on you, your relationship with your family, and of course the intensity of your desire to unschool. You may also want to see if you can change schools, perhaps enrolling in an alternative school or a magnet school related to your interests.[1]

---

[1] A good sourcebook is Jerry Mintz's *Almanac of Education Choices: Private and Public Learning Alternatives and Homeschooling.* You may want to check into the truly radical Sudbury Schools.

When you sense the timing is right, ask them to reconsider.

Beyond yes

After they say yes, you want to live with them in harmony. Try to be tolerant of your parents' worries, especially at first. If they are a bit overbearing, don't panic—they'll relax. If they ask you to study in a fairly rigid way at first, try to cooperate—many unschooling families start this way and then slowly come to their senses, abandoning arbitrary structure. You might show them this bit of wisdom, written by Donna Richoux in *GWS* #52:

> Over the years I've had a few long phone calls from parents who are concerned about the lack of academic interest shown by one of their children. Among other things that cause them worry is the fact that the child will show an interest in something and the parent will arrange for a chance to follow up on it—lessons, a visit—and shortly thereafter the child loses interest.
>
> Somewhere in these conversations I've said something like: how would *you* feel if someone older than you—say your mother, or mother-in-law—lived with you now and always worried about whether you were OK, whether you read too little or too much, and whether she should do something to fix you up? Suppose she got upset because you signed up for a course somewhere and then dropped out? Suppose she *made* you continue?
>
> The parents laugh ruefully in recognition. "That would be awful. I'm always signing up for things and dropping out," they say.
>
> There are many good reasons for dropping out of an adult education class—the brief exposure was enough to satisfy one's curiosity, something about the teacher turns one off, one has less time than one expected because of other changes in one's life. Aren't we lucky that, as adults, we *can* quit? Nobody tells us we have to finish what we begin, or worries about what that says about us. So maybe it's reasonable to extend that same privilege to our children.

Or show them Gwen Meehan's comment on working with her son Pat, fifteen:

> I was all full of the things I was going to help Pat explore academically this year, but it has been abundantly clear that that route would lead nowhere. He might cooperate wanly in order to placate his father and me, but he wouldn't really learn anything.

If your parents just can't relax, find yourself an adult advisor, mentor, or tutor whom your parents respect. Chances are, once they see that this adult doesn't get bent out of shape over your choices, they'll back off.

If they *still* watch you too closely, turn the tables on them with a friendly (if possible) sense of humor. Watch them back. Take notes on how well they seem to be learning, and how well they use what they learn. Give them progress reports. Once they get the message, stop.

Most importantly, continue to do all you can to support and encourage *their* dreams. If your independence inspires them to dramatically change their own lives, don't freak out. Stand behind them and beam. ❖

11

the Not Necessarily Difficult Legal Issue*

As I write, homeschooling is legal in all fifty states of the U.S. and many other parts of the world, and each year, the laws become less bothersome. Though the legalities could still stand a lot of improvement, growing numbers of people support homeschooling. When homeschoolers are so obviously living intelligently and happily, and when their average test scores are higher than school students' average test scores[1]—even though these tests narrowly reflect *school* methods of learning— legislators and courts look rather silly requiring them to go back to school "for their own good." Truth is on your side, and for most families at least in the U.S., it is now easy and quick to get out of school.

However

In a few states and many countries, homeschooling is quite regulated, and homeschoolers are still working for better laws. They could use your help. There's no better way to learn "citizenship" or "government."

Even where homeschooling is now easy, it wasn't always. In the seventies and eighties, schools and courts harassed a lot of families. Lucky for you, homeschoolers did not give up. Instead, they banded together, spoke the truth, suffered, and eventually won supportive laws. Thanks to their very hard work, Americans and most Canadians (and many others) are unlikely to face any serious hassle from schools, let alone a court trial. Don't take their struggle for granted—and be ready to stand up for your freedom if you need to.

If laws can change for the better, they can also change for the worse. If hundreds of thousands of people quit school all at once, schoolpeople would panic about losing their jobs, and would therefore lobby for tighter restrictions on

---

* The information in this chapter is as accurate as I could make it. However, it is not intended as *official* legal advice, which I am not qualified to give. Legally, only an attorney has the right to give legal counsel. Also, laws change frequently, so some details might be out of date by the time you read this.

[1] A nationwide study conducted by Dr. Brian D. Ray in 1990 found that homeschoolers scored, on average, at or above the eightieth percentile in all subjects on standardized tests. (The national average is the fiftieth percentile.) A second, larger study in 1994 found that homeschoolers scored, on average, in the 77th percentile on the Iowa Test of Basic Skills. Information on both studies available from National Home Education Research Institute.

homeschooling. There are millions of schoolpeople, and they might win....then again, homeschooling is now widespread enough (in English-speaking countries, anyway) that major backsliding seems unlikely.

This chapter will give you some basic pointers and information on the legal aspects of homeschooling. Please note that much of my commentary pertains mainly to the U.S. You'll also find a section specifically devoted to international homeschooling, and most of the general principles apply to everybody everywhere. Yes, I am shifting my terminology a little. In this chapter, I will mostly use the euphemism "homeschooling" rather than "unschooling." *Unschooling* is not a legally recognized term, and probably never will be. Don't use it when you talk to schools, courts, or legislators; it will anger or at least confuse them.

("Homeschooling" implies that *somebody* is teaching you, even if it's "only" your parents. That's easier for arrogant professional educators to swallow. Of course, you *do* have guiding adults in your life, but no one should be bossing you about. Gradually, tactfully, start letting people know that you are responsible for your own education. But don't strut around acting as if you don't need no help from nobody. It's not true, and it will earn you enemies.)

General stuff you need to know to understand homeschooling legalities

The more you know, the more powerful your position. That's one major purpose of anyone's education, of course—but as an unschooler living on the edge, you have a real chance to put this truth into action, *now*.

1. The best way to find out how things really work, and what's really allowed, is to contact a local homeschooling organization. These groups can share the lessons learned by all of their members and contacts. They have had experience dealing with laws and school boards, and can offer you invaluable advice. Many groups even publish legal guides.

If a group helps you and doesn't charge for their materials, pay their membership fee or find some other way to contribute. The homeschooling movement has come as far as it has because the people in it are generous, involved, and incredibly helpful.

There are homeschooling groups in every state and in many countries, and you can communicate by mail or email if not in person. (Find out about local organizations in the annual *GWS* directory, by asking a reference librarian, or by searching the Internet.) Some of the groups near you may be so strongly opinionated as to religious or other "truths" that you feel alienated by them. However, even some fundamentalist Christian homeschooling groups are helpful to less dogmatic unschoolers. *Don't* waste your time asking your school or school board about homeschooling laws. These people are often completely misinformed.

2. In the U.S., education laws are the business of each state, not of the federal government. Californians and Iowans, for example, face completely different sets of regulations. Every state has statutes, or written laws, on compulsory education. Most of these laws now have specific provisions for homeschooling. (In some cases they define homeschooling as a type of private school.)

3. No law is an issue until someone tries to enforce it. The vast majority of homeschoolers are perfectly legal. However, in restrictive areas, some people do break laws in order to homeschool. Sometimes, schoolboards ignore them. Sometimes, schoolboards simply don't know about homeschooling families. Until

Mr. Mint registers Junior Mint for kindergarten, they don't know he exists. If a schoolboard does get upset over your actions, it may first ask you to return to school, and then perhaps try to take you to court.

Often, by the way, school administrators and boards think they have much greater power than they do. If worse comes to worst and you are taken to court (perhaps most likely if your parents are separated and if they disagree about homeschooling), one thing you can do in preparation is attend a few other trials—not necessarily homeschooling trials—just to demystify the whole thing a bit.

4. Most of us do, supposedly, live in democracies. In the U.S., the people who pass the statutes are your local elected representatives—not the state senators and representatives who work in Washington D.C., but the state legislators who work in your state capitol. These people are supposed to represent the choices of the people who elect them. Technically, that's not you, because you're not old enough to vote. However, any politician with foresight pays attention to the opinions of thoughtful future voters. Obviously, your parents' voices count too. See the end of this chapter for suggestions on changing legislation.

What do the U.S. statutes say?[1]

Laws change somewhat frequently, and they are different in every state. Within state laws, separate districts have varying policies and attitudes. Therefore, I cannot tell you exactly what you are expected to do in your particular district this year, and whether you should cooperate with or defy the authorities. [2] Instead, I'll mention a few common aspects of current statutes, and in Appendix D you can find access to information on homeschooling organizations.

Most statutes specify that you must register with the state or a local board, be in "homeschool" for a certain number of days and a certain number of hours, and that you keep attendance records. Some statutes ask that you keep records such as logs, portfolios of written work, and even written evaluations of progress (like grade reports); in some states, you must show these records to certain officials. (Be creative with unsavory regulations. If your state requires a progress report, write it yourself and have the parents sign it.) None of these requirements should cause problems. Attendance in school can certainly include educational field trips, such as your kayaking expedition around Prince William Sound.

Other requirements may be more bothersome.

1. One requirement in most states' homeschooling laws is that parents provide instruction in the same areas schools do—math, language arts, science, art, history, health, etc. Don't panic when you read this stipulation. By pursuing your interests, you will automatically include some of these subjects. If any get left out, you can either ignore them and probably not get caught, or study them in ways that you find interesting. There are so many ways to explore any subject that you can almost certainly end up with a legal program that you like, even if it includes subjects you

---

[1] Note to non-U.S. readers: Though this section discusses American laws, some of the suggestions are relevant elsewhere too.

[2] Information on the laws of all fifty states is available through the Home Education Press Web site. You can also request copies of the statutes from your state department of education or your local representatives, or look them up at a law library.

used to hate. See the rest of this book for ways to design a program you can love and everyone else can accept.

And remember: the laws don't ask you to imitate school *methods*. Textbooks, for instance, are not required; nor are grades, marks, or book reports. School activities take most of their shape from rigid schedules, bureaucratic logistics, and limited access to the outside world. There's no point in lowering your intellect to that level.

2. Because people just don't get it about self-directed education and insist on believing that homeschoolers are taught by their parents, some statutes say a lot about parents' qualifications. In some states, one parent must hold a high school diploma or GED certificate. In others, a bachelor's degree is required. In a few states, if neither of your parents has a teaching certificate, you must consult occasionally with a certified teacher. Sometimes, these states pay for this by technically enrolling you in school and paying a teacher-consultant.

3. Many states require you to take standardized tests, either once a year or once every few years. In some other states, you are required to submit some type of annual "assessment"; standardized testing is one of your choices, but you can also elect an alternate method, such as having a certified teacher evaluate your progress, or assembling a portfolio of your work. Other states have no assessment requirements at all.

In some states that require testing, very low scores can send you back to school. In Colorado, for instance, if the composite score on your test is at or below the thirteenth percentile, you are first given the chance to take another test; if your scores are *still* below the thirteenth percentile, you may be required to go to school until the next testing period. (The average test score is in the fiftieth percentile.)

Some homeschoolers refuse to take standardized tests, since they believe on principle that tests are unfair (maybe not to them personally, but in general) or misleading. It does seem rather absurd to require testing as an evaluation of homeschooling—after all, if you're in school and you do badly on the standardized tests, the guidance counselor is unlikely to say, "School doesn't seem to be working for you; why don't you quit and learn on your own?" In *GWS* #100, Oregonian Ann Lahrson writes:

> I had been a schoolteacher before I began homeschooling. In school, I and other teachers knew that there were kids who could do the work but couldn't perform well on the test, and kids who got a high score on the test but didn't remember any of the material afterwards. I had been one of those kids myself, and I think doing well on tests gave me a false sense of self-worth, because although I did well on tests, I didn't magically have an understanding of what I could do or wanted to do, and when I graduated I remember feeling like a phony. Also, when I was a student, I remember that there were some kids in the class who clearly had a real grasp of the material, they really connected with it, but they didn't do as well on the tests . . . In some way, I learned that truly understanding the material *wasn't* necessarily the best thing . . . When I began homeschooling . . . I didn't like the idea of [my children] judging themselves, or limiting themselves, according to what the test said.

Ann explains that when her youngest daughter was eleven, she chose to take the required standardized test one year. But the following year, she chose not to. Ann asked her why, and she said, "It doesn't tell you anything useful. If it was a test about butterflies, I could study about butterflies and then find out how much I remembered. But that test isn't *about* anything."

Of course there is some legal risk to test-resisting, but many homeschoolers have had no problem either quietly ignoring or openly resisting the "required" tests. If you think test resistance is right for you, be sure to order *GWS* back issues #92 and #93, which include several detailed stories about people who have at least partially avoided testing. You may also want to suggest alternate forms of assessment rather than refusing assessment altogether.

4. In some states, there are clear-cut statewide guidelines; follow them and you have automatic legal approval. In others—such as West Virginia—you are supposed to request permission, often from local or county boards. However, these boards usually have specific guidelines to follow in granting approval, and their decisions can be challenged.

5. In California, you can easily register your home as a private school. Also, in many districts you can homeschool through an independent study program (ISP), which is a branch of the public school system. (In some districts, these programs allow great freedom; in others, they are rigid and inflexible.) Many Californians also enroll in umbrella schools or other private schools with programs for homeschoolers. Also, you can take the CHESPE (California High School Proficiency Examination) and thus exempt yourself from school and homeschooling regulations too. The CHESPE certificate is legally equivalent to a diploma; employers are not allowed to discriminate against people who have one. The California Homeschool Network publishes a *California Homeschool Information Packet*, with comprehensive information on legal options and much more.

6. In some states, you can start homeschooling and then notify your local authorities. In others, you must first notify them and wait for their response before leaving school.

7. And in Kansas you must conduct a tornado drill three times yearly. There's no place like home.

An Ounce of Prevention

If you live with a bit of diplomacy, you shouldn't have to actually deal with courts or hostile school boards. Legal technicalities, after all, are not the only factor which affects your right to homeschool; unspoken social rules are even more important and fundamental. The following suggestions are especially important if homeschooling is difficult where you live. However, they can help maintain peace and goodwill anywhere.

1. Trust, as much as you can.

Don't turn a peaceful situation into a war. Until they prove otherwise, assume that the people in your school are your allies. Assume that they want you to have the best possible education, and that therefore they will cheer you on. Teachers and even administrators will likely support you unless you make them feel defensive.

Most of the teenagers I heard from said they'd never been hassled, and that the schools basically ignored them as long as they fulfilled local requirements. In most cases this involved little more than sending in a short statement every September outlining their plans. Some reported that their local schools were not just neutral, but helpful and supportive. Thirteen-year-old Anne Brosnan, for instance, wrote me: "The school is perfectly happy with us, and we've never been to court. About twice a year a lady comes from Babylon Schools to visit us, and she's really nice and we like her. We don't take tests and she just makes sure we are 'pretty smart'!!"

A California mother wrote in *GWS* #35 about what happened after she explained to the local principal why she planned to take her daughters out of school:

> The principal agreed with me completely about my observations and said he would support my endeavors in any way he could. His support was not just official, but warm and genuine . . . The district agreed to send me any non-consumable materials I needed. The principal said my children could partake of school activities if they wanted as long as full-time students weren't bumped from the class and the teacher was agreeable.

Of course, there is no guarantee they'll be nice. A few teenagers wrote me about minor trouble they'd had: "'They' still feel they own us," wrote Todd Brown, fifteen, about his school district in Virginia, "The local principal has forbidden us and some other nonschooling friends from taking driver's ed. Also in the past he has been unreasonable and even downright rude." A parent wrote me that local school officials "enjoy control and power, and their lack of awareness and support causes problems."

Sometimes schoolpeople simply talk arrogant nonsense—"We . . . were informed that no parent could teach a child to read," Californian Bonnie Sellstrom told me about the early stages of homeschooling her sons, "We did put Gary in the independent [homeschool] program with the principal's approval and he was able to complete second and third grade while his schoolmates completed first grade."

2. If you live in a state or country with difficult laws, keep your ship together. At the same time that you radiate friendliness and expect your schoolpeople to be nice, *give them every reason you can to hate the idea of messing with you.* Some of these reasons could be:

- Get your community on your side. If the schools think you're all alone, they might move in for the kill. But if they see that your community supports you, they'll realize the odds are against them and stay off your case. And your community *will* support you if you give them the slightest reason to do so. In most situations, people love to root for any underdog with the guts to beat a system.

    How to win that community support? Be visible. With some of your free time, start a project that is terrific for everyone—a tree planting campaign, a theater production for kids, a teen-to-senior-citizen adoption program, a neighborhood newsletter. Smile. Take lessons from neighbors, in exchange for work. If you keep to yourself, your community may think you are arrogant and standoffish, that you consider yourself (but not other people) "too good" for the schools. That will get their hackles up for sure. Of course, if you *do* consider yourself better than other people, no amount of fakey goo will make your neighbors like you.

- When you start homeschooling, write a very detailed, typed paper explaining your actions, your plans, your reasons, a brief history of homeschooling, and a summary of local laws and recent national court decisions. Mail it to the schoolboard. (In some places, you are required to submit a written plan anyway; by making it long and detailed, you help establish yourself as a force to be reckoned with.)

Forget everything you ever learned about good writing being direct and simple; make it as long and flowery as you can. Unfortunately, bad confusing writing impresses most bureaucrats more than clear writing does. Toss in plenty of jargon like "learning style," "individualized education program," "experiential education," "writing across the curriculum," and "neuro-linguistic programming." Don't say you've been growing mushrooms; say you've been "learning mycology through experiential education." Borrow a textbook on educational psychology from a college library to get some juicy terms, or have a teacher-friend help.

In *GWS* #44, Lisa Boken wrote about working with and learning from boatbuilders, day care centers, an herb shop, and a health food store. "We call this," she explains, "for the benefit of the public school authorities, Reality Centered Learning. We give everything we do with the kids a buzzword like that."

Follow up by keeping a detailed portfolio of everything you do—your writing, your art, extensive lists and journals of books you read and places you go.

- Join a local program that combines some of the elements of a private school with homeschooling. There aren't yet many successful organizations of this type, but more crop up each year. The one I most respect is Pathfinder Learning Center, in Amherst, Massachusetts. Maybe you can convince your favorite ex-teachers to quit school and start up their own center.

- No matter where you live, one simple way to deal with rude legal requirements is to enroll in a long-distance umbrella school. Unlike correspondence schools, umbrella schools usually encourage you to learn as creatively and independently as you wish. They do not require you to study anything in particular and don't provide set curriculums or correspondence teachers; their function is mainly to help you keep records and to handle negotiations with your local schoolpeople when necessary. The better programs do also give good advice when you ask for it. Usually, they charge a flat fee which can seem expensive—but if it solves your legal worries and thus sets you free, it's money very well spent.

  The Home Based Education Program of Clonlara school, in Michigan, is probably the best and most widely used umbrella school. It offers as much or as little structure as you want, although it does not actually provide textbooks. It can give you copies of the same curriculum guidebooks public schools use, formats for record keeping, and—if you complete the reasonable, flexible graduation requirements—an accredited high school diploma. Clonlara has had a campus-based school since 1967, and the international home-based program since 1979. Another reputable umbrella organization is the Pinewood School.

- If you are legally old enough, you can simply drop out of school. For all real purposes, you can still be an "unschooler" or homeschooler. Good colleges and employers won't notice the difference, especially if you *call* yourself a homeschooler.

- Stay informed on homeschooling issues. If you have to attend meetings with school officials, take the initiative for politely educating them on homeschooling—don't let *them* preach to *you*.

Understand what the schoolpeople have to lose: money and pride. Don't carelessly say or do things that increase their losses.

Money: if you quit by the dozens or hundreds, teachers and other schoolpeople will panic about their jobs, reasonably enough. Schools are given money based on the number of students who attend each day—somewhere around $5,000 to $10,000 per year per student (but the amount is greater in affluent suburbs and lower in depressed rural areas and inner cities). Therefore, each person who quits causes his school to lose that much money each year. In the U.S. and Canada, some states and districts work out programs where they continue to enroll homeschoolers, giving them access to certain classes and services in return. These programs could be developed much further, helping both the schools and homeschoolers financially, though many homeschoolers prefer to avoid such programs since "government money comes with government strings." Regardless, if the homeschooling movement continues to grow rapidly, teachers *will* eventually lose jobs.

Pride: quite aside from the homeschooling movement, the teaching profession has long suffered from a general feeling of not being respected or taken seriously enough. Teachers do face injustice—they are not trusted with enough independence or creativity in the classroom, they are swamped with inane clerical details, students and parents viciously blame them for things that are beyond their control, and their pay is low compared to other careers that require similar qualifications. All of this discourages teachers from living with healthy humility and honesty; instead, it encourages them to be generally defensive and overly concerned with their reputations.

To teachers of this unfortunate mentality, homeschooling feels like an additional slap in the face, even a challenge to do battle. After they wear themselves out convincing the public that they are knowledgeable, indispensable professionals, homeschooling families come along and say, "We don't need you. Our kids will have better educations without you."

(Of course, there are many earnest teachers whose self-esteem is intact enough that they can see clearly. They are not puffed up with superficial pride, and will be glad to see you escape to learn freely, even though they may nevertheless worry about money.)

American teachers have formed several very powerful unions, which not only work for higher salaries but also lobby for laws which help them. Obviously, favorable homeschooling laws do *not* help them. So far, the NEA (National Education Association) and other unions have not felt threatened enough by homeschooling to really fight hard. But as homeschooling continues to rise and shine, they *will* fight hard. Already, for the past several years they have included a head-in-the-sand statement in their annual resolutions: "The National Education Association believes that home schooling programs cannot provide the student with a comprehensive education experience."[3]

If I belonged to the NEA I would be embarrassed by such a careless declaration. Nationwide, homeschoolers' standardized test scores are above school kids', even though these tests don't reflect the variety of learning methods and subjects available

---

[3] NEA resolutions passed at the NEA annual convention, Washington, DC, 1996.

to homeschoolers.[1] Then there's that term "comprehensive." Of *course* homeschooling can't offer a comprehensive education. Neither can school. "Comprehensive" is a huge word. It approaches infinity. No one should toss it around so glibly.

Furthermore, in order to try to get comprehensively educated even in their confused understanding of the term, you can't have time to be comprehensively *alive*. The underlying message is that schoolpeople prefer quantity over quality. Their statement implies, "Homeschoolers cannot be trusted to force enough worksheets, textbooks, and multiple choice quizzes on their children, in the fields of English, biology, chemistry, algebra, geometry, art appreciation, history, health, geography, French, and Physical Education." Anyway, if those NEApeople themselves were "comprehensively educated," they would have done their homework and learned that homeschoolers are far beyond their petty ideas of education.

But of course the NEA has to make their statement, silly as it is. If we had somehow gotten ourselves into a nutrition predicament similar to our education predicament, by this time all kids would be eating three meals a day at state run cafeterias, where millions of cooks, waitresses, and other cafeteriapeople earned salaries. If sad parents suddenly got wise and brought their kids home for blueberry pancakes, those cafeteriapeople would lose no time issuing proclamations that parents without degrees in nutrition are unfit to feed their own children.

Teachers' money and pride panics are not your fault; they are the natural and fitting consequences of an arrogant profession which has preyed for a century on the planet's young. However, you may want to generously do something to alleviate the problem. With tact, you can make things easier for both you and the schoolpeople, at least in the short run. If you want to ease the money panic, you can look for a way to stay partially enrolled in school so they get their dollars (Chapter 19). If you want to ease the pride panic, you can avoid making public statements that accuse teachers of incompetence. In your conversations, focus instead on the structural problems of schools, and point out that the system prevents teachers from teaching to their best ability. No honest teacher will disagree with you there.

How to work for better U.S. homeschooling laws

Contact your representatives: write, phone, email, visit. Make specific suggestions on legislation, or simply help teach them about homeschooling by describing your own life and education. This is one of the main ways homeschoolers have so far had legal success: by getting to know their representatives and showing them how wonderful homeschooling is.

If you're up for more, write a bill that would make homeschooling more possible, and then ask your local representative to sponsor it. If your state has difficult laws, homeschoolers are probably already working on a bill. Hook up with them and see how you can help. An important, radical change that most statutes need is an acknowledgment that homeschooled teenagers have the right to teach *themselves*—so the Authorities won't poke their noses into your parents' qualifications and schedules. See *The Kid's Guide to Social Action*, by Barbara Lewis, which is informative enough for activists of all ages.

---

[1] See the journal *Home School Researcher*.

Related statutes would also be helpful. For instance, consider writing (or supporting) a bill that allows people of any age to take the GED. Or, consider working on "educational choice" legislation that gives tax credits to people who want to educate their children outside of the public schools. (Minnesota has such a law, and Oregon had a bill on the 1990 ballot, though it didn't pass.) Make sure that these credits are available to homeschoolers as well as private school students. The way this works is that if you choose to homeschool (or go to private school), the state tax people return to *you* most of the money they would have otherwise passed along to the public school. You use this money to help pay tuition at a private school, or to buy supplies for homeschooling. Through legislation like this, you and everyone else who leaves school could get several thousand dollars a year—which could obviously make a substantial improvement in your attic laboratory.

A potential drawback: schools may become more reluctant to share their resources with you. Consider aiming for a compromise, where homeschool students might give up part of their rebate, and then be legally entitled to use certain school resources. Also, many homeschoolers think that this sort of legislation is dangerous because if the government "gave" (returned, actually) money to homeschoolers, it might attach rules and regulations and expectations to the cash... and maybe even to the whole practice of homeschooling.

If you plan on working on homeschooling legislation, see *The Story of a Bill*, by Howard Richman, which tells how Pennsylvanian homeschoolers won a good homeschooling law. You could base your own efforts on Richman's detailed account.

Free the planet!

If you're not a U.S. citizen, lucky you. Unschooling may be more difficult, but yours is the chance to make history. Depending on where you live, you may have to fortify yourself with a big bottle of courage vitamins, but your actions are truly important. Your example will open the door so a big blast of fresh air can blow into the brains of your friends and classmates.

If you are a U.S. citizen, please read this section. The world needs you! In South Africa, the previous government actually imprisoned two parents for homeschooling their kids, but American homeschoolers wrote hordes of letters to the South African embassy and the parents were set free. In Russia, many educators have been trying to develop a new education system that suits their new democracy. They looked to U.S. schools and were surprised to find that our schools didn't have much to do with democracy. Fortunately, a delegation of teenage homeschoolers (led by alternative education activist Jerry Mintz) visited Russia and demonstrated, by talking about their lives and giving workshops related to their interests, what was possible for self-directed young people. Homeschoolers in Japan, wanna-be homeschoolers in Germany, and people in other restrictive countries crave contact with U.S. unschoolers. Sometimes this contact feels like their lifeline. If you're interested in traveling, consider visiting homeschoolers in difficult places and offering to speak to their organizations about your own activities and those of your friends.

Conversely, if you live in a country where it's hard to homeschool, and can't find other homeschoolers, contact any Americans living in your area—such as missionaries or military families—and ask if *they* know of local homeschoolers.

The unschooling movement in many countries—especially in the Western world—resembles that of the U.S. in the 1970's and 1980's. That is, there are few homeschoolers, so they feel isolated. Laws are ambiguous, and there are proportionally fewer unschooling *teenagers*. It's my guess that in ten or twenty years, the numbers, laws, and attitudes in these countries will catch up to where the U.S. is at the turn of the millennium. That makes for an awesome and hopeful vision, and you can help make it come true.

When a law is unclear, homeschoolers attempt to interpret the law as it applies to them. In some ways this ambiguity can be a blessing—that is, a law may not state that homeschooling is *allowed*, but neither does it explicitly *prohibit* homeschooling. Usually, though, homeschoolers prefer to push for specific legislation, hoping that this will clearly establish their rights. The U.S. has gone through this process during the past twenty years—there are still a few states where homeschooling rights are a bit fuzzy, but that doesn't stop people from doing what they believe in.

In most regions of most English-speaking countries, it's legal to homeschool, and there is a thriving, rapidly growing unschooling movement, with numerous support groups, a few nationwide organizations, and newsletters. (The terms "deschooling" or "natural learning" are used more than "unschooling." Also, like in the U.S., many people use the terms "homeschooling" and "home-education" to mean self-directed education.) Barbara J. Smith, who directs the Calgary Montessori Home Education Program in Alberta, Canada, gives advice which is realistic for teenagers in most English-speaking countries:

> Take advantage of the flexibility. Find a mentor or an apprenticeship. Do job shadowing. Let your program be interest based—you can't do it all. Aim for good research skills, good critical thinking skills. Be entrepreneurial. Value informal learning. Look in your own community. Travel when you can. Have fun learning. Learn a foreign language—go there!
>
> Within our program, I facilitate special projects for teenage students—such as work experience in an eye clinic, construction and decoration of a family room, travel in Greece with interviews of relatives and documenting the sites, an equestrian project training a miniature horse, food studies and menu design.

In most other European countries, it is legal or semi-legal to homeschool but quite rare, and somewhat difficult, and often frowned upon. Katherine Hebert, fourteen, holds both Swiss and American citizenship. Her unschooling experience reflects that of many Europeans:

> Once you've settled in and have sunk into routine, you realize [that homeschooling in Switzerland] has quite a few advantages. The main one is that you are in the Centro of Europe, culture capital of the world. To make my point I'll give you a few statistics: if you aren't scared to fly and have an extra two hundred bucks saved up from the last bake sale, why not go to Stockholm? How about Russia? Turkey? Greece? England? The places are limitless. The Italian border is four hours away by train (considering I can't drive yet I take the train everywhere), Rome five and Venice six. Germany is an hour and a half, the French border twenty minutes and Paris two hours. Get the picture? Only two weeks ago I was doing volunteer work in Sarajevo, Bosnia, a half an hour plane trip away . . .
>
> The resources are more difficult to get than in the States. The local library is only accessible to adults, my mother's World Health Organization library is only for W.H.O. workers and the U.S. embassy library only for embassy workers. I get around this problem by posing as an eighteen-year-old at the local library, as my mom at the W.H.O. library, and as a secretary at the embassy under a fake name; I hope they never actually check to see if I work there. I also get a lot of my information off the Net.

If someone is interested in homeschooling here, I think it's a great idea. If you have a strong drive for learning and like to get out and do stuff this is the perfect place for you.

There's little information available on unschooling in most parts of Africa, Asia, and Central and South America. That doesn't mean it's not happening—undoubtedly, there are young autodidacts in every nation, though they may feel alone and not realize they're part of a worldwide movement. If you live in an area where no one has heard of unschooling, it's truly up to you to be the bright ray of brave hope. Aleta Shepler's advice for unschooling teenagers in Venezuela would be well adapted to most of South America and, in fact, to much of the world:

If you are interested in a traditional book-centered type of education, you will need a lot of money for such an endeavor in Venezuela. There are public libraries, but you may not check out the books. One can use the Internet now but sometimes the phone system doesn't work and in the interior the electricity only works certain hours of the day. However, if you are interested in experiential education, there is a great deal of freedom and opportunity to explore your passion.

Our children have observed Cappachin monkeys in their native environment, interviewed Bolivian women regarding their traditional strategies of family planning, worked with street kids, directed a neighborhood theater group, built a recycling center, studied the impact of subsistence farming on the rainforest, learned to write a proposal, a petition, and make power phone calls, run an import comic book business, learned to ride and train a horse, raised rabbits and dogs, trained a parrot, etc. . . . They have learned a great deal about cross-cultural conflict resolution.

If you learn best with a mentor, there are many possibilities. In the capital city, there are many artisans who can serve as mentors in ceramics, clothing design and construction, carving, painting, etc. With the help of an agent there are opportunities in theater, movies, and commercials . . . In the interior, there are still people who can show you how to build a grass roof, carve a canoe, observe and identify the flora and fauna of the rainforest.

Most of the kinds of activities which are extra-curricular but school-related in the U.S. (such as sports, music, drama, and art) are done in social clubs in Venezuela. For example, our daughter Halee belongs to a horse club and spends every afternoon riding with her Venezuelan friends. Our son Os attends a comic art institute every morning, where he meets with his mentor and shares his work and imported comic books with his fellow learners (ranging in age from 18 to 48).

I would highly recommend that you design your home based educational endeavor around a big problem or question that needs to be solved. Venezuela is a country which is in crisis and it is our family's experience that you can learn most academic subjects and many skills by making the resolution of a social problem the focus of your study. Our children have devoted 85% of their educational budget to social problem-solving expeditions. We believe that this is the true meaning of "public education."

While there are many opportunities and legal freedoms in Venezuela for homeschoolers, it is not always easy. You will have to develop the skills of a detective to sniff out mentors, apprenticeships, and other learning resources. And you will have many well-meaning Venezuelans and expatriates who will try to direct you to traditional schooling. Non-conventional educational in Venezuela is for risk-takers, social change agents and the passionate. It is not for followers or the faint of heart.

General Resources
- *Growing Without Schooling* magazine publishes articles on international homeschooling, and lists homeschooling organizations around the world.
- The annual directory issue of *Growing Without Schooling* includes the latest

addresses for dozens of international homeschooling organizations.

- Clonlara's Home Based Education Program. If you are not sure about the laws in your country, or if homeschooling seems to be illegal or semi-legal, or if you'd simply like some long-distance support, enroll with Clonlara. These people are amazing! They provide a legal structure for homeschoolers in twenty countries so far, as well as in all fifty states of the U.S. They are expert at dealing with school officials all over the world, and have even been able to help people homeschool in Germany and Japan. Very few of their client families outside the U.S. are American citizens.

- The Internet. Search for "homeschooling" and you'll find heaps of information pertaining to many countries. Jon Shemitz's "Jon's Homeschool Resource Page" and Karl Bunday's "School is Dead, Learn in Freedom" Web sites provide worldwide information and link to other international sites. Also see The Homeschooling Zone, which includes a worldwide directory of homeschoolers.

The Countries

In Appendix D you will find a list of many countries' largest or broadest organizations, which can put you in touch with smaller groups near you. Almost all of these organizations are run completely by volunteers—sometimes it's just one dedicated family. So when you write, be sure to include a large self-addressed stamped envelope, and it's also nice to send a little money to cover costs of photocopying, etc. If no organization is listed for your country, you may be able to find one via the general resources listed above—and no matter where you live, Clonlara can likely help you homeschool legally.

What if your country isn't listed? I don't have information about homeschooling everywhere, and I don't have room here, anyway, to go into detail on all the countries that I do know about. In addition to the countries discussed below, I heard from and about homeschoolers in Bermuda, Brazil, Haiti, Hong Kong, Israel, Malaysia, Mexico, Nigeria, Saudi Arabia, and Taiwan. Do your best to find other homeschoolers, or just sniff out the local laws and give it your best shot. Then, write and tell me about your adventures so I can talk about them in another book!

Americans (and others) living abroad
form a large, though dispersed, homeschooling community. *Military* families have practically no problem homeschooling anywhere—even in Germany—and most other expatriates have no problem in most countries. Valerie Bonham Moon, an American military mom in Germany, says that "any military personnel can consult DoD Manual 1342.6-M, and also read UR 10-12." She is beginning to form a network of military families homeschooling abroad, and you can contact her for information.

Australia
Despite—or because of? —difficult laws in some states and territories, Australia has a thriving, though small, community of homeschoolers who are politically active and alert. Officials put the total at somewhere between five and twenty thousand among the country's population of eighteen million. "As in the U.S.," says Janine Banks of New South Wales, "there are restrictive laws in a couple of states, but many people continue to home educate as they wish. To the best of my knowledge, no-one has

ever been jailed for home educating in Australia . . . Most of the general population do not know it is a legal alternative to school, and there is a lack of awareness of home education and its advantages. This means there are very few resources specifically for home educators and most of the support literature I have read comes from the U.S. or Britain. We are a growing movement but still in our infancy."

The worst state is Queensland, where if your parents aren't registered teachers, they're supposed to hire one to teach you or else enroll you in a correspondence school. Yet, at least two hundred homeschooling families—in Brisbane alone—do not comply with these regulations; it seems that most Queensland homeschoolers simply don't bother to notify the authorities, and they get away with it. Eleanor Sparks remarks in her (funny and comprehensive) Web site, "The Education Department seems to be putting a lot of the home schooling issues into the 'too hard' basket." (And anyway, as Eleanor says, "The list of criteria spelled out in the Information Booklet [of Queensland] can be used against the Department. It would be fairly easy to prove that the State schools did not meet the standards set down by the Education Department that home schoolers' curriculums must meet in order to be approved.") If you want to unschool yourself in Queensland, you should definitely get in touch with a local homeschooling group, and *not* with the Education Department. At the other end of the Australian legal spectrum is Victoria and the Australian Capital Territories, where the law clearly allows people to homeschool without permission from the Education Department.

In between the heavy-handed laws of Queensland and the cheery freedom of Victoria, the other states and territories at least seem to have more homeschoolers than rules and regulations *about* homeschooling. Jo-Anne Beirne of Homeschoolers Australia Pty Ltd writes in *Growing Without Schooling* #101:

> The lack of a national approach to education has been good for homeschooling . . .
> Because some states do not have a process for certifying that a student has completed high school, access to jobs has not traditionally been predicated on the school examination process, but rather on workplace examinations and interviews.

Belgium

Karen Maxwell runs a homeschooling discussion group in Brussels, and reports:

> Homeschooling is a legal option in Belgium, but it is a fairly well-kept secret. A family who wants to homeschool runs the risk of hearing that it is not legal from a variety of sources that should be reliable. I write a letter to the school inspector of my district once a year from each of my two boys [ages ten and fourteen], stating that I take the responsibility for their education for the coming school year. For the last five years, that has been the extent of my contact with the educational establishment.
> As there is no legal restriction on homeschooling, the individual school inspector seems to sometimes feel obligated to "interpret" the law and the reasonable restrictions. I have also known families that had their family allowance stopped, as someone who handled their benefits felt that family allowance was only provided if the children attended school, but in both cases the money was paid after legal proceedings.
> All of my community contacts know that I homeschool, and I have not been secretive about it and have had no trouble. It is an option that is used by a very small minority here, and I have no idea what the statistics are. By contrast, in France the option is much better known, although the percentage of homeschoolers may not be much higher than here.
> Compared to the U.S.: As I have *no* restrictions to follow, and as we "unschool" rather than following lesson plans, I would say that is the biggest difference from any states that require planned lessons or testing at the end of the school year.

Canada
Each province and territory has its own laws governing homeschooling, and as I write the official count of homeschoolers is about ten thousand. British Columbia has the best legal climate for unschooling, with a vital, warm "deschooling" community; I met dozens of independent, bright unschooling teenagers during speaking trips to Vancouver and Victoria. British Columbians, in fact, are better off than most U.S. citizens. Homeschoolers must register with a public school, through correspondence courses, or with an independent school of their choice. (Some of these independent schools are operated *by* unschoolers.) These institutions receive a small amount of money from the government, based on the number of homeschoolers registered with them, and in turn they provide resources back to their "enrolled" homeschoolers.

Nova Scotia, Alberta, and Saskatchewan are pretty good too. Alberta is similar to British Columbia in that homeschoolers are supposed to register with a school board; they can register with any board in the province. Registered Albertans also receive a small amount of cash for learning supplies.

Laws have improved considerably in the past few years in Ontario, so that school boards no longer have much authority over homeschoolers. Each year, Manitobans must register, submit an educational plan, and then submit two progress reports. Quebec is "way down near the bottom of the list" when it comes to a good legal climate, with an ambiguous, indefinite law that allows hostile school boards to cause a bit of pain and suffering. Some families stay underground and choose to have nothing to do with the Commission Scolaire; many others enroll with Clonlara or other long-distance umbrella "schools." Nevertheless, homeschooling is clearly legal and parents do not need to be certified teachers. Elizabeth Edwards, who publishes a bilingual homeschooling newsletter, writes:

> The question of language creates its own problems, as many resources for homeschoolers here in North America are available only to English speaking families. We have the highest rate of drop-outs for Canada and enormous pressure because of our demanding language laws. Our advice to teenagers is to get close to a computer and to not worry. Our unemployment is so high presently that a piece of paper (a degree) is practically worthless. Job finding is an archival term, what we need is business creation. Our system allows for anyone to enter CEGEP [the equivalent of college in the U.S.] by writing a grade 11 equivalency exam. My suggestion is that students prep for that if they are sure they wish to enter the system of college and to by-pass secondary entirely. Of course even CEGEP could be avoided depending on the area of life your interests lie in. I strongly advocate the apprentice system and encourage my kids to look upon their natural talents as the doors of opportunity in life.

England
Homeschooling is unquestionably legal and well established throughout the U.K. Roland Meighan, director of Education Now, estimates about twenty to twenty-five thousand teenagers, but other homeschooling leaders guess under one thousand. Some people feel it's easier to homeschool in the U.K. than in the U.S. —the regulations are the same throughout the whole country, and therefore easier to communicate and understand. Few people homeschool for religious reasons, so British homeschoolers don't quarrel much among themselves. Formal testing is not required. Homeschoolers do not have to follow the National Curriculum. And homeschoolers *can* take GCSE's and "A" level exams at home.

On the down side, school officials have the right to visit homeschoolers to ensure that their educations are "suitable" to the "age, ability, aptitude, and any special educational need" of the learner, and in a few areas these visits are intrusive and aggressive. It's difficult to attend school part-time in Britain, though on that front the visionary Roland Meighan is working to raise awareness and bring about many improvements. He advocates "Flexischooling," sort of a combination of homeschooling and using schools part time. And, at this point, it may be harder for homeschoolers to gain admittance to universities in England than in the U.S., but homeschoolers *have* been admitted to Cambridge, Oxford, and York Universities.

France

Homeschooling in France is a little-known option, but explicitly legal since 1882. Your family needs only to announce your decision to homeschool two weeks before the new school year starts. You give one declaration to the mayor of your town, and another to the inspector of the regional academy which represents the board of education. The "authorities" may look into a homeschooler's education at ages eight, ten, and twelve, and the academies can require a detailed description of how you plan to reach academic goals. In reality, homeschooling is easier for some families than others. Sophie Haesen, of Alsace, reports:

> Very much depends on the regional academy and their former experience with homeschoolers. If they have been dealing with others before, it should be easier for you as they already know that this possibility exists. If you are the first family in your region, they might be inclined to make administrative problems as they themselves do not know too well how to deal with homeschooling. (In France, usually the first reaction to the fact that homeschooling is legal is surprise and disbelief, even with teachers.)
>
> I know of about two hundred families who are homeschooling in France, because they are members of the homeschooling network. How many "independent" homeschoolers there are, I do not know, and it is almost impossible to estimate.

Germany

The Bad News: Germany is the only nation I know of where homeschooling is definitely illegal. Foreign military families are exempt, but all school-aged Germans and non-military foreigners are required to attend school. A few families have homeschooled and fought hard for their right to do so, but have been so harassed and prosecuted that they eventually fled the country. Valerie Bonham Moon, an American military homeschooling mom, has also heard of families who have had their children obviously leave the country and then quietly return so they could homeschool in secret, but she has not personally known anyone who has done that. Margy Walter reports that another family "managed to keep their kids at home a good part of the year by writing them 'sick' for weeks on end, but they were also harassed and had to hide the kids inside from the neighbors, etc. — pretty ghastly."

The Good News: Clonlara can help even Germans homeschool, through its connections with alternative schools. And some would-be homeschoolers enjoy the comparative freedom of Waldorf schools, which are numerous and large.

Ireland

The Irish Constitution says that the family is the main educator, so homeschooling has long been legal and relatively problem-free, and the trend is growing. In *GWS* #84 (1991) Mary Delmage Sheehan writes, "Now that we are starting to organize a homeschooling group, the full extent of homeschooling is becoming apparent and it is clear that it has been going on quietly and successfully for many years . . . The reaction of school-going children to homeschooled children usually seems to be, 'Lucky thing!' and the reaction from adults is similar—'Good idea.'"

Jamaica

In Jamaica, apparently no one restricts homeschooling because officials don't recognize it as an option, and because there are already many kids who don't go to school. "There are many children who just don't go to school mostly for economic reasons," writes Sally Sherman, an American citizen living with her teenaged son Theo near Ocho Rios. "Many times, they don't go if they do not have lunch money. And very few go when it rains . . . There are no truant officers." Schools are also overcrowded and lack supplies. After Theo finished grade school he didn't go back, and nobody official said anything.

Nevertheless, says Sally, "The social pressure on parents to send their kids to school is tremendous." Perhaps that pressure, along with lack of awareness about unschooling, explains why, despite the freedom, "Only a few of us take advantage of this incredible opportunity." Many Jamaican homeschoolers are Rastafarians. As Sally says, "Their religion teaches them what Babylon (the system) does to their children. Also, most schools are insensitive to culture differences (or purposely want everyone to be the same) and require that children keep short hair, though Rastas wear dread locks." Sally points out several good opportunities for Jamaican unschoolers:

> There are lots of accomplished tradespeople here and apprenticeship is a natural occurrence. Most carpenters, electricians, plumbers, and masons need helpers and pay them very little, but it's easy to work with someone for a while and then move on.... Also the music industry is big here and there is probably opportunity within that.

Japan

Press stories from Japan offer wake-up stories:

> A ninth-grader depressed by school discipline hangs himself. A teacher slams a school gate on a student, crushing her skull. Another teacher beats a student to death on a school outing, just for carrying a hair dryer... Typically, children are hit on the head, punched in the face, kicked or beaten with sticks for missing homework deadlines or breaking the rules.[1]

> A [fourteen-year-old] teenager who confessed to the brutal murder and beheading of an eleven-year-old acquaintance may have been responsible for earlier attacks on two schoolgirls, police said on Sunday....While police have not disclosed a motive, a letter sent to a local newspaper ten days after the killing blamed Japan's authoritarian education system. "I am not forgetting revenge for the compulsory education that has produced me as an invisible existence and on the society that has produced this compulsory education," the rambling note read in part....

> Residents said on Sunday they were glad there had been an arrest but many voiced concerns about a system that puts so much pressure on students to succeed. "Although the suspect was arrested, the problem remains to be resolved,"' said Yoshihiro Kubota, 41, a Kobe resident.

> "This case exposed the ugly aspect of school life," said Kubota, the father of three schoolchildren in Kobe. Since the killing, children have been escorted in groups on their

---

[1]"Japan's brutal schools: Discipline fosters culture of violence," by Mari Yamaguchi, Tokyo, Associated Press, March 1994.

way to school and armed with noise emitting devices.[2]

Thanks to an incredibly stressful and abusive system, around 180,000 "school refusers" from ages six through fifteen have stopped going to school. Because Japan places such a high value on schooling, these kids suffer greatly, and they have little or no support for their attempts at saving themselves. Dr. Pat Montgomery, director of Clonlara, says:

> Last year the suicide rate of young boys hit an all time high . . . When school refusers quit going to school, there are not many places they can go. Their self-esteem sinks to a low because they are disgracing their families . . . I must emphasize that they do not make this decision gleefully; they are usually physically ill leading up to it and afterwards . . . I was shown a hospital in Tokyo where all ten floors held children with school phobia . . . The idea was to rehabilitate them so that they could go back to school.

Fortunately, a few people have responded with compassion, setting up "free schools" to help school refusers meet and learn outside of the system, and the government has basically averted its eyes. This brave beginning has led to interest in homeschooling also.

In 1994, 889 people attended a full day Tokyo symposium on homeschooling featuring Pat Montgomery. And in 1997, Clonlara enrolled 150 families and has even opened a Japanese office in Kyoto, with a Japanese contact teacher, Konomi Shinohara Corbin. This program is adapted for the needs of Japanese homeschoolers, which differ in some ways from those in other countries. "Now is the time for homeschooling to wax," says Pat, "while its existence is officially ignored by the powers that be. Another case of 'When the people lead, the leaders follow.'"

Of course, being *allowed* to homeschool is only half the battle in Japan. Whether a homeschooler will grow up and be accepted as an adult member of Japanese society remains to be seen. "There may be a serious risk of not being able to access higher education, or problems getting a job without the Junior High school graduation certificate," writes Kyoko Aizawa of Otherwise Japan. She reports that the Japanese advisory panel for education recently proposed that school refusers and homeschoolers should be allowed to take an exam in order to receive that certificate, but they would still not be able to say on their résumés that they had actually graduated from junior high school. Kyoko, attorney Sayoko Ishii, and other homeschooling advocates are hoping instead for better legislation that clearly allows and recognizes homeschooling as a worthy path into responsible adulthood, and they feel that equivalency exams are not the answer. In the meantime, Clonlara has some hopeful news:

> Several of our Japanese students have graduated with our Clonlara diploma and have entered colleges and universities there—even the renowned Waseda University. So, we have no problems on that score. Others have used their Clonlara credentials to go into the work force or to TV and theatre work.

At this point, some Clonlara students may still have to take Japanese exams to earn their graduation certificates, but at least they can prepare for those exams outside of the school system.

"The legal position of homeschooling is unclear," says Leslie Barson in *GWS* #106, "and until this is clarified, the present homeschoolers are frightened and

---

[2] "Japanese Teen Confesses to Beheading," by Noriko Yamaguchi, June 29, 1997, Kobe, Japan, Reuters.

cannot join together. Nor can they advertise homeschooling as a choice for Japanese families." Of course, since compulsory schooling stops at age fifteen, theoretically it's possible for older teenagers to find some way to take charge of their educations outside the system, but independent learners cannot necessarily expect to be accepted by employers or universities.

The Netherlands

Homeschooling is legal, but not well known; it took one mother almost six years to track down information. In 1988, a homeschooling family won an important court case, partly through proving their seriousness—they said they'd leave the country if forced to attend school. In *GWS* #102, Liz Meyer Groenveld writes about her seven-year-old daughter:

> My worries have always been about the higher grades. Academic standards are very high here; for example, to enter university, one must know not only Dutch but English, German, and French. And in Holland one must have a trade diploma even for work such as flower arranging . . . But reading *GWS* never fails to reassure me that where there's a will, there's a way. I think that as long as we can meet the academic requirements, Lizzy should have no more trouble passing a state exam to enter university here than any transfer student from another country would have. Now that she is . . . quite fluent in English and Dutch, I am working on finding someone to teach her German . . . I plan to ensure that Lizzy can homeschool as long as she wants to . . . I do think people assume that we are doing things very officially, with tutors and textbooks, when in fact we are unschooling. I also ask the school children regularly what they're working on, and in most areas we're way ahead of Lizzy's class despite the minuscule amount of time we set aside for actual lessons.

New Zealand

There are about five to seven thousand homeschoolers in New Zealand. This accounts for more than one percent of the school-age population, so homeschooling is definitely well known and increasingly popular. Your parents do have to fill out some detailed forms, outline how they intend to address various subjects, and then provide annual reports. Homeschooling mom Debbie Bennett says, "I don't think the laws are particularly restrictive. As long as you tell the authorities what they want to hear you can be fairly relaxed in your approach. It's up to the individual really—just as long as you play their game." Homeschooling families receive several hundred dollars each year for educational supplies. Jan Brownlie says, "It is very easy for teenagers to homeschool, especially if you apply for an exemption (from enrollment at school) and emphasize the work experience angle. In fact, if a teenager over fourteen or fifteen can say they have a job, they can leave without applying for an exemption." Jill Whitmore of Auckland notes that:

> It is accepted that children may learn informally as well as formally . . . Our own teenagers were able to attend a local school part time during the later part of their home schooling careers; this was by agreement with the principal and teachers. Some other teenage home schoolers that we know of have enjoyed similar arrangements.

The Philippines

Candace Thayer-Coe, the mother of a Canadian/American homeschooling family living in the Philippines, reports that "A Filipino family who has homeschooled one of their sons through high school has told me about the Filipino law on schooling. They said the law is: School is mandatory at seven years old but if your child is not in school there is no punishment enforced. People do tend to ignore the law here."

But as in many parts of the world, Candace says, "There are not many homeschoolers here because it is socially unacceptable. Who you are here in the Filipino community . . . has a lot to do with where you went or go to school . . . We are considered brave by our peers and fellow employees at Asian Development Bank to courageously keep our children out of any group's system."

Norway

Norway had its first national homeschooling conference in 1996. Homeschooling is controversial but legal.[3]

Portugal

"Parents here are very dissatisfied with the state of public schools," writes Gloria Harrison in *GWS* #80 (1991). She knew of no homeschoolers besides her own Portuguese/American family and a few Americans, English, and Canadians.

> As far as homeschooling my own children, I have never met with any hassle . . . Portuguese schools . . . function in two shifts. Children go to school mornings only or afternoons only. That means that one always sees children around in the streets, and my children and I don't stick out like a sore thumb when we go out. No one has ever asked them why they're not in school . . . My brother-in-law told me that homeschooling in Portugal is not against the law, but he didn't think many people would do it, because of the stigma attached to it.

Russia

Interest in alternative education is definitely increasing. In *GWS* #97, Natasha Borodachenkova wrote about the experience of homeschooling her young daughter, Natasha. Though the legal system was very rigid at the time (about 1988) and required that all children attend state (public) schools, the headmaster of her school made an exception for Natasha at her mother's request, with the agreement that she would take exams in some subjects.

South Africa's

homeschooling movement is alive and kicking. The old government vehemently opposed homeschooling, and the present Parliament is not exactly eager to dispense freedom, either. But with the new, more democratic government, activists have won major improvements—and continue to fight for more. Our star is Kate Durham, who says, "I was your average housewife except that I knew what had to be done and how to do it." Kate organized an association, helped motivate homeschoolers in other provinces to also organize, and then traveled repeatedly to Cape Town to educate politicians.

As a result of her work and that of other dedicated people, South Africa now has national legislation which allows homeschooling, though you still have to register and then hope that the government will grant approval. Many families homeschool openly without registering, though, somewhat fortified by a growing public resistance to state interference in private matters. How many homeschoolers? "A guesstimate puts the figure at about 1,300 . . . with the majority underground," says Kate, "Our association's membership grew close to one hundred percent in 1996." The public schools are terrible, and the private schools are expensive, so Kate

---

[3] Information from Karl M. Bunday's Web site, "School is Dead, Learn in Freedom."

expects the trend to continue. (Ironically and obnoxiously, the old South African compulsory school laws did not apply to black kids. In a letter to *GWS,* Kate says, "White children especially were herded into schools. It is my personal belief that this was an effective way of perpetuating the myths and fears on which apartheid survived.")

Spain
The laws are ambiguous, but homeschoolers are pretty much allowed to do as they please; as Bippan Norberg points out, the law "has basically been used to force poor families to bring their kids to school instead of using them as labor." In one court case a judge condemned 150 such families, but said that the problem was not the lack of schooling, per se—it was a larger issue of neglect and abuse. He said that legal consequences would probably *not* apply to homeschoolers, because "in a case like that, the parents do not let go of their obligations towards their children, but the opposite—they take responsibility for choosing the best educational method."

As far as Bippan knows, no family has had serious legal problems for homeschooling, and there is a nationwide homeschooling movement of at least a few hundred families. "But we know that a lot more people would do it if it was completely legal," she says, "Lots don't even know it is semi-legal. Some families are completely open about it, like we are, and have not had any problems at all . . . Others do it completely in secret and are afraid. From our point of view they are afraid of things that they absolutely have no reason to be afraid of." Bippan's family holds national meetings and week-long camps for homeschoolers, and usually about fifty people attend. They also send out an information packet on request.

Bippan's son, Lomi Szil, fifteen, is one of few teenage homeschoolers in Spain. Most of his friends hate school, but don'tt see homeschooling as an alternative since they've never had much chance to decide *anything* for themselves. But Lomi says if any Spanish teenagers *do* choose to homeschool, there are plenty of opportunities to take courses and try out all kinds of things. "Even when the rules say that you have to be a certain age or show that you are in school, here in Spain you can always go around the rule. Many courses have an age limit of sixteen or eighteen, but only because there is nobody under that age who *can* take part, since they are all in school." Despite the lack of unschooling peers, Lomi manages to educate himself with amazing vitality. Among other things, he juggles, contemplates going to circus school, studies Aikido, is a boy scout, plays basketball, and much more:

My father is Hungarian and my mother is Swedish and we live in Spain, so I speak Hungarian, Swedish and Spanish fluently. I also speak some English, as I hear English a lot as my parents speak it with lots of their friends. We live in a very international town (51 nationalities!), but my friends of my age are all Spanish and go to school.

Do you lay in bed or watch TV all day? is a question I often hear from other teenagers. But I only lay in bed the few hours I sleep and we don't have TV, and even so I don't have enough time to do all the things I want to do!

About a year ago I was interested in radio and wanted to try it out so I took a radio and TV speaker training, and right after that I took a short course in how to make radio programs for young people. Then I took part in a training in rural tourism in this area, where we mostly studied tourism and its impact on nature. These courses were supposedly for adults, but I had no problem participating.

I have always liked vegetarian cooking and I also like to eat! I cook quite a lot at home. A couple of years ago I volunteered at a vegetarian restaurant and I learned a lot . . . A year ago I cooked lunch once a week for the staff at an alternative center.

Once in a while I go with one of my parents to give talks about homeschooling, as I'm one of the very few homeschooled teenagers in Spain at this moment . . . I will be part of the team producing the homeschool newsletter, as I know lots about layout, how to make a newsletter, printing etc. (I started a newsletter in my scout group and also worked with others doing one for an ecology group. Right now I have offered to do the layout for a pamphlet for a new group working against the traditional Spanish torture of animals, bull fighting.)

With the world as it is, there is no other option than to be involved in projects for peace, human rights and ecology. I have mostly concentrated on ecology. I'm a member of big groups like Greenpeace, as well as small local groups, and I participate however I can. For instance, I promote recycling in my scout group, through a battery-collecting campaign. When there are volunteer jobs that need to be done, like a study of coastal contamination or signature collecting, the local ecology groups contact me—unless I'm already involved!

In this part of Spain there are many alternative festivals related to ecology, peace, alternative medicine, crafts, organic food, etc. My mother and I organized the first one in our town last year. It was a big success so we put on another one this year. It's a lot of work to organize such a big event: more than fifty stands, twenty talks, twenty workshops, live music, etc. My mother and I shared all the work, but as I'm not an adult she had to do all the contacts with the town hall and TV stations. But the radio stations phoned to interview me, as they had no idea what age I am!

My mother has been selling her homemade cosmetics at these festivals. I started helping her, and then I got my own organic popcorn stand next to hers. Now I go without her to sell at the festivals, and I'm thinking of starting to make and sell more complicated food. The only problem is that as I'm too young to drive, it's difficult for me to get to the festivals with all the materials.

Recently I got into a project with some others: to start a food co-op, where I hope to work halftime in the future. The dream is to open a vegetarian lunch place next to the food co-op. I already have some experience selling food from wholesale distributors to friends.

Most of these activities are about fifty kilometers from my home, which means that I spend a lot of my time on my bike, on the train, and on the bus.

Sweden

Homeschooling parents Ywonne and Gunnar Jarl write:

In all of Sweden (an elongated country of nine million heads) only one hundred children are doing homeschooling . . .We were told, and believed, that Sweden was among the worst nations in the world in its intolerance of homeschoolers . . . One year ago we got ourselves a computer and connected to the Internet. Within a few weeks our isolation broke and we discovered we were members of a global community . . . As our knowledge grew we became aware that things are not so bad after all. Swedish laws are in fact much more liberal than many local state regulations in the U.S.A. . . . Since it after some time has become clear to me that grown-ups with kids very often show assent to our ideas, but very rarely take any action, I came to the conclusion that if homeschooling will ever become a well-known opportunity in Sweden some other group of people will have to be the spear heads. Teenagers are made to be spear heads!

According to the Jarls, the School Law states that children aged seven to sixteen must be educated, but can receive permission, one year at a time, to learn via an "adequate alternative." This "adequate alternative" can include homeschooling, but only at the discretion of the local municipal committee of education or the board of a private school. Because of these regulations, some people homeschool in secret. The Jarls advise: "Get in touch with Ywonne and Gunnar Jarl. Get yourself a copy of *Hemskola for Nyborjare* by Ywonne and Gunnar Jarl . . . Stand tall—do less!"

Switzerland
Local authorities have some veto power over your choices, and only a tiny handful of people have chosen to homeschool, let alone *un*school. Essentially, some parts of the country allow homeschooling, and others don't. Homeschooler Marie Heitzmann reports that Ticino is the worst place: "When people from there want to homeschool, I tell them to move." In the Vaud Canton, where Marie lives, and in Geneva, homeschoolers have to take a fairly simple exam each year. Katherine Hebert, fourteen, an American with dual citizenship, reports that

> Homeschooling is not really encouraged in Switzerland and to tell the truth homeschooling is more or less considered by the Swiss and French as something of a hippie movement, associated with high school dropouts and drugs. The only children who are informed of their right to homeschool are those with two or three hours commuting to and from school, where homeschooling is considered to be 'beneficial' to their education (implying that in other circumstances it isn't beneficial). Swiss students inquiring into homeschooling have doors slammed in their faces; the people are kept ignorant of the educational possibilities . . .
>   Yet, homeschooling is legal under Swiss law if you follow the rules . . . These rules restrict homeschoolers and keep them within neat boundaries. I enrolled in Clonlara, which is mainly a school on paper. I have practically nil correspondence with them and am left free to my studies. I have an exceptionally open-minded school district officer, who after a few Sundays over at our home to have tea and cookies, warmed to the homeschooling idea and then gave me full support, offering tutoring, classes at the Swiss school, and great project ideas.

Ironically, the very rigidity of the school system in Switzerland makes it easy for *teenagers* to homeschool, even without their parents' approval. As in many European countries, the schools are based on a tracking system. Uninterested students finish when they are fourteen or fifteen, and then usually go into apprenticeships. Though this rigid system certainly has its drawbacks—the Swiss suicide rate is the world's second highest, and the apprenticeship track is stigmatized—at least it also provides a loophole through which fed-up teenagers can escape. As Marie points out, "Most Swiss parents would not accept homeschooling, but would have no choice if the kid didn't have the grades to stay in school."

Venezuela
The good news: school is not compulsory, and the lower classes have a thriving apprenticeship system. The bad news: societal expectations are very, very powerful, and for people who can afford to go to school, it is definitely not considered cool to take charge of your own education. (School is free through eighth grade, but nevertheless, many families cannot afford the necessary books, uniforms, and supplies.) "For an upper class family to decide to educate their children at home, using the apprenticeship model, is unthinkable!" reports Aleta Shepler, a U.S. citizen and mother of three unschoolers. Even so, people's minds can change. Aleta says that Venezuelan acquaintances "were critical of our choice until they saw that Kirsten was able to attend college, Halee was published in a magazine, and Os was accepted to a Venezuelan university art program at age fifteen. Now there are very few open criticisms." ☀

12

the importance of The Vacation

Every day I went to school was a constant attack on my self-worth. I learned not to believe in myself. It was bombardment from all directions; the teachers were saying how bad I was doing in their classes, my family was ashamed of my grades, and the students were attacking me about everything under the sun! I was like a plant trying to grow in darkness—it doesn't. It all left me afraid to dream my dreams—afraid to be my true self! Who wants to show their true and beautiful face if they're just going to get a rock hurled at it?! The real question is: how do we undo the damage done? We have to take time to dream again. Like the sculptor who removes everything that is not a part of the sculpture, we have to remove everything that is not a part of us. We have to dream our dreams again, not other peoples, but our own precious dreams that mean everything to us. Our dreams are our life maps.

—unschooler Jenny Smith

We start out thinking of what we won't *have to do when we stop going to school, and it takes a while for us to think about what we* do *want to do.*

—Eva Owens in *Growing Without Schooling*

BEFORE YOU START your new life, you have to let go of the old one.

There are loud cruel voices you must banish, before you can hear the sweet faint muses. There are harsh schedules you must cancel, before you can coax your natural rhythms back into place. Otherwise, no music.

Learning in school is swimming upstream against the current of your natural curiosity and rhythm. It takes exhausting effort, but it can be done. Unschooling is swimming downstream, still kicking and paddling and crossing over to investigate the shores, but without fighting. *If you don't give yourself time to turn around in the river, unschooling will be a miserable confusion. If you don't give yourself time to adjust, this book will not work for you.* Still facing upstream, you'll drift downstream. In other words, you'll be neither here nor there... and maybe you'll end up wanting to be back *there*, in school, because at least you know it's someplace.

The vacation I hereby suggest is your time to turn around—and rest—*before* you make any effort to steer your course. If you *don't* take a vacation, you may start unschooling with the same frenzied guilty complexes that you've been schooling with. No fun. Jessica Gray, thirteen, who convinced her mother to let her out of school in fifth grade, writes in *GWS* #93:

My original hopes for homeschooling were that it would allow me to be free, to grow, to expand my knowledge of what really existed in this world through my own experiences. During that first year, as we traveled the bumpy path of having to keep the school system content and carried with us my old thoughts and beliefs that education consisted of books, pens, papers, early mornings, bad food, and at least six hours of sitting at a desk, I lost the sense of what homeschooling really meant to me and what I had wanted it to be from the beginning. Out of insecurity and fear of being "not enough," I spent a whole year working with a program that was set up exactly like school. The program had many textbooks, tests, a requirement of six to eight hours of work each day, and an incredible amount of stress. The one year I spent with this program dragged itself out to feel more like five dreadful years. I came out of that program with not much knowledge except for one valuable piece, which was that I would never put myself through that again . . .

When I received the books and curriculum from the program at the beginning I thought they looked fun, but that's because they looked *safe* . . . I felt pretty miserable for a long time, and that robbed me of any remaining energy. Once again I was judged only by tests, not by the hike I took in the mountains or the research I did on a subject that meant something to me.

After Jessica figured out that she did not want to waste her youth doing school at home, she changed her approach completely. Among many other things, she volunteered with Habitat for Humanity and traveled widely with her mother.

Your vacation

When you quit school, do nothing academic for at least, at the absolute minimum, a week. If you wish, however, write stories or journal entries about your past and your future. Dream, dream, dream. If you crave TV, watch it. If you crave sleep, indulge. Allow yourself to go through withdrawal. Pass no judgments. If you want to "work" on anything, work on forgiving and forgetting. Forgive yourself for everything. Forgive your teachers for everything. Forgive your parents for everything. Forget the lies school taught—forget that learning is separate from your life, that you can't teach yourself, that you are defined by your grades, and all other such nonsense. Detoxify. Purge.

Obviously, your parents need to know this vacation is coming. If not, they may anxiously pile textbooks around you and assign essays on The Reign of Queen Elizabeth. I don't know about you, but that sort of well-intentioned concern would certainly drive *me* back to school. If they don't think they can handle watching you do nothing for a week or so, visit your grandmother.

And after the vacation

Unfortunately, I can't promise that all your school wounds will heal in one short week. The complete process of unschooling your spirit could take a month or even years—not that you should wait months or years to get on with life. Anthony J. Hermans, seventeen, reflects, "It's not easy to learn to deal with excessive freedom—especially when you're used to something else." Judy Garvey, homeschooling parent and author of *How to Begin Homeschooling*, calls the transition process "flushing out." She points out in *GWS* #70 that it can involve a period of hating the mention of anything remotely connected to academics, or even a temporary lack of interest in *everything*.

A few enemies may lurk in your gut, waiting to make life difficult. Fear, for example, may overwhelm you at first. Most of the structure in your world has suddenly evaporated, and not just for the weekend. Your time is yours, and you may feel dazed by the responsibility of that concept. Expect to be afraid; just don't give in to that fear. Where there's fear, say some wise women I know, there's power. No one feels afraid when they walk into a boring job for the fourteenth year, which is a sorry reason to do a boring job for fourteen years.

Another enemy is the guilt that blocks your natural curiosity. People who have never gone to school have never developed negative attitudes toward exploring their world. Unfortunately, you probably have. It's not your fault if you don't immediately want to run out and watch ladybugs with a magnifying glass. It might take time before your desire to learn surfaces from beneath the layers of guilt—the voices insisting *I should learn this, I have to learn that*. Give yourself that time. Don't push. You'll recover. Homeschooling father Dan Raymond told me he thought it would take a year before a new unschooler could do anything "real" and start going forward on his or her own.

Impatience, too: in Chapter 3, I pointed out that schools helped eighteenth- and nineteenth- century factory owners by forcing people to shift from a natural, agricultural way of scheduling their lives to an artificial, industrial way. Quitting school, you can ease back into a healthy tempo, but you'll have to be more patient with yourself than factory owners are with their employees. Allow yourself to find a natural pace, even though that means you may slow down, stare into space more often, breathe easier. You won't necessarily accomplish less—many homeschoolers accomplish far more than their schooled peers—but it's O.K. if you *do* accomplish less. The meaning of life has to do with quality, not quantity. After Adrian Deal, fourteen, quit school, she created a wonderful pamphlet entitled, "Isn't there school today?" Part of it goes like this:

What do you do all day?
I hear this from my grandmother who wonders if I just "flop around all day eating chocolates." Well, no I don't. But I also don't do as many things as they do in school: for example, in one day I might do one or two things enjoyably at my own pace instead of cramming in huge amounts of seven different "subjects."
After being out of school for a short while, I realized that a day is not very long—you just can't do that much in a day. Therefore, it is impossible to fully absorb (much less enjoy!) large amounts of algebra, chemistry, history, English, Spanish, biology, and health in one day. My point? School teaches you that you must do, do, do all day. So the first thing you must do when you quit school is relax, don't make yourself do anything, and realize that it's okay if you don't do those seven subjects every day.
Now, on to some of my daily activities: reading a book (fiction or nonfiction), watching a movie, writing to one of my many pen pals, doing office work for my mom, listening to music, working in my scrapbook, making this brochure, cooking something delightful, painting with watercolors, making jewelry, taking art classes, browsing the library, and just having fun.

The worst thing that can go wrong with your unschooling is lack of trust.

If your parents don't trust you, they will nag or look like they want to nag. If they see you watching TV they may assume that's all you'll ever do. It will drive you crazy. You'll wish you were back in school, where everyone *expects* you not to want to learn anything. Tell them how important their trust is. Continue to educate them about homeschooling. Share the stories in this chapter with them. Introduce them to other homeschooling families.

If the schoolboard doesn't trust you, that's not so bad because you don't have to see them every day. Still, it can force you into more structure and more subjects than you think are healthy. Don't worry too much about the school board. Learn to be diplomatic. Nod and smile and then go right on doing what you do.

The worst disaster by far is *you* refusing to trust yourself. You can suffocate yourself under a stack of guilt trips. If parents and teachers have not trusted you through a lot of your life, it is not your fault that you finally stopped trusting yourself too. It's their fault, but there's no point in revenge. Instead, work through it.

Help

If anyone is still on your case with things you "should" be doing, or nasty demonstrations of no trust, or if you find yourself tormented by guilt, school nightmares, or an inability to relax, *get some help.* Perhaps all you need is contact with other unschoolers. Maybe you need more intensive care, such as work with a counselor. On behalf of wise friends, I recommend co-counseling, or Re-Evaluation Counseling ("RC"), although I am not myself a co-counselor.

I mention co-counseling because it is far less judgmental than some other forms of counseling and therapy; a traditional psychiatrist might start with the unhelpful assumption that your unschooling is the cause of your problems. Also, co-counseling is empowering. Co-counselors work in pairs; each person performs two roles—counselor *and* client. (A session goes like this: first, one person is the counselor and the other the client. After a designated time period, such as an hour, you switch roles.) Furthermore, after you take a short, inexpensive[1] introductory course, it is free. According to co-counseling literature, it "assumes that everyone is born with tremendous intellectual potential, natural zest, and lovingness, but that these qualities have become blocked and obscured in adults [and teenagers] as the result of accumulated distress experiences (fear, hurt, loss, pain, anger, embarrassment, etc.) which begin early in our lives."

After you complete the "Fundamentals Class," available all over the world, you can participate in any group of co-counselors. Co-counseling is open to all ages, and has special youth chapters and newsletters in some places. Get more information and find out about a group or class near you by contacting The International Re-Evaluation Counseling Communities.

An issue related to this business of guilt and trust is the question of structure—but we'll deal with that in Chapter 16. One relatively uncomplicated solution to some of these psychological difficulties is suggested by Judy Garvey and Jim Bergin, who have a thirteen-year-old son, in *GWS* #76: An apprenticeship or job outside the home, they say, is the best way to make the transition to unschooling. Because it is a structured use of time out in the world, it combats any feeling of "dropping out" or "failure."

Hey, Miss Llewellyn, if it's so complicated and difficult for some people to heal from school, why are you so optimistic? How do you know I can recover?

Partly because I've heard enough success stories. Partly because like many adults, I have recovered too. It wasn't until I was in college, but my brain did finally boomerang back from the land of grades, SAT scores, harried paper writing, boredom, obedience school, and busywork. The revival, by the way, happened

---

[1] Some scholarships are available.

mainly through conversations with friends, and mostly *not* because of any official college curriculum.

These stories and comments will help to illustrate the process:

Katrina Dolezal, fifteen, writes in *GWS* #76: "I think the best way to make the transition from public school to homeschool is to be allowed plenty of time to forget some of what was learned in school about how you should learn."

Sylvia Stralberg describes her vacation in *GWS* #80:

Things finally got so bad this year in eleventh grade that I said, "That's it—I'm not going back to school anymore," and I didn't. I had a few months of recuperation, which meant doing *whatever* I felt like doing, be it baking, reading, cutting recipes, or watching a movie. I had a lot of guilt feelings during that time about not being in school, but fortunately I have wonderful parents who reassured me that what I had done was OK.

Rosemary Risley writes about her daughter in *GWS* #76:

Lora only read what she was forced to read when she was in school, and I would sometimes coerce her by reading one chapter out loud to her and then having her read the next to me. All of a sudden, during the summer between school and homeschool, she became an avid reader . . . I don't know how many books she read that summer, but I was amazed—it was as if now that she didn't have to, and she was free, she wanted to read. She has read over sixty books in each nine months of homeschooling. If we did nothing else these two years, I consider that a major accomplishment.

Judy Garvey writes in *GWS* #76:

Before children go to school in the first place, all of their natural learning systems are intact. This is what we can see in families who have homeschooled their children from the very beginning. However, once children are in school for about three years, they are forced to shift over to a very unnatural system to survive the emphasis on memorization and the daily stress, rigidity, and humiliation of classroom life . . .

Most children are very hurt and angry about what has happened to them and to their peers in school. As long as they stay in school that anger must remain under control. When they come home, it all begins to come out. It may show up in extreme highs and lows, negative emotional outbursts, or long periods of apparent depression.

Kathleen Hatley writes in *GWS* #45:

A change that pleases me very much this year was to watch our son Steve (twelve), who spent four years in public school, and who spent his first year of homeschooling asking for "assignments," become a more self-motivated learner. He became interested in mechanical drawing when I gave him a beginning drafting set and he spends a lot of time designing cars and space ships. He has discovered science fiction and reads Asimov, Bradbury, Heinlein and others with great enjoyment (he has always read a lot, but despises the school-type reading programs where one must answer questions to prove comprehension). We both enrolled in the IBM Systems computer course at the state Vo-Tech school and he thoroughly enjoyed that—the perfect classroom situation, in my opinion, no tests, no grades, just people voluntarily coming to learn about something which they were interested in, from a helpful expert in the field. Since Steve's career goals tend toward the technical at this point, he works real hard at mathematics, and at his request we added the Key Curriculum algebra and geometry series to his regular sixth grade math. He surprised me this year by informing me that he didn't want to take a summer break from his schoolwork!

Darlene Graham, a mother, started to feel like homeschooling was working after three years. In *GWS* #37, she advised, "Don't feel discouraged if your school program doesn't work like magic from day one. We have found that the longer our children were in public school, the harder it was for them to re-develop their own natural curiosity and creativity."

In *GWS* #64, editor Susannah Sheffer relates a conversation with Emily Keyes, fifteen. When she was in school, says Emily, she hated it and always got in trouble for not doing her homework. After eighth grade, her parents heard of homeschooling and decided to try it with both Emily and her younger brothers. After her mom took a class in homeschooling, she decided to try "natural learning," with no curriculum. Emily was lost at first:

> I still didn't know what to expect, or what I would want to do with the time, because back then I wasn't interested in much of anything. We decided to start homeschooling on the day that school started, and it should have been like any other day, except we didn't know what to expect of one another. We didn't know what mom was going to do, if mom was going to assign lots of stuff. My attitude was still so rebellious. I was so fed up with school that I felt I didn't want to learn anything. There was so much tension that first week.
>
> The change was very gradual. Your whole thinking changes. In school, everything's programmed for you, this is how you have to think, and then all of a sudden you're on your own, and you don't know what you want to do. It was so hard at the beginning, but I knew there was no way I would go back to school, and I think we all knew it would get better if we stuck it out.

Emily goes on to explain how eventually she discovered that she thinks mechanically and logically, and how she learned to fix machinery, to work with sound equipment, and to enjoy, among other things, early American history.

Arlean Haight writes in *GWS* #28:

> When we took the children out of school nearly two years ago, we had advice from several people, among them Dr. Pat Montgomery [director of the Clonlara Home Based Education Program]. She told us if we would let the children follow their own interests, and just help them when they needed help, they would learn more than if we put them on a pre-planned curriculum.
>
> I respected Dr. Montgomery, and was grateful for her help. But I just couldn't see any glimmer of hope in Becky [fourteen]. It seemed that seven years of public school had successfully stamped out any inclination she might have had to learn. By her own admission, she had learned to cram for tests, make A's and B's on her report cards, and promptly forget almost everything she had "learned." Whenever I allowed her free rein on "school," her one interest was mindless fiction—nothing of any value that I could see. Pat tried to encourage me, but I had the misgivings and insecurities that I see in so many other parents new to home-schooling. I was afraid Becky would learn nothing at all. So—we embarked on a "curriculum." It turned out to be just a duplication of the old public school pattern. So I went pretty easy with it, still allowing her freedom, and limiting her fiction reading to what I felt was least objectionable.
>
> But, Pat was right. It finally happened. This year Becky progressed from Louis L'Amour Western fiction to an interest in Western history, then to the history of the United States, and is now in the process of memorizing the Constitution word for word.

Fifteen-year-old Maya Toccata, of British Columbia, says:

> Most of my time is taken up by living. Which involves rock climbing, writing, reading, working at a hat store, researching massage, aromatherapy, shiatsu, reflexolgy, and doing the layout and editing of a teen section in a small home learning newsletter.
>
> I have been home schooling for two and a half years now and it has been an interesting process. Now I feel comfortable with what I'm doing and feel I'm doing enough, but I

didn't feel that way at first. I had a hard time persuading my parents to let me unschool. So when I started I was trying really hard to make it look like unschooling was working for me and that I was learning a lot, but I didn't really care about what I was trying to learn so I just sort of hung around all day. I felt like I was a big fake. I thought I wasn't learning anything, but now when I look back I see that I learned more about myself in those few months than I have in nine years of school, in fact in school I was trying to ignore my true personality to be like every one else.

How not to get stuck in la-la land

After I published the first edition of this book, I began to feel that there was something incomplete and overly simplistic about my advice on vacations. Jennifer Louden's *Woman's Comfort Book* helped me understand what was bothering me. In a chapter called "The Shadow Side of Comfort," she says:

> It is possible to use comfort and being comfortable as excuses to limit or negate ourselves . . . For instance, when I started paying attention to how I comforted myself, I realized that staying home weekend nights and ordering Thai food and watching videos was comforting and safe, but it also could be limiting and boring. It made me uncomfortable at first, but I found when I made unusual plans for the weekend, I almost always came away stimulated and enriched.

Yep indeed, it may not always be enough for a new unschooler to simply take a vacation from academia in which absolutely anything is permissible—any amount of TV, any number of potato chips. I'm still certain that most people need a relaxed time in which to heal from the pressures of school, and to reclaim their own internal motivation. But some ways of vacationing are healing and rejuvenating, while others may be more likely to *worsen* the feeling of being out of control of one's life. I now think the unschooling process requires not just two essential steps (vacation and then *do something*), but three.

I still think an "anything goes" vacation in which you indulge some of your petty cravings is crucial. But it's just as crucial to recognize when you've had enough of that—and move on to phase two which is *still a vacation*, but a much more rejuvenating one, and will probably need to last anywhere from a week to a year. During this time, do not strive to meet academic goals, but *do* actively experiment and play—no more excessive TV, eating, sleeping, video games, or hanging out with unexcited people. During this time you might experiment with transition rituals, or find other ways to engage with the world such as making new friends, changing your wardrobe to reflect your true personality, or visiting a variety of churches or other religious services. The general point is that such activities can take you beyond *both* 1) the pressure, chaos, and stress of being schooled, and 2) the boredom and self-loathing that can result from too much lounging around, from a lack of creative release. ❉

Unschooling Transition Rituals

These suggestions are based mostly on my own experiments. I hope they'll spark you to make up activities that meet your particular needs.

Try these rituals when

- you've just quit school.
- you feel guilty or nervous about being out of school.
- you believe you should be doing some kind of academic work, but you feel unmotivated.
- you have no desire to learn about anything.
- you've been out of school for a long time but still don't really feel in control of your own education.
- you think of yourself as unintelligent because you got bad grades in school.
- you've been stressed out because of preparing for a test or working on some difficult academic project.
- you are still in school and not happy about it.

1. Reclaim your past

Get out your favorite childhood toys, hobbies, collections, books, and old photos—whatever evidence remains of your early life. Arrange these things around you and take some time looking at or playing with it. Does any of it still entice you? How might you invite your early interests into the present? How could you pick up where you left off?

2. Purge school

Throw darts at photos of your school, or build a bonfire with useless worksheets or homework assignments, or take a report card and rip it to shreds and stomp on it. Write down all the ways school has harmed you and limited you. Burn the paper... and then write down the ways you want to grow beyond the limits of your past. Post your list by your bed or computer.

3. Make a scrapbook

Supplies: Back issues of *National Geographics* or other magazines (from thrift shops, garage sales, library sales, etc.); any other postcards, photos, or other flat paraphernalia; a scrapbook or any looseleaf binder, construction paper, and a three-ring hole punch.

The point here is to play with a topic that intrigues you, by collecting and arranging pictures, postcards, poems, quotes, maps, whatever. *National Geographic* alone is a great source for many topics —I have one scrapbook showing traditional costumes of a variety of different cultures, another one in the works showing traditional architecture worldwide, and still another called "pastorality" —worldwide markets and farming methods. Let your scrapbook remind you to always keep your education beautiful and personal.

4. Comfort with children's books

Have a children's book party. Invite a few friends to bring stacks of their favorites. Ask each person to briefly describe the books they bring, and to read a chapter aloud from one. Then put pillows on the floor and let everybody hang out and read all afternoon. Serve bread and jam. Finish with a pillow fight.

Or give yourself a day at the library. Take a notebook to the children's non-fiction section and skim lots of books. Make a list of subjects that intrigue you. Make another list of specific questions that your reading generates. You don't have to follow up on either of these lists... but you can if you want to.

5. Report Cards

Find an old school report card. If you quit school recently, get your latest report card or progress report. Read it carefully and notice your feelings. Are you proud? Depressed? Competitive? Angry? Nervous? Ashamed? Confused? As the feelings subside, invite your logic-brain to join in. Think about what your report card is: a subjective evaluation of your tests, papers, and "participation" *in classes which you didn't freely choose to take*, given by people who don't know you very well, are overworked, have too many students, don't have nearly enough information to judge you accurately, and are themselves probably not great examples of joyful, purposeful learning.

Ask yourself: which of these subjects are important to you? Why? How successful was each course in helping you learn about its subject? (Grades deflect the pressure off of the school, onto the student. In my dance classes, if a student doesn't get something it's up to *me* to teach it in a different way—and of course up to her, also, to go home and practice, and to articulate her questions as clearly as possible. At school, all the emphasis is on evaluating *you*, but sometimes it would make more sense for students to grade their teachers.) How much do you really know and understand about the subjects you got good grades in? What subjects do you feel you *would* be good at, if only you had more time or if the material were explained differently? What things are you good at that aren't even listed on the report card? What things would you like to be good at that aren't taught in school?

Write your own report card based on your knowledge, skills, and personal qualities. Include not just grades, but explanations. Then project yourself into the future and write a report card for where you'd like to be a year from now.

6. Inspiration Cards

Cut out magazine images you like or that inspire or haunt you. Use rubber cement or a glue stick to attach them to heavy paper or cardstock. On their backs, list the questions and activities they suggest. Play with them, sort and arrange them in different ways, make patterns or mosaics. Put them in a bag and draw one out whenever you feel sluggish.

7. Keep an unschooling journal. Starters:
The time I got an F.
I am curious about...
Why I cheated:...
A list of questions:
I hate math/science/history because...
I love math/science/history because...
I feel alive when...
What I want to contribute...

8. Learn with your body.
Take a day for each of your senses: explore with your ears, your eyes, your hands and skin, your nose, your tastebuds. .

money, bicycles, and other Technical Difficulties

There is no wealth but life. —John Ruskin

We haven't the money, so we've got to think. —Lord Rutherford

MONEY

IF YOUR PARENTS were paying full tuition at some gourmet private school before you quit, no problem. You can have plenty of private lessons, lab equipment, a library all to yourself, a high fashion set of drums, and money left over to vacation in Jamaica.

But you needn't be rich. Some homeschoolers spend under a hundred dollars per year on supplies. That's less than many school kids spend on *school* supplies.

Of course, if money is scarce at your house, you might not get lots of toys and the high fashion drums. On the other hand, you won't clutter up your life with things you end up feeling obligated to use.

The best money advice I can give, in fact, is to use your lack of money to help you. Let it help you focus your life around a few things that matter most to you. If you decide to be a naturalist and a photographer, spend your money there, not on a bunch of fancy math books you don't need. That way, you won't end up wasting *time* doing more math than you need.

Another way scarce money can be a blessing: you will be more creative and develop a clear understanding of what is necessary and fundamental to your interests. By figuring out what you don't need, you will also figure out what you do need. That's some of the best learning you can do about anything.

Also, remember that although you may lose a stingy little pond-full of "free" education—use of textbooks and equipment and such—you get an ocean of time in exchange. If you want, you can look at time as money. You can use it as an investment in your future (by volunteering in a field you dream of working in later) or as a way to get cash now (a job).

Strategies to make your money go as far as possible

Use school facilities and books. You may encounter the least resentment if you work out an arrangement where the school gets to officially enroll you (so they get money for you) in exchange for providing equipment and even allowing you to take the classes you want or attend events. For details on this sort of arrangement, see Chapter 19.

Buy only books you will use again and again. Get others through libraries; use interlibrary loan. Borrow textbooks from your school district. If your district is not cooperative about loaning you books even though your parents' taxes support the schools, talk with individual teachers you trust. If they think you are going to run to the Authorities and say, "Miss Pickle loaned me a chemistry book, so there!" they won't do it, because they don't want to get in trouble. Be diplomatic and low-key.

Trade your time for lessons or equipment. Try to do work that you learn from and enjoy, not just slave labor. For instance, Seth and Vallie Raymond earned free pottery classes by running a kiln. Their mother told me, "Art and music teachers usually like kids who barter for lessons. If they're willing to work, they're more invested in what they're doing." Along the same line, *GWS* #70 mentions a violin student who "is cataloging his [teacher's] records in exchange for the lessons the man is giving him."

See Barbara Sher's book Wishcraft *for great ideas.* One is holding a barn-raising, where people get together to tell what they have and what they need, and then team up to make each others' dreams come true with minimal cash.

Use someone else's lab equipment for labs that require microscopes or other expensive equipment. (See Chapter 21 for access to lab equipment.) However, about half the labs in most science books don't require expensive equipment, just beakers, graduated cylinders, graph paper, etc.

If you want to learn to play the piano and don't have one, practice in a school or university practice room, or at someone else's house.

Earn money in a way that brings you into closer contact with what you love. Finance your photography education by taking portraits of senior citizens and selling them, for example. If you take this approach rather than working at McDonald's, you win doubly—you not only earn money, you also gain experience. That way you won't feel resentful about having to "pay" for your own education—paying for your education can be part of it.

Find used books and equipment at university and college used book sales, thrift stores, flea markets, and garage sales.

Work for legislation that would give tax credits (like $3,000 per student per year) for education outside public schools, including homeschooling. Minnesota passed a similar measure. Oregon had one on the ballot but turned it down. Most people who oppose it do so because they think it discriminates against poor people whose parents couldn't afford to send them to private schools even with a $3,000 discount. But for homeschoolers, $3,000 would make a tremendous difference, *especially* for poor people. In other words, this legislation gives your parents a tax refund to be used for equipment and resources for your homeschooling.

Get a grant. A grant is when someone else gives you money to carry out a project. Look up "grants" at the library, and try especially to find an up-to-date book in the reference section. The government (that is to say, your parents' and friends' tax dollars) is one source of grants. See J. Robert Dumouchel's *Government Assistance Almanac.*

Transportation
If you are not old enough to legally drive:
- ride your horse, bicycle, or feet.

- if your area has good public transportation, use it.
- carpool with other unschoolers.
- if you volunteer or work on a regular schedule, ride with an adult who works at the same place.
- put up notices at the places you spend your time, explaining that you need rides. Contribute gas money. If strangers offer you rides, be sure you know enough to trust them before you accept.
- invent an alternate means of transportation, preferably one which will not contribute to global warming and lung cancer.
- speak up for your right to drive.

If you *are* old enough to legally drive:

If you live in a state with one of those disgusting laws preventing "dropouts" from driving until they're eighteen, do what you can to change it. But don't worry on your own behalf—the law shouldn't affect you if you're a "homeschooler." Kathryn Blount, fifteen, in Texas, found that all she needed was a letter from a parent or tutor saying she was homeschooled.[2]

Adults only
Vita Wallace writes in *GWS*:

> I am in a figure drawing class for adults . . . partly because I just couldn't stand the idea of being in a class labeled "for teenagers." My mother called the teacher before the class began to see if it would be all right if I signed up for it. He said that as long as I thought I could concentrate for two hours straight, I was welcome to try it. No one there has ever asked me how old I am, and I don't think they'd mind if they knew.

To be a Compleat Self-schooler, start developing some assertiveness. You will need it as you look for unorthodox ways to find things out, get things done, and join classes or groups that teenagers aren't usually part of. Realize that rules are usually flexible.

For example, a Middle Eastern dance troupe I belonged to had a rule that members had to be at least twenty, but a nineteen-year-old danced blithely in our midst, and no one ever thought about it. When we got around to reviewing the troupe's constitution, we canned that rule. Many organizations have obsolete rules that no one cares about. If you set about your business believing (politely) that anything is possible, you will prove yourself right.

And other Technical Difficulties
One *GWS* reader had kids who were hassled when they hung out in the world during school hours. "Why aren't you in school," everybody's cousin wanted to know. The mom solved the problem by printing up "passes" that explained the kid was on an independent educational errand, complete with her administrative signature at the bottom. No more harassment.

Chapter Summary
Where there's a will, there's a way. ☀

---

[2] From *GWS* #73.

14

getting a social life without proms

But, good gracious, you've got to educate him first. You can't expect a boy to be
vicious till he's been to a good school. —Saki (H.H. Munro)

WHENEVER I MENTION my work, hardly anyone says, "But how would people learn anything without school?" Instead, they say, "But how will they make friends?"

The question kills me. Teenagers make friends in *spite* of school, not because of it. There is only one reason schools can claim to enhance social growth: thanks to compulsory education, schools are full of *people*.

Well. A good slice of birthday cake surpasses its beginnings in flour, sugar, milk, egg, and vanilla extract. Likewise, a healthy social life goes far beyond mere contact.

A healthy social life requires much more than indifferent daily acquaintanceship with three hundred people born the same year you were. It starts with a solid sense of self-esteem and self-awareness. It builds in *time*—time to spend with other people in worthwhile, happy activities where no one loses, no one is forced to participate, and where conversation and helping one another are not outlawed. In other words, school fights hard to keep your social life from happening, even though defensive schoolpeople preach loudly that school is important for socialization.

(Actually, they're right. While school has little to do with social *growth*, it has everything to do with *socialization*. I think it was in *Growing Without Schooling* magazine that I read someone's clear explanation of that term: socialization means bringing an individual under the control of the group. School-style socialization makes a group of people obedient and easily manipulated by peer pressure or "authority"; it makes a nation of idiots who wish they were people on TV since they don't know who they themselves are.)

As for romance. Affection, intimacy, and passion really are not encouraged to take root in a linoleum room smelling of chalk-dust. A mystery-relationship belongs out in the big mystery-world.

So. School is detrimental to friendship and other social joys, insists your author. But where does that leave you? To have a social life, you at least have to start with raw material—other human beings. Since most of the people near your age are shut up in school, you do face a challenge. Now, you are not alone in your aloneness—*most* of the social structures of our society have broken down. Streets are seldom neighborhoods; family members rarely know each other well; adults' work environments require so much conformity that people cannot see who their colleagues are. Friendship and community do not happen automatically. But with a little effort, you *can* make them happen, just as adults do. Don't sit home and mope, and don't be unimaginatively convinced that you need school to have friends. Instead:

Create a new and better social structure.

When school is the structure of your life, you run into people all the time. When school is not the structure of your life, you can build a better social structure instead of inventing each day from scratch. This approach frees you from having to make a continual effort to spend time with people: if you always meet Josefina and Nazir to play music on Thursdays, then on Thursday you don't have to say to yourself, gosh I feel kind of like spending time with someone but I don't know quite whom, or what I feel like doing. Here are a few of the many possible strategies.

Set up regular, scheduled contact with friends. Start an important project with schooled or unschooled friends, and set regular times to work together two or three times per week. These projects could be anything—writing a book, cleaning up a beach, starting a health information library, making a music video, rebuilding the engine of an old pickup.

If you prefer to work independently, you can still share space with friends. Your arrangement could be simple: school friends coming to your house to do their homework while you do your academic work, unschooled friends bringing a novel and lounging on your bed. Or your arrangement could be more complex: a workshop or other definite space in one of your homes where each of you kept ongoing projects and worked in the warmth of each others' company, with sunlight streaming through the windows and music in the background.

Start a business that puts you into frequent contact with people—like custom-painting skateboards or tutoring Spanish.

Join clubs or organizations for people with similar interests. There are infinite possibilities, especially in a city: the Society for Creative Anachronism (see Chapter 23), the Sierra Club, outdoor programs of universities, performance guilds, ultimate frisbee teams, Amnesty International, drum circles, mountain search and rescue, city planning committees.

There are worthwhile non-school organizations specifically for teenagers, too. Look into 4-H, church or temple youth groups, YMCA activities, hockey or soccer teams, scouts, youth symphonies and other musical groups, teen hotlines and support groups. For a big list, see the latest edition of *The Directory of American Youth Organizations*, edited by Judith Erickson.

Start your own club—to work on environmental issues, cook desserts, undertake big projects, whatever. Advertise your first meetings by posting fliers at or near a school, or by having friends post fliers, or by placing a classified ad in a school newspaper.

Get involved in a regular work situation that provides contact with the kind of people you like to be around.

Take a class outside of school—dance, martial arts, bicycle repair.

Start a weekly study circle to explore a subject you're interested in—Zen Buddhism, Shakespeare, the history of your region. A book to check is Leonard

Oliver's *Study Circles*. Also see Chapter 17, on salons.

Remember to bond with other unschoolers!

Come to Not Back to School Camp. Organize an unschoolers' study group or hiking club; ask a local newsletter to help get the word out. Hook up with other unschoolers' activities. Adrian Deal, fourteen, writes, "It's so easy to make friends with unschoolers! There's no popularity contest to win and you don't feel like you're being graded for your looks, the makeup you do or don't wear, and the number of guys you've gone out with." Sarabeth Matilsky answered a classified ad in *GWS* and then spent a summer with a homeschooling family in Alaska.

Join or organize a retreat or trip

Here and there unschooling teenagers have organized their own retreats. Selina Hunt and Emily Houk of New York planned a weekend for 33 people (about seven adults and the rest teenagers) at a Victorian mansion on a nature preserve. They played music, talked, walked along the beach, went hiking at night, cleaned up part of the salt water marsh, and made waffles for brunch.[1]

Corinna Marshall, Zoë Blowen-Ledoux, and Damon Holman of Maine also planned a weekend gathering at Corinna's house, for about ten unschoolers. Corinna writes in *GWS* #112:

> A lot of people don't know how many options are open to them, and we thought that if we all talked to each other about what we were doing with our lives, each of us could make our own lives more exciting as we learned about our opportunities. Another goal we had was to spread the word about unschooling, because it's a very misunderstood concept.

Join or organize an unschooler's club or study group. Emily Linn, of Michigan, organized a successful, long-term older homeschoolers' group. She began by placing a notice in homeschooling newsletters and magazines. At first, the group got together for monthly events, which included private workshops at a science institute, swimming and dining at a yacht club, skiing, attending a Pow Wow, camping, and attending a member's harp recital. Over a period of several years, it evolved and added academic activities. They organized a five-session French class, with the participants sharing the cost of the teacher. Later, they set up programs in biology, physics, a Great Books discussion group, and more. Emily's mother, Diane Linn, reports in *GWS* #94:

> [Emily] sent out a survey to the group, listing some topics that she thought were interesting, and asking for feedback. Every September the group gets together for a business meeting, and at that meeting last fall they brainstormed a list of things that they wanted to study but didn't feel they could easily study on their own and would enjoy studying with a group. Many people mentioned foreign language, but they wanted different languages, so that wouldn't work well. The two other topics that emerged were science and the arts. So that led us to organize a fifteen-session biology program, and then we had a ceramics program at a century-old historic pottery in this area...
>
> There are about forty kids in the group all together, and they come from within about an hour's drive of Detroit. Of course, not everyone participates in every activity. Some activities have to be limited in size, and not everyone is interested in every activity anyway. Sometimes we only get three or four people, and that can be fun, too. A lot of friendships have grown among kids in the group. Emily now feels that she has a good

---

[1] From *GWS* #112.

group of pals. She has made it a point, in all the flyers she sends out, to say that this is a nonsectarian group, that we don't favor any one philosophy, in order to welcome all homeschoolers. Consequently, the group is really a mixture of people—we have people homeschooling for religious reasons, people homeschooling for academic or other philosophical reasons. The group has become racially integrated, too, which we're very grateful for. The kids are meeting people from many different backgrounds, with many different kinds of life experiences, and the friendships really cross those lines.

In an interview in *GWS* #85, Emily says, "One thing that really worked was having an information sheet ready to send to people who called asking for information, because I couldn't tell them everything on the phone, and this way I could follow up right away when they were really interested."

Some things that happen to many unschoolers

They keep up their friendships with school friends, doing the same kinds of things with them that they used to. Adrian Deal writes, "My social life is so fabulous! I'm becoming even better friends with some of my schooled friends because I have the *time* to talk to them and do things with them." Sometimes, they feel frustrated because their school friends don't have as much free time as they do. Cafi Cohen writes in *Home Education Magazine*:

Our kids had friends when they attended school. But after a year of homeschooling, I realized they had more friends than they had had while in school. Of course, this was contrary to my expectations . . . Watching Jeff and Tamara, though, it all became clear. Our homeschoolers had more friends because they had more *time* and *energy* for friends. That's what friends take—time and energy. As homeschooled teenagers, they had an abundance of both. No longer were my kids hobbled eight or more hours each day by busy work and educational administrivia. Instead, they worked on academics, generally completing them in the morning; both had *much* more time to make and be a friend, to socialize.[1]

They grow closer to their families and start liking their parents and siblings more than they used to.

They have fewer acquaintances. They develop stronger, closer friendships. They appreciate not having to spend time around hordes of people they don't have a lot in common with.

Their friends include adults and children as well as people their own age. They get over any former feelings that they can't talk with adults. Jeremiah Gingold wrote in *GWS* #74:

I am friends with the adults who live in the house next door to us . . . Dick is interested in bicycling and philosophy and Crunch is interested in word games, movies, and sports. These are all things that I am interested in, which is one of the reasons I immediately became friends with them. The other reason is that they take me seriously and respect what I have to say about things. There are a few things that I talk to them about that I don't talk to most of my friends about who are closer in age to me (I'm thirteen) —for instance, politics and education.

I don't think my friendship with them is very different from my friendships with other teenagers, except for the fact that we have better conversations. We often fool around with each other the way I would with friends my age. I think there are many things that I can learn from them, but that doesn't make me feel that they are necessarily superior to me.

---

[1]*Home Education Magazine*, March-April 1997.

There are probably things that they can learn from me also. I do think that we have a very equal friendship, most likely because they respect me in the same way that I respect them.

Anne Brosnan, thirteen, wrote:

My social life is much more rounded than school kids'; I talk to anyone and everyone the same. I've noticed that most kids will talk to anyone younger than them but only superficially, and hardly talk to adults at all except when spoken to. I don't believe in that and make a point of showing that I'll talk to anyone about anything. On the track team there's all ages and I'm friends with all equally. I don't make a point of talking to someone just because of closeness in age. For example, I talk to the little boys in kindergarten because we share a common hatred of the rock group "New Kids on the Block." And the coaches ask me quite important things such as make sure so-and-so is standing in the right lane, and sometimes they get so mixed up I have to remind them what they are supposed to be doing (they're grateful for it).

I have about thirty pen-pals and they range in age from about ten to fifty. I consider these my friends and my social life because you can be "social" through the mail. I may not have as *many* friends or acquaintances as other kids but it is not the amount but the quality of friendship that counts.

I've heard a whole lot about homeschoolers going back to high school for various reasons and the main one was to have more friends. But school isn't supposed to be about friends—the purpose of schools is to learn, or to be taught. However I never heard of a homeschooler going back to high school to get an education, because that is what they were doing before they went back to school. The stupidest reason I've heard of was a kid who wanted to go to high school so she could go to her prom. This, I think I shall refrain from commenting on...!

Anthony J. Hermans, seventeen, was out of school during seventh and eighth grades, though he went on to a private high school. He wrote me that unschooling "allows an individual to meet (and learn to deal with) a wide range of people rather than being largely restricted to one's 'peer' group . . . Homeschooling can provide an incredible boost in self reliance and esteem which all but eliminates peer pressure. I feel very little pressure from my peers as do other homeschoolers with whom I have conversed."

Younger unschoolers—around twelve and thirteen—often appreciate not having to deal with the pressure of having "boyfriends" or "girlfriends" just to fit in and be popular. Older teenagers frequently feel that most of their schooled peers are immature, inexperienced, and uninteresting. They fall in love and make friends with people slightly older than themselves. Their relationships and friendships are strong and honest. In general, unschooling allows teenagers to stay "young" as long as they want, but also to "grow up" as soon as they are ready.

They exchange letters and email with unschoolers and other people around the world. Sometimes, they travel to meet these people.

Their friends are mostly people who share their interests. When I asked about the greatest advantages of unschooling, fifteen-year-old Michael Severini said, "I can spend more time with people who have the same interests I have."

They grow more secure and feel better about themselves as a result of leaving the social world of school, a world which is often cruel, judgmental, and nosy. (One researcher has even "proved" that homeschoolers have significantly more positive self-concepts than do school students.[1] Another study concluded that homeschoolers are less peer-dependent than public and private school students.[2] Suzanne Klemp, fifteen, comments, "My confidence has grown immensely—I am not judged for reasons such as clothes, money, or my looks . . . My social life is better than it ever was at school. I meet people at the YMCA [where she teaches ballet], ballet class, and I have adult friends."

They do sometimes feel excluded from the bustling social activity at school. Most of them, however, feel that this social activity is shallow and unfulfilling. They don't *really* want it, but sometimes they do fantasize about it.

What else can you do if you feel lonely and isolated?

Take your feelings seriously. Human contact is crucial. Don't try to tell yourself it's not important to have friends. If you want to be in love, don't tell yourself that's silly. It's not.

In fact, our social needs are more important and basic than our intellectual and creative needs. If you let your social life end when you quit school, pretty soon you won't care much about learning and exploring the world. You'll want to get right back to your locker, because Tatiana will be rummaging in her locker next to you. Psychologist Abraham Maslow pointed out that people have a hierarchy of needs. Each of us has to feel a sense of belonging, love, acceptance, and recognition, *before* we can set out to fulfill "higher" needs such as intellectual achievement and complete self-fulfillment.

Don't romanticize your memory of school. School does provide contact with masses of people. It does not make friends for you, or even provide an environment that is good for making friends. Everyone who goes to school, and everyone who doesn't go to school, has times of overwhelming loneliness. Being in a crowd doesn't necessarily help.

Take responsibility for your own social life. Make an effort to stay in touch with former friends. If you aren't invited enough, do some inviting. Throw a party. If you're lonely, don't blame the universe, me, or yourself. Instead, do something about it.

Be sensitive to your friends' feelings about your changing life. If they stay in school, they may watch you with envy. They may overly romanticize *your* life, or feel intimidated by your independence and growing maturity. Quitting school *will* make you smarter and happier than you used to be, but it will not make you superior to your friends. Don't be arrogant; don't think that unschooling makes you the most interesting creature in the universe.

Don't feel apologetic for your happiness, but do reinforce your friends' trust in you by showing your interest in their activities. Go out of your way to let them know what you enjoy and admire in them. Don't talk more than you listen. But if they become hostile and defensive, and you can't work through this stuff together, it's time to seek out new friends who are not threatened by your growth.

Involve your old and new friends in your most important activities. Don't think

---

[1] Dr. John Wesley Taylor's doctoral dissertation on "Self-concept in home-schooling children" and his article on the same subject in *Home School Researcher*, as described in Dr. Brian D. Ray's booklet, *Marching to the Beat of their Own Drum: A Profile of Home Education Research.*
2 Delahooke, 1986, quoted in the National Home Education Research Institute's *Fact Sheet 1.*

of friendship as something that takes place only during French fries and mall shopping. Don't settle for boring, predictable friendships. Challenge each other. Get a little more honest as time goes by.

Go to school sometimes. Eat lunch there, be in the choir, be a teacher's aide, go to assemblies. See Chapter 19 for ways this can be worked out. If it can't be worked out, who will catch you if you eat with your friends? I know of a college student, majoring in sociology, who routinely eats in a high school cafeteria just to watch people interact in their high school ways. No one has ever noticed that she doesn't belong. And you can always hang out at other schoolteenager hang-outs, if that's your style.

See your family in a new light. Cultivate your siblings and parents as friends.

Free yourself of schoolish prejudices. Don't cheat yourself out of potential friends because of the clothes they wear or the makeup they don't wear. A shared sense of taste and style is a legitimate part of some of your friendships, but there's no reason *all* your friends have to look like you, is there?

The best solution of all: *Get your friends out of school!* Let the vision spread... ⊛

15

adults
in a new light

You cannot teach a person anything; you can only help him find it within himself.
–Galileo

Now that you don't have to *obey* teachers and principals and hall monitors with walkie-talkies, maybe you can start some healthy relationships with adults. Adults can be your friends, buddies, jogging partners, and other "equals." Since you already know about friendships among equals, I see no point in explaining How to Make Adult Friends. If you spend time around adults—in chess clubs or during political campaigns or wherever—you will make adult friends. Thirteen-year-old Mylie Alrich points out that when you don't go to school, "the line between 'kids' and 'grownups' is almost not there."

It is also valuable, however, to have *unequal* relationships with adults. To reach your fullest potential, you need mentors, role models, and teachers. That's not just because you're a "kid." Adults also need mentors, role models, and teachers in order to reach *their* fullest potential. No one should be bossing you around or giving you unsolicited report cards, but these guides *can* help push and encourage you to do things you might not be gutsy, determined, or skilled enough to do on your own. If you're seeking any type of guidance, Susan Shilcock's experience may be helpful:

> We almost always start new experiences as experiments. That helps us define more clearly what we want and what parts of the current arrangement are on target . . . Though many of our short-term experiments have ended up lasting much longer, proposing the idea as short-term makes it easier for the adult to say yes . . .
> We look for people actively involved in their area of interest. We look for an artist, not an art teacher, a Spanish-speaking person, not a Spanish teacher, a wood worker, not a shop teacher, a chemist, not a chemistry teacher. (Of course, sometimes these are one and the same.) Second, we look for people who see themselves as learners. Generally, if someone believes that he has a complete body of knowledge, he tends to be less enthusiastic and more rigid about how he shares his information. On the other hand, people who view themselves as just further along the spectrum of learning about their subject will share not only their expertise but also their own challenges and confusions . . . [1]

Teachers (and tutors)
are a fairly obvious role—people who explain their knowledge in a specific area. You may or may not admire them as people-in-general. You *do* need to admire their

---

[1] From *GWS* #112.

expertise in whatever they're teaching you, or else find a new teacher. Some teachers become more than teachers—mentors or role models or friends. But it is fine to have a teacher simply in order to learn a particular set of skills. Teachers may not actually teach a class or formal lessons, of course. Jonathan Kibler writes in *GWS* #74:

> Besides my dad, there are three people in particular who have helped me learn more about computers. First, Mr. Warner was my 4-H Club instructor. He taught me the most commonly used BASIC words. He explained what the commands "PRINT," "GOTO," and "INPUT" meant. Also, he taught me about flow charts. Knowing about flow charts helped me to write my own programs. He also introduced me to some new programs. Before I met Mr. Warner I knew nothing about computers; I am very glad that I met him through 4-H.
>
> Second, Mrs. Penn is a computer instructor at a school. She goes to the same church as I do. When she found out that I was interested in computers, she invited me to work on them with her. Almost every Sunday after church I go over to the school with her and work with the computers in the classroom. I play computer games and write programs. I enjoy these Sundays very much. Mrs. Penn has also lent me books about computers. Through her, I have gained more appreciation for what computers can do. I am happy that she takes the time to allow me to work with her.
>
> When I first got my own computer, I didn't know how to work any of the software. I found out that one of the dads in my YMCA Trailblazer group, Dr. Loader, had the same computer and printer as I did. He offered to help me figure out some of the software. I had a lot of questions about word processing programs in particular. Dr. Loader happened to have a word processing program that was easy to use and he copied it for me. He also spent a lot of time answering questions for me over the phone—and in the beginning I had a lot of questions! He invited me over to his office so that he could better explain how the programs worked. Once he even came over to my house on his lunch hour to help me print a file. I'm really grateful for all the time he has given to me.
>
> I'm really fortunate to have all of these friends who know about computers and are willing to help me.

Role models

are people you admire from afar. You watch what they do and how they do it. You study them to see what you can learn from them. You can have role models in the career you hope to go into, or role models for life-in-general. By giving you a picture of what's possible, they help you to challenge yourself. They can be people you know—like your parents, or people in the news—like Sinead O'Connor or Sandra Day O'Connor. Role models don't have to know you exist in order for you to learn from them. Of course, other young people can be role models too.

Other adult guides

Adults play many other helpful roles also. They can be spiritual leaders like gurus or rabbis or priests or priestesses, experts you can ask for occasional advice or information, counselors, advisors. They can be teachers in unusual senses of the word: Australian unschooler Alex Banks-Watson says, "One of my favorite things to do is listen to adult conversations." In ancient Greece, philosophers wandered through the streets and countrysides with teenaged boys, engaged in dialogues about truth and beauty. In a talk at my college, Barry Lopez spoke about the Eskimo people, who have no word for "teacher" or "wise man" but instead recognize people who play the role of "isumataq." The *isumataq* does not teach or preach, but in his presence, wisdom is *revealed*. I mention these roles because they can help you to see and encourage nuances in your own relationships.

Mentors

Are people who pay a lot of attention to you and give you long-term help, advice, guidance, and support. Depending on their style, they might also kick your pants when they think you're not challenging yourself enough. In the *Karate Kid* films, Mr. Miyagi—the trainer (*sensei*) —and his student Daniel show mentorship in action. Eileen Trombly provides another example in *GWS* #18:

> Amy, fourteen, has taken ballet lessons from an older woman in town and has developed a unique, warm relationship with her over the years. The woman is now in her eighties, still participates in dance, and has a very interesting past which she shares with Amy. The lesson is one-on-one so there is always much time for sharing and feeling relaxed in each other's company. The teacher was once a ballerina in the New York Ballet Troupe; owned a theater with her husband, who was in vaudeville; was daughter-in-law of a former Connecticut governor; and was acquainted with Anna Pavlova. She has much to offer in the way of experiences, and her polished yet friendly manner has served to influence Amy in a very positive way.

And seventeen-year-old Sarabeth Matilsky, of New Jersey, writes:

> It was the autumn of '95, and my mother and I were sitting at our dining room table with the hateful blue book in front of us. Sighing with frustration, I was trying to understand active and passive verbs and what makes an object "definite." These daily sessions with *Warriner's English Grammar and Composition* were definitely not introducing me to the joys of the English language. Though we continued to work with the book for a while more, after a month or so of discouragement I wrote to Susannah Sheffer [editor of *GWS*]. I asked her if she had any ideas for me—books to read, stuff to do, anything besides that dreadful book. She wrote back with suggestions, and she also offered to critique my writing if I wanted her to.
>
> So, for over a year now I have been sending her my essays and articles, and she has been sending me her comments, suggestions, and answers to questions. I have written more in the past year than I ever did before, and think that is partly because I always had someone to show my work to. It's great to be able to do that, I discovered, because even if I never end up doing anything with an essay (like getting it published), I learn a lot in the process and I have an audience of at least one thoughtful person. She is always respectful, and in return I truly value her comments. I've been having so much fun writing to her, and now when people ask me how I study English, I can truthfully tell them that I do it by "correspondence"!

You don't *need* a mentor to have a nice life. Furthermore, not everyone who wants a mentor finds one. However, people who do have mentors say that the relationship helps them grow and succeed much more than they could on their own.

If you'd like to have a mentor, how can you find one? Patiently. Mentors are not as easy to find as adult friends, teachers, tutors, and role models. You can't just advertise in the help-wanted section—anyone who thinks of himself as a ready-made mentor is quite certainly *not* one. Likely, a mentorship will develop naturally out of other types of relationships:

If you have an intense interest in music, perhaps you take piano lessons, and over time, you grow closer to your teacher. Eventually, he may begin to take a more personal interest in you, and one day you realize you have a mentor. After you've been leading tours at the science museum for a few months, the director asks you into her office for a cup of tea. It turns out she knows all about stars, and when you tell her you have been learning to identify constellations, she invites you on her next telescope outing. Two months later, you realize she has become your mentor.

There is no quick formula to follow; like most important human relationships, each mentorship will develop uniquely and at its own pace. In *Professional Women and Their Mentors*, Nancy Collins cautions:

> When you find the right mentor, you never actually say: "Will you be my mentor?" This is the number one rule of beginning the relationship . . . Mentor relationships take time to develop . . . The relationship seems to begin when the mentor is both supportive and demanding, and the mentoree feels stretched and appreciated.

However, if you know someone whom you think would make a good mentor, you can certainly *encourage* the relationship in that direction. Tell them you admire their work. Show your appreciation for any time they spend with you. Ask for their advice. Watch for small ways to help them out. If they teach classes, sign up—and put focused energy into your work. If they enjoy the role you are quietly creating for them, they will soon start to take initiative for developing the relationship. If not, they'll back away. Be sensitive. Don't force.

If you don't yet know anyone you'd like to have as a mentor, get more involved in what you love. This way you can meet lots of adults—potential mentors. Take a pottery class; volunteer at the zoo; join a writers' guild.

An ideal mentor is good at what she does, and other adults respect her. *Your* feelings toward her, however, are the most crucial. Nancy Collins writes, "In selecting your mentor, you should try to choose someone for whom you feel admiration, affection, respect, trust, and even love in the broadest sense."

Some of your former school teachers have excellent mentorship potential—as long as they have the time to develop an individual relationship with you. Also, of course, they must have some expertise. Forget teachers who are obsessed only with "teaching" itself, and not entranced with their subject. Avoid attaching yourself to someone who wants mainly to "help you grow up" or some such slobbery vague condescending controlling rot.

Don't forget old people. With time on their hands and a lifetime of experiences behind them, they make splendid mentors, enriching their own lives and yours.

Also, mentors need not be sugary touchy-feely types who always encourage you to do what you feel like doing and who tell you everything you do is wonderful. I often work best with very demanding people, like Pat, my flamenco teacher, who snapped, "Again! Lift your chin! Bend your knees! Faster! Don't look at the floor!" But if you prefer the sugary touchy-feely type, that's fine too. Encouragement, recognition, and warmth may be exactly what you need.

Once you have a mentor, relinquish a little bit of control. Remember, you picked somebody you trusted, so now try what they suggest. Take the risks they ask you to take. Let them push you onto your tightropes.

Finally, think about your end of the bargain. How can you return some of your mentor's generous energy? Offer to help by cleaning her house or typing her novel. Realize that you will never completely pay her back for her gifts, and that she won't ask you to, but that someday you can obliquely return the favor by sharing your own white-haired expertise with some wild teenager. ❁

starting out—
a sense of
the possibilities

I do not believe much in education.
Each man ought to be his own model,
however frightful that may be. —Albert Einstein

A DIFFERENT KIND of Time

Don't be a factory. Do a few things well instead of everything poorly. Big undertakings—like starting a town orchestra or trying to find the ultimate physics theory—do take time. If you love your big undertakings, that time is never wasted.

A Different Kind of Structure

The homeschooling community talks a lot about structured education versus unstructured education. Although there is no such thing as a completely structured or a completely unstructured education, these terms are convenient and can make it easier for you to think about how you want to organize your unschooled life.

In a mostly "unstructured" education, you *let* life happen to you, keeping your eyes open and learning from whatever you happen to do. In a mostly "structured" education, you *make* life happen, setting goals and making plans. Which is best? That's a philosophical and religious question, and there are plenty of respectable votes on both sides.

An unstructured education frees you from unnecessary boundaries between life and learning. It allows you to calm your mind and to live on a healthy schedule, reading only when you are hungry. It invites you to soak up the universe by swimming in the river without telling yourself, "I should be thinking about the natures of the currents, and the names of the potential fish near my feet, and the dead poets who wrote about water." It meshes with the teaching of Zen masters, Indian gurus, and ancient Chinese philosophies, which ask their followers not to strive, not to battle life, but to let themselves be shaped and carried by its flow.

A structured education, on the other hand, is what you want if you are goal-oriented or if you enjoy being methodical. After all these years of living with other people's curriculums, you can get a big thrill designing your own personalized education. It can be as formal, rigorous and organized as you want, far more so than school. You can set big or small goals for yourself—such as finishing a math textbook by a certain date, writing a letter to your newspaper every week, writing and illustrating a children's book during October and November, completing an inventory of local tree species before Earth Day, phoning three people each day until you find an apprenticeship you like. If you take this approach, you *will* get things done. Barbara Sher's book *Wishcraft* can help you set epicurean goals and reach them, although she writes about life, not just education, which may confuse you if you don't yet realize they're the same.

One more point about structure versus unstructure: don't assume that structure has to be *school*-style structure. Personally, I despise the idea of school-at-home, and the kind of schoolish schedule that would entail. But you can build your own structure centered around whatever you like. For some homeschoolers, structure consists of five or more hours of daily music practice. For others, it consists of a full-fledged computer programming business, or nonstop reading, or tinkering all day long with electronics.

One valuable kind of structure is goal-setting, which is explained in profound detail in the aforementioned *Wishcraft*. This is the sort of structure which serves your desires (I want to build a windmill so I will do this, that, and the other thing) instead of your sense of guilt (I should study chemistry every day for 45 minutes). Obviously, you are going to learn plenty by setting out to achieve your goals; in the windmill department that's going to include physics, carpentry, geography, and probably history. If your goal is writing a book on unschooling, you're going to learn about the homeschooling movement, the publishing industry, word processing, library research, original research, law libraries, words, and fear. If your goal is to restore the neighborhood swamp to health, you'll learn about chemistry, biology, politics, economics, your own muscles, and organizing people. Reanna Alder, fifteen, says, "Most of my learning is done in the name of *life* or challenging myself rather than *education*. For example, I think I would be happier and would feel more capable and presentable as a writer if I knew I could spell better, so I work on it."

If you are completely confused as to how to start structuring your life, here's one way: do "academics" for two hours each day—not necessarily lots of subjects, or the same ones every day; you are not going to dry up if you don't do 45 minutes every day of "social studies." Do some kind of work or project for four hours. In the rest of your time, read, see friends, talk with your parents, make tabouli. Take Saturdays and Sundays off. Sound arbitrary? It is. I made it up, although it is based on a loose sort of "average" of the lives of a hundred unschoolers, most college-bound. Once you try this schedule for a month, you will know how you want to change it.

If you like participating in programs and doing academic work in groups with adult leaders, consider thinking of your summers as hardcore "education" time. During the summer, there are lots of interesting "enrichment" academic opportunities which are more fun and productive than school. See *Free and Almost Free Adventures for Teenagers* and *Student Science Opportunities*, both by Gail L. Grand, and *Peterson's Summer Opportunities for Kids and Teenagers*. Then, spend the winter making holiday feasts, hibernating with a stack of epic novels, ice skating, visiting favorite uncles, painting murals on your ceiling.

Quite possibly, you may need a structured plan because your state laws require that you submit one. If so, read Chapters 17 through 30 for ideas and then try two brainstorming techniques:

1. Make a list of the subjects you have to cover. Write down all the ways you can think of to "study" each one, and a list of related books you think you might like to read. Also ask your family and friends for suggestions.

2. *Make a list of your most important interests.* Then look at each one and consider how academic subjects could be related. For instance, if you love horses, your horse list might look like this:

Language Arts/English: Read *National Velvet.* Write a profile of a local horse breeder. Write poetry or stories from a horse's point of view.

Social sciences: Conduct a study of careers related to horses. Look into why so many young girls are intensely interested in horses, by conducting a survey or another type of study. Read about the profound influence horses have had on cultures around the world, such as the culture of Plains Indian tribes. Stay on a working cattle ranch for a week.

Science: Learn about horse anatomy, diseases, and biology. Find out about the evolutionary history of horses. Learn to use a microscope to diagnose horse diseases.

Art: Draw horses. Make a saddle or other tack. Produce a documentary video on horse care or horse races.

You get the idea. Here are some comments and morsels of advice from unschoolers on their experiences with school-style structure and other kinds of structured and unstructured learning. In *GWS* #22:

This past year, we got away from correspondence schools altogether, ordered our own texts (for math only), and really got unschooled . . . My daughter (thirteen) now studies totally independently, with only occasional help in algebra, or help with a Spanish conversation. Her progress is really astounding, too. She reads more than ever, and does about three times the work that she did in regular school—by choice. I guess that once we eliminated all the busywork, she discovered how much *fun* learning can really be. She is once again eager, sets her own schedule, and still manages to get so much done that it is truly astonishing. The changes in her have also been very beneficial, because, as she controls and uses her own time, it has matured her and made her very responsible and sensible.

In *GWS* #35 a brave mother writes about her teenagers:

What do they do all day? Why is it that I don't know? *Why is it that I don't care?* We don't keep journals or go on field trips or categorize the day's activities into subject areas. I can't stand the dead smell of all those fakey thought-up things.

And Borgny Parker writes about unschooling her daughter Abigail:

We started off thinking that we would be following the public school day at home. That did not work well at all. Both David and I saw the need to keep our distance because we were putting Abi under the same pressures she was seeking to avoid. What evolved was our own blend of non-schooling, I guess. We saw Abigail take off in different directions by herself.

Halee Shepler, eleven, of Venezuela, writes:

The way I do my schooling is by answering three questions each year:
1. What skill do I want to learn?
2. What question do I want to answer?
3. What big problem do I want to solve?
    Usually one thing leads to another. For example, one year I wanted to learn how to train my horse. This led to the big question: "How do individuals and cultures change?" One day when my instructor and I were working with my horse, she asked another rider to

jump him without my permission. When my horse refused the jump, the rider beat my horse. So I wanted to solve the problem of animal abuse. I started to search for resources. In *Horse Illustrated* I found an article about Tellington Touch Equine Awareness Method. I wrote and I got information.

This led to a new problem that I want to solve. Linda Tellington-Jones wrote about the work at the Paralympic Games. I told my friend who is blind and does jumping about the Paralympics and she was interested in entering the next competition, but there is no committee in Venezuela. I am helping her in this. So you see how one thing leads to another. I hope to be a TTEAM practitioner some day, after completing the two-year program for horses and companion animals, and work in therapeutic riding.

After Eva Owens left "one of the so-called top public high schools in the country" after ninth grade, she wrote in *GWS* #105:

I am by nature very unorganized. I decided that with homeschooling, I wanted to be somewhat organized to learn what I wanted to learn. Also, when I wrote up my homeschooling plan, the school wanted me to set objectives that they could follow up on. So way back in September I set goals for myself for the year. By December I decided that I needed a little more guidance than that. So I sat down with Leslie [an adult friend], and with her assistance I set my goals for the coming month. Ah, but that was not enough for Eva, the procrastinator. Now in April I've become quite content with the routine of, after eating breakfast, writing down what I want to accomplish that day, with thought to my monthly goals. This has turned out to be best for me. At the end of the day I can see the results of my work and can see what I have not done. It's very clear cut that way.

Christian McKee, of Wisconsin, writes:

At the age of eighteen and as one who has never gone to school, I realize that somewhere during the past five to six years I've come to think of myself not as a homeschooler or as an unschooler, but simply as who I am, Christian McKee, citizen and community member. My life, except for the few times my parents doubted their own belief in unschooling, has essentially been mine to structure and live as I have chosen. In the past eighteen years I've dabbled in a little bit of everything: radio engineering, juggling, skate boarding, cross country skiing, foreign language, singing, make-up design, fly fishing, all sorts of unusual things. While it seems that unusual things interest me, I think it could be said that I am pretty intellectual by nature. When I'm interested in something I study it in detail. For the past four years I've focused my life around my interests in choral music, fly fishing, radio engineering, and the study of foreign language. While each of these endeavors has taken on a significant role in my life, I'm not sure that any one of them will become the way I make a living for myself. My fishing has offered me opportunities—my own small business, travel and work in Montana, instructing beginning fly tiers, being a demonstration fly tier at regional conclaves, served as a board member for a regional chapter of the National Federation of Fly Fishers—but I'm not sure that I will continue to center my life around chasing the elusive trout with a stone fly nymph. Fishing has expanded my outlook on life and offered me opportunities to experience what a less traditional life style might offer, but my experiences with singing and foreign language have also opened unimagined doors. Through my work with singing, German and French, I've been able to travel (locally and internationally), teach young students German and study at the university. My small taste of university life (I've taken German courses, a literature and a writing class) has whetted my appetite for more concentrated academic studies. As a result, I've applied to and been accepted at Kalamazoo College. My plans for the immediate future are to continue, for one more year, as a special student at the university of Wisconsin, possibly live in my own apartment and then move to Michigan for college. What can I say, this is just how my life fits together. As I said earlier, it has little to do with unschooling, homeschooling or schooling of any kind and more to do with being myself and how I choose to live my life at the present time.

Gwen Meehan, mother of unschooler Patrick, writes:

> Last year was licking wounds and healing time. We both put much more emphasis on structured learning. We "did History, English, Algebra" and other "school" things. It was fine and necessary for that time.
>
> Over the summer, however, I read all my back issues of *GWS* which highlighted homeschool information for older students. By the time I had finished, I realized the overwhelming consensus was: get off the formal education road entirely. Every parent and every child backed up the idea of simply letting the student direct his/her own education. My role would be "facilitator." I did not have to worry about "teaching a curriculum," no matter how loose.
>
> This has been the proper direction for us. Patrick is developing wonderfully.

Other parents wrote:

"The only books we steadily use are math books, because math is easier to stick with if we use a specific book. I really prefer the Saxon method and he does too."

"Throw away the textbooks, tests, and timesheets."

Teenagers wrote:

"We study reading, math, language, spelling, social studies, and science. We stuck close to [our] textbooks for our first two years. This was no different than being in school, and caused a lot of stress for all of us. It was also *boring!*" (The writer now uses textbooks only for math.)

"If the school sends you a curriculum guide, ignore it. You'll learn a lot more going at your own pace."

"Don't try to imitate school. Take areas you are interested in and learn from there. Find adults who know about subjects you are interested in and learn from them."

"Don't schedule yourself too tightly. In school a lot of time is spent just moving from class to class, being counted, disciplined, organized. You don't need to structure everything. Be relaxed. Take time to talk. Take time to think. Do nothing sometimes. Ask questions. Don't force learning. Some days you're just not in the mood, other days you don't want to stop."

Don't sink to the level of school.

Dream the biggest dreams you can, and then follow them. Start a cultural exchange program for Japanese and American teenagers. Build a log cabin and furniture to go inside it. What you lack in skill and experience, you can make up for with time and patience. Don't rush.

Remember your adolescent power and magic.

Don't spend all your time on mental stuff. It's not natural. You have your whole life to be academic. You have only seven years to wiggle and pray in a teenaged body.

Life doesn't get worse, but it does get less intense. Things become less new, and hormones stop raging. So honor and treasure your passion while it peaks. I'm not telling you to act on your every whim or to do stupid things like get pregnant when you're not ready to be. I am telling you to cling stubbornly to your spiritual yearnings, not to be talked into any imitation reality, to fall in love with people, and, as Thoreau put it, to suck all the marrow out of life.

A Small Dose of Chinese Philosophy

Before I suggest specific things to do with your precious time, I want to throw the spotlight on the concept of balance.

Some things we do are *outward*—giving, producing, working, speaking, taking action. Others are more *inward*—receiving, consuming, relaxing, listening, being passive. To be healthy we need to balance both in our lives. No one speaks wisely without having first listened. No one can listen happily if they aren't heard also.

When it comes to structuring your life, people of any age need to combine what our society calls "working," or "real life," with "academics." I am going to redefine these general areas as *giving out* and *taking in*. Learning, or education, happens equally in both, to the degree that you are fully awake and present. It happens most, though perhaps subconsciously, when you are happy. It happens rarely in school. That is, learning about history or how to talk in Spanish happens minimally in school. Learning how to take orders and sit quietly—that happens continually.

Most people your age are forced into too much *taking in*. Restricted from working or otherwise contributing to society, forced to read and listen all day, young people are desperately dependent, useless, powerless, and passive. Your lives are out of balance.

On the other hand, many adults feel pressured to do nothing *but* give out—the workaholic executive who feels like a failure if he doesn't advance continually in his career, the classic-tragic mother who drives her four kids to ten kinds of lessons and cooks three color-coordinated, balanced meals daily and scrubs Junior behind the ears but has no time to take a photography class or digest her own food or soak in a bubble bath. These lives, too, are out of balance.

People *need* balance. If they don't find it in a good way, they'll get it in a superficial way that hurts themselves and the world around them. We call some of them yuppies—people who work at stressful, nice-money jobs but don't feed their minds and spirits enough, so they switch into another mode—buy, buy, buy. Bad for personal growth and bad for the planet, which is what gets used up when people buy things they don't need or even deep-down want.

Conversely, teenagers who aren't allowed to affect the world or achieve independence in a good way often resort to vandalism, insulting their teachers, joining gangs, killing cats, yelling at their parents—anything to make a difference. School denies your basic need to touch the world, to contribute, to matter.

Many activities seem to cross the line between giving out and taking in. Traveling, for example, is active and takes work, but is usually more "taking in"—absorbing, enjoying, looking, listening—than "giving out." On the other hand, learning to write is considered academic, and schools rarely encourage you to direct your writing to a real audience, but actually, writing is essentially a way of speaking out and affecting the world.

The Chinese concept of Yin and Yang nicely expresses the relationship between these two ways of being. Yang contains the outward, aggressive, giving aspects of the universe and one's life. Yin contains that which is inward, passive, receiving.

The sun is yang and the moon yin, a candlestick yang and a bowl yin, hardness yang and softness yin.

What society calls "education" is mostly a yin activity, while "work" is yang. And you may prefer to think of adolescence as a more yin time in your life than adulthood. Nevertheless, both ways of being are necessary for health and satisfaction. In fact, according to Chinese philosophy, most of our troubles—global, health, and societal—result from a stagnant imbalance of yin and yang.

It boils down to this: you need to have both of these kinds of activity—"giving out" things like starting a business, directing a play, or volunteering at the local soup kitchen, and "taking in" things like watching the news, reading, or going to hear a historian speak at a museum. Also, realize that "academics" are only one part of the yin you need. Leave yourself time to stare at the fishbowl or linger at dinner. When you escape school you'll undoubtedly want a more outward, active life that affects the world around you, but don't starve yourself by shutting off the inward flow. The *Tao Teh Ching* reminds us, "For all things there is a time for going ahead, and a time for following behind; a time for slow-breathing and a time for fast-breathing; . . . A time to be up and a time to be down." If you were a bike, you'd have at least ten speeds. Shift gears as needed.

What's Ahead

Part Three, Chapters 17-31, talks mainly about what you can soak up, or "education," or the yin part of your unschooled life. Part Four, Chapters 32-38, talks about touching the world, "work," yangish stuff. Mix and match.

Finally: I give you a lot of suggestions in order to bridge the gap of fear; you're so used to being told what and how to do everything that I figured I would hold your hand a bit. But only if you want your hand held. If you're ready to say, "I can figure out what I want and how to do it on my own," that's *fine*. Hesitate not. After all, you are the heroines and heroes on the edge of a frontier. Your choices will inspire the unschoolers who follow. Hold your heads high, and ride off into the sunrise. ☀

Part 3

The Tailor-Made Educational Extravaganza

17

Your Tailor-Made Intellectual Extravaganza

On your learning depends the welfare of the world. —The Course in Miracles

Fᴿᴏᴍ ʜᴇʀᴇ ᴛʜʀᴏᴜɢʜ **Chapter 31**, this book puts access to academia in your lap. Before you ignore this advice, or—worse—before you approach it with determined despair because you "should," please listen: intellectual fervor is for everyone. Maybe you don't think so, because when they made you do worksheets in history, biology, or English, they stole from you the desire to investigate the past, marvel at caterpillars, or hear a good story. *Don't let them get away with it.*

Or maybe you don't think intellectual fervor is for you, because you think you know where your territory is, and it's anywhere—under the hood of a pickup, in the cosmetics section of a department store—except in academia. Wrong! The *universe* is your territory. You don't have to take a test to be allowed into the community of intellectuals. It doesn't matter whether you used to get A's or F's. If you read slowly or have a small vocabulary, you can read slowly and like it, and you can ask a person or a dictionary about words you don't know. If your father does nothing after work but drink beer and watch TV, that doesn't ban you from the poetry section of the library. If *you* do nothing after school but drink beer (or Dr. Pepper) and watch TV, that doesn't ban you from the poetry section of the library.

Now that you're out of school, why bother at all? Why not just lie and write in your log book that you spent two hours yesterday reading *The Mind's I*, and that you collected coyote poop all morning today to see what they've been eating?

Because if you find out and soak up some of the conflicting mesmerizing shocking funny logical illogical beautiful sparks we call "knowledge" or "information," you will grow a broader mind, more capable of seeing the connections and relationships between things that make the world and life so mysterious and wonderful.

Because knowledge mixed with wonder shapes your mind into the interesting, lively kind of place you'd like to inhabit for the next eighty years, maybe even eternity.

Because if you don't know what's been said and thought and tried before you walked in the door, you may repeat someone else a few times before you contribute anything new. The world does need new contributions, which is one *good* reason the schoolboard has for wanting you to be educated.

Because it is not fun to be ignorant and confused.

Because if you know things and think about them, you'll free your mind of narrow prejudices and cruelties. (Another reason you do the rest of us a favor by getting educated.)

Because if you know why the Trojan War, the French Revolution, World War II and Vietnam were fought and what changes they led to, you can form your own opinion about what justifies war, and what kind of war can be justified. Being informed improves your citizenship.

Because if you're a budding pianist, you need to understand the tradition behind you—not only the great pianists and composers, but also the roots of music in fire and ritual and mystery. Whatever you love, you will love it more truly when you understand its history.

Because certain skills—especially reading, writing, arithmetic, and simple algebra—can give you control over your own affairs. You can write to friends, businesses, congresspeople, the public, the planet. You can read about whatever you want to know, you can manage your money. (This basic stuff was supposed to be "taught" thoroughly in grade school. Chances are it wasn't, so you may want to work more on it.) If you can also draw and do physics and advanced math, you can design buildings, bridges, airplanes, computers.

Maybe, also, because you have to prove to the parents that your brain isn't mildewed from snooping around in the forest instead of sitting in Miss Enquist's biology class.

How does it work?

Getting educated in the big beautiful sense needn't ruin your day. If you devote two hours each night to reading and sometimes writing, conducting Scientific Experiments, or tackling other mental exercises, you will certainly learn far more, and far better stuff, than you have been learning in school. Of course, you may wish to spend more time on "educational" activities you love. But don't feel obligated. After all, you never spent a lot of time learning in school. As Micki and David Colfax (whose homeschooled sons went to Harvard) point out in *Homeschooling for Excellence:*

> The child who attends public school typically spends approximately 1,100 hours a year there, but only twenty percent of these—220—are spent, as the educators say, "on task." Nearly 900 hours, or eighty percent, are squandered on what are essentially organizational matters.[1]

Academia in what you love

There are seven big fat chapters in this book which tell you how to study all the school subjects without school. They can help you both learn things you are already interested in and also discover that you like more intellectual stuff than you ever thought you did.

But at the same time, you can sweeten your life by giving your brain to the things that already have your heart. It's mostly a matter of realizing that there is no cement wall between the things we do and the things we learn. Rather than look for things to do that fit into a "subject," look at the things you already like to do and

---

[1] David and Micki Colfax, *Homeschooling for Excellence*, p.46.

think about where they might take you if you didn't stop them.

For instance.

I have always loved ethnic textiles and costumes. I used to not have time to do anything about it, but now I keep a hefty scrapbook of pictures cut out mostly from *National Geographics*, showing the traditional costumes of cultures all around the world. I also collect textiles and costumes when I can afford to, and I make replicas of folk costumes, slowly. I don't think of this as anything academic—it's just something I enjoy—but if I were a teenager I would most certainly point it out to the schoolboard and colleges as an eminently respectable way of fulfilling my social studies requirement.

After all, this activity has put me into contact with all kinds of knowledge. For example, after I noticed that Apache moccasins resembled the footwear of the tribes who live along the Amur River in Siberia, I went to the library and found out that the ancestors of the Apache had supposedly migrated across the land bridge and down to the American southwest quite directly, without dillydallying along the way or mingling much with other people. Later, as I read folktales of the Amur tribes and heard people talk about Apache religion, I noticed more similarities between the two cultures, subtle things I wouldn't have picked up on if not for the earlier moccasin clue. I keep this connection in my head as one of the questions I'm going to investigate when I have time. Meanwhile, I used a book on Native American footwear to design a pair of Apache-style moccasins which I decorated with a fishy Siberian motif.

Also thanks to my interest in costume, I know the whereabouts of all kinds of countries and regions within these countries. (Throughout high school and college, I'd barely heard of these places—Tunisia, Bosnia, Sardinia, Turkestan, Rajasthan.) Through costume, I've learned a lot about history and the relationships between countries. Women's dress in Southeastern Europe, for example, reflects centuries of Turkish rule. An intense interest in folk and ethnic dance has grown up beside my love of costume. The way different cultures dress has taught me many things about the way they perceive the roles of men and women, and about the relationship between people and nature. My interest has also invited me to reflect on the value of the industrial revolution, which is largely responsible for the drab factory-made clothes we wear now—and for other carelessly built aspects of our lives. I could fill a few more pages with things I've pondered and learned about in connection with ethnic costume.

My interest in costume is not any more inherently cerebral than your interest in airplanes, skiing, Pink Floyd, cute boys on TV, church, baseball, computers, or dogs. Your scrapbooks, obsessions, daydreams, collections, conversations, questions, and reading can all bring you into contact with the lushest, most meaningful kind of academia.

Jaywalking in the Milky Way

Along that line, be aware of interdisciplinary studies. What are interdisciplinary studies? Usually anything with "studies" tacked onto the end—American studies, Asian studies, bioregional studies, environmental studies, ethnic studies, urban studies, women's studies.

A single discipline provides *one* language, or set of questions, through which to look at ourselves and our surroundings. Chemistry looks at them in terms of molecules; physics looks at them in terms of atoms. Sociology examines people's behavior in terms of cultural patterns and relationships; psychology examines their behavior in terms of their minds and emotions. Conversely, an interdisciplinary "field" looks at one thing with a lot of languages. For example, in women's studies you might 1) read and criticize literature by women and about women, 2) study women's roles in history, 3) look at women's bodies from a biological point of view, and 4) look at contemporary female roles through sociology.

I encourage you to apply the interdisciplinary idea to whatever you love. Consider history, geography, literature, art, science, etc. as they relate to your interest. If you love cars, maybe you would like to find out the history of cars and other transportation, about the significance of cars in literature and movies, about the symbolic role of cars in our culture, or even about the environmental damage they cause.

Who will screen your calls?
Your teachers used to. Some did a good job. Most were lousy. You need to decide how it's going to happen now.

Huh?

The unpleasant flip side of living in an information age is that it's hard to know what matters and what doesn't. With millions of books to choose from, which one are you supposed to read? With millions of Web sites at the poke of a button, which should you summon to your flickering screen?

One of the best things a good teacher does is bring you the worthwhile stuff instead of the worthless crap. However, teachers are not usually very good at this role. First of all, they are bombarded with even more information than most people, and a lot of it is very cheap-imitation-style unappealing stuff the educational publishers want them to buy. They have little way of knowing what's worthwhile and what's junk, and little time to make thoughtful choices. Educational publishing is *mostly* junk, so they're likely to go wrong.

Also, the best books on any subject are hardly ever textbooks. Since teachers are supposed to live in the land of textbooks, they often don't read the best books or even think profoundly in their own fields. Too many social studies teachers, for example, really only care about coaching football and have little feel for the life of other cultures or for the kinds of forces that go into national elections.

Teachers are often out of touch with the real innovations in their field, and have no sense of how their field connects to the world. (Remember, most teachers have done little besides go to school.) Teachers are not necessarily experts in their field. They do not even necessarily love their field. For these reasons, most teachers are not the best people to trust with the task of helping you choose resources. Every school has exceptions, of course, and some schools are full of exceptions.

Who or what, instead of teachers, can help you make sense of the heaps?

This book provides a start. It tells you a few good resources to get your hands on, both in general (Chapter 20) and in specific subjects (Chapters 21—30). It also tells you about reference works for each field—books that point out other good books. Sometimes the best reference works include the mail-order catalogs of specialty stores. In Chapter 21, for example, you will be guided towards the catalog of The Exploratorium store.

Another most excellent friend you can have is *The Millennium Whole Earth Catalog* or one of the earlier editions of the *Whole Earth Catalog*, which seductively describe pretty much the best books in nearly every field, ranging from evolutionary biology to cheesemaking to boardsailing to Western spirituality.

If you become especially interested in a particular subject, ask for help from an adult who has a passionate relationship with it. See Chapter 15.

Fortunately, the Internet tends to organize itself fairly well, and offers helpful "hotlist" sites like those of the Franklin Institute. Hotlists recommend the best sites in a particular field, like art, Africa, space science, literature, American history, or math.

Librarians can give penultimate advice.

After you've been independent for a while, you'll develop a knack for scanning your eyes over dozens of library books and magically choosing the one or two that will most reward your efforts.

By the way, if you are addicted to babytalk, you'll have to get over it. School textbooks are mostly written in babytalk, because their writers know you're not interested, and babytalk is the only possible way to keep your patience. Most popular books, high school textbooks, and newspapers are purposely written at about eighth-grade level. When you get into real books, some of them will be tough. As long as you're interested in the subject, the toughness will be worth it.

Of course, a lot can be said in simple, straightforward language, but complex subjects often require more difficult language. School tends to assign novels at higher reading levels, but otherwise doesn't challenge you much. Therefore, college reading comes as a big shock for a lot of freshmen. Most of the books I recommend in the next chapters are not especially difficult, but some do go beyond eighth grade level.

An eye on your college future

Many, if not most, new unschoolers plan to go to college. (Many later change their minds—when it becomes obvious that directing their own educations is great fun and terribly effective, some of their upstart brains say, "Why spend the next four years taking orders and the following four—or more—in debt?") If you *are* unschooling with the plan of college in the back of your head, note that in Chapters 21-25 you'll find advice from college professors on what they would like their new students to already know. I am grateful to these professors for sharing their views, and for the most part I think their advice is useful, but as you read these comments please keep a few things in mind.

- Most of these people teach in highly selective schools, and their expectations are higher than those of professors at more typical institutions.
- Note whether the professor is talking about students who expect to major in her subject, or simply to take a basic course. You definitely do *not* need to be an expert in every academic subject in order to go to college—even a selective college.
- I asked these people what the ideally prepared student would be like, as well as the minimally prepared student. The ideally prepared student is rare—mostly a creature of professorly fantasies. When you read about the ideally prepared student in a subject you love, pay attention, but don't worry if you don't exactly match the profile. Honor the goals discussed by the professors, but not

necessarily the methodologies. College professors can be expected to know a great deal about their subject matter, but they don't necessarily know anymore about homeschooling than your pet iguana does. So if a professor says, for example, that in order to take a college level course in history you need to have already taken at least two high-school level history courses, translate that to the *equivalent* of taking two history courses—which might mean studying history books on your own, or writing a few thoughtful essays and a research paper, or participating intensely in an e-mail discussion list, or watching five movies about the civil war and analyzing their different biases. Approach any focused history activity with complete attention and patience, and you'll be better prepared than your peers who have merely passively taken "at least two high-school level history courses." Keep this "equivalent" principle in mind when you talk or correspond with any professors or other academes.

- The opinions of one or two professors, while certainly valuable, do not necessarily represent the opinions of most professors in that subject.

Some unschooled ways to learn anything

Throughout the upcoming chapters, you'll find heaps of specific suggestions for ways to learn without school. Chapter 18 lists resources you can find in your community. Here, I'll mention a few activities and strategies that can enhance your learning in any subject but don't fit in the "community" category.

Create a small museum that relates to your interest—natural history, local art, archaeology, skateboarding. A helpful book is *Exhibits for the Small Museum: A Handbook*, by Arminta Neal. In college I lived in a natural history interest house. We kept a little museum in a back room full of a charming disarray of rocks, shells, fossils, and dilapidated iridescent taxidermed birds. In other words, you don't have to be rich or famous or hired by the government to start your own museum.

Write papers. The "What I Did on my Summer Vacation" essay is usually rot, especially since when your teacher reads it she doesn't have time to care what it says. Writing a mandatory essay comparing and contrasting the French Revolution and the American Revolution is also usually just busywork. But when you get interested all by yourself in the similarities and differences between the two revolutions, writing a paper can be one of the best ways to develop and clarify your knowledge and opinions. Writing can be a sharp tool that helps you reflect and draw conclusions on any experience or topic. You can write much more precisely than you can talk, because you have time to organize and think through complicated arguments and ideas. For inspiration, find academic journals in fields you like.

If "papers" and essays are too formal or strenuous, write your thoughts about what you learn in an informal journal. Or make a zine.

Read academic journals, but only if you're ready to be patient. These journals (magazines) are written by and for specialists—they do not attempt to entertain the general public or to explain anything in easy language. If you're interested nevertheless, look in a college library, where you'll find magazines like *The Journal of Psychohistory; The Ukrainian Quarterly; Sport and Exercise Psychology; Energy Economics; Work, Employment, and Society; Asian Music; Research in African Literatures;* and *The Journal of Medicine and Philosophy.*

Write letters to people and organizations, asking thoughtful questions big or small. Especially write letters to people you admire. Be polite, but not self-deprecating. Enclose a SASE—self addressed stamped envelope. (That means with *your* address on it.) If they respond and invite you to write again, go ahead. If you write to people who aren't terribly famous your chances of a thoughtful response are better—not because famous people are heartless, but because they are already swamped with mail. Unschooler Chelsea Chapman writes in *GWS* #69:

> I write to a former U.S. Olympic Equestrian Team trainer who writes to help me with training and riding our horses. I started writing to her last fall when we were having trouble with the training of our Norwegian Fjord colt. I got her address out of a newsletter put out by the Norwegian Fjord Horse Registry and sent her a letter asking how she dealt with *her* Fjord horses. She mostly writes and tells me stuff about her horses and training methods and tack.

If you have a computer, find software to help you learn. It need not be expensive; you can download all kinds of free and inexpensive stuff off the Internet, or buy commercial programs together with friends or other homeschooling families. Ask your computer-geek friends for advice.

Through the Internet, you can research an astounding variety of topics, find out the latest sports scores, participate in discussions on the Middle East or read tips on finding nude beaches. The Internet will undoubtedly continue to change, expand, and multiply, so ask those computer-geek friends or a computer shop or Internet service provider for suggestions.

Don't forget how to communicate without a computer. Form a study group to investigate a particular subject. Host or join a salon—a regular discussion session with friends or acquaintances, somewhere comfortable with good tea and scones. The *Utne Reader* proclaims:

> Salons may be the antidote to the atomized and over-mediated lifestyle that prevails in pre-millennial America. We need to get together and talk with each other about the things we care about and believe in. It's fun. It's hip. And it can change the world.[1]

If you want to develop serious expertise in any academic area, find a copy of Ronald Gross's excellent book, *The Independent Scholar's Handbook.*

Look for outstanding people and organizations that aren't famous or popular. Instead of asking Alice Walker for criticism on your writing, send a copy of your best short story to a young novelist who has just published her first book—which you think is great, but which hasn't (yet) won any awards. Instead of competing for an internship at Spike Lee's company, check out the work of local filmmakers.

Keep your antennae unfurled.

Most young children have a pretty good sense of what they like—but only in a *general* sense. They can't know about all the *specific* things they might like because they don't know about everything out there that coincides with their tastes. Long before I was six I loved ballet lessons and dressing up like a Gypsy and swirling around at home. I grew up taking ballet and occasional jazz and tap lessons, and I enjoyed them. But it wasn't until college that I discovered international folk dancing, which hit much closer to home—and it wasn't until after college that I found belly

---

[1] You can read the whole excellent series of articles on salons in the March/April 1991 issue of *Utne Reader.*

dancing, which hit *all* the way home to my Gypsy heart.

The moral of the story, of course, is *keep looking*. Hela, a teacher and one of my heroines, says "Take a bite of everything so you don't miss something you could have loved." Ava, also a teacher and another of my heroines, makes a point of trying something new every year. Last year, when she was nearly sixty, she took up sea kayaking.

Be all that you can be.

Your brain doesn't exist all by itself. In school your body got used to sitting still and suffering in the name of education, but you'll live a lot longer, smarter, and happier if you deprogram that habit right this minute. Make sure your muscles and your skeleton feel good while you flex your intellect. Wear clothes that make you comfortable and happy; eat food that gives you bliss and energy; stretch a lot and take breaks to sprint around the block or dance to a Bob Marley tune; wear perfume just for yourself. And nurture your spirit too. I try to wake up early every day and walk down to the river while I reflect on life and make wishes for the day ahead. Find your own way of centering, preferably in the morning or before you begin any academic work—read your Bible or your Ram Dass, meditate, tiptoe through the tulips, weed the watermelons...

A little Sermon

Probably it's sad if you quit school and don't read any challenging books, but it's not the end of the world and certainly not enough reason to despise yourself. How many adults you know find two hours each week, let alone each night, to edify their souls through "education?" OK, some of them went to college and supposedly learned everything they ever needed to know there, but how much of that do they actually remember?

I hereby proclaim that you are nearly guaranteed to improve your intellect by quitting school—even if you don't make the slightest effort. With a healthy, relaxed (unschooled) brain, you will pick up useful and captivating knowledge about the universe simply by keeping your eyes open, watching some good movies, reading magazines in the dentist's office, and asking people to explain things they say that you don't understand. Most adults have forgotten what they learned in school, don't attempt to organize their education any more than this, and get along all right in the world. You don't have to be "educated" just to keep your heart beating and your car running.

Each person has her own clock. Though I got mostly A's in high school, I learned little. I forgot things soon after tests because most of the curriculum meant nothing to me. So much for informed citizenship. However, as my interests have broadened in the few years since I've been out of college, I've effortlessly amassed quantities of useful knowledge in widely varied subjects. In other words, I suffered from a poor education when I was a teenager, but this poor education did not prevent me from opening my eyes and getting on with things a few years later. If you don't read now, you can read when your hormones wane. ❂

18

beyond "field trips": using cultural resources

No student knows his subject; the most he knows is where and how to find out the things he does not know.
—Woodrow Wilson

IN ORDER TO go about acquiring this tailor-made intellectual extravaganza thing that you will call an "education" when talking to the school superintendent, you'll want to draw from a variety of cultural resources, including libraries, museums, and other palaces of wisdom. If you live in a big city your largest trouble will be choosing the prettiest palaces from a kingdom full of them. If you live in a rural area or smaller town, your choices may seem limited—you have more natural and rural resources instead. But no matter where you live, information abounds. Once you know some ropes, you can find whatever you need.

The Public Library
is the most valuable resource for most people's educations. When this planet gets itself together, it will have much less school and much more library. In a library, you can learn whatever you want, but no one will try to make you learn anything. You can find treasure in even a small library; with either a librarian's guidance or a small dose of courage, desire, and knowledge, you can find *real* words: novels or poems that awaken your spirit, non-fiction that explains how to do anything—blow up a dam or build solar panels or make cream puffs or get a children's book published or choose a tennis racket or sew a seam or write a bill and find someone to help turn it into a law.

There are two ways to use the library: with an agenda and without an agenda. *I cannot overly stress the importance of having no agenda*, at least occasionally. School makes you think of the library as a place to go when you want specific information about a specific subject. That's one thing the library is for, of course.

But the library is also a smorgasbord of surprises. Sometimes, go to the library and walk into the shelves and see what's there. Forget the catalog, and don't try to think what subjects you might be interested in. You don't have to read any books you find, or even check them out, but pick them up and read their back covers and flip through a few. Also, if your library has an oversize section (for large, tall books) poke around in them—that's where you find lavish art books, photographs of Balinese dancers, and other surprises.

Using the library *with* an agenda takes more skill. Unfortunately, if you're like most teenagers and many adults I've worked with, you don't know how to use the library, even if you think you do. You'll spend a lot of time there, so check out the territory thoroughly:

Sign up for a tour. If you don't see one advertised, ask. That way you'll find out about all the things you'd otherwise never realize your library has. Ask whether your library has an introductory handout or a map. In school you are used to being kept in the dark as to the way things work. There is no particular reason for schoolpeople to want you to know how school works. Sometimes information is deliberately withheld from you—for instance, teachers have "teacher's editions" of textbooks, with all the answers and with background information to make them sound more intelligent than you.

The library is the opposite; it is all about access to information. Librarians *want* you to know how to use the library. It makes their jobs easier and more rewarding.

Become intimate with the library catalog. Most libraries now use a computerized system (rather than the old-style card catalogs), and some are better than others. Generally, you can look up books by subject, title, or author. When you're searching by subject, get good at brainstorming for related terms—especially narrower or broader terms. For instance, if you type in "snakes" and don't want to plow through all 943 listings, try "snakes mythology" or "snakes natural history" or "snakes pets" or "snakes North America." Conversely, if you type in "polka" and nothing comes up, try "folk dancing." Also, try different forms of the same word. If "runners" yields nothing, try "running." If nothing works, ask the librarian.

Get familiar with the cataloging system. (Smaller libraries—which means most public libraries—use the Dewey decimal system; larger libraries—most college and university libraries—use the Library of Congress system.) This way, when you want information on a general topic, you can ignore the catalog and march straight to the right shelf. When I want to look over a library's supply of books on dance, embroidery, folk songs, folktales, international costume, Native American history, or gardening, I simply smile sweetly at all the people hunched over their computers and head right for the proper shelf. Since these are some of my main interests, I know where to find them, just as you know your best friends' phone numbers by heart, and can find their houses without maps.

Many libraries have handy little cards with the Dewey decimal system all broken down. Another way to do it is to use the catalog to look up one book on the subject that interests you, and then go look at all the books shelved in that area.

Peruse the periodicals (magazines) frequently. Periodicals are more useful than books in many situations, especially when you're looking into a subject that changes or develops rapidly, like political issues or fabric dyeing techniques. Learn to use the *Magazine Index* (on microfiche), as well as *The Reader's Guide to Periodical Literature*. (In many libraries, *The Reader's Guide* is now computerized.)

Does your library have a local history section? If so, it may include books by and about interesting people in your community, law records, old yearbooks—your parents'?, photographs, newspaper clippings, and tape recorded interviews. When my brothers and I were dirty barefoot kids visiting my grandmother we used to love to make our way into the elegant local history wing of the public library to look at photos of our ancestors and a blueprint of my grandmother's house before she tore it up to make more room for her animals.

Check out the reference section. Don't lose by assuming it's just shelves of encyclopedias. A reference section is an opulent microcosm of bookish delights. The only way to know what it has is to slowly inspect it. While hunting down books like *The Guide to Alternative Colleges and Universities* and *The New Improved Good Book of Hot Springs,* I've chanced upon *The Encyclopedia of Unbelief, The Art of Maurice Sendak, The World Guide to Scientific Associations and Learned Societies,* and *A Dictionary of Chivalry.* If you find a reference book you love, check to see if there's another copy on the regular shelves that can be checked out.

Don't be embarrassed to use the children's and young adult sections. Smart adults use them all the time. Not only do they yield some of the most charming stories of all time, but they also provide a splendid introduction to any subject. When you have gaps in your knowledge, like you've heard of Joan of Arc but don't know why people make such a fuss over her, chances are you don't need to read *Joan of Arc: The Image of Female Heroism.* Instead, find a children's biography and get an understanding of the big picture. When the big picture tickles your curiosity, *then* pick up something dense and intense—you'll be ready for it. (You can also read encyclopedia articles for introductions to anything, of course. But children's books are brighter and often about the same length.)

Realize that there are books about everything, not just "bookish" things. (Actually, I don't know what "bookish" means. Good poetry, for example, isn't bookish— it's life-ish.) There are books about car repair, winning teenage pageants, and saving the world. There are books about everything you've thought of plus everything you haven't thought of: books of Maori folktales and Zulu chants, Scottish folk songs and Southeast Asian recipes. Books by and about people who talk with gorillas and dolphins, books full of joyous reports by "survivors" of "death." Whatever it is, if people have put a name to it, then someone has written a book about it, and your library can get it for you.

Even if the book you want doesn't appear in the Catalog, your library can probably get it for you through Interlibrary Loan. Ask at the reference desk. You'll have to fill out a form and probably pay a small bit of money.

Don't overlook the library's other treasures—CD's, video movies, computers, pamphlet files, career files, phone books of New York City and other exotic ports, newspapers, and bulletin boards. Be sure to know where the new books sleep, and glance over them from time to time.

To become an advanced library user, use *Find it Fast,* by Robert Berkman.

College and University Libraries

If you live near a college or university, don't be afraid to use its library. Remember, you *live* there. If it's a state university, your parents' taxes pay for it. College students are just visiting for four years or so—it's not their territory any more than yours. These libraries offer far more in the way of scholarly journals (in case you have the patience necessary to bushwhack through mortifying terminology), academic studies of things, art books, and literary classics. Most have separate libraries for math and science; some have separate law, architecture, art, map, education, or music libraries. Most also have special collections—books from a particular country, or on a particular subject.

These libraries tend to skimp on how-to books, children's books, *Teen*

Magazine, mysteries, Harlequin romances, Gothic novels, and science fiction. They probably won't have a copy of *The Lorax*. Instead, they might have something with a convoluted title like *Speaking for the Trees: The Lorax and Environmental Debate in Oregon Schools*.

In an academic library, you can also use the CD-ROM databases. These are huge indexes which can help you access very specialized information.

Don't get freaked out if you go into a college library and find call numbers like LB.138 instead of good old Dewey decimal numbers. Most academic and other large libraries use the Library of Congress cataloging system, which is just as easy to use once you're used to it. Basically, books are shelved in alphabetical order according to their call numbers. AR books come before ZT books. LB books come before LM books.

Courses

Find out what's available by checking dance and martial arts studios, museums, art centers, community education listings, foreign language or culture centers, college and university catalogs, community colleges, and as many other sources as you can think of. Also, see Chapter 19, School as a Cultural Resource.

Local colleges and universities

A college or university provides not only courses and libraries, but also a continual array of lectures, concerts, and workshops open to the public. Find out about them by reading college newspapers or checking college bulletin boards.

Professors can also be wonderful resources. They are busy, which means they may not have time to sit around chatting. On the other hand, they might love to have your help—preparing microscope slides or running down articles in journals, and in connection with this help you may find yourself a mentor or guide. (If you learn to use academic CD-ROM data bases, you can be a valuable research assistant.)

You can also study or hang out (and meet people) at the student union, or eat in the cafeterias (for social, not gastronomic, pleasure). You can join groups such as animal rights organizations, dance troupes, and outdoor programs. No one advertises these as being open to the public, and technically sometimes they're not, but in truth the people who run these organizations often welcome participation from anyone who is interested. You just have to hang around a bit, look friendly and inquisitive, and ask if you can join in. Don't let one "no" keep you from finding a "yes."

You can often take courses at junior or community colleges through high school enrichment programs. Be sure to present yourself as a homeschooler, not a "dropout." *GWS* #49 tells about thirteen-year-old homeschooler Daniel Lewis, who took an ancient Greek course at Fort Wayne Bible College in Indiana, earning full college credit. Unfortunately, since so many homeschoolers have enrolled in community colleges, some colleges are now installing cumbersome regulations. As Julie Castleberry Nuñez writes in *Homefires* Magazine, "A good many teachers were having a hard . . . time getting comfortable with the notion that fourteen- and fifteen-year-old students, who had never been to school in the conventional sense, were appearing in their classrooms and occasionally out-performing their college classmates. The backlash was inevitable: college placement tests became mandatory, the interviewing process was made more stringent, and finding a ten-year-old on campus is pretty much a thing of the past."[1]

You may occasionally have use for a correspondence course or an online or video course—see *The Independent Study Catalog* and *The Electronic University,* both published by Peterson's Guides.

Lessons

Vanessa Keith wrote in *GWS* #32:

> *I'm fourteen. I've never been to school (except one day with my cousin). I have been trading with neighbors for two years. I trade babysitting, washing dishes, and money for lessons. I have four lessons a week: sewing, weaving, botany, and piano. It works great if you have friendly neighbors.*

You can find private lessons informally—in Vanessa's style—or formally. Music teachers put up their cards in music stores. Sewing teachers put up their cards in fabric stores. Foreign language tutors hang fliers around college campuses. Also check the classified section of the paper.

TV and Radio

Relying on either too heavily will make you into a passive un-person, but do consider checking the TV guide and phoning your public radio station to ask them to mail you a program guide. PBS and The Discovery Channel present informative programs; most don't treat subjects with the depth that good writing does, but the visual component often makes up for that. It's especially good for spying on the lives of wild animals and for learning about dance, Shakespeare, opera, and such. Rosie Moon, an American homeschooler living in Germany, writes:

> I am fourteen years old and in my third year of high school. The way I like learning is by reading magazines and watching TV because I want to be either a fashion designer or cosmetologist. I like seeing different makeup techniques and different hairstyles in the magazines and on TV. In real life people don't do their hair or makeup as well because they aren't professionals and so it's harder for me to learn by observing them. I also like seeing the way different designers style different types of clothes . . . I like watching *Style* on CNN because they talk to the designers and ask them about the collection that has just been shown and what they were thinking when they designed it. That's my favorite way of learning. It may not be like reading textbooks or watching documentaries but it has worked very well for me.

Radio programs are great for getting easy brainfood while you're making jam or sewing a tent. Public, college, or alternative stations often have interesting local shows and also provide the excellent programs of National Public Radio and Pacifica.

Also, there are a wide variety of programs called "instructional TV," designed especially for teachers to use in school. They include "courses" on foreign language, science, math, and many other academic areas. These programs are sort of like super-teachers, because the people who put them together have much more time and money at their disposal than regular teachers. Regularly using one or two might be nice; regularly using four or five would probably feel like an impersonal hi-tech version of school. To find out what's available in your area, call the local PBS

---

[1]"Homeschoolers in the Community Colleges: Keeping the Doors Open, Part II," by Julie Castleberry Nuñez, in *Homefires*, December 1996.

station and ask them to mail you an instructional TV guide.

Events and Resources for Schools

Homeschoolers are often just as welcome as school students to attend stuff like science fairs, young writers' workshops, spelling bees, and some athletic events.

For instance: the National Geography Bee (with a $25,000 scholarship for first prize) is open to people ages eight through fifteen, and homeschoolers are welcome. And the 1997 winner of the Scripps Howard National Spelling Bee was thirteen-year-old homeschooler Rebecca Sealfon of New York.

Events and Resources for Homeschoolers

Resource centers for unschoolers and homeschoolers are popping up here and there, and I predict they'll start popping up faster. They range from basic to elaborate. One example is The Resource Center for Homeschooling, run by Deb Shell, the mother of four unschooled teenagers, in Vermont. Deb's center is mostly an information clearinghouse with a helpful newsletter that lists apprenticeship opportunities, adult tutors and resource people, etc. Others are The Pathfinder Learning Center in Massachusetts, and the *drop out* resource center in California.

Sometimes unschoolers set up learning exchanges. In *GWS* #113, Luz Shosie of Connecticut writes:

> I started by sending a questionnaire to all the families listed on the mailing list of our group, Unschoolers Support. I asked them to list things they'd like to learn, teach, share, or exchange. Now we have Connections, a list of people from all over Connecticut who want to share their knowledge, ideas, goods, services, activities. A crucial difference between Connections and school is the matter of choice. In Connections, whatever is learned is at the learner's request. It's a voluntary arrangement. We list what is being offered and what is being sought, and then it's up to each person to use our mailing list to contact someone. People then make their own arrangements about time and place to meet, methods to use, compensation, etc. I don't take responsibility for anything beyond listing the names, and I made that clear both because I didn't want to be in an administrative position and because I believe people can be responsible for whatever they choose to do. That means that I can't guarantee that anyone who is offering to teach something will indeed be a good teacher. That's up to the learner to figure out.

Luz's exchange list includes people willing to share skills in everything from architecture to local access cable TV to desktop publishing to farm skills.

Homeschoolers also organize conferences, conventions, workshops, study groups, retreats, and much more.

Museums, Art Centers, and Science or Technology Centers

are more than exhibition halls, though when you're not in field-trip mode the exhibits themselves can blow your mind. These institutions also

- need volunteers
- have internship programs
- give demonstrations (like blacksmithing at a Colonial museum)
- give classes, workshops, and events which are open to the public
- have private libraries which they might let you use if they know you (maybe after you've volunteered for a while sorting dead butterflies into different trays)
- have staff who are experts in their fields.

Bulletin Boards

Every community seems to have at least one place where people put up notices and fliers telling about events, lessons, used flutes for sale. Try natural foods stores or co-ops, laundromats, cafes where college students or granola-eaters eat, and independent bookstores. Also, when you want to get your own message or advertisement out, make a flier and hang it up.

Newspapers

Once a week, most newspapers list classes, cultural opportunities (auditions for a musical, for example), and events. In addition to these listings, they sometimes include more detailed information about "educational" opportunities. If your community has alternative newspapers or free newsletters published by various organizations, they will often list different *types* of opportunities.

Small, specialized retail stores

The people who sell outdoor equipment, weaving supplies, garden tools, South American folk art, solar panels, or ballet shoes often have considerable expertise in their fields. You can also learn a lot by walking through such shops and glancing through any magazines or books they sell. When a particular store owner helps you, return some goodwill by buying your supplies from him or her. Sometimes small shops have higher prices than huge chain stores, because they can't buy in huge bulk quantities and have to pay higher prices for their goods in the first place. Just remember that when you spend your money, you vote for the kind of world you want to live in. Would you rather live in a world full of K-Marts and Wal-Marts, or a world where Mike owns his own friendly bike store down the street?

The Internet

"I use the 'net for just about everything," writes sixteen-year-old Nick Blanchard-Wright,

> I receive around fifty e-mail messages a day, from friends, teachers, and people looking for my help. If something interests me, or I want to know more about it, I can look it up online. I followed the '96 election live on the Internet. I've become somewhat of a computer guru, making around $200 a month teaching a small class on the Internet for the local library, designing Web pages, and fixing people's computers. My typing, spelling, and writing have all improved—the Internet provides anyone the opportunity to publish their work, and since the whole world can see it, you want it to be as good as possible.
>
> I even found out about unschooling through the Internet. I was fed up with public school, and decided to research alternatives on the World Wide Web, and came across an unschooler's homepage. Like a lot of people, I had always pictured homeschool as being the same as public school, but with your parents handing out the work instead of teachers, and was amazed by how wrong I was. The page mentioned *The Teenage Liberation Handbook*, which I read, and within a month I was free!

The magic of the Net has to do with its lack of hierarchy and with empowerment. Nine or ninety, working class or upper class, Ph.D. or dropout—anyone with access to a modest computer and modem can both use the Net and express themselves on it. Anyone can use it both to learn directly from experts, and to share their own expertise.

The magic of the Net also has to do with incredible generosity. Many, many people eagerly share their knowledge, whether it has to do with the Net itself or their other interests. For instance, on the Middle Eastern dance mailing list I subscribe to, many of the top national performers and seminar teachers cheerfully and unpompously answer, often in great detail, the questions of people who just took their first dance lesson last week. Yet the welcoming atmosphere also encourages less experienced dancers to add their perspectives.

I'm no Internet maven, but my Webwise friends collaborated with me to bring you these suggestions and possibilities:

- If you're new to the Net, find out everything you need to start by contacting a local service provider (look up "Internet" in the yellow pages). Or sign on with one of the corporate giants such as America Online or Compuserve.

- Don't feel you need the latest and greatest computer gadgetry to take advantage of the Internet. An inexpensive computer will do; put your extra techno-budget toward a fast modem. A good monitor is nice for viewing graphics on the Web, but you'll do OK with an older model. I've had the same computer for seven years. It was an IBM-PC compatible 286 when I bought it; my brother helped me inexpensively upgrade it and add more memory and a fast modem, and it does a splendid job of bringing the Web-World to my screen.

- Don't give up if you don't find something the first time you look. Realize that the Net is always changing. If you try something and it doesn't work, phrase your question another way. Search for the name or subject of what you want instead of its specific (maybe outdated) address (URL).

- Collaborate on an electronic project—sound, video, text, pictures, animation. The possibilities really are endless. With enough equipment, you could
  ◆work on a piece of art with a Japanese pen-pal
  ◆write a book with a friend who's moved away
  ◆create a comic strip with your cousin in Alaska
  ◆get quick feedback on your choreography from your dance mentor
  ◆design a co-housing community with your friend from summer camp.

- Create or expand a business on the Web, anything from consulting to mail-order shopping to showcasing your artistic or musical talents.

- Learn to ask. The Net circulates an incomprehensibly huge mass of data, so it requires—and fosters—question-creating-talent. Clarify your curiosity, define your interests, pinpoint exactly what you want to know.

- Exercise good judgment. The Net is not censored or screened—and I hope it stays that way—so the information you unearth is not necessarily stamped with approval by Experts or Boards or Academies or Presidents. Develop your own crap-detector so you don't waste brainspace soaking up pseudo-facts. It helps to find one Web site you trust and then jump off to other sites it recommends.

- Check out the Web's hotlists, like those of the Franklin Institute. These are organized lists of links to good resources in specific fields—like art, Africa, space science, literature, American history, and math. They'll help you avoid wading through thousands of not-so-hot presentations. "To make the list," says Franklin Institute, "a resource needs to stimulate creative thinking and learning."

- Create your own Web page, full of Great Teachings on that which you know best, or full of dark humor or psychedelic fractal art, or otherwise find a way to express yourself on the Net. Personal home pages are one of my favorite proofs that some people are really alive, that they don't wait for grades and gold stars and sticks and carrots to motivate them into action. If you're proud of your page, tell Jon Shemitz and Reanna Alder about it. Jon's extensive labor-of-love homeschooling page has a list of links to homeschoolers' personal pages, and Reanna's page has a directory of unschoolers ages thirteen to nineteen.

- *Play.* By clicking on links, you can effortlessly glide from one topic to the next. In that respect, the Web resembles a relaxed conversation among interesting friends, or an afternoon staring at the sky, thinking in long interconnected thoughts. Furthermore, on the Web you can also, miraculously, follow your brainstorms backward, by simply retracing your steps. I love this combination of right-brain free thinking, and left-brain precision and accuracy.

- If you start to feel frustrated or overwhelmed, like there's no way you can ever keep up with the software, the hardware, the technology, the jargon...*stop!* Keep the Internet and its heady wonders in perspective. It's a great tool, but it's not your whole life. And if the Internet or other computer-related stuff disgusts you, you're not alone. Some people consciously choose not to get on the Internet or even to use computers for anything... and they have great reasons—having to do with balance, valuing face-to-face community over electronic disembodied community, and many other issues. No matter how technologically oriented this world gets, we still live *in our bodies* and need people who do things besides sit at computers—i.e. grow food (preferably without poisons, i.e. organically, which requires a lot of human attention), make disturbingly beautiful art, deliver babies by hand, rescue ducks from oil spills, and build houses.

- See Bill Henderson's funny, wise book, *The Minutes of the Lead Pencil Club.* (The Club is an informal, international organization dedicated to raising awareness of how computers and other electronic inventions harm our lives. "Each time you give a machine a job to do you can do yourself," writes Henderson, "You give away a part of yourself to the machine . . . If you drive instead of walk, if you use a calculator instead of your mind, you have disabled a portion of yourself. On the other hand, every time you remove a technology from your life, you discover a gift.")

- Watch the clock. Don't ignore your body, or the passage of time, or the part of your being that does not relate to the Net. Sometimes we sit too long at our monitors, our cells bombarded by enemy particles. Our eyes strain and grow myopic, our wrists cramp and develop carpal tunnel syndrome. The sun goes out in a green and pink bath without our attention; crocus season comes and we forget to watch; our buddies go dumpster diving without us; the fetus down the street turns into a soccer player while we crawl from one site to the next. Our bodies wilt while our screens display new sites, each fresher than the last.

Unlike TV, the Web really is intellectually (and even socially and emotionally and artistically) engaging and rewarding. But like TV, it weaves a timewarp of its own and if you don't watch out, it will suck up days and weeks and the seasons of your life. The planet won't cease to spin, and your body won't cease to wrinkle, while you sit in the apparently timeless realm of the Net. So pay attention, and make sure you don't let the Web Spider cast a spell on you in which one day you decide that's enough browsing, so you reach over to turn off your monitor. As your eyes refocus from the screen to the shifting pattern of afternoon sunlight coming through the leaves, you realize that your room is full of decades' worth of dirty dishes and your gray hair is tickling your thighs.

Personally, I like to set a timer, and every time it goes off I walk outside, feel my breath, check for a newly opened rose, turn my eyelids toward sunlight or starlight, remember who I am, who We are.

- And *don't worry.* If you don't have access to the Internet now, or if you're just not interested in it, *that's OK.* The information age will not leave you behind. One of the best things about the Net is that as it develops, it gets increasingly easier to use, and shows every sign that it will continue to do so. When and if you do want to get wired, it will take you only a couple afternoons to get used to it, and a few weeks to get truly proficient at navigating. If you decide someday that you want to get involved at a more intense level—say, by designing elaborate Web sites or software—then *at that time* you can learn the skills you need, whether that is programming in a particular language (perhaps not yet invented as you read this) or some skill that we don't yet have a name for.

  The computer manufacturers, magazines, software companies, Internet providers, and the rest of the gigantic computer industry very much want you to be afraid that if you don't get on the Net yesterday, you'll be left behind. I very much want you to stand up to that fear. Ironically, you have not only your own brains to trust (and that's plenty), but also the Internet itself. Yes, every day it gets richer and more complex. But every day it also gets more intuitive, better organized and interconnected.

Your government

can do a lot for you, which makes sense considering that your parents give it a big chunk of their money. For instance, by reading *The Encyclopedia of U.S. Government Benefits*, I found out that the U.S. Travel Service can arrange through its Visitor Services Division for travelers from overseas to visit your home. The government can also help you get small business loans, obtain aerial photographs, and find access to many other surprising things.

Summer camps, overnight workshops, and retreats

At elaborate slumber parties, you can learn to do anything from physics to stained glass to massage to rockclimbing to building houses out of straw. I love learning new skills in these intense short-term communities. To find out about them, get on the mailing lists of local conference and retreat centers, or read the ads in magazines related to your interest, or participate in a related Internet news group and ask for recommendations.

And don't forget

zoos, ports, workplaces, the YMCA, the phone book, churches, city governments, factories, ethnic festivals, arboretums and gardens, hobbyists, parks and pools, clubs and organizations, and travel agencies. ☀

19

school as a cultural resource

THIS BOOK HAS said a lot of nasty things about school. Now it's going to say something nice. Schools have darkrooms, weight rooms, computers, microscopes, balance beams, libraries. They have choirs, bands, track teams, maybe even a Spanish class you like. Many enterprising homeschoolers have found ways to use the school resources they want without having to endure everything else.

This chapter tells about a few of these ways schools can cooperate with homeschoolers, and gives examples of particular homeschoolers who have taken advantage of school resources. If the schools in your area have never tried anything like this, you can pass this information along to them, and assist them in setting up a program that helps both you and them. Yes, them.

How do you think schools get the money they need to pay teachers, buy chalkboards, and shop for new math books? The state tax people give it out, based on the number of students who attend. If they have to take you off the rolls, they lose dollars—from 4,000 to 15,000 or so per year, more or less depending on where you live.

If someone works out a way to keep you on the rolls—full-time or part-time— then your school can keep some of that money. As the homeschooling movement comes of age and sweeps the U.S.—and then takes over the whole world— arrangements like this can help schools save face and keep giving salaries to people—a far better use for tax dollars than nukie bombs. [1]

Some school districts already have elaborate homeschool programs which can help you by lending textbooks, allowing you to take certain classes, and/or paying a certified teacher to see you each week (to fulfill any state requirements about certified teachers). In Port Townsend, Washington, Seth Raymond participated in a program like this. To fulfill legal requirements, a group of unschoolers and a certified teacher, Marcie, spent two hours together each week, engaged in some type of class or activity. Also, Marcie was available to work with each homeschooler for a

---

[1] Many homeschoolers think it's a mistake to be connected with any state agencies or schools whatsoever, that that only empowers schools and makes it more likely that *all* homeschoolers will end up more controlled by the schools. I definitely see their point, but I'm choosing to provide information on these possibilities and leave the decision-making up to you.

few hours at the beginning of each semester to set goals and decide what to call their activities. If they wanted her advice or guidance during the semester, she gave it. At the end of each semester she looked at their completed log books and gave credits in various subjects. For the people who requested it, she gave grades based on whether they had fulfilled the goals they set for themselves.

Students' main official task was to keep track of their activities, using a daily log book. Seth's log book had places for math, reading, biking, Spanish, science, drawing, history, occupational education. Some of the entries went like this:

Occupational Ed: "Stacked firewood, cooked breakfast, mowed lawn."
Biking: "Edited music tapes for biking," "bike competition—placed 4th."
Science: "Watched and identified birds."
Reading: "Read *Of Mice and Men*."

Some families have convinced their districts to not only provide access to school buildings and textbooks, but also to give an allowance for supplies. You can likely negotiate a similar situation; after all, you have leverage. The school will make more money off of your enrollment than it will spend on you, even with a substantial allowance.

For instance, Susan Swecker of California wrote in *GWS* #76, 1990, about what happened after an administrator approached her homeschooling group. It was his idea to set up some kind of partnership. Before the group met with him, they met together and decided what conditions they would agree on. They knew they could be assertive since they were five families strong, and for each of their kids the district would gain $3,000. They presented the following list of requirements to the administrator.

1. No testing unless someone [a homeschooler] requests it
2. Use of the school library and computers at specific times
3. Use of audio-visual materials, darkroom, and supplies
4. One field trip each month
5. Access to school psychologist, speech therapist, nurse, and other specialists
6. The right to research and order our own academic and art materials
7. $400 per child per year to purchase academic and art materials
8. The right to use the building housing the gym, home economics room and restrooms for bimonthly meetings and potlucks on Saturdays, especially during the winter
9. The right to attend summer school and other school functions and workshops
10. Home visits by the homeschool coordinator as needed

The administrator wisely agreed to the whole list, and as far as I know everyone lived happily ever after. With $400, you can buy a lot of good books and a tall stack of silk shirts to paint.

Other homeschoolers decide to attend school part time, and convince local officials to cooperate. In *GWS* #33, Pennsylvanian Janet Williams describes her "seventh grade" daughter Jenni's new schedule after previous years of pure homeschooling:

Her schedule is as follows:
Monday - 1st period Computers, then home.
Tuesday - 1st Industrial Arts, 4th Recess, 5th lunch, 6th Science, 7th Phys. Ed, 8th Art.
Wednesday - 1st Speed Reading, 4th Recess, 5th lunch, 8th Chorus.
Thursday - 1st Spanish, 4th Recess, 5th Lunch, 6th Science, 7th Phys. Ed, 8th Bi-weekly

clubs.

Friday: home all day.

. . . Periods when she is not in a class, she works independently in the library or computer room.

Nick Blanchard-Wright, of Washington, writes:

> Despite its other shortcomings, I'm lucky to have a school district that is very open to letting homeschoolers attend public school classes. I'm currently taking my high school's technology class, and my little sister is in the middle school orchestra. I'm one of several homeschoolers in the technology class, which works out well for the school since we can spend more than the class's one hour period keeping the school's computers running.
> Once I was sent to the office twice in fifteen minutes—the first time was to be lectured for having too many absences that month, and the second time was to show them how to use the school's network. Later I solved the absences problem by having my mother write a permanent excuse saying that throughout the year I would be absent for various educational reasons. I then laminated it and gave a copy to the secretaries to keep on file, and now when I've been gone I just show them the note. I had my technology teacher sign a similar hall pass, so I can enter and leave campus whenever I want.
> No longer having to worry about grades, I can concentrate on actually learning something instead of just mindless busy work. The teachers and staff are friends, mentors, equals - and when I help them with the computer systems, my students—instead of just state funded babysitters. Schools aren't all bad, they are a great resource for homeschoolers as well as public schoolers. You just learn a lot more when you're there by choice.

In California, most districts have an independent study program, which can sometimes be adapted to fit homeschoolers' needs. Thirteen-year-old homeschooler Mylie Alrich told me that thanks to her participation in her district's independent study program, she belongs to a school gymnastics team and has a pass so she can go to school dances.

As time goes by, more states and districts are instituting official rules and regulations. For instance:

In 1985, the Michigan Supreme Court ruled that public schools had to "open their elective and supplemental classes to private school students [including homeschoolers] who get their basic education elsewhere." The court said, "Public schools are open to all residents of the school district...This statutory right to public education is not conditioned upon full-time attendance."[1]

In Washington, homeschoolers have the legal right to enroll part time in school, and also to participate in school activities including interscholastic sports.

Oregon, Florida, and some other states also have policies that guarantee homeschoolers' right to play on school sports teams. And many homeschoolers participate in school sports in states and districts that have no such policy. Homeschoolers continue to work hard to win the official right to participate in school sports, and their efforts are paying off. One heroine is Nicky Hardenbergh, who has worked with other Massachusetts homeschoolers. They have put together a thorough, useful packet for homeschoolers in other states, and if you contact Nicky she will also attempt to put you in touch with other people in your state who are working on those issues.[2] Ask local homeschoolers what's been tried and what has worked. If

---

[1] From *GWS* #44.

[2] Contact information in Appendix E.

their answers are disappointing, don't give up.

Homeschoolers in Maine got a bill passed that gives them access to schools in all districts. Each district, however, can form its own policy, so some will be more open (sports, classes, extra-curricular stuff) than others (merely library and textbook use). [1]

Even if you are not officially enrolled in school, schoolpeople will likely give you what they can, especially if you're sweet. Fourteen-year-old Pat Meehan of Florida wrote, "The schools here are very helpful. We get a lot of our videotapes from the county teachers' professional resource center through the school I would attend if I were going to school. Everything is very cordial. Some of the teachers are watching how we do because they are thinking of home schooling their own children."

Leonie Edwards, sixteen, of Minnesota, quit school in seventh grade. She has access to the school library, and every fall she helps with the high school musical.

Many other unschoolers report on good relationships with schools—they attend on special days or to give presentations. For instance, *GWS* #70 mentions a homeschooling puppet club in Vermont that performs for schools.

Another way to get access to the school things you want is to skip the administrators as well as the legalities and quietly go straight to the people who have what you need. The choir director just may be overjoyed to let you use a music practice room during lunch. Can't hurt to ask. Eva Owens of Massachusetts left school after ninth grade, and in *GWS* #105, she said:

> I wanted to continue taking Latin with my wonderful high school Latin teacher. I also wanted to be free to take an elective or two at the school if I ended up choosing to. The school administrators seemed to think I was crazy for believing I could get a better education outside of their prestigious school than in it. Even worse, I had the further audacity to assume that the school people would agree to be an academic side dish to my educational feast. As it has happened, I have been taking Latin all year without the school's official permission, although they do know I'm doing it. It wasn't until March that we made any sort of headway in communicating with the administrators. I've learned that clear, straightforward persistence is the best way to go. I've also found that talking to a lot of the teachers around the school instead of to the administrators is the best way of drawing support . . . I now take both the Latin class and a public speaking class at the high school. ☺

---

[1] From *GWS* #115.

the Glorious Generalist

Culture is activity of thought and receptiveness to beauty and human feeling. Scraps of information have nothing to do with it. A merely well-informed man is the most useless bore on God's earth.

—Alfred North Whitehead

*W*HAT, *M*ISS *L*LEWELLYN, *is a glorious generalist?*

A generalist, in general, is someone who knows about a lot of things. But a glorious generalist must be distinguished from the heap of ordinary generalists.

The cheap flash generalist merely knows a lot of trivia. If he is especially flashy he can also recite amusing quotes by famous people. Nothing wrong with that, but the glorious generalist goes way beyond.

The almost-but-no-cigar generalist knows about a lot of things. He may even know a lot about a lot of things. But it stops there.

If the glorious generalist has a lucky tricky verbal mind, he can also spew trivia and quotes. I often wish I could do that. Pretty likely, the glorious generalist knows a lot about a lot of things, but not until he has been in business for a while.

The glorious generalist sees the world whole.

Because he sees the world whole, the glorious generalist can communicate thoroughly with people of every profession, religion, or background. He can pick up any book or magazine and find in it a connection to his own interests. If he is an all-the-way-there glorious generalist, maybe he can do mystical/scientific things like read the meaning of the galaxies in a fistful of sand.

How does the glorious generalist operate?

He starts with faith that the universe has meaning. This faith comes in two varieties—he can trust that a God, or an otherwise entitled Ultimate Reality, exists and created all this or guided it into place. Or, he can trust himself and other humans enough to believe that he can *make sense* of it all, that even if there is no *actual* collaboration between the pattern of a spider's web and the lyrics to that Led Zeppelin song, he can still weave it together in his mind so that it has harmony and order, like a stained glass window in a French cathedral.

Also, he trusts language. He believes that with language he can bridge almost any chasm between himself and another person.

Once you trust enough, you are a glorious generalist. You are not afraid or bored to be trapped in a stalled elevator with a nuclear physicist, an Eskimo shaman, an opera singer, or a milk delivery person.

What if the universe looks like a complete junkyard, and you *don't* trust it to make sense? Well, chaos shapes reality too; nothing *real* is as uniform or predictable as the rows of offices in a tall building. As long as your mind is honest, your understanding of the universe will be in flux: an ocean, not a sidewalk. But you can't even ponder or acknowledge change or chaos until you have some order in your mind, a canvas for that wildness to burn its image into.

Anyway, if your universe is a junkyard, don't be afraid. A lot of that is just school-scars, so much flying at you so fast that any basic understanding of anything seems completely elusive. Once you recognize your confusion, you can start to relax. It doesn't take a special IQ level to be a glorious generalist; *everyone* could be one. In fact, I think we all come into the world as glorious generalists. Most four-year-olds aren't fundamentally bewildered, and it's not for lack of questions and wonder.

Confused or not, go ahead and initiate yourself into the society of glorious generality. The fear will wear away; the cosmos will take shape in your mind.

How to become a glorious generalist

Become a student and observer of a glorious generalist. First, you'll have to find one. (A lot of full-time mothers, by the way, are closet GG's, though they probably haven't noticed.) You can check your candidate out to see if she meets some of the following criteria established by the nonexistent Criteria Board of the Universal Committee of Glorious Generalists. But if she fails the test, that doesn't rule her out. I hope you have some intuition, because you'll need it for this and later in life also.

1) Does the suspect take you seriously? If she knows you, does she ask you questions that go beyond mere politeness? The glorious generalist wants to learn from *you.*

2) Does she exhibit a wide range of interests? This sometimes shows up in a tattered, diverse library, or in scrapbooks or menageries or cluttered projects.

3) Are her friends a motley crew? Are they a mixture of young and old, this profession and that, three religions and five philosophies, hippies, yuppies, and rednecks? (Not that the glorious generalist herself would describe them so slickly. She tends not to slap labels on people.)

4) Does she attend to the basic structure of her life—what she eats, how she cares for her body, how she treats her plants?

5) Is she unintimidated by specialists? Does she judge people on their capabilities rather than on their degrees? Is she brave enough to decorate her own house, raise her own kids, without worrying that she's not an "expert"?

6) Have you ever heard her laugh and say, "*Every*thing is connected!"?

Once you find this person, try to hang around and notice how she thinks, talks, and finds out things. But don't worship. Glorious generalists are usually humble people who don't wish to be fussed over.

Read the biography of a Glorious Generalist. Or read a book written by one. Here are a few of my votes. Yes, there are cookbooks in the list as well as books about physics. Often, the glorious generalist has written one or more books that make an ordinary subject seem wonderful and infinite, or a complicated subject seem understandable and fascinating. The glorious generalist can zoom up and down on the scale of broad to specialized knowledge. A good way to find out about glorious generalists' books is to perk up your ears when someone says, "Well, it's a book about baking bread [or about political campaigns, or whatever] but it's really a book about life."

Christopher Alexander, *A Pattern Language* and *The Timeless Way of Building*
Gregory Bateson, *Steps Toward an Ecology of Mind*
Julia Cameron, *The Artist's Way*
Joseph Campbell with Bill Moyers, *The Power of Myth*
Fritjof Capra, *The Tao of Physics* and *The Turning Point*
Lewis Carroll, *Alice in Wonderland* and *Through the Looking Glass*
Annie Dillard, *Holy the Firm*
Richard P. Feynman, *Surely You're Joking, Mr. Feynman*
John Fire and Richard Erdoes, *Lame Deer, Seeker of Visions*
Natalie Goldberg, *Writing Down the Bones* and *Wild Mind*
Molly Katzen, *The Enchanted Broccoli Forest* and *The Moosewood Cookbook*
Barry Lopez, *Of Wolves and Men*
W.A. Mathieu, *The Listening Book*
Brad Matsen and Ray Troll, *Planet Ocean*
John Muir, *How to Keep Your Volkswagen Alive*
Theoni Pappas, *The Joy of Mathematics*
Michael Phillips, *The Seven Laws of Money*
Robert M. Pirsig, *Zen and the Art of Motorcycle Maintenance*
Tom Robbins, *Even Cowgirls Get the Blues*
Laurel Robertson et al, *The New Laurel's Kitchen*
Rudy Rucker, *Mind Tools: the five levels of mathematical reality*
William Upski Wimsatt, *Bomb the Suburbs*

Get your hands on the best resources for Glorious Generalists. Subscribe to *Whole Earth Review* magazine. Buy a copy of the latest edition of *The Whole Earth Catalog*, and get the earlier out of print editions at a used bookstore. The people who put them out are the most glorious bunch of generalists at work in the U.S., and their catalogs and magazines are the ultimate tool and text. Mostly, they review books on every imaginable subject. But you don't have to actually track down the books and other resources they recommend in order to have fun; just reading the reviews and excerpts is a vivid journey through the big universe. It is a glorious mind indeed that describes the *Tao Te Ching*—the classic book of ancient Chinese philosophy—on the same page as a book about sewage treatment. The page heading is "Whole Systems: Water," and it all fits. I used to read *The Next Whole Earth Catalog* every night before I went to bed, though it made sleep difficult. After about six months of that, I started finding and using books they suggested.

Cultivate the habit of browsing. Make it a point of view and a way of life. If you deliberately sniff out the territory, you will have constant fun knowing new things, and every once in a while you will run into something unexpected that changes your perspective.

Browse in the realm of words: Sometimes when you are in a library, just wander into the shelves and look at what's there. Look at the piles people have left sitting around on tables. Notice the variety of magazines; investigate a couple. Do the same in bookstores, preferably strange and atmospheric bookstores. Look to see what books friends have on their shelves. Ask which are their favorites. Take a mental bubble bath in the children's library. Flip through the telephone book yellow pages at home and the college catalogs at the library. Read the newspaper now and then. Know what's on TV and radio, and tune in when the moon turns blue.

Browse in the material world: walk somewhere new every few days. Go into a different store, take a different trail, look in the pet food or cookware section of the supermarket, swim in a different stretch of the river.

Ask big questions of people you meet. Find out what they do (even if they go to school—what else do they do?) and trust that they can explain their interests and work to you. See if you can grasp the essence, the ultimate point, of what they do. Some good questions to ask are:

What got you interested in what you do?

What were the first steps you took to get involved?

Why does your work matter? Where does it fit in the world?

What questions are you asking in your work? (Or, what problems are you trying to solve?) How are you trying to answer or solve them?

This last one, by the way, is my magic wand question, one I kind of learned from reading the twentieth-anniversary issue of the *Whole Earth Review.* I don't always need it, but when someone refuses to believe that I am truly interested in his master's thesis on environmental economics or in her work as an electrical engineer, it opens doors. Clement, my friend the biology research assistant, kept saying, "Well, it's complicated" when I asked him exactly what he was up to. Finally, I said, "What questions are you busy asking in that esoteric laboratory?" And he told me. He was asking what role a certain hormone played in the life of a certain caterpillar. He hoped that the answers would give a clue as to the role of other hormones in human epilepsy. Not only does conversation like this dissolve barriers between seemingly different people, but it also reveals the beauty and meaning of things we call "academics." In my rather unacademic approach to life, I learn more from conversations with people like Clement than I ever did in school, college included.

Sometimes you will run into people who really can't explain for you what they do. Put on your suspicious hat. If it can't make human sense, does it make any sense? Some people in government bureaucracies don't seem to know anymore where the ground is. That's the kind of out-of-touch mentality that's going to blow up the world, if anything is going to. The good (and strenuous) book to read on this subject is *Standing By Words,* by Wendell Berry, very glorious.

Be ye not frenzied. (Teachers in school cannot easily be glorious generalists because they are frenzied. In this sense they are deplorable role models, although their frenzies are not their faults.) The idea is not to fill your mind up like a crowded refrigerator. The idea *is* to weave a prayer rug out of everything that comes your way.

Pay attention to the details of your own life, such as what you eat, how you speak to your friends, how you walk down the street. The better you understand yourself, the better you understand everything else. You stand at the center of your prayer rug; you can't leave yourself out.

Let yourself cross boundaries. Be prepared, while you are reading Blake's poetry, to come up with a physics question you want answered. Entertain yourself with treats that stir it all up, like the artwork of M.C.Escher—as Stewart Brand describes it, "Geometry set at its own throat via the images of dreams."

I suppose while we're here in the generalist chapter we might as well talk about the trendy concept of Cultural Literacy. Sigh. The idea is that we don't get enough inside jokes. When someone mentions the Wright brothers (who did quite nicely without much school in their teenage years, thank you) or the Sistine Chapel, you won't know what they're talking about if you're not culturally literate.

I have no argument with the basic concept—even if we don't always need these terms to understand each other, we do need them to understand our past and a lot of the best books. But please don't get all bent out of shape about it. First, whenever someone says something you don't "get," you can ask them what they're talking about or write it down and look it up when you go to the library. Second, if you keep your eyes open in a Glorious way, you'll be plenty culturally literate. I don't recommend hyperventilating your way through a book on cultural literacy as if you were studying for the Ultimate Exam called Living in Western Culture. Living in Western Culture is *not* an exam. It's a feast.

Ultimately, education is about our connection to the universe, our place in it. The bigger that connection, the bigger our lives and dreams. Through what we undertake to know and understand, we can be as immense as the milky way— glorious indeed. ☀

21

unschooling science and technology

You care for nothing but shooting, dogs, and rat-catching. You will be a disgrace to yourself and all your family. —Charles Darwin's father

SCIENCE IS ONE of the best reasons to quit school.

It took me a while to understand this. Several college admissions directors told me that their unschooled applicants had weak science backgrounds. Among the teenagers who wrote me about their unschooled lives, a few said they felt like they skimped on science. Coming from an unscientific background myself, I felt as if I were encroaching on forbidden territory. In a bit of panic, I thought about changing my title to *The Artistic or Literary Teenagers' Liberation Handbook.* Instead, I researched extra hard and called extra loudly on the expertise of my scientific friends—and I ended up believing that a mass unschooling movement could inject new life, responsibility, and genius into the world of science.

No doubt, science presents special challenges to the unschooler. Lab equipment is expensive. Lab equipment is *intimidating.* This chapter tells you how to get around these difficulties, as well as how to make scientific use of the big wide world that schoolteenagers miss out on.

Why do unschooling and science go together? How should you approach science without school?

You have the whole universe, not just a grey room, for your laboratory. Use it. "Most people, most of the time, learn most of what they know about science and technology outside of school," says the National Science Foundation.[1]

School treats science all wrong. It usually allows no play and is afraid to ask you to do serious work. But real science is made out of play and very hard work, mixed together. It's a shame that we think of sciences as the most austere and forbidding of the academic disciplines, because the only way you can start right is to mess around. Tease your mind with inspiring books and trips to beaches and roadcuts. Make questions: why are clouds shaped like billows of ice cream? Why are all the cottonwoods in the park dying? Go on a mental picnic at the Exploratorium in

---

[1] quoted by Roger L. Nichols, President and Director of the Boston Museum of Science, in a letter to the editor of *The Boston Globe*, 10/12/87.

San Francisco or another innovative science museum.

My brother noticed people in his freshman class at Caltech whose actual knowledge base was scanty—perhaps they hadn't yet studied calculus or much physics—but something had inspired them strongly enough that they craved the scientific tools with which to continue exploring their universe. This "something" had varied—for one it was staring at the night galaxies, for another reading a rather poetic book called *The New Physics*. What they ended up holding in common was *questions* and *desire*, two of the best beginnings for anything. Einstein's play went like this:

> Someone . . . asked Einstein how he had got started on the train of thought that led to the theory of relativity. He said that it had begun with two questions that he had asked himself, and couldn't stop wondering about. One was, "What does it really mean to say that two things happen at the same time?" The other was, "If I were riding through space on the front of a beam of light, what would I see, how would things look?"[1]

Science also demands intense, serious work. Scientists have immense responsibility to handle information carefully and honestly, in order to tell the truth about their subjects. Without a school schedule, you can take all the time you need for careful scientific investigations. You can wait for the right weather; you can observe the growth of molds for years instead of one lonely Friday in the lab.

Outside of school you have the chance to get involved with real scientists and real scientific work. My friend Heather, currently a Watson scholarship finalist and senior biology major at Reed college, suggests helping scientists with their research. Scientists always have more ideas than they have time to follow through on, she says. A biologist, for example, might need someone to catch aquatic invertebrates, record information from climate gauges, check traps, or collect water samples.

Phone up graduate students—who cannot afford to pay research assistants—and ask if you can help. Or put up neon pink notes in university science buildings. If you live near a college without any graduate programs, approach seniors, who often have a labor-intensive project to complete, or professors.

If you try this, expect to be inspected. Although you are offering to provide free labor, you could completely ruin someone's research by being irresponsible with data. Heather says it's a good idea to do an inventory of your past before you contact anyone. List all the experience you have which shows that you can be precise and systematic. This could be descriptions of scientific work you've done on your own or in school. It could include recommendations from previous teachers. Work as a surveyor's assistant is the ideal background; certain kinds of cooking—candy making, for example—require precision too. So do woodworking and drafting. If you have little experience with anything of this nature, be ready to explain convincingly that you *know* you'll work carefully. If your scientist feels you aren't yet qualified, ask what you can do to become that way.

Teri Jill Mullen writes in *GWS* #78:

> I am acquainted with a homeschooler who is interested in chemistry, and I have a good friend who is a chemist. I asked my friend if she would allow an eleven-year-old boy to just hang around while she worked. She asked her boss, who was once a college professor. He was *very interested* and now this eleven-year-old homeschooler has access not only to

---

[1] *John Holt, "Einstein's Questions," GWS #9.*

a chemistry lab, but to a very educated, friendly chemist. Certainly a boy his age in school would not find time for just hanging around and watching someone work.

Along the same line is an article in *GWS* #29 which quotes liberally from a paper entitled "How Children Can Become Experts," by Dr. David Deutsch, a theoretical physicist and founder and director of a small computer company. Deutsch writes about a hypothetical twelve-year-old who has a keen interest in physics. School won't help much, he says. Books will, but only for so long:

> The point here is not that he will run out of facts to learn: he will not. The point is that factual knowledge from such sources actually constitutes only part of what a physicist needs to know. The more important part is a complex set of attitudes and ideas concerning, for example, the recognition of what constitutes a physics problem, how one goes about solving it, and what might be acceptable as a solution. One can learn such things in only one way: by participating in the physics culture. That is how graduate students learn physics when they are finally permitted to participate in real research. And this—research alongside real physicists—is what I think our hypothetical child should be doing.

Deutsch goes on to say that school is not the way to become a scientist, any more than it is the way to become a carpenter. The adult physicist would first benefit from having the apprentice do small problems—"sub-tasks" that did not require overall physics knowledge, but which nevertheless contributed to his work. The young apprentice would benefit from watching the physicist think, and from being able to ask questions. Eventually, however, the relationship would intensify:

> [The apprentice] would begin to "think like a physicist" as he unconsciously assimilated inexplicit knowledge simply by observing a physicist solving problems. He would begin to enjoy more and more the inner rewards of doing physics. At the same time he would become steadily more useful to me in an ever wider range of sub-tasks. Factual knowledge would come to him without specific effort, as a side-effect of pursuing his interests. Later he would begin to grasp the details of specific problems which I was working on, and he would begin to find research topics of his own. I would find myself learning increasingly from him, both directly and because one always learns by explaining things to a willing listener. And because we would naturally have many problems and interests in common, he would be a particularly helpful colleague for me. Finally the apprentice would be such no longer, having overtaken his teacher-colleague in knowledge and skill. This is perhaps the greatest long term benefit which would accrue to both parties.
>
> I must stress that I am not thinking of "child prodigies" in the above example. I am convinced that arrangements such as the one I describe can and ought to be the normal way of entering any profession.

If you are artistic, or if the grey smelliness of most school science classrooms dismembers your enthusiasm, you can do lush colorful sketching unschooled science, particularly as a naturalist or geologist.

the anti-propaganda note

Don't be brainwashed by government education people when they emphasize science and math over other subjects. This way of thinking is based on a dangerous, narrow sense of economic competition; it is much more likely to lead to an unbalanced, neurotic society than to any life-sustaining technological breakthroughs. I decided to bother to mention this because the U.S. Government spends lots of money to push schoolstudents to believe that science and math are gods that can fix anything. They're not. Furthermore, even if you *are* a big science or math fan, school is not where it's at.

What is science, anyway?

Science is not, of course, planets and zygotes, but rather a careful, imaginative yet methodical process of studying them, which involves seeking facts that can be proved again and again, in the same way. At normal atmospheric pressure, water always freezes at 0° Celsius. That's Science. It's predictable. It's been tested, but if you don't believe it you can test it for yourself. If your water freezes at 15° C, phone the newspaper.

An important early task, in doing any kind of science, is knowing what this scientific method business entails. Unfortunately, school courses don't necessarily impart this understanding to you. They didn't to me. However, you can read about it in almost any science textbook, in the first chapter or thereabouts. Or in any encyclopedia article on "science" or "scientific method."

While you're figuring out method, also think about the limits of science. Some things can't be understood with science, because they will never react the same twice. People are a good example. That boy you like, for instance. If you send him red roses tomorrow, he might reward you with a grin that puts you on a cloud. If you had sent him red roses last week, he might have fed them to his pet caterpillars.

Science has plenty of previously discovered "facts" for us to learn, but the heart of science is the process of *finding* facts through experimentation. Please recognize, therefore, the difference between reading the results of others' experimentation and conducting your own experiments. Both are important, and some books are wonderfully inspiring, but to actually practice science, you must use the scientific method for yourself.

What sciences, and when?

One little side benefit of unschooling is that when you hear about intelligent research on education, you can put it to work for you *now*. Russian, Chinese, and Japanese students generally do much better in science than Americans, and one likely reason for this is that they study all branches of science at once. In other words, they might study biology on Mondays and Wednesdays, physics on Tuesdays, and chemistry on Thursdays and Fridays, for four or five years, instead of one year of each all separated out. Absorbing it over a longer period of time, they remember it longer.[1]

Eventually, American schools may follow their example, but first, the Experts will have to argue about it in fourteen meetings, and then the textbook companies will have to develop new curricula, Ph.D.'s. will have to test the new curricula on nine school districts and write dissertations on the results, your school district will have to "allocate funds" (fork over money) for the new textbooks, and the science teachers will all have to go to workshops that tell them how to adapt to a new schedule. That's bureaucracy. It will take a while.

In the meantime, consider approaching your own scientific work in a spaced-out way. Or not. As you like it. At any rate, biology, chemistry, and physics are standard preparation for majoring in science in college. Geology and subcategories of the others, like field zoology, are optional.

---

[1] Sharon Begley, "Not Just For Nerds," *Newsweek*, April 9, 1990, p.61.

Finding Lab Equipment

If you look hard enough, you will find the lab equipment you need. Some ways unschoolers find access to microscopes and other toys:

- by making arrangements with a teacher or school to come in and use equipment. This might work especially well if you offered to grade quizzes or wash beakers in return. Also, if you find an inspired teacher-scientist, you might end up with a mentor too.
- by becoming involved as a volunteer, apprentice, student, or indefinable presence at a museum or science center. *Hostex News* says:

  An eleven-year-old boy conducts regular research projects at the Museum of Natural History in New York. He is one of the few living "protozoologists" to observe the rare act of a paramecium forming a protective wall around itself as the surrounding water dries up. [1]

- by using lab equipment at a parent's college or place of work.
- by buying equipment. Aside from a good compound microscope, most isn't expensive, unless you want to have better facilities than schools do. If you want to buy, you can decide *what* to buy by making a list of necessary equipment for the labs in your textbooks.
- by always mentioning their needs when they meet people. Gwen Meehan, mother of unschooler Patrick, wrote in *GWS* #73, "I happened upon a marine biologist with a Ph.D. that included some education credits. He has invited Pat to come use his microscopes and ask questions any time he likes." In *GWS* #113, Diane Metzler writes:

  One of the fathers in Luz's unschooling group [Unschoolers Support] has his own lab at Yale University, and my daughter was able to work with him several times a month. They did dissections, and she was able to ask him questions when she came across something in her biology textbook that she didn't understand. His focus is studying brain cells, looking for clues to how to cure epilepsy, so they did some work together on culturing brain cells, and he showed her how to keep a lab book and take notes. We had looked at a list of labs that the ninth graders were going to do at the local high school, to see if we should try to do any of the same ones, but most of them were things like using colored paper clips to simulate DNA sequencing. I think that Danielle's experience of seeing how a real scientist worked was much more beneficial to her.

Do you really need lab equipment?

Probably, but maybe not as much as you think. Most lab experiments in high school textbooks don't demand much in the way of supplies. The most serious equipment any of them require is a compound microscope, Bunsen burner, and triple beam balance. In the dozen-or-so textbooks I investigated, however, the majority of labs required little more than beakers, test tubes, crucibles, petri dishes, medicine droppers, graduated cylinders, and for physics a lab cart, recording timer, pulley, connecting wires, and dry cell. My friend Clement-the-biology-research-assistant points out that you can make do, in many cases, with substitutions. Use a candle instead of a Bunsen burner, any sort of scale rather than the triple beam balance, random plastic containers instead of official petri dishes, etc.

---

[1] From *Hostex News* (Britain), May 1982.

Mail order science equipment

Carolina Biological Supply Company. This *fat* catalog costs a lot but is worth it if you want a huge selection of scientific supplies. In 1,200 pages, you can shop for a real human skeleton (or the bones of dozens of other animals—a gorilla skull, a rattlesnake skeleton), chemicals, plant and animal tissue cultures, living things: amoebas, paramecium, centipedes, termites, silkworm eggs, salamanders, African clawed frogs, fertile quail eggs. Carolina also sells physics, chemistry, and other science and math supplies.

Edmund Scientific Company—ask for their imagination-stimulating *Annual Catalog for Technical Hobbyists.* Edmund provides everything from microscopes (their specialty) to dry ice makers to Geiger counters to telescopes to science fair guide books to a model kit of the human tooth, along with raucous fun like "moon blob," "magnetic marble magic," plastic spiders, and such.

American Science and Surplus will not only sell you all kinds of industrial and military surplus, but make you laugh too. Solar panels, pipets, and lots of unscientific weirdness like gold metallic jackets and a scratch 'n sniff book about three-course business lunches.

The *Science/Math/Technology* catalog from *Learning Things* sells an "Ultrascope," which is a very inexpensive microscope. According to people who use it, its quality is excellent, although since it magnifies only up to 300X, it won't do for certain kinds of advanced work. Also a wide variety of supplies for biology, physics, laboratories, chemistry, technological projects, etc.

Nasco Science catalog. One of the major school suppliers, with therefore a wide variety of school-type science equipment—dissecting tools, lab books, model rockets, soil testing kits, microscopes, lab furniture, the works.

General science reference books:

Concise Science Dictionary, edited by Alan Isaacs: useful if you want to do a lot in one science without studying the others. While you are reading about marine mammals and run into chemistry words, look them up fast here. If you have textbooks for all the sciences, you shouldn't need it.

The Art of Scientific Investigation, by W.I.B. Beveridge, is old but still relevant, clear, and wise. Written in the 1950's by a Cambridge professor and researcher of infectious diseases, it thoroughly explains how to go about scientific experimentation on a serious level. Also, it acknowledges that scientists are people, not machines, and that their personalities affect their work.

Other general resources and ideas

Read popular books on science. I've recommended a few under each branch of science, but there are many others. If you've never read this sort of thing before (schools rarely assign the stuff), be prepared to get amazed and inspired. Or read any of the inexpensive, charming children's science books published by Usborne (like *Electricity and Magnetism, Ornithology,* or *Planet Earth*).

Check out some children's experiment books from the library, like *The Thomas Edison Book of Easy and Incredible Experiments,* by James G. Cook, or Usborne's *Science in the Kitchen.* There's nothing wrong with simple experiments; without lots of complicated equipment and procedure, nothing distracts you from the strange beauty of scientific reality.

(If you want to seduce your reluctant self into science, try forgetting textbooks for a while and combining the previous two ideas—popular books and kiddie experiments.)

There's no law against using high school textbooks and working through them at home, just don't let them rule your life. Try to choose one after looking through several, comparing the way they organize material and especially how clearly they describe laboratory experiments. Advantages of textbooks: they cover all the basic territory and provide a good overview and broad understanding. Usually, they are easy to understand. They have glossaries and thorough indexes; they make great reference books when you have a question. Disadvantages: using them *slavishly* is unnecessary and usually boring. They can't provide cutting-edge, completely up-to-date information. Also, textbooks are expensive, if you can't borrow them. One way to use them: skim through, read the instructions for the labs, and carefully do a few labs that interest you. Save most of your scientific energy for better stuff, like playing with wires or hatching a crop of ant eggs.

If you like textbooks, you can use college texts too. Try your local university bookstore to see what current classes are using, and then save money by finding these texts at libraries, used book sales at colleges, or by posting notices saying what you're looking for.

Write the Exploratorium Store for their booklist. It describes great books in all scientific departments, for all ages.

If you consider yourself an environmentalist, put your scientific efforts to work for a local or national conservation organization. The Audubon Society, for example, needs volunteers from time to time to do things like count salamanders and monitor acid rain. Local groups sometimes conduct restoration projects, such as rehabilitating a polluted stream. To become involved, watch the newspapers for stories of such projects, or phone up all the local conservation groups. Your library undoubtedly has a list, or you can contact the national offices of these groups and ask for addresses and phone numbers of local groups. For lots of ideas and examples of environmentally healthy work going on in science and other fields, see the *Whole Earth Ecolog,* edited by J. Baldwin, or *Helping Nature Heal,* edited by Richard Nilsen.

Form a science co-op with other unschoolers or friends of any age. Buy equipment together, share ideas, discuss projects openly. As you become better scientists, eventually you may want to apply for grants together.

Read scientific magazines. Science News is especially good: short, up-to-date (published weekly), clear. Look for other magazines at your library.

The Earthwatch Institute is a bunch of scientists who conduct research all over the world—and let people pay to help them out. I've heard from and about many homeschoolers who have fabulous experiences on Earthwatch expeditions. Spending the money to go along on one of their projects seems to me like a better educational expense than tuition at a private school or college; however, they do also give scholarships. Some of their work relates to textiles, folklore, etc., but most is scientific. Projects last from two to three weeks. Examples: studying moths in Papua New Guinea while staying in a tribal guest house, training sea lions in California, doing lab work (which will contribute to a map of the Pacific Ocean) on a research ship. You must be at least sixteen.

If you might major in a science in college

Do all the math you can. Get comfortable with the scientific method by conducting experiments and being as precise as possible. Read the work of other scientists, both popular and scholarly. The detailed advice of professors at the ends of the sections on biology, chemistry, and physics might interest you, but it essentially boils down to math, method, inspiration, and perseverance.

In the long run, college itself is not necessary for the development of a great scientist, but graduate school is definitely valuable. (No law says you must have a B.S. to go to graduate school. You *will* need plenty of knowledge and solid, inspired scientific experience.) Going to graduate school, say my scientific friends, is the first really valuable level of education, more or less equivalent to an apprenticeship. Many of them—including my Caltech graduated brother—feel that with a few good books and lab equipment, they could have taught themselves all they learned in college.

Scientists and engineers without school

William Lear, 1902-1978, founder of the Lear Jet Corporation, quit school after eighth grade to work as a mechanic. He studied radio in the navy during World War I, and went on to invent hundreds of electronic devices, mainly various navigational aids for private aircraft. Later, he developed the Lear Jet, as well as stereo tape systems for cars and the first lightweight automatic pilot for jet planes.[1]

A 1980 UPI story from Eight Dollar Mountain, Oregon, reports:

You wouldn't expect to find a space-age scientist living with computers and telescopes atop a roadless hill on the edge of the Kalmiopsis Wilderness, thirty miles southwest of Grants Pass, Oregon.

But then, Paul Lutus is a man who's spent his 33 years doing things in different ways.

. . . As a bookwormish "extremely precocious and arrogant twelve-year-old," he idolized Albert Einstein. Believing school would "lead to ruin," the seventh grader dropped out to study astronomy and electronics on his own.

When his parents didn't accept that decision, he moved out. Under the wing of a foster family, the twelve-year-old became a television repairman. At sixteen he qualified for a Federal Communications Commission radio-television license and later worked as a radio announcer in San Jose, California.

At twenty he launched a career as a "street person." He earned a panhandler's living in San Francisco by sketching portraits, singing folk songs, strumming his guitar, holding bubble-blowing classes.

He switched to a research associate position at Mt. Sinai Medical school in New York. Then he pedaled his bicycle from New York to Colorado where he took a job designing research equipment for the molecular biology department at the University of Colorado.

In 1974 Lutus began work as a NASA consultant in San Francisco. He moved to his hill at the base of Eight Dollar Mountain a year later. He designed computer programs that helped the Viking spacecraft fly to Mars, and he's the electronics engineer who invented a new kind of lighting for the space shuttle.

And the *Christian Science Monitor* describes Vincent J. Schaefer, one of the world's top atmospheric scientists, who left high school after two years. At seventeen, he and three other teenagers started their own small archaeology magazine. The New York State Department of Archaeology noticed it, and the state

---

[1] Information from *Current Biography Yearbook 1966*.

archaeologist invited Schaefer along on a month-long field trip.

In order to help his family earn money, he took an apprenticeship at General Electric. At GE, Schaefer found a mentor who encouraged him to conduct his own experiments in the laboratory. Eventually, without any college or university training, Schaefer discovered the first method of seeding clouds. In 1961, he founded the Atmospheric Sciences Research Center in New York. For the next fifteen years, he directed it as the leading professor. The newspaper article passes along Schaefer's "secret of success":

♦Work on your own.
♦Learn by doing.
♦Seek out worthwhile people and make them your friends.
♦Read books.
♦Take advantage of every good opportunity to learn something.
♦Remember that mature people enjoy helping young people who are trying to find themselves and realize their potential.

Shaefer insists that anyone with the desire could do what he has done. "You have to have a sense of wonder," he says, "and be aware of everything that goes on. You have to develop what I call 'intelligent eyes'—be intrigued with the world and everything in it."[1]

Unschoolers doing science

Britt Barker followed her interests in wildlife and classical music instead of going to school. Starting at age sixteen, she traveled with naturalists in Canada, assisting them while they wrote a book on endangered species. Later, she received a grant to participate as a team member on an Earthwatch Institute expedition to study wolves in Italy. You can read about these experiences in her booklet, *Letters Home*.

After "high school" age, Britt kept up her independent style rather than attending college. She again volunteered for Earthwatch, this time at the Bodega Bay Marine Lab in California. At nineteen, she was offered a three month position as an intern at Point Reyes Bird Observatory in California, working with a biologist and four graduate students. Next, she spent six weeks tagging elephant seals for the Farallones National Wildlife Refuge near San Francisco. By that time she had been offered a winter job in Arizona monitoring bald eagles from land and air, using radio equipment.[2]

Kathleen Hatley wrote in *GWS* #53 that her son Steve, thirteen, had

developed a strong interest in freshwater fish. Aside from actually going fishing, which is his very favorite thing to do, he managed to read every available book in the library, including five volumes of a fish encyclopedia. He worked out a deal with a friend who is a graduate student in fisheries, to supply him with worms and perch fillets for his specimens. In return, Steve received a large, fully-equipped aquarium, in which to keep his own specimens. A highlight of the year was when he got to "seine" a local river (drag the river with huge nets to bring up small fish to study) with the curator of the University Life Sciences Museum. Next week, he starts an apprenticeship with the ranger at a nearby lake (who happens to be one of the most knowledgeable naturalists around). He will be learning, among other things, how to manage a camping and fishing facility. This interest

---

[1] From Emilie Tavel Livezev, "Self-Educated Scientist's Formula for Life-long Discovery," in *The Christian Science Monitor*, 12/20/1982.

[2] Britt Barker, *Letters Home*.

in fish led into many other areas, as a real interest always does—climate, pond and stream ecology, life cycles of insects, etc.

My older children continually reinforce my belief that when a child has an interest in something, they have a real need to plunge much deeper into the subject than a normal school curriculum ever allows.

In *GWS* #102, Madalene Axford Murphy writes about her son Christian, attending Williams college:

Early on, our son Christian began to reach the limits of his father's and my knowledge in science and math, and it became obvious that these would be major pursuits in his life. At first I cheerfully expanded my own knowledge, learning along with him, but finally I had neither the time nor the interest to keep up with him. We met this situation in a number of ways.

Several years earlier, we had bought a good basic telescope on the advice of an expert at the Buhl Science Center in Pittsburgh. Later, we added a good microscope. The cheap models available in discount department stores and many catalogs are difficult or impossible to keep in focus and seem designed to frustrate kids' attempts, particularly if they want to work on their own . . . [Christian] became fascinated with astronomy, read all the books by Asimov he could get his hands on and anything else on the topic the library had to offer.

Eventually he began to feel he needed some help. We discovered an astronomy group that met one evening a month, and he began to attend meetings. He discovered that one of the founders of the group was giving a twelve-session seminar on astronomy for adults at our local nature center. On the recommendation of the naturalist there (a friend of his) he was allowed to sign up, though he was only eleven . . . I was concerned, but Christian wasn't. He plowed through the reading and was disappointed when the classes were over. Did he understand everything? No, nor did many of the adults in the class, but words like "parallax" and "gradient" had become part of his vocabulary and he knew a whole lot more about telescopes and the science of astronomy than he had before.

Another group, the Audubon Society, helped open up several aspects of biology for him . . . When they started planning their annual Christmas Bird Count, Christian and I decided to participate. Of course we could recognize chickadees, cardinals, and nuthatches, but beyond that, neither of us were sure of our identifying skills. One of the Society's more active members was a biologist who worked at a nearby fish research lab, and I asked if we could tag along when he went on the bird count . . .

The biggest success of the bird count was the friendship that developed between Christian and Bob, the biologist. Bob invited Christian on other bird counts and for the last two years has taken him along as a timekeeper/recorder on an intense five-hour government sponsored survey of birds . . .

The summer after the original bird count, Christian discovered he could volunteer at the fish research lab where Bob worked, and he ended up working two eight-hour days a week. He worked on computers in one section and on a project in another section where Bob worked that involved sampling the number of fish eggs in various streams in the Northeast. Christian learned a lot about lab techniques and about the amount of tedious work required to get accurate results for a study.

All of these biology activities took place during Christian's "high school" years, a time when homeschooling parents and sometimes children often begin to get a bit more nervous about whether they need to become more traditional, particularly if the children are planning on college. Christian did decide to use textbooks to fill in gaps in his knowledge of science, and activities like those I just described made the textbook knowledge real and useful.

Chemistry was never a major interest for Christian, but for a long time he thought he might be a physicist, fueled by his love of astronomy and his readings of biographies of fascinating people like Richard Feynman. He heavily used a textbook for physics, perhaps because I was little help beyond the beginning basics and we could find no living resource nearby . . .

Christian supplemented his textbook knowledge of physics with wide reading in periodicals like *Science News, Scientific American,* and a host of others that were much more current than any textbooks could be. And he did finally meet a nuclear physicist, the father of his older sister Emily's roommate her freshman year at St. John's College. Christian had a number of long conversations with him . . .

Physics ended up being the preferred topic of any of Christian's science fair projects. Up until two years ago, a science fair was an annual event at our house, with lots of other families participating. No prizes were given because our science fairs were not meant to be a competition but rather a sharing of interests and discoveries. They provided a reason to delve a little more deeply into a subject and offered a patient and understanding audience with whom to practice communicating ideas . . . Christian's projects ranged from rockets to lenses to pendulums.

Of course, not all of us need or want to focus on science as Christian did, but we are all better off if we pay it some attention. Christian's sister Emily, interested in a career in museum studies, wanted

to be literate enough in scientific terminology and techniques to understand newspaper articles and issues that might affect her daily life. Her own voracious reading, which included books like Lewis Thomas's *The Lives of a Cell,* accomplished that. She also dabbled in a chemistry textbook long enough to learn about chemical formulae, the table of the elements, and other basic information.[1]

Biology

If you plan to give your brain to biology, even partially, think carefully about what kind of animal experimentation is okay with you, and for what purposes. Although you'll start small, it's a good idea to keep your ethics married to what you do. A biology student I know is fed up with most biological work. Too much of it, she says, reflects no purpose beyond feeding scientific egos, at the expense of (for instance) frogs who get genetically engineered to have mashed up faces, mashed up legs, mashed up brains. Also, think about *manipulation* versus *observation.* Often, you can find scientific knowledge by carefully recording your observations, rather than actually interfering with whatever you're studying.

If you're interested in medicine, consider working with a veterinarian. There's a great deal of overlap between human medicine and animal medicine (after all, humans are animals too!), and as you can imagine, it's far easier to get permission to watch a cat being spayed than to watch a human being being spayed. Lots of unschoolers volunteer with, or apprentice to, veterinarians. In *GWS* #103, twelve-year-old Caitlin Fahey of New Mexico describes some of her volunteer work at an animal hospital:

I clean cages, feed animals, watch and help with surgery, monitor animals under anesthesia, draw up saline solution from bags of IV water for moisturing purposes, scrape tartar off teeth, take temperatures, prepare Betadine and alcohol sponges for surgical prep, clean up animals that have just gotten out of surgery and return them to their cages) . . . clip nails, brush tangles out of fur, help get the surgical instruments and drapes ready for the autoclave, and I get to look at x-rays or radiographs, usually with an explanation from

---

[1] From *GWS* #102.

someone . . .

What I love about working there is the variety. You never know what is going to come in that you haven't seen before. Usually, apart from all the regular spays and castrations, there will be a ligament repair or an amputation or some kind of bone surgery or tumor removal. Animals come in with all sorts of complaints: seeds or thorns in eyes, ears, and paws, tails that need to be amputated because they have been closed in doors, respiratory infections, bad breath and dirty teeth, hematomas (ruptured blood vessels), purebred puppies that need their tails docked or puppies that are polydactyl (having more than the normal number of toes) and need to get their extra toes cut off (or else they can't be shown when they're older) . . .

I learn about a lot of this stuff from the doctors, who lend me textbooks that they used in school and also give me magazines. I have gotten experience and knowledge, and even my cat, from the animal hospital.

Popular reading

Anything by Stephen Jay Gould or Lewis Thomas.

Ernst Haeckel, *Art Forms in Nature*. A psychedelic picture book to make you fall in love, even with tapeworms.

James D. Watson, *The Double Helix*. Tells the story of the discovery of the structure of DNA. Reading it, you watch scientific method, minds, and friendships in action. In that respect, it is like a mini-apprenticeship. "As I hope this book will show," writes Watson, himself one of the scientists, "Science seldom proceeds in the straightforward, logical manner imagined by outsiders."

Jane Goodall, *My Life With the Chimpanzees*. I mention this book because you can read it fast and it tells, briefly, how Goodall set up her famous project in Africa without benefit of college training. (Instead, she found herself a mentor.)

Mail-order

A cleverly designed, inexpensive, origami-like skeleton construction kit—sturdy cardboard, anatomically correct—is available from National Teaching Aids. Their catalog also has posters and models of dissected frogs, worms, etc.—visual aids which could partly replace actual dissection.

Beautiful anatomy charts available from the American Map Corporation and from The Anatomical Chart Company.

Unschoolers learning biology

With the help of *GWS* editor Susannah Sheffer, unschooler Emily Ostberg found an apprenticeship on a 35-acre farm, Ix Chel, in the rainforest of Belize. In *GWS* #96, she writes:

> Ix Chel is on the bank of a swollen yellow river and consists of about twelve little buildings, a trail of medicinal plants, and lots of greenery watched over by a tall radio antenna. The electricity is solar-powered, the water is from rain, food is from the garden, and the bathrooms are latrines.
>
> Here at Ix Chel there is a short trail through the rainforest full of naturally occurring medicinal trees which the tourists guide themselves through. Ix Chel also works to find new medicines by sending samples to the New York Botanical Garden for positive identification and then to the National Cancer Institute for testing. Twelve plants so far have shown promise in treating cancer and AIDS. Ix Chel makes and sells rainforest remedies. We make them right here from tinctures of plants and alcohol with very simple equipment . . . When I'm not busy I help [Jay the plant man] press plants, fill in data, do

calculations, weigh bark. I'm learning a lot about botany just by hanging around and helping out.

Emily Linn organized a group of teenagers who got together for numerous academic (and other) activities. Her mother, Diane Linn, reports in *GWS* #94:

The biology program was one of the best activities. It really worked splendidly. We started with five kids, and by the end we had twelve because the word spread. Emily had asked her father if he would be the primary leader of the group, and then I was sort of the academic coordinator. The three of us spent many hours talking about the structure of the program, who would assume what responsibilities. We continually checked with Emily and asked her how she thought things were going.

Early on, we decided to run it as a co-op. We asked each family to have at least one adult participating in some way. Several families were in charge of getting materials—we gave them catalogs, and a lot of materials just came from the hardware store or the grocery store. One mother was in charge of getting research articles from the library for the kids to look at . . .

Every other week, Tom [Emily's dad] would present the material from the textbook and answer questions about it, and maybe have some sort of lab work. On the alternate weeks, we did mostly lab work. That became more and more flexible as we went along, but we did make sure that Tom had the opportunity to sit down with the kids and talk about their readings. We had a textbook that we used to cover all the basics in an efficient way, but because textbooks are so boring and so often overloaded with superfluous details, we supplemented it with other books, many of which were more elementary than the textbook. We told the kids not to sit down and memorize terms, but just to read for understanding, and if the terms were important enough and if they used them enough, they would eventually find that they had memorized them.

By the spring, we were getting into physiology and anatomy. A friend of ours who is a biologist told us that he had to order specimens in bulk, and that we could have the ones that he didn't need, for free. This might be useful for other homeschoolers to know: biologists or biology teachers have to order this stuff in bulk, and so often they end up throwing things away, so if a homeschoolers group contacted their local high school, they might get just what they were looking for. It's also easy to order specimens through biological supply houses . . .

Two of the parents were in charge of field trips and speakers. When we studied bacteria, for example, we went to the Detroit sewage treatment plant and learned how bacteria are used as a natural purifier of sewage. We had a prominent geneticist come and speak to us, too, and give a slide show. The mother who organized this called a hospital and asked about how to arrange for a geneticist to speak. We've found that if you say, "We're a group of homeschoolers and the kids are highly motivated and very interested in this topic," it's as if "motivated" and "interested" are magic words. People couldn't do enough for us; we had so much time donated. They're so impressed by a group of teenagers who are truly interested in learning.

We didn't run the program like a traditional classroom. We had made it clear at the beginning that we were not a school and were not in charge of how much the kids learned. It was very informal, and there were no tests, except at the end we had a final exam which we held by pretending we were on a TV game show. Everyone was slamming on bells and screaming out answers, and the whole group aced the complete exam that was in the textbook.

Be a naturalist

The naturalist is the one with a butterfly net, a carefully labeled collection of abalone shells, an aquarium, a miniature museum, two pet boa constrictors, a field diary full of sketches and notes, a worn pair of hiking boots, and quartz crystals from a trip to Wyoming instead of the corner New Age Shoppe. The naturalist makes science rich, beautiful, and personal, rather than dry and remote.

Natural history (the naturalist's path) is an ideal scientific avenue for an unschooler, since you have all the time you need outside in "the field," and it can be very inexpensive as well as rigorously, respectably scientific. Naturalists are usually well-rounded scientists—geologists and climatologists as well as biologists—but they deal mostly with botany and zoology.

"What really makes a naturalist?" asks Gerald Durrell, in *The Amateur Naturalist*, ". . . A naturalist first of all has to have a very inquiring mind. He seeks to observe every little variation in nature and to try and discover its origin and function . . . A naturalist should also be an assiduous note-taker, recording every detail of his job with accuracy and neatness." Durrell, by the way, famously collects animals for zoos and conducts other naturalistic adventures. As a child, he rarely went to school.

Resources

Gerald Durrell's *Amateur Naturalist* covers botany and zoology—no rocks and such. Clear, beautifully illustrated, and comprehensive. Sections on techniques, equipment, and setting up a workroom—all you need to know to turn your love of nature into science. Also, Durrell points out cheap or free ways to get the job done—like substituting a razor blade for a scalpel.

If you want naturalistic help with rocks and minerals or climate study, Vinson Brown's *Amateur Naturalist's Handbook* is good. It's great for plants and animals, too, just not as lush as Durrell's book.

To help you draw beautiful pictures in your naturalist's diary, see *Nature Drawing: A Tool for Learning*, by Clare Walker Leslie. If you are hopeless like me, start with *Drawing on the Right Side of the Brain*, by Betty Edwards.

You will eventually want field guides, such as the Peterson series, which will help you identify birds, animal tracks, mushrooms, etc. The *Sierra Club Naturalist's Guides* don't have lots of pictures, but each one gives a clear, thorough background to the geology, botany, and zoology of a particular region like the Pacific Northwest or Southern New England.

Popular reading

Edward Abbey, *Desert Solitaire*
Annie Dillard, *A Pilgrim at Tinker Creek*
Aldo Leopold, *A Sand County Almanac*
Barry Lopez, *Arctic Dreams*
Edwin Way Teale, *The Insect World of J. Henri Fabre*

Preparation for college biology

G.J.C. Hill, professor of biology at Carleton, says that laboratory experience in chemistry, physics, and biology is expected background for potential biology majors. He is frustrated with students

> that have had lecture/seminar/discussion group experience but lack involvement with the equipment and visual observations, data analysis, and understanding of experimental design. Problem solving in the biological disciplines is a necessity; biology is an empirical science not a theoretical one.

Professor Hill would also like (but not necessarily expect) freshmen to have

> a general familiarity with the major sub-disciplines of biology: genetics, physiology, organismic, anatomy/morphology, evolution and cell/molecular in both animals and plants. I am not suggesting Advanced Placement courses, just a one-term general survey at the high school level. One of the problems we face is that many high school teachers use their biology courses for single sub-discipline presentations (primarily genetics, for example) or as a platform for socio-biology (personal hygiene, AIDS, greenhouse effect, pollution, etc.) without providing the fundamentals of biology. This may give the student problems at the college level when he/she is expected to spend a full year in introductory courses learning a massive vocabulary of basic terms and concepts. The problems are not insurmountable but they do add to the burden of initial adjustment and may foster a sense of inadequate preparation.
>
> As to the "ideal student": someone with an enthusiastic curiosity about what makes nature "work" without the preconceptions or prejudices of "that's impossible" or "I don't believe in... " or "You can't do... " This must be combined with the intelligence to know the difference between improbability and sheer fantasy. Biology is a discipline filled with many levels of discovery, all of which pertain directly or indirectly to how we live in the world and how we perceive it. Anyone who continues to experience a sense of awe about the natural world is the "ideal student" as far as I am concerned—*as long as it goes beyond the mere "gee whiz" stage.*

Chemistry

Popular reading

Chemistry seems to have fewer bards than other sciences. Maybe you will write the book that does for sulfur dioxide what *Cosmos* did for the big bang theory. In the meantime, read the excellent but partly outdated *Asimov on Chemistry*, by Isaac Asimov.

Preparation for college chemistry

Marc S. Silver, Chairman of chemistry at Amherst, advises:

> I would suggest that a freshman needs to know very little chemistry to do well in beginning chemistry at Amherst. We *like* them to know some of course—understand the implications of the Periodic Table, know the common ionic species, etc—but that is not essential for success. Those who do best have the ability to solve word problems and to do algebra. These are certainly the skills I should most emphasize. Of course, being smart helps too.

The chemistry chair at an ivy league university says:

> Some of our freshmen place out of our general chemistry on the basis of their high school experience, which I suppose is my ideal for the way freshmen should be prepared. Based on what I am told by my students and my own experience, I have concluded (unhappily)

that many high school chemistry courses are pretty thin . . .

In my experience, the troubles students have in general chemistry, if they have trouble, usually stem from mathematical problems, not from lack of prior knowledge of chemistry. Many students have difficulty converting ideas they "know" at a verbal level into algebraic expressions they can solve to get answers. This skill is essential for success in all the physical sciences.

The algebra needed for general chemistry is elementary. Students see it as high school sophomores. The crew we get undoubtedly passed the math courses in question with all A's. What many of them did not come away with, however, is facility at using the math they "know" to do useful things for them. They never really internalized it.

It follows that the preparation students need for college chemistry is any preparation that enables them to use algebra as a tool. They can get that skill in math courses, physics courses or chemistry courses, but just so long as they get it, I can teach them general chemistry successfully. It certainly makes it easier for me and for them if they had some chemistry before I see them, but it is not absolutely essential.

Physics and astronomy

When Buckminster Fuller was in the navy, he asked himself why the bubbles in a boat's wake were round. This might sound like a "dumb" question, but it led him to geodesic domes and hundreds of other discoveries.
—Paul Hawken, *The Next Economy*

A dream was the best physics lesson I've ever had. It was the first day in a physics class. The professor said, "Your first assignment is to roll a ball. No writing, no reading. Roll your ball everywhere and always watch it. Roll it in the park, roll it in the street, and roll it in the kitchen."

Good textbooks, etc.

Particularly for people with weak math backgrounds: *Conceptual Physics*, by Paul G. Hewitt. You *do* need math for advanced physics, but you can get a surprisingly substantial start without math, thanks to this profound book. At the end of each chapter, rather than ask you to work equations, it gives you exercises to test your understanding, like: "Imagine a super-fast fish that is able to swim faster than the speed of sound in water. Would such a fish produce a 'sonic boom?'"

Exploratorium Cookbooks and *Snackbooks*. These give detailed instructions for building replicas of the famous fun exhibits at the Exploratorium museum in San Francisco. Most of the "recipes" relate mainly to physics, and explain such delights as 3-D shadows, a harmonograph, a Bernoulli Blower, a person-sized kaleidoscope, and a pendulum table. Check your library or access many of the recipes on the Exploratorium's excellent "ExploraNet" Web site. The Exploratorium will mail free tables of contents if you ask. Also see their quarterly magazine, *Exploring*.

If you want a traditional textbook, try Saxon's *Physics*, by John Saxon, which (like Saxon math books) is praised for its clear presentation and its integration of review throughout the text.

Popular reading

David Macaulay, *The Way Things Work*. Explains the physics of cars, guitars, parachutes, stereos, spacecraft, etc. with fantastic drawings and a sense of humor.

Stephen Hawking, *A Brief History of Time: From the Big Bang to Black Holes*. A terrific and understandable book about the ultimate physics question: the origin of the universe and all the related orbiting big issues.

Richard P. Feynman, *'Surely You're Joking, Mr. Feynman!': Adventures of a Curious Character.* A wonderful, funny collection of autobiographical essays by a Nobel prize winning physicist, which turns up on many unschoolers' "favorite books" lists thanks to Feynman's contagious love of life and learning.

Richard P. Feynman, *Six Easy Pieces: Essentials of Physics Explained by Its Most Brilliant Teacher.* The transcripts of six brilliant and accessible lectures given only once to freshmen at Caltech. (You can also get audio recordings of the lectures.)

Preparation for college physics

Alfonso M. Albano, chairman of Physics at Bryn Mawr, describes the background needed for his introductory physics courses:

> Minimum: a working knowledge of plane geometry, algebra and trigonometry. The student must be able to follow simple geometric arguments, to solve linear and quadratic equations, as well as coupled linear equations in two variables. She must be able to graph simple functions as well as infer information from simple graphs. She needs to have some familiarity with exponentials, logarithms and trigonometric functions, and be able to perform some rudimentary manipulations with them.
>
> Calculus is neither a prerequisite nor a corequisite for the introductory course, but the basic notions of calculus are introduced and used. The textbook is calculus-based. It is not essential for the student to have had previous exposure to calculus (or to physics, for that matter).
>
> Ideal: In addition to the basic mathematical skills listed above, some exposure to calculus would help. Beyond these, of far greater importance perhaps are curiosity and an open mind and a capacity to keep being surprised and awed by the realization that some aspects of the universe do seem to be understandable. And yes, we do get some of these students every now and then!

The chair of physics at another highly respected liberal arts college says:

> Apart from general things applicable to all disciplines, like the ability to think, write, and speak clearly, the main thing [a beginning physics college student] needs is a solid background in high school mathematics, up to but not necessarily including calculus.
>
> What else would I like such a freshman to know or have? Some prior exposure to physics at the high school level is probably useful, but we do not require it even in our introductory course for potential majors. The same goes for computer experience; the ability to use a word processor and to write simple programs in a language like Basic or Pascal can make things easier but is not necessary. Our most exciting students are often those who have read widely and enthusiastically in the popular literature about physics and astronomy, though they may have little in the way of special or advanced preparation.

Gary Wegner, professor of physics and astronomy at Dartmouth, writes about astronomy:

> A freshman interested in a career in astronomy at Dartmouth majors in physics. There are astronomy classes that one can take that satisfy the requirements for the major. All of these have the first two general physics courses as the minimum prerequisite. Thus in principle a student can take astronomy after arriving with little or no physics background.
>
> The ideal students, however, should have calculus, high school physics, and knowledge of computers. In general, I recommend that an undergraduate get as strong of a background as possible in these areas in order to go on to graduate school. Generally speaking, a Ph.D. is required to do professional work in astronomy.

Geology

Geology challenges you to look at the earth, wherever you are, and ask how it got the way it is—it's a great science for detective-types.

Popular reading

Any of John McPhee's "geology" books: *Rising from the Plains, Basin and Range, In Suspect Terrain.*

Dance of the Continents: Adventures with Rocks and Time, by John W. Harrington.

Earth Magazine—a glossy magazine mostly focusing on geologic issues, for interested beginners. Good, well-illustrated articles on stuff like deep earthquakes, Antarctica's ice sheets, how brontosauruses may have defended themselves, how Balinese farmers have used their volcanic geology to produce large yields of rice, etc.

Good textbook

Understanding Earth, by Frank Press and Raymond Siever, latest edition. This clear, broad introductory college text is aimed at the beginning student without any specialized science background. Nevertheless, it contains lots of detailed information. It is not a lab book, but it describes landforms that you can go looking for in your own territory.

Technology and computers

People who work with technology are usually called "engineers." (William Lear, described previously, was an unschooled and uncolleged electrical engineer.) Another word for technology is "inventions," scientific knowledge put to work for people—whether in the form of space shuttles, wind-powered laundromats, or snowboards.

Appropriate technology

Two terms which aren't mentioned enough in school are "appropriate technology," or "sustainable technology," meaning the kind of machines and tools that use energy and other resources efficiently and wisely, things that run on solar, wind, or human power (like bicycles), and stuff like sewage recycling plants and organic agricultural methods.

We need all the innovation we can get in this department. A lot of it will come from people who find out how civilizations did things before the industrial revolution, and then adapt these old-style methods and tools to fit our present needs. You can be one of these people; *The Millennium Whole Earth Catalog* suggests plenty of excellent books and other resources to start with. A living history farm or museum is also a good way to become intimate with such technology, as is a "primitive skills" or "aboriginal skills" event or workshop. Solar technology, by the way, is an area whose leaders have mostly learned all they know from independent experimentation and sharing ideas—not from college or other school programs.

Centers and organizations

The Green Center does technology that is inexpensive, human and beautiful rather than expensive, cold and sterile. They research food, energy, water and waste treatment systems on a farm in Massachusetts, and have also built a nature center, organized a community farm, and a specialized ecological library. They offer a number of detailed publications on topics like "composting greenhouses" and "how to make a solar algae pond," as well as back issues of the excellent magazine, *New Alchemy Quarterly.*

The *Aprovecho Research Center*, in Oregon, is famous for designing efficient, inexpensive wood-fired cookstoves which help prevent over-cutting of forests in third world countries. They offer three-month internships in sustainable forestry, organic gardening, and appropriate technology. Their stove designs are used in at least sixty countries, and Aprovecho is also responsible for numerous other inventions including bread ovens, water heaters, solar cookers, water pumps, composting toilets, etc. Most interns are college-aged, but there are no official age restrictions. The internships do cost a small fee, but include room and board and the chance to learn a great deal and to live with other interns and staff. They also allow lots of freedom if there's something particular you're interested in doing.

The *International Human Powered Vehicle Association* encourages development and sharing of inventions and sponsors annual competitions. Among its members' accomplishments: the Gold Rush bicycle which has gone 65 miles per hour, a man-powered airplane which has flown 72 miles across the Aegean Sea, pedal-powered hydrofoils.

See if your community has some kind of cycling center, like (in Oregon) Eugene's exceptional Center for Appropriate Transport or Portland's Community Cycling Center. Centers like these offer free and low-cost repair classes, apprenticeships, information on cutting-edge bicycle designs, inexpensive used bikes, etc. If there's not a center, start one. If there is, check into apprenticeships and volunteer opportunities.

Computers
Everyone already seems to know that there are a lot more self-taught thirteen-year-old computer whizzes than knowledgeable adult "computer teachers," so I won't bother preaching that computers can be your unschooling friends. A recent article in *US News and World Report* reports on the increasing trend of teenagers who run successful computer businesses—offering technical support, consulting, graphic design, and Web site design—some of whom have graduated from high school early in order to concentrate on their work.[1] And an article in *Business News* encourages small business owners to hire young computer experts to help them break into the high tech world. "An increasing number of whiz-kid consultants are making their voices heard, and the businesses that are best able to listen to what they're saying will come out on top. Whether it's surfing the Net, designing Web pages, programming for interactive systems or working in other high-tech sectors, employers are learning that the kids are more than all right."[2] If you have a computer or access to one, consider learning to program. There are all kinds of realms to get into—creating games or other software, hacking, Web site design... but you will discover these and more for yourself. Barb Parshley writes in *GWS* #32:

I am presently apprenticing in the most positive sense of the word, under someone who

---

[1] Susan Gregory Thomas, "Mini Computer Moguls," in *US News and World Report*, May 19, 1997.

[2] Jeff Reid, "And a Child Shall Lead Them," in *Business News*, Fall 1996.

designs computers . . . One day, as I expressed my regret to him for my not having gone to college for a degree in this field so I could work better for him, I asked him what his degree was in. He chuckled and said he didn't have one. Being sure he misunderstood my question, and also sure he must be progressing toward his doctorate, I restated my question. He said once again that he didn't have a degree, not even on a high school level. In fact, he never went past eighth grade. He is self-taught, and is designing computers for companies both here and abroad.

Noam Sturmwind, fourteen, of British Columbia, writes:

As an adult I plan to be involved in the field of computers, electronics, or both. I have not chosen (up to this time) to take a computer course. I am entirely self-taught; I have been unschooling since I was 7 years old.

My learning has all been hands-on; I use computer manuals and books from the library to assist in my learning, but also do much experimenting and playing around to find out what I want to know. I've taught myself several programming languages – C++, Visual Basic, and HTML, as well as designing many small programs to do specific tasks. Some examples of the programs I've designed:

♦A math program where you can input any number, the program finds all the numbers that divide into your number evenly.

♦Another math program that finds all the prime numbers up to a number that you specify.

♦A program that interfaces with an electronics project hooked up to the computer. It controls 3 LED's (small bright colored lights); the program gives you the option to flash them at a specified rate, allow them to turn on and off in sequence, or let you turn them on and off individually.

♦Another program that interfaces with an electronics project: a door alarm. When someone opens my door, the computer greets them (out loud over the speakers), with whatever phrase I have entered.

Over the last few years, many people have asked me for computer consultations and help with problems, including my dad! I love the challenge of being able to sort out their problems and show them how to proceed.

I have been the Victoria Systems Operator for a British Columbia homeschooling bulletin board called "WonderNet" for a few years now. This has involved setting up message areas and files, keeping the long distance gateway to the bulletin board in Vancouver operational, adding new users, and upgrading the software.

For many years, my dad & I have done our own computer upgrading at home, adding and removing equipment or making changes to our existing hardware. We've taken our computers apart many times, and miraculously, they actually work when we're done!

Two possible volunteer positions I plan to create for myself involve working with computers. I plan to work in a used computer shop helping with repairs and problem solving; I've also thought about teaching computer skills to young children. This would allow me to combine my love of computers with my enjoyment of young children. I will also continue volunteering my time as a computer consultant to friends and family.

I am certainly the 'computer expert' in my family — when I started exploring the world of computers, no one in my immediate family knew anything about them. Homeschooling has allowed me the freedom to totally immerse myself in my computer learning as much or as little as I choose to, at any given time. Because I have such tremendous flexibility and control over my own time, I have been free to pursue this passion, while still following my other interests such as karate, swimming, skiing, my love of nature, and avidly reading any and all books I get my hands on! ☼

unschooling math

The world is colors and motion, feelings and thought... and what does math have to do with it? Not much, if "math" means being bored in high school, but in truth math is the one universal science. Mathematics is the study of pure pattern, and everything in the cosmos is a kind of pattern.
   —Rudy Rucker, *Mind Tools: The Five Levels of Mathematical Reality*

Most people leave school as failures at math, or at least feeling like failures.
   —Sheila Tobias, *Overcoming Math Anxiety*

In the last few years my math paradigm has shifted, thanks to profound thinkers like Aaron Falbel, who writes occasionally for *Growing Without Schooling*, and Seymour Papert, author of *Mindstorms: Children, Computers, and Powerful Ideas.* I've come to question why so many homeschoolers feel they should use a textbook approach for math, when they feel textbooks are intrusive, misleading, limiting, and uninteresting for other subjects. Being a little bit math-phobic myself, it's taken me a while to open up my thinking, but that's part of the point. So many of us *are* math-phobic (thanks to school and to math-phobic lineage), and that phobia prevents us from approaching math with the same objectivity, independence, and courage that we exercise when we decide, say, to learn about European history—itself no simple or straightforward task.

Many of us don't even know what math *is*—we confuse it with arithmetic and forget that it's more about logic, and about analyzing and recognizing *patterns.* As Patricia Clark Kenschaft says in her wonderful book, *Math Power*, "Computation (routine calculation) is to mathematics as spelling is to literature. It has value in itself, but it is no substitute for the real thing." And in *GWS* #107, Aaron Falbel says, "School math is very different from real math. School math is mostly about computation (arithmetic) and symbol manipulation techniques. By themselves, these things can be awfully boring. Real mathematicians do not sit around all day doing school math. School has concentrated on this one tiny part of mathematics because: a) it can be graded easily, and b) most school teachers are not mathematicians and have little or no idea what mathematics is really about or what real mathematicians do." In *GWS* #78, William Higginson, a professor of mathematics education at Queen's University in Ontario, says:

Rather than thinking, "I can do these marvelous, open-ended, creative activities with my child in music, art, and language, but for math I have to go back to the textbook," parents should realize that mathematics has the same potential as these other disciplines . . . We're in a transitional stage, though; there's a tendency to overplay the fun elements, the motivational elements, without following up on them or understanding the powerful ideas that are embedded in those activities.... One way to look at this is to ask, "What are the problems that face the world today, and what do I need, as a citizen of the world who is trying to cope with these problems?" People wonder how calculus is used. Well, at the root of many of our environmental problems, for example, lies a fundamental misunderstanding of the concept of growth. If calculus is about anything, it's about how things change over time. Another example is that it's very easy to be misled about all sorts of things if you don't understand some statistical ideas.

In *GWS* #107, Aaron Falbel writes about his experience working on math with two teenaged unschoolers. He suggested they focus on logic puzzles, paradoxes, topological puzzles, geometry, probability, and recursion puzzles.

For our first session, I brought in some books by Raymond Smullyan (*The Lady Or The Tiger* and *What is the Name of This Book?*) consisting of all sorts of logic puzzles. These books are about as far away from math textbooks as you can get. They are chock full of amusing puzzles—pure mathematical candy. The puzzles are not meant to illustrate important mathematical principles; they are simply fun. But they are incredibly rich, mathematically speaking. The puzzles escalate in difficulty as the book progresses, and solving them requires careful, rigorous, systematic thinking—in other words, mathematical thinking...

I hope [the unschoolers] came to see mathematics less as the sort of necessary baggage school people say one ought to carry around and more as a way of looking at and exploring the amazing variety of patterns in the world around them, as an experience that can be as fun, as fulfilling, and as beautiful as art, drama, or music.

(Falbel also notes that the author Raymond Smullyan was "largely a self-taught mathematician who dropped out of school several times.")

"Real math" books, from very simple to very challenging

Anno's Math Games (I, II, and III), by Mitsumasa Anno. Anno's books are for very young children, but they vividly convey what math is really about.

Mathematics: The Language of Science, by George O. Smith. You can read this wonderful kids' book in an hour. Like many simple explanations, it is quite profound. It zips through math history and the purposes and definitions of different branches of math, including strange events like the discovery of zero.

The I Hate Mathematics! Book, by Marilyn Burns, delightfully written for people aged nine to twelve.

The Joy of Mathematics, by Theoni Pappas. In short chapters (on snowflake curves, infinity, nanoseconds, comets, crystals...), Pappas shows how math connects to nature, art, science, music, architecture, philosophy, history, and literature.

The Mathematical Tourist: Snapshots of Modern Mathematics, by Ivars Peterson. Sparkling essays on fractals, code breaking, prime numbers, labyrinths, higher dimensions...

Mathematics Made Difficult, by Carl E. Linderholm. This hilarious book takes simple things and makes them incredibly complex. It starts by challenging your idea that you know how to count. It reminds us that math has more questions than answers, and that whenever we add, subtract, even *count*—we operate on a heap of assumptions. With Linderholm, we get a chance to look underneath these assumptions into the labyrinth.

Remarks on the Foundations of Mathematics, by Ludwig Wittgenstein. "The mathematician is an inventor, not a discoverer," says Wittgenstein, a dead philosopher. This difficult book is heavy on logic and profundity.

A few other holistic ways to enjoy math

1) Read "Harper's Index," in any issue of *Harper's* magazine. The index is about the world in general—with a sociological emphasis—but it gets its points across with eloquent numbers. For example, the October 1990 "Index" included the following tidbits:

Percentage of Americans who believe in ghosts: 25.

Years it would take Jim Bakker to earn enough to pay his federal fine at his current job cleaning prison toilets: 2,331.

Average number of words in the written vocabulary of a six- to fourteen-year-old in 1945: 25,000.

Average number today: 10,000.

2) Do logic problems—find them in crossword puzzle books, as well as in logic problem books.

3) Play chess, Set, Mastermind, and Pente.

Math Panic

often goes hand in hand with low math skills. When we're scared of anything, it's impossible to learn. Books that can help you understand your fear and do something about it are *Overcoming Math Anxiety,* by Sheila Tobias, and *Mind Over Math*, by Stanley Kogelman and Joseph Warren.

Basic arithmetic and simple algebra skills

are extremely helpful if you plan on keeping track of your finances, gas mileage, or calories. Of course, you can use a calculator for most of life's necessities, but you're much better off if you cultivate *understanding* also. If grade school didn't help you to adequately develop these skills, you can practice them on your own in a relaxed way. Try *All the Math You'll Ever Need*, described later in this chapter.

Higher math

That is to say, advanced algebra, advanced geometry, trigonometry, and calculus. Why bother? If you want to do anything scientific or understand theories about the nature of the universe, or if you want to design structures or invent technologies, math is your necessary tool. It is also the way a lot of people search for beauty. The *Encyclopedia Americana* says math can "woo and charm the intellect," and that "the symbols can be employed neatly and suggestively, just as words are used in poetry." Bertrand Russel said, "Mathematics possesses not only truth, but supreme beauty—a beauty cold and austere, like that of sculpture."

Does everyone need to study higher math? Certainly not. Too many of us school-educated people end up with more math theorems in our heads than we'll ever use in our lives, yet not enough to help us really *do* anything like build a bridge. On the other hand, we would *all* be better off with at least a rudimentary understanding of each of the major branches.

College? You may need math to get in. How much depends on how selective the college is, what you plan to major in, and whether your other academic accomplishments are thick enough to balance out lack of math. Once you are in, you likely won't need to take any if you major in humanities or arts. If you major in a social science, you will probably take some statistics. Even in colleges that require a balanced diet of general courses, you can probably avoid math. For instance, at Carleton we were required to take any three courses in math and science, which meant you could take three science courses and skip math.

Textbooks and other instructional math books
In the past, many homeschoolers had a difficult time with math. Textbooks didn't explain things well enough, or include enough review, to help most people learn on their own. Now that several popular instructional books and a few good textbooks have arrived on the scene, however, those days are over.

- Many homeschoolers—and schoolteachers—feel that the Saxon books are the best in-depth math textbooks. They have led to phenomenal increases in test scores and numbers of school students who choose to take higher math. They make sense because they are written very clearly and are based on the principle of review. Therefore, instead of learning something and forgetting it, you do it again and again throughout the book until it becomes second nature, a living language rather than a forgotten vocabulary list. (Some unschoolers, of course, *dislike* them because of the emphasis on review—different approaches work for different people.) You can buy Saxon homeschool packets which include the regular text plus an answer key.

  Saxons can guide you through arithmetic, algebra, geometry, trigonometry, and calculus, as well as physics. You may be able to borrow the books through a school. Or for a catalog, contact Saxon Publishers directly. Inexpensive used Saxons are often available from the Budget Text Home Education Catalog.

  Saxon offers free diagnostic tests, so you don't need to guess where to start. As a general principle: if you've been confused in the past, start where you feel comfortable, even if that means in a book supposedly several years behind your grade level. I took math through calculus in high school. I got a C once in eighth grade, an F the last semester of twelfth grade calculus, and the rest B's and A's. In other words, I supposedly learned something. But I couldn't have told you then, and I can barely tell you now, what any of that math was about. I never had any idea what the quadratic formula was for or how we got it. I don't remember how to find logarithms or do differentiation. If I ever decide to learn math again (and there's a good chance of that), I'll start with John Saxon's *Algebra 1*.

- *Mathematics: A Human Endeavor (A Book for Those Who Think They Don't Like The Subject)*, by Harold R. Jacobs, is another great textbook. Although it *is* a serious textbook, it is also good enough that most public libraries have a copy. People like it because it is fun and clear. I recommend it instead of the Saxons *if* you want to do some higher formal math and love it, but not in great depth. It includes (in just one volume) algebra, geometry, statistics, and trigonometry, getting its points across with generous use of jokes, games, puzzles, paradoxes, and magic tricks, as well as problem sets.

- *Mathematical Snapshots,* by H. Steinhaus,. This innovative book uses visuals—photos and diagrams—to explain math concepts and equations. It is not simple material, but is good for people who prefer to learn visually and spatially rather than with words. It is also helpful training if you want to start thinking more visually and spatially. You need some experience with algebra and geometry to understand it.
- *All the Math You'll Ever Need: A Self-Teaching Guide*, by Steve Slavin. A superb, friendly, clear workbook that (for most people) lives up to its title. In logical progression, Slavin covers multiplication and division, percentages, fractions, areas of triangles/circles/rectangles, simple algebra, interest rates, statistics, personal finance, business math, etc. Designed for adults who want to relearn everything they forgot from their schooldays, but also the perfect tool for unschoolers who don't want to waste a bunch of years in the first place.
- *Everyday Math for Dummies: A Reference for the Rest of Us*, by Charles Seiter—another good self-contained workbook, emphasizing business and money math.

The chairmen say
The chair of a very selective liberal arts college math department says,

> If the freshman wants to major in math or science he/she should be able to get a grade of 4 or 5 on the advanced placement BC-Calculus exam. The ideal preparation for a normal student includes math courses from some colleges. This should be easier for a "homeschooler" who does not worry about fitting college courses into a high school schedule.

Frank Morgan, chair of mathematics at Williams, simply informed me that algebra and trigonometry are necessary for freshman-level courses, and that the ideally-prepared student has also studied calculus.

A math unstudent
Amelia Acheson shows a bit of what's possible when she writes about her son in *GWS* #42:

> Alazel (sixteen) loves math—he bought a set of accounting books from a local high school teacher and hurried through them. When he asked her for more, she was amazed at how far ahead of her classes he was. He also got a college supplementary text in trigonometry, and covered most of that between November and March. Then he set that aside and did no math for several months. About two weeks ago, he found his dad's analytic geometry book. It took him about three days to work through most of it, and demand a calculus course. In one and a half weeks, he has devoured about half of what college professors turn into a year's hard work for freshmen. His dad has promised to coach him through physics when he gets integration under his belt.

Andy, sixteen, of Germany, writes:

> Even though I have liked math since I was seven, I couldn't do much about it until we started unschooling when I was eleven. Before that the class only went as quickly as the teacher let it, and the teacher wouldn't let us finish the math book in half a year. When we started unschooling I was able to work at my own pace and not the teacher's. Now, I am sixteen and am in Trigonometry and Algebra III, having finished Algebra 1/2, Algebra I, Algebra II and Geometry by myself.

Dan Casner, twelve, of Wisconsin, gives a behind-the-scenes view of what it's like to *use* math for enjoyment and other real purposes, rather than simply learn it for some vague future:

Recently I made a probability chart of the odds of a given number coming up on several different combinations of dice. I thought it would be neat to do for its own sake and also thought it would be useful for a game that I like to play with friends. Prior to this, I had watched a PBS program on combinations, and tried several other models. The first one I did on the computer--I created a Pascal's triangle, though in this case it was shaped in a rectangle. (Pascal's triangle is a mathematical formula that my dad taught me.) I wrote some basic instructions and printed them out. After I tried to use it in real life, I realized it wasn't quite as good as I'd thought, and I did a little more research.

I did the next probability chart as a combination spread sheet and word processor program. And when I went at it still another time, my dad showed me how to use a computer program called Mathcad, which is designed to help math professors make diagrams, etc., for their presentations. But it is also useful for doing your own calculations. My latest chart showed probability for up to five dice, each with up to thirty sides.

I did a lot of the calculations in my head with help from my dad, during our walks with my dog. We talk a lot when we go on these walks, and I do a lot of my thinking that way. And I get a chance to ask questions about science and electronics and chemistry and engineering and other things. On this particular excursion we worked out the mathematical formulas to use Pascal's triangle to calculate the probability of any given number coming up on the dice. I did the math, but he suggested some of the approaches and helped turn me around when I went the wrong way.

I've never in my life sat down to work on a math text book, although I have used books *about* mathematics. In this case, *Math Wizardry for Kids,* by Kenda and Williams, was useful as it showed Pascal's triangle. ✸

unschooling
the social sciences

My grandmother wanted me to have an education, so she kept me out of school.
—Margaret Mead, anthropologist extraordinaire

THIS CHAPTER DESCRIBES ways to study "social sciences"—history, anthropology, sociology, geography, political science, economics. Most of these fields are quite related to each other. In writing this chapter, it was hard to decide whether to stick some resources under geography or anthropology, under political science or history. In the end, I decided to not get bent out of shape over it. All these "separate" fields can grow more meaningful when they are allowed to merge a bit, as you can tell from reading the following accounts. Kathleen Hatley writes in *GWS* #45 about homeschooling her sons:

> We have been very active this year in the peace movement, and this has provided the older boys with a very direct type of learning in the area of "social studies." We have constructed a section of the Peace Ribbon, regularly met with and written to our representatives (they were quite thrilled to get their first correspondence from their Congressmen), viewed numerous films and attended lectures on Central America, and met priests, nuns, and refugees for some first-hand information about U.S. involvement in Latin America. Because of these experiences, they follow the news and current events with great interest, enjoy reading about the geography and history of Central America, and even practice their Spanish.

Jenny Smith, fourteen, of Alberta, writes:

> About a year ago, my twin sister Dawn, our unschooled friend Christy and I started to work on a model of a space station. We named it "First Rising Moon" and all of us take it really seriously; i.e. exactly what *would* you need to survive. We set the location on the moon and our ideal plan was to have no help from earth once we got there. This meant that we had to plan food (figure out how much one person would eat in a year), clothing, working, and homes for 1,000-2,000 people. We also had to decide such things as a limit on the number of children, what to do with the dead, and how to make everything. The only one we really stumbled on is what to do for toilet paper since all things must be recycled!
> We have done floor plans, investigated solar energy, and written up a list of requirements for those wishing to apply, and our work isn't even close to being done. It is one of those projects that just keeps growing. We decided that all people would have to go vegetarian

as bringing up from earth thousands of cows didn't add up. We have had to contact the local market garden, B.C. fruits, and Alberta Agriculture to find out how many plants grow per square footage of soil. Finding out how to organize up to 2,000 people has proved to be a great challenge.

When we get bored of First Rising Moon, we read Shakespeare, act, and read world history. Last year we each took two countries (Russia, China, England, Mexico, India and France), researched their history from the birth of Christ on and made a comparative timeline.

History

History is not merely what happened in the human past, although school doesn't usually point this out. It is rather the *study* of what happened in the past, and it is full of opinions, arguments, and inconsistencies.

History goes far beyond dates, names of presidents, and wars. Although that should be obvious, I mention it because it wasn't obvious to me until after I'd endured high school and taken an enlightening college course. History asks all kinds of questions about relationships and patterns: What role did Christianity play in the rise of the medieval European medical profession? How did art influence peasant life in eighteenth-century Russia? Why are there wars? How did the experiences of early European explorers in America change European attitudes toward the natural world? How has the etiquette of warfare in Japan changed over the centuries? How did our current prison system develop? How did the structure of villages change during the industrial revolution? Where did compulsory schooling come from?

Understand the difference between primary and secondary sources: a primary source is a document (or sometimes a painting, etc.) produced by someone at the scene of the crime. A letter home from a soldier in the Civil War is a primary source. A secondary source is a historian's interpretation of a variety of primary sources, like a *textbook* about the civil war.

Since history is based mainly on written documents, it usually looks back only as far as a culture's written heritage goes. Archaeology—a branch of anthropology— looks further into the past, since its clues are found more in physical objects than in words.

Primary Sources

Eyewitness to History, edited by John Carey. Truly a history book you can't put down, *Eyewitness* bulges with primary sources from all over the world and all throughout history. A caliph of Baghdad describes a tenth-century Viking funeral, telling mostly about the girl who volunteers to be cremated along with the Viking and his ship. Tales of death and destruction are thankfully interspersed with treats like an eighteenth-century English lady's description of a Turkish bath, and Neil Armstrong's description of his first moments on the moon. A soldier at Gallipoli (WWI) writes about burying his friends in the sides of the trench, and how parts would stick out:

> Hands were the worst; they would escape from the sand, pointing, begging, even waving! There was one which we all shook when we passed, saying, "Good morning," in a posh voice. Everybody did it . . . We couldn't stop shitting because we had caught dysentery. We wept, not because we were frightened but because we were so dirty.

Mine Eyes Have Seen, edited by Richard Goldstein, is a similar collection, but focused on U.S. history.

Great Speeches of the Twentieth Century is a wonderful set of audio recordings; it includes live excerpts from 78 landmark speeches by people ranging from Amelia Earhart to Gloria Steinem, from Joseph McCarthy to Adolf Hitler, from Martin Luther King to John F. Kennedy.

The Penguin Book of Twentieth Century Speeches, edited by Brian MacArthur, is a similar collection in book form.

Twentieth-century primary sources—here's a short list, not intended to be comprehensive, only to give a few good ideas:

- James Agee, *Let Us Now Praise Famous Men* (with photos by Walker Evans). Agee tells about sharecroppers in the South during the depression of the 1930's. People read it in English class too—it is a moving and beautiful piece of journalism.
- Anne Frank, *The Diary of a Young Girl*—Jewish life in hiding, Holland occupied by the Nazis during World War II.
- John Hersey, *Hiroshima*. A journalist's detailed 1946 story of six survivors of Hiroshima, starting from just before the bomb dropped and following through with exactly what happened to each of them during and after the explosion.
- Anne Moody, *Coming of Age in Mississippi*. The firsthand account of a black woman who grew up during the Civil Rights movement and took part in sit-ins and other history-making events.
- Aranka Siegal, *Upon the Head of the Goat: A Childhood in Hungary 1939-1944*. Another Jewish tragedy—though at least she lives to tell the story from an adult perspective.
- Studs Terkel, *Hard Times: An Oral History of the Great Depression*. Studs Terkel is a master of recording oral histories. In this book, all kinds of people tell of their experiences during the depression.
- Studs Terkel, *The Good War: an Oral History of World War Two*. A variety of Americans give their viewpoints—women at home waiting for news of their sons and husbands, eighteen- and nineteen-year-old soldiers in Europe.
- Elie Wiesel, *Night*. Just about as terrible as it gets. *Night* tells about Wiesel's boyhood in Nazi prison camps; his family dies, his faith dies. With anti-Semitism rearing its head once again all over the world, it is extremely important that people read books like this one.

Find autobiographies in the 921 section of your library, along with other biographies, in alphabetical order according to the subject's last name. Browse around in the section, and you'll find something good you didn't know you were looking for. I found *Blame Me On History*, the wonderfully written, fast-paced autobiography of Bloke Modisane, a black activist who fought for freedom and human rights in South Africa.

Secondary Sources

Millennium: A History of the Last One Thousand Years, by Felipe Fernández-Armesto. This globe-sweeping epic is much praised for its scholarliness, relevance to the present, and liveliness. With hundreds of fascinating tales, the author weaves together a larger story about the ways that different cultures have influenced each other back and forth across the planet.

A History of US, by Joy Hakim. This ten volume set, written for people ages ten and up, is an exuberant, multi-faceted, open-minded history of the U.S. Easy to understand and fun to read without oversimplifying.

A People's History of the United States, by Howard Zinn. Zinn's highly acclaimed book gives a much broader picture of U.S. history than you'll find in most textbooks or school history courses; it includes the perspectives of women, labor leaders, war resisters, fugitive slaves, and many other poorly understood groups of people.

Lies my Teacher Told Me: Everything Your American History Textbook Got Wrong, by James Loewen. A fascinating exposé. The author surveyed twelve leading high school textbooks and found them an embarrassing collection of bland optimism, blind patriotism, and misinformation.

The One Hundred: A Ranking of the Most Influential Persons in History, by Michael Hart. Hart ranks and profiles the people who have most influenced the course of history. His list includes such diverse personalities as Queen Elizabeth I, Gorbachev, St. Augustine, Stalin, Aristotle—as well as autodidacts like Thomas Edison, the Wright Brothers, Michael Faraday, John Dalton, Antony Van Leeuwenhoek, Nikolaus August Otto, Henry Ford, and Alexander Graham Bell.

The Times Atlas of World History, edited by Geoffrey Burraclough. If you want a solid overview of world history, this book will meet your needs. Try reading a two-page spread every day. Each of these spreads is a self-contained unit, with maps and illustrations, with titles like "From hunting to farming: the origins of agriculture," "The ninth and tenth century invasions of Europe," and "East Asia at the time of the Ch'ing Dynasty." You can also skim through the glossary, not memorizing, just finding what you like and thinking, "Oh! So that's who Alexander the Great was!"

Any library will have interesting history reference books including atlases and dictionaries, such as *A Dictionary of Chivalry,* by Grant Uden.

The Concord Review is an outstanding journal of high school students' history essays. It is both more scholarly and more entertaining than any middle school or high school level texts you are likely to read.

Biographies and autobiographies can bring it all alive. The 921 section in a Dewey decimal library is packed with them, alphabetized according to the subject's last name. Choose carefully. Try a couple of my favorites: *Maus,* by Art Spiegelman (Pulitzer Prize winning memoir of Jewish survival during the Nazi holocaust) and *Red Azalea,* by Anchee Min (a young girl growing up in China during Mao's cultural revolution).

Libraries also have heaps of books about particular historical problems or events. Many are dull or written in very academic language. Others are terrific, such as:

• Fernand Braudel, *Civilization and Capitalism.* This three volume set takes a long time to read but is fascinating, detailed, and not especially difficult if you start at the beginning and go slowly. It covers fifteenth- to eighteenth-century Europe—the rise of capitalism in the preindustrial world. One nice bonus is that it doesn't pretend to be a *comprehensive* European history; rather, it acknowledges its focus on economic themes. (Most school textbooks also focus on specific themes, such as wars, governments, and white men's exploits, but they pretend to be general history books. By pretending this, they imply that other perspectives, and other stories, don't exist.)

- Dee Brown, *Bury my Heart at Wounded Knee: An Indian History of the American West*. The side of American history we don't often hear. Broken treaties, murders, other foul play.
- Susan Griffin, *Woman and Nature*. Griffin gives us a strange, terrible, powerfully eye-opening account of the way that men have thought about women and nature over the past several thousand years. The book's style helps to get the message across, written in a combination of prose and poetry.
- Suzanne Massie, *The Land of the Firebird*. A lavish, colorful history of Old Russia, focusing especially on the arts. Full of sensuous descriptions of feasts and parties and weddings and church services and palaces, and dramatic narrations of the lives of tsars and tsarinas.
- *Foxfire*—volumes 1 through 10, edited by Eliot Wigginton. The outstanding Foxfire series is based mostly on interviews with old people in the Appalachian hills. They include detailed information on fiddle making, burial customs, snake handling, ghost stories, and dozens of other "affairs of plain living." High school students in Georgia conducted the interviews.

Historical Novels
Some people think of historical fiction as being a skewed, subjective view of the past. They're right, of course. But the same is true of any other source, primary or secondary. Historical novels can give you a greater feel for a time period than textbooks can. Usually, their authors are historians in their own right who do extensive research—reading all those textbooks and primary sources and visiting the setting of their work. Their novels often include notes in the front or back that tell about their research and other background information. Before you read a historical novel, you can increase your understanding of it by reading a brief description of the time and area in a good encyclopedia or atlas, such as *The Times'* described above.

If you want a variety of short pieces, look for an anthology of historical fiction, such as *The Undying Past*, edited by Orville Prescott.

For novels, the following authors and books are known both for historical accuracy based on careful research and for great entertainment:

- Marion Zimmer Bradley, *The Mists of Avalon*—based on the King Arthur Legends but also reflecting the early Celtic world and religious tradition.
- Pearl Buck, Asia. Especially *The Good Earth* (rural China before and after the Maoist revolution). Buck's parents were missionaries in China and, by the way, she didn't go to much school.
- Forrest Carter, Native Americans, *Watch for Me on the Mountain* (about Geronimo and the Apache nation), and *The Education of Little Tree*.
- Willa Cather, *My Antonia* (Bohemians on the Midwestern frontier), *Death Comes for the Archbishop* (nineteenth-century New Mexico).
- James Lincoln Collier and Christopher Collier, early American history, American revolution. *My Brother Sam is Dead*, etc. Collier's books were popular with my students and are easy to read.
- Stephen Crane, U.S. Civil War—*The Red Badge of Courage*.
- Charles Dickens, *A Tale of Two Cities*. Paris and London at the time of the French Revolution, quite the tearjerker.
- Esther Forbes, the American Revolution—*Johnny Tremain*.
- Ernest Gaines, *Autobiography of Miss Jane Pittman*—a century of African

American life, starting in slavery and progressing through the Civil Rights movement.

- Robert Graves, the Roman Empire and ancient Greece—*I, Claudius*; *Claudius the God*; *The Golden Fleece*; *King Jesus*.
- A.B. Guthrie, Cowboys, Indians, and the American West—*The Way West*, etc.
- Nathaniel Hawthorne, Puritan New England—*The Scarlet Letter*.
- Irene Hunt, the Civil War—*Across Five Aprils*.
- Morgan Lywelyn—novels set in the early Celtic world. *The Horse Goddess*, for example, takes place in the eighth century B.C. in what are now the Austrian Alps.
- Mary Mackey, matriarchal Europe, 5,000 B.C.—*The Year the Horses Came* and *Horses at the Gate*.
- James Michener, mostly U.S. history—*Chesapeake* is considered his best. Also other subjects such as Palestine and the Jews—*The Source*.
- Margaret Mitchell, Georgia in the 1860's, during and after the Civil War—*Gone with the Wind*.
- Naomi Mitchison, Ancient Greece and Roman Empire. Her best are supposedly *The Conquered*, *Cloud Cuckoo Land*, and especially *The Corn King and the Spring Queen*.
- Katherine Paterson, Japanese history. *The Sign of the Chrysanthemum*, *Of Nightingales That Weep*, *The Master Puppeteer*.
- Mary Renault, classical Greece. Especially *The King Must Die* and *Bull from the Sea*.
- Irving Stone, biographical novels—about the Lincolns, John and Abigail Adams, Michelangelo, and others.
- William Styron, *The Confessions of Nat Turner*. This story of the only major black slave revolt in America won the Pulitzer Prize.
- Gore Vidal, U.S. history—*Empire*, *Washington D.C.*, *Burr*, *Lincoln*, *1876*. Lots of people say Vidal is the very best historical novelist.

Movies can be historical fiction too.

Just don't be brainwashed. Recognize that any movie has an editorial perspective, no matter how objective it seems. As with historical novels, you can make more sense out of what you see by first checking an encyclopedia or historical atlas. A little background knowledge on the *Ballets Russes*, for instance, makes the movie *Nijinski* far more interesting.

You can find excellent documentaries (*The Atomic Cafe, Hoop Dreams, Paris is Burning, Woodstock*) as well as hundreds of good movies based on actual events— *All the President's Men, Amistad, Andersonville, The Ballad of Gregorio Cortez, Beyond Rangoon, Brother Sun, Sister Moon, Gandhi, Get on the Bus, Glory, The Killing Fields, The Last Emperor, Malcolm X, The Mission, Nixon, Panther, Schindler's List, Silkwood, Titanic...* Also, movies can give you a feel for another time and place even when they are not based on actual events. Filmmakers go to great lengths to recreate authentic settings, bringing us outstanding movies like *At Play in the Fields of the Lord, Black Robe, The Color Purple, Dances With Wolves, Farewell my Concubine, Good Morning Vietnam, Jeremiah Johnson, Once Upon a Time When We Were Colored, The Razor's Edge*, and *The Seven Samurai*.

Living History

Living history projects are one more proof that learning-in-the-world is far thicker and richer than learning-in-school. All over the world, you can join groups of people who make a hobby, an education, or a vocation out of recreating a particular period of history, in lifestyle, costume, language, and skills.

In the Rocky Mountain states, "buckskinners" run rampant—mountain men with muzzle loading rifles and tipis. When I taught school, two of them invaded our social studies class for an afternoon, spinning yarns and wearing moccasins.

All over the world, you can find enclaves of medieval enthusiasts who belong to the Society for Creative Anachronism. They joust in authentically crafted suits of armor, embroider stunning fourteenth-century-style dresses, dance the really old dances, teach each other to play music on ancient instruments, throw brightly colored festivals, and publish fascinating information on things like "Early Scandinavian Culture," "English Domestic Architecture 1200-1500," "Falconry," and "Leathercraft for Common Usage."

Many living history projects revolve around farms, and that fact brings me to one of my little sermons. Living history goes way beyond mere academia. It even goes beyond being a creative way to have a raging good time. Living history projects could help fix this planet. We now realize that many aspects of "Progress," or "the industrial age," or whatever you want to call it, hurt the planet and our lives. For instance, most American agriculture now depends on petroleum-powered machinery and on incredible amounts of chemical pesticides and fertilizers. Organic farmers are leading the way back toward health, but they don't know everything that farmers did in the Good Old Days.

When the world got industrialized, few people thought that the "old ways" would ever be important again—and much of this complex lore was lost. Historians recorded dates of wars and names of governors, but few people had the vision to write down the ways that people *did* things—herding cattle, growing vegetables, tanning leather. As the world grows once again less consumptive, more human, and healthier, it needs to recover this information. And when living history fans spend their time working with ox teams and water-powered wheat mills, they reclaim for all of us the knowledge of how such things work. From there, we can go on to adapt them to our twenty-first-century lives and beyond.

Resources

- Society for Creative Anachronism: call the information desk of a local college or university, ask around at a renaissance fair, or contact the national office. While you're at it, request a free catalog (of well-researched books, pamphlets, and costume patterns you'll find nowhere else).
- *The Book of Buckskinning*, several volumes, edited by William Scurlock. These books overflow with lore and give detailed instructions on making equipment, using muzzle loaders, and acquiring skills for the "black powder" movement. To find other mountain men and women, contact the National Muzzle Loading Rifle Association.
- Find out about hundreds of living history farms, festivals, museums, magazines, suppliers, and organizations around the country in *The Living History Sourcebook*, by Jay Anderson. This book tells you everything you need to start participating in a group, or to simply find an event and watch other people make history out of themselves.
- Check out the excellent web site of The Living History Re-enactor Network.
- If there are no living history sites or programs near you, consider starting your own— carefully, with the guidance of experts. If you can present your idea charmingly, you will find businesses or foundations to help pay for the project.

Seventeen-year-old unschooler Andrew Endsley describes his involvement in a program called "Living History Units" in *GWS* #77:

> We dress up in a costume or uniform from a period in history, and then spend time at historic sites, or do reenactments of battles, for the enjoyment of the public and also for our own enjoyment. A lot of work goes into the historical accuracy of the uniforms. Being involved with this now takes me all over the country . . . Since the unit I was in was known for its special attention to historical accuracy, we were asked to be part of the battle scenes in *Glory*.

Other History Activities

- At the basic level, you might want to know a sort of timetable as to what "major" events happened when. I see no reason why you should memorize this information unless you want to—however, it can be so constantly thought-provoking that you might like to decorate your bathroom wall with it. You could make a timeline, based on one from a book or historical atlas.
- Visit places near you where the past is visible—an official historical monument, a restored house, a cousin's attic, a rusty ghost town. Often these places reek of tourism; you may need to spend several hours just sitting, slowly conjuring up images of what happened there, letting the tourists fade, almost slipping into a trance. It also helps to visit historical places when few people are present—dawn, Monday mornings, maybe even if you're lucky when a museum is closed to the general public. Remember, you are not on a school field trip. Don't be in field trip mentality. Stay as long as you like. Be quiet and dream into the scented past.
- Submit your very best historical writing to *The Concord Review*. If your work is published, consider yourself honored. (Editor Will Fitzhugh, former teacher, says, "I would welcome essays of around 4,000 words, typed, with endnotes, on any historical topic, from secondary students learning at home or on their own, or wherever.")
- Conduct your own historical inquiries. There is plenty to be found, interpreted, and presented to the heap. You might record oral histories in the style of Studs Terkel, soliciting the stories of the elders in your community or city. A helpful short book is *The Tape Recorded Interview*, by Edward Ives, which clearly discusses equipment as well as subtleties like the dynamics of interviewing a husband and wife together versus separately.
- Your own family history would surely love to be investigated and written down by you. In turn, researching such personalized history can make *general* history more meaningful. The library has useful books, such as *Genealogy: Finding Your Roots: How Every American Can Trace His Ancestors at Home and Abroad*, by Jeanne Eddy. Search the Internet and you'll find helpful Web sites. In *GWS* #36, Virginia Schewe writes:

  > Quite by accident this summer, I opened the doors to genealogy and suddenly history became very interesting to the youngsters. After we discovered that a great-grandpa had been in the Army during the Civil War, did a little research in the service records, traced his path, and read about the battles he had taken part in, the Civil War wasn't just some old dumb scrap anymore.

- To share your original research, start a publication like *Foxfire*. (See above under "secondary sources, specific information".) If you want to start a similar project, you'll want companions (*get your friends out of school!*) and you may want to contact the Foxfire people. Since so many teachers have been inspired by their work, there is now a wide variety of published material available to help new groups get started, available from The Foxfire Project. By the way, in my always-humble opinion, Foxfire-type projects are important partly for the same reason living history is: they can help us reclaim the wisdom that we need in order to live abundantly in an ecologically healthy way.
- If you become enamoured of a specific branch of history, you may want to

travel to the appropriate setting to look at ruins, meet the locals, meet other scholars, and inspect special collections of documents and artifacts at libraries and museums.

- Combine history with something else you love. See Chapter 33 to read what Anna-Lisa Cox did with her interest in costume. If you like cars, get involved with the local antique car collectors' clubs. Or collect old jewelry, knives, books, tools, horse tack, gramophones. You can do this for free by keeping a scrapbook collection instead, cutting out pictures of such things in magazines, and labeling them with any notes you wish to add.

- If you become a serious collector, open a small museum. House it in a spare room or even in a corner of your bedroom. You could open it to the public occasionally or only to friends and fellow enthusiasts.

- Make a timeline for the subjects that interest you—team sports, the Protestant church, anything.

Unschoolers learning history

Leigh Pennebaker organized a group of homeschooled teenagers, and after they experimented with various activities, they decided to study the Civil War together. She explains in *GWS* #94:

> We began by having a Civil War re-enactor come, dressed as a union soldier and carrying all the paraphernalia that one would have carried as a foot soldier during the Civil War. He stayed for an hour, and that was really interesting. On the same day, an author of a book on the Civil War and southern life came and read parts of the book and talked to us. At that time, I was vice-president of the group, and the president and I had found these people by calling around to historic places and getting in touch with people who knew a lot about history.
>
> The next week I wasn't there . . . but the others went to a Civil War era house and museum, and the people gave them a tour and explained what life was like on the home front. That was one of our big interests—we didn't want to find out just about the major battles and the famous people, because you can read that in most books. We wanted to learn what it would have been like to be a regular person, or a regular soldier, during that time. On that same day, the group also talked to a historian about the politics of the Civil War, and they said that the event was just wonderful and enthralling and that the historian just loved our group. That was one of the amazing things . . . whenever we had someone speak to us, the instructor or lecturer would be shocked at our maturity and interest.
>
> Another activity was going to a Civil-War-era plantation and mansion—which is not, of course, a plantation any more. I had the idea to dress up in authentic costumes, and I thought I would be laughed at because the kids would think the idea was ridiculous. But everyone jumped on it and thought it was a neat idea, and everybody worked hard on their costumes and had a great time.

Reanna Alder, fifteen, of British Columbia, writes:

> I learn an incredible amount from reading stories. I read a lot of historical fiction and stories from different wars. I've read many, many Jewish World War II stories, like Anne Frank and *Maus*, and lots of lesser known ones. Also many Cambodian, Korean, Russian, Native American and Japanese war stories. War stories tear me apart, they are fascinating and painful. I'm not completely sure why I read them. I gravitate towards them, and I often have a hard time sleeping afterwards. It seems very important to me to know all the stories, to understand.

Preparation for College History

In general, U.S. colleges will expect that you have some general knowledge of U.S. history and Western history. For more specific guidance, here are the words of the experts. Alice B. Robinson, Chair of History at Wellesley College, suggests:

A freshman needs to know how to read, reason, and think analytically. She needs to realize that just for something to appear in print does not necessarily mean it is true or useful. She has to have some idea about what constitutes evidence; of the relationships between fact, inference, and opinion; of why the historian selected certain facts to include and ignored others. If she does not have that minimal degree of sophistication, she at least needs to be open to learning about and appreciating it . . . In terms of knowledge, a student needs to have just plain general background information about this country and the world at large. For example, I've been floored to have students without a clue as to what a bishop is (i.e. not even know it has something to do with religion), or ignorant that there are "books" in the Bible, or with no geographical knowledge (i.e. mixing up Poland and Belgium).

Ideally, students who are well-read, who have had travel opportunities or other interaction with people different from themselves, and who are intellectually and socially at the more mature end of the seventeen- and eighteen-year-old spectrum make the best history students. Aptitude and attitude are probably more important than lots of specific knowledge. Self-discipline, intellectual curiosity, willingness to work, enjoyment of study, ability to accept and profit from constructive criticism all make for an ideal student. Probably the "unschoolers" are not as grade-conscious as many schooled are, which would be a great big plus, as far as I am concerned.

. . . For schooled students, success in Honors classes and A.P. classes allow them to by-pass introductory work and take courses with greater depth and more challenge. If homeschooled do something similar they should be well-prepared for college, too.

Clifford Clark, professor of history and American Studies at Carleton, shared the following advice:

Minimum expectations for a Carleton freshman's success in Carleton history courses: Carleton history professors expect their incoming students to have various kinds of preparation. First and most basic, they should have the reading and writing skills that are essential for survival not only in history courses but in college in general. On the reading side, they must be able to identify the argument in an essay and restate it briefly in their own words. They should be able to test the argument in terms of its logic, internal consistency, and reference to the sources. And every student of the historical record needs to be able to read quickly and to skim if necessary so that they can get the main arguments out of a two-hundred page book in three hours or less. On the writing side they need to be able to compose an expository essay that sets forth their question or thesis in the introductory paragraphs, develops an argument with reference to their source materials in the body of the paper, and draws their conclusions at the end.

In addition to these basic reading and writing skills, a good student should have a sense of the basic chronology in American history and some preparation in European history, Asian history, or some other major historical literature. They need to have taken at least two history courses, have read some interpretive books or articles beyond the basic textbook, and have been exposed to some primary sources, i.e., materials written in the time period being studied. They also need to have the minimal research skills that will enable them to look up material in the library using more sources than simply an encyclopedia.

Finally, the minimally prepared student should be able to recognize the complexity of studying the historical past and to frame his or her arguments about the past in such a way that they recognize and evaluate the merits of different interpretations before choosing the one they most favor.

The Ideal Preparation for a student: In addition to the background and skills mentioned above, the ideally trained incoming student would come to college with a burning fascination with the past and an intense desire to understand it. This frame of mind might, in some cases, be likened to a detective mentality. An inquiring mind, full of questions, is a rare commodity and is much prized by teachers.

The best students add to this quality of mind a greater degree of sophistication in reading and writing than his or her minimally prepared counterparts. The ideally prepared students will not only be able to identify and paraphrase an argument from an essay or book, but would also be able to decipher the assumptions upon which the argument rested. They will also have enough self-consciousness as writers to recognize the position of their audience and choose the writing strategy designed to make their arguments most effect. For most people, these will be skills acquired only through substantial contact with reading and writing historical studies of various kinds.

Anthropology and sociology

Anthropology is the study of human beings as creatures of society. It fastens its attention upon those physical characteristics and industrial techniques, those conventions and values, which distinguish one community from all others that belong to a different tradition.   —Ruth Benedict, *The Patterns of Culture*

Sociology is the same thing, except a sociologist investigates her own culture. Thus, unlike the anthropologist, she can use introspection as a major tool.

In the unromantic opinion of my little brother Richard, a Reed anthropology-major dropout, anthropology means going out and looking at exotic people and writing down what you see so you can preserve them in libraries so that no one feels guilty for sending Progress in to destroy their traditions. However, Richard also acknowledges that some anthropologists use their knowledge to help restore cultures, like scientists who use their knowledge to heal devastated ecosystems. Such anthropologists sometimes work with the governments of developing nations to save as much of a threatened culture as possible, at least preventing their complete destruction. *Cultural Survival Quarterly*, described below, exemplifies this movement.

General resources

For a fairly general beginning, try Ruth Benedict's *The Patterns of Culture*. Start with Chapter Two, which is full of stories. Then go back to Chapter One, which is more abstract. Pages 24-30 give a glimpse of strange powerful versions of adolescence.

Funk and Wagnall's Standard Dictionary of Folklore, Mythology and Legend, edited by Maria Leach—contains more than 8,000 short fascinating articles on topics like blues, Chinese folklore, eating the sacred animal, hanging, Robin Hood, wolf society, and zombies.

Cultural Survival Quarterly is an anthropology magazine with a political agenda. In its own words, "Since 1976, *Cultural Survival Quarterly* has addressed issues of both immediate and long-term concern to indigenous peoples throughout the world. The *Quarterly* serves to inform the general public and policy makers in the U.S. and abroad to stimulate action on behalf of tribal people and ethnic minorities." Find it in a college library or subscribe.

Archaeology and indigenous skills

Archaeology is a branch of the anthropology tree, with lots of ripe fruit ready to be slurped up by unschoolers. Two possibilities: 1) dig 2) do archaeology "living history" style or learn indigenous or "neo-aboriginal" skills. For opportunities in both categories, subscribe to *Archaeology* magazine. To dig, you can also contact Earthwatch (whose expeditions unearth guns in Bermuda, excavate a prehistoric Asante site in Ghana, etc.) or your state parks people, or the National Park Service. *National Geographic* also covers archaeological discoveries, if you want to just read about them and look at pictures.

Living history and indigenous arts and skills

Grown up unschooler Kyla Wetherell comments:

> We live in a society that is becoming more and more technologically advanced while its individuals are becoming less and less technologically capable. People in indigenous societies knew how to gather materials for, make and maintain everything they used, whereas today, for example, we can turn a knob on the stove or strike a match to produce fire, but take away the manufactured matches and mass-produced propane stove and most of us would die before we could start a fire to keep us warm and cook our food. This is why I've spent days turning rawhide into buckskin and hours at a time chipping away at a piece of obsidian trying to make a knife blade. It's exciting and empowering to know how to make your own tools, shelter and clothing. And it gives me a more intimate ecological consciousness.

To learn indigenous arts and skills, or to turn yourself into a part-time cavewoman or a Viking-style voyager:

- Contact natural history museums; they may need interpreters.
- Find likeminded companions and organizations through *The Living History Sourcebook*.
- Jim Riggs, one of the world's greatest experts on "aboriginal life skills" (i.e. foraging, making buckskin, using stone tools, weaving baskets and mats, making fires with bow and drill) gives two-week courses in Oregon's high desert. My brother went on this course—he ate packrats and jackrabbits and learned heaps. He says that once you acquire some basic abo skills, as you would in this course (or could on your own), it's also fun to drop in on the annual Knap-In in March, a no-cost two-week campout where he met Jean Auel and lots of interesting, knowledgeable people. The pamphlet for Riggs' course says, "Drawing from disciplines of anthropology, archaeology, experimental archaeology, primitive technology, natural history and ecology, participants master documented aboriginal processes and technologies, replicate and use important material culture tools and implements."
- You don't need an organization to learn abo skills; go ahead and experiment on your own. Early in his teens, my charming little brother Richard took to refining his archery skills and riding horseback into the hills with nothing to eat except what he could find. He learned local edible plants; he digested grubs; he grew one fingernail very long and sharpened it—a "digging" tool. None of this was intended to be especially academic, but it reflected and enhanced his fascination with cultures who live—and lived—closer to the land. (Several years later, he temporarily abandoned his

exchange student host family in Ecuador to sneak into the Amazon and drink ayahuasca with the natives. That was anthropology too.)

- Other resources:
 ♦The Stone Age Living Skills School in Colorado
 ♦*Earth Knack: Stone Age Skills for the Twentieth Century*, by Bart and Robin Blackenship
 ♦The Society of Primitive Technology
 ♦Paleotechnics: Art and Technologies of Early Peoples, a company which offers books and videos for sale.

An unschooled archaeologist

In *GWS* #82, sixteen-year-old Amber Clifford of Missouri writes:

I've been interested in archaeology since I was a little girl. One of my favorite books was David Macaulay's *Pyramid* . . . Somehow I managed to choose a subject my parents didn't know much about.

In the beginning, archaeology was just a casual interest. I read books by classic archaeologists, the discoverers of King Tut and Troy. Later I kept a scrapbook of all the newspaper and magazine articles about archaeology. It was during that time that I saw my first Indiana Jones film. Even though the movies were over-romanticized, Indiana Jones inspired me. I dove headlong into archaeology.

At that time I was living in Lubbock, Texas. I began to study classical archaeology in Europe and Asia heavily. I read volumes of mythology, from Greek to American Indian. I went dozens of times to the Texas Tech University Museum, that had an entire hall devoted to the archeological history of Lubbock. I also became on a first-name basis with the directors and workers at the Lubbock Lake Site. The Lake Site is an archaeological site, and I was there at every field day talking and working.

I was able to do the reading and studying on my own, but my parents helped me find the resource people that I needed and took me to the places that I needed to see. We're in a town with a university, so when I was interested in fossils, my mother called the geology department and got the professor to talk to me. I didn't know how to go about finding someone, and she did, so this is where she was really helpful, to me.

It wasn't until last year that I became really interested in United States archaeology. That year I wrote a paper on the uses of neutron activation analysis (NAA), and one of the sections was on NAA's use in archaeology. I got on the mailing list at Kampsville Archaeological Center, and I have kept in contact with the scientists I used as references.

Since that time I have done a lot of things. Last year I submitted a grant proposal to the National Endowment for the Humanities for a paper on NAA uses in archaeology. The NEH has a Young Scholars Program for high school and college students. I needed an advisor, and found an anthropology professor whom my 4-H leader knew. I sent him a paper that I had written, and he said that on the basis of that he was willing to take me on.

If you get turned down by the NEH you can request a critique and they will tell you what you can do to improve your proposal and resubmit it. I got turned down but I'm going to resubmit my proposal in November. The director of the NEH said they were very interested in the fact that I was a homeschooler and willing to put so much time into this.

This past year I also visited the Etowah Mounds Archaeological Center in Georgia. There is a museum and three burial mounds there. I began heavy research into the archeological record of Missouri. Now I have a list of sites and museums to visit in the area, and I hope to go to an archaeological camp this fall.

Cultural Survival, the organization which publishes *Cultural Survival Quarterly*, also has a broader goal: "to promote the rights of indigenous peoples in their relations with national and international societies." They seek independent scholars for their "scholars' network" and sponsor special projects worldwide, such as a weaving project in Pakistan, and literacy and health-care education in Zaire. Most of their projects are staffed by volunteers. Also, they have unpaid internships available at their Cambridge office.

Popular reading
The following books are profound and surprising, though most are also less formal and analytic than textbooks or scholarly works:

- Carlos Castaneda, especially *The Teachings of Don Juan: a Yaqui Way of Knowledge* and *A Separate Reality: Further Conversations with Don Juan*.
- Robert Coles, M.D., *Children of Crisis*. In five compassionate volumes, Coles looks mostly at the lives of poor children in the United States.
- Kenneth Good, *Into the Heart: One Man's Pursuit of Love and Knowledge Among the Yanomama*. Good, an anthropologist, spends twelve years with some of the world's most remote indigenous people in the Amazon rainforest. His book stands out because he let himself get personally and emotionally involved, rather than staying removed from the experience in the proper academic way. Not only did he live in a large communal house with the Yanomama (unlike most researchers who stay in separate buildings), but he also fell deeply in love with a Yanomama woman. A truly powerful, vividly told story with a strange, bittersweet ending.
- Jacob Holdt, *American Pictures: A Personal Journey Through the American Underclass*. Holdt, from Denmark, hitchhiked through America for several years in the seventies, staying with very poor families and selling blood to earn money for film. The result is this book and a long slide show by the same name, phenomenal unflinching works of compassion. You need a strong stomach to take it—photos of dead bloody people on the street, families living in incredible poverty, black men eating from tin trays in prison... next to pictures of rich white girls in velvet bedrooms.
- Theodora Kroeber, *Ishi in Two Worlds*, insightfully describes the life of Ishi, the last survivor of a Californian Indian tribe who was "adopted" by anthropologists in the early twentieth century.
- Barry Lopez, *Of Wolves and Men*. The mind-blowing difference between the way Eskimos and other native peoples relate to wolves and the way white Americans relate to them. And, all of Lopez's books are books about the whole universe.
- Richard Nelson, *Make Prayers to the Raven*, reveals the relationship between the Koyukon people of the Alaskan boreal forest and their surroundings.
- Studs Terkel, *Working: people talk about what they do all day and how they feel about what they do*. Read the words of a prostitute, a farmer, a strip miner, a hotel switchboard operator, a bar pianist, a policeman, a lawyer, a gravedigger, and many more.
- Colin Turnbull, *The Forest People*. The BaMbuti pygmies of the Congo rainforest live in amazing harmony with their environment. As far as they are concerned, the forest is their father and their mother, and it likes them. When

anything goes wrong, they figure the forest must be sleeping—so they wake it up with lots of music. This moving book turns a lot of people on to anthropology.

- *The Portable North American Indian Reader*, edited by Frederick Turner. Native Americans' experiences in their own words.

Movies

Look for movies that increase your understanding of other cultural groups, or your own cultural group for that matter. I especially recommend *Pow Wow Highway* (a Native American fairytale), *Romper Stomper* (skinheads in Australia), *Menace II Society* (one of the most powerful inner-city gang movies), *City of Hope* (inner city conflicts), *Secrets and Lies* (family dynamics, racial issues), *Once Were Warriors* (a New Zealand Maori family trying to adjust to city life).

"Advanced" reading in anthropology and sociology

Ethnographies are anthropologists' studies of particular cultures. Written mainly for other anthropologists, they're densely academic and not intended to be especially entertaining—but they *can* be fascinating. One of the most enjoyable is *Pigs For the Ancestors*, by Roy A. Rappaport, about the natives of New Guinea.

To find other ethnographies, look under "ethnology" in a college library catalog.

Read anything by Claude Levi-Strauss—difficult and worth it. Especially *The Savage Mind.*

Also read anything by Clifford Geertz. You might start with *The Interpretation of Cultures: Selected Essays*, especially "Deep Play: Notes on the Balinese Cockfight" and "Thick Description: Toward an Interpretation Theory of Culture."

An unschooled and uncolleged sociologist

Eric Hoffer wrote *The True Believer*, an extremely influential book about fanaticism and mass movements. He had no formal education, but rather a "hunger for the printed word." He worked at various jobs—mainly as a longshoreman on the docks of San Francisco—and wrote several other highly acclaimed books.[1]

Geography

The drumbeats we listen to, the earrings we wear, the fruit we eat—it all reflects the richness of a thousand cultures' traditions and talents. Geography is one of the most fun and lavish thoughts you can immerse yourself in, especially when you are out beyond the limits of school.

General knowledge

National Geographic magazine. Buy cheap back issues at thrift stores and library sales. There's nothing like it, though it conveys a strange subtle arrogance and sexism.

Gaia: An Atlas of Planet Management, edited by Dr. Norman Myers. One of the better tools for saving the world, this enticing book investigates global crises involving land (ocean pollution, rainforest destruction) and people (illiteracy, poverty). Lots of photos and charts and illustrations.

Choosing an atlas is an education in itself. Inspect all the choices in your

---

[1] Information from *Current Biography Yearbook 1965.*

Local Geography: Bioregionalism

Bioregionalism means living *where* you live, which is surely as important as living *when* you live (as opposed to in your memory of the past or in your fantasy of the future). Bioregionalism means knowing and caring about the landscape and the people near you. It means cultivating the perspective that where you live is the most beautiful place on earth, even while you realize that every other place is also the most beautiful place on earth—for other people. If anything saves this planet, it will be people who love where they are—ceasing to live in abstract fantasies, plugging in and talking to their neighbors, noticing the first leafing out of trees in the spring, climbing the nearest butte to get a look at the lie of the land, going out dancing to local bands instead of being seduced only by the faraway stuff on MTV, reading poetry by local authors, snacking on hometown blueberry muffins instead of on Ripples potato chips.

The best national magazine for bioregionalists is probably *Raise the Stakes*, published by Planet Drum Foundation. Through this magazine you will also find news of bioregional events like the annual North American Bioregional Congress. Every so often one of their magazines includes a directory of bioregional groups; you may order the latest directory separately. Also have a look at *Home! A Bioregional Reader*, edited by Van Andruss. Search the Internet for local activities and mailing lists. Another excellent resource is the *Essential Whole Earth Catalog* (look up "bioregions" and "reinhabitation" in the index). See issue #32 of *CoEvolution Quarterly* (in many libraries). Important writers and spokespeople include Gary Snyder, Stephanie Mills, and Wendell Berry.

A bioregionalist perspective will influence everything you do, from eating to reading to making friends to deciding whether and where to go to college. In your library, look up books on various aspects of your particular area—its history, the lifestyles and cultures of people who lived there first, its geological background and agricultural products. More importantly, go for walks in your neighborhood, eat in a cafe that is not a McDonald's or other international chain, bicycle around the outskirts of town, get to know the pigeons or the homeless people in the park.

library's reference section. Especially look for a local atlas.

See the Atlapedia Online Web site for profiles on just about every country on the planet, with information on climate, culture, religion, language, economy, history.

Man in Nature, by renowned historical geographer Carl Sauer, is a detailed yet simple book about Native Americans living with the land. Native American nations themselves have chosen this book for their schools, and the poet Gary Snyder thinks it's great too.

Specific knowledge

In the 900 shelves of your library, you can find dozens if not hundreds of books about specific parts of the world and people who live there. Especially watch for unpretentious stories told by the natives themselves. A terrific example is *The Land I Lost: Adventures of a Boy in Vietnam*, by Huynh Quang Nhuong, and my favorite is *Dreams of Trespass: Tales of a Harem Girlhood*, Fatima Mernissi's evocative recollection of growing up in 1940's Morocco.

See the *Insight* Travel Guides series. With photos and fascinating cultural and historical information, they make great geography books as well as travel guides with depth. Countries and regions range from Bali to Alaska to Israel to the American Southwest.

Check back in the "anthropology" section of this chapter for information on ethnographies. Ethnographies overlap from anthropology into geography.

Watch movies set in cultures different from yours, fiction and non-fiction. Outstanding examples: *The Emerald Forest, Salaam Bombay, Babette's Feast, The Milagro Beanfield War, The Gods Must Be Crazy, Local Hero, El Norte, Wedding in Galilee.*

And read novels that take place in places you know nothing about—like *Mirage*, by Soheir Khashoggi, set in several Middle Eastern countries, or *Possessing the Secret of Joy*, by Alice Walker, which involves the Olinka people of Africa, or *Barefoot Gen*, by Keiji Nakazawa, a comic book novel set in 1940's Japan, after the bomb.

Activities

Keep a scrapbook. Focus on pictures of worldwide dwellings, farming practices, celebrations, whatever. Those cheap *National Geographic* back issues come in handy.

Find out what music from other cultures you like. Most libraries have some international music. The *Explorer Series* by Nonesuch Records is especially good for instrumental music, including Japanese flutes, African drums, and Indian sitars.

Also check the "worldbeat" or ethnic sections of music stores. Some great international pop artists whose music strongly reflects their ethnic heritage are Ofra Haza (Yemen), Clannad (Ireland), King Sunny Ade (Nigeria), Queen Ida (Cajun territory U.S.A.) and Sheila Chandra (India). Dynamic traditional music includes Sweet Honey in the Rock (African-American spirituals), Jean Redpath (Scottish folksongs), The Chieftains (Irish), Miriam Makeba (South Africa), and The Bulgarian State Radio and Television Female Vocal Choir, which will stop your heart or break it.

Notice that a lot of your favorite music probably has strong ethnic influences.

Peter Gabriel, for example, has been especially innovative in weaving global sounds into his work.

And if you are a musician, enrich your work by soaking up some faraway sounds.

Learn to cook and eat the foods of a new culture. You'll find a smorgasbord of ethnic cookbooks in the 641.5 shelves of the library.

Hang a map of the world or your state on the wall.

Throw a party, combining several elements of a culture that interests you. You could recreate an entire traditional celebration, such as a Russian New Years' festival, complete with an ice slide, costume workshop and authentic games. Or you could simply serve the right food and play the appropriate funky music.

Have a pen-pal. International Youth Service provides names and addresses for people between ten and twenty years old. Some Web sites help pen pals hook up with each other, too.

Go international folkdancing. I can't imagine a more interdisciplinary thing to do, since you'll end up not only whipping your feet through incredibly complex patterns, but also learning about geography, international music, and costuming. More importantly, I can't imagine many things that are more *fun*.

And travel if you can and want to.

Map resources
Road maps and atlases of the whole world are available from the American Map Corporation's free catalog. They also sell a wide variety of bilingual dictionaries, guidebooks, and beautiful up-to-date wall maps of the U.S. and the world.

Economics

Always remember that the economy is the relationship between living beings and the earth—another living "being."   —Paul Hawken, *The Next Economy*

Unfortunately, too many economists are narrowly entrenched in their field, interested only in money and stocks and such. They fail to see that the workings of money itself are abstract, taking their meaning from the reality beneath them: land, food, water, soil, air, sunlight, and human creativity, diligence, and wisdom. From that perspective, I recommend the following books, whose authors see the big picture and give a sense of the connections and movements in economics:

- Barbara Brandt, *Whole Life Economics.* Brandt shows how activities like caring for children, planting gardens, and helping friends are as integral to the economy as are "allocating resources" and shuffling money around.
- Paul Hawken, *The Next Economy.* Hawken describes our current transition from a Mass economy to an Information economy.
- In *The Next Economy*, Hawken himself says, "If I could recommend a single book on the economy that might lift the veil of our economic crises, it would be Fernand Braudel's *Structures of Everyday Life.*" The human activity which has the greatest effect on economics, says Hawken, is the everyday tasks that make our lives move—baking bread, doing laundry, catching fish.
- *Home Economics*, by Wendell Berry. This brilliant collection of essays focuses on the way that the health of individual households and farms makes up the economic health of the whole planet. It also discusses the relationship between

the industrial economy and the greater global economy—the economy that goes beyond money.

Bend and update your idea of economics by learning about effective alternative-money systems like Ithaca Money or Time Dollars. These are complex bartering systems that encourage more local spending, increase local wealth, help start new businesses and jobs, build community, reduce consumption of petroleum products (because fewer items are imported), and even help to reduce the gap between rich people and poor people. For example, in Ithaca, New York, you can use Ithaca Money to buy anything from air conditioning to bank services to carpentry work to dance classes... and you can earn Ithaca Money by doing or selling anything that other people want. Both Ithaca Money and Time Dollars publish information that people in other areas can use as inspiration.

If you want to read about economics in the more ordinary, narrow sense of the word, try the 330 section of your library, or these:

- *Econ 101½*, by Elaine Schwartz—an excellent, clear explanation of terms, concepts, and patterns
- *Economics in One Lesson*, by Henry Hazlitt
- *Whatever Happened to Penny Candy?* by Richard Maybury
- The children's library, of course. *How to Turn Lemons into Money: A Child's Guide to Economics*, by Louise Armstrong, is fun.
- Read *Forbes*, or *Money*, or other gold-watch fast-car magazines about money. It will probably take some time before you understand all the jargon.

Political science
When I first wrote this section, it was January 1991, and the U.S. had just gone to war against Iraq. The world felt dark and small; there was talk of a draft. If the worst continued, I thought, some of my readers would be sent to fight. In a letter to a former student, I wrote:

> If teenagers had more say in the world, the world would be a much cleaner, more peaceful place. The people who wage war and destruction have so little to lose, it seems... they're no longer young, they won't be around to see garbage dumps and nuclear waste blot out the face of the earth, they're not the ones who have to meet the "enemy" face to face and shoot, they spend far more time with their documents and diplomats than with their grandchildren. It seems tragic and unthinkable that you are so alienated from the actions of your government.

Later, as I finished this book, the war was over; a cherry tree blossomed outside my window. We all breathed easier, though across the world a country was ruined. My sense of urgency about all this had diminished, but the political structure of the world had not changed or improved. It *still* seems tragic and unthinkable that you are so alienated from the actions of your government.

How can you begin to make sense of it? I suggest 1) getting involved, and 2) getting informed.

By getting involved, you can start to build a bridge between you and what happens in the world. You can't vote, but you can go out in the streets with a sign or a flag, or play your guitar at a rally, or organize a vigil. You can work to get a city ordinance or a statewide or nationwide bill passed. Plugging yourself in will empower you and give you an unbeatable education. For a bit more on activism, turn to Chapter 38.

By getting informed, you can share the thoughts of the world's greatest political philosophers, and build your own twenty-first-century thoughts on top of their wisdom. You can then keep this thinking quietly inside yourself, or else begin to talk about it or take action on it. By staying in touch with current events, you are better able to decide what changes need to be made in the world. Knowledge is power.

Current events

Read a local paper—not necessarily every day, but perhaps once a week. Better yet, read at least two papers with different editorial viewpoints or agendas—even if that means you only read them twice a month. Pay special attention to local news and politics, because locally your voice can easily make a difference. Read the editorial page especially, to find out how your community feels about things, and to clarify your own opinions. For national and world news, read the *New York Times* or the *Christian Science Monitor*. Your library probably subscribes.

National Public Radio and Pacifica Radio have excellent news programs and thoughtful in-depth interviews and commentaries. They can usually be heard on college, "alternative," or public radio stations.

Know who your local and state representatives are; keep their names, addresses, email addresses, and phone numbers handy in case you should want to tell them your opinion or ask them for information. If you contact them frequently and thoughtfully, they will start remembering you and taking you more seriously as time goes by. Politicians need this sort of regular contact with a few people so they don't start living in a dream world where all their constituents are barely real.

Political theory

These are the works which have most influenced and/or thoughtfully criticized Western political systems:

* Plato, *The Republic*
* Aristotle, *Politics*
* Thomas Hobbes, *Leviathan*
* John Locke, *Second Treatise of Government,*
* John Stuart Mill, *On Liberty*
* Karl Marx and Friedrich Engels, *The Communist Manifesto*
* Niccolo Machiavelli, *The Prince*
* George Orwell, *Animal Farm, 1984*
* Alexis de Tocqueville, *Democracy in America*
* Henry David Thoreau, *On the Duty of Civil Disobedience*

By the way, most of these are described invitingly in Clifton Fadiman's *The New Lifetime Reading Plan*.

Also read the *U.S. Declaration of Independence* and especially the *U.S. Constitution*, or your country's political documents. The constitution itself and books about it can be found in the 342.73 section of your library. Look for a collection of short bits of important political writing, such as *Great Political Thinkers*, edited by William Ebenstein.

If Thoreau's idea of non-violent civil disobedience interests you, you might research further into the practice. See the writings of Martin Luther King, Jr.; watch the movie *Ghandi*. Your library may have a related anthology, like *The Quiet Battle: Writings on the Theory and Practice of Non-Violent Resistance*, edited by Mulford Q. Sibley. See Chapter 38 to find out how to get training in non-violent action.

Also, pay attention to the important new political theories and models springing up. Many of them come out of the peace movement, the women's movement, and new religious traditions. One of the most important and visionary new political writers is Starhawk, whose books *Dreaming the Dark, Truth or Dare*, and *The Fifth Sacred Thing* present a radically fresh, empowering way of looking at politics.

Miscellaneous activities and organizations

To better understand the judicial system, attend trials.

The World Game Institute, inspired by the work of Buckminster Fuller, conducts powerful workshops for high schools, universities, and organizations—including United Nations Representatives. In their World Game Workshop, one hundred participants play a game on a huge map, trying to solve the world's problems. Contact the Institute to get a schedule and find out about your chance to get involved.

Read AWOL, *a brave and well-researched zine* by and for teenagers "about peace, war, rock, rap, 'n roll."

Amnesty International is one of the few organizations that is at least as interested in your participation as in your money. Also, it draws support from people of all political persuasions—you don't have to be right wing, left wing, or center wing to believe in what they do. Their work consists mainly of writing letters to governments worldwide—Turkey, Malaysia, South America—on behalf of prisoners who are being tortured. It focuses on nonviolent "prisoners of conscience"—people who are imprisoned for their beliefs, color, sex, ethnic origin, language, or religion—and the letter writing campaigns are remarkably effective; many prisoners are released as a direct result, and others are at least treated more humanely. ☀

unschooling "English"

THE BEST ENGLISH teacher in the world would hardly say a word, especially to the whole class at once. She would stay out of your way, let you read all you wanted, and not try to organize any cute conversation about the motivations of the characters or the relationship between the setting and the theme. She would not keep you from writing by "making" you write. She would sit peacefully at her desk, reading *Pride and Prejudice*. If you went to her, she would put her book down, smile, and consider your questions.

Unfortunately, if this teacher ever existed, she is surely fired by now, because every time the principal came in to check on her, she was not busy asking you the difference between Metaphor and Simile. She was violating the first law of teaching, which is Thou Shalt Be Busy.

Fortunately, since you are out of school, her nasty luck need not distress you. Instead, you can go sit under the persimmon tree with your literary treasures. If you want conversation about setting and theme, or more intricate matters, you can go find it in the company of other people who want it too.

"English," as they call it, generally means reading and criticizing literature, and also writing—expository and "creative" writing. This chapter covers these territories and also touches on mythology.

Literature

Literature is words telling us our lives. Our lives are funny, profound, and tangled. So are the good stories about them. The study of literature happens two ways. The first and most wonderful way is simple—reading something because you like it. If you don't read for enjoyment, you lose.

The second way, which is also wonderful as long as it stays honest, is literary criticism. That's when you first read something, and then talk (or write) about it. Unfortunately, dull and insensitive approaches to criticism ruin a lot of people's love of reading, let alone their potential enjoyment of criticism. Too many college English majors end up burying their former favorite books, after nailing them into caskets made of words like "denouement," "flat character," and "narrative voice."

Sometimes literary criticism seems utterly ridiculous, a way to make insecure

English professors feel as scientific as scientists, even though they're not and shouldn't be. At its best, however, criticism can deepen your relationship with literature, enabling you to be twice as moved.

Criticism, by the way, does not mean saying *bad* things about literature. It means saying analytical, thoughtful things about literature, after asking questions: What does Shakespeare's use of the word "nature" reveal about the relationships among Lear and his daughters? Can a feminist appreciate Edward Abbey? What does the barometer in *Surfacing* show about the relationships between the men and women in the story? What effect does the concept of royalty have on Hamlet's fate? What does the film version of *The French Lieutenant's Woman* show about the relationship between reality and fiction? How do "The Miller's Tale" and "The Franklin's Tale" complement each other? What is implied by the differences in Mrs. and Mr. Ramsey's language, in *To the Lighthouse*?

Some people—could be you—can love this. Others can only laugh or run. There is no shame in feeling either way. It *is* a shame to turn against reading stories just because you don't like to publicly dissect them afterward. It is a worse shame to perform literary criticism if you can't also simply enjoy reading for the fun of it.

Do you *need* to analyze the books you read? *No, no, no,* a thousand no's! You don't need calculus to use long division and basic algebra, or to get along marvelously in the world. And neither do you need to get into heavy criticism in order to love and be changed by great books.

How can people who hate to read study literature?
They can watch movies.

Movies, like books, can be "classics" or cheap laughs. You can criticize a good film just as academically as you can criticize *The Tempest*. Ask your local art film house for a schedule; search the video rental store (Sundance and Cannes award winners are always good bets); see *Videohound's Independent Film Guide.*

Always watch a movie for pure enjoyment the first time. (Watching for enjoyment doesn't mean you won't notice things like symbolism and plot structure, just that you shouldn't force yourself to think this way.) If you plan on deeply understanding any movie, the second and thereafter watchings can be as analytic as you like.

Of course, it is a sorry state to hate to read, but that's beside the point.

Exactly which of the 2,472,003 books should read?
There is no single answer to this question. Nobody except a vampire has the time to read all the great stuff. That's good news for you, since it means your answer to the question "What have you been reading, young man?" is potentially as good as anyone else's.

Of course, there are a lot of books that count as classics, and a lot more that don't. What counts? Why is *Sweet Valley High* out and *Romeo and Juliet* in? No one quite agrees, but we have several generally accepted definitions: good literature is made up of works that have endured the test of time and offer something of value to our present culture. It is made up of stories that take us beyond mere entertainment, raising questions about the way we live and die. Ezra Pound wrote, "A classic is classic not because it conforms to certain structural rules, or fits certain definitions (of which its author had quite probably never heard). It is classic because of a certain eternal and irrepressible freshness."

Why bother to read the stuff? Mainly for enjoyment. Also to be lifted out of yourself, to fly, to cry. To broaden your perspective and to learn about human nature. We can look to literature when we face a dilemma or crisis, because literary works show different ways of handling all our situations—birth, coming of age, falling in love, losing love, failure, success, betrayal, loneliness, watching parents age and die, wanting money, getting money, hating money, losing money, enduring war, facing death.

Introductions

Be aware that most of the "classics" you usually hear about have been written by white men in England or America. Don't *avoid* their books—after all, they are the people who have had the most opportunity and encouragement to write in English during the last few hundred years. Therefore, they have written a lot of the greatest stuff. But also make an effort to find some of the other greatest stuff—literature by women, literature from all cultures and colors. Most newer literary anthologies are pretty well balanced. If you get an older (cheap, used) anthology—pre-1982 or so—at least look in a newer one to notice what you're missing.

If you might want to read a lot of English literature, especially the delicious magical old stuff from *Sir Gawain and the Green Knight* through Malory, Chaucer, Spenser, Milton, Shakespeare, and Blake, you'd best prepare yourself to get its inside jokes by reading the Bible, some Greek mythology, *The Odyssey*, and *The Iliad*. If you don't want to read the whole Bible, read *Genesis, Exodus, Job,* The *Song of Songs, Isaiah,* the four Gospels, First and Second *Corinthians,* and *Revelations.*

If you're learning a foreign language, don't miss out on reading its best literature. One of the peak experiences of my life-so-far was sitting in the late afternoon sunshine of the winter solstice at Macchu Picchu's stone solar dial reading *The Heights of Macchu Picchu,* by Pablo Neruda, in Spanish.

For companionship, join or start a book discussion club, or just read to each other. You might want to consult *The Reading Group Handbook,* by Rachel Jacobsohn.

Bibliographies

A bibliography is a list of books. It helps when you're confused and lost in the literary universe. You've heard of Shakespeare, of course, but then you've also maybe heard of Danielle Steele. Why should you read Shakespeare? And how do you know what else you should read, if you don't have an English teacher? (Once you've been out of school a while, you will not feel insecure without teachers. At first you might. Therefore, the bibliography.) You can ask your librarian for a list of books, or you can try these lists:

The New Lifetime Reading Plan, by Clifton Fadiman and John S. Major, introduces 130 "classics," including plays, novels, essays, poetry, and biographies. For each, it gives a description of the author, of the piece itself, and its social and historical context. Also, the book includes a list of critical works you can read if you want to take anything deeper. To actually read the recommended literature, you'll need to go to the library. Fadiman also recommends a few other books on history, math, art, etc. If you are one of the nervous college-bound, know that reading some of the books described here will make any college admissions department happy.

Five Hundred Great Books by Women, by Erica Bauermeister et al, gives wonderful descriptions of "thought-provoking, beautiful, and satisfying" books representing many countries, cultures, time periods, and themes.

Miss Llewellyn's miniature teenage bibliography

This list reflects my conviction that the teenage years are a time of powerful personal transformation and vision. As a teacher, I noticed that most teenagers seemed to especially enjoy literature which put them in contact with the bizarre and visionary, the wild, the edges, the unexplained sides of human nature. Through literature, they sought assurance that no matter how saran-wrapped the adults tried to make things seem, reality remains big and weird. My friend Keith said he liked being around his friend Mary because she made him feel like he had a place in the universe. I didn't ask him what he meant, but I translated his comment into my relationship with literature. No matter how strange my thoughts or hopes, I can always count on literature to mirror them, and to assure me that I am not alone. *Most good literature can do this for you, but here is a short list especially tailored for searching teenagers.*[1]

Novels

Maya Angelou, *I Know Why the Caged Bird Sings*

Hal Borland, *When the Legends Die*

Ray Bradbury, *Dandelion Wine*

Rita Mae Brown, *Rubyfruit Jungle**

Lewis Carroll, *Alice in Wonderland*

Dante, *The Inferno* (not really a novel, but a very long poem)

David Lee Duncan, *The Brothers K*

William Golding, *Lord of the Flies* (I vehemently disagree with Golding's pessimistic view of human nature, but this is nevertheless a compelling, provocative psychological novel.)

Jean Hegland, *Into the Forest*

Keri Hulme, *The Bone People*

John Knowles, *A Separate Peace*

Ursula LeGuin, *The Word for World is Forest*

Everything by Madeleine L'Engle, starting with *A Wrinkle in Time*

C.S. Lewis, *The Chronicles of Narnia, Out of the Silent Planet, Perelandra, That Hideous Strength*

Carson McCullers, *The Heart is a Lonely Hunter*

Tom Robbins, *Even Cowgirls Get the Blues**

J.D. Salinger, *The Catcher in the Rye*

Sapphire, *Push**

Lynne Sharon Schwartz, *Leaving Brooklyn**

Ignazio Silone, *Bread and Wine*

Tom Spanbauer, *The Man Who Fell in Love with the Moon**

J.R.R. Tolkien, *The Lord of the Rings* trilogy

Alice Walker, *The Color Purple**

Richard Wright, *Native Son*

---

[1] Bear in mind that some of this stuff would never in a trillion years make it past the claws of the school censors—some of it deals with harsh (but real) stuff like rape and child abuse; some of it is considered "adult" literature. I've asterisked the more controversial written works so you can avoid them if you wish.

Short Stories

Sherwood Anderson, *Winesburg, Ohio*
Shirley Jackson, "The Lottery"
D.H. Lawrence, "The Rocking Horse Winner"
Ursula LeGuin, "The Ones who Walk Away from Omelas"
Barry Lopez, *River Notes, Desert Notes, Winter Count, Field Notes.*
Edgar Allen Poe, anything—especially "The Masque of the Red Death"

Essays and non-fiction

Edward Abbey, *Desert Solitaire* (start with "The Dead Man at Grandview Point")
Annie Dillard, *Holy the Firm*
John Fire Lame Deer and Richard Erdoes, *Lame Deer, Seeker of Visions*
Kahlil Gibran, *The Prophet*
Peter Matthiessen, *The Snow Leopard*
Henry David Thoreau, *Walden*, also "On the Duty of Civil Disobedience"
Revelations (in the *Bible*, preferably New International Version or other easy to read translation)

Plays

Arthur Miller, *The Crucible*
Shakespeare, *Hamlet*
Sophocles, *Oedipus Tyrannus*

Movies

Dead Poets' Society
Equus
Harold and Maude
Jesus of Montreal
The Last Wave
One Flew Over the Cuckoo's Nest
Picnic at Hanging Rock
Double Happiness
Fried Green Tomatoes
Lone Star
My Life as a Dog
The Piano
Priest
Quiz Show
Romeo and Juliet

Poetry

William Blake, anything—*Songs of Innocence and Experience* (not as innocent as they seem), *The Book of Thel, America: A Prophecy, The Marriage of Heaven and Hell*
Allen Ginsberg, *Howl*
The lyrics to your favorite songs, such as those by Pink Floyd, U2, Led Zeppelin, Tori Amos, Ani Difranco, the Indigo Girls, Ferron, or Bruce Cockburn.

And a short list of great **love literature**, in case you should need it:
* *The Song of Songs,* out of the *Bible*
* Emily Brönte, *Wuthering Heights*
* Any poetry by Robert Herrick, especially "Corinna's Gone a-Maying"
* Edgar Allen Poe, *Annabel Lee*
* poetry by Sappho
* Shakespeare's sonnets
* Various dusty old books in any college library—track them down by typing "love literature" or "love poetry" into the computer. At the University of Oregon, I found old leather-bound collections of Chinese and Arabian love poetry.
* *Into the Garden,* edited by Robert Hass and Stephen Mitchell—an imaginative, eclectic collection of short romantic readings, including songs and poetry from traditional cultures (ancient Egyptian, Australian Aboriginal, Navajo, native Hawaiian) and bits by passionate, profound people like Emily Dickinson, Rumi, William Blake, and Ralph Waldo Emerson.

Anthologies
An anthology is a collection of literature—a lot of stuff in one book. Cheap and handy. If you want to own one general anthology, own *The Norton Introduction to Literature,* any edition.

If you want to own two or more anthologies, own some Norton Anthologies, like *The Norton Anthology of American Literature.* These are fat books with fine print, wrinkly thin paper, and tons of treats. They are cheaper, more fun, more serious, and less censored than high school literature textbooks. Also, you can buy them at university used book sales, or by posting a notice that says what you want on a college campus. Your many choices include anthologies of English literature, American literature, world literature, women's literature, poetry, short stories, and essays—just to name the ones I've used and loved.

Technicians of the Sacred and *Shaking the Pumpkin,* edited by Jerome Rothenberg, are my favorite translations of traditional poetry from primal ("primitive") cultures. *Technicians* covers the whole world, *Pumpkin* just Native North America.

Eye of the Heart, edited by Barbara Howes, is a rich collection of Latin American short stories.

Words in the Blood, edited by Jamake Highwater, is a collection of contemporary Native American writing from North and South America.

Resources for critics
You can get a gentle start in criticism by reading the commentary throughout *The Norton Introduction to Literature* or another good text.

A Glossary of Literary Terms, by M.H. Abrams, gives you all the language you need, along with lots of examples, to talk like an English professor. It explains terms like *elegy, irony,* and *Russian Formalism.* Required in many college English classes.

If you want to be hardcore, start reading criticism and writing your own. If you like C.S. Lewis and medieval English literature, start with C.S. Lewis's criticism—it is as clear and wise as his fiction.

Hit the scholarly journals. Read a few to get an idea of whether you want to major in English or another literary field in college—the dense difficult papers in them are just the type of thing you'll be writing, again and again, in any English de-

Making Contact With Literature

It's human nature to want intimate connection with whatever we're attracted to. It's more gratifying to hike through wilderness, drinking snowmelt and acquiring blistered feet, than to drive a scenic mountain route. It's nicer to kiss somebody than to stare at a photo. My father told me once that he thinks some men hunt because it is the only way they know to be close to wild animals, more than watching them on TV or in zoos. In many ways I catch myself trying to establish relationships with things I like—cutting up *National Geographic* to rearrange it into my own scrapbooks, inventing variations on my favorite recipes, taking my own photos of favorite landscapes though postcards are cheaper and more perfect.

Same thing with literature. It's not always enough to simply read stories and let them work on us in their deep, unspoken, mysterious ways. Sometimes we need to meddle, to build a bridge between ourselves and someone else's writing. Unfortunately, the only way most of us are encouraged to do that—in high school and college English courses—is by performing left-brained, even cold-hearted, acts of literary criticism upon the pieces we love. The further you go up the "English" ladder, the less acceptable it becomes to make any comments about how literature affects you *personally*, or how your own life reflects its themes. Instead, you must analyze, define, compartmentalize. At times, this gets absurdly abstract and detracts from literature's ability to work on us in those deep, unspoken, and mysterious ways. Therefore, here are a few other ways of becoming involved with literature, ways which I think are respectful of yourself and of what you read, ways which let it keep living and growing inside you:

1. Make a commonplace book—a personal collection of quotes lifted from your reading—from novels and poems and essays, *not* from other people's books of quotations. W.H. Auden's *A Certain World: A Commonplace Book* is a nice example, though the fact that it was *published* is a bit misleading: the most important value of such an undertaking is intimately personal, although it could easily feed into more public projects. For instance, the "education" section in my own commonplace book is getting long enough that I sometimes consider turning it into a book of its own someday—but I would not try, or *want*, to publish my whole collection. You can organize your quotes by themes ("honesty," "dogs") or leave them in an amorphous, poetic lump. Your quotes can be as short as a phrase or as long as a page... or more. Because the important thing is your involvement, it's best not to photocopy or use a scanner to lift quotes, but rather to type or write them out yourself.

2. Memorize your favorite bits of literature. Some people memorize quotes so they can sound urbane while chewing hors d'oeuvres at snobby parties, but that's not what I mean. Twelve years ago I spent half the summer at a field camp in Northern Minnesota studying zoology. I walked alone in the evenings, and sometimes I'd be overwhelmed as the fireflies came out and the loons called and the frogs sang and the warm wind moved inside me and tossed in the alder thickets. I wanted to have some way of *touching* this beauty, and one thing I did was to memorize part of Barry Lopez's story "The Search for the Heron." Then I would walk along at night reciting it in a quiet voice. Yes, I do know that sounds cheesy, but I'd be much more pleased with myself if I had a bigger supply in my cheesy brain of memorized poems and paragraphs, and not such a big supply of college English papers upstairs in my file cabinet.

3. Read aloud to someone you love, or take turns reading aloud. If you make reading itself into a full experience, you won't feel so much that you have to do something else (i.e. write papers) *to* the experience to appreciate it.

4. If you're trying to get to know someone, trade reading "assignments," so that you each read each other's favorite literature. That way, you get to build a shared inner landscape and enjoy good books along the way.

5. Write essay-length book reviews, like those in *Harpers, Audubon, The Nation, Ms.* Writing long reviews is a great balance between criticism and just-plain-reading. You actively participate in the reading—watching for ways the book relates to what you know from other reading, from personal experience, from stories in the news, from your understanding of history, from eavesdropping in the park. You keep your eyes peeled for good quotes, and you try to both capture the overall gist of the book and to highlight a few points or themes which strike you as especially interesting. It's often fine to weave in relevant personal stories or current events, certainly to give background information about the author or subject, and to point out the book's limitations or to suggest unusual applications for it. For instance, I wrote a review of Susannah Sheffer's *Writing Because We Love To: Homeschoolers At Work* in which I pointed out how classroom teachers could use the book's ideas; my piece was published by *English Journal,* a magazine for secondary English teachers. That's another advantage of writing reviews: it's one of the easier ways to get published as a beginning writer.

6. Host a poetry reading. Read your favorite poems, and invite a few friends to read their favorites. Honor the poems by making it a gala event, candles and dress-up.

partment. If you do like these journals, read them and become a precocious expert. Write your own criticism in the same vein. Eventually, send in an essay and see if they'll publish it.

College?

The possible majors are usually English, Classics, or comparative literature. Also, if you major in a foreign language often you can "concentrate" on reading literature in the original. The best departments, especially for a traditional English or Classics major, are mostly at small liberal arts schools. The best preparation is reading the Bible and Greek mythology, developing strong writing skills, getting your heart broken at least once, and coming prepared to learn to read all over again.

Mythology

Mythology is a lot bigger than they tell you in school. It is not just a bunch of cute stories about why the moon changes shape. It has to do with the deepest dreams, hardest questions, and ultimate destinies of the human race.

Resources

The Power of Myth, by Joseph Campbell with Bill Moyers. Watch it on videotape or read the book. Afterwards, anything else by Campbell.

The children's library, for gloriously illustrated versions of the myths themselves.

Funk and Wagnall's Standard Dictionary of Folklore, Mythology, and Legend, edited by Maria Leach.

Parabola: the Magazine of Myth and Tradition. Published quarterly, available by subscription and in many college libraries. Each issue centers on a topic like ceremonies, guilt, mirrors, or the tree of life. This wonderful magazine proves that scholarly work can stay meaningfully connected to life.

Edith Hamilton, *Mythology.* Often considered the standard, though it focuses mostly on Greek myths and leaves others out.

What you can do

Try to write for journals like *Parabola.*

Incorporate myths into your artistic work—poetry, art, music. Make up your own mythology—as have William Blake, J.R.R. Tolkien, Ursula LeGuin, and other authors.

If the myths of a particular culture fascinate you, find out more about that culture's history, geography, etc. Consider learning the language.

Write your own retellings of myths, adding details, personal interpretation, and perhaps illustrations. Two outstanding examples are *Till We Have Faces,* by C.S. Lewis, and *Prince of Anwyn,* by Evangeline Walton.

Writing

First, the acquisition of basic writing skills, so that you can communicate without blocks and fears and confusions. Second, the further development of literary talent— journalism, essays, poetry, plays, short stories, novels. And a quick mention of storytelling.

Basic writing skills

We learn by example. Therefore, the best writing teacher for most people is lots of reading.

Common sense, too, will take you a long way. I've had several students who spoke articulately, but who panicked and fell apart when they had to write, because school had coached them to believe writing was difficult and mysterious. Together we found that all they needed was to slow down and imagine themselves talking, and then write what they heard themselves saying in their heads. Simple? Yes. Silly? No. School doesn't often advocate common sense solutions, because if everybody trusted their common sense, they'd stop feeling they needed school "professionals" to learn.

Don't expect anything to come out perfectly the first time. At first, brainstorm, jot down your thoughts, and just spill everything out freely. Don't bother about spelling, perfect word choices, punctuation, etc. You can organize and reword things the second time around. On the third pass, you can finesse it, use a thesaurus, get rid of passive voices, check spelling, worry about commas. Writing is a *process*; for most people, it requires several steps. If you try to get it all right in one step, you'll set yourself up for failure. The basic idea is that most of us can't both create and censor at the same time. So first you write and create, *then* you censor and structure and limit.

Three excellent books on learning to write expressively through this process are Gabrielle Rico's *Writing the Natural Way*, and Natalie Goldberg's *Wild Mind* and *Writing Down the Bones*. You can also get a splendid audio recording of one of Natalie Goldberg's live workshops, *Writing the Landscape of Your Mind*.

For no-frills, concise step-by-step guidance, turn to *How to Write*, by Herbert and Jill Meyer.

If you want criticism on your writing, ask your friends and family. Ask what confuses them or repeats itself. Also invite them to give you any other feedback they think of. What some of your readers may lack in "professional" expertise, they will more than make up for in the amount of time and energy they can devote to critiquing your work. Even in my tiny 26-student school I was too swamped with my students' writing to give enough response to any of them.

If writing skills—especially punctuation, usage, mechanics, etc.—don't come naturally, then arm yourself with a few helps: Strunk and White's *The Elements of Style*, and possibly a good general textbook. I recommend *English Composition and Grammar*, by John E. Warriner.

If you want to work on grammar—for foreign language study or whatever—Warriner's texts are excellent for that too.

Beyond basics: developing literary talent

Of course, to be a writer, all you really have to do is write. Frills like writers' conferences are unnecessary. And if you *don't* write, no amount of writing instruction will pull a novel out of your navel. Once you are writing, however, outside stuff can help.

There are lots of books about how to write in any library. Most are abominable. Several are outstanding. For non-fiction, try William Zinsser's *On Writing Well* and *Writing to Learn*. For creative writing of any kind: *Writing Down the Bones* and *Wild Mind*, by Natalie Goldberg. For poetry: *The Practice of Poetry: Writing Exercises from Poets who Teach*, edited by Robin Behn and Chase Twichell. For word choice, fun, the writers' lifestyle, and fiction writing—especially novels and screenplays: *Starting From Scratch: A Different Kind of Writer's Manual*, by Rita Mae Brown.

Attempt to apprentice yourself via mail or in person to a writer you admire. Send him something short you've written, typed neatly, revised and without spelling mistakes and as good as you can possibly make it. Enclose a SASE. Politely ask for his feedback, *if* he has time. Make sure to point out that you'll understand if he doesn't have time. If he's famous (which means busy), or if your work is sloppy, he'll likely not be able to respond or at least not in detail. Try someone else. Several teenagers, including Tabitha Mountjoy, fourteen, and Kim Kopel, sixteen, do writing apprenticeships through the mail with Susannah Sheffer, editor of *Growing Without Schooling*. (Her wonderful book on the subject of homeschooled writers, *Writing Because We Love To*, tells how this has worked.)

Or anonymously apprentice yourself to a great writer by studying her work carefully. Some techniques: copy passages of her writing into a notebook (to help yourself understand her style). Try writing in her style. Read her best works again and again. Memorize parts of her works. Read her biographies, letters, anything you can find that tells *how* she wrote. Eventually, try the same process with a different writer.

Start or join a writers' guild or support group. C.S. Lewis, J.R.R. Tolkien, and other friends met to share and discuss their writing in a group they called The Inklings.

Attend writers' conferences. There are real ones intended for adults (but without age requirements) and sometimes okay ones for school teenagers, which you can get in on too.

Take a course in writing—*if* you trust the teacher. It only makes sense to be taught by real writers. What right most secondary school English teachers (like yours truly) have to pretend to teach "creative writing" is beyond me.[1] Teachers need not be *professional* writers, as long as they are willing to share their work and you think it is good. A lot of writers do teach, particularly in occasional college courses. If you don't find a writer-teacher, skip it.

If you are interested in a course, you might consider looking for one in writing *creativity*, or journal writing, or something along that right-brain line. While I sit at my computer endlessly day after day, my housemate Caroline is taking a wonderful weekly class called "Women's Journal Writing Workshop." They start with guided meditations, like imagining wandering through a big house and meeting a wise old woman. Then they spend half an hour or so writing poems or prose—or drawing— based on the meditation. They finish class by sharing their work with each other in a supportive atmosphere.

See your writing as a way to make a difference in the world—join Amnesty International and write letters on behalf of tortured prisoners, write your members of congress or parliament thoughtful letters about injustices that steal your sleep, write the utilities company outlining your ideas about ways they could encourage energy

---

[1] This probably seems contradictory, so I thought I should explain: Although I've wanted to be a writer (among other things) ever since I was 13, I was much too self-conscious to show most of my writing to *anyone* until the publication of the first edition of this book. So, when I was a schoolteacher, I never shared any of my own writing with my classes.

Journalism: the neighborhood newspaper

Living fully at home is as important—and sometimes as difficult—as living fully in the present. Just as many people imagine that their lives will begin in the future—after they graduate, get promoted, marry, or retire—many also act as if events downtown, or in New York or Paris or South Africa, are more important than what happens in their own neighborhood. Yet, if more people cared about where they lived, we'd all have less to worry about and more to celebrate. And that's one place where your writing talents can step in and make life fuller for everybody who lives within a few square miles of you.

Every neighborhood would be made happier and healthier by a small, sincere, well-written newspaper or zine that celebrates local people and events. Give the behind-the-scenes story of the bed and breakfast inn down the street, or a profile of the old lady who adopts stray cats, or an explanation of where your neighborhood's sewer goes after it leaves each house.

Focus on the personalities and details behind your stories; merely printing what-why-where-who-and-how won't satisfy people's desire to understand their neighbors. Better to publish one significant issue each month or season than a poor-quality, rushed weekly. For examples, read profiles and feature articles in all kinds of magazines and newspapers. You could also encourage letters to the editor, and include an editorial page.

Don't think of your project as a "kid-produced" newspaper, or it will probably end up matching people's expectations of kid-produced things—dumb and cute. Just think of it as an important way to tell the truth and bring your neighborhood closer together.

A typewriter (or neat handwriting) and paper is all you need. If you have a computer, work with any word-processing program or go high tech with desktop publishing software. Black and white photos can add interest. For other graphics, use your friends' artistic talents or check Dover's pictorial archive books for a bizillion copyright-free illustrations. Photocopy your creations on recycled paper... and distribute them. You might give the first issue away free, but then ask people to subscribe for money. If you write decently, neighbors will gladly pay for your paper. You can probably get local businesses to buy advertising space, too.

Of course, your paper could have a focus other than your community, such as city-wide teenagers' lives and activities, or news of your extended family.

Don't invade anyone's privacy by publishing embarrassing facts about their personal lives. And be careful that what you write is true. Generally, however, as long as the focus of your paper is positive, and as long as you write it yourself or with friends, you'll have no need to worry about legal issues. Investigative reporting, or a paper that questions local issues, can be important also, but that's a whole different ballgame. If you might make anyone angry, you'll have to be certain not to make any legal mistakes; research carefully before starting anything controversial or "political." An excellent start is *Author Law and Strategies*, by Brad Bunnin and Peter Beren.

You probably won't need books to tell you how to make your newspaper; mistakes and experiments (i.e. *experience*) will guide you. But you might have a look in the 070.5's at the library or check the library catalog. One excellent help is *Editing Your Newsletter: How to produce an effective publication using traditional tools and computers*, by Mark Beach.

Craig Conley, a fifteen-year-old former homeschooler attending Louisiana State University, wrote about his newspaper in *GWS* #30:

> I first got interested in writing newspapers five years ago when I was present at the collapse of an historic old hotel in Joplin, Missouri. I wrote an article about the history of the hotel and how it collapsed, trapping four men under the rubble. I added other articles about what my family was doing, and what was going on in town. Soon I had a whole newspaper . . . Now my paper is read by forty families, in fifteen different states. It is called *Craig's Quarterly* and each issue ranges from twelve to thirty pages. It contains book reviews, news articles, artwork and stories. Subscribers send in articles they have written . . .Reporting on activities . . . is good training for life. It makes me more observant and analytical. I try to look at people I know and new people I meet as possible subjects for an interview and sometimes this leads me to ask questions I might never ask otherwise. The most fascinating people are really in your own backyard.

conservation.

And use writing to make a difference *in your own life*, and in your relationships with friends and family. Keep a journal or diary. On birthdays and holidays, give written gifts. Pour yourself into correspondence with pen-pals or even with nearby friends. Write your own autobiography, or the biography of your great uncle. Write love letters, apologies, a book of family customs for your new niece. For great ideas, I highly recommend:

- *The New Diary: How to use a journal for self guidance and expanded creativity*, by Tristine Rainer.
- *Put Your Heart on Paper: Staying Connected in a Loose-Ends World*, by Henriette Anne Klauser.
- *Families Writing*, by Peter Stillman.
- *Writing Your Life: Putting Your Past on Paper*, by Lou Willett Stanek.
- *Writing Family Histories and Memoirs*, by Kirk Polking.

If you want to get published

See *The Market Guide for Young Writers*, by Kathy Henderson, for a description of over one hundred contests and magazines that buy specifically from people under eighteen.

Merlyn's Pen is a high quality, competitive magazine for teenaged writers.

Start your own zine, or contribute to someone else's. Zines range from raw and chaotic to refined and elegant. For a sampling, see *The Book of Zines*, edited by Chip Rowe.

Homeschooling teenager Dori Griffin edits a nice literary magazine, *The Inkwell*, and actively seeks dedicated writers.

Post your best writing on your personal Web site.

There's no reason you can't also attempt to get published in mainstream "adult" publications. (Helpful directories: *Writer's Market, Novel and Short Story Writer's Market, Children's Writer's and Illustrator's Market, Songwriter's Market,* and *Poet's Market*, all updated annually.) Just keep in mind that there is intense competition for the well-known publishers and magazines, and it often takes serious adult writers many years to break into print. If your ego isn't ready for rejection, stick with less competitive forums.

Storytelling

The ancient art of storytelling has been with us always, but recently it's enjoying more recognition. As the brochure for the National Storytelling Association points out, "Through storytelling we have preserved our heritage, passed on traditions, learned skills, and — most importantly — developed our limitless imaginations . . . Whether we spend our days harvesting corn or selling real estate or ministering to a congregation, we share our knowledge and experience through storytelling — and in the process we gain a better understanding of ourselves and our world."

The National Storytelling Association sponsors an annual conference and an all-out annual festival. It also publishes the bi-monthly *Storytelling Magazine* and the *National Storytelling Directory,* which lists storytellers, organizations, events, educational opportunities, periodicals, production companies, broadcast programmers, and Internet sites. The magazine and directory are free with membership.

The Annual Storytelling Festival, in Tennessee, offers three days of tales by both professionals and amateurs. Information free from the National Storytelling Association.

Unschoolers in English Unclass

Reanna Alder, fifteen, of British Columbia, writes:

This freedom I have puts me in an excellent position to grow and evolve. I can see what I want to do, who I want to become, how I want to live, and I can go straight towards it.

Today, just before getting in the shower, I opened *Wild Mind* by Natalie Goldberg somewhere in the middle and read a bit. It's a writing book that is also about life. I read the book a few years ago and learned a lot, I skimmed it today hoping for some inspiration. Nothing particularly grabs me. I put the book down and hopped in the shower. Internal conversation time:

"Maybe I should go to one of her seminars so I can ask her about my writing... Natalie, I would say, I'm really frustrated about my writing, it seems detached and ungrounded these days, and it doesn't sound like *me* speaking, even though they are my ideas. Natalie, you say you write from your body, how do you write about ideas and philosophies from your body?"

"I guess you would use body language, (heh heh) instead of mind language. I guess you would find a way to communicate ideas and philosophies through feelings and everyday real lives."

"That's true, I'll try that."

My mind wanders onto other topics and then I realize something really funny. It's true, what they say, I really do have all the answers inside me, just waiting for me to ask the right questions. It's like in the movies, when the protagonist finds out something really important, that their companion knew all along. "You never told me!!" the protagonist yells. "You never asked," the companion responds coolly.

Jade Crown, fourteen, of Washington, writes:

When I was in seventh grade, Jodi, an old elementary school teacher of mine, started a teen writing group which I joined. We met in a cafe every week, surrounded by a full-fledged hippie and skateboard punk scene, and the smell of coffee. Jodi hardly talked at all, mostly we just wrote. We'd make up a topic like, "my first pair of shoes" or "chamomile tea" or "what matters" and write our first thoughts for five minutes, even if it was stupid or disturbing or uncomfortable. Then we'd each read what we wrote aloud. Sometimes the topic got buried by what was on my mind, and my writing came out about something totally different. But that was all right. The topic was just a tool for getting started on writing what you really wanted to write about, without having to think, "I want to write about my grandma dying. Let's see, I'll start off talking about before she got sick, and I need a beginning, middle, and end, so I guess I'll end with her death, since that's pretty much the end. No, that's too depressing... " Because after you've figured all that stuff out, you sit down and write something totally shallow and cut-off from how you wanted it to be. Or you never write it because come to think of it, you suck at writing and it's a cheesy topic.

Instead of giving feedback about each other's writing, we gave "recall." Recall is simply saying back something you remember from the piece. Not: "I liked that part about the guy's hat" but actually repeating as best you can, the words, lines, or paragraphs you remember most. No comments. Jodi has been totally supportive of my decision to unschool, and although she doesn't do writing group anymore, she's agreed to keep helping me with writing on a one-on-one basis.

In *GWS* #40, Evelyn Tate said that her teenaged daughter Amy had several younger pen pals. She illustrated her letters to them, and planned to start writing stories for them in response to their letters. Janey Smith wrote about her daughter in

GWS #43:

Lindsey (almost thirteen) decided to enter an essay contest for a women's fair at the University. She was to pick a contemporary woman who she thought would find a place in future history. She chose Margaret Thatcher, read a difficult biography of her, had to figure out lots of stuff about British government, wrote the essay, and won first prize. This consumed her interest for a couple of weeks.

Katherine Houk describes her fifteen-year-old daughter Tahra's literary endeavors in *GWS* #43:

She worked with some film-makers as production assistant on a HUD film about housing discrimination.

The rest of her time was devoted to reading a tremendous variety of books, writing her poetry (five volumes!), and working on her music (guitar and bamboo flutes).

In November of this year, Tahra's poetry brought her a paid job! She was one of sixty New York State poets who read their work at the State Museum in Albany. We went to hear her and listened to some of the other poets as well. From what we could see she was the only "child" reading . . . She . . . met some interesting people . . . She puts in countless hours on her writing because she loves it.

English In-Spite-Of-School

Katherine McAlpine is a successful freelance writer who mostly does commercial work. In *GWS* #66, she writes:

Two things made those [high school] years bearable. First, literature. I'd play sick every chance I could so I could stay home and read. Or I'd play hooky and hide out all day in the county library. (Bless those librarians. They never reported me, though they must have realized that I was truant from school.) I read widely and wildly, whatever captured my interest, without direction or guidance. When I happened upon "The Waste Land," there was nobody to tell me what it was supposed to be about, how I was supposed to evaluate it, or that it was supposed to be very difficult. So I read all of T.S. Eliot's notes on the poem, then half a dozen critical studies, then a bunch of stuff on the Grail legend, and drew my own conclusions.

Unschooled writers

Ernest Hemingway said that Beryl Markham, author of *West With the Night,* "can write rings around all of us who consider ourselves as writers." The book describes Markham's experiences as a pilot in Africa, as well as her childhood and teenage years on a remote farm in Kenya. There are occasional allusions to "lessons" to be done—apparently Beryl was more or less "homeschooled" by her father. However, her youth was dominated by more exciting things—hunting boar with spears, being attacked by lions, listening to Murani legends, watching Kikuyu dances, apprenticing with her father as a horse breeder and trainer. At seventeen, when her father moved to Peru, she stayed in Kenya and trained race-horses. Later, she learned to fly. Her writing is graceful and direct, and full of good stories.

Jack London, author of *White Fang, Call of the Wild,* and lots of great outdoor stories like "To Build a Fire," quit school at fourteen to seek adventure. ☀

25

unschooling
foreign languages

WHY STUDY A language? 1. In order to be able to communicate when you travel, 2. To communicate with immigrants and foreign travelers in your area, 3. In order to read (for example: science in German or Russian, literature in Greek or French or Japanese), 4. Because you like words, or 5. To get into a selective college.

Foreign language is not really a discipline of the same intensity as the study of molecules or epic poems until you are far past fluency. As a beginner, you don't study the language from an academic perspective; you merely try to speak and understand it, to use it as a tool. But as you learn, you may wish to flirt with interesting academic questions, like: how does a language reveal or shape the culture it belongs to? For instance, in Russian, the verb "to get married" is different for men and women. For women, the term literally translates, "to go behind a man." In Cantonese, the symbol for "angry" breaks down into symbols for two men and a woman. (If this sort of inquiry interests you, get yourself a good etymological dictionary and investigate your own language. Also read Mary Daly's controversial books—full of fascinating word origins—or Bill Bryson's *The Mother Tongue: English and How it Got that Way*.)

How we learn languages

There may be a lot of mystery about how we learn languages, but we don't necessarily need to solve this mystery any more than we need to know out why we like chocolate. By thinking for a few minutes about how children learn to talk, you will understand all you really need to know about learning a new language.

Any natural language learning starts with lots and lots of listening. Before most people can actually learn a language they need to hear it constantly for days or months. If you decide to start by working with a textbook, fine, but at the same time expose yourself to the sound of the language, through foreign movies, subway rides, college language clubs, whatever. That's the way babies do it, and they're the experts. Don't worry that you can't understand what you hear. Don't try too hard. Relax. Don't worry, be happy.

Along the same lines, many people find it much easier to converse in a strange tongue after a little wine. Under a bit of influence, the conscious mind gives up some of its control; intuition and the subconscious mind rise to the surface. Sentences filter in as a whole rather than as a set of separate words. That's why I thought Russian dinners, soaked in vodka, were so much fun in college.

Of course, I would never advocate Breaking The Law so you absolutely mustn't drink any alcohol ever until you're 21 unless you visit or live in a barbaric nation that doesn't monitor teenagers' morality in this way. I *do* advocate finding other ways to attain the same relaxed, soft brainscape that alcohol can induce. Deep breathing can help. Trance can too, if you know how to do that. Or you can try simply listening to music or dancing rhythmically or staring at a candle flame. In general, you want the linear, logical left brain to recede, so the fuzzy, intuitive right brain can rise. Once you're in that frame of mind, go ahead and talk.

Language for travel

If travel is your reason for learning, you don't need to learn until you actually arrive in a new country—if you have plenty of time, that is. Certainly the most exciting and vivid way to learn a language is to use it because you need it. If you like this idea, you can try several approaches:

- Find out about language schools in the country you will visit, and plan to enroll as soon as you arrive. Often these schools will arrange for you to live with a family, if you wish. You can find out about trustworthy schools by checking travel guides in the library. Some areas are famous for their language schools. For instance, many people begin a journey through Latin America by spending a month in one of the many Spanish schools in Antigua, Guatemala. One good source of information is the annual language learning programs directory published in *Transitions Abroad* magazine.
- Learn how the basic sentence structure works and how verbs are conjugated. Memorize a few key phrases like "thank you" and "Where's the bathroom?" (This should take a few hours, using a book, tutor, tape course, CD-Rom software, and/or video cassette.) Then take a dictionary with you and go. Panic on the plane and do some more last minute studying. Make a complete idiot of yourself for a while. Don't hang around with other English speaking people. From personal experience, I highly recommend this method. In third world countries, it's cheap. It's fun. It's life. It works.
- Spend a year or more learning a language through books or other resources (as described below). Once you feel comfortable with your skills, plan a short trip. This method demands self discipline, and is definitely less romantic and effective than the previous two ways. But hey, it's safe. Your school board will approve.
- Enroll in a foreign exchange program. The obvious trouble is that you may have to go to school, which won't be any more fun, after the first few weeks, than school in your hometown. But you can always try a *summer* program so you don't have to go to school.

Language for other uses

If you decide to learn a language for college, "the future," or another abstract reason, choose carefully. This can be one of the more important choices you make in life, since it can strongly influence what you are capable of doing, where you travel, and what you can read. Consider these factors: Are there countries you hope to visit? What languages are most widely used? (Spanish is an excellent choice for that reason.) What are your interests and possible future plans? (If you know you want to conduct research in the jungles of Ecuador and Indonesia, you may want to learn Quechua and Penan.) What languages are easiest? Do you want to learn the language of your ancestors? Will you need to read in a specific language? (For example, German is nearly necessary for many scientists. Russian, French, and Latin are great for literary scholars.) What cultures fascinate you?

Resources

I hope you don't rely solely on books or programs to learn a language; removed from actual human communication, it's no fun and a little bit insane. But in combination with a native tutor or a foreign friend, good resources can help you organize and practice your learning.

- Bookstores and music stores offer a variety of cassette programs that help you to learn a language through listening and repetition. Two programs widely recommended by unschoolers and others:

  1. The Learnables cassette program, developed by the International Linguistics Corporation teaches languages (French, German, Mandarin Chinese, Russian, Spanish, English, and Czech) by having you listen to words and phrases again and again, following along in a *picture* book. After ten lessons, you begin speaking gradually. The program never asks you to read or write, trusting that these skills can be learned easily after you absorb the spoken language. Many young children use the program successfully, which is a good sign that it makes sense—after all, young children are the experts on natural language learning.

  2. Audio-Forum Courses, based on listening, understanding, and repeating. Mostly developed by the U.S. State Department's Foreign Service Institute, these courses come in three lengths depending on how much time and energy you want to invest. Ninety-one(!) languages are currently available. Audio-Forum also sells foreign language games, books, musical records, and videos—language instruction courses, foreign movies, French operas, Tai Chi instruction.

- Instructional TV runs video programs like *España Viva.*

- Bookstores and college bookstores also have various texts for learning languages. You might check to see what books local colleges are using and then look for a used copy.

- A cheap way to get an introduction to almost any language, from *Growing Without Schooling* #70: Contact the American Bible Society in New York and get a Bible from them in the language you want. The reader who sent the idea liked using Bibles because they were inexpensive and full of good stories. If you are familiar with Bible stories already, that will help. If not, find an English Bible (try Revised Standard Version or New International Version) and read them both together. Go for the story parts, like in *Genesis, Ruth,* or *Matthew.* Or get a copy of the $1 Dover edition of *Peter Rabbit* in English, and another in Spanish, Italian, Russian, German, or French.

- For a free lesson in Esperanto, and information on learning Esperanto, contact the Esperanto League of North America.

- If you're interested in learning Latin or Greek, request a catalog from Bolchazy-Carducci Publishers.

- Two excellent books to help you pull together your own foreign language "program" from a variety of techniques and resources: *How to Learn any Language*, by Barry Farber, and *How to Learn a Foreign Language*, by Graham Fuller. Both are packed with useful advice, such as this tidbit from Farber:

> Most phrase books offer too few of these "crutch" phrases. When you meet your first encounter, pull out pen and pad and fatten your crutch collection. Learn how to say things such as, "I'm only a beginner in your language but I'm determined to become fluent," "Do you have enough patience to talk with a foreigner who's trying to learn your language?" "I wonder if I'll ever be as fluent in your language as you are in English," "I wish your language were as easy as your people are polite," and "Where in your country do you think your language is spoken the best?" Roll your own alternatives. You'll soon find yourself developing what comedians call a "routine," a pattern of conversation that actually gives you a feeling of fluency along with the inspiration to nurture that feeling into fruition.

- *Transitions Abroad* magazine includes well-researched listings of good language programs around the world, intended for travelers.

Activities

- Host a foreign exchange student for a year—homeschooling families *can* do this, though the exchange student will go to school. If it seems a bit odd to live with a student when you are not one, you can just befriend an exchange student, or try to set up an unschooling exchange by writing to *Growing Without Schooling*. Danielle Metzler, of Connecticut, writes in *GWS* #106:

> I found learning Japanese without a teacher or textbook to be both challenging and enjoyable. The key was having the right attitude. This included realizing that learning is sometimes hard work. However, it is fun, it is much easier and has a more lasting effect. It also included looking for *every* opportunity to use what I was learning. My family hosted at least six Japanese exchange students over the course of eighteen months. Between their visits I reviewed what I had learned and took in some more information from my CD ROM program and my grammar book . . .
>
> The exchange student program provided a sheet of survival phrases with a pronunciation guide. This sheet was not enough, so one of the first things we did was pick up a very good English—Japanese dictionary. I made sure it was small enough to carry around wherever we went. It had phrases and a pronunciation guide. We also bought a book on Hiragana, the primary Japanese alphabet. Even though there is also another alphabet and pictogram system with thousands of characters, I was still thrilled to be able to recognize a few words now and then.
>
> The one thing that helped me the most was talking with someone who is Japanese. It is essential to understand how words ware pronounced right away. This helps eliminate a lot of confusion . . .
>
> I think homeschoolers benefit by sharing what they have learned, so I did just that. I prepared a three-hour hands-on presentation on the Japanese language and culture for homeschoolers in my support group. Some of the things I shared with them were origami, basic Hiragana, introduction to conversational Japanese, some of the gifts we received from our various students, and the Tea Ceremony . . . Giving this presentation allowed me to review what I had learned about the Japanese and their language.

- Another possibility is to house or simply befriend a foreign *college* student. Contact the foreign student support services at local colleges to see if they can help with arrangements. In *GWS* #87, Nicky Hardenbergh of Massachusetts writes:

If any homeschooling families are looking for ways to get to know people from around the world, they could investigate the International Student Office at their local university or college. Three years ago, my family volunteered to be a host family to a foreign student through the Harvard University International Office. We were delighted with our student, Hiroshi, a young linguistics student from Japan. At our mutual convenience, we invited him to our house several times over the course of the year, or met him in Cambridge. Because he was in a graduate program, he had little time for socializing; my initial misgivings that being a host family would be overly time-consuming quickly evaporated.

When Hiroshi returned to Japan, we enthusiastically signed up to host another student. This time we were matched with a mathematics student from Paris. Once again, we were delighted with our student. My husband particularly appreciated being able to receive mini-tutorials in various aspects of mathematics from Eugene. Since Eugene is in a Ph.D. program, we have been his host family for two years now.

Even though Eugene was still in Cambridge, we discussed with the coordinator of the program the possibility of getting another student this year. When we heard that she had a young man from Beijing, China who was coming to the East Asian Studies Program, and that he liked to cook, we signed up for him. Once again, we were delighted . . .

When ZhenZhou, the Chinese student, came to our house, I could not get over the fact that I had, in my kitchen, someone from Beijing. China has been such a closed place during my lifetime. Now I could actually find out about it firsthand. We have learned so much from him about Chinese history, ancient civilization, and life in Communist China.

The entire host family experience has been incredibly valuable to us. Having someone from another culture for a friend is a wonderful experience, and an immense enrichment to our homeschooling program. You can imagine that we use the visits as times to learn more about the students' countries. Equally valuable, we have become more conscious about the structure of our own culture as we answer our students' questions about American life. At the same time, we have a connection to academia and can find out more about he subjects our students are pursuing. . . .

The coordinator of the Harvard host family program . . . tells me that most universities and even smaller colleges have programs of this type.

- Find out if your city has a foreign language center. Some of these centers not only offer classes, but also host regular lunches where people—both fluent and stumbling—talk informally.
- Find out when a local college or university has language tables. This means that during lunch or dinner in the cafeteria people who want to speak Japanese (or whatever) sit together and try to make sense. Again, some may be native speakers and professors, others will be beginners or merely curious. If you're like me, you think you'd feel way too stupid waltzing into unfamiliar territory populated by people older and smarter than you. Ignore this feeling. All the other students probably feel just as self-conscious as you do, regardless of their age.
- Go to foreign films, with or without subtitles. Better yet, rent a foreign video and watch it many times.
- In *Homeschooling for Excellence*, David and Micki Colfax report that their son Reed (who later went on to Harvard) "joined the local Spanish soccer team, developed an ear for the language, and has had the easiest time of [their three

older sons]."[1]

- Explore the different ethnic neighborhoods of a city. While you're there, eat at inexpensive restaurants that don't look touristy, and watch for opportunities to strike up a conversation.
- As you approach fluency, you can read literature in the original language. You can listen to exotic radio stations on a shortwave radio. You can begin to make linguistic forays into the structure of the language itself. You can work as a tutor or translator (maybe as a volunteer at first). You can work as an American representative on a Russian fishing boat, like my friend Laurachka. You will think up plenty of your own ideas for ways to use and deepen your language skills.

The professors say

In general, they say that *if you want to learn a language in an academic setting, you have to know English grammar.* If yours needs help, use a good text like Warriner's *English Grammar and Composition.* (For most people there's no reason to bother studying English grammar *unless* they want to learn a foreign language in a methodical, academic way.) Nancy Saporta Sternbach, Assistant Professor of Spanish at Smith College, writes:

> What we like best in our first-year students is the ability to think, the motivation to study and the desire to learn Spanish. Generally we find that a student who writes well, and is well-read, in English has less trouble translating those skills to a foreign language than the ones who also have trouble writing in English or whose grammar background in English is weak.
>
> Of course, we teach many levels of Spanish, even to our first-year students, depending on how much Spanish they've had before and how well they do on the placement exam (which consists of a grammar section, a listening comprehension and a composition) they take when they arrive. Some, who have studied many years of Spanish, go directly into a literature class. Others find a review of grammar useful. Still others will want to perfect speaking and writing skills in a conversation class. But, for beginners in the language we recommend a good grasp of the concepts of grammar (i.e. knowing what verb tenses and the parts of speech are, and how to use them correctly) in their own language, and the willingness to study in order to learn.

Richard Sheldon, of Dartmouth's Russian department, advises:

> I would say that the most important thing for success in our Russian classes is a knowledge of English grammar. I'll never forget the day I was talking blithely about direct objects only to have a student raise his hand and ask what one is . . . We have noticed over the years that students who have studied Latin in high school have a minimum of difficulties. Getting used to a language with cases and inflected verbs is a big help. ☻

---

[1] David and Micki Colfax, *Homeschooling for Excellence,* p.93.

unschooling
the arts

There is a vitality, a life force, an energy, a quickening that is translated through you into action and because there is only one of you in all time, this expression is unique. And if you block it, it will never exist through any other medium and be lost, the world will not have it. —Martha Graham

On Halloween I wanted to be Max from Maurice Sendak's *Where the Wild Things Are*. I got sidetracked and sat down marveling at *The Art of Maurice Sendak*. On page 22, I ran into the commentary on My Subject:

"I hate, loathe, and despise schools," [says Sendak] . . . To this day, he tends to look on all formal education as the sworn enemy of the imagination and its free, creative play . . . "School is bad for you if you have any talent. You should be cultivating that talent in your own particular way."[1]

This chapter can't teach you to draw gnarly monsters or sing like the wind. Instead, it aims to help you decide how to start cultivating that talent of yours in your own particular way, and to inspire you with descriptions of other unschoolers' artistic work. It can't give in-depth help with everything; it can't even *mention* everything. The arts are endless, especially because artists are always making up new kinds of art.

General advice and resources

Find out what your city offers. Call your city council or chamber of commerce and ask them to mail you information on local arts. If you have a center for the performing arts, put your name on their mailing list.

Don't divorce art from the rest of your life. Remember that decorating your bedroom, planting a garden, playing your harmonica at sunset, making cards for your friends, painting a mural on the garage, singing a lullaby to your sister, making up dances in your basement, and arranging vegetables on a plate are all worthy of your most impassioned artistic efforts. If art does not serve to make life more meaningful, it is empty.

If you have talent, dedication, and a unique approach, you may want to consider going into business as an artist—a photographer or drummer or candlestick maker.

---

[1] *The Art of Maurice Sendak*, by Selma G. Lanes.

Most of this book's relevant information is in Chapter 36, but if you want to look for nationwide jobs or contracts, you may also want to use one of the market guides published by Writer's Digest. They include *Photographer's Market, Artist's and Graphic Designer's Market, Songwriter's Market,* etc. Each is updated annually and lists thousands of publishers, magazines, movie makers, poster companies, and others who buy art. Also, these guides give valuable advice on marketing (selling) your work.

The various editions of the Whole Earth Catalog do an exceptional job of pointing out excellent books and magazines for artists and craftspeople.

Write Dover for their free art catalogs. Dover publishes dozens of cheap copyright-free books of design which you can use to inspire your pottery, quilts, greeting cards, etc. A couple that I use and love are *Ancient Egyptian Designs for Artists and Craftspeople* and *Traditional Japanese Crest Designs.*

See if any universities or colleges near you have arts programs open to the public. The University of Oregon, for example, operates a wonderful Craft Center with high quality, low cost classes in photography, jewelry, woodworking, stained glass, etc., available to the public. (And remember, even when programs and opportunities are *not* officially open to the public, persistent unschoolers often manage to find their way in.)

Art Camps

Spending a week or so with other people who love the same art or craft that you do, working with a skilled teacher, is an ecstatic way to develop your talents whether you are a beginner or professional. There are hundreds of arts, performing arts, and crafts camps and retreats. Find out about one related to your interest by browsing the Internet, reading the ads in arts magazines, asking in art stores, asking local artists and performers. Here are a few examples of highly regarded camps, to give you a sense of what's available:

- The War Eagle Seminar, Arkansas—summer craft programs mainly for adults, teenagers with special approval. Focuses on woodcarving, with classes in carving songbirds, caricatures, animals. Also classes in knifemaking, scrimshaw, stained glass, quilting, etc. Very reasonably priced, with camping possible on the farm where the classes are taught.
- The Clearing, Wisconsin—a wide variety of arts and crafts courses, such as watercolor painting, woodblock printing, oil painting, outdoor photography, and journal writing.
- Augusta Heritage Center, West Virginia—week-long classes mostly in traditional American folk arts, like Mountain Dulcimer, Cajun Dancing, and Blacksmithing.
- International Music Camp, North Dakota—a respected, inexpensive camp for teenagers.
- The Country Dance and Song Society, Massachusetts—traditional and historic English and Anglo-American folk dance, song, and instrumental music.
- The Middle Eastern Music and Dance Camp, in California—teaching and live music by some of the world's best Middle Eastern musicians and dancers. Participants range from absolute beginners to seasoned professionals.

Studio and fine arts

Check out local art museums or art centers. Art supply stores are good places to find out about classes and lessons. Art supply stores are also good places to wander and get inspired by the colors and textures of paints and pens.

Art History

For every reader of books on art, 1,000 people go to LOOK at the paintings. Thank heaven!   —Ezra Pound

Art history means studying other people's art, not doing it yourself. The two activities go hand in hand, of course. Take a cue from Ezra, and look more than you read. Go to museums. If you don't have any museums in Dinkytown, go to the library and look at the oversize books in the 700's section, like *Two Thousand Years of Japanese Art, The Early Comic Strip, The Art of Jewelry, Italian Painting, Turkish Carpets,* and *Picasso: The Artist of the Century.* At a poster store, buy yourself a couple nice prints to hang above your baseball card collection.

Drawing

Realistic drawing skills are necessary for many forms of art, from architecture to sculpture to fashion design as well as making portraits.

For starters, try *Drawing on the Right Side of the Brain* by Betty Edwards, which can turn any patient artistic failure into a modest artistic success.

If you want a class, find one with a live model, preferably nude. Artists need this training to develop a clear sense of the human form.

Os Shepler writes:

I'm sixteen years old and I've been unschooling in Venezuela for six years. Right now I am working towards becoming a full-time comic artist. My Journey began when my mother brought home *The Teenage Liberation Handbook.* This book lead me to Barbara Sher's *Wishcraft,* which helped me to name my goal —to create my own comic book— and to break it down into steps and get the support I needed.

I started my search for resources. At first I took general art classes at a small local art studio (in Venezuela extracurricular activities like art, music, drama, and sports are not offered at public schools but through private clubs). I was really dissatisfied with the results of my artwork and the amount of discipline I lacked. So, I began writing letters searching for other resources and therefore discovered a series of videos produced by Stan Lee. These videos gave me access to such comic artists as Jim Lee, Todd McFarlane, Rob Liefeld, and Will Eisner. I studied these videos inside out and purchased any materials they suggested. I also spent a lot of time studying other comic artists' work. Through this study, I became a comic collector and eventually I started my own business importing comics for other Venezuelan collectors. (Legally, my visa does not permit me to have a paying job, but I may be self-employed.)

Still, my artwork, at the time, was very poor and disappointing. I knew I needed a mentor. Some unschoolers are very independent and don't depend on the 'mentor' aspect of learning. However, I have discovered that my personal style of learning is very visual and I don't learn very well through reading books or lectures. I needed someone to show me the process of creating comic art. I tried everything. I wrote a letter to Jim Lee for an apprenticeship, I contacted graduates from Joe Kubert college, I spread the word that I was looking for a mentor in the comic arts. Finally, by some act of God, a fellow missionary friend of my parents found a comic institution in the heart of the city while riding a bus (very *Wishcraft*ish!). She contacted me right away and I immediately put together a portfolio and showed it to the director of the comic institute. They were somewhat impressed and enrolled me in their Venezuelan equivalent of a B.A. program. When I started my classes, I discovered that I was the youngest student at the age of fifteen while most of the other students were between eighteen and thirty years of age.

All my academic subjects are integrated by my endeavor to create my own comic book. I unschool Writing by participating in the on-line X-Men Role Playing Game (Uncanny X-MUSH), I learn Spanish by daily use, I learn math through my import business, I created a cartoon character for my Boy Scout troop for Environmental Science, I do Social Studies by resolving cross-cultural conflicts in the multi-cultural classroom of my comic school, etc. And Clonlara Home Based Education takes care of documenting all these credits.

At this time, I am pursuing an internship with Marvel Comics because I desire to be familiar with the entire production process. While the industry is experiencing tough times in the United States, in Venezuela it is in crisis! As a student in the Comic Art Institute in Caracas, Venezuela, I and my fellow learners are preparing for careers in an industry which does not exist in this country. Our director and my mentor, Julio Lopez, has told us that the hope for our future depends on a few of us becoming risk takers and starting a Venezuelan production company and thus providing employment for our fellow artists. I hope to contribute to such an effort.

Beatrix Potter said, "Thank goodness, my education was neglected... I was never sent to school... The reason I am glad I did not go to school—it would have rubbed off some of the originality (if I had not died of shyness or been killed with over-pressure)."[1] Instead, Potter spent her time writing, drawing, and studying nature.

Photography

If you're serious, find access to a darkroom. Start your search by visiting local photo shops and telling them what you're looking for. If you can't find one, consider setting up your own and renting time to other photographers, or forming a co-op.

Aside from reading good books and magazines, you'll want to look carefully at the work of other photographers. Every once in a while an outstanding photographer writes a book explaining exactly how he or she made certain photographs. One such book is Ansel Adams' *Examples: The Making of Forty Photographs*. Ansel, by the way, wrote in his autobiography about the end of his school career at age twelve:

> Each day was a severe test for me, sitting in a dreadful classroom while the sun and fog played outside. Most of the information received meant absolutely nothing to me. For example, I was chastised for not being able to remember what states border Nebraska and what are the states of the Gulf Coast. It was simply a matter of memorizing the names, nothing about the *process* of memorizing or any *reason* to memorize. Education without either meaning or excitement is impossible. I longed for the outdoors, leaving only a small part of my conscious self to pay attention to schoolwork.
> One day as I sat fidgeting in class the whole situation suddenly appeared very ridiculous to me. I burst into raucous peals of uncontrolled laughter; I could not stop. The class was first amused, then scared. I stood up, pointed at the teacher, and shrieked my scorn, hardly taking breath in between my howling paroxysms.[2]

At this point, the Authorities invited Ansel to leave school. His completely excellent father bought him a year's pass to the 1915 Panama-Pacific International Exposition. He went every day, enchanted by an organist, paintings, sculpture, and science and machinery exhibits. His first photos—about a year later—disappointed

---

[1] From *The Tale of Beatrix Potter*, a biography by Margaret Lane.

[2] From Ansel Adams and Mary S. Alinder, *Ansel Adams: An Autobiography*.

him, so at age fourteen he persuaded the owner of a photofinishing plant to take him on as an apprentice. He went on to become perhaps the world's greatest photographer, as well as an expert mountaineer and avid conservationist.[1]

Pottery, sculpture, and painting

Again, try to find a way to share the equipment and space you need, through an artist's co-op or through city art programs. Art supply stores are a good place to start asking questions. If you're just starting out in a field, consider taking a class—especially one that lets you come in to use studio space during non-class hours. Once you know what you're doing, consider an apprenticeship.

Filmmaking and video production

An apprenticeship, as usual, is a great way to learn. So is experimenting on your own and analyzing other people's films and videos. An excellent opportunity is your local cable access (or "community") TV station, which provides free training and access to equipment in exchange for interesting work. Like zines, personal Web pages, and other labors of love, public access TV productions are one more proof that some people are really alive, that people take on great projects just because they want to, and not only when they get paid money or when they are competing for prizes and trophies. In *GWS* #25, Eileen Trombly writes about her unschooled daughter:

> Lori had taken a video course at Connecticut College at the age of eleven. Her intense interest in this area caused her to volunteer her services in the filming of several political campaigns in New London, and also for the annual March of Dimes Telerama. She has continued this volunteer work for the last seven years and is now number-one camera person and assistant director for the Telerama. The director from New York phones to be assured of her participation each year. As a result, Lori received a job offer at the Eugene O'Neill Theatre here in Waterford, via the theater director in New York.

A year and a half later, Lori is in college and Eileen writes again *(GWS* #33):

> Lori has already been offered a position at O'Neill for next summer and was given her *own studio* this summer. Even though we're fifteen minutes from the theater she sleeps nights at the mansion provided for the convenience of the N.Y. critics, etc. She often works late hours and is completely immersed in what she does.

Unschooler Andrew Endsley writes in *GWS* #77 that his work as an extra in *Glory* and *Dances With Wolves* led to a greater interest and involvement in film:

> I like behind the scenes work, and I'd like to continue working on the technical aspects of film . . . You meet people who remember you, and they give you a call when they need you on another project. A week ago I got a call from our contact out in Montana. He wants me to work for three and a half months as a production assistant.

A trio of filmmakers who dropped out of high school

Claude Berri, responsible for over a dozen films including *Jean de Florette*, *Manon of the Spring*, and *Tess*. Because he was Jewish, he spent WWI in hiding, an experience which later inspired his first film. Afterward, he had to go back to school, but says, "I was literally allergic." He dropped out at fifteen and worked as a furrier while he took an acting class. At seventeen he got his first bit part in a movie.

John Boorman, maker of *The Emerald Forest*, *Deliverance*, *Hope and Glory*,

---

[1] Information from *Current Biography*, 1977.

and *Excalibur*, dropped out at sixteen and went into the laundry business. After a year he started writing for women's magazines.

David Puttnam, producer of *Chariots of Fire, Local Hero, The Killing Fields,* and *The Mission*, dropped out at sixteen and began working at an advertising agency.[1]

Architecture

Serious learning comes not only from reading and looking at pictures, but also from walking through the streets of your city and as many other cities, towns, and villages as you can get to. Apprenticeships, too, can be invaluable.

In Arizona, you can visit Paolo Soleri's Arcosanti, a visionary, futuristic-looking energy efficient town built on the concept of "arcology," which combines architecture and ecology. People from all over the world pay to take workshops and help with the work there. You can sign up for an introductory seminar; to continue in a longer workshop your parent must participate also unless you are eighteen.

If you're interested in architecture, you'll naturally find out about the work of famous architects and about cathedrals and Greek temples and such. (At the library, try the 720's shelf.) But don't miss out on the beauty and wisdom of "vernacular architecture"—more humble buildings like yurts, log cabins, and English cottages. An outstanding book for starters is *Shelter*, edited by Lloyd Kahn.

Also, for a unique, beautiful, human approach to architecture, see the works of Christopher Alexander, especially *A Pattern Language* and *The Timeless Way of Building*.

Finally, don't miss the "children's books" of David Macaulay—*Cathedral, Castle, Pyramid*, etc. Each shows, in fascinatingly detailed drawings, the designing and building processes that went into these monuments.

In his autobiography, Frank Lloyd Wright writes (about himself), "What he was taught in school made not the slightest impression that can be remembered as of any consequence." Wright dropped out of high school to take a drafting job with a professor of civil engineering, and went on to become one of the world's most innovative and admired architects.[2]

Crafts

The thousands of possibilities include decorating eggs Ukrainian style, knitting sweaters, carving wooden boxes, marbling paper, making jewelry, weaving a rug or Scottish kilt, making a patchwork quilt. You can often find free or inexpensive classes through yarn supply shops, bead stores, etc.—you buy their stuff and they gladly show you how to use it. Be inspired by looking at local craftspeople's work at fairs, and if someone's work moves you, ask if you can take lessons from or apprentice with them.

The library, Dover catalogs, and any edition of the *Whole Earth Catalog* can give you all the bookish support you need to start any project. If you're into funky jewelry or arty clothing, look for the magazine *Ornament*.

Craftspeople often find inspiration in collections of folk art. Some museums have good collections. If you're ever in Santa Fe, New Mexico, don't miss the

---

[1] Information on Berri, Boorman, and Puttnam from *Current Biography 1989*.

[2] From Frank Lloyd Wright, *Frank Lloyd Wright: An Autobiography*.

chance to feast for a few days in the overwhelming Girard Wing of the Museum of International Folk Art.

Aside from the visual art forms I've mentioned, there are many other applications of artistic skills I don't have room or expertise to discuss. For instance, you can design clothes, decorate hotels, be a graphic designer, create animated films, or design wallpaper or fabric.

Liz Claiborne, fashion designer and founder of Liz Claiborne, Inc., escaped school because her father considered formal education unimportant. Instead, she studied fine arts in Belgium and France. She entered the world of fashion at age 21, when after winning a design contest sponsored by Harper's Bazaar, she began doing assorted jobs in New York's garment district.[1]

Dan Casner, twelve, of Wisconsin, writes:

> For Halloween I made a full tracking mask. The mask had a long snout because it was a lizard mask, however I designed it to follow my facial expression and speech. I designed a tensioning mechanism to allow the lower section of the jaw to follow the movements of my jaw both vertically and horizontally. For instance, if I stuck out my chin, it stuck out its chin. If I opened my mouth, it opened its mouth. Also, I've been working on designs for a ventriloquist's dummy and several marionettes.

Performing arts

Good performing arts opportunities in school are the exception, not the rule. However, if your school has one of the exceptions, I know better than to tell you it doesn't matter. My school had one of the exceptions, and despite the rest of the drudgery I endured, I am still thankful for having belonged to the Capital High School Concert Choir and the Capital Singers. When I think much about it, though, I get angry anyway. Music wasn't my first love; dance was. Because I didn't like my school's trendy-girl-boofy-hair dance program, I sang instead. It was a terrific music program—but I wonder how my life might have gone differently if I had quit school and danced my heart out. If your school does have programs you want to participate in, go for it—many states now allow homeschoolers access to extracurricular and arts programs.

Or, find a program elsewhere—a city youth symphony, a good dance school, a little theater, community musicals, an arts summer camp, run away and join the circus. And don't rule out college groups. One of my college's modern dance troupes included two high school students. No one made a fuss out of their age or the fact that they weren't Carleton students; they were welcome because of their seriousness and talent.

Of course, you can study or perform by yourself—break dancing on street corners, giving a violin recital, performing stand-up comedy, playing piano in a restaurant. Or you can team up with friends—as a chamber orchestra, reggae band, tap dance troupe, or theater company. In *GWS* #108, fourteen–year–old Jenny Boas of Florida writes about her interest in circus arts:

> Ever since I was ten, my main hobby has been circus skills, things like juggling, unicycling, etc. Over the past few years I have become quite a good juggler . . . I have

---

[1] Information from *Current Biography* 1989.

gotten to the point where I can keep five balls in the air at the same time.

This summer I had the opportunity to go from where I live in Florida to Rhode Island to be part of a real circus. My family has a friend who lives in Rhode Island, and he asked me if I would like to come and stay with him and his family and be a juggler in the circus that he was producing. . . .

There were people at the circus from all over the world . . . There were about nine performers in the circus—trapeze artists, acrobats, stilt walkers, clowns. There was even one other person who could juggle five balls. He and I would have contests to see who could go the longest without dropping a ball. It was great to have all that competition and my juggling skills improved immensely.

Music

Learn by practicing, experimenting, taking lessons, joining a band, playing your viola with your favorite songs on the radio, composing, singing in the church choir.

Your library probably has books of Beatles songs, Beethoven's piano concertos, and seventeenth-century English folk songs, as well as a wide variety of CD's and tapes.

Don't be stuck thinking the only instruments to play are the ones in school bands and orchestras. There are also pan pipes, organs, dumbeks, harmonicas, marimbas, ocarinas, ouds, mizmars, lyres, sitars, and hundreds of other implements of bliss.

Consider the possibility of creating your own instruments. An excellent resource is Bart Hopkin's book, *Making Simple Musical Instruments*, and his delightful quarterly magazine, *Experimental Musical Instruments*. Fifteen-year-old Saeward Stone of British Columbia writes:

Several years ago I began to experiment with making musical instruments. My primary resources were books and imagination. I also began playing the flute. I then found someone in the community who used to make musical instruments professionally, who was happy to work with me. My first project was a mandolin which I was immediately inspired to play. I then made an acoustic guitar. Presently I am working on a violin, a mandolin for commissioned sale, a rebec, an octave mandolin, another guitar, and numerous repairs for people.

I play flute, whistle, mandolin, fiddle and some guitar. My thirteen-year-old brother plays guitar, piano, five-string banjo, and some fiddle. My ten-year-old brother plays fiddle, and my seven-year-old sister plays fiddle also. We play a lot of music at dances, song circles, Celtic festivals and at home, calling ourselves "Stone Circle." We play folk music—so far, Celtic, Ukrainian, and American fiddle tunes.

In the summer we often make $150 an hour busking at the summer market. We are planning to travel to Cape Breton to participate in music there. My future goals are to build a harpsichord and to travel Europe to learn more about violin making and music. I am also working towards a self-sufficient lifestyle with a small farm and workshop using old-fashioned methods and hand tools.

Stretch your ears by listening to different kinds of music. Try a classical music radio station on Sunday mornings. Public radio stations often offer a wide variety of programs, from traditional Celtic music to Brazilian rock. Phone them and ask for a program guide in your mailbox. Go to concerts. Explore "alternative" music stores.

Learn about music theory and composition, through books or tutors or classes. Try Usborne's simple *Music Theory for Beginners*. The unschooling Wallace family found creative ways to study music in addition to taking lessons from local teachers. Nancy Wallace, the mother, writes in *GWS* #30:

Ishmael . . . is studying music composition with a recent composition graduate from

Cornell. Ishmael adores him, although I have grave reservations because he gives Ishmael so much homework that he has hardly any time to compose. In any case they are analyzing music from Gregorian chants to Debussy to Ravi Shankar, and Ishmael is getting a full scale graduate course in melody and harmony. Mostly, I have no idea what they are doing, with their sequences, modulations and chordal structures, but Ishmael seems extremely happy during lessons. He also takes music theory lessons from a woman up the street and she is teaching him "solfege," among other things.

Ishmael later moved to Philadelphia, where he studied music at a conservatory while earning money by working as an accompanist and stage manager. His sister Vita taught younger children to play violin in order to earn money for art supplies. (Ishmael endured school until part way through second grade, when his parents couldn't stand any more to watch him suffer. Vita never went to school. As the two grew up, both developed a strong love of music. During the year that they were fourteen and eleven, they earned over a thousand dollars for playing recitals and winning competitions. At ten, Ishmael wrote a musical play, *Love's Path is Lumpy, or, Eat Your Spaghetti*, which was produced in Ithaca, New York; Ishmael was the pianist. For more on the Wallaces, see Nancy Wallace's two insightful books, *Better Than School* and *Child's Work*.)

Canadian artist Carey Newman, fourteen, writes in *GWS* #68:

I have taken piano and theory lessons for ten years. While I don't plan to become a professional musician, I have reached a level such that I could work at it if I decided to. My mom has encouraged me to write piano and theory exams before quitting lessons for the purpose of using these certificates as stepping stones to get into the field of music if I were to choose to do so at some future date.

GWS #37 ran a reprint of a newspaper article about an unschooled musician, Gunther Schuller, head of the New England Conservatory of Music. Schuller had quit high school, and commented, "I have the feeling I would not have been a very good music student in, for example, the rigid programs which allow for almost no electives, which some of our schools demand."

Irving Berlin, composer of over 1,500 popular songs including "God Bless America" and "White Christmas," went to school for two years, then quit at the age of eight and took various jobs to help support his family. Some of the jobs had nothing to do with music, but he also sang for tips, sang in shows, and worked as a singing waiter.[1]

Bo Diddley, legendary blues guitarist, dropped out at fifteen and began playing guitar on the streets for tips.

Keith Richards, lead guitarist for the Rolling Stones, was expelled at fifteen for habitual truancy, but went on to an art college where he was introduced to blues music.

Randy Travis, country singer and songwriter with three Platinum records, two Grammies and numerous other music awards, passionately hated school. He dropped out in ninth grade, worked at various jobs and began singing in bars, often with his parents chaperoning from the audience.[2]

---

[1] Information from *Current Biography* 1963.

[2] Information on Diddley, Richards, and Travis from *Current Biography* 1989.

Music books

Mickey Hart, *Drumming at the Edge of Magic: A Journey into the Spirit of Percussion.* An inspirational autobiography—Mickey Hart was a Grateful Dead Percussionist, among other things.

John Holt, *Never Too Late: My Musical Life Story.* A funny, wise, moving account of the way John learned to play the cello in his forties and fifties, revealing a great deal about the process of becoming a musician—*and* blasting away cultural myths about old dogs and new tricks.

Diane Sward Rapaport, *How to Make and Sell Your Own Recording: A Guide for the Nineties.* This book covers just about everything, from cassette duplication to choosing a CD manufacturer to cover design to using microphones and mixers in recording to working with a studio to finding investors to selling your stuff in local music stores and through nationwide distributors.

Acting

The classic book is Constantin Stanislavski's *An Actor Prepares*, designed "to prepare the actor to present the externals of life and their inner repercussions with convincing psychical truthfulness."

Get involved in local theater, of course, but also think about staging your own play. Libraries have books that explain all the necessary aspects, including directing, set design, lighting, costume design, and business. One such book is *Practical Theater: How to Stage Your Own Production*, edited by Trevor Griffiths.

If you're seriously interested in improvisational or stand-up comedy, consider taking classes from The Second City in Chicago, Toronto, or Detroit.

See *A Dictionary of Theatre Anthropology: The Secret Art of the Performer*, by Eugenio Barba, a detailed, bizarre, densely illustrated, fascinating encyclopedia.

Unschooler Emma Roberts writes in *GWS* #68:

> I act a lot in our local community theatre . . . This past March I was in *Brighton Beach Memoirs*. I was the only kid under sixteen in the cast. Being with all those adults really gave me a professional feeling. The adults were so serious and fifty kids weren't running around making noise. I felt that the play was more realistic than a bunch of kids on stage standing around waiting to say their lines. When I am in a play with other kids I want to hang around and play with the other kids and not really watch the play and pay attention. That is nice too, but I don't feel professional.

Georgina McKee, fourteen, writes:

> I have been homeschooled all my life. In the last fourteen years I've done so much stuff I can't even remember it all. I do remember swimming for about six years. I was pretty good and I won a lot of ribbons. Then it was off to singing and I'm still doing that. My choir just returned form a ten-day tour of Italy, where we sang twelve concerts in Florence, Rome, Pisa. . . .
>
> Right now my main passion is acting. I've always been interested in it but never did anything about it until last fall, when I auditioned for a play called *The Snow Queen*. I got the part I wanted! Pretty cool for a first time around. During *The Snow Queen* I wrote a play with my neighbors. I showed the script to my director and she liked it. Later she asked me to help her revise her script for her spring production of *A Little Princess*. (I also got the opportunity to serve as the assistant to the assistant director.) During *The Snow Queen*, I got an offer to take acting lessons from the woman who was the assistant director of the play, but that would have to wait until the summer. In the meantime I auditioned for an opera put on by The Madison Opera Company. I got into that too and got asked to try out for the lead part! I didn't get the lead, but I did sing in the chorus

which was just so exciting! The biggest thing was yet to come. I got a pamphlet about the Children's Theatre of Madison Summer Drama School and was able to get my way paid with a scholarship. So, I got to spend four grueling yet fun and educational weeks learning about Theatre—voice, dancing, singing, the works! The result of our work was a production of *Jane Eyre.*

What do I love about acting? Well, I love having all eyes on me! But most of all I love taking on another person's character. I love watching people and trying to be them. I love being able to do things on stage as someone else that I would not be allowed to do as myself. Most of all, I like the people, the smell of backstage before a show, and the sound of applause when you've done it right. I someday hope to be a Broadway star, then move onto The Big Screen, and maybe even have my own sitcom called "GEORG!"

A few allies

Eddie Murphy, according to *Current Biography* 1983, was an "indifferent student," and said school was "a never-ending party, just a place to get laughs."

Roseanne Barr, comedian and star of the TV series *Roseanne*, dropped out of high school at sixteen. She worked as a dishwasher and eventually started performing in comedy clubs.[1]

And Mel Gibson told journalist Roy Sekoff, "School bored me. I graduated, but just barely."[2]

Dance

Almost half of the unschooled girls who responded to my questionnaire were involved in dance to some degree, and many of them took three or more classes a week. Aside from taking dance lessons, you can audition as a dancer in musicals, start your own troupe, or move to New York to chase the dream of the ballerina.

Instructional videos are one of my favorite ways to keep learning new dance material. Look in magazines or newsletters devoted to your dance form, or ask other dancers if they know of good videos. Unfortunately a lot of videos are really bad and expensive, so try to get a recommendation, or find one with good reviews, or better yet, preview or rent before you buy. My favorite, which is appropriate for dancers of all genres as well as for people who have never danced before, is Gabrielle Roth's *The Wave: Ecstatic Dance for the Body and Soul.*

Don't miss great dance movies like *The Turning Point* (ballet), Carlos Saura's *Carmen* (flamenco), *Blood Wedding* (flamenco), *A Chorus Line* (jazz), *White Knights* (tap and ballet), *Strictly Ballroom* (ballroom), *The Tango Lesson* (tango), and the old musicals, like *The Bandwagon* and *Singin' in the Rain.*

GWS #30 reprinted part of a newspaper article about Cathy Bergman, former unschooler and president of the National Association of Home Educators:

> Bergman said that as a teenager her goal in life was to be a ballerina. "I had to practice six hours a day in order to be a ballerina, which I couldn't do if I was in school. In a home school I could put all my energies into dance. That doesn't mean I didn't do anything else. You are inspired when you have so much free time to learn and grow. Your interest will lead to another interest. My ballet led to reading about ballet, and that reading gave me history. Reading that history led me to study great figures in art."

Of course, there is more to dance than ballet, tap, modern, and jazz. You can

---

[1] Information from *Current Biography* 1989.

[2] "Mel-o-drama," by Roy Sekoff, *Seventeen*, January 1991.

also learn flamenco (fiery controlled passion), international folk dance (lots of intricate footwork), Capoeira (Brazilian martial art/dance combination), Tai Chi (not strictly dance but a graceful Asian movement focusing on the flow of energy throughout your body), belly dancing (sinuous undulation and intricate hip isolations), classical Indian dance (complex everywhere, especially hands and face), square dancing, ballroom dancing, West African and hula—just to mention a few. ☀

sports teams
and otherwise athletics

UNSCHOOL YOUR BODY! What you can do with it in school is nothing compared to what you can do with it on an icy hill or a surfboard or a green field or a horse or a bike or a dance floor. Plus, your muscle tone will automatically improve now that you're not spending all your daylight hours on a chair.

If you're looking for a new activity, don't think that your only choices are the things you used to do in gym class. Consider walking or skipping or running or biking to work, yoga, gardening, hiking, climbing, skiing, rollerblading, kayaking, dancing, tai chi, horseback riding, martial arts, trapeze swinging, and feisty teenage sports like skateboarding, snowboarding, or freestyle biking.

If you are serious about an individual sport (as opposed to a team sport), you will improve more outside of school, unless you have a truly outstanding school coach who has plenty of time for you. *GWS* #17 reports that tennis player Bjorn Borg taught himself to play in his childhood, stubbornly (and wisely) refusing advice that he didn't agree with.

Your library has books on fitness (aerobics, yoga, etc.) in the 613 section. The 796 vicinity is sports territory.

Need a team?
Don't go to school but do play on the team.

Many state laws now specify that homeschoolers can participate in school sports and other extracurricular activities. Even when they don't, exceptions are often made or found. *GWS* #69 tells about an unschooled sixteen-year-old in Vermont who participated in his district's cross country meets. At one point, he ran up against a legal technicality which prohibited his involvement, claiming private schools (including home schools) had an unfair advantage (they could have an intensive training program). The coaches, who liked the kid and thought the rule stupid, started working to change it. He skied too. Since the ski coaches also liked having him around, they let him participate through another technicality in the rules—a special guest category.

In *GWS* #78, Gretchen Spicer writes about her daughter Jessie's involvement in a high school gymnastics team. In ninth grade, Jessie decided to go to school for the first time, in order to be on the team. She did well in school, but decided not to return for tenth grade—among other things, she felt alienated from her family, and had to drop piano lessons and some of her ballet lessons in order to make time for school. The Wisconsin Interscholastic Athletic Association refused to let her participate on the gymnastics team as a homeschooler, but they finally worked out a compromise. Gretchen explains:

> They are willing to consider her a transfer student. She can transfer to the school one week before the first meet, take twenty hours of electives, and thereby be there for the time needed to be allowed to play on the team. She doesn't have to take core subjects, and she can arrange it any way she wants—three full days a week, or four hours a day, five days a week. She'll continue this through the gymnastics season and then leave, and for now, she can go to practices without going to school at all.
>
> At first we were angry about this. It seemed ridiculous for her to have to spend all that time there doing things that have nothing to do with being on the gymnastics team. But she feels OK about it for now, because it's better than going full-time, and she'll take some things she wants, like an art class and driver's education, and she can take study halls. We're not finished fighting this, but for the time being we can live with this compromise.

Jesse Schwerin, fifteen, ran on a school cross country team. His mother Virginia writes in *GWS* #77:

> I ended up writing to the school and telling them what we were going to do—I didn't ask permission. I just wrote the athletic director of the school and said, "My son is a home-study student in the Lenox School District, and he's qualified for sporting events, and he will be joining the cross-country team." The people in the athletic department were encouraging—there was no problem at all.

If yours is an individual sport, like tennis, maybe you could train on your own but join a school team for tournaments.

Join a non-school team—through a community league, community college, private school, or church league.

Start your own team of unschoolers and dropouts. If there are enough of you, start a league. Experiment with coaching yourselves and each other—an excellent experiment in self-directed learning. *GWS* #97 reports that Oskars Rieksts of Pennsylvania, a homeschooling father with a fifteen-year-old son, formed a homeschool basketball team because they found no other available opportunities. It developed gradually—the first year they had seven people aged eleven to seventeen, with a wide range of abilities. "We only practice about once a week," wrote Oskars, "Not as often as a regular high school team, but I like the homeschooling aspect of it—I tell them things they can practice at home, and many of them are very self-motivated about that." By the team's third year, they had enough players for three teams—one for seven- to ten-year-olds, one for ten- to thirteen-year-olds, and one for high school aged people. They played small Christian schools and planned to organize a homeschool basketball round-robin. "We chose basketball primarily because it was my son's interest, but we also liked the fact that you only need five players for a team. So you don't need too many kids to get something like this going."

Another Colorado family, with an eighth-grade aged son, started a volleyball team and then added other sports too: soccer, softball, and basketball. They played in a Christian schools league—"Although we were playing in a Christian schools league, it wasn't a requirement that the players be Christian . . . We got involved with Denver Parks and Recreation, and when we used their gymnasium, we used it at a kind of low point in the day, when they didn't ordinarily get many people, so they didn't charge us anything for it . . . We practiced twice a week, and played games once a week. That can be demanding, and we did have families drop out, but we always had enough for a team."[1]

Unschooled athletes

In *GWS* #43, Janey Smith writes about her teenaged son:

Seth did an interesting thing recently. He became interested in cycling and joined a bike club last spring. He's the youngest member by far. He trained for a race and did well last spring, goes on long rides with them (25-70 miles, 100 this Sunday), bought some needed equipment . . . This was getting expensive for him, so he made a deal with the owner of a local bike shop to work out purchase of things at cost. He won a summer race and came in third out of fifty (some experienced racers) a week ago. He reads biking magazines and books and plans his training and strategy.

Erin Roberts, fourteen, has played on an AYSO (American Youth Soccer Organization) team for the past few years, and works as a youth referee and a co-coach for a team of four- and five-year-olds. "This fall," she writes, "I will be playing for Boonesboro's Junior Varsity High School team. Everyone involved was very helpful about giving me the opportunity to play on this team even though I don't go to the school."

In 1979, a fourteen-year-old unschooled boy lived at a ski resort over the winter ski season alone in his father's camper, technically under the guardianship of other adults but actually on his own. He was able to ski as often as he wished, and his father commented in *GWS* #12 that he "spent an interesting, difficult, exciting, productive winter there." ☀

---

[1] From *GWS* #97.

the call
of the wild

*Oh yes, I went to the white man's schools. I learned to read from school books,
newspapers, and the Bible. But in time I found that these were not enough. Civilized
people depend too much on man-made printed pages. I turn to the Great Spirit's book
which is the whole of his creation. You can read a big part of that book if you study
nature. You know, if you take all your books, lay them out under the sun, and let the
snow and rain and insects work on them for a while, there will be nothing left. But the
Great Spirit has provided you and me with an opportunity for study in nature's
university, the forests, the rivers, the mountains, and the animals which include us.*
— Tatanga Mani, Stoney Indian

I HAVE ALWAYS been grateful for the trust my parents have given me and my siblings.
My younger brothers started backpacking, hunting, and camping without adults in
junior high. I first backpacked without adults at sixteen—me and the two little
brothers in the Sawtooth range. Richard dropped a big rock on his foot so Ned and I
took turns carrying his pack. We all drank the water without purifying it; we spilled
propane on our shortbread cookies; we brought enough trail mix to feed the world.
We had a great time.

The freedom and encouragement my parents gave us led us all further into the
wild. I took a mountaineering course in the North Cascades and I backpacked alone
in a remote corner of Peru. Ned and Richard spent weeks kayaking through the Sea
of Cortez in Mexico. Richard sneaked around in the Amazon when his AFS host
family thought he was in Guayaquil. He took two National Outdoor Leadership
School courses and now considers teaching for them. Ned kayaked around Greece
and biked through Turkey. My mom worries a lot, but she always gives her blessing.

Most people associate outdoor activities with the heat of summer. In summer
school's out anyway, of course, so people who want to walk boulderfields can do
that and also be a Star Pupil. There are already good books that tell about these sorts
of opportunities, because most teenagers (and college students) can already have
access to them.

However, the summer wildernesses get more crowded every year. You may as
well take advantage of September, October, and the other seven best reasons to quit
school. If you live in a northern climate, it helps to have a big mind like John Ruskin,

who said, "There is really no such thing as bad weather, only different kinds of good weather." Even if you don't want to camp in a snow cave because you're a cold-wimp like me, you will find that spring and fall are enchanting backdrops for outdoor activities, with their slanted light, mating elk, colored leaves, wet flowery meadows. Of course, if you have the money you can always head south.

If you are lucky enough to have parents as trusting as mine were, there's no limit to what you can do. I do have a couple words of encouragement and warning.

First, encouragement

Generally, young people growing up now seem far more sophisticated in some ways than my peers and I were. For instance, they know and care much more about the world, the environment, and people who starve.

On the other hand, I see distressing signals that young people are increasingly softer, more cautious, overprotected by parents and other adults who don't know them well enough to trust them. I suppose it's also a reflection of our society in general, which at the moment reeks of a squeamish "better safe than sorry" mentality, with mandatory seatbelt laws, with lawsuits and sanitary codes and endless restrictions. Gumption and bravery are not especially in fashion.

Ignore fashion. Think for yourself. The wilderness does not come in a Styrofoam package, and you may never make "sense" of it, but so what? If you proceed with care, you are not going to die or get hurt outside. Well, you *might*, of course—but it's far more likely you'll die or get hurt in somebody's Chevrolet. Anyway, neither dying nor getting hurt are anywhere near as unhealthy as avoiding life.

Now, a warning

Do it, but don't make trouble for yourself by going unprepared. If you don't already have outdoor skills, learn them in the company of people who know what they're doing. Take a first aid course. Choose equipment and clothing carefully, so you don't get hypothermia in wet cotton jeans. Don't confuse stupidity with bravery.

Companions and guides

You don't have to take a "course" to learn outdoor skills any more than you have to go to school to learn history. You can simply tag along with experienced outdoorspeople. If you don't know any yet, you can find them by posting a note on bulletin boards of outdoor equipment stores, or by contacting local mountaineering clubs. You can meet them more indirectly by attending local Sierra Club meetings or participating in other conservation organizations. For planning trips and finding companions in other states or regions, use the Internet—especially news groups and mailing lists.

Don't rely completely on your companions' knowledge; read up a bit on your own also. An excellent starter is *The National Outdoor Leadership School's Wilderness Guide*, by Peter Simer and John Sullivan, or *Wilderness Basics*, by the San Diego Chapter of the Sierra Club.

Organizations

If you have difficulty finding informal guides, consider going on a trip with an organization. There are two excellent national schools, as well as hundreds of local ones all over the country. These programs vary from very cheap to very expensive. Some teach beginners; others organize experienced climbers for an "assault" on

Acongagua or Annapurna. Nationally speaking, the two old-timers are still considered the best. They are not cheap but sometimes have scholarship money:

NOLS (the National Outdoor Leadership School) is probably the best national organization that teaches wilderness skills. Through courses that last approximately a month or a semester, you can learn to backpack, cross country ski, ice climb, kayak, etc. The courses themselves are usually extended wilderness trips through stunning areas like the North Cascades, Alaska, or the canyons of the Southwest. You have to be sixteen for most courses, but there's also a course especially for fourteen- to sixteen-year-olds.

Outward Bound is also a good place to learn skills; it is equally known for emphasizing "personal growth"—deliberately pushing the limits of your endurance and courage. Again, opportunities range all over the place, from backpacking and climbing to rafting.

NOLS and OB are terrific, and their instructors have finely tuned skills and charisma. However, you can spend far less money by taking a course close to home, through the outdoor program of a university, the YMCA or YWCA, your community parks and recreation department, or local mountaineering (etc.) clubs. Also look for fliers in outdoor equipment stores. The Sierra Club runs outings both nationally and through local chapters. (If you're an experienced outdoor adventurer and live in or near a big city, you may also want to volunteer to help lead the Sierra Club's Inner City Outings for urban youth, disabled people, and seniors.)

The Hulbert Outdoor Center runs camps and wilderness adventure trips specifically for homeschoolers. Its various programs offer rock climbing, backpacking, journal writing, lots of natural history stuff focusing on forest and pond communities, new games, trust and team building activities, and a ropes course.

For outdoor volunteer opportunities in tree planting, trail maintenance, living history farms, etc., see *Helping Out in the Outdoors: A Directory of Volunteer Work and Internships on America's Public Lands*, updated annually. You do have to be eighteen for some positions, and sixteen for others.

The academic wilderness

You can combine your love of the outdoors with "academic" study; you could spend a whole year strolling the Appalachian trail with Spot and give the school board nothing to complain about. Here are some ideas, but first I must preach:

I have this horrible vision of wandering through the Chiracahua mountains and stumbling on some teenager who read this book. All around him are strange towers of volcanic rock. The sun going down splashes eternity everywhere. He sits hunched under a tree, reading a geology textbook, memorizing terms. Then he gets out his *Appreciating Art* book and dutifully studies the paintings of Monet and Van Gogh. Please don't be him.

Remember that a lot of the beauty of spending time outside is the beauty of simplicity—stripping your life of miscellaneous distractions and conveniences so your soul lies naked, ready to be *touched*. If you are a receptive enough adventurer, you will learn far more from quiet observation than from any contrived academia. Keep these things in mind as you read through the following ideas. If you try to incorporate one or two of them into a trip, you may enhance your adventure. If you try to do it all, you might as well just stay home and nail a poster of Yosemite on your door.

Conduct field research; be a zoologist, ornithologist, botanist, or geologist. Collect, observe, experiment. Ask questions: what does the blackbird do if you come closer than fifteen feet to its nest? Closer than ten feet? (But don't harass.) Record your findings in a notebook. See the section on being a naturalist in Chapter 21.

Read background information on the area you're in. The Sierra Club Wilderness Guides are excellent companions, since they tell all about the plants, animals, and geology of one region. Ask a local ranger station for other suggestions, or check the bookshelves in a local mountaineering store.

Make art. Paint or sketch what you see, or work on another project. I bring embroidery—it's small and it's a nice meditation while I'm sitting on a rock.

Write. Of course, you don't have to write about "nature" just because that's where you are; you can just as easily work on your science fiction novel. However, there are some great role models out there for inspiration—people who write based on their outdoor experiences. Many of the more contemplative "nature" writers, such as Barry Lopez, Annie Dillard, Ed Abbey, and Peter Matthiessen, successfully combine tales of high adventure with profound commentary on life, the universe, and everything. These people do not necessarily do the actual writing while they're out, but they do generally take notes or keep detailed journals. Otherwise, memory fails.

Read. "Nature writing" like that mentioned above is an obvious choice. But you can stick anything in your backpack: Thoreau, Emerson, Blake, Gary Snyder, the *Tao Te Ching.* Anything Native American—*Lame Deer: Seeker of Visions, The Portable North American Indian Reader,* Jerome Rothenberg's poetry anthologies— is particularly appropriate companionship in the wild. In general, go for profundity. Jane Austen's world of social etiquette, delightful as it is, may seem petty in contrast to the mountains surrounding your tent.

If you are interested in the relationship between people and wilderness, maybe you want to conduct a bit of sociology during your trips. When you meet someone on the trail, introduce yourself and get permission to ask questions. Carry out a survey on whatever interests you—why are they there? Do wilderness experiences make them Nicer to their Kids? When they are in an empty canyon is their belief in a God strengthened or diminished? How is their attitude toward wilderness different from their attitude toward their own backyard? Write up your results and look for a place to have them published.

Along this line, you may wish to first check into other people's wilderness sociology. For instance, Joseph L. Sax's *Mountains Without Handrails* questions the notion that wilderness vacations are a privilege of the elite.

Finally, don't shut yourself off to other ways of learning—quiet meditation, fasting, prayer... *stillness.*

Helpful Reading

- Don't miss the *NOLS Wilderness Guide,* or *Wilderness Basics,* mentioned above. For any outdoor activity, these books give important information on safety, technique, and equipment. Also, they teach minimum-impact camping— how to not hurt the wilderness while you enjoy it.
- *Outside* magazine covers a wide range of outdoor activity. Its yuppified, slightly sexist attitude irritates me a bit, but its information is high quality, inspiring, and usable. Also, you can locate all kinds of outdoor schools, expeditions, and

equipment through its advertisements.

- *Backcountry Bikecamping,* by Mike Sanders.
- *Mountaineering: The Freedom of the Hills,* edited by Ed Peters.
- *River Camping: Touring by Canoe, Raft, Kayak, and Dory,* by Verne Huser.
- *Ski Camping,* by Ron Watters, includes the obvious, plus information on building and inhabiting snow caves.

Other excellent books tell about other people's wilderness adventures, explaining in enough detail that you could base your own trips on theirs. Examples:

- *Rivergods: Exploring the World's Great Rivers,* by Richard Bangs and Christian Kallen—exciting descriptions of ten river trips. Stunning photos.
- *Miles From Nowhere: A Round the world Bicycle Adventure,* by Barbara Savage—a young married couple bikes around the world.
- *Tracks: A Woman's Solo Trek Across 1,700 Miles of Australian Outback,* by Robyn Davidson, in which the author travels through the bush with four camels and a dog—inspiring and wonderfully written. Also see the companion book of stunning photos, *From Alice to Ocean: Alone Across the Outback.*

Unschoolers without walls

British unschooler Shawn Hargreaves, thirteen, joined with five other teenagers to organize a sailing trip. At last report they were sailing with the boat's two adult owners, but they themselves were sharing responsibilities for planning expeditions. He wrote, "The experience of sailing 1,300 miles and taking responsibility for the ship and its crew has changed me a lot. I am much more confident and self-reliant, and can work better with other people."[1]

Dan Casner, twelve, of Wisconsin, writes:

Last winter a friend, my brother, and I decided to go out into the woods near my friend's house (they're not much of a woods, just uncut lots) and see what animals we could find. Along the way we learned a lot about other things—plants, and we found a fox den and lots of other tracks including deer tracks. But through all the weeks we went out there we never actually saw a fox, although we always found fresh tracks and other evidence, like leftovers of uneaten rabbit from a kill. We learned a lot about animal tracking. But we didn't do nearly as much as we would like to because my friend goes to school. This year we think it will be fun to try again, and fortunately the lots are still uncut.

So I've started researching. Sleds, survival, camping, winter ecology, the study of snow and ice, animal tracking. My mom still helps me to find people to talk to who have experience in these fields. And I've also looked for information in four libraries, including our home library. Learning to *do* the research has been as big a part of this undertaking as the research itself. Narrowing the search on computer catalogs to headings that were useful—at first I went through 193 titles because I didn't know how to narrow the search I wanted. Asking reference librarians for help and finding out how to ask the real questions, finding that some reference librarians were more helpful than others, learning to skim books and other materials to find what was wanted without wasting time on entire books that did not hold the kinds of information required. The range of books has been quite broad: from *Owl's Winter Fun* to the *Boy Scout Camping Badge Book* to *Winter: an Ecological Handbook.* ☸

---

[1] Information from British magazine *Education Otherwise,* reprinted in *GWS* #72.

worldschooling

*Something hidden. Go and find it. Go and look
behind the Ranges—
Something lost behind the Ranges. Lost and waiting
for you. Go.*

—Rudyard Kipling, "The Explorer"

UNFORTUNATELY, THE WORLD is not a classroom. It is difficult to find *An Introduction to Geography* and other marvelous books like that when you are changing trains in Bolivia or setting up camp in the Canyonlands. Without a chance to do lots of homework assignments on latitude and longitude, unschooled teenagers are surely handicapped and will be uninformed throughout their lives. Some of them bravely try to make their way through the world anyway. It's a wonder they're not all drowned or lost.

One of the more outrageous unschooling stories is that of Robin Lee Graham, who quit school in 1965 at age sixteen and sailed around the world alone in a boat named *Dove*. It took five years and the whole world paid attention. His book, *Dove*, tells of all kinds of things no teenager should be allowed to face—battling loneliness and storms, losing a mast, falling in love in the Fiji Islands, feasting on shellfish in the Yasawa Islands and on roast pig and papaya with Savo Islanders, traveling with dolphins and cats, motorcycling through South Africa. "Was I different just because history didn't turn me on and boats did?" he asks. At the age of thirteen, he had already spent a year sailing in the South Seas with his parents. Then,

> At fifteen I was back in a California classroom, my spelling still lousy, but I was almost as useful with a sextant as a veteran sailor. On our 11,000-mile voyage I had seen lands of unbelievable enchantment.
>
> It is hard to believe that my parents, having allowed me to sail the South Seas at a most impressionable age, could ever have expected me to be a typical American schoolkid, to go on to college and graduate to a walnut office desk, a home on Acacia Avenue and membership in the local golf club.
>
> I am sure Corona del Mar's high school is a good one. For me it was a return to prison. Beyond its asphalt playground and wired fences there were sun-splashed, palm-fringed shores waiting for my shadow.
>
> [Later that year, while making secret plans to sail away with friends, Robin says:]
> School became almost unbearable. It wasn't so much that I disliked learning—for I

realized the need to be at least partially civilized and my grades were average—but that I detested the routine of school days, the unchanging pattern from the brushing of my teeth to learning English grammar. I came to hate the sound of the bell that summoned me to class, the smell of tennis shoes and sweat in the gym, the drone of history lessons, the threat of tests and exams.

Down at Ala Wai harbor it was all so different. I loved the smell of rope and resin, even of diesel oil. I loved the sound of water slapping hulls, the whip of halyards against tall masts. These were the scents and sounds of liberty and life.

[When he actually sets sail for his global voyage a year later, he reports on the first day at sea:] At nine o'clock I forced myself to eat a can of stew and then tuned the radio to my favorite Los Angeles rock music station. It was interesting to hear the news announcer report that I was on my way—"the first schoolboy ever to attempt to sail the world alone." The announcer audaciously guessed a lot too, and guessed wrong when he added, "The most important piece of Robin's luggage is a shelf of schoolbooks."

"Like hell," I told the cats.[1]

When Robin completed his voyage, Stanford invited him to enroll. He tried it, but quit after a semester to start a life of homesteading in Montana. (You can read about that in his second book, *Home is the Sailor*.)

I know people are not used to the idea of teenagers roaming on their own, despite the examples of occasional Robin Grahams. If you totally panic at the thought of exploring strange territory without your mother, independent travel is probably not for you. But if some excitement surges with the panic, maybe you should start fantasizing with maps. No significant legal barriers prevent teenage travel, and if you think you're ready, you are. Yes, tragedy could strike, but no more likely to you than to an adult, and far less likely than if you walked through the halls of most inner city high schools in the U.S. of A.

What does she mean by travel?

She means something in between going to the airport to pick up Aunt Matilda and stowing away on a space shuttle, that's what she means. A drive to Oklahoma or a train/bus/pickup truck/walking trip through South America is exactly the sort of thing she has in mind.

She does not mean going to Kathmandu on a week-long package tour during which you stay at the Sheraton, because she is not enthusiastic about such sorts of travel, and she has read lots of advice which warns her against writing about topics which fail to enthuse her. She figures, anyway, that the travel agents in your yellow pages are quite enthused about this topic, and that you can ask them.

Why to travel and why not to travel

Why to travel: It's cheaper than private school and far more educational. If you choose your destination carefully or stay close to home, it can be no more expensive than public school plus the food and electricity you consume at home. In *The Next Whole Earth Catalog*, Kevin Kelly wrote, "The drifters of Europe in the sixties invented a contemporary form of education: extended world travel. At about $3,000 per year, all adventures included, it is still the cheapest college there is."

---

[1] *National Geographic* ran stories on the voyage in October 1968, April 1969, and October 1970. Also, you might look for the out-of-print movie, *Dove*.

I will spare you a big gushy sermon about the joys of travel, since you can make one up for yourself while gazing at any poster of a market in Marrakesh. I *will* say that international traveling is an especially timely thing to do as we shift into a more global economy and awareness. The U.S. is no longer The World Power. We have no excuse for arrogance. We need to learn from and about the rest of the world.

Why not to travel: because I said to, or only in order to learn about people in other countries because the United States is no longer The World Power. Or because you think it's better and braver than staying at home and paying attention to your carrot patch, 'cause that ain't necessarily so.

Organizations that coordinate teenage travel

- The Center for Interim Programs and Time Out, both described in Chapter 33.
- The Council on International Educational Exchange, which publishes the *High School Student's Guide to Study, Travel, and Adventure Abroad* and also runs various programs and publishes other literature. If you plan to travel abroad, request their free publications list and their free *Student Travel Catalog*. Among their publications are *Volunteer! The Comprehensive Guide to Voluntary Service in the U.S. and Abroad*, and various brochures—on scholarship programs, work abroad, educational programs in the third world, workcamps, etc. They also have a scholarship fund which awards money for transportation costs of selected young people who write a project proposal. (Ask for their brochure on The International Student Identity Card Scholarship Fund.) The CIEE exists "to develop, serve and support international educational exchange as a means to build understanding and peaceful cooperation between nations."
- American Youth Hostels, Inc. Through AYH membership you can stay in worldwide hostels very cheaply, though you are supposed to be at least fifteen to use hostels on your own. Also, they sponsor trips, especially bicycle trips. Write for their catalog and membership information.
- Once you are eighteen, you can go on a short or long seminar trip with the Center for Global Education. This organization runs travel programs completely unlike others; its goals include "introducing participants to the reality of poverty and injustice, examining the root causes of those conditions, and reflecting on the role and responsibility of North American citizens to enter into public debate on foreign policy concerns." Seminars go to Latin America, the Philippines, the Middle East, South Africa, and Hawaii. If you are younger than eighteen and especially mature, you *may* be able to go on a seminar, particularly if a parent goes too.
- Volunteers for Peace "International Workcamps." You must be sixteen or over to participate in a workcamp (and over eighteen in many cases). Workcamps involve construction, restoration, agricultural or environmental work—like landscaping a public park in Morocco, or renovating an old church in Spain. These projects bring together ten to twenty volunteers from many different countries, and last from two to four weeks. VFP states:

> Workcamps are an inexpensive way to travel and a very effective way people can promote international goodwill.... Your readers can live and work in one or several of sixty foreign or American communities for two to three weeks at each site. Our focus is primarily all of Western and Eastern Europe. We offer additional programs in Ghana, Tunisia, Morocco, India and Turkey in the "third world." [Many] people volunteer with

VFP by registering for a number of consecutive workcamps in the same or different countries and thereby spend several months abroad . . . Through tangible work projects, and the challenges of group living, you can create a more positive and hopeful vision for the world and our future. In short, workcamps are places where the power of love and friendship can transform prejudice.

Send for information and a free copy of the VFP newsletter, or purchase the complete workcamp directory, which is published in April of each year and lists over eight hundred programs. Register early—in April or May—to get the camps of your choice.

- To find out about more organizations that sponsor volunteer programs around the world, see Bill McMillon's *Volunteer Vacations*. You'll find opportunities for world-wide archaeology and science as well as chances to help handicapped people vacation in Britain, and a whole range of other choices. Some are restricted by age.
- Willing Workers on Organic Farms is a networking organization that operates all over the world, though mostly in Western, developed countries.
- The Traveler's Earth Repair Network is a networking service for travelers looking for work and volunteer positions in reforestation, forest preservation, sustainable agriculture, permaculture, etc.

Travel companions and other informal arrangements

In the travel department, like any other department, GWS *can be most helpful.* Advertise for unschooling travel partners; make arrangements to stay with people in the directory who list themselves as hosts; simply read the magazine and stumble across occasional opportunities. For instance, in *GWS* #35, sailboat owners wrote in seeking a crew member on a long sailboat cruise through the Caribbean islands, Panama, Seattle, and Hawaii.

Use Internet mailing lists, newsgroups, and Web sites to find traveling companions. Check them out carefully, of course, before you make concrete plans, as the Internet is notorious for its potential in hooking up sweet naïve people with dangerous tricky people.

If you have pen pals, arrange to visit them. See *Geography*, in Chapter 23.

You can always start traveling on your own, staying in hostels, and then link up with other travelers. If you're female, think carefully about the hazards of being female and alone. However, know that in many third world countries you will likely be verbally harassed but not physically harmed.

If you're heading to South America, be sure to join the South American Explorers' Club. The club not only helps people find travel partners, but also produces an excellent magazine, answers detailed questions, and provides maps. Also, they keep cozy offices in Lima, Peru, and Quito, Ecuador, where members can hang out and go through files on tropical butterflies or on recommended local guides for remote areas or on just about anything else.

Mixing travel and academics

First of all, get it through your head that traveling is certainly enough education all by itself. You don't need to cram in scholastic stuff in order to make it meaningful. But a few deliberately added cerebral endeavors *could* intensify your pleasure. Such as:

Go to museums, wherever you are. Art museums, cultural museums, science museums, history museums. Take your time and remember to forget school-field-trip mode.

While you travel, read about the history, natural history, culture, politics, art, or anthropology of the country or state you're visiting. Buy a few books before you leave home, while you're in planning and organizing mode. But also be ready to find more specific good books once you're in a particular area.

Keep a record of your trip in a journal. Consider sharing the journal or adapting it for letters or essays. While unschooler Britt Barker traveled, she described her adventures for her weekly newspaper column back home in Ohio. These columns eventually became a booklet, *Letters Home.*

Keep a naturalist's journal of the plants, animals, weather, and geology of the areas you visit. Make collections of rocks, feathers, etc.—if you feel it's ethical to do so.

Take photographs. Be an artist and pay attention to composition and other beyond-snapshot concerns. Be an eye-opener and capture scenes that most people wouldn't think of recording. Or sketch people, buildings, etc. Always ask for permission before photographing or sketching people. Timbuktu is not a zoo.

Bring a tape recorder, and conduct oral history interviews. Or, simply use your tape recorder to record the sounds of your trip—a train ride shared with goats and farmers, an evening in the town square with kids and music playing.

If in a foreign country, speak the language. Avoid English and speakers thereof.

Before you go, read novels or watch movies which take place in your destination.

Resources: *how* to travel

- *Transitions Abroad: The Guide to Learning, Living, and Working Overseas.* This outstanding magazine is "a bimonthly guide to practical information on the alternatives to mass tourism—meeting people, places, and cultures on their own terms through active engagement in the life of the host community." In-depth, practical articles, resource listings, even helpful advertisements. In a recent issue: over two hundred of the best employers for short-term overseas jobs, how to teach abroad without certification, Tasmania, worldwide travel bargains, the Dingle Peninsula of Ireland, a directory of training and placement programs for teaching English as a second language, eco-education in Wales, conservation volunteer work in the Caribbean, working on Caribbean boats. Highly recommended.
- *The High-School Student's Guide to Study, Travel, and Adventure Abroad,* by the Council on International Educational Exchange. This book focuses on international *programs* that you can participate in. It also talks briefly about traveling independently, and gives excellent details on the logistical headaches of traveling—flights, passports, international student I.D. cards, etc.
- *Work Your Way Around the World,* by Susan Griffith. Covers the regulations for working in various countries, and includes information on volunteer positions too.
- *Classic Walks of the World,* edited by Walt Unsworth, gives directions for walking hut to hut in Italy, circling Annapurna in Nepal, etc. Details and photos.

- *Transitions Abroad Alternative Travel Directory: The Complete Guide to Work, Study, and Travel Overseas.* Extensive resource listings for volunteering abroad, language study programs, high school level exchange programs, much more.

Guidebooks
A guidebook tells detailed information about a particular country or area, including logistics. There are many series and publishers; these are excellent:

- Lonely Planet Guidebooks help with adventurous off-the-beaten-track travel, though the off-the-beaten-tracks are getting rather well-beaten lately. Titles range from *Bushwalking in Australia* to *New Orleans City Guide* to *West Asia on a Shoestring.* (The "Shoestring Guides" help low-budget travelers.) With a nice sort of hippie mentality, the Lonely Planet people view travel as a vehicle for positive social change and learning. At bookstores and libraries, or information and a wonderful free travel newsletter direct from Lonely Planet Publications. Check out their excellent web site also.
- The *Insight* Guides have lots of photos and substantial cultural and historical background, as well as detailed practical advice.
- *South American Handbook*, edited by John Brooks. Fine print, fat, an *incredible* amount of information.

Other People's Trips
- *Maiden Voyage*, by Tania Aebi. At eighteen, sailing instead of going to college, Aebi became the first American woman, and the youngest person ever, to sail the world alone.
- *A Walk Across America*, by Peter Jenkins. Sort of a Jesus-hippie perspective. Jenkins did just what the title says.
- *Across China*, by Peter Jenkins. Then he traveled across China.
- *Blue Highways: A Journey into America*, by William Least Heat-Moon. Heat-Moon went in a car. The literary critics loved his book.
- *Secret Corners of the World*, by The National Geographic Society, describes actual trips to out-of-the-way places such as northern Afghanistan and Tierra Del Fuego.
- *A World of Villages*, by Brian M. Schwartz. Six years through back roads of Africa and Asia, emphasizing encounters with village people.
- *A Book of Traveller's Tales*, edited by Eric Newby. There are lots of anthologies of travel writing, and many are good. This one seems to have the widest variety. For instance, in the section on Africa, you find the words of fifteenth-century Portuguese explorer Vasco da Gama as well as English writer Cecil Beaton describing his 1967 encounter with the Rolling Stones in Morocco.
- *Music in every Room: Around the World in a Bad Mood*, by John Krich. Funny and articulate, focuses on Asia.

Miscellaneous resources
- *The National Homeschoolers' Travel Directory* lists homeschoolers all over the U.S. who welcome homeschooling visitors.
- The American Map Corporation's free catalog offers road maps and atlases for everywhere, as well as a wide variety of bilingual dictionaries, guidebooks, and other products.

- *The National Audubon Society Expedition Institute Program Catalog.* The institute offers a unique alternative college program, or you could simply draw inspiration from their work—they drive a bus all over the country, visiting migrant farm workers in Florida, working on the Green Island restoration project in Texas, talking with Lakota Indians about their political activities, hiking in Yosemite, etc.
- The 917.3 section of your library has an incredible variety of books with American trip ideas. You'll find all manner of books about American exploration—stories of people who've done it and advice on how to do it, general and specific—*Great American Mansions; National Park Guide; Discovering Historic America; Cavers, Caves, and Caving.* In fact, all through the 910's and the 930's—990's you will find books about worldwide travel and geography.

Unschoolers at large
In *GWS* #52, Dick Gallien writes:

Just got a call from Linda Salwen of New York . . . Her homeschooled fourteen-year-old son found the money, which included $500 from the local paper, to fly with his bike to California where he has started biking *alone* back to New York to raise money for either peace or world hunger . . . Next year he is planning on biking in Russia.

In *GWS* #87, Jo Anne Noland of Kentucky writes:

My oldest son, Greg (sixteen), is spreading his wings as we watch in wonder. Last summer he spent a month in France with a French family. This was a wonderful experience for him and his French improved greatly . . . He traveled to northern France visiting castles, tried new foods, and enjoyed vacationing in the south of France with his family. He earned all the money for this trip from babysitting and bussing tables where I am a waitress. At fifteen he flew by himself without a group or chaperone. He missed one plane connection from Paris to Lyon, but solved the problem by catching a later flight and calling the French family to alert them of the change . . . His friend from the French family is coming to stay three weeks with us [this summer] and Greg has been invited to visit them again in August.

Unschooler Anita Giesy, of Virginia, spent her "senior" year working in a grocery store to make money for the next stage of her education, a year-long trip driving around the country. In planning the trip, she writes

When all my friends were trying to decide what they were going to do after high school, I started doing the same thing. Among my friends, there seemed to be three choices going around: go to college, get a job, or join the military. I decided that the military wasn't for me. I thought about college, but decided that this wasn't the right time for me. Looking at where I wanted to go and what kind of career I might want, and thinking of all the people I've heard about who changed their jobs halfway through their lives to do what they always wanted to do, I decided that if I want to do something that takes a college degree, I can get one later.

So I looked at what I wanted to do with my life now and I decided the answer was travel. That is when I conceived my plan to see America . . . Different lifestyles, cultures, and ways of doing things interest me.

I have a good friend in Massachusetts who I met through *GWS*. In the summer of 1987 I went up to her farm for a week and became a part of her family. She taught me about taking care of her horses and I helped out, including cooking, and I went with her to various community activities. After that visit I went up two more times. Five days after I got my driver's license, I started on a two-week driving trip to Massachusetts and back. That's the kind of thing I'd like to do with other families across the country, to come in and live as a useful member of the family. [1]

After this letter appeared in *GWS*, about forty families wrote to invite Anita to stay with them. Midway through her journey, she stayed with me. She told me about other unschooled families and teenagers she'd met—Michael, nineteen, now in college to become a Greenpeace-style lawyer, paying his way through by working in a camera shop and doing photography on the side... Matt, sixteen, a computer hacker and programmer who entertains fantasies of breaking into NASA. And she told me about the structure of her trip. She takes time every evening to write in her trip journal, with the idea of possibly writing a book about her experience. The pace of her journey has worked well—five or six days with each family gives enough time to get to know them. To other young travelers, she advises that the most important thing is to be adaptable, to consider it all an opportunity to learn. "As long as you don't have any particular expectations," she says, "Everything that happens is a bonus." Anita gave me an article she'd written for another homeschooling newsletter. Part of it says:

So I planned it all out and on September 8, 1990 I set off on my great journey. From Virginia, I went criss-crossing the south out to California, staying with homeschooling families all the way. I've been as far south as Florida and New Orleans. Before I'm done, I'll go as far north as Vancouver, Canada. The families have been wonderful and I've been able to live, work and play with them. The first family I stayed with, the father was a potter. The day after I arrived was clay mixing day and I helped mix one ton of clay. I stayed with a midwife and got to go along on a birth. I stayed with a college art teacher and got to model for his art class. Every family is a new learning experience and a new friend. And I guess you could say, I've gone from a homeschooler to a worldschooler. ◉

---

[1] *Growing Without Schooling* #74.

other school stuff turned unschool stuff

WHAT ABOUT THE rest? Health, typing, drivers' education, home economics, woodshop, and of course graduation... Information to help you with all of it waits patiently at the library and in your community. This chapter is just a quick road map. Like the rest of this book, it doesn't try to show *all* of the roads—an impossible task.

Health and sex education

If you have ovaries, look at *The New Our Bodies, Ourselves*, by The Boston Women's Health Book Collective, an empowering, detailed, easy-to-understand book written by women for women. Although its information is not quite the latest available, it is nevertheless one of the best books to turn to for overall information on the female reproductive system, sexually transmitted diseases, pregnancy, childbirth, abortion, birth control, etc. I also highly recommend Christiane Northrup's *Women's Bodies, Women's Wisdom*, and her cassette tape set, *Creating Health*.

If you have testicles, I'm sorry no one has yet written a book as good as these for you. But *Changing Bodies, Changing Lives*, edited by Ruth Bell, is a good sex education book for all teenagers, full of straightforward quotes from teenagers as well as sound no-nonsense medical information. You may also want to see *The What's Happening to my Body Book for Boys*, by Lynda Madaras.

Before you become sexually active, learn about safe sex so you don't become an AIDS statistic. Helpful books are *The Complete Guide to Safer Sex*, by The Institute for Advanced Study of Human Sexuality, and *Risky Times*, by Jeanne Blake.

For a general understanding of the human body see one of the terrific, simple kids' books, like *The Magic School Bus: Inside the Human Body*, by Joanna Cole, *Blood and Guts*, by Linda Allison, or *The Body Book*, by Sara Stein.

If you want to look at hundreds of detailed colored drawings of every human body part and system (skeleton, blood vessels, etc.), see *Gray's Anatomy* or the *Atlas of Human Anatomy*, by Frank Netter. Or get a copy of the excellent *Anatomy Coloring Book* by Wynn Kapit.

For more, the 616 section of your library has books on drugs, AIDS, skin care, alcoholism, and dozens of other health topics.

Drivers' Education

Many homeschoolers contact a local school and easily arrange to take a course there. Most school districts offer summer drivers' education classes which should not be difficult for you to sign up for. You can also learn on your own (with an adult present) by getting a permit and then passing a test. Or take private lessons.

Autoshop, Woodshop, etc.

I'm not lumping these together because I think they're not important; I'm lumping them together because they never fit in school in the first place. Far better to get out and apprentice yourself to a mechanic or a cabinetmaker. Also, there are heaps of books, and classes offered through various community programs. In *GWS* #38, a mother writes:

> My son (twelve) and I are taking a small engines repair class two nights a week, through adult education. This is the same class taught to the junior high kids, but in the evening. We bring our own engines to repair. It is attended mainly by retired gentlemen, but this time my 72-year-old mother-in-law and my son and I add a little variety to the class. We've really learned a lot in spite of all the help we got from these very nice old men who couldn't believe we were capable. So far we have repaired three lawn-mowers and a go-cart. This includes grinding valves and installing new piston rings and gaskets.

John Boston writes in *GWS* #42 about his son Sean, fifteen:

> When the high school would not let him take Auto Shop without signing up as a full-time student, he enrolled in a Regional Occupational Program auto course, even though he was below age sixteen. He now attends a weekly class session, with hands-on training on our old truck and car, and spends three mornings a week at a local auto parts house.

Business classes

Again, far better to learn by doing it. Start your own business or work for someone else's. Good books described in Chapter 36. Plenty more in the library. Good courses on bookkeeping and such through community colleges.

Typing

Typing how-to books in any library; computer programs are also available. It doesn't matter whether you learn on a typewriter or a computer, except that since a computer is easier most people like it better. It *does* matter that you learn the standard finger positions, since you can never get fast with the two-finger hunt-as-you-go method. Yes, it's annoying and slow at first. So was learning to talk, and aren't you glad you didn't settle for a ten-word vocabulary?

Once you can type, learn to use a good word processor.

Home Economics

Home economics, in my ever-humble opinion, suffers unforgivably in school, which ought to keep its dirty hands off. Home economics is about as basic and important as anything gets; it deals with the fundamental workings of our lives: the way we spend our money, what we eat, how we heat our homes, what clothes we wear, the skills we have to help us take care of these things.

Your library has plenty of how-to books to help you learn all the skills of home economics, from bread baking to making your own leather jeans. For instruction, look not only to the community education people but also to the bulletin boards of fabric (etc.) shops and to 4-H groups.

Furthermore, two thirds of the counties in the United States have an official county home economist, paid by the government to help people solve homemaking and community problems. Call your county administration office (in the government pages of the phone book) to find out if you have an economist, and what services he or she offers.

Home economics really is *economics*, in the deepest sense. Which is to say, home economics is about the way your life, food, garbage, and consumption fit into the world. All those popular new books about thousands of ways you can help save the earth are really home economics books—when you decide to recycle your newspapers, buy locally organically grown fruits, and eat less beef, you are making home economics decisions that help the greater economy—the economy that is bigger than your home and far bigger than money.

Maybe you'd like to build a house or two.

To develop one of the ultimate "life skills," learn to shelter yourself. Pick a standard method, such as timber frame building, or an innovative method using renewable resources, such as straw bale or cob or tires. Rosie Records, thirteen, of California, writes:

> My mom was (I think) the first one in the family to hear about natural building. She had become interested in strawbale and told me about it; I'd made a mental note of it as something interesting to try out later, then pretty much forgotten about it. It was still something of a wish to eventually have my own, well-insulated, hopefully strawbale, as-naturally-built-as-possible house, but I didn't start to think about it as something I could actually do (outside of the hazy future) until I went to Not Back To School Camp '96. I went to Kyla Wetherell's natural building discussion and heard about building codes and rebar and R-value, most of it for the first time. And I was inspired by Kyla's solar oven (and the delicious taste of the cookies from it!). I bought a how-to book and constructed my own solar oven out of salvaged plywood, glass, screws, and cardboard, and realized that building was something that fed my heart.
>
> In June of '97 I went to the second annual Women's Natural Building Symposium. With fifty other women I plastered, thatched and sculpted on a lovely, small clay-earth-and-straw (cob) house, and fell in love with the atmosphere of mutual creativity and strength. As a woman, I find the sense of power and self-confidence that comes with building very rewarding. To possess the skill to make shelter is something very special, and it ties in with my love of nature. Unfortunately, I live in the suburbs, so my opportunities for building are few, but I know that one of my main goals is to make a cob/straw-bale/wood/salvaged materials house on my own piece of land, or more immediately to apprentice and learn more of the ropes about it.

Resources

- The annual week-long Women's Natural Building Symposium, an outstanding opportunity open to women of all ages. Information available from Becky Bee at Groundworks.
- Search the Internet for information on natural building to locate nearby organizations and whizzes, as well as listserves and much more.
- The Shelter Institute in Maine offers highly renowned one- to three-week courses, in which you can learn to design and build your own timber frame house—everything from climate considerations to engineering to foundations to framing to electricity.
- At Heartwood, in Massachusetts, you can learn to build a beautiful, traditional energy-efficient home, in courses lasting from one week to several months. Apprenticeships are available also.

Graduation

is one of the closest things our culture has to a rite of initiation. In public school, it's often impersonal and boring, but nevertheless an important ceremony. As an unschooler, don't neglect to find some way of celebrating your passage into adulthood. Of course, your options are endless and potentially far more meaningful than an ordinary "commencement exercise." You could create an elaborate ritual, or plant a tree, or simply let your family and friends take you out for dinner and make a toast in your honor.

In inventing your event, you might research the rites of passages of other cultures, such as vision quests and potlatch feasts. Don't neglect to look into your own ethnic or religious heritage for ideas. Find ideas in anthropological books or see *The Book of the Vision Quest: Personal Transformation in the Wilderness*, by Steven Foster. Or ask a trusted adult or friend to put together a ceremony or ritual *for* you.

Of course, you could "graduate" at sixteen or nineteen—there's no reason it has to happen at eighteen. You might plan the timing around a natural transition, such as completing some major project, or starting to apply to colleges, or choosing to move into your own apartment. In *GWS* #77, Dawn Bowden describes her ceremony:

> It was just my best friends and my relatives and neighbors. Manfred and Barbara [of The Learning Community, a private school that helps homeschoolers] stood up and talked, and presented me with a diploma, and they each gave me presents.
>
> It was so nice, because it was even more recognition than you get when you graduate from a normal high school. They both said something to me; they didn't just say something in general to a class of five hundred.

By the way, there is probably no reason you can't go to a local senior prom, if you are a prom-going type. But there is also no reason you can't organize your *own* elegant romantic dance—an unschoolers' ball. ✸

31

college
without
high school[1]

I IMAGINE THAT Grant, Drew, and Reed Colfax are tired of being invoked as proof that you don't need grade school, middle school, or high school to get into Harvard. So I won't mention them, or Grant's post-Harvard Fulbright fellowship, or the list of other colleges such as Yale, Princeton, Amherst, and Haverford which also admitted them.

Yes, unschoolers can go to college.

We don't hear about them when they go to the University of Montana, and they no longer make a media splash when Harvard welcomes them. Lots of people saw the Colfaxes on TV, but few know of, for example, unschooled Elye Alexander who was accepted both to Harvard and Middlebury College. (His interests included writing poetry and studying insects and birds. Also, he was a state medallist and a black belt in Tae Kwon Do.)[2] There were no talk shows or big headlines when Dawn Shuman was accepted by Bennington, Carleton, Hampshire, and Reed colleges. It no longer an exception or an unusuality when unschoolers get into the most elite institutions, hardly even worth mentioning anymore in homeschooling magazines. Some colleges now actively recruit homeschoolers. Indeed, it's now commonly understood in the unschooling community that unschooling does not, in itself, harm your chances to get into selective colleges. In many cases, it seems to improve the odds: *perhaps* by making an application unique, but more likely just by making it possible for people to get really smart, and moreover to get to know themselves, before they apply.

The hundreds of colleges and universities in the U.S. that have admitted homeschoolers include Amherst, Antioch, Boston University, Brigham Young University, Brown, Caltech, Carleton, Carnegie-Mellon, The College of William and Mary, Colorado College, Duquesne University, Evergreen, Harvey Mudd, MIT, Michigan Technological University, Northwestern, Oberlin, Princeton, Rice, St. John's, Sarah Lawrence, Swarthmore, Texas A & M, Wellesley, West Point, the U.S.

---

[1] Note to readers outside the U.S.: I use the term "college" in the American sense: like a university, it is an institution for higher education usually attended by people approximately 18-22 years of age. (Colleges are generally smaller and sometimes more specialized than universities.)

[2] From *GWS* #75.

Naval Academy, the U.S. Air Force Academy, the University of California at Davis, the University of Pennsylvania, the University of Pittsburgh Honors College, Williams, and Yale. In the U.K., York University and colleges in Oxford and Cambridge have admitted homeschoolers, as have at least two universities in Japan. And homeschoolers have gone on to various four-year colleges, two-year colleges, and art and trade schools in many other countries, including Australia, Canada, Ireland, Mexico, and New Zealand.[1] As our movement picks up speed, good news continues to trickle in from around the globe.

Indeed, the question is no longer "Can unschoolers get into college?" but rather "How can unschoolers best and most clearly present themselves to college admissions departments?" The cutting-edge pioneers in college admissions are no longer mere unschoolers, but rather unschooling test resisters—that is, unschoolers who also refuse to take standardized entry tests. I'm expecting new frontiers in the next decades; for instance, I hope to hear soon from people who are admitted to *graduate* schools without having completed undergraduate degrees.

If you want to go to a very selective college or university and you're nervous about being admitted, I hope the next few pages will ease your mind. First, you should simply know that unschoolers who want to go to "good" colleges and are inclined toward academic study and who are willing to document their work in order to demonstrate their experience and skills to college admissions departments *rarely have significant trouble getting in.* Like their schooled counterparts, they are not always admitted to their first choice college, and on some occasions they are asked to take a class or two at a community college before their application (to the more selective institution) is completely approved, but by and large college admissions just aren't a big stumbling block anymore. If you'd like to see how some admissions directors think about unschooled applicants, read on. In 1990, I put the following question to the admissions directors of fifty of America's most selective, respected universities and liberal art colleges:

> If an applicant to (Barnard, etc.) had completed little or no formal schooling, would you still consider her? I am not talking here about the stereotypical teenage dropout, but rather a creative, enterprising individual who has done one or several interesting things with her time, such as started a business, played in a jazz band, traveled, written comic books, volunteered in a Sierra Club office, or raised boa constrictors. I also mean someone who has taken care to meet your admissions requirements other than attending school—studied English, math, foreign language, science, and social science on her own or with a tutor, and taken AP or achievement tests [now called SAT II's] as well as SAT's demonstrating that she performs as well as your successful applicants.

Of the 27 admissions directors and officers who responded, none said no, although three were skeptical. Most said they would be completely open to such applicants, but that they didn't want their openness to be misinterpreted as welcoming people who had merely "done their own thing" for several years and not bothered to learn math or strong writing skills. Some were already accustomed to the idea and warmly positive. But all agreed, with varying levels of enthusiasm, that

---

[1] Sources: *Growing Without Schooling*, personal correspondence and conversation, the Clonlara Home Based Education Program, various colleges' literature, Karl M. Bunday's Web site, "School is Dead/Learn in Freedom."

they'd willingly consider such an applicant.[1]

Worst first. One rather pessimistic response came from Grinnell. The admissions officer pointed out that he was open to reviewing any candidate, but that the homeschoolers he had previously considered had been poorly prepared. On a similar note, John A. Blackburn, Dean of Admissions at the University of Virginia, said:

> We will consider students who have not completed a high school diploma in a traditional setting. The burden of proof that one has become educated in the areas we consider important is on the student, and it is a difficult task to accomplish. To be quite frank, the students who have been home schooled are often well versed and well read in a few areas, but there often are blank spots in their education. In the cases we have seen, the students usually are well prepared in terms of literary criticism, the use of a foreign language, the study of government or history, but in most cases, their background in science and math is quite lacking.
>
> As we both know, there are not many examples of self educated people in history; Benjamin Franklin is the person who jumps to my mind first, and in his case, I would say that it was because of his strong intellect, intelligence and perseverance that he was able to accomplish what he did. I doubt that the average person in this world could do the same. For that reason, I believe that public schools are essential, for the association with fellow students and teachers and the stimulation that comes from that experience is extremely beneficial for most people. But, there certainly are cases in which home schooling can work and work well.

What shall we do with these responses?

First, avoid the mistakes that the previous unprepared applicants made. If you want to go to a selective college, know what it takes. Just being unschooled doesn't make you Harvard material. It's not that you might not be *good* enough, just that you may not have chosen to fulfill their kind of college requirements, or that you may not be ready or willing to submit to that type of an environment. Also, even if you *are* Harvard (or Princeton, or Pomona...) material, you may not get in. At Harvard, only about one out of every eight applicants gets in, and most of the *applicants* (let alone *accepted* applicants) have quite the list of accomplishments, despite the time drain of school. It may be safe to say that being unschooled makes your application stand out, but it will *not* make up for what they consider a weak academic background.

Second, be ready to educate confused or hesitant admissions people. Tell them explicitly what you have been up to, and take the initiative to politely correct misconceptions. Benjamin Franklin, for instance, is only one of *many* self-taught successes in recent history. Furthermore, most people experienced with unschooling stress that they (or their children) are mentally way ahead of their peers not because of their "strong intellects," but because they have room to grow. Remember that the homeschooling movement is still in its childhood, so college people haven't yet had the chance to see much of what it's about.

And on behalf of these few nervous admissions directors, let me feed you some words of caution. Notice what kind of person I described in my letter. I did not merely say someone who didn't like school and quit. Having been to one of these

---

[1] Also: In 1994, Patricia M. Lines, a Senior Research Analyst with the U.S. Department of Education, conducted a telephone poll of selected admissions officers from large universities and colleges. In her "Homeschooling" pamphlet, she reports that they "indicated willingness to consider applications from homeschooled students. ...some estimated that they admit a handful of undergraduates each year without a transcript."

colleges myself, I knew better.

Most admissions people were quite positive. Robert E. Gardner, Dean of Admissions and Financial Aid at Davidson College, said:

> Like most institutions, we have rules for the masses, and we break rules when it seems just and proper to do so. It really depends more on the individual than anything else; we would consider, and probably admit, a strong person and refuse to consider a weak one . . . Let me add that if a student had been "schooled" at home by one or both parents, presumably in a way that resembled a formal education, although not in a typical "school setting," we would be very interested, indeed. Such individuals are often the yeast that leavens the bread and would be a welcome addition to any educational environment. . .
>
> Good kids are wherever you find them, and it is really too bad so many colleges look in the same places. Given the general state of many schools today, it is not at all clear that all of the bright, highly qualified kids are found within the halls of accredited institutions. For an adolescent to pursue knowledge on his/her own, outside school, speaks very highly for his/her motivation, genuine interest in learning, and willingness to take risks in a good cause. Seems to make sense to me.

Larry Clendenin, Director of Admissions at St. John's College in Santa Fe, wrote:

> It just so happens that St. John's has admitted students such as you describe and will continue doing so given certain essential reassurances that they are capable of succeeding in our rigorous program.

Bates College Director of Admissions William C. Hiss says:

> Bates, like most colleges, has a set of printed admissions requirements that include a high school transcript and a number of recommendations . . . But the faculty gives to the Dean of Admission the right in any particular instance to forgive requirements, including that of a high school diploma if we are convinced the student has proved themselves ready for Bates in other ways.

The Senior Admissions Officer at an ivy league university responded:

> Candidates who have, as you describe, "taken care to meet your (our) admissions requirements other than attending school" and who are presenting compelling admissions cases, in their own right do very well in our admissions process and throughout their undergraduate careers at [our college].
>
> . . . For the majority of admitted students there must be something else [beyond academics] that sets the student apart from the rest. It certainly can and often does fall within the nonacademic realm—a musician, an actor, an athlete, an artist, a community worker, an employee (to name only a few) who puts forth distinguishing credentials within the context of our applicant pool. None of these activities must be school sponsored at all; thus, I do not see the candidate who is not trained within the school setting to be placed at a disadvantage in our process.

The director of admissions at one of the nation's most prestigious technological institutes cautioned that he wouldn't want to mislead anyone, and didn't want the school's name mentioned directly. Nevertheless, he said,

> The hypothetical candidate you have described in your letter . . . would be a viable candidate here . . . Whereas the prerequisites for candidacy expressed in our literature include a year of chemistry and physics at the high school level, and so on, the Admissions Committee will review the credentials of anyone proposing to study here. That is, a diploma is not a requirement and, given adequate basis, other formal requirements could be waived.

Some admissions officers were downright enthusiastic, like Thomas S. Anthony, Dean of Admissions at Colgate University:

I have little doubt that I would be delighted to admit a person [like that] described [in] your letter. Besides, I would like to see a large number of them in any class. In addition to the normal skills required for success in college, people like this would have a degree of initiative, independence, self knowledge and philosophical perspective that would make them desirable college students indeed. I suspect they would also have a degree of maturity not often encountered in typical college first-year students . . .

It may interest you to know that we have had students who bore some of these characteristics over the years. I recall particularly one young man who did attend high school, but he might as well not have been there. After leaving school, he spent three years working on a tug boat in the Gulf of Mexico where he wrote a book *a la' Pascal's Pensees* and went into business selling Mexican food with a member of the Dallas Cowboys. He enrolled at Colgate and after some initial struggles ended up doing very well.

Duke University's Senior Associate Director of Admissions, Harold M. Wingood, says:

Our experience with students educated in this fashion has been very positive. In many cases, they are among the strongest students in our applicant pool. They are usually very well read with eclectic tastes and unusual sensibilities. Because they have been out of the academic mainstream they usually have a different perspective, and can be a positive influence in the classroom. While I was working at another institution, we enrolled a student who had been entirely educated at home. She managed a highly competitive academic setting with aplomb and graduated with high honors. We have admitted to Duke students who have been educated at home, but in the last four years, we have not been able to enroll any of those students.

. . . There is no inherent bias against students whose academic profile or educational environment do not conform to the norm in our evaluation system. We welcome diversity in every form. Our goal is to enroll those students who have the greatest potential to contribute positively to the university.

Mark F. Silver, Associate Director of Undergraduate Admissions at Washington University, writes:

My first response to reading your letter was: "Where is this student? Does he or she exist? How can we get him or her to apply to Washington University?" I am being somewhat facetious; however, the short answer to your question is that we would most definitely be interested in hearing from a student such as you describe in your letter. We have never stood on standard, traditional preparation as the sole criterion for admission. As a matter of fact, a number of [such] students, many from home-schooled situations, have been evaluated and admitted . . .

There are many factors that indicate success in college for prospective students, and academic achievement in a traditional setting is but one. Leadership skills, ability to cope with new and different situations, the ability to synthesize information in creative ways, and a person's intense interest in a specific field all add to the likelihood of their success in college. I often encourage students with whom I speak during my recruiting activities to consider taking a year off between high school graduation and beginning college to enhance just those skills.

Boston University has recently begun initiating contact with unschoolers. *GWS* #79 prints a letter written by the undergraduate admissions office, part of which reads:

Boston University welcomes applications from homeschooled students. We believe students educated at home possess the passion for knowledge, the independence, and the self-reliance that enable them to excel in our intellectually challenging programs of study.

Two homeschooled students currently attend Boston University. One is a sophomore in the College of Liberal Arts, the other a freshman in the College of Engineering. Both students are doing very well. Their educational and personal transitions from homeschooling to the University are a proven success.

If you are a homeschooled student interested in attending college or simply concerned to know more about your options in higher education, we would be pleased to talk with you.

Will unschooling affect your ability to get into college? Probably not. If you were on the path to the Ivy League when you were in school, you can stay on it out of school. If you were planning to go to a state university or community college, those doors remain open also. What may change: you will likely become a more interesting, skilled, and knowledgeable person outside of school, one whom selective colleges will find more enticing. Or, your values may change, and you may decide to work toward something besides college. The worst danger is that your values change and you can't forgive yourself. You may become immersed in new directions and loves which consume your time, but remain tied to the idea that you "should" prepare for college. If your interests and loves are compatible with college, you will have no trouble. But if they are irrelevant to college—say, you spend all your time carving cabinets but you believe you want to go to college and get a degree in chemistry—good luck. You have some serious stuff to solve.

College *now*

An interesting tangent of the unschooling/college issue is the possibility of beginning college at an early age. If you plan to go to college eventually, maybe you would like to go to college *now*. Many unschoolers find that while high school is indeed a waste of time, college skips the busywork and has time to get to the point and beyond it. In fact, this was a recurring pattern among the teenagers who described their lives to me. They frequently led very unpressured lives without school, which gave them freedom in which to develop one or several intense interests. Thus, by the time they were fourteen or seventeen or so, many wanted to be in a challenging, meaningful (not high school) academic environment.

Homeschooler John Waldowski of Maryland, for one, took the GED at sixteen because "he felt it was a waste of time to continue with his high school curriculum if he was capable of doing college level work, especially since his goal is to become a clinical psychologist, which will require several years of school."[1]

Some teenagers begin their college careers by taking one or two courses through universities or community colleges, while otherwise continuing their unschooled lives. Leonie Edwards, who began working as a dental assistant at age fourteen, also began earning college credits through correspondence courses which will apply toward her pre-dental coursework.

Dalila Droege, fifteen, of Indiana, was accepted as a "special student" to Indiana University at South Bend, where she receives full credit for the classes she takes. In *GWS* #84, she writes:

> College is a lot different (and better I might add) than the other formal school I remember. In a way, it is more relaxed and lenient. No teacher watches me to make sure I'm doing what I'm supposed to and being a good little girl. I'm responsible for my own learning. In that way, college is more like my homeschooling than elementary school was.

Some colleges have a "dual enrollment" program, in which regular high school

---

[1] From *GWS* #71.

juniors and seniors (with GPA's above a certain level) take classes both at high school and at a public university. Unschooler Bronwyn Jackson, sixteen, was admitted to a dual enrollment program at Florida State University on the basis of an interview and portfolio. She was allowed to take two classes per semester for credit, and audit as many as she wanted. "The administrators at the dual enrollment office at FSU all know me by my first name," she writes in *GWS* #84, "I've persuaded them to let me enroll in an honors course, and they have offered to write letters of recommendation to the private colleges with higher academic standards I want to attend in another year." (Bronwyn went on to Wellesley College.)

In *GWS* #84, Bettie House of Texas writes:

Recently, my son's education has taken an unusual and interesting turn, which may prove encouraging—even inspiring—to other self-educating young people. About a year ago James, now sixteen, began an earnest, intense study of math and physics. Up until that time, he had proceeded no further in math than long division. In a matter of days, he was well beyond any point I had reached in my formal, traditional schooling. He was definitely on his own. He worked through college algebra, plane, solid, and analytic geometry, trigonometry, all levels of calculus, differential equations, gamma and bessell functions, Fourier analysis, calculus of variations, vector analysis, Laplace transforms, as well as going deeply into the study of physics, including mechanics, thermodynamics, sound, fluid dynamics and statics, electrostatics, light and optics, gas laws and statistical mechanics, magnetism, and other related topics. In his studies, he relied on books he checked out of the public library, the Buffalo Creek Community School library, and books he bought.

After several months of work, James expressed an interest in finding some way of earning credit for his studies as well as finding someone who could guide him further along. About that same time, we read an article in a local newspaper regarding the Texas Academy of Math and Science, a state-funded program whereby students with a deep interest in and a talent for math and science can, by invitation to the program, complete their first two years of college simultaneously, while attending the University of North Texas. About two hundred students per year are accepted into the program.

In spite of the fact that James has had no graded courses, transcripts, etc., since sixth grade, he was accepted by TAMS on the bases of his SAT score, letters of recommendation from three teachers, an essay, a letter from me, a personal interview, and a diagnostic math test designed by TAMS. Instead of a transcript of grades, or any other record of scores and evaluations, TAMS accepted a letter from James outlining his method and course of study along with his extensive reading list for the year. TAMS looks for students with self-motivation. James has thoroughly demonstrated that quality.

Other unschoolers enroll as full-time students in state universities. Mark Edwards enrolled as a freshman at California State University, Hayward, at the age of sixteen, after being homeschooled since eighth grade. His younger brother Cliff entered Chabot college at fifteen, and his brother Matthew was a freshman at Holy Names College in Oakland at fourteen, simultaneously working as a pianist and organist.[1] Homeschooler Amy Hovenden enrolled at Brigham Young University at fourteen. A newspaper clipping from the *Provo Utah Herald* says,

She feels no major qualms about starting college at an age younger than most. "I feel excited and a little nervous," she said. "But I don't see any problems with it. The other students are just people, too." . . . Amy had to undergo nearly three months of intense scrutiny by college entrance boards to determine her social readiness as well as her

---

[1] From *GWS* #8.

scholastic ability. She was thoroughly checked for emotional stability, and was found to be very "balanced."[1]

M. Coleman Miller, who had been homeschooled until he was ten, graduated at fifteen from Hillsdale College in Michigan with degrees in math and physics. "One of the most sought-after graduate students in the nation," he was also "adept at basketball and karate."[2]

GWS #50 reports on homeschooler Alexandra Swann, who completed her bachelors' degree from Brigham Young University at age fourteen in 1985 through independent study. She had started at age twelve and worked for about three hours each day. After graduating, she began work on her masters' degree.

If you want to be at college with people your own age, try this: get about two years of college under your belt while you still live at home and hang out with your old friends. Do this however you want—through a community college, correspondence courses, whatever. Then, when you are eighteen, go off to college along with your peers—but as a transfer student sophomore or junior, rather than as a freshman.

How your mature, unschooled perspective will influence your college experience

First of all, it will help you get into college. Maturity always does. But it will also help immeasurably once you're there. In *GWS* #89, Emily Murphy—enrolled at St. John's college—comments:

> I also found that homeschooling helped me tremendously in my schoolwork, because I have the self-discipline to get things done early. I have a couple of friends at college who pull all-nighters to get essays done that are due at 9:00 the next morning. I find out what my assignments are for the next three days or the next week, and I make goals for myself and decide what I need to do first. That's just the way I work. In my homeschooling, we would make a curriculum at the beginning of the year and then every week we would sit down and look at what I had done and what I needed to do. I would sit down by myself and make daily goals, and figure out things like whether or not I was doing volunteer work that day and would have to get things done around that. So that was very helpful at college, when I was involved in fencing, chorus, and I had a work-study job, and had to work around that schedule.

Colleges increasingly encourage freshmen to take a year off for work or travel after high school and before college. They feel that such a break gives the student a much wiser perspective and greater self-knowledge, as well as a better understanding of why they want to go to school. Also, several admissions officers pointed out to me that their "non-traditional" students almost always do very well. These are older students who have been working or otherwise living normal adult lives for several or many years after high school, and then decide that they want a degree. In these cases, their high school background has almost no relevance to either getting admitted *or* doing well once they're in.

By leaving school ahead of the crowd, especially if you take yourself out into the world, you give yourself a most valuable clear head, a feeling for truth and reality that just doesn't happen until you're away from the world of intellectual guidance for a while. Coming from that perspective, all your decisions will be wiser—including

---

[1] From *GWS* #37.

[2] From *GWS* #40.

the major decisions whether to attend college, where to attend college, and what to study.

But do you really want to go to college?

I wish someone had asked me this question, in a serious tone of voice. At our house it was assumed that one goes to college, and Not Just Any College, but a Reputable and Highly Esteemed one. Had I noticed that I didn't have to go, maybe I wouldn't have. Maybe I would have, but with clearer expectations.

This is how Native Americans answered the question, after Maryland and Virginia colonists offered to educate six of them for free at Williamsburg College in 1774:

> We know that you highly esteem the kind of learning taught in those Colleges, and that the Maintenance of our young Men, while with you, would be very expensive to you. We are convinced, therefore, that you mean to do us Good by your Proposal; and we thank you heartily. But you, who are wise, must know that different Nations have different Conceptions of things; and you will therefore not take it amiss, if our Ideas of this kind of Education happen not to be the same with yours. We have had some Experience of it. Several of our young People were formerly brought up at the Colleges of the Northern Provinces; they were instructed in all your Sciences; but, when they came back to us, they were bad Runners, ignorant of every means of living in the woods, . . . neither fit for Hunters, Warriors, nor Counsellors, they were totally good for *nothing*. We are, however, not the less oblig'd by your kind Offer, tho' we decline accepting it; and, to show our grateful Sense of it, if the Gentlemen of Virginia will send us a Dozen of their Sons, we will take Care of their Education, instruct them in all we know, and make Men of them.[1]

Why do you want to attend college? Will college give you what you want? Are there other ways to get what you want? There are certainly excellent things about college, and many uglinesses of high school have no twins in college. Nevertheless, if you go to college without ever thinking about the possibility of not going to college, it takes on most of the same negative qualities as "compulsory" middle school or high school. *Don't enroll just because it's expected of you.*

Many unschoolers tell me that college is a possibility for their futures, but only if they find themselves specifically interested in a field they could learn best in college, or if they truly need a degree to do the work they've chosen. They often say that they would *not* attend college to learn in a general sense, because they already know how to do that no matter where they are. If they want to write, program computers, act, farm, make music, gain sustainable living skills, or run almost any kind of business, they know they don't depend on an institution for training.

Before you decide, I highly recommend reading *The Question is College*, by Herbert Kohl. Though it is directed toward parents, it discusses teenagers' futures—collegiate or otherwise—with respect and originality. I wish my parents and I had read it when I was seventeen. Another interesting book is Charles Hayes's *Proving You're Qualified: Strategies for Competent People Without College Degrees.*

Here are a few other perspectives to encourage you to think about whether you want a degree. Anne Brosnan, thirteen, writes:

> I really don't know if I'm going to college or not. I might win a scholarship somewhere. I

---

[1] From *Touch the Earth*, edited by T.C. McLuhan, p. 57.

might be busy. I might be canoeing in Canada, or selling hammocks in Hawaii. It all depends. My plans for the future are to maybe be a pianist (therefore I might go to a music college) or a writer/poet (therefore I don't really need to go to college). I could do a lot of things. I'd also want to have a farm. That's easily accomplished without a college education, especially if you can teach yourself through college just like you did high school and grade school.

In *Dove*, Robin Graham tells about being invited to enroll at Stanford after he finishes sailing around the world. He and his wife Patti stick it out for a semester, but then can't take anymore:

> What surprised us most was how little we had in common with our peer group because most of them had grown up in a different world. I had had the advantage of experiences that most people don't gain in a lifetime and I'd seen horizons far beyond the local ball park and movie theater. It was sad to see how some students straight from high school were ready to believe anything and were so easily duped by cynical professors, especially by one Maoist who was passionate about his bloody revolution. The students who applauded this professor loudest were the ones who owned the Porsches and the Jags.
>
> We made some good friends among the faculty and the students. Most of the students genuinely wanted to see society changed for the better. Like Patti and me, they wanted to expose hypocrisy and they despised the brainwashing attempts to persuade my generation that the dollar buys the only important things in life.
>
> It certainly wasn't Stanford's fault that Patti and I couldn't fit into the campus life. It's a great school and we knew how lucky we were to be there. But right from the start we had a feeling of claustrophobia. The walls of the classroom boxed me in so that I could hardly breathe. I began to fear that even if I saw through my years at the university I would be sucked into a life style which Patti and I were determined to avoid—the nine-to-five routine, membership in the country club and that sort of thing. That first semester at Stanford seemed as long as two years at sea.[1]

Anne Herbert writes in her "Rising Sun Neighborhood Newsletter" in *The Next Whole Earth Catalog*:

> I've noticed that when I meet people my own age who seem to have had a truly incredible number of adventures, they turn out to have not gone to college, so instead of doing one thing for four years they started doing two or three things a year as soon as they left high school.

In *GWS* #109, Sarah Shapiro writes about her decision to leave Brown University:

> I was angry at the way [schoolwork and classes] were intruding on my life. I hated them bitterly, and sometimes felt that I just couldn't keep it up . . . I read and reread some of the writers who articulated feelings I have had about schooling, like John Holt and James Herndon. And I heard echoes of many a summer's end: walking into a bookstore or a library as if it were a candy store, glancing longingly at all the books I wanted to read, and knowing that school would take up all the time instead.

Sarah chose to leave college, reassured by meeting people like Susannah Sheffer at *GWS* "who cared about what they were doing." She comments:

> Seeing people who had found 'work worth doing,' as John Holt called it, reassured me that this was a reasonable and possible goal . . .
> Even now, outside of school, I still don't always get to read as much as I'd like, but now it's only because I'm *choosing* to do something else. As an apprentice at a small New England farm last summer, I worked long, hard hours, got to know and care about the people I was working with, caught up on sleep whenever I had the chance, and didn't read

---

[1] Robin Graham, *Dove*, pp. 194-195.

much beyond organic farming journals. Now, working with a group that is trying to set up farms near New York City, planting bulbs in urban gardens, juggling, helping a friend with her Jewish after-school program, sitting in on geology lectures at Columbia University, helping my parents move to a new apartment, and staying in touch with far-flung friends, I don't have infinite time either, but I have managed to sit down with some good books, from Russian novels to treatises on geology.

I feel very lucky to have this time in my life, without many responsibilities, in which to learn about things I care about. I've found that most of the people I want to learn from don't care a bit about whether or not I'm in school or have a college degree and are happy that I'm interested in their work. When I called to offer my help to Just Food, an organization trying to promote community supported agriculture near New York City, they were mainly interested in my farming experience. They did ask me if I was in school, and I told them I was learning in a different way, by finding people who were doing work that I thought was important and trying to make myself helpful. I was plagiarizing from John Holt, but under the circumstances I didn't think he'd mind at all.

I'm considering the possibility that it might be useful to me someday to have that piece of paper that says I have been through college and that it would make my family feel more comfortable about my choices. I may hold out on moral grounds, though; one way to delegitimize unfair and ridiculous credentialing systems is to boycott them, and the reverse is also true—taking part in them lends them your tacit support. If I decide to get a degree I may try a program at the Regents College of the Statue University of New York, which I first read about in Holt's *Instead of Education*. This program gives college credit for taking all sorts of standardized tests. Since that happens to be one of the meaningless kinds of games I'm good at, I figure I might as well take advantage of it . . .

Meanwhile, I'm trying to make up for lost time in my reading life. Recently, I've been jumping around from Tolstoy to George Eliot to Hardy to Flaubert. One writer I keep coming back to, though, is Henry Thoreau. I vividly remember sitting in a college dorm room, avoiding pressing schoolwork to read him and being struck by the force of a line from *Walden*: "Did you think you could kill time without injuring eternity?"

Sarabeth Matilsky, a seventeen-year-old unschooler taking several college dance classes in New Jersey, writes:

The more I see of college (while taking my dance classes and talking to friends), the more disillusioned I'm becoming. Now that the semester is half over, it seems as though the instructors are trying to cram as much knowledge into everyone's heads as possible, in preparation for those Looming Final Exams. Even in my classes it's happening, as our exercises take on a rushed quality as we start to focus on our equivalent of an exam—a final project. I hate the whole grading thing, too, that everyone is so wrapped up in. I feel so mixed up, because (especially in my Rhythm Analysis Class) my classmates roll their eyes if I say that I like what we're doing. "As long as you get the 'A,' that's all that matters," their comments imply. And I can definitely see how one could be sucked into it all. But I am determined to stay true to myself, and *not* look at a letter as the product of my work. I never looked to see what grade I got on my class last semester. The knowledge that I took away from the class was my reward. I think that if I ever find myself relying solely upon my teacher's grade to show what I've learned, I'll need to completely re-evaluate my reasons for doing that thing. So right now I'm looking deeply into this whole college business. I see many good things, and many not-so-good, and if I ever go I don't think I'll go full time—just take the courses I'm interested in and allow myself to become wholly caught up in them.

Realize that while a college degree definitely makes many *jobs* easier to get, unschooling all the way through your life probably makes it easier for you to make a living out of the things you love. Almost anything can become an independent business, whether in environmental consultation or in teaching and performing with steel drums. If you open up your head you can open up your life. Rather than go to college and graduate school to become a marine biologist, for instance, you could go straight to the coast of British Columbia at the age of eighteen, begin conducting your own research on salmon spawning (investing far less money than you would in college), and by the time you were 22 or 23, you'd probably look far more appealing than laboratory rat-people to the powers who hire marine biologists. Of course, by that time you might have come up with ways of making your research pay you without having an employer. You might even be hiring your own laboratory rat-people.

A degree-crazed society like ours, in fact, is a big cop-out. It discourages true expertise. People are unlikely to ask, "What makes him a knowledgeable person? What is he good at? How is he good at it?" Instead, they ask, "What's his degree? Where did he get it?" That's all they think they need to know. As an unschooled and/or uncolleged person, you will frequently butt up against the assumption that you know nothing. I figure you can nobly accept these situations as opportunities to clarify muddy minds. And after enough of you refuse to play the degree-crazed game, the rules will change.

Instead of college, you could just get on with life—or you could design your own course of study, unschooling your way through college. Kendall Hailey did just that, and wrote a book called *The Day I Became An Autodidact*. If you want to unschool on a high academic level, I strongly recommend using *The Independent Scholar's Handbook*, by Ronald Gross, a thorough guide to conducting intellectual projects without being a student, professor, or research assistant.

If you are interested in the humanities, the most intense college learning usually happens when you write papers. You might want to take a course or two to get a feel for writing papers, and then keep it up on your own, using scholarly journals as a gauge of your own work, sending your papers to scholars you admire or to journals, for possible publication. Also, you could ask a professor for guidance in designing a college substitute program.

Of course, saying yes to college is perfectly fine too, as long as you *think* about it first. Anna-Lisa Cox wrote in *GWS* #74,

> The last time I wrote I was still undecided about going to college. I knew it wasn't my only alternative. I could keep on giving the historic fashion shows I've been giving, or take an internship in a museum leading to a job. But in the end I decided that college would give me a chance to do more exploring, and I knew that's what I wanted to do. So I went through the rigors of college applications and got accepted at the college of my choice. An interesting note: I found that my homeschooling, far from being a hindrance, was an asset. With colleges looking at clone high school students, a homeschooler really stands out and gets noticed. It is true that applying as a homeschooler takes extra work, and just being a homeschooler doesn't mean you'll get into Harvard, but it can give you a valuable edge.

Finally, just as there are lists of people who accomplish all manner of wonders without going to school, there are even longer lists of people who succeed spectacularly without college. As you'd expect, many of them are artists and writers, but they also include scientists such as Jane Goodall, who had no university degree, nor any formal training in ethology, when she began her work with chimpanzees in

Tanzania. (After she'd been at it for five years, however, she wrote a thesis and Cambridge University awarded her a doctorate.) Steve Jobs and Stephen Wozniak, founders of Apple Computers, dropped out of college. Physicist/architect/generalist extraordinaire Buckminster Fuller was expelled from Harvard. A few other people on the uncolleged list include Ernest Hemingway, Paul Gauguin, Amelia Earhart, Eleanor Roosevelt, Harry S. Truman, Lewis Mumford, Ralph Lauren, Robert Frost, Walt Disney, Charles Schultz, and Roger Tory Peterson.[1]

And do you really want a college *loan*?

I am appalled that young people are routinely encouraged to go into significant debt in order to earn a piece of paper, and that practically no one raises any questions as to whether this is a good thing. Many, many people go to college with the idea that they'll be able to explore, discover what they're interested in, and pursue it— only to find themselves far too stressed out and overworked to really enjoy themselves and learn happily, *and* only to graduate and find themselves in desperate need of a tedious job that will allow them to pay off their loans. So, as it turns out, instead of meeting their goal of learning and exploring, they've locked themselves into a straitjacket.

Maybe you *especially* shouldn't go to college if...

You think you might want to run your own business, or work as a freelancer, in which case college is probably the worst possible use of your time and money. Based on my experience, the ideal preparation to succeed in business is:

- Expertise in the field—gained by independent study, apprenticeships, jobs, reading, observing, volunteering, perhaps carefully chosen classes.
- Experience running the business for a year or three, *without* yet needing to support yourself with it.
- Bookkeeping skills—you can get out of them by using simple accounting software, like I do, but it's better to have a solid understanding of how your finances work.
- Experience using, saving, and spending money.
- Decent math computation skills and good "numbers sense." You don't have to be born with it. Devour *Everyday Math for Dummies*, by Charles Seiter, or *The Only Math Book You'll Ever Need*, by Stanley Kogelman and Barbara Heller.
- Experience working (or volunteering, apprenticing, or interning) in someone else's business, not necessarily in the same exact field as yours.

Darlene Lester, of California, writes about her son Ely in *GWS* #100:

> During his years at home he discovered and developed his talent for drawing. He took art lessons, drew every day, and delighted us with his increasing skill. He had a great love for Disney-style art and spent a lot of time drawing Disney characters. He got astonishingly good. At twelve he was earning money doing "quick sketch" portraits at parties. He learned how to do this from a retired artist who had worked at Disneyland . . .
>
> [Later, when Ely started researching art schools,] He found out that they were all horrendously expensive. Finally he discovered a life drawing class in L.A. that was taught by a retired Disney animator. He signed up and made the two-and-a-half hour trip once a week. He met some people in the class who told him about an ROP animation class held at a high school in the area. He signed up for that, too, and said he felt like he was in the right place . . .

---

[1] Sources: *Current Biography, 1979 Book of Lists, GWS* #17, *GWS* #59.

This ROP program funnels talented people into the animation industry by creating internships with the various animation studios. Ely just recently interviewed to become an intern at Film Roman, an animation company in L.A., and he got the internship. He will train there for about a month, and if they like him, he'll be put on the payroll . . .

The beauty of all this is that while Ely's artistic peers are grinding away in universities or expensive art schools, with no guarantee of work in that field, Ely will be busy training in the nitty-gritty of his chosen career.

Steve and I have always told the boys that we've both had a wonderful life, each of us doing what we love to do (and getting paid for it), without having attended college. Instead, we move directly toward our goals with as few middlemen as possible. It was definitely a quicker and more enjoyable way to go, and it always seemed much cheaper. We are clear now that many kinds of work can be entered directly through some kind of apprenticeship arrangement, or through a trade school, or by simply working on your own, getting tips from mentors or books when you get stuck. We are more sure than ever that college is not for everyone, that for many kinds of work it is not the best route, that it is shamefully overpriced for what you get, that it doesn't guarantee you a good-paying job (or any job, for that matter), and that its hard sell given routinely in high school is not deserved.

Mae Shell, of Vermont, writes in *GWS* #109:

When I began volunteering at the library two years ago . . . I didn't realize that it would lead to my first paying job. At that time, volunteering was simply a way of getting out into the world and interacting with other people . . . I already knew a few of the librarians, having spent quite a bit of time in the library as an avid reader. Before long I felt I had carved out a little niche for myself and I enjoyed having a place to go away from home where I felt so comfortable.

Mae also started taking classes at a community college, decided that she wanted to work in a library as a career, and began thinking about pursuing a degree in either library science or literature. But as it turned out she enjoyed her volunteer work so much that she didn't want to put it on hold in order to concentrate on college—nor was she sure she wanted to take on the huge debt that going to college would require. So she kept volunteering—and soon she was offered a temporary paid position, filling in for a vacationing librarian. Soon after, another librarian broke her hip and Mae was paid to fill in for her for another six months. When that librarian was able to return to work, another part-time librarian left for good, and Mae was given her job. Plus, she continued to volunteer, was given many more opportunities to fill in for vacationing librarians, and was also paid to make posters for library events. She writes:

At this point, I see no reason to go to college . . . When I decided to pursue becoming a librarian, I knew that in order to really succeed, I would have to get at least a B.A. and probably an M.A. as well. I didn't really want to go to college; academia has never appealed to me, and after taking the classes at the community college, I saw how diminished my usual creative writing became when I was being assigned papers to write. I got burned out doing the assignments, and had little or no energy for writing essays and poems on my own. I have always loved to read and write, but somehow, being forced to do those things and to do them within rigid guidelines took all the fun and adventure out of it. As a lifelong unschooler, I have always felt that it is real skills, and not a piece of paper, that defines how much a person knows in any particular area. I felt that going to college to get a degree so that I could work in a library was backwards; wouldn't I surely learn more about how libraries work by working in a library?

[Mae explains that she nevertheless considered taking a few courses one semester at

Burlington College.] But as September rapidly approached, I began to realize that I really didn't want to take classes; what I really wanted was to continue working and volunteering at the library and to pursue writing on my own time. Things have turned out wonderfully—that is exactly what I am now doing . . .

I have seen in the last few years how good hard work, commitment, and dedication can show people that I am genuinely capable of doing the things I enjoy and of being successful as well . . . I hope to find success without going into debt paying for college. So far, I have. In this day and age, when people who have Ph.D.'s write into Ann Landers and Dear Abby complaining about not being able to find work, I wonder how much a college education means anyway. If you learn from it, then it is worth something. But if it is just a piece of paper, then it means nothing . . . My idea of utopia is a society in which people are judged by their expertise, by what they have actually done and what they can do.

Some collegiate options

Even if you are certain you want a degree, you need not earn it in the standard expensive age-18-to-22 method. Here are a few alternative paths you might consider:

Investigate the tricky underground ways to get a degree with far less time and money than most colleges require. You can replace from one to four years of normal college with independent study—correspondence courses, colleges that give credit for life experience, and passing tests that earn you credits. If you want to look into these alleyways, see *Bear's Guide to Non-Traditional College Degrees,* by John Bear, which is updated frequently, steers you away from scams, and probably waits this very moment in the reference section of your library. You may also want to earn credits or a whole degree via the Internet, in which case you should search the Internet itself for information; also see *The Electronic University,* published by Peterson's Guides.

GWS #18 tells about Emil Berendt, a sixteen-year-old who finished his B.S. before he graduated from high school, by studying at home and passing exams. Kirsten Shepler of Venezuela was accepted to Goddard college in Vermont, even though she refused to take the SAT. In *GWS* #106, she writes:

When I made the decision to homeschool, my views on many subjects changed, one of which was my view on college. After having the freedom of designing my own education and learning through experience, I just couldn't see myself choosing to go back to an imposed curriculum . . . Goddard College's off-campus program combines experience with academic study and offers the security of a degree. Students use campus facilities and resources only during the week-long on-campus residencies that begin each semester. At those residencies, students plan large-scale full-semester independent study. After the residencies, they carry out their study plans in the field, keeping in touch with their faculty members through correspondence every three weeks. Goddard College uses student- and faculty-written evaluation reports instead of grades.

[Goddard normally admits only people over 25, but Kirsten explains:] Goddard was willing to consider me for their off-campus program because of my homeschooling endeavors. Therefore, I stressed my homeschooling philosophy when applying . . . At the end of my interview, the interviewer told me that letting a seventeen year old enter the off-campus program was very unusual but she felt that I was prepared.

If you have no idea where you want your life to go, put college on hold. In the meantime, travel, work, continue to learn on your own. You might want to use the help of the Center for Interim Programs.

Make a point of knowing about all kinds of colleges. Coming from your unschooling perspective, you may want to look into "alternative" schools such as

Evergreen, Prescott, Antioch, St John's, Naropa, Deep Springs, or The Audubon Society Expedition Institute. (None of these, by the way, have much in common with each other.) Also, look into specialized colleges like technological institutes (Caltech, Harvey Mudd, MIT), art schools (San Francisco Art Institute), music schools (Juilliard, Oberlin), unique opportunities like the outstanding international folk music and dance group at Dusquesne University in Pittsburgh. Look for specialized guides at the library, like *Peterson's Top Colleges for Science: A Guide to Leading Four-Year Programs in the Biological, Chemical, Geological, Mathematical, and Physical Sciences.*

In choosing the type of college you attend, think about this statement, written by the dean of admissions of a very competitive liberal arts college:

> We have admitted two [unschooled] students, and we may admit another this year . . . We are a rather traditional college of Liberal Arts and Science with an enrollment of two thousand, all undergraduate and all in residence. I mention this because I do not believe we represent a good choice for these kids. We have found that they are accustomed to doing what they want to do and only what they want to do. They have not had to make many of the daily adjustments that kids in public schools have been forced to make, so they have no experience in adjusting to rules, regulations and procedures with which they are not sympathetic. One of these students is leaving to try out a larger university and we will be surprised if she returns. The second student seems to be having similar problems but the jury is still out as to whether he will stay or leave. We are admitting another such student for next September and he appears to be so bright that they are hardly able to measure him! We do not yet know if he will attend, but we suspect that he will not. So the bottom line here is that while we are very high on these kids, we tend to doubt that we are a good choice for them.

Testing and refusing to test

Kirsten Shepler, a student in Goddard College's off-campus program, writes in *GWS* #106, "Because I am a compulsory-school refuser, I chose not to take the SAT. Along with my application, I submitted a letter stating my reasons for not sending the scores." Part of that letter says:

> I believe that schools should not constantly test and measure us in order to rank us. By doing so, they teach us to believe that we *can* be tested and measured, or at least that everything important about us can be measured and the rest must not be important. The SAT *might* measure technical intelligence well. However, tests like the SAT can't measure important intelligence, like our insightful knowledge or our sense of wonder.

There are at least 241 schools in the U.S. that don't require SAT or ACT scores, including the California State Universities and many other public universities, many Christian colleges, and numerous private colleges including Bard College, Middlebury, St. John's, and Juilliard. For a complete list of these schools and a good common-sense pamphlet on standardized testing, contact The National Center for Fair and Open Testing.

Scholarships

Yes, homeschoolers can qualify for scholarships. I've heard of several cases in which homeschoolers were considered for sports scholarships. Unschoolers are as eligible for National Merit Scholarships as anyone else—Joshua Berger, for example, was one of five Vermont National Merit Scholarship winners in 1991, and was admitted to Dartmouth College, where he planned to major in math or physics.[1] In 1997, Adam Grimm of Oregon won a full National Merit scholarship to Rensselaer Polytechnic Institute to study electrical engineering.[2]

Jamie Smith, homeschooled all her life, spent her "senior year" of high school at a community college, took the PSAT and SAT, and then applied for and received two scholarships which paid for her complete tuition and books at the Honours College of Maryland University, where she planned to major in English before going into a career in journalism. In Canada, Eugenie Daignault was homeschooled until Grades 11 and 12, after which she graduated and received a scholarship and two bursaries to the College of the Rockies, where she planned to study medicine.[3]

Getting into state universities and community colleges[4]

Admission to most state universities and community colleges is a fairly cut and dried process. In addition to filling out a regular application and possibly taking the SAT or ACT, you may also have to take the GED and pass it. If that worries you, coach yourself with a book like Barron's *How to Prepare for the GED*—your library should have a recent edition.

Each state has a minimum age requirement for the GED, often eighteen. Homeschoolers are working to abolish this minimum age requirement, but in the meantime you can often get special permission from a schoolboard to take it sooner. Ask local homeschoolers whether they know of anyone who has been able to take it at an early age. *GWS* #27 offers this story:

> Last February, our daughter (sixteen) became impatient at having to wait till she was eighteen to take her GED test and start her course at the Technical Institute (she has decided she wants to be an astronaut!) So she talked me into appealing to the school superintendent for permission to take the GED before reaching the required age . . . As soon as he understood our request he said he would be happy to oblige, and that was that.

For information on taking the GED in your area, contact a library, high school, or community college, or for more general information contact the GED Testing Service of the American Council on Education.

You may not need to take the GED. Most big universities do have some kind of clause in their admissions requirements that leaves room for admitting students with "special circumstances." Of course, if an epidemic of unschooling breaks out (Go team!), your circumstances will no longer be special. I figure having to take the GED is painless compared to having to take six years' worth of school, including a few too many unimaginative exams.

If there's a specific university you hope to attend, write their admissions

---

[1] From *GWS* #82.

[2] David Smigelski, "Teach Your Children," *Willamette Week*, June 11, 1997.

[3] Information on Jamie Smith and Eugenie Daignault from *CHEA News* (The Newsletter of the Canadian Home Educators' Association of B.C.), Vol. 9 No. 2, April 1996.

[4] Note to non-U.S. readers: The information in this section and the next section ("Getting into selective colleges and universities") is written from a U.S. perspective. However, many of the same principles will apply to homeschoolers in other countries. You should also speak with local homeschoolers, who may know more about the situation where you live. If you are confused or anxious about this issue, one of the best strategies is to enroll with Clonlara, the respected international long-distance "school" for unschoolers. Clonlara's diplomas and credentials are accepted and legal in many countries.

department and ask whether they have any specific guidelines for homeschoolers.

Getting into selective colleges and universities

Traditional colleges want their incoming students to have a broad, thorough education. Normally, they measure this education mainly by looking at high school transcripts. Their verdict also depends heavily on recommendations from teachers or other adults, on an application essay, on the strength of one's "extracurricular" interests and achievements, on standardized test scores, and sometimes on an interview.

Do your best to see the admissions process through the eyes of admissions officers. When an admissions officer looks at your unschoolish application, her job will instantly grow both more interesting and more confusing. Without the standard transcript of courses and grades, she will need assurance of some other variety that you are a strong candidate. The more clearly you show what you know, what you can do, and how you've spent your time, the sweeter her job will be. As Carleton Dean of Admissions Paul Thiboutot points out, he prefers students with traditional backgrounds because "The simple matter is that this background gives us the easiest means for evaluating readiness to pursue college study." Admissions people have incredible paperwork, and if tons of you descend on them all at once, it will be difficult for them to be happy about it. Don't be their logistical nightmare.

Nevertheless, colleges are increasingly prepared to deal with nonstandard applications. If you know where you want to go to college, write to the admissions department—even if college is five years away—and ask how they would like you to organize your application. Increasingly, colleges and universities are preparing guidelines for homeschooling applicants. Stanford sends out a form letter that reads in part: "[Homeschooling] students are no longer unusual for us, and several are usually admitted and enroll at Stanford each year. They are, of course, still a small minority in our applicant pool. We are scrupulously fair in evaluating these applicants, and they are not at any disadvantage in the admission process. At the same time, as you may already recognize, these applicants present us with some special challenges, and in what follows I will suggest how your students can best address these issues when they apply."

In a talk to homeschoolers, a senior admissions officer at Harvard was asked, "What is the easiest format for you to review?" He responded, "The easiest for us to review would be some sort of a booklet. It would be like 'My Career in Homeschooling,' something like that."[1]

The admissions director at Washington University says:

> Our only concern in evaluating such individuals has been: Are they prepared to meet the academic demands of Washington University? So, assuming your hypothetical person to exist, we would rely on standardized testing, AP or Achievement tests [now called SAT II's] to evaluate their academic preparation. On those rare occasions that students approaching your description have applied to us, we have often requested a formal interview on campus.

Of course, despite the headaches you will cause, you can also delight admissions people. Set yourself apart from the masses who are only applying to college because it's the next step in a routine they've never thought about. Make the people who read

---

[1] From *Talk About Learning* #10, published by Earl Gary Stevens, 1989.

your application feel honored that you *want* to be at their institution—even though you know from experience that you could choose to learn independently instead.

And make their fears go away. Unless they have had some positive experience in the unschooling department, admissions people may be full of all the worst stereotypes about homeschoolers. They may suspect you of not having any social skills, or of never having heard of Darwin, or of not being able to work algebraic equations.

More reasonably, they may be concerned that you will have a difficult time adjusting to a structured learning environment which is directed by someone else. Delsie Z. Phillips, Director of Admissions at Haverford, speaks for many when she says,

> The academic program at Haverford is structured, and the faculty give grades. There are not other options. It would be important to us to know that the student understands this and is truly seeking the kind of educational framework we provide.

If you don't want to be in college, you *will* have a difficult time making peace with structure. Or an impossible time. Don't be mistaken as to why these colleges exist. Don't feel that they owe you places in their classrooms and laboratories. They don't—but neither should they discriminate against you because you don't have a conventional background. Don't think they should accept you because you're an interesting person and then let you do whatever you feel like doing. By enrolling, you are agreeing to play their game. Their game is a good one. But there are other good games.

There are books devoted to each of the following aspects of college admissions. My purpose here is only to point out the *difference* unschooling will make in each of these areas. If you need more information, see Cafi Cohen's excellent book, *And What About College? How homeschooling leads to admissions to the best colleges and universities.*

Testing

The more confused an admissions committee feels about your day to day academic preparation, the more it will be forced to rely on standardized test scores to decide how smart you are and what you know. Your test scores will definitely be more important than the average school-student's. One dean of admissions writes about unschoolers' tests, "the stronger the better, and the more the merrier." John Blackburn, Dean of Admissions at the University of Virginia, recommends the following:

> My advice to [unschooled] students is to take as many different achievement tests [now called SAT II's] as they can. The normal number is to take three in one sitting, but I would suggest that the student take English Composition, Math (preferably Math Level II), a foreign language, American History, at least one of the sciences and literature. AP tests would be helpful, but since most students take them in the spring before they enroll in college, the scores are not usually available for evaluation. If a student can take a sizeable number of AP tests in the spring sixteen months prior to matriculation, then the admissions office would have the AP scores available for the normal period of evaluation.

You might as well establish a friendly relationship with tests at your earliest convenience, by taking them more than once. Consult books on SAT's, and ACT's at any library—you will find sample questions as well as basic information about the tests. There are many books on studying for these tests. One with a creative, effective approach is *Cracking the System*, by Adam Robinson and John Katzman, which helps you to understand the brains of the people who write these tests.

Some people swear that test preparation courses improve your scores. I wouldn't bother, but then I've always thought standardized tests are fun. It probably boils down to whether they scare you or not. If they do, by all means take all the courses and practice tests you desire.

If you want to be automatically considered in the National Merit Scholarship program, be sure to take the PSAT in October of your "Junior" year.

In any case, be certain you register for the tests you need in plenty of time—by April of your "Junior" year for the SAT, May for the ACT. You can get registration forms through any high school or by requesting a Registration Bulletin directly from The College Board.

References

You will need at least two letters from adults who know you and believe in you. If you were in school, these people would probably be teachers. If you're not, they won't be. Instead, employers or mentors do nicely. Probably, no one in your family will qualify, although many colleges will *also* want to hear from your parents regarding their role in your education. (If your parents have mainly supported you in your own decisions and activities, they shouldn't lie and say they've been teaching you at home. That only preserves the dangerous misconception that people can't teach themselves.) Harvard-Radcliffe sometimes asks for a detailed autobiography in lieu of teacher recommendations. Unschooler Sarah Pitts, of Georgia, went to Boston College. In *GWS* #96, she advises:

> It's a good idea to plan ahead and get letters from anyone outside the family with whom you have extended contact, even when you're young. If you get involved with an activity when you're fourteen and do it for a year, it may be hard to find that person years later when you're applying to college. When I was in ninth or tenth grade I worked as a counselor with my county 4-H group. At the end of the summer the counselor wrote me a letter thanking me, and we copied that and sent it to the colleges. It would have been hard to track her down later if I hadn't gotten the letter at the time.

Interview

Some colleges don't require interviews for everyone, but they may require an interview of you. Again, you'll have to give them a full, convincing picture of yourself and your strengths to compensate for your missing transcript. Also, you may have to get it out of their heads that people who don't go to school are social misfits. Don't cry for your mother, even as a joke.

Interviews don't necessarily have to take place on campus. Colleges who want students from all over the country send admissions officers to travel all over the country and recruit students. During this time, they also conduct interviews. You can ask any local high school counselor for a schedule of college recruiters. Or, if you know which colleges you want to apply to, write them directly and ask about their recruitment schedules.

The application essay

will not be much different for you than for schooled people, except that it will count more. Since you can't show them A's in English, they will want to see for themselves how well you write. Unless you spend your unschooled life writing articulate things that get published, that is. Be sure to write about something that matters.

Outside interests

Colleges want to know what you do with your time besides textbook academics. (Part of the reason for this is they consider their student body part of their curriculum. They figure if you're an interesting bunch, you'll learn neato things from each other and more people will want to go to school there.) If they see that you know how to love something and chase it and do it and be it, great. Harvard is especially explicit about wanting students who not only fulfill standard academic requirements, but also demonstrate expertise in an additional area of almost any kind. This is your showcase, since unschooling is all about doing what you love.

In lieu of the high school transcript: college coursework

After hearing from both admissions officers and unschooled teenagers, I strongly advise: before you apply to a selective college, take at least one course through a local university or community college. This way, you both prove that you can handle college-level, structured coursework *and* find out cheaply whether you *like* doing it. Certainly, success in a college class shows your readiness for college better than success in high school can. You may be able to do this through a high school enrichment program, or you may have to first get your GED and then enroll. Phone them up, explain yourself politely ("I would like to take your course in Beginning Japanese"), and ask how to go about it. You may not *have* to do this, but it will reassure nervous admissions officers tremendously. Bowdoin Director of Admissions, William R. Mason, commented:

> We have two entering freshmen this year . . . who were completely home schooled. Each of them did take local college courses and the support from teachers was exceptional enough to convince us that both these students possess superior academic ability.

If your application is especially scanty, a selective college may even *ask* you to start by enrolling elsewhere full time. For instance, Delsie Phillips of Haverford says, "In some cases we have asked students who lack formal education and testing to enroll in an open admission college to prove their ability to excel in a structured situation. When they have presented appropriate grades, we admit them." And David Illingworth, a senior admissions officer at Harvard, told a group of homeschoolers:

> Something that I think could help the application of a homeschooler to highly selective colleges is some kind of participation in a summer enrichment program. I think that would give the student a chance to perform in a university environment, see what life is like *away* from home, live on their own, and also give us a chance to [get a look at] some grades and college courses. Many colleges offer summer school programs for, say, high school juniors, people who are arriving seniors, to go and spend six weeks on that college campus and take courses . . . If you can afford it, it would be a very good way for a homeschooled person to begin to prove himself in a greater context outside the home.[1]

Your daily bread

The main part of getting ready for college is becoming a well read glorious generalist with knowledge of literature, history, political structures, math, science, and foreign language. (This doesn't mean you need to get it from textbooks or lectures.) The more selective the college, the more of all this you need. Also, admissions people expect that you have strong reading, writing, and math reasoning

---

[1] From *Talk About Learning* #10, published by Earl Gary Stevens, 1989.

skills, and some degree of comfort with scientific process and laboratory equipment.

You will most likely end up writing, in detail, exactly how you have approached your academic studies. Therefore, you need to keep careful records with dates. List the books you read and the textbooks you use, the lectures you attend, the specialists or professors with whom you converse, the letters you write to senators or scientists, the trips you take, the experiments you conduct. Hold onto any writing you do.

To be a strong candidate, you'll probably need to be reading, writing, conducting scientific experiments, and working math problems for two to four focused hours, five days a week, eight months of the year, for three or four years. If I'm sounding grim and you're grossing out, just remember that to do college prep the school way, you'd spend at least six hours daily in school, plus homework, for *twelve* years, and not learn as much. More importantly, remember that it should be fun, and needn't orbit around textbooks or worksheets. If you hate it no matter how you approach it, put your life on a different path and get happy.

Actually, this is a key to your happy future. If you enjoy *preparing* for whatever kind of college you want to attend, you'll probably enjoy college itself and the kind of life it pushes you towards. On the other hand, if you have to force yourself to work trigonometry problems and read heavy books, you can also expect major frustration during college. Don't sacrifice your present for your future, because your present mirrors your future. All times, say the mystics and the physicists, are now.

Therefore: throughout your years of college preparation, stay in close touch with yourself. Don't get knocked off balance, don't forget who you are, and don't get frenzied or unhappy. Michael Phillips, in *The Seven Laws of Money*, talks about wanting to be rich: "Say you've got the $100,000 that you desired. You are now the process that it took you to get there. If you had to sell dope, you're a dope dealer with $100,000."

Translate that right into the world of college preparation. You want to get into Dartmouth. You do get into Dartmouth. You are now the process that it took you to get there. You could be a narrow, harried geek with cramped muscles, or you could be a perceptive, questing, lively human being. Test your motives every few months. If the U.S. of North America sent you off to war on your eighteenth birthday and all the colleges shut down before you came back—*if* you came back—would you bitterly regret all that time you'd "wasted" studying for it? Or would you rejoice over what you'd already learned? As they say, life is not a destination but a journey.

Getting-into-college stories

In *GWS* #89, Emily Murphy recalls her admission to St. John's College:

I applied to just two places: Penn State . . . and St. John's. Penn State said they couldn't consider me because I didn't have a diploma; I suspect it was because I didn't fit into their computer system. But just at the point that they said no, St. John's said yes, and St. John's was really the place I wanted to go, so I decided not to pursue Penn State any further. If I had wanted to, I could have gotten a diploma from the State Department of Education or somewhere else. But St. John's didn't care about the diploma at all. They were excited that I was a homeschooler. They kept contacting me, and I felt that they really wanted me there. You do have to provide two letters of recommendation from teachers, so I got letters from teachers in classes I'd taken. My practice had been to get a letter of reference whenever I took a class or did a volunteer project.

I didn't have a traditional transcript or a regular grading system, but St. John's doesn't give you grades anyway. My mother did what St. John's does once you're a student there: she provided a detailed list of what I'd done. Fortunately, I also scored pretty high on the SAT, so that probably helped. For the St. John's admissions application, you have to write three major essays: one on why you want to go to St. John's, one on your experience with books, and one on an experience that changed your life.

(Several years later, Emily's mother, Madalene Murphy, writes in *GWS* #109:

Emily graduated from St. John's and now has a year's contract to write a pictorial history of the college, based on her own proposal and her work in their photo archives. Soon after her book proposal was accepted, she was offered a full-time job as assistant registrar of special collections at the Maryland State Archive in Annapolis, which means she is head of their extensive photo archives and is responsible for preservation, acquisition, research, etc. . . . She will probably go to graduate school at some point but is now pleased and very busy.)

Laura Gelner focused on math and science at Colorado College. In *GWS* #89, she writes:

Colorado College had had a few homeschooling applicants, so it was somewhat familiar to them. My mom wrote a pretty detailed letter about what we had been doing, explaining why I had no transcript, in place of the usual counselor's letter. We had the normal test scores to submit, and we had a neighbor who is a public school teacher write one of the teacher's recommendations. She's someone I've known for four or five years, and I've talked with her a lot about homeschooling. I talked about homeschooling in one of the essay questions that asked what you thought of the block system. I said I had been learning that way all along. The way I tended to work, in homeschooling, was to throw myself into one subject for a month or two. When I was reading *War and Peace*, for example, I just put everything else by the wayside and read that book for a month. I was about fifteen or sixteen at the time. It was my own choice to work this way; I wasn't doing assignments from my mother.

Bronwyn Jackson, at Wellesley, writes in *GWS* #96:

I am a Sophomore at Wellesley College. I started to write and call colleges in what would have been my sophomore year in high school. In the beginning of my senior year I decided to apply to three women's colleges: Converse, Hollins, and Wellesley. I was admitted to all three. All of these schools were interested in homeschooling. Hollins and Converse didn't know much about homeschoolers but Wellesley had had several apply each year for a while and knew what to expect.

Aside from the usual applications, I sent lists of books that I had read, my music repertoire, poetry I had memorized, books that I had written over the past four years, activities that I had participated in that I would not have been able to had I gone to regular school (a stained glass apprenticeship, an archaeological dig, the Florida State University bands and orchestras, etc.), a tape of me playing the harp, and pictures of the quilts I had made. In addition to regular essays I submitted articles I had written for a high school newspaper and *GWS* about homeschoolers and what being a homeschooler meant to me. My harp teacher, professors at FSU, and my high school physics teacher (I took a class at the high school) wrote letters of recommendation. The Wellesley admissions department says that these kinds of letters are very important for homeschoolers because they help the admissions board decide if the student will be able to do well at the college.

Hollins and Converse both said that I needed to take a lab science before coming to their schools, so I took physics at a high school in Tallahassee. Wellesley, too, suggested that I take a science class, but also said that if I wanted just to homeschool my senior year, it was OK with them. A homeschooler applying to a college should find out what that school's policies are regarding credits, GED's, and diplomas. No Ivy League school requires a diploma. Less prestigious schools, especially community colleges and state schools, since they have to follow state guidelines, tend to get caught up in unproductive rules.

Sarah Pitts writes in *GWS* #96:

I applied to five colleges, and Boston College was my first choice . . . The application focused heavily on activities, and in one section you had to write what activities you were involved in and any awards or honors you had won. Since I'm homeschooled I couldn't list activities like president of the French Club or member of the Honor Society. Instead I listed things like my involvement in community theatre and the leadership positions I've held there, and my involvement in 4-H. Also, I was in charge of registrations for our state homeschool conference, and I listed that to show that I had organizational skills. Finally, I listed the jobs I had had, including my internship with a bookseller, doing shipping and receiving . . . Most applications ask for at least one teacher recommendation in addition to the counselor letter. We were a little stumped at first, but I ended up asking my employers to write letters. I had worked for a year and a half at a computer consulting firm, and I was also working at one other job, in retail. Then, the president of the theatre group I was involved in sent a letter for me as well. ◉

Part 4

Touching the World: Finding Good Work

beyond
fast food

*Nothing is really work unless
you would rather be doing something else.*
—James M. Barrie

EQUIPPING YOURSELF ACADEMICALLY certainly won't take all of your time unless you want to go light years beyond your schooled peers, and *this world needs you.* We are starved for people who work with not just their hands and their minds, but also with their hearts. Most humans, including teenagers, crave the chance to do real work—something that makes a difference in the world—instead of just sitting and taking notes all day. Some work brings money, some doesn't. Try to think of work as something that *matters*—not just a way to sell your time, body, and soul in return for cash. John Holt came up with a healthy definition in *Teach Your Own*: "By 'work' I mean what people used to call a 'vocation' or 'calling'—something which seemed so worth doing for its own sake that they would gladly choose to do it even if they didn't need money and the work didn't pay."

Now versus later
When I was a teenager I hated the nonsense question adults asked: "And what do you want to do with your life?" Like the other standard, "Do you like school," it made no sense to me. It referred to some abstract future instead of my present. I always had answers, but my heart wasn't in them. At the time, all I really knew was that I had to go to school, supposedly so that I could later apply my school knowledge to whatever I did. Unfortunately, it didn't occur to me that I could also have begun doing the things that I dreamed about doing "someday."

In your unschooled life, the question of good work is a question about your here and now, not just a speculation about your future. In ten years, you may change your mind completely about everything, including what work you want. If that happens, you can get the skills and knowledge you need then. Your task now is to use your time beautifully *now*. Your life isn't something that's going to start happening when you're 21. It's happening today.

In fact, one of the great things about unschooling is that it makes healthy future work much more likely. It allows your present to blend with your future, with no forced split. Many unschooled teenagers wrote me with a clear sense of this connection between their present activity and their future work. Michael and Christin

Severini, for instance: At fifteen, Michael takes flying lessons. He envisions later work as an airline pilot. Christin, thirteen, now dances with a ballet company and belongs to PETA, and she says, "My future plans are to become a professional dancer and to help animals in some way." The Severinis' plans ring with truth because their everyday lives are consistent with their future fantasies.

How to be psyched for Monday

Do work you love. You *can* do work you love.

This topic needs a couple hundred pages to itself. Fortunately, an entertaining, wise, and extremely knowledgeable woman named Barbara Sher has taken care of that, by writing a book called *Wishcraft*. Read it, and you will see clearly what it is you most dream of doing, and furthermore, how to make it happen. Probably, without the clarity her book brought to my life, *this* book wouldn't be happening, I wouldn't be teaching and performing Middle Eastern dance, and I might even still be teaching *school*. She'll get you out of ruts, pronto.

But I shall also add a few comments on the relationship between unschooling, money, and good work. No matter who you are and how much money you don't have, if you are an unschooler you can do work (now and all your life) that both fulfills your spirit and also pays your way. One huge reason many working class people have so little chance to get out of the working class is lack of time. Generally, creative, fun work pays better wages than mindless minimum wage or unskilled stuff. However, before you can make a living by making earrings, coordinating advertising for the community performing arts center, or producing seminars on ecological restoration, you need time to develop expertise. Once many working class people are out of high school, their parents can't afford to support them through college or any other kind of transition. They have to scuttle right from high school into full time unskilled jobs, with no time to gradually become involved (without pay) in something challenging that they really *love*.

By unschooling, however, many people could break out of poverty. Instead of squandering their teenage years in school drudgery, they could invest that time in learning skills that will later provide interesting work, or in gradually building up a business or getting started in a field through volunteer experience. While they are teenagers, they can *afford* to volunteer or start a slow-growing business, even if they also have to bag groceries twenty hours a week at Spaceway.

In this regard, whether you are poor or not, enjoy your distinct advantage over adults. Unless your parents are the vindictive kind who say "go to school or get a job and pay your way," you aren't yet pressured to be financially independent. (If your parents do hint in that direction, remind them that the whole idea of education, in school or elsewhere, depends on children not being forced to earn money. You need time to explore, which is why you quit school in the first place.) In other words, part of your education can be doing terrific work even if it doesn't pay for your meals. Adults who have to buy the tofu don't have that luxury.

Of course, you might start a silkscreening business at fifteen which succeeds spectacularly. Or you might begin volunteer work which directly leads to happy employment a year from now. But you can also do work that might *never* bring dollar bills—spending Tuesday mornings at a battered women's shelter, organizing a talent show, writing letters to senators, planting trees or a garden, teaching your mother how to use a computer.

Start short

When you approach businesses or adults—looking for apprenticeships, internships, volunteer opportunities, or jobs—sometimes you're more likely to coax a "yes" out of them if you suggest a trial period. As Emily Bergson-Shilcock says in *GWS* #95:

> Most everything we do, we say, "Let's try it for three weeks first." It's easier for people to say yes that way. If you walk into a store and say, "I'd like to volunteer here," and they've never had volunteers before, it's more likely that they'll say no. Just because they haven't had volunteers, that doesn't mean they can't, but it's easier for them to say yes to something short term. Then if it works out, you can keep going . . . In a lot of ways it's easier to go into a smaller business, and easier if you already know and like the people.

Try a class or program

If suggesting a trial period doesn't work, sometimes it helps to enroll in a class or other program at the business or organization where you'd like to volunteer, work, apprentice, or intern. That's just another way to get your foot in the door, and to get to know the staff and let them get to know you.

Doing it

The possibilities are exhilaratingly endless, but to help you begin thinking I've grouped them into categories: apprenticeships, internships, volunteering, jobs, businesses, farm-related work, and activism. There are several good books on each of these topics. One that covers many types of teenage work is Ruth Lembeck's *Teenage Jobs*. Old but not outdated, it gives hundreds of good ideas and real-life examples.

Remember, you don't have to copy typical adult working patterns. For one thing, you can consider your work part of an *education* helping you build skills and experience for your ultimate career goal. It's up to you to draw the experience and learning you want from any situation. Working in a bookstore, for instance, doesn't mean you're going to work in a bookstore for the rest of your life. It could be a superb stepping stone toward a career as a bookstore owner, author, illustrator, librarian, publisher, book designer, graphic designer, customer service consultant, or business interior designer. (Or, maybe you *do* want to keep working in someone else's bookstore, which certainly has its own rewards.) Emily Bergson-Shilcock opened her own store when she was seventeen, and several volunteer jobs helped provide her with the experience she needed. At fifteen, for example, she wrote in *GWS* #95:

> When I was thirteen, I wanted some kind of job. We know a lot of the storeowners in our town because we homeschool and we often walk around during the day. We especially liked Janet, who runs a store called T-Shirt Tunnel, because she was very friendly, she wasn't pushy, and she accepted homeschooling. We suggested the idea of having me volunteer there, and we suggested trying it as a three-week experiment at first. She said that that was fine, and it worked out really well. Since then it's really blossomed. At first, because I was only thirteen, I wasn't getting paid, but then I was doing a lot of work and even bringing stuff home to do, so Janet started giving me five dollars each time. Then when I turned fourteen she started paying me a regular wage, and now that I'm fifteen, I'm getting paid five dollars an hour. I work there about four hours a week, and more around Christmastime when she needs extra help. You need to be sixteen to work the heat presses, which we use for putting transfers on T-shirts. I know how to use the presses, but I don't use them when customers are there because technically I'm not supposed to. So right now Janet can't leave me in the store alone, but when I turn sixteen she'll be able to.

One of the best parts has been the way Janet has taken a lot of my suggestions and used them. When I first started, the store was just kind of staying where it was; it wasn't improving a lot. The signs were all hand-done, and the cardboard would fade from being in the windows. I took all those signs home and typed them up on the computer. Last Christmas we had coupon books, and that was my idea. Then I suggested that Janet put other stuff in the window so that people in the neighborhood would realize that she sold more than T-shirts. After that people would come in and say, "I never knew you sold anything besides T-shirts, and I've lived here for years!" . . . When I started, Janet was very open to having me come, but she said, "What would you do?" That was just because she'd never had a volunteer before. I started out helping her stock shelves. Then I started using the cash register, because I have one in my bedroom and I've always loved working it. She had a couple of buttons on her cash register that she'd never used because she didn't know what they meant. I showed her what they meant, and then she was much more willing to show me things, like how to use the Visa machine.

Also, remember that you can combine several jobs or activities; you needn't do just one thing for forty hours a week. Here are a few stories that show the variety that's possible. Lavonne Bennett writes in *GWS* #18 about her son, a "mechanical and electronics genius" described as a "stupid dummy" by a high school teacher:

> We took him out of high school in the middle of his junior year . . . He's seventeen now and has managed two stores for an electronics-product firm, parlayed a $150 clunker car up to a classic sports car, has bought equipment for his recording studio, has been a mentor for an eight-year-old boy, helping him to organize model-train layouts, and has given guitar lessons.

Ann Martin of England tells about her son Nicholas, fourteen, in *GWS* #21:

> He spends one afternoon [each week] in a shoe workshop where he helps out in exchange for tuition and will bring home his own hand-made shoes next week! He has been on a residential sports course, goes on trips with a local theater company, and he helps in a shop owned by a friend of mine, who is teaching him the basic skills of running a business.

Kandy Light wrote about her children in *GWS* #47:

> Dawn (sixteen) is in New York right now helping some friends while they have their third baby. They live and work at a health reconditioning center. Dawn has been helping in their various programs, learning massage, hydrotherapy, etc. She has also worked in their vegetarian restaurants. They want her to come live and work there . . . She also met some doctors while there, who have invited her to come work and learn with them at their health center in the South. Last year she was a full-time babysitter for a local school dean. The dean recently moved and called this week to ask if Dawn could come to live with them and teach *their* children at home (in California).
>
> When here at home she is hired as a secretary for a local businessman, besides apprenticing with the Barkers at their Country School [see Chapter 37] . . . She has also been asked to learn lay midwifery, train as a colporteur, gardener, etc. . . .
>
> Our fifteen-year-old twin boys, Tim and Dave, are apprenticing with an Amish man learning engine repair. They are learning first-hand how to repair tractors, lawn mowers, chain saws, etc. A neighbor has bartered two calves with them in exchange for them helping him do hay, plant corn, and occasionally milk his cows. Every day they work for another neighbor for four hours, landscaping his picture-perfect lawns and gardens and doing maintenance work. When our local principal moved, he hired them . . . They've earned $75 a day helping to move people. They, too, are apprenticing with the Barkers in Millersburg. ◉

33

apprenticeships and internships

If you know what kind of work you want to do, move toward it in the most direct way possible. If you want someday to build boats, go where people are building boats, find out as much as you can. When you've learned all they know, or will tell you, move on. Before long, even in the highly technical field of yacht design, you may find you know as much as anyone, enough to do whatever you want to do.

—John Holt, *Teach Your Own*

A great many of the people who are doing serious work in the world (as opposed to just making money) are very overworked, and short of help. If a person, young or not so young, came to them and said, "I believe in the work you are doing and want to help you do it in any and every way I can, will do any kind of work you ask me to do or that I can find to do, for very little pay or even none at all," I suspect that many or most of them would say, "Sure, come right ahead." Working with them, the newcomer would gradually learn more and more about what they were doing, would find or be given more interesting and important things to do, might before long become so valuable that they would find a way to pay her/him. In any case, s/he would learn far more from working with them and being around them than s/he could have learned in any school or college.

—John Holt

THE SITUATIONS HOLT describes above are usually called apprenticeships or internships, and are based on the concept of mutual benefit. The apprentice or intern gives labor in exchange for the chance to learn about a certain kind of work. The labor itself may seem repetitive or boring to someone experienced in the field, but should be interesting and challenging for a newcomer. By the same token, the "master" or supervisor should not have to take a lot of time to stop and explain how to do things, because the apprentice will learn mainly by watching and doing. Sometimes the apprentice or intern is also paid in money. Sometimes the apprentice or intern pays. Often, no money is exchanged.

What's the difference between internships and apprenticeships? Internships often involve office or administrative work, while apprenticeships usually focus on learning specific skills in a craft or trade. But many people use the terms interchangeably.

Apprenticeships can take place in any field, from chemistry research to interior decorating. They've been around for millennia, though in recent decades they've been somewhat forgotten in the U.S., or at least restricted to certain trades. But homeschoolers have rediscovered them as a superb learning arrangement, and more recently, some schoolpeople have even started to set up apprenticeships for school students.

In some countries, apprenticeships have always been the way that people learned certain types of work, but these fields are often stigmatized as the fate of people not brainy enough to become doctors or ambassadors or such. I'm excited that unschoolers are reinventing apprenticeships for their own purposes—not only completing long-term apprenticeships to become electricians or midwives, but also arranging short or long term situations that may have nothing to do with their career goals, or that involve an academic field rather than a "trade." Unschoolers apprentice themselves for a week or five years, to chemists and museum curators and windmill repairpeople and poets. So, if you live in an area where people define apprenticeships or internships unimaginatively, don't let them limit you—dream up the best situation for you and for a skilled adult whom you admire, and then explain your dream and suggest a trial period.

Organizations that offer internships

Thousands of organizations offer positions in fields including communications, arts, human services, public affairs, science, and industry. You might work on costume and scene construction with a ballet company, conduct a research project for the Peace Corps, do camera work or lighting for TV stations, write and conduct surveys for a newspaper, or do office work for a publisher. Some internships offer stipends. Many provide room and board, free classes, college credit, and help with finding employment. If you want to apply for a particular position, do keep in mind:

- Some programs are rather rigid; others are flexible enough that you can adapt them to fit your particular interests.
- Some internships are in high demand, and difficult to get. You will compete for them with other people, most older than you.
- Many internships will be officially off-limits until you are eighteen or so, though others are open to high school and even middle school age people. Furthermore, almost all organizations are open to "independent" inquiries. In other words, they will consider ignoring normal requirements, creating special positions for people who wouldn't fit into their usual slots. And anyway, persevering unschoolers often find that age requirements are not written in stone.

Check with businesses, non-profits, and other organizations near you, or go to the library for a reference book such as *Internships: on-the-job training opportunities for college students and adults, America's Top Internships, Peterson's Internships,* or *Student Advantage Guide: The Internship Bible.*

If you use one of these reference books, remember that the less famous organizations will be easier to break into. A small town newspaper, for instance, won't have as many applicants as *The Washington Post.*

Your library may also have more specialized internship guides, like Ronald W. Fry's *Internships: The Travel and Hospitality Industries,* or the *National Directory of Arts Internships,* or the American Association of Botanical Gardens and Arboreta's *Internship Directory,* which lists over five hundred summer jobs and internships at botanical gardens and other horticultural institutions.

Services that help to arrange apprenticeships and internships

Don't waste your time with a mediocre service, because you can probably do as well on your own and save money. However, a really excellent consultant can open up opportunities you never dreamed of, and turn out to be well worth the expense. In this really excellent department, the main player is Cornelius Bull.

Cornelius Bull runs the Center for Interim Programs, which maintains a list of around three thousand opportunities all over the world. Bull is expert at matching clients with situations that reflect their interests. Not all of them are technically "apprenticeships" or "internships," but most involve some kind of interesting work. Many are inexpensive, providing room and board; others cost more due to travel, tuition, and other expenses. Most clients are college students looking for a way to take creative time off, or high school graduates wanting to do something meaningful for a year before they go to college. However, Bull has also worked with everyone from burned out lawyers to "empty-nested mothers," and is willing to work with teenaged unschoolers as well. In a talk at Choate, a highbrow prep school in Connecticut, he told the following story about one of his clients:

> I have a young kid who was totally allergic to school. He got through his sophomore year of high school, and he said, "Forget it, I can't do any more." He went off to Nepal. This kid is a magical climber. He is a human fly. They didn't care about that in high school. Why should they? That doesn't matter. It's irrelevant. So, he had never gotten any good strokes . . . Mountain Travel, the foremost trekking company in Nepal, watched this guy and was so impressed that they offered him a job and then discovered he was sixteen. They said, "Hey, go home and come back when you're eighteen and work with us."

Bull enjoys working with clients in person, but often does all the arranging during long phone conversations and through the mail. Some of the programs in his files are those of other organizations like the National Outdoor Leadership School, but some are unusual, out of the way opportunities he's personally tracked down through his huge network of friends, former classmates (Princeton), and former students (he taught and was headmaster of private schools for thirty years). Possibilities include working on organic farms in Spain, interning in wildlife rehabilitation in New York, doing whale research in Maui, and learning to conduct tea ceremonies in a Japanese castle.

Another organization, Time Out, "arranges enriching opportunities worldwide." Time Out is run by David Denman, a former teacher, headmaster, director of admissions, etc. Denman has worked successfully not only with college students, but also with teenaged unschoolers and "dropouts." Like The Center for Interim Programs, Time Out arranges a wide variety of experiences, not just apprenticeships and internships. Watch for new local and regional organizations, as both homeschooling and apprenticeships become more popular. For instance, the new Gateway Apprenticeship Program in Boulder, Colorado, is eager to work with both homeschoolers and schooled students, "linking up masters in their fields with young people who long to do certain kinds of work."

How you can arrange and design your own apprenticeship or internship

You may need perseverance, but all you really have to *do* is decide what kind of a position you want, and then talk to everyone in your area who works in that field until you find someone you like who will take you on for at least a trial period.

A very helpful book is *The Question is College,* by Herbert Kohl. It discusses apprenticeships as an alternative to *college,* but is relevant for people of any age.

You'll have it easiest if you already have adult friends you might like to apprentice yourself to, or if your parents know someone who might work out. Tad Heuer writes in *GWS* #98:

> During the spring of 1993, the legislature passed an education reform act, which included provisions for homeschoolers. My parents worked with Rep. Gardner to give her the perspective of a homeschooling family. This provided me with a "bridge" to introduce myself. When I met with Rep. Gardner, I told her of my interest in politics and asked if there was any way I could help her at the State house. She was very receptive and said that I could intern in her office.

Of course you can approach strangers too. After all, apprenticeships and internships help everyone involved. You learn by watching people who know what they're doing and by actually doing many of the same things they do. They get free or inexpensive help, as well as the joy and pride that comes from sharing what they love with an excited newcomer. Chances are, if you phone all the dog trainers in the yellow pages, at least one will let you try a one-day experiment, and that may lead into a week-long volunteer job, and then a three-month apprenticeship. Don't give up after one "no-thank-you."

Be sure to talk about your ideas and goals thoroughly enough that both parties have similar expectations. Write them down. If you envision three hours on weekday mornings of laying out newspaper copy, but Mr. Mendoza sees you sweeping floors and running errands, it won't work. Discover that *before* you commit yourself.

If you want to set up a position away from home, you may have success—as others have—placing a classified ad in a homeschooling magazine or newsletter. In *GWS* #87, Judy Garvey reports on what happened after her teenage son Matthew wrote a letter to *GWS* seeking an outdoor apprenticeship:

> I wanted to let people know about the worlds that have opened up for him as a result. He received many generous offers for apprenticeships or visits... Matt just left for Mexico, where he will be working on a ranch in the Sonora high desert area for two months. This first apprenticeship actually came about from contacting Donn Reed, author of *The Home School Source Book,* who happened to know the homeschooling family who owns the ranch. Matthew will be using many of the skills he has learned already, plus he will be working as a cowboy and general ranch hand. He is very happy there, making friends with the Mexican people he works with and in awe of the beautiful country around him.
>
> In July, he will be leaving for at least a three-month stay in Alaska. He will work with a homeschooling family who has a hunting guide business both on the peninsula and north on the Yukon border. This family apprentices a young person every couple of years who could eventually be trained as an Alaskan guide. Since that is Matthew's goal at this point in his life, this opportunity is a great one for him. When his time with them comes to an end, he may go to stay with another family closer to Anchorage but also quite remote. They raise huskies and, in fact, their sixteen-year-old just won the Junior Iditarod . . .
>
> Besides the letter which was printed in *GWS,* Matt prepared a résumé in which he listed all of his experience, skills, and interests, his size (which was important to his work), date of birth, parents' names, and a couple of references. He has had to write many

letters to his prospective mentors to make arrangements. The result of all this is first-hand experience in how to go about finding work in his chosen field.

GWS also runs occasional notices or ads from people *offering* work situations, apprenticeships, and internships. For example, someone wrote in *GWS* #27, "Wanted: apprentice to learn microcomputer programming. My ideal would be an unschooler, ten to fifteen, who can commute to my small software company. I envision the apprentice spending about one day a week at first, later maybe about three days a week." And a midwife wrote in *GWS* #25,

> If there were a young person who wanted to learn about the body, birth, and babies, I'd be glad to have them spend time here with me going on home births, and being present for the pre-natals, etc. I won't put any age limit on it, because I've learned from Wendy [her eight-year-old daughter] that if there's an interest, anyone can learn it. My daughter often knows more about what's happening than some of the mothers I work with!

Homeschooling organizations themselves may offer positions, too, and are often more inclined than other businesses to accept young interns. *GWS* sometimes has openings, which could be a valuable start for someone interested in magazine production or general business management.

You can use an internship sourcebook like one of those listed previously as an important source of information even without applying for one of the internships it describes. Find a position that sounds ideal, *except* for its location or age requirements, or whatever. Write the sponsoring institution for more information. Then, find a similar institution closer to home. Write up a thoughtful but flexible proposal, and approach them. To help reduce any reluctance, point out that you have based your ideas on an organization similar to theirs.

Apprenticeships can and should happen in academic fields too. See Chapter 21 for a description of Vincent J. Schaefer, who became a engineer mainly as a result of an apprenticeship at General Electric. Also in Chapter 21, see the bits of Dr. David Deutsch's paper, "How Children Can Become Experts." In *GWS* #96, Susannah Sheffer tells how she helped Emily Ostberg set up an apprenticeship related to botany in Belize.

> Last winter, when Emily was seventeen, she told me that she was interested in doing some kind of botanical work in Asia or Central America. She had already spent a month in Nepal, visiting family friends, and had loved that adventure. She had also studied for a while, though not very extensively, with a university botany student. Emily asked me for help in researching possible opportunities and making some of the necessary phone calls.
> I knew almost nothing about this field, but I had heard of the Rainforest Action Network in San Francisco, so I began by calling them. They had no information about volunteer opportunities in the rainforest itself, although they would have been happy to have volunteers in their office. Next I thought of Cultural Survival, an organization here in Cambridge [Massachusetts] that is dedicated to the survival of indigenous populations. I called and learned that they had a database of organizations looking for volunteers, so Emily and I visited them and she went through the computer files, copying down organizations that looked interesting. She later wrote letters to several of them, and received a couple of interesting responses, including one that she considered pursuing. Meanwhile, I asked [a colleague's husband] if there was anyone he could suggest calling at Harvard ([he] worked at the Harvard Museum of Comparative Zoology . . .), and he told me about the Harvard Herbaria. After speaking with several different people on the phone, I finally reached a graduate student who was willing to talk to us about the work that students and researchers were doing out in the field. Emily and I met with him and learned

that there were a lot of fairly tedious jobs with which a researcher might appreciate help. The difficulty was that most of this year's projects had been set up long before, and Emily was interested to begin this work in a few months (that summer or fall). Still, it was interesting for Emily to get a sense of what sorts of people were doing what sort of work. In the process of seeking out an apprenticeship or internship, very few letters or phone calls are wasted, I found, precisely because they help the young person understand who is doing what and to gain a clearer sense of where he or she might fit in.

At around this time, Emily saw an article in the *Whole Earth Review* about Ix Chel Farm in Belize. She wrote to the magazine asking for the address of the Farm, and then wrote to the Farm itself saying that she was very interested in working there as a volunteer. She said she had little or no experience in this area but she was willing to work hard and was interested in botany, biology, and horticulture. She received a fairly quick response telling her that she was welcome to come and giving her some idea of what she might be able to do. After Emily and her family did some further investigating about Ix Chel and about what working there would be like, Emily made plans to go there in early July.

And reading books can be a bit like an apprenticeship, if you choose carefully and approach it that way. Some books really invite you inside to observe a person's work. For instance, *The Double Helix*, by James D. Watson, brings you behind the scenes to watch the process of the scientific discovery of DNA.

Make the most of your internship or apprenticeship.

Ask your master or supervisor for reading suggestions. Milk her brains. Do extra work. Be proactive. Keep a journal. In *GWS* #79, an adult piano technician apprentice writes:

At the beginning of my apprenticeship, I found that I wanted to be completely directed by my teacher. I wanted to be told exactly what to do, in complete detail, without any necessity on my part for any form of decision-making or any prerequisites of knowledge other than that supplied by my teacher. Perhaps this seems cowardly, but as a beginning learner in the field, it was how I felt . . . Specific directions for assigned tasks, and the freedom to observe the teacher performing more complex work, were all that I needed and wanted at the time.

So I would call that phase one, and now, six months later, I have noticed that I am entering a second, slightly different phase of learning. I have, for the most part, been given what I wanted—careful directions, appropriate jobs for my level of skill, and a good deal of freedom to observe and listen and learn without having any expectations to perform placed on me. Now I feel that I am ready to take on some things myself, to make some decisions for myself, to see a job that needs doing and to feel able to do it, maybe with a few questions asked but with a fair understanding of the basics at hand. I still have so much to learn, and I still need by teacher to direct me, but not in the totally dependent way of the beginning learner. I now feel the surety to begin to function, in a small degree, on my own.

Examples

Anna-Lisa Cox writes about the process of developing an interest in historical costume and finding a related internship. In *GWS* #68:

I am seventeen, and until I became a part-time student at the local college a couple of years ago, I had been schooled at home all my life.

My main passion in life right now is, and has been for the last three years, social anthropology and history. Antique clothing has been the context which brought these subjects alive for me. I became interested in antique clothing when I was living in England for a year with my family. I stumbled upon the Victoria and Albert Museum in London, which has one of the best costume collections in Europe. I was instantly fascinated by it, and I determined to find out more about the subject.

Now, three years later, I have a large costume collection of my own (acquired through hours of rummaging through charity shops, garage sales, and local estate sales), which I use in historical fashion presentations for local clubs, churches, and businesses. I am also the costume collection consultant for the local historical society. I find what I do very exciting. It's wonderful to be able to help friends date their grandmother's dress, or to teach them how to clean and preserve it.

[A year later, Anna-Lisa writes in *GWS* #74:] My true love is museum work, tied to an intense interest in antique clothing. Luckily, my parents have been an incredible help and encouragement, patiently supporting me in my exploration and decision-making . . .

With the help of friends I was able to find [a museum internship], which I will be going to in April. Some friends arranged for me to get together with the curators of a costume museum near them. I was a little hesitant about even trying, as I had been disappointed so many times, but I decided to go ahead, and I'm so glad I did. The curators are three young women, all as excited and interested in costume as I am. When I first met them we talked for two hours straight. Around the end of our conversation, the head museum curator asked what museum I was in charge of! I decided to tell her the truth, that I had no museum experience, but she said she was very impressed with my expertise and would still love to have me come and work with them.

It all sounds so easy as I write about it, but getting to this point has taken enormous amounts of time and energy. In fact, last summer, when I was in England with my family, I went through an intensive search for an internship. I wrote and called museums. I even had a friend who used to be a costume curator helping me, writing letters of recommendation to old colleagues. But even so, not one internship came out of it. So I guess all I can recommend is to keep trying. There's an internship out there just waiting for you, if you have patience.

Elaine Mahoney writes about her daughter in *GWS* #23:

Kendra, thirteen years old now, is an apprentice in a sewing machine repair shop. A family friend owns a repair shop and has been graciously sharing her knowledge and skill. Kendra enjoys spending time at the shop and is learning by doing. She answers the phone, waits on customers, makes bank deposits, and is learning the general maintenance and repair of sewing machines.

[The next year, she adds in *GWS* #28:] [Kendra] is in Tennessee at present [with 4-H], attending the World's Fair . . . One of the exciting parts about the trip is that they also plan to go to Kentucky to go to a sewing machine convention, which ties in nicely with her apprenticeship.

In the fall, Kendra plans to take a correspondence course in sewing machine repair to acquire a certificate.

Lisa Asher writes in *GWS* #45:

I am a twelve-year-old homeschooler presently living in Barnstable, Massachusetts. My father is an architect, and I am, too. I am his apprentice.

I first became interested in architecture a year ago, when I began homeschooling. I made floor plans (the overhead view of a house without a roof). My plans were not very good, not even buildable, but they were a start.

About two months ago I got serious. I began to design buildable plans that took weeks instead of days to complete, and included sections and elevations.

My father looks at all my designs and shows me where I need to fix something. When I have a good plan, my father blueprints it.

I also help my father. When he has a completed design, he pays me to trace it. He also asks my advice sometimes. I even help design.

Right now, I just design contemporary houses, because that is what my father designs, but I would like to design rustic houses also someday.

Gretchen Spicer writes in *GWS* #53:

Jacob (fifteen) and Tom, my husband, are working at an outdoor Shakespeare Theater. Jacob started as an intern at $100 a week, but within two weeks was filling the position of two interns and is now getting $200 a week . . . We get to see lots of plays and now the kids are quoting Shakespeare constantly. Our house has become a very dramatic place recently.

Judy Garvey and Jim Bergin write about their thirteen-year-old son Matthew Bergin in *GWS* #76:

Shortly after leaving school two years ago, Matthew began working with a man who has a landscaping business. He loves the work and because of his energy and enthusiasm he has now become a real asset. This summer he will begin earning a wage for his labors. What he has already received from this apprenticeship—new self-esteem, real skills, and an awareness of how the world works outside of school or his family—could never be measured by salary.

In *GWS* #76, fourteen-year-old Emma Roberts writes about the process of choosing and setting up a theater apprenticeship:

I don't remember how I got the idea to have a theater apprenticeship. The whole idea really appealed to me. I love theater, and spending a few days every week working on it sounded great. It would solve my problems about wanting to go somewhere every day, and it would be fun. So I began thinking about what would be the ideal situation for me. I concluded that, say, three days a week working backstage, in the box office, anything to do with theater would be great. I was sending out some headshots and resumes for auditions for myself, so I sent along a cover letter saying that I was interested in volunteering in their theater, explaining I was a homeschooler and very flexible. At first I felt kind of strange asking to be an exception, but I got used to the idea.

I hadn't heard from the places I had written to in Boston when one day my Mom and I were talking to the scenic designer at Mount Wachusett Community College, Patrick Mahoney. I do a lot of theater at The Mount . . . so I know everyone pretty well. Mom happened to mention that I was looking for an apprenticeship in Boston, and she asked him if he knew of any places I could write to. Patrick said yes, he thought he did. Then he asked if we had considered The Mount as a possibility. We hadn't, because it hadn't occurred to us as being a real theater, but of course it is. I had recently had a chance to have a tour of two professional theaters in Boston and Worcester, and afterwards I realized how really professional the theater at The Mount is. Patrick said he would mention it to Gail Steele, the head of the theater department. I called Gail after about a week and we set up a meeting.

When I went to the meeting, Gail and Pat asked me what I would be interested in doing. I told them two or three days a week helping where I was needed would be great. They were really excited. Then Gail said she had talked to the head of the humanities department and he suggested I might like to take a few courses at the college. I couldn't believe it!

We set up for me to take two classes, The Fundamentals of Acting and Scene Tech, and get college credit. Going through the process of being admitted was a riot. You could tell they'd never heard of such a thing: a fourteen-year-old-girl who doesn't go to school wanting to come to their college and take classes. I finally got accepted, and I'm going to begin the whole thing in the fall. They offered for me to start the apprenticeship this summer, but I am so busy with a theater in Wilton, NH that I told them the fall would be better.

So I finally got a change, and if I ever want to go on to Boston to do an apprenticeship there, I can say, look, I've already had experience!

Tad Heuer of Massachusetts, now a student at Brown University, spent his fifteenth summer working as a legislative intern. Tad did his share of grunge work—typing names and addresses into databases, sorting the mail, etc. But many aspects of the work were interesting. In *GWS* #98, he writes:

> When people had questions about bills, I would get a copy of the bill and additional information from the committee where it had been sent for review. This information went to Rep. Gardner, who gave me her position and an outline of a possible reply. I then wrote a letter to the constituent. When people requested information about laws, I would call the department that was most likely to have jurisdiction.
>
> The Senate Legislative Education Office sponsored intern seminars almost every day. These were one of the best parts of my internship. They were given by representatives, senators, lobbyists, press secretaries, etc. They spoke on a variety of issues and always gave us a chance to ask questions. One speaker discussed Hydro-Quebecois II's plans to flood Cree Indian land to create a massive power grid for the Northeastern U.S. Another told us about the first bill he introduced. It called for all deer killed by cars to be frozen and distributed to homeless shelters for stew meat! (It passed overwhelmingly.) The seminars were also a good place to meet other interns. Before each seminar, we had to stand up and introduce ourselves. Although all the other interns were college students, they were very friendly and didn't treat me differently because of my age.
>
> Working as an intern was a wonderful introduction to the world of politics. Besides learning about the day-to-day life of legislators, I also improved my communication skills.

In *GWS* #112, Zoë Blowen-Ledoux writes about her puppetry apprenticeship. During parts of her apprenticeship, Zoë actually lived in the home of her mentors, John and Carol Farrell—live-in arrangements were typical of apprenticeships in the past; they're not so common now:

> For the past year, I have been doing a puppetry apprenticeship at the Figures of Speech Theater . . . I've been learning about the Farrells' theories about puppetry, and I find that I accept and identify with them. I'm learning that, for me, puppets reflect some part of us that's not visible without some symbol to illustrate and illuminate it . . .
>
> The intensive training part of my apprenticeship began in September as I worked with John on wood carving. I began by reading through many books with photos of different puppets to get ideas of what style of puppet I wanted to carve. I spent four weeks making a clay head, a model of the one I was going to make in wood, and learning to sharpen carving tools. In October I went to a craving workshop that John was teaching at Haystack Mountain School of Crafts in Deer Isle, Maine. That weekend was the first time I'd done anything with wood, and I found I really loved it . . .
>
> In the month after Haystack, I continued carving. I loved seeing the figure and the personality emerge from the wood. I completed carving the head and set it aside in order to move on to pattern drafting. This shifted my time from being with John to being with Carol. I learned to sew on the machine and did many sewing exercises to make straighter, faster seams and have better control. I took on a project of drafting a set of clothing that I will be able to wear.
>
> I've also been reading collections of myths and stories and the book *The Power of Myth*, by Joseph Campbell. I began this reading to find a story I could adapt into a character sketch for my puppet, but I've found myself really intrigued by mythology from all the different regions of the world. This has led me to the idea of writing my own myth, by incorporating aspects from different cultures, rather than choosing only one to use.
>
> Overall, my apprenticeship has been a great chance to do focused reading. I've read many articles in theater and puppetry magazines, and lately John and Carol and I have had discussion about articles and theories. I enjoy talking and thinking with them about the ideas that the articles pose, and I find that I absorb much more this way than if I just read

them myself.

Overall, very few problems have come up in my apprenticeship. Those that have come up, we have managed to solve in a creative way. For example, earlier this winter I was frustrated with the way the schedule was set up and how short the periods of time were in which I could work. We adapted the schedule to allow me to stay at the Farrells' home for longer, more intense blocks of time.

At times, I've felt frustrated by how long it takes me to complete something I'm working on. When carving last fall, it seemed that I was taking too long to finish. Thinking about it now, I can see that in fact I was absorbing a lot, both of the more obvious quantifiable skills (like carving and tool sharpening) and also of the less obvious adjustments I was making to fit into the Farrells' lifestyle.

I've been challenged creatively in many ways throughout this year as I developed new skills and ideas. My training here pushes my boundaries of familiarity and presents many new possibilities to pursue. ✺

volunteering

"Volunteer work is a tremendous use of time," seventeen-year-old former unschooler Anthony Hermans told me, "It accomplishes a useful task, allows one to get away from the norm and provides many longlasting friendships. I have volunteered in community service clubs, at the local library, our wildlife sanctuary, and a local history reenactment park. My sister has helped at a local homeless shelter for women and children."

Two big thrills come with volunteer work: the knowledge that you are helping something you believe in, and a huge realm of possibilities. Volunteering can be *anything*, a free ticket into any world you want to explore. Also, you can set your own schedule, working as much or as little as you wish. Few groups will turn you away because of your age. Volunteer experience looks great on a résumé, and furthermore, volunteer jobs often turn into paid jobs.

In cities where I've lived, a variety of organizations are run mainly by volunteers: senior citizens' support systems, soup kitchens, the Humane Society, a non-profit Latin American import shop. Every city has its own counterparts to these, and also chapters of environmental, social, and political action groups—Greenpeace, the Sierra Club, Amnesty International, the Greens, the Republicans, the Democrats, Students Against Drunk Drivers.

But you're not restricted to the groups that actively search for volunteers. You can always go to an organization, person, or business you like and speak your piece—"I'd like to get involved with what you're doing—is there something I can do to help, for free?" or "I'm a mime; I'd like to teach a free weekly class at the Immigration Center." In *GWS* #100, Earl Gary Stevens writes about how his son got a volunteer job at a Maine radio station, and how that job developed:

Jamie was eleven when he decided to go to WMPG [a local community FM station affiliated with a university] and volunteer his services, any services. He walked the four blocks to the station and told them that he was available and willing to do any kind of work—sweeping, filing, talking into microphones, whatever they had. A little while later he called to tell us that he wouldn't be coming home for a few hours because he was working at the station . . . After a week or so, during which Jamie was filing and labeling and getting to know everybody, the woman who co-produced "Chickens Are People Too" asked him if he would like to try hosting the show. With the bravery of the young and the non-schooled, he immediately nailed down a date and floated home to tell us about it. From clerical work to hosting "Chickens" in less than a month!

[Chickens is a children's variety hour, normally hosted by kids. Jamie hosted a few shows.] Before long he was also helping out with spot announcements and making guest appearances on other shows. As he worked in front of the microphone he became interested in learning how to use the production studio and the equipment for splicing, mixing, and recording. He took a production studio course offered by the radio station and in due time was presented with his own key to the studio.

Jamie's interest in radio entertainment led to an acting part in a radio play and then to parts in four productions of the Mad Horse Theater Company's Children's Theater. Jamie performed in *Matilda, The Prince and the Pauper, East of the Sun and West of the Moon,* and *Charlotte's Web.* Now, at age thirteen, he is talking about the possibility of producing and hosting his own community radio show . . .

Almost a year after Jamie's first day at WMPG I happened to run into the station manager while he was standing outside the station. When I introduced myself as Jamie's father, he smiled and began talking about Jamie's first visit. "It isn't often that we get a kid his age begging us to put him to work. We could see that he was very passionate about wanting to be one of us, so we gave him a tour and found him a job. We all appreciate his spirit; he has energized us, and he has made a difference at the station."

What a wonderful experience this has been for Jamie! He has hosted more than thirty radio show broadcasts, met interesting young college students who became his friends, found a niche for himself on the university campus, became involved in theater, and made many positive discoveries about himself. Occasionally he meets an adult who isn't respectful to kids there, but nearly everyone has been glad to meet and work with him.

Lots of unschoolers have volunteered successfully and happily at libraries, food co-ops, museums, radio stations, cable access TV stations, with veterinarians, Habitat for Humanity, and—ironically—in schools. Though strange, the idea makes sense. First, a volunteer, being *voluntary*, is far more empowered than a compulsory-school-student. Second, part of the unpleasantness of many schools ties to overcrowded classrooms and overworked teachers; therefore, a willing helper can make some difference. By participating in school in a new role, you the unschooler can gain a new perspective on your own childhood and the whole issue of School and Society. Finally, children can only benefit from being exposed to the calm, fresh perspective of an unschooler, a person who isn't going to harass them about the usual things. *GWS* #26 tells about a fourteen-year-old who spends two and a half hours every afternoon in an elementary school, and a thirteen-year-old who takes an hour each Thursday to read to elementary schoolkids and correct papers. And unschooler Jade Crown, fourteen, of Washington, was invited to a public school to speak about children's rights.

If you'd like more advice getting started, see *Lend a Hand: The How, Where, and Why of Volunteering,* by Sara Gilbert, *A Student's Guide to Volunteering,* by Theresa DiGeronimo, or *The Kid's Guide to Service Projects,* by Barbara Lewis. *Making Things Happen: How to Be an Effective Volunteer,* by Joan Wolfe, is excellent for volunteers who want to take an active, leadership role. Also, you can find resources for volunteering outdoors in Chapter 28, and for volunteering around the world in Chapter 29.

Looking down the road, you may also want to consider volunteering as a way to continue your education at the college level. Once you're eighteen or twenty-one years old, many more opportunities will become available, particularly if you have useful skills. One good resource is *Alternatives to the Peace Corps: A Directory of Third World & U.S. Volunteer Opportunities*, edited by Phil Lowenthal.

And remember that volunteer work can lead into other opportunities. In *GWS* #118, Emily Murphy writes:

> Because of the flexibility of my schedule, at an early age I was able to volunteer at a local museum, one of the most exciting and valuable experiences I have ever had. In addition to its being simply a fun experience, I was able to parlay this early experience into more jobs during my high school [homeschooled] and college years in libraries, museums, and archives. Because of this experience, when I applied for the position I now hold, as Assistant Registrar and Curator of Photographs at the Maryland State Archives, I found that all those jobs I had had since I was fourteen added up to four and a half years of full-time experience in my field—more than enough experience to exempt me from the M.A. requirement for my position!

Examples

A parent writes in *GWS* #36:

> Since spring, our thirteen-year-old daughter has been volunteering at a science museum two days a week. To say that she loves it is an understatement! She's been doing a great deal of work in the museum's "mount room," cataloging their collections and learning names (in scientific as well as laymen's terms) of many birds and mammals in the process . . . She's becoming quite the birder. Occasionally she gets to go on a field trip with the museum's naturalist. And we all got to go (at special staff rates) on a whale watch sponsored by the museum . . .
>
> The naturalist, by the way, has been very impressed by both of our children's obvious love of and knowledge of nature. He said that he'd be more than happy to take them out into the field any time. All the museum staff thinks that it's wonderful that our daughter had the chance to be doing this and have been very supportive, giving her a range of things to do to broaden her experiences there. Occasionally she will take over for the receptionist, and the accountant wants to teach her some of that. She can use the cash register and she helps get out mailings at times. Everyone has found out what a good worker she is and the demand has become high! Her major focus is and will be, at her request, the natural history work.

At thirteen, Alison McCutchen began volunteering at a library and in a vet's office. Her mother Ruth writes in *GWS* #32, "She enjoys both but favors the vet. During her first week she saw a dog spayed and our two ten-month-old kittens neutered. She described it to us in *glorious* detail and we all found it fascinating. She wasn't fazed by any of it."

A year and a half later, Ruth McCutchen sent this update to *GWS* #41: "Alison's (fifteen) latest volunteer job is at the local legal aide office where she is filing and summarizing social workers' case notes."

Alison's sister Deborah was sixteen when her mother wrote in *GWS* #46, "Deborah's latest volunteer jobs have been at the zoo: one in the Metazoo, an indoor exhibit with small animals, reptiles and microscopes, the other in the commissary where the diets are prepared."

Theo Giesy writes in *GWS* #26:

> Darrin (fourteen) and Susie (twelve) volunteer three days a week at the Cousteau Society. They do all sorts of things, like work in membership. Darrin works mostly in the warehouse, packing things members have ordered (books, T-shirts, etc). He also drives the fork-lift.
>
> Since they work there so much they were invited to the $50-a-ticket reception the night

before the Calypso sailed. Darrin couldn't go so I got to go in his place. I met Jacques and Jean-Michele Cousteau. Darrin has made friends with Jean-Michele's son Fabien—they are about the same age and have many common interests.

I like the Cousteau's attitude toward their employees and volunteers. They appreciate Darrin and Susie very much. They were worried about the lack of work permits and the number of hours spent, so I wrote a letter on Brook School letterhead saying that they were working there as part of the Brook School Curriculum and under the responsibility of Brook School. That satisfied everyone; it looks official.

Darrin runs the spotlight for Tidewater Dinner Theater, $40 per week (six shows). That is why he couldn't go to the Cousteau reception. He hopes to be able to run the light board soon, $115/week. He enjoys doing spotlight and is treated as an adult around the theater.

Frank Conley, twelve, writes in *GWS* #30:

I am presently taking a veterinary medicine course at Louisiana State University. (This course is being given for "gifted and talented" junior high and high school students—I had no trouble registering as a homeschooler.) I became interested in learning more about it and decided to ask a local veterinarian if I could help out at his clinic in return for the experience of watching them work.

It has been very worthwhile. The three vets who work there have been very kind and helpful to me. They explain everything they do and not only allow me to watch but actually let me perform certain duties. They say I'm "indispensable."

So far some of the most interesting things I've done are: watch an autopsy on a cat, learn to draw blood from animals and prepare slides, take temperatures and fecals, watch surgery performed, and go along on emergency calls.

I go to the clinic nearly every day now, for several hours a day. I plan to take an animal science course next.

I recommend this way of learning to everyone. At first I was afraid no one would want my help, since I'm only twelve, but the people I talked to were happy to have free help.

A mother writes in *GWS* #35:

My oldest decided she would like to do volunteer work at a nursing home so we found one nearby that would take her at age fourteen. She works two days a week from 10:00 A.M. until 3:00 P.M. The residents adore her and the feeling is mutual. The nurses have only praise for how well she has fit right in and all think she must be eighteen. She talks to residents, takes them for walks, holds hands, feeds them. The residents look forward to her coming. Most of all, Lauren loves to hear their stories of the old days. (We also like to talk about the criticism I heard that if my children don't learn to get up to go to school every day, they'll *never* be disciplined to get up and go to a job when they are older! Balderdash.)

Karen Franklin of Florida writes in *GWS* #72:

Adam, our twelve-year-old, spends a lot of time at the Science Museum . . . Adam's big interest is marine biology, especially sharks. The director of the museum is an expert on this, has worked with the top people in the field. The main exhibit this summer was about sharks, so Adam, already quite an expert, led many tours and answered many questions.

Seventeen-year-old Sarabeth Matilsky, of New Jersey, writes:

There's definitely never a dull moment at the George Street Co-op, the store that has been the hub of my family's community since before I can remember. The co-op has been much more than a food store for us—it has been a place to meet people, to socialize, to network, to learn. I started working in the store by myself when I was nine (to fulfill my family's work requirements), and when I was thirteen I got my own membership. Over the years I've worked hundreds of hours in the co-op, doing my own hours, other people's hours, and sometimes just working all day when there were no volunteers and the coordinator was going crazy. I have always felt respected while working in the store, if not always by strangers shopping ("You're WHAT?... Only *twelve years old??"*) then certainly by the staff and most of the other members I've worked with.

As I've gotten older and more experienced, I've been offered more and more responsibility. On any given day that I come in to work I may stock shelves, price grocery items, package bulk food, stock from the overstock areas, package produce, fill pasta bins, bring food down from the upstairs freezer, scrub the floor, check in orders, run the register, organize refrigerators, process special orders, or do any other of the million and one things that need to be done in order to operate a retail store. While doing these things I've learned many varied and useful skills, such as: understanding the math that's involved when members get their various discounts at the register, dealing with fussy shoppers, understanding the behind-the-scenes stuff that happens in a food store, including budget management from year to year and the nuances of profit margins, plus countless other things. The co-op has been an invaluable part of my education—not just because it's taught me about politics or social studies or math or geography, but because it's helped me learn *all* of that and more. It hasn't been my grade school or high school or college education, but rather a part of my *life* education.

Luba Karpynka of California writes in *GWS* #87:

My twelve-year-old son, Joaquin Gray, has volunteered at our public access TV station, KCTV, for about a year now, about twelve or more hours weekly. And he has just completed a six-month internship (among adults!). His prime interest is computer graphics, but his functions are directing (the entire crew as well as audio, technical, and floor directing), and doing computer graphics, camera, and lights. He produces a show for a local political group, meetings of which he attends with his dad. And he's in the process of creating his own science fiction mini-series.

All this has been possible because of his having been always homeschooled and having the time to focus on his various interests. He virtually taught himself everything about the Commodores 20 and 64, and as we can't afford an Amiga 2000, he familiarized himself with it at the station. Now he'll be giving paid lessons to crew volunteers (adults) on this Amiga.

Carmen Nolan of Florida, fifteen, writes in *GWS* #106 about volunteering in a zoo:

I have always loved animals with all my heart; I can't remember not caring for animals. My Mom deserves credit for getting me involved at the local zoo. She called to see what kind of volunteer opportunities were available there, and as a result I was enrolled in an eight-week, mini-zoology, docent training course. I graduated from the course in November and began volunteering as a docent immediately. Many people believe that volunteering at the zoo is mainly shoveling animal waste, but it is not! As a matter of fact, I don't do that at all! A docent as a volunteer teacher and, in that capacity, I have had to learn a great deal about a wide variety of animals, as well as about public speaking, in order to conduct tours, provide animal encounters, and participate in community outreach programs. I was very honored to receive the Central Florida Zoo's "Rookie of the Year 1994" award . . . I am the youngest docent the zoo has ever had.

As a direct result of volunteering at the zoo, I have been able to affirm the career I would like to pursue. I started working with the licensed rehabilitationist there and have decided that I would like to do that type of work. Animal rehabilitation would be a very fulfilling and rewarding field for me. In addition, I am also interested in the study of primates and the use of sign language with them.

As of this date, in addition to being a docent at our local zoo, I am also a paid employee. I have been hired as a teaching assistant for one of the many educational programs for children that the zoo offers. This opportunity is especially thrilling because I feel that I have earned it through my volunteer work and dedication, and because I am still pretty young. I feel very privileged to have the adult world believe in me enough to give me a place in the working environment that I enjoy so very much!

Anna Barnett, fourteen, of Oregon, writes:

We first found out about WISTEC when my brother started homeschooling. The local science museum, Willamette Science and Technology center, isn't huge, just a few large rooms, but I loved and *still* love it.

It hosts traveling exhibits, and has several of its own permanent ones. WISTEC has a nature room with gemstones, a colony of bees, and all kinds of critters. It has a different theme each season, bubbles or physics or photography or whatever. I started taking Saturday Science classes. Once I took a summer class in photography and discovered that WISTEC had a darkroom, too. (Whoa, cool!) Mark Dow taught both Saturday Science and the photography class.

I think at this point that I had started homeschooling/unschooling. I had decided that I wanted to see what it was like doing volunteer work, and I chose WISTEC because I thought it would be fun to work there and I knew they needed volunteers. I called Mark Dow because he was the WISTEC person that I knew best, and my favorite teacher. I filled out a form and became an official volunteer.

The first thing I did was to help set up a huge exhibit from the Exploratorium in San Francisco. It was called "Finding Your Way" and it was all about navigation. I screwed and unscrewed things, and moved things around for people, but I generally got the hit that somebody else could have done the things I was doing, maybe better, and people were figuring out jobs for me to do. Around then I wrote a letter to *GWS* about my job. I think I was eleven or twelve at this time.

The next thing I did was help at the huge annual Eugene Celebration. This Celebration lasts two or three days and spans all of downtown Eugene, blocks and blocks. They had a booth there promoting Finding Your Way and WISTEC in general. I was all over the celebration with my friends and every now and then I'd come by and work for an hour or so.

My work at the WISTEC booth was a different story than setting up the exhibit. The booth had activities for kids to do, flyers and coupons for the exhibit, and a couple people explaining how to do the activities, what WISTEC was, and what the exhibit was about. The volunteers manning the booth were very busy and grateful to have my help. I gave away a lot of coupons and got a lot of kids and parents interested in WISTEC.

I don't think I did any other jobs for a while after that. Mark never had any jobs for me when I would call him, and I got occupied with other things.

Then I took a class called WISTEC Apprentice through Saturday Academy. It was with Mark and we designed exhibits and built test models in the shop. After the class was over I continued to come in once a week to work on leftover ideas. It was great fun, and I also got over my phobia of power tools.

But after a couple months I started to get bored. I didn't feel like going to work to the shop anymore. Then my mother suggested that I take some samples of my computer graphics in and see if I could do that for volunteer work. I did and was immediately put to work on Superpaint (graphics paradise). Mark had me make an explanation, with diagrams, for an exhibit at the science corner. The next week I started work on an explanation for an exhibit for a conference. It took a month and I worked really hard on it.

Now I do a lot of computer graphics and I'm also generally a sort of museum elf. Once I helped Mark experiment with some different dye indicators for a Mr. Wizard appearance at a WISTEC birthday party. Another time I made a huge freehand scale drawing as sort of a poster explanation for an exhibit. I hang science photos, make copies, feed Beastmaster the iguana and Rock the tortoise . . . it would take pages to tell all the odd jobs I do, but you get the picture. And the other job, the one I was saving for last, is helping with Friday Night Science.

Friday Night Science is a weekly class for elementary school kids. Each week the topic is different. I help with setting up, supervising the kids, and I do more odd jobs, which range from passing out freeze dried food on a "space shuttle mission" to pointing out signs of animals on nature walks. There's usually about a dozen wild kids so Randy, the teacher, can always use all the help he can get. A while ago I brought a friend, and she wants to come back and help again. And one of the best parts is that I get to do all the activities, too!

I really like being at WISTEC. I like my work and the place in general. I get along well with the other people that work there, and they appreciate my help.

As for my plans for the future, I guess WISTEC doesn't really have much significance. My career plans seems to be changing about once a month at this point, but right now I think I'd like to be a chef, or maybe an actress or a psychologist. I do plan to try volunteering at some other places once I get more time.

My advice for anyone who wants to try volunteering: Go for it! And, wherever you choose, don't be afraid to ask, either. You'd be surprised at how many different places, from the library to the hardware store, could use some help. ☻

jobs

I was like many other fullbloods. I didn't want a steady job in an office or factory. I thought myself too good for that, not because I was stuck up but simply because any human being is too good for that kind of no-life, even white people.
—John Fire, *Lame Deer, Seeker of Visions*

DON'T BE LIMITED by the stereotypes that tell us what kinds of jobs teenagers can do. You can do much more than babysit, flip pancakes, and wash cars. Jobs in specialty retail stores, for example, are one of the best ways to get involved in a field that you love. Consider comic book stores, pet stores, book stores, jewelry stores, imported clothing stores, antique stores, feed stores, bike shops, cheese stores, bakeries, natural foods stores, piano stores, music stores. The people who work in these places are often very knowledgeable, and you will learn from being around them and the stuff itself. Also, retail stores frequently hire teenagers.

Know about the child labor statutes in your state or country so you can figure out how to work around them, and know when you need to be low key. Generally, in the U.S. you have to be fourteen to get a work permit; employers are supposed to keep these permits on file for any employees under eighteen. You may have to get a permit through the counseling office of your ex-school. Some homeschoolers' employers, however, have only requested written permission from parents. In general, both state and federal laws influence your situation. For more information, contact your state or region labor (employment) department (look in the phone book), or call local representatives and ask them to mail you copies of the statutes.

Look for work through your parents' network of friends or through the homeschool community. *GWS* often runs advertisements or announcements of homeschooling families who want a teenaged live-in nanny, for example.

If you are especially young or have difficulty getting a job, consider offering to work for very low wages—but only at first. Once you're good at what you do, don't feel embarrassed to ask to be paid more; if you work as well as an adult does, you deserve an adult wage. If you are legal and have a work permit, then in many countries you are entitled to a minimum wage, no matter how old you are. If you feel you're being taken advantage of, discuss it with your boss. If that doesn't work, contact your state department of labor for information and help.

Another alternative is to work for trade—that is, in exchange for something other than money. If you are quite young, this would make the whole situation easier on your employer, who could call you an apprentice or a volunteer rather than an employee, and thus avoid trouble with tax and labor department people.

As an unschooler, you have an edge on the best summer jobs, including jobs at camps, resorts, and national parks, because such places prefer people who can work the whole season—often May through September, not just June through August. Check the library for books on summer jobs for teenagers and college students.

Unschoolers and their jobs

Rosalie Megli writes in *GWS* #20:

New opportunities are opening up for Lora, our thirteen-year-old daughter. She has made arrangements to begin part-time work at the local veterinary clinic, feeding animals and cleaning cages. She has also been made welcome to accompany the vets on farm runs and with office work. Since Lora loves animals and may be interested in veterinary science as a vocation, we are delighted with her arrangements. Lora got her work permit from the superintendent of schools with *no* stipulations regarding working hours . . .

Lora also has a small craft business (she makes herb-filled potholder mitts) and is going to buy a microscope with proceeds from pre-Christmas sales.

Eileen Trombly writes in *GWS* #24:

Amy was interviewed and accepted and jumped into the Avon world with both feet . . . She has done a good deal of baby-sitting and house cleaning . . . in recent months. She has been in great demand due to her reliability and dependable qualities. Her duties as sitter expanded over the years and she was called upon by parents of newborns as well as older children. During the summer months she even went on family sailboat cruises to Block Island, Newport, etc. . . . Alas, burnout at age fifteen set in and wages became insufficient for an ambitious ballerina who went through toe shoes faster than she could pay for them.

. . . Her first five days as an Avon representative were highly successful and she grossed a personal income of $100 within that time. Additional calculating indicates that she is working approximately two hours daily (at her convenience) and earning $7.50 an hour. Not bad for a fifteen-year-old. If she chooses to work more hours, she'll make more—it's her choice . . . Most of her customers are older people and are impressed by her confidence. In figuring out her finances even further she finds she is able to take additional ballet lessons, as well as save.

Pam Robinson writes about her twelve-year-old son in *GWS* #25:

Jared has overhauled a lawn motor mower, truck rear-end, and transmission. He works summers for a neighbor driving a tractor that pulls a hay chopper and large hay wagon. He is paid very well because he is one of the most responsible, dependable employees in the area. This year at twelve he had the job of training and breaking in all the new help, seventeen- and eighteen-year-old young men. He is not required by us to work, yet he often chooses to work long hours, Sundays, and holidays.

Erin Roberts, fourteen, wrote me about her work with horses. She has worked part time at a riding stable for four years, guiding trail rides and otherwise helping out. She also works at an Arabian farm, Windsor Arabians, as an assistant trainer. "I especially help break their three- and four-year olds," she explains, "but I also help out with halter breaking the young ones as well as miscellaneous tasks around the farm." She recently bought a three-year-old halter broken Arabian gelding and trained him to ride. When I heard from her, they had just entered their first show and Erin said, "We didn't win any ribbons, but we had a great time."

Scott Maher, thirteen, writes in *GWS* #37,

In September I went down to the Wakefield Pet Shop and asked the owner Steve, whom I already had known, if there would be any way I could come down and help. I told him how I was a home schooler and that I could come down in the mornings. Steve said we could try it out for a while and see what we think.

I went down on a Monday at 10:30 and first he showed me around and showed me how things are done . . . I started off feeding the birds and cleaning their cages. Next I swept the floor and fed the fish. Then I fed and watered the small animals, lizards, rabbits, guinea pigs, and cats. Some days I clean filters in the fish tanks and test the pH of the water; other days I clean the cages and clean the glass. I have helped unload shipments and put stock away.

I have been working there almost four months now. I have waited on customers, given them advice, taken inventory, and I even take care of the shop if Steve has to leave. Soon I will be learning how to use the cash register . . .

I think the best part of it is learning about all of the different animals, fish and birds and learning how to take care of them. I have been put in charge of lizards and small animals. It is a lot of fun to help out customers.

A year later, Mary Maher, Scott's mom, sent an update to *GWS* #43:

There have been many times when Steve, the owner, has called Scott at home and asked him to please come down for the day because he very much needed his help. On several occasions, Steve has had to leave the store for several hours and he has left Scott alone, in charge. When Steve opened a second pet shop in a nearby city, he often took Scott with him at night to get things unpacked or to set up displays or even to have Scott help put up paneling and install ceilings. Once in a while, Scott travels with Steve in the evenings to service or set up very large fish tanks for restaurants or private residences.

Customers don't seem to mind that Scott is so young. They will engage him in lengthy conversations on how to take care of a particular pet or how to go about properly setting up a fish tank. One fellow, an older man, took all Scott's advice on what fish were compatible for his new tank.

Recently, Steve has decided that he would like to sell pet supplies at a Sunday flea market in another town, and Scott will be in charge of the whole operation.

Eleadari Acheson, fifteen, writes in *GWS* #76 about her work at a used bookstore and as a coach at a gymnastics club:

During the past two years the store moved to a larger location and my hours have increased to three five-hour days per week. My income and responsibilities have increased as well. I now buy and price books, clean, organize displays, make business calls, write business letters, conduct book searches, answer questions, and restock shelves. In addition, when the owners are on vacation I handle mail and banking.

At first I was the only employee, but a few months ago three more employees were hired . . . As senior employee, I am paid more per hour than the rest even though I am the youngest. When the owners are unavailable, the other employees call me when they have questions . . .

[About her gymnastics work:] When I started I wasn't strong enough to spot even a front limber with the older kids. Now I'm spotting the older kids' back handsprings by myself. I also lead warm-ups and teach the less complicated tricks while the head coach teaches the harder stuff . . .

I consider my jobs the most important part of my homeschooling education.

Kristine Breck had been out of school six years by the time she wrote in *GWS* #70:

My main interest is animals. I recently had the opportunity to go from my home in Alaska to an exotic animal breeding compound in Florida, where lions, tigers, leopards, and other rare animals are raised. It was a dream come true for me because I had always admired the big cats and now I was going to live with them.

No doubt, I had worked for it, and it has been work I have loved doing. I trained several winning obedience dogs and a performing sheep, raised a musk ox, tamed a fox, trained and raced the World Champion racing reindeer, and taught my best friend, a horse, to do 35 circus tricks (so far).

Last summer when the Florida big cat people brought their educational exhibit to our small town in Alaska, I gave them a copy of my resume/portfolio. They said I had talent, and they came to our farm to give me an audition.

In February, I boarded the airplane for Florida . . . Since I was working with very special animals, some endangered species, the owners trusted me a whole lot to take good care of the young baboon, the llama, the lion cubs, and the baby leopard. I tried very hard and used all my knowledge to be worthy of their trust. And I must have been a good "nanny," because I never had any problems, and they invited me and my mom to come back and live and work on the compound permanently.

People I met were very surprised at my adventure. They usually guessed, "And you're only sixteen or seventeen, right?" Actually, I'm fourteen, but under my circumstances, age was not important. Qualities such as knowledge, interest, and desire to learn were what mattered. It was a wonderful experience, and I think homeschooling is excellent preparation for the real world, because we live and learn right in it.

A year later, Kristine wrote in *GWS* #79:

This last summer I spent five months on the road, working for the Big Cat Show. I'd had other jobs before, but this one was intense, and in it I learned and practiced responsibility, financial management, and taking care of myself away from my family. I really enjoy traveling, and a person can learn a lot from the many situations and environments encountered. It seems like adjusting and making changes comes more easily after you've traveled.

. . . My next job was through people who knew me and said I was a mature, hardworking, ambitious young person, which I have always tried to be . . . In this job I handled camels and Nativity animals in the Radio City Music Hall Christmas Spectacular. It was a very impressive place to work and required staying in New York City for two months, which is truly an enlightening experience for anyone from a small town.

Kristine went on to live and work at an animal park in Maine, saving her money "to buy a vehicle and equipment to take my performing animal show on tour independently." By the time she was nineteen, she had indeed performed throughout the U.S. with her horse, Magic, including appearances on the David Letterman show and Radio City Music Hall, and had moved to California. There, she started her own business which included an educational animal program, and also organized horse-drawn sunset dinner rides and children's pony rides.

Randall Kern writes in *GWS* #67:

I am twelve and have been a homeschooler all my life. I have been programming computers for six years. A year ago I started going to an IBM computer club, even though I didn't have an IBM yet. When we got one, last June, I became the consultant for our group.

The last meeting I went to was held in a newspaper office, because the computer they use for their accounting needed to be set up. When we got there we found out that the program they had bought didn't do what they wanted. So they hired me to write an accounts receivable and account maintenance program for the newspaper.

GWS #43 tells about Jeff Gold, who at sixteen had dropped out of high school and was earning $2000 a week helping companies safeguard their computer programs.

Leonie Edwards, sixteen, loves her full time job as a dental assistant, and plans to become a dentist. She began working at fourteen as a sort of assistant-to-the-assistant. At that time, she wrote in *GWS* #64:

> I work mainly with the dental assistant. I started doing things like cleaning rooms, sterilizing instruments, setting up trays, preparing the rooms for the next patient, and watching how the dental assistant did things. After a while they gave me more to do, such as getting the patients in and putting a movie on for them, filing, preparing syringes, making sure the rooms are stocked, and developing x-rays. Then I started assisting the dentist with several patients. Now the dentist calls me, instead of the dental assistant, to help with fillings and sometimes root canals.

"Thanks to homeschooling," she writes now, "I can put 'two and a half years of dental assisting experience' on my college application." At the same time, she's working on a correspondence course from the University of Kentucky on Human Biology. The credits will build towards her pre-dental bachelor's degree. ☀

36

your own business

STARTING A BUSINESS can mean freedom, creativity, self-expression, and fulfillment of your unique talents and interests. It can involve nearly anything: breeding and selling tropical fish, cleaning attics, running a bead store, mending old books or jeans, starting a mail-order book club for teenagers, training horses, designing Web pages or giving computer consultations, recording language instruction cassette tapes if you have a native tongue other than English. For the most part, any business run by an adult could also be a teenage business. And just because you've never heard of anyone who made a business out of helping kids build treehouses and forts doesn't mean it can't be done. Of course, you can try any kind of work as part of a job, too—working in someone *else's* bead store, for instance.

In a business, you answer to yourself and your customers (or clients) instead of a boss. Naturally, running your own business means you have to stand on your own two feet, and that nonexistent boss can't give you a salary. If you act wisely and love what you do, you'll probably *eventually* make a profit. If the worst happens, you could lose your investment of money; if your business is something like childcare or petsitting, you could possibly even be sued if a court held you responsible for damages. However, if you take care with whatever you are doing and don't make empty promises, you should have no trouble.

There are two reasons starting a business especially suits itself to teenagers. First, you don't yet need to support yourself financially. You needn't worry about making fast money, so you can enjoy a slow start, learning gradually from your mistakes.

Many adults cannot easily afford to go into business, because they can't take the time off their original jobs to get started—and they have to keep those jobs to support themselves. Many businesses make no profit or even lose money their first year or so. This is mainly because most businesses require an initial investment—large or small depending on the type of business, your standards, and your ingenuity. Generally, a retail business requires the greatest initial investment—renting a store and buying all the things you plan to sell. (You can creatively cut costs anywhere, of course. I have a small retail business with almost no overhead expense; it consists mainly of toting a box of instructional videos and sequined veils with me every time

I teach a dance class or workshop.) At the other end of the spectrum, a service business requires little capital. To be a tutor, freelance photographer, guitar teacher, or typist would require only advertising and transportation costs plus the tools of the trade—camera, guitar, or computer.

I do not wish to imply that your business *can't* make a profit in its early stages. Especially if it's your major goal to make money, you can do it. My friend Laura made bread and cookies every day when she was a sophomore in high school, and by selling them to teachers and students, she paid for her trip to Scotland the following summer.

The second reason starting a business is a great idea for teenagers is that it's one of the few legal, exciting money-making opportunities for people under the age of eighteen. Many places can't hire you until you're sixteen, but no one can stop you from running most kinds of businesses. Even if you're sixteen, finding fun work isn't necessarily easy. There's always McDonald's, but a degrading job like that is for someone who's too tired out—by school, for instance—to do anything better.[1]

Make a plan

After six years making a living running my own businesses (teaching and performing bellydance, publishing my own books, directing a summer camp, and operating a mail order book catalog), I suggest that you set up a clear set of financial records, right at the start. The office of your secretary of state can send you information on legalities and taxes. And do write a business plan:

- List your start up costs. (A new software program? fliers to post around town? a boom box to use when you teach hip hop dancing?)
- List your ongoing costs. (Postage? subscriptions to special magazines? advertising? transportation? phone bills? office supplies?)
- Estimate your net income potential (all the money you expect to take in).
- Estimate your potential profit (all the money you take in, minus all of your expenses).
- Identify the competition (or you may prefer to think of the competition in a more friendly way, such as your "colleagues") and consider how their business will affect your business. It doesn't have to be a negative relationship—perhaps you could share subscriptions to expensive trade magazines, or refer customers to each other when you're overworked.

Books to get you started

There are many terrific books which both tell about the legal and paperwork side of a business *and* give a general overview of the possibilities. These are my favorites:

- *Growing a Business*, by Paul Hawken. (Also a PBS series.) Helps you design and start a business that reflects your own interests and skills. An original, conscientious economist and businessman, Hawken has no college degree or other "qualifications" to interfere with his common sense.
- *Small Time Operator*, by Bernard Kamoroff, gives you all the information you need on record keeping, taxes, and other technical headaches. Kamoroff writes

---

[1] My brother Ned didn't like my using the word "degrading" here, for excellent reasons. I'm not saying it's necessarily degrading to cook, sweep floors, or serve food. I do feel a large corporation whose main motive is profit inevitably steals vitality and meaning from the lives of its workers.

in a friendly, clear style. In my office, his book is indispensable.
- *The Teenage Entrepreneur's Guide: Fifty money-making business ideas*, by Sarah L. Riehm. Gives a clear introduction to setting up a business and taking care of paperwork, marketing, etc., and gives detailed plans for fifty kinds of businesses, ranging from auto detailing to bumper stickers to catering. My only hesitation: this book might influence you to fit yourself into one of these businesses, rather than *invent* a business that fits *you*.
- *Wishcraft*, by Barbara Sher, helps you get *anything* together in your life, but it's especially terrific for a project like starting a business, which can be overwhelming if you don't know how to break it down and get the support you need.
- *Running a One-Person Business*, by Claude Whitmeyer and Salli Rasberry, an overall guide to everything from bookkeeping and time management to publicity and having fun.

When are you ready to start?
Depends on what you want to do. You probably already have skills that could lead to a business without further training. The people I taught in school, aged eleven to fourteen, already had the expertise necessary to operate dozens of businesses, such as:
- giving skateboard lessons
- decorating and painting skateboards
- teaching or tutoring Japanese or Hebrew
- writing newsletters on various issues
- sewing and designing clothing
- forming a band
- giving figure skating lessons
- coaching hockey or tennis
- teaching sailing
- picking up neighborhood recyclables (with help of a bike trailer or older friends with drivers' licenses)
- making tie-dyed and batiked clothing
- producing videos
- making and selling food—catering, cookies, etc.
- raising and breeding various animals

Or, perhaps you'd like to do something you're not yet skilled in—but could be with some practice, guidance, and/or good tools. A job related to your interests is valuable training for a later business, especially when you're fairly new to the field. Or design a more independent training ground. Maybe you're a good tap dancer and would like to start a small professional troupe, but first you want to spend a year taking more lessons, giving amateur recitals, and studying all the old Gene Kelly and Fred Astaire musicals you can get your hands on. Good. Do it.

Yes, it's best to hold out long enough to be sure you're offering your buyers a quality product or service, but don't wait too long just because you have stage fright. Sometimes there comes a point when your interest can't develop any further until you put yourself on the line and start sharing your skill with the world. That happened to me.

After I'd taken a year of Middle Eastern dance lessons, I knew I'd found one of my callings, and I set a goal of performing professionally in two years. I'd moved to a new city and had an impossible time linking up with other dancers for lessons, so I practiced on my own every day and studied videos of other dancers. Finally, I reached a plateau where I felt dead-ended and frustrated at the lack of contact. I took the big plunge and nervously phoned up a local Moroccan restaurant—a year and a half before I had planned to start my "career." To my surprise, they thought I was pretty good. In fact, after my first performance I was signed on for a standing Friday and Saturday night engagement. Furthermore, although the first two shows were pure panic, in my bones I knew that the timing was right. A live audience was exactly the challenge that my dancing needed in order to progress.

To make your business successful on the most ultimate terms, be sure it is not only something you love and that the public will buy, but also something *good* for people and for this battered planet. I mean not only the *type* of business, but also your approach to it. As a belly dancer, I bring joy, cultural awareness, affirmation of womanhood, and friendly entertainment to my audiences. I help them celebrate, and that is good work. If I perceived my art differently, I might instead bring silliness, mild pornography, gimmicks, and cheap flash.

Run your business under the scrutiny of your own moral code. Mainly, just *think* about what you're doing and take time to do it right. If you open a catering service, consider an alternative to polystyrene foam (Styrofoam, etc.) packaging. As a fabric painter, you can find dyes and paints that don't harm water systems after you dump them down the drain. When singing for a crowd, aim not just to impress your listeners, but also to warm them and make them feel good.

Also, remember that a lot of situations that we think of as teenage "jobs" are really small businesses—when you're babysitting or shoveling snow there's a fine line between "clients" and "bosses." While this sort of work may not be as glamorous as designing rock gardens, you can make it more meaningful simply by *thinking* of it as a business, and becoming more creative and proactive in your approach. Of course, unschooling can give you an advantage even in these typical teenage "jobs." Lora Risley mentions in *GWS* #76, "I was allowed to babysit at children's homes and I earned quite a bit of money because I was available when the other babysitters were at school."

Unschoolers in business

At age fourteen, Carey Newman of British Columbia wrote in *GWS* #68:

Right now I am working towards becoming a full-time artist. My parents have played a big part in my progress up to now.

When I was twelve my Dad asked the Sooke Museum about me having a solo show of my wildlife sketches in their gallery. The museum approved and said that I could have a show…. A lot of my time during the months before the show was spent preparing for the opening night, which close to ninety people attended. Through the next two months over half my drawings sold. I thank my mom and dad for pushing me to get everything ready for that show.

[Later] I started on Northwest Coast Indian art. My dad, an Indian artist himself, was very helpful in showing me the rules of Indian design. Soon after, my father received an application form for the Sooke Fine Arts Show, a juried show that takes place in Sooke every year. Jokingly, I said that I should enter my Indian designs and silk-screen-print them. My parents turned it from joke to matter and said that I should try. They supported me financially by lending me the money to enter the show, and to buy silkscreening material. An artist friend of mine helped me to do the silkscreening. Two of my designs were accepted and I went on to sell 59 prints over a period of ten days, bringing in just over $2,000, from which I paid back my parents and bought more equipment and supplies to continue with this art form.

My mom later found out about the Okanagan Summer School of the Arts, got the application form, helped me apply for a bursary to cover expenses, and assisted me in composing a letter with samples of my work so that I could get accepted into a course that didn't normally accept anyone under sixteen.

At thirteen, Vita Wallace began earning money giving violin lessons (see *GWS* #64 and #70). *GWS* #64 pointed out that young teachers are sometimes actually *better* than older teachers since they know freshly what it feels like to be taught.

Amelia Acheson writes in *GWS* #42 about her twelve-year-old daughter:

She picked up a clowning book at the library last summer. Her first decision was to duplicate one of the costumes and gags she saw there for a Halloween costume. It turned out so delightful that she was invited to bring it to a day-care center to "show-off" and entertain the little kids. Over the year, that has grown to a business, and now includes all three of our kids. They have been paid for their clowning—they have their own business cards—they brought home a huge first place trophy from a parade—and, mostly, they have a lot of fun at it. They ride unicycles, juggle, do gymnastics. Tia does magic tricks (one of her magic books says that magic is a trade like no other—you have to learn it yourself at home). They sometimes work in partnership with a fourteen-year-old clown from another town who makes balloon animals—as a result, he is learning to unicycle, and they are learning to make balloon animals.

In *GWS* #24, a mother tells about her family's unschooling. They'd spent the first year with the Calvert curriculum (a correspondence school), and not especially enjoyed it. So they changed:

Into the second year, we started the family business. We sell and repair bicycles. We also sell all accessories associated with bicycling. The kids and I manage the store while Dad works his full-time job as a carpenter. (Unless you are very rich, outside income is necessary the first years in business.) He has an active role in the store evenings and weekends. Our fifteen-year-old son, who has the bike knowledge (from books and other places) manages the repair department, doing all repairs (training dad), keeping stock of parts and working with customers. Our sixteen-year-old daughter is the family organizer, keeps us clean and orderly, manages the store, selling and keeping up with the accessory inventory. Mom's (that's me!) main job is to keep the office going, books, etc. . . . Sounds simple? It's not. But somehow it all works!

At sixteen, Carmen Rodriguez-Winter and her seventeen-year-old brother Javier opened their own shop, Back Alley Peddlers, in Toledo, Ohio. They sell vintage clothing, concert T-shirts, skateboards, hats, their own handmade jewelry, incense, hair dye, poetry written by their friends, lava lamps, and such. Carmen had fantasized about opening her own store ever since fourth grade, and a few years after she left school in eighth grade, she felt ready to do so. With their mother's help, Carmen and Javier decorated and renovated the building and launched their dream, traveling to Los Angeles, New York, and Chicago for fashion shows. "Without homeschool this wouldn't be a reality at all," she says, "I'd still be at school, just sitting there, being really super bored, and doing nothing with my life, just being a bum."

Emily Bergson-Shilcock, seventeen, of Pennsylvania, also opened her own shop, The Destination of Independence. She explains:

I was homeschooled all of my life. The basic philosophy of my homeschooling education was "learn in the process of doing real work" (as opposed to "make work"—like math worksheets instead of purposeful measurement in the wood shop or kitchen) . . .

Just after my seventeenth birthday, I reached my life long goal and opened a retail store. I have always been interested in money and business, and my parents have supported my interest—for instance, when I was ten they gave me a real electronic cash register. Also, starting at age seven I was involved in numerous volunteer opportunities. Consequently, my life dream was to discover how I could combine business and helping others into a feasible career.

The Destination of Independence, selling products to make everyday living easier for people with disabilities, was born in April of 1995. My products include wall-mounted jar openers, reachers, long handled shoe horns, ergonomically designed garden tools, Arthritis Foundation award-winning kitchen utensils and doorknob grips and extensions; all designed and chosen to help people with Multiple Sclerosis, arthritis, Carpal-Tunnel syndrome, etc. Owning and managing my store has helped me to broaden my world and educate me in hundreds of ways: researching manufacturers and products, public speaking through demonstrations, writing business letters, handling State and Federal taxes, using a financial management system on the computer, increasing my sensitivity to the needs of the elderly and disabled, practicing continuous improvement, and realizing that with hard work and a positive attitude, anything is possible.

I have loved being a homeschooler not because it is the only way I think one can learn and flourish, but because I think it was the best way for me. ☀

pigs
and honey:
farm-related work

WHY?

1. FOR YOUR edification. Getting involved with the lives of the plants and animals that we eat fills a big gap in our "educations," a gap the schools can't possibly fill. The field trip to look at cows doesn't cut it. Nor does the photograph of cornfields on page 361 of your *American Heritage* book, or chopping up rats in biology. I may overly romanticize this one, because I am not *yet* a small farmer. But no one ever argues convincingly against the goodness of contact with the fundamental building blocks of our lives. Undertaking any sort of agricultural project will be good for your brain. The Colfax family found that

> At home, our efforts to restore the land, to plant gardens, and to improve our livestock, stimulated interest in biology, chemistry, and, eventually, embryology and genetics. Clearing the badly damaged land provided lessons in ecology, and the construction of a house and outbuildings showed the boys the relevance of seemingly arcane subjects such as geometry. Drew, at seven, understood that the Pythagorean theorem was invaluable in squaring up his sheep shed foundation. Grant, at nine, discovered a Pomo Indian campsite on the ridge and was inspired to delve into North American archaeology, an interest which later broadened into studies of Mayan and Aztec cultures.[1]

One of the most delightful unschooling families I heard from was the Fallicks, from a small community near Davenport, Washington. They live without any conventional utilities, generating most of their own electricity from solar panels. They grow much of their own food, use an outhouse, and get water from a creek. Jj, the mother, described the family's education in part as follows:

> Our activities have a yearly sort of cycle, tied to the seasons and seasonal/climate factors. The kids spend more time during the winter in indoor activities and most of their time the rest of the year outdoors. Just living here is an education . . . about electricity (why do you disconnect the solar panels from the house/batteries during electrical storms?) and wildlife (the list of what lives here that Kate is compiling is over a page and includes a bear and cougar) . . . We play instruments (between us all piano, guitar, clarinet, recorder, mandolin, and percussion/washboard) . . . [We] read aloud, . . . sing, etc. The kids are involved in 4-H, mostly home economics projects and the arts, plus church, a gifted kids group and the homeschool community.

---

[1] David and Micki Colfax, *Homeschooling for Excellence*, p.5.

In *GWS* #28, Lynne Hoffman wrote, "I've drawn up a chart of common farm chores and checked off which academic subjects each suggests to me." Her chart included "plan garden," "plan pond," and "carpentry" under geometry, "make cheeses" and "freezing" under chemistry, etc.

Of course, no one in their right mind does anything wonderful merely in order to be academic. There is something rather unsavory about growing red hot chili peppers in order to learn agricultural science. On the other hand, there is something savory indeed about growing red hot chili peppers because you want to grow red hot chili peppers, and accidentally catching a lot of biology, sunshine, cooking skills, and agricultural science—whatever that means—along the way.

2. To Heal the World, or a small bit of it anyway. Agriculture is in a bad way. Your breakfast eggs were probably the work of a hen who's never been outside; she lives in a wire pen barely big enough to turn around in, and the lights in her factory stay on all night to stimulate faster egg production. The grapes your boyfriend brought on Sunday's picnic were dangerously dusted with chemical pesticides that threaten the lives of field workers. The steak sizzling in the pan oozes hormones.

The modern agricultural expert, unlike the old-fashioned farmer, has forgotten the health of the rivers and wildernesses and small towns and—above all—of the people who eat plums and spinach, milk and bacon. He sees only chemicals, yields, efficiency, and giant new tractors.

In order for everyone to keep eating, say wise farmers like Wendell Berry, many more people will need to start farming, organically and on a small scale. Yet, we are *losing*, not gaining, farmers. According to an article in *Harrowsmith*, "The average age of farmers is 52 . . . There are now twice as many farmers who are over the age of 60 as there are under the age of 35. Over the next ten years, farmers will be retiring in record numbers."[1] So, I admit, I kind of hope you will check out farming and get hooked. I figure that would help save human life on planet earth.

3. I also figure you might just plain have fun drying herbs, milking goats, baking bread, and carrying chicken shit to the compost pile—not to mention having room to *move.* Anne Brosnan, thirteen, of New York, laments,

> We live in the suburbs and have so far for seven years, but before this we lived in Minnesota in a rural cabin. We don't like it here in New York and we're selling our house to move back to a farm in Minnesota or a farm in Kentucky. I think that for homeschoolers the ideal place to live is in the country, because if you have freedom all day you should have a nice place in which to vent it. It seems so closed in here and we walk off our property in about fifteen short steps. The kids here go to school for most of the day and when they come home they just roam about on skateboards or talk on phones, because there aren't really opportunities for anything when people live close together like this. It seems like kids here know about a lot of things but they've never tried doing them.

So what do you do, buy yourself forty acres? Hassle your parents to quit their jobs and move to the sticks? Knock on the doors of all the farm houses in Lane County? Nah. Exercise some initiative instead. Your brain may storm up a plan. Here are ideas and resources to get you going:

---

[1] Craig Canine, "A Farewell to Farms," in *Harrowsmith Country Life* May/June 1991.

Go away and stay on a farm.
Go for two weeks, three months, or a year.
Place a classified ad in GWS, *explaining what you're hoping for.* Be willing to work, of course, in exchange for room and board. Given the warm, open nature of the people who read and write for *GWS*, I suspect that this tactic would land you with multiple invitations. You could probably find a situation with other unschooled teenagers, or one with younger children (whom you might help to care for). You could probably find an organic apple farm or a cattle ranch. Or place ads in regional or state homeschooling newsletters.

Of course, you would want to communicate very clearly with the family ahead of time as to your and their expectations, especially if you plan to stay a while. Be sure they know how inexperienced you are. Be sure you know how cold it gets, and what time you will have to rise and shine. Be sure you can coexist with each other's religious choices. Be sure you know how much freedom they feel like giving you. Rural homeschooling families run the complete range, from fundamentalist Christians who will not appreciate the Rolling Stones raging in your bedroom, to extremely flexible people whose own teenagers live next door in a converted barn and completely control their own academic, personal, and social lives.

Discuss whether you will mainly help with preexisting chores, or whether you might be allowed to undertake a new project, such as designing and planting an herb garden or building an outdoor solar shower.

Every once in a while, a family writes in to *GWS* to make an offer along this line. In *GWS* #18, for example, one rural family was looking for a live-in babysitter who would work ten hours each week. They offered to pay $50 per month plus room and board. In *GWS* #20, a family offered a small wage plus room and board for help with haying and gardening on an organic cattle farm.

The Homeschooler's Travel Directory lists and describes many rural and farm families who welcome homeschooling visitors.

Place a classified ad in Mother Earth News, Back Home Magazine, Whole Earth Review, or another magazine that attracts rural subscribers.

Or plug into a preexisting program, such as a living history farm, which you can locate through the *Living History Sourcebook.*

Check out The Country School, run by the homeschooling Barker family on their Ohio farm. Visitors spend five to eight days participating in farm life—working with animals, an organic orchard and garden, field crops, maintenance, and food preparation. The Barkers also run wilderness programs in Michigan, Idaho, and Montana.

See Healthy Harvest, *a directory which lists* over six hundred organic farms, organizations, apprenticeships, courses, and related information.

But Miss Llewellyn, I don't want to leave home. I'd miss my little sister.
Well, I didn't say you had go away for keeps. You could try it for a week and come back. Your little sister will be right where you left her, exploring the contents of your underwear drawer.

But, of course, you can also indulge in Earthly Pleasures right where you live.

Local farmy things to do

Rather than live on a faraway farm, find a local one, by putting up notices in feed stores, talking to the farmers at the farmers' market, or asking everyone if they know a farmer who might like an apprentice. Ask around in natural food stores if there's a regional directory of organic farms. Tabitha Mountjoy wrote about her work as a farm apprentice in *GWS* #68:

> I first met Ms. Chaffin, who owns the farm, by buying a horse from her. My new horse, Shari, is now boarding there, so I help out around the barn. I sometimes feed, which includes graining, haying, watering, and anything else that each horse needs. I might clean stalls or lead horses to pasture for their exercising. I am also learning to give the ill horses penicillin injections.

Join a 4-H group. I am sorry to admit that when I was a teenager, some nasty terms like "hick" ran through my snooty little fashion-conscious brain when I heard that term 4-H. If you think that way too, get past your stereotypes and get big. You can wear purple hair and angry black boots and still shear a sheep. According to the *World Book Encyclopedia,* 4-H is the "largest informal education program for young people in the United States." Elaine Mahoney wrote in *GWS* #28 about her daughter:

> Kendra is a 4-H teen this year . . . The 4-H teen boys and girls work on community projects, organize dances, go on trips together, and study animal care, health, nutrition, gardening, and energy . . . Kendra went to the State House with 4-H and is going to Washington D.C. with them in July. She also has a proposal application to request funding of a community awareness project that she has in mind, sponsored by Reader's Digest, through 4-H.

If you have a big yard, try a project or two right there, on your own. Maybe your parents even already have a garden, but you consider it their thing, not yours, or maybe they dump lots of chemicals on it. Ask if you can make your own fun. Due to city codes and neighbors with noses, you probably can't have piglets. You probably *can* have rabbits, kiwi fruit, blue corn, and a greenhouse full of gourmet salad things in the winter. Entice yourself with books from the 630 to 640 region of your library: *Cultivating Carnivorous Plants, Raising Your Own Turkeys, A Horse in Your Life, Growing Food in Solar Greenhouses...*

Learn to do cool stuff like save your own seeds, and trade them with other people. The Seed Savers Exchange has eight thousand members who are devoted to rescuing old varieties of vegetables, fruits, grains, flowers, and herbs from near-extinction.

For help with gardening pests, soil testing, or other local issues, contact your county agricultural extension agent. A good use of your family's tax money, this agent is paid to help farmers, gardeners, and homemakers solve agricultural and family living problems. He should know about healthy, organic solutions for problems, as well as conventional unhealthy, poisonous solutions. Be sure to specify your preference. (Or, he may refer you to a local "master gardener," who is a regular person who took a bunch of classes and now knows the answers to your questions. Maybe *you* want to become a master gardener? You get free classes in gardening, in exchange for volunteering a specified amount of time to answer other gardeners' questions.) Call your county information number listed in the phone book government pages.

Start a small organic agricultural business—growing and selling strawberries or specialty vegetables (edible flowers, for instance, bring $28 and more a pound), raising chickens and selling eggs, selling honey, drying and arranging flowers, raising milk goats or exotic animals like miniature horses, growing basement mushrooms, raising sheep and dyeing their wool... the possibilities are endless.

Rent a spot in a community garden. Ask your amazing librarians for information.

Organize an effort to convert your city into paradise, with more fruit trees, community gardens, even mini-farms amidst the shopping zones. See *The Edible City Resource Manual,* by Richard Britz, or *Eco-City Dimensions,* edited by Mark Roseland.

Examples

GWS #15 reports on unschooler Grant Harrison, then fourteen years old and living in rural England:

> He has a small business running 100 head of poultry, selling the eggs to callers who come to his egg-grading room. Surplus cocks, etc, he will calculate to the last pence for their rearing costs and add his percentage for his time, and these are sold to the house. He has ten different pure breeds. He experiments with cross breeding. He is in need of a metal turning lathe which we [his parents] will help him obtain. He wants to make parts for the clocks which he mends, make a steam engine, parts of spinning wheels, etc. Already he has shown that he has tremendous aptitude in wood turning.

More stories from *GWS*:

> We live on a working ranch in central New Mexico . . . Our children (sixteen, fourteen, and seven) have been homeschooled their entire educational experience . . . Living on a livestock ranch, the girls have ample opportunity to practice some veterinary skills, drive tractors and trucks, and operate small machinery. There's also time for observing wildlife and plant life and learning something about their immediate environment. We often take "field trips" to various historical and interesting locations around our state. –Donna Spruill, *GWS* #45.

> Since we are a farm family, quite a number of our science projects are closely tied to agriculture. The latest project is a fish farm—complete with ten-gallon-aquarium for the showy stuff and a five-gallon nursery tank . . . Both boys did a man's work in the fields this past farming season . . . We put them on the payroll and they did a swell job . . . Mark (fourteen) learned how to operate the combine and he also drilled (planted) over one hundred acres of wheat this fall. Bill (thirteen) did most of the disking and field cultivating just ahead of the planter, plus hauling the harvested grain. –Virginia Schewe, *GWS* #35.

> The girls (Star, thirteen; Deva, almost six) have been going visiting a woman who lives twenty miles from here. This woman invited two other girls of similar ages to share four days with her; she expects them to cook and care for themselves and help her with her gardening and other projects. She is a talented artist with fabric and crochet and plans to share her skills with them. Star brought her wool, etc., and was very excited . . .
> Star was very involved with horses (more in imagery than reality, although she had her own pony for several years) and thought she would become more involved when we moved. But as she has grown she finds craft work, reading and gardening much more appealing to her than working with animals. She had a hard time letting go of her "images," even felt guilty that she didn't want to own a horse (as though she were betraying herself!). After much tearfulness, she gave away her six geese and their goslings when she realized the inefficient set-up she had and that she was not really that interested or attentive to them. She has been much relieved and happy now that they are gone and has put much energy into her garden, which is thriving. –Laurie Fishel-Lingemann, *GWS* #30.

Kirsten Rowe, of New York, tried a three-week experiment on a dairy farm and ended up staying for more than a year. In *GWS* #108, she writes:

When I started homeschooling, the summer before I would have been in eleventh grade, I thought it would be neat to try spending three weeks on the dairy farm that family friends owned in Earlville, New York . . .

I found farm life to be completely different from the suburban life I grew up in. When I got to the farm, the farmers told me about how they get up at 4:30 in the morning, and when I asked them about days off, they looked at me strangely, saying that they didn't get days off.

Nonetheless, I became enamored with life on the farm. The births of the calves were breathtaking to me. I loved feeding the calves and bedding down the heifers in the barn. Seeing the milking operation was also intriguing. During my visit I became even closer with our friends, and they invited me to live on their dairy farm as part of my homeschooling experience.

This farm is a 480-acre registered Holstein farm. We milk eighty cows and grow our own replacement heifers. My main jobs are feeding at the heifer barn and cleaning the horse barn. I relish the time I spend with my six-month-old registered Holstein calf, "Hop Along Cassidy."

Though it's been an incredible year and a half, the plan does have its disadvantages, including the separation from my best friends in Ithaca. I try to get back every other week so that I can see my friends and go to parties. All of my friends from school think it's so cool that I just moved to a dairy farm on sudden impulse like that . . .

When I wanted to be able to share my growing excitement and knowledge about the dairy industry, I ran for the '95-'96 position of Chenango County Dairy Princess. Since winning this position, I've made many presentations at schools, camps, day care centers, senior nutrition sites, retirement homes, and area clubs. One big project involved producing a documentary on osteoporosis. I've learned a lot about this debilitating disease through the research I've done. It has even made me rethink some of my own dietary choices, and I wanted to be able to share what I've learned with other kids. As a teenager myself, I know that teenagers aren't always open to suggestion, so I decided that instead of standing in front of a class and spouting out facts, I could better reach kids through a documentary that could put a face on the disease.

I found a video production company nearby that was willing to film and edit the documentary at cost to them. My parents and I made up the remainder of the cost. I filmed interviews with people and spent a lot of time working on the editing. Then I decided that before the title page, I wanted the image of hands breaking a bone. I went to the pathology lab at Cornell University and was able to obtain the femur of a dog who had actually had osteoporosis . . .

In conjunction with my dairy princess activities, I will be going to Honduras in November. The group I'm going with is called Heifer Project International. We will be giving area families a cow and asking that they pass on their cow's first born heifer to a neighbor. Because the villagers are new to farming, we will be building a milk dumping station and teaching the people how to care for and grow food for their animals. In the area where I will be going, 75% of the children are severely malnourished. The milk they will be able to get from the cows will drastically help to improve their nutrition.

Jesse Williams, twelve, of Washington, writes:

I gained a lot from doing the farmers' market this year: experience in growing fresh market produce, doing business, and dealing with various people.

We have always had a large garden at home. I have also grown mini pumpkins to sell. Two years ago when my pumpkin business was at its peak I sold four thousand pumpkins, supplying our two local grocery stores.

Early last spring when I was planting vegetable starts I had no idea I would be doing the market. I did know that I was getting tired of growing pumpkins for the grocery stores and I had become more serious about growing fresh produce on a marketable scale. Although I was unsure of where I would sell them, I began to start a succession planting of standard vegetables.

The best place I found to sell my produce was a newly started Friday farmers market in our town. I was quite ill-prepared on my first market day. For one thing I only had spinach and two types of lettuce for sale. I had a table but no awning and there were very few customers. I had paid for my space at the market through the end of the month; otherwise I might not have gone back.

With my first month I made many improvements. I built an awning, got a more effective display system, and got better at keeping the produce fresh in hot weather. Another plus was that as the season progressed I had a much wider variety of vegetables.

On market days I would get up around 6:00 A.M. My dad and I would drive to the farm and pick the produce. My dad would help me set up. Then I was on my own until the market ended.

By the end of the season I was doing fairly well. I had made enough money to pay for several major additions to our gardening equipment. I also had a 36-name mailing list compiled of customers who signed up at the market.

I want to keep farming in the future. I'm not sure if I want to keep doing a market. I might try another distribution method. I also have a bit of interest in producing fresh market meat and dairy products. I do know that growing good food will always be a part of my life. ☀

38
fixing the world:
social and political
activism

BEING LESS THAN eighteen doesn't make you less than human. Nor does it deprive you of a voice in the world, unless you let it. *Growing Without Schooling* #68 tells about twelve-year-old Andrew Holleman, a Massachusetts school kid who saved a woodland in his community from turning into condominiums. Andrew researched zoning laws and other information, wrote letters to legislators and TV anchor people. He got his neighbors together and told them what was going on, won their support, and circulated a petition. The developers' permit was denied.

Activism: Political Science in Action

If you see that something's wrong in the world, you can help fix it by working through or "at" our political system. You can contact congresspeople, distribute fliers for political campaigns, knock on doors to ask for Greenpeace donations, and help other people register to vote—though you yourself can't yet vote. [1]

Here are two major ways you can become more deeply involved—one working through the legal system, the other working more or less outside of it. However, these can be combined—for example, you can use civil disobedience to help raise people's awareness, which can then lead to changed laws.

1. Get a new law passed.

Most bills (potential laws) are supposedly begun by senators and representatives, but they can also be written by ordinary citizens. Even if you don't want to go through the headache of writing an actual bill, you can write a detailed proposal, get other people to support your efforts, and urge your representatives to develop a bill.

First, identify a particular law that needs changing—does your city have fair guidelines for skateboarders? Does your state need a better recycling law, or a law that allows people of any age to earn their G.E.D. diploma? Should sixteen-year-olds

---

[1] How to contact your U.S. senators and representatives in Washington: write them c/o U.S. Senate, Washington DC 20510-3701 or c/o U.S. House of Representatives, Washington DC 20515.

be able to vote in national elections? Should congresspeople face penalties for breaking promises to their constituents?

Then, with the help of likeminded people, write down what you think the law should say. Attend city council meetings, or contact your representative and senators until you find someone who will consider developing and sponsoring your bill. For practical information about working on legislation, contact the League of Women Voters, in the phone book.

If your issue is a popular one, then undoubtedly other people are already working on it. Plug into their efforts rather than start from scratch. Likely, the League of Women Voters can tell you who's working on what. Also, of course, contact relevant organizations—the Sierra Club for environmental issues, Planned Parenthood for birth control issues, and so on.

2. Participate in non-violent direct action or civil disobedience—otherwise known as sit-ins, blockades, marches, demonstrations, rallies, protests, and political street theater.

Non-violent "direct action" usually refers to a dramatic act done in public in order to call attention to a societal wrong. Direct action can be legal or illegal.

Civil disobedience is the illegal version of non-violent direct action, meaning deliberately breaking a law that you consider wrong. The tradition has thousands of years behind it—remember all those Hebrew boys in the Bible refusing to worship kings' idols? Thoreau gave it new life in the 1800's when he refused to pay taxes that supported slavery and the Mexican War, and then wrote about his convictions in the classic essay "On the Duty of Civil Disobedience." As the story goes, Emerson came to see Thoreau the night he was in jail. "Why are you here?" asked Emerson accusingly. "Why are you not here?" countered Thoreau.

Whether you want to go all the way and risk arrest or become more softly involved by chanting in a peace march, my activist friend Heiko strongly suggests that you take a free workshop in Non-Violence, offered frequently in almost every city by peace groups. How to find these groups? Check local alternative newspapers (usually available at natural foods stores or co-ops) and bulletin boards. Contact Unitarian and Quaker (Friends) churches, or college peace groups. If you find nothing, contact the national War Resisters League to ask for local phone numbers.

Non-Violence workshops last about six hours. They cover 1) the history and philosophy of non-violent civil disobedience, 2) consensus process—how to reach agreements, not just majority-wins/everyone else loses, 3) what to actually *do* when you're involved in civil disobedience—how to deal with police, how to let your body go limp when they carry you off, what not to say, etc.

Heiko further advises: don't try to do tough political work on your own. Surround yourself with support, both practical and emotional. At times, all your efforts will seem a failure. Don't give up—your role is small but essential. Drop by drop, water makes an ocean.

Speak for yourselves

Overwhelming issues like the environment, world hunger, and world peace certainly deserve your attention, but *your* rights are important too. Consider: the voting age, driving ages, draft laws, school and homeschool statutes, birth control and abortion issues, legal drinking ages, and child labor laws. I encourage you to speak up and let your voice be heard.

You, the world

Thanks to changes in public attitudes and popular books like *Fifty Simple Things You Can Do To Save the Earth*, you probably already know that your own actions count. In the big picture, it helps when you don't eat tuna caught in dolphin-killing nets, when you use your junk mail instead of new notebooks for scratch paper. The *Fifty Things...* book and many organizations and people can help you decide what changes to make in your own life. But I have a couple things to add. Some people acquire strange military pious personalities when they first start changing their lifestyles for political/environmental reasons, temporarily losing touch with the things they care about most in the first place. So:

As you work to make the world a better place, don't turn into a robot. Keep it personal. Clean up a roadside pond and then go fishing there. On your way to the recycling center, give your apple to a bag lady. Gestures will not, in themselves, get the work done, but they feed the spirit and keep the motivation alive.

Also, now that you live so correctly and sacrifice your time to Good Causes, don't condemn less perfect people. Remain humble. Recognize that no matter how good your intentions are, as a twenty-first-century industrialized-nation human being, some of *your* activities harm the earth. If you wear cotton, especially if it's not organically grown, you support cotton fields full of pesticides rather than habitat for diverse wildlife. If you wear polar fleece or polyester—petroleum products—you support a petroleum-dependent economy and global warming. If you use electricity, you are part of the reason the power company plans to damn another river. Don't kick yourself for what you can't do, but don't kick other people either. Kicking, in fact, *prevents* other people from getting involved—just like when your mom used to nag you to do your homework it made you want *not* to do your homework.

In the company of your parents, remain *especially* humble. Recognize that not only did they invite you into this world at great cost to themselves, but they also exercised tremendous patience when you went through your shop-till-you-drop years (*real* good for the planet), your three-page-long Christmas wish-list years, your "But Jonnice's mom bought *her* a new TV" years. Exercise a little patience and acceptance in return, and remember that they grew up in less enlightened times than you did. (Twenty years ago, vegetarians were the cutting edge; they read Frances Moore Lappé's *Diet for a Small Planet*. Now, the nutritional activists have moved on to veganism and organically grown produce; they read John Robbins' *Diet for a New America*. We can only speculate where the nutritionally correct will lead us twenty years from now.) You can talk *with* your parents, of course, but don't preach *at* them.

You can also combine your political convictions with your other work. Make a business out of recycling or planting organic gardens for busy people. Volunteer to do research for Greenpeace. Find an internship with a shelter for the homeless.

Resources
- *Fifty Simple Things You Can Do to Save the Earth*, by the Earth Works Group. Short and sweet.
- *In the Tiger's Mouth: An Empowerment Guide for Social Action—Acting Effectively, Enjoying it, Keeping at it*, by Katrina Shields. Practical and insightful advice to help keep you from burning out; Shields shows you how to

Heiko's brainstorm

The following lists are based on a wonderful chart my activist friend Heiko made. They can both help you generate your own ideas *and* see how to address huge issues through concrete goals, which break down into small, do-able subtasks.

Examples of large issues that people can work on

Afro-American, Latino, Asian American, or Native American awareness and rights; Central America; consumer protection; the environment; farm issues; gay/lesbian rights; homelessness; human rights; handicapped access; hunger; labor; old people's rights, young people's rights; organic agriculture; peace; racism; religious freedom; social justice; women's rights.

Major ways people can address any of these (or other) issues

1) Change people's attitudes through education (not necessarily *school* education, of course—getting media attention is often helpful).

2) Change laws—which can include electing decent congresspeople, working to get certain laws passed, and making certain that laws are enforced.

3) Change structures *directly*—support labor strikes, force companies (and colleges) to divest their stock in inhumane countries and corporations, start recycling programs, help people install solar hot water heaters, support boycotts, create shelters for battered women, etc.

Some options people (and groups of people) have in their approach to accomplishing these goals

* be straight or be controversial
* be egalitarian or be hierarchical
* vote or use consensus process
* hire staff or be volunteer-only
* work on a grassroots level and/or make friends in the "establishment"
* work with a group that already exists or start your own group

Some specific strategies people can use to accomplish their goals

(Choose a few that most reflect the talents of your group and that will use your energy most efficiently. Don't try to do all these or you'll do none of them well.)

Make phone calls to representatives, write letters to representatives, plan and carry out projects, make leaflets, distribute leaflets, staff offices, work at information tables during fairs and events, organize fundraising events, do library research, do original research, create Web sites, host e-mail listserves, write press releases, call newspapers, help put together alternative newspapers, organize meetings, write proposals, attend public hearings, attend rallies and marches, get arrested, design and make posters or banners, perform guerilla theater, help prepare mailings, talk to your friends, go door-to-door and talk to your neighborhood, do coalition building with similar groups, volunteer at soup kitchens or women's shelters, write books, make videos, publish a zine, etc.

care for yourself while you care for the world.

- *Common Cents,* by Representative Timothy Penny, shows how decision making and power playing goes on behind the scenes in Washington, and tells how regular people can improve the system.
- *The Kid's Guide to Social Action: How to Solve the Social Problems You Choose,* by Barbara Lewis, is a great resource for organizers and law-changers, and despite the title is not condescending or over-simple.

Organizations

Band together. Working with others makes it all possible, not to mention fun. Working alone gets meaningless fast. You may want to see the short booklet written by and for teenagers, *Student Action Guide: how to have a successful environmental club,* by YES! (Youth for Environmental Sanity). Although it focuses on environmental issues, you could also use it to form other types of action-oriented groups, too. Among other things, it explains how to work around interfering school schedules and policies if you want to start a *school* club. (Even as an unschooler you might choose to get your club *started* through a school, in order to reach as many interested people as possible. Then, hold continuing meetings at someone's home or a coffeeshop—somewhere more joyful and comfortable than school.). By the way, YES! is a group of dynamic young people who tour internationally, raising environmental awareness at school assemblies everywhere. They run highly praised, life-changing week-long summer camps for people aged fifteen to twenty-one.

Or, plug into somebody else's organization—by volunteering locally or interning in a national office. Here are a few of the hundreds:

- *The American Friends Service Committee* is an old, well-organized, tremendously effective organization that works for social justice and peace in 23 countries. Like the Quaker religion from which it springs, the AFSC believes that "there is that of God in each person." Hundreds of volunteers, who need not be Quakers, help in the work of supporting the rights of immigrants, refugees, and small farmers. They advocate on behalf of people who are hungry, homeless, unemployed, and otherwise in need. They build health clinics, feed Somalian orphans, build housing for homeless people, offer information and support to gay and lesbian youth, produce documentaries, etc.
- *Amnesty International* works to end torture and free "prisoners of conscience".
- *Equality Now* is an international human rights organization that works for the civil, political, economic, and social rights of girls and women.
- *Greenpeace* and *Earth First!* are known for visionary environmental activism.
- *Homeschoolers for Peace and Justice.* People aged twelve to seventeen can join as members and contribute to the newsletter; people of any age can subscribe. Each issue has a focus, such as Black History, The Power of Song, Native American Treaty Rights, The Struggle in South Africa, and "What is True Patriotism?". The focus is announced in advance so that members can contribute relevant articles, essays, book reviews, poetry, artwork, and political cartoons. But HFP&J is more than just a good newsletter; it's a long-distance community. Members carry out projects together, such as making a peace quilt and sending school supplies to Nicaragua; some have traveled to meet each other; and for many, the community and newsletter has served as a springboard to more social activism.

- *The Listening Project of the Rural Southern Voice for Peace* is a grassroots opportunity to build community and to help opposing groups understand each other.
- *The National Child Rights Alliance,* which supports youth liberation, publishes a fascinating newsletter, and seeks to change economic, social, legal, medical, cultural and parental practices that harm youth.
- *Oxfam America* fights global poverty and hunger by working with grassroots organizations in Africa, Asia, the Americas, and the Caribbean. They sponsor a large anti-poverty and hunger campaign, "Fast for a World Harvest." Oxfam also has support materials to help you organize an event such as a "hunger banquet" or a group fast, in order to raise awareness and money.
- *Peace Links* is an organization founded and run mainly by women, with the goals of increasing communication between Americans and people in the former Soviet Union, of preventing nuclear war, and reducing military spending. They have thousands of Russian and other pen-pals (who write in English) waiting for American pen-pals. Also, they provide information which can help you organize a group of teenagers or people-in-general to work for peace.
- *PETA* (People for the Ethical Treatment of Animals) works to stop unnecessary animal exploitation.
- *The Rainforest Action Network* works to protect worldwide rainforests and support the rights of their inhabitants through education, grassroots organizing, and non-violent direct action.
- *The Sierra Club* is the oldest and largest non-profit environmental organization in the world.
- *The War Resisters League* offers, among other things, free youth workshops on topics like organizing groups of people, publishing zines, nonviolence theory and history, and anti-militarism. They also run week-long training programs. ❀

Part 6

The Lives of Unschoolers

the
guinea pig
chapter

Tʜɪs ᴄʜᴀᴘᴛᴇʀ ɢʀᴇᴡ stubbornly out of my mailbox.

The book in your hands is spiked all through with stories of unschooled teenagers—where they work, what they think about learning, how they play soccer, which musical instruments they love. But I wanted to describe more of the people who wrote me about their lives, just to assure you they're real, just to give you a bigger idea of what's possible. In the next pages, therefore, I throw a party to introduce you to a few dozen of these teenagers, and toss in morsels of *GWS* articles along the way. Each teenager here deserves a whole celebratory chapter to herself, but that's another book for another year.[1]

Most of the people you're about to meet study a fairly traditional curriculum, including math, science, literature, history. I do not explain their academics in detail, but most use textbooks for math, and textbooks or library books for other subjects. Some also use PBS, tapes, computers, and museums. Many learn from adult friends. Some take courses through junior colleges, correspondence schools, or even public high school. Some have parents who are intimately involved with decision making and checking work; others work and make choices independently. Also, they don't necessarily study a lot of subjects at once—they might read biographies for a few weeks and then spend a month having a Relationship with a microscope.

However, some of the people here do not study *anything* formally. Even these completely "unstructured" teenagers usually find out about "academic" subjects in more depth than schooled teens do; they just don't do it on predetermined schedules. Most are avid readers, probably because nobody forces them to read.

Introductions will be made in alphabetical order. After they're finished and you've found someone to sit by, your author will make a few comments.

Tom Adams, twelve, of Pennsylvania, pursues a variety of hobbies—collecting and cataloging stamps and football and baseball cards, collecting rocks, drawing, carving wood, reading mysteries, and playing baseball and football with friends.

---

[1] The book is *Real Lives: eleven teenagers who don't go to school,* and the year was 1993. Among the eleven teenagers are some of the guinea pigs in this chapter: Anne Brosnan, Rebecca Merrion, Erin Roberts, Patrick Meehan, Tabitha Mountjoy, and Kevin Sellstrom, as well as Jeremiah Gingold, who is quoted elsewhere in this book.

Eventually, he'd like to go to college and perhaps become a professional baseball player or a lawyer. He points out that living in a university town offers great advantages, since he has access to the university library, cultural events, and "knowledge bank" of professors.

Joseph Anderton, fifteen, of North Carolina, uses textbooks; he tests at two years above grade level. He spends much of his time working with his father, who is a heating and air-conditioning serviceman; he plans to earn a license in this field and maybe also go to college. Also, he plays football with friends and collects baseball cards.

Britt Barker, of Ohio, now a 22-year-old pianist and bush pilot, grew up passionately interested in wildlife and classical music. You can read more about her field biology and travel experience in Chapter 21 (or in her own booklet, *Letters Home*), but I wanted to mention other aspects of her life here. Unschooled and surrounded by a close farming family of seven, Britt began writing for publication at age twelve with an article for *Mother Earth News* on ponies. Two years later she began selling weekly word-search puzzles to a local newspaper, and wrote a second article for *Mother Earth News* (on dairy goats) at fifteen. An accomplished classical pianist and integral member of the family's farmsteading operation, she decided at age sixteen to spend time away from home in search of new adventures, described in *Letters Home*. In 1986, she was chosen as one of *Teenage* magazine's "one hundred most interesting teenagers in the country."[1]

Britt's mother Penny sent me an update on her other kids. **Maggie**, seventeen, is a dedicated dog musher who keeps thirty dogs—Alaskan huskies and border collies. In Michigan, she conducts pack dog trekking and dogsledding workshops for people ages eleven and up. In a newspaper clipping about a fifty-mile race that she and her dogs won, a sheriff comments, "You could see the joy in her face....She was smiling when she came over the hill and crossed the road."

Other unschooled Barkers are sixteen-year-old **Dan**, "the cellist," fourteen-year-old **Ben**, "the kayaker and boat builder," and twelve-year-old **Jonah**, "the mechanic." "All so different," comments Penny, "It's great fun." All of the Barkers work together to run The Country School, a summer program at their farmstead, where children and teenagers visit for five days at a time, participating in farm activities.[2]

Benjamin Israel Billings, sixteen, of Massachusetts, wrote,

I like to fish. I read a lot (Vietnam). I really like my music (progressive rock, classical,

---

[1] See Britt Barker, *Letters Home*, and *GWS* #49.

[2] A later Barker update—among many other things:

At 27, Britt continues to play music, write, and fly as a private pilot. She also works as a brakeman on the Wyoming Railroad and runs Suzuki piano studios in both Wyoming and Colorado.

At 22, Maggie has become well known in Europe as well as all over America for her dog sled racing. She also trains dogs for Search and Rescue, teaches other people to train their own border collies for livestock work, and runs dogsledding programs in Michigan and Montana.

At 21, Dan is a cellist with the Missoula (Montana) Symphony and leads outdoor programs. He also attended Oberlin college, where he performed with the Oberlin Chamber Orchestra.

At eighteen, Ben works as a herd-riding cowboy in Montana, and runs canoeing and mountaineering expeditions in Michigan and Montana.

Jonah, at seventeen, has also lived in Montana for a year, where he has his own mechanic's bench in a shop and is saving money for helicopter training.

mens' choral, new age, folk and some Irish also). One of my favorite things is bike riding (I did 96 miles in an afternoon last summer). I play Dungeons and Dragons. Boy Scout activities are always favorites as well as church activities . . . I am receiving my Eagle Scout in April. I am currently serving as a Junior Assistant Scoutmaster.

Django Bohren, thirteen, of Louisiana, lives "on the road" with his family since his father, Spencer Bohren, is a musician. One fall, for instance, he traveled through Louisiana, Yellowstone Park, Washington, Oregon, Montana, Wyoming, Colorado, Arizona, Michigan, Illinois, and Kentucky. He *did* attend school once for two and a half weeks and enjoyed it, but his unschooled life is full. Constant travel, obviously, exposes him to worlds most teenagers don't get the chance to see.

Anne Brosnan, thirteen, of New York, wrote a lot worth repeating. In her words, I catch glimpses of the unschooler I might have been:

I learn by living and doing. At home we can do anything we want, anytime. Mom doesn't make us do any reading or schoolwork. Kids go to school to learn how to do things, but it wastes a lot of time and you can get by doing whatever it is and learning as you go along. I learned to play piano by playing it. I found out how to read music just from finding the note for middle C on the music and on the piano, and all notes followed. I learned how to read by reading, how to type by typing, etc. It goes on and on, and it's a very simple concept, really . . .

[Anne lists her interests:] classical music, folk, ragtime, early American (classic) jazz, piano, banjo, harmonica and other instruments . . . I pursue the study of music by listening to it and playing it.

Mythology and folklore, legends and beliefs of all cultures, deep ecology, philosophy, the Gaia Hypothesis. (These following people I study and/or admire) Albert Einstein, John Muir, Robert Frost, Charles Dickens, Amos Bronson Alcott, Leonardo Da Vinci, Ludwig Beethoven, Wolfgang Amadeus Mozart, Johann C. Bach, Abraham Lincoln, the Tree as a Being.

Nature, ecology, wolves, etc. The Lives and Personalities of Wolves and Whales in Relation to Humans as a Study of Environmental Peace, archaeology, anthropology, genealogy, geography, lexicology, bibliophilism, auto-didactism. Books such as Charles Dickens', Shakespeare, Scott O'Dell, *Watership Down* (Richard Adams), *My Family and Other Animals* (Gerald Durrell). Fishnetting, knitting, cuckoo clocks, running, basketball, badminton, Famous Homeschoolers, poetry, calligraphy, philately, postcards, animal skeletons, geodes, owls, Carl Larsson, typing, Galapagos Islands, Sierra Club, newsletters, history, simple living, farming, treehouses (for permanent living), vegetarianism, African wildlife, composting, recycling, bicycles, Native Americans, canoeing, camping, and hats. I use no textbooks except one or two workbooks for occasional math, and no correspondence courses.

[Anne explains what she does with her time:] I go to track and basketball practice for a total of about three days a week and games and meets on weekends. That's in the evenings. In the daytimes I practice piano for about 45% of the time (a lot, anyway), write letters, read, knit, practice basketball, track, tennis, etc., do some gardening or composting, make hammocks, clean house, sort books, knead bread, etc. I have a lot of projects going too such as writing articles and cleaning and stamp collecting.

Todd Brown, fifteen, of Virginia, says the greatest advantages of never having gone to school are "choices" and "freedom." From what his friends tell him, school sounds "hostile, barbaric, and monotonous." Todd approaches his many interests from a thoughtful, profound perspective. For instance, he says that *Star Trek* is "an extension of our dreams and a realization of our limitless capabilities." In addition to watching the show, he reads books and attends *Star Trek* conventions. His other major interests are entomology—"I love insects and arthropods of all kinds"—and making electronics devices—"I can't even begin to describe the joy of designing and testing a circuit." Also, he sails, uses a computer, draws, uses a microscope, makes jewelry and models, and reads. Included in his academic work is Latin and philosophy. His father teaches him electronics. College? His sights are set on Virginia Tech. He enjoys his Boy Scout troupe and marine biology camp. He is curiously hard on himself for one gap in his "education": "I hate history although I firmly believe that history will repeat itself if not studied. This is a flaw I am *not* proud of."

Sharma Buell, sixteen, of Maine, uses no textbooks or tests. "We just sit on the rim of the big melting pot, stirring, throwing stuff in... tasting what looks good." A free spirit with a thoughtful outlook, she does "a lot of art," hitchhikes, and thinks constantly. "I've learned most things the hard way," she says, "from actual experience which, I suppose, does the trick—but nothing like a clean, safe textbook with a time limit to 'learn' controlled information."

Becky Cauthen, fourteen, of Georgia, spends her non-academic time playing piano twice a month for a homeschool group and three times weekly for church. A candy striper, girl scout, and member of her church youth group, she helps run a cattle and goat farm, sews some of her own clothes, bakes, and plays guitar. She says she would not consider returning to school: "I would be gone from home for seven hours or more and that's a lot of time wasted. Now I can take a break from a tough English assignment, go help doctor cows or walk in the woods, or play the piano and come back to my work refreshed."[1]

Chelsea Chapman of Alaska is taught by her parents, though not school style. She explains in *GWS* #74:

> Let me try to describe our homeschooling. My mother teaches us culture, history, literature and things like that, while Dad teaches us math, chemistry, some history, and physics. We do schoolwork from about 8:00 A.M. to 12:00 or so. Often we don't do any at all, and we never do it in the afternoon. My Dad works one week and then has the next week off. When he is home, we talk about math and chemistry, and he gives us some problems to work out. Often he just draws us pictures of protons, neurons, etc. to look at and study. Today I wrote short essays on Pythagoras, Archimedes, and Avogadro. Knowing about their lives really helps me remember their respective theorems, principles, and laws.
>
> I love physics and things like that! I have always thought that I was just not a smart enough person to understand these things and that they were deadly dull anyway (something I got from school). But now I have discovered that they aren't hard or dull or stupid, and I am finally getting over the thought that "hard stuff" isn't for everyone.
>
> Now, I said my mother teaches us history and literature. We mainly read for history. In fact, we read all the time. My eleven-year-old sister and I will read anything and everything. We are really allowed to study what we choose here. In fact, it reminds me of Summerhill school sometimes. I love poetry and read masses of Blake, my favorite. Shakespeare is all right; I like *The Tempest* best. In contrast, I have been reading DOS

---

[1] Several years later, Becky's mother wrote to *GWS*: "I am happy . . . for the opportunity to affirm homeschooling, especially organic, unstructured, interest-directed styles of learning. We had no grades, diploma, etc. but merely wrote descriptions of Becky's character, how she learned, areas of interests, etc. This, along with proof of the GED, SAT scores, and applications, was sent to three colleges (two state and one private) and [Rebecca] was accepted and awarded scholarships in piano at all three. She is now attending Shorter College in Rome, Georgia, and is doing well."

(Disk Operating Systems) and doing a lot on our computer. We really just work on what we are interested in. Often schoolwork is nonexistent, like when there are more important things to do like going to watch the start of the great "Yukon Quest" dog sled race!

I'm going to be a naturalist/writer/artist/poet when I grow up. These all, I think, can be combined.

Alex Clemens was thirteen when his mother wrote to *GWS* #16,

Alex now programs the Apple II, works at the hardware store, helps our Supervisor at city hall, takes math from his former public school math teacher, writes journal and book reports for me, passed his karate green belt in June, and cooks his own meals.

Christopher DeRoos wrote to *GWS* #32 when he was sixteen,

Two years ago . . . my mother started taking me to sit in on college courses. I am at Holy Names College in Oakland [California], where a friend also attends. He started there when he was fifteen . . . I am in computer sciences and economics. I'm going to be taking an auto engineering class . . . I am serving on a Planning Commission—Sign Committee, reviewing the Alameda County sign ordinances . . .

My motto is from *Auntie Mame*, "Life's a banquet and most of you poor suckers are starving to death." Being home taught has been the best!

Jonas Diener, thirteen, of Virginia, studies nothing formally. Instead, he spends his time biking, reading what he wants to read, working on a computer, and playing around with electronic things—"lights and wires and stuff."

Katrina Fallick, fourteen, of Washington, is interested in ecology action, fashion design and merchandising, and sociology. "Ecology action" means she plants trees and reads a lot to find out what else needs to be done. To pursue her interest in fashion, she investigates clothing stores and then designs and sews clothing which she predicts will fit the next trend. Also, she works on a steering committee which organizes a local homeschool fair (she helped to film a commercial for the fair), reads, hikes, writes to pen pals and—oh yes—studies academic things like math and history. She plans to take the GED at sixteen, so that she can take college classes. However, she emphasizes that she will go to college for "knowledge, not a diploma," and that she will "take whatever classes [she needs] at whatever college has the best program for what [she wants] to learn."

Katrina's mom Jj later sent me the following update:

She is in Spokane attending a high school level vocational program in fashion merchandising—living with friends and "home schooling" for her regular subjects. At fourteen, she is enrolled as a high school junior . . . it will give her entry-level job skills at fifteen and she hopes to get a job at sixteen, take a few classes at the junior college and begin a career in fashion design . . . making her own designs.

Zachary Field, fifteen, Maine, plans to become a professional juggler soon, and practices for well over an hour each day. He says his academic studies are "very informal." Like many unschoolers, when he first quit school five years ago, he and his family attempted to set up a fairly rigid home program, which later grew very unstructured. His interests include extensive reading, riding his unicycle, and spending time with his friends, most of whom are fellow jugglers.

Benjamin Flagel, twelve, Maryland, belongs to two 4-H clubs, reads a lot, plays baseball, basketball, and soccer, keeps a garden, and collects butterflies and baseball cards.

Nicole Flores, of California, wrote in *GWS* #52,

I dropped out of high school when I was fifteen and in the ninth grade. My mom and her boyfriend made it legally possible by turning our home into a private school.

It's great. They've been providing me with resource materials and three years later I've become interested in subjects I would have shrieked about if I was still in high school. I'm writing science fiction stories, reading physics, and most importantly I've learned how to think for myself and make my own decisions. Basically, the freedom I lacked in school has enabled me to grow up.

Elise Foxton, fifteen, of Washington, is enrolled in both a general homeschooling correspondence program and also in an algebra course through the University of Nebraska. She echoes most of the homeschoolers I heard from: "You have more time to do things not related to school. I ride the horses I take care of while other kids are still in school." Last year she started successfully showing her two horses, and she takes weekly riding lessons.

Theo Giesy, of Virginia, was one of the first homeschooling *moms* in the seventies. Her grade-school-aged kids kept asking if they could stay home from school, pointing out that they got more of an education at home. Theo took them seriously and took them out, though at the time she had no assurance that it would work out legally. All four of her kids started taking ballet, and Theo recalls their experiences in *GWS* #58, ten years after they'd started. By that time, her kids were fourteen, eighteen, twenty, and twenty-two. Theo writes:

Shortly after she started taking ballet, **Danile** [the eldest] began to be interested in a career in dance. When she was thirteen, she started performing with a small modern dance group that performed in schools. She has been performing with similar groups ever since. She got her own apartment before she was eighteen, since she was dancing with a group based in Williamsburg, forty miles from our house. When she was eighteen she told us that she didn't need our financial support any more and that she would tell us if she needed help. Besides dancing she teaches ballet and jazz classes. She has never felt the need for a diploma. When filling out the "school attended" slot in job applications she writes Brook school, grade completed: twelfth.

Darrin also took ballet, and since he was not in school he could watch rehearsals and help by running the tape recorder. That led him into theater technical work. He kept taking ballet but was more interested in tech work as a career. He went to Antioch College for two years [beginning at seventeen], and during that time he began to think that he did want to dance. He left college and spent the past year studying at Boston Ballet. He recently signed a contract with Nevada Dance Theater for next year.

Susie enjoyed ballet but never planned to be a ballerina. She has considered musical theater and modeling. She has worked in the groups that Danile worked in, both as a dancer and as a tech person. Now she is dancing in a lounge. Next year she and Danile will both dance with a group that performs in schools and for other community groups. She doesn't know what she wants to do beyond that.

Anita is writing poems, a teenage romance, and moving notes to friends and family. She babysits for ten families, though she is cutting back to have time for other things. She makes beautiful earrings which she gives to special friends and occasionally sells. Had she been in school, I'm sure she would have been labeled "learning disabled" because she was a late reader . . .

It has been wonderful to watch all four children grow, learn and develop with no curriculum, no artificial schedules and no comparison with "the norm."

At eighteen, Anita took a year-long road trip around the U.S. When she came through Eugene and stayed with me, she told me more about the Giesys' lives. As a teenager, Anita developed a very strong interest in children, and held several long term daytime babysitting jobs with different families. Also, she was involved in 4-H, worked as a counselor for 4-H camps, taught workshops in earring making, did technical work for dance productions, and lobbied against a law requiring parental consent for minors' abortions.

Danile, 25, continued to dance with the company Ballet Tidewater and to teach ballet as well as jazz and character dance. Also, she performed as a "heartbreak dancer," doing fifties style rock 'n roll dancing. Darrin, 23, danced as an apprentice with the Ballet Met of Columbus, Ohio, and considered auditioning for other dance companies or going back to college. He had also been a volunteer fireman and an EMT. Susie, 21, had just returned from six months of traveling on her own in Europe. Before that, she danced with Ballet Tidewater and taught ballet to inner-city kids.

Darlene Graham of Texas wrote in *GWS* #37 about her sons **Grant** and **Graham**,

> Grant is seventeen now and works as a carpenter while preparing to take his G.E.D. test. Graham, fourteen, has taken a breather from his violin lessons . . . He does quite a lot of auto repair with my husband, and is becoming very skilled and responsible. At his age, he loves anything to do with cars, and never complains about unloading livestock feed since it involves driving to the barn, backing up, etc., and maybe going once or twice up and down the driveway for good measure.

Ashia Gustafson, thirteen, of Washington, is extremely involved in dance, and is in fact considering a dance career. Currently, she studies ballet, jazz, tap, and modern dance. Also, she pursues a fairly "traditional" academic program through the Calvert School, a correspondence school described in chapter 11. She plans to attend college, and considers her academic knowledge and skills more well rounded, and generally higher, than that of her schooled peers.

Andrea Harrison, of England, became a member of Ludlow Orchestra at age sixteen. *GWS* #15 reports:

> She plans to go on to Dartington to study music when she is eighteen. Until recently she has run a small business from one of the buildings [at home]. She obtained organic whole wheat from a neighbor friend, made bread and sold it from her little shop, but has now found that the demands were too great on her energy and time for her to do justice to her musical study. Some days this can be in the region of eight to ten hours of intensive study.

Gordon Hubbell, fifteen, of California, is a new unschooler studying Russian, English, and math. He spends as much time as possible skiing and mountain biking. He participates in ski races, reads books on ski technique, and skis "the Extreme" frequently. "With mountain biking," he explains, "I ride eighteen miles everyday at a high cadence through varying terrain."

Jud Jerome, rather famous poet, essayist, playwright, etc., wrote way back in *GWS* #1 about his daughter, from age twelve onward:

> To avoid the law [in the early seventies] we enrolled her in a 'free' school in Spokane, Washington, run by a friend who carried her on the rolls, though she has not yet, to date, seen that city or that school. She spent most of the first year here at the farm, pitching in as an adult, learning from experience as we were all learning. While she was still thirteen we went to help another commune, in northern Vermont, with sugaring, and she loved that place—which was very primitive and used horse-drawn equipment—so asked to stay. This was an agreeable arrangement on all sides—and she has lived there now for over five years, except for one, when she was sixteen. That year she and her mate (ten years her senior) went to Iceland (Vermont was not rugged enough for them) to winter, working in a

fish cannery. The next Spring they traveled, camping, to Scandinavia, hiked the Alps, then flew home—coming back with $3,000 more than they left with after a year abroad. Last year, she wanted to apply for a government vocational program, for which she needed a high school diploma, so went to an adult education class for a few months, and took the test, passing in the top percentile (and being offered scholarships to various colleges). She "graduated" earlier than her classmates who stayed in school. I think her case illustrates especially dramatically the waste of time in schools. She is by no means a studious type, would never think of herself as an intellectual, has always been more interested in milking cows and hoeing vegetables and driving teams of horses than in books, and in her years between thirteen and eighteen moved comfortably into womanhood and acquired a vast number of skills, had a vast range of experiences in the adult world, yet managed to qualify exceptionally by academic standards. By comparison, her classmates who stayed in school are in many ways stunted in mind, emotionally disturbed, without significant goals or sound values in their lives—in large part (in my judgment) specifically because of their schooling.

Clarissa Johnston, fourteen, of Georgia, who has been out of school for five and a half years, takes gymnastics four days a week. She studies most academic subjects using textbooks, but also attends a Spanish class at a high school and studies nature on her own. In addition to her fairly rigorous academic coursework and intense involvement with gymnastics, she appreciates the time she has (after chores) to be with friends, spend time outside, and read. She has already decided on a college, and hopes to become a botanist or P.E. teacher.

Vanessa Keith, now 21, of New Hampshire, never went to school. She never studied much, either, except algebra when she was eighteen, and some Montessori-style reading, writing, and math around the ages of six and seven. Neighbors gave her occasional lessons in typing, French, math, and writing. Mostly, she followed her interests in crafts, weaving, and sewing. At eighteen she took the GED, her first test ever, without studying, and passed. Growing up, she spent four months of every year at work, picking apples and pruning apple trees with her parents.

John Keller, nineteen, of Minnesota, is currently a freshman at Carleton College. As a teenager, he learned under the guidance of his parents, who work with Wycliffe Bible Translators. He grew up living in Vietnam, Cambodia, and France as well as the U.S.; last year he spent five weeks traveling with his father in Europe. A potential French, English, or political science major, John is an Eagle Scout, a Boundary Waters canoe guide, and hockey player. He comments:

> In the eighth and ninth grades I used a prepared curriculum. Once we realized we could do a better job on our own, we bought texts and other materials, and planned grades 10 through 12 independently.
>
> Now that I am in college, I am more sure that I was prepared for it as well as anyone else. Also, I feel that I am a stronger individualist because of home schooling, and am less likely to just go with the flow of popular opinion on campus.
>
> Socialization was never a big worry for me, but all the same it is reassuring to see that I have made many good friends, that I feel comfortable participating in classes and discussions, and am involved in extra-curricular activities.

Suzanne Klemp, fifteen, of Wisconsin, has been out of school four years. "It was my idea," she writes, "because I didn't like the negative environment in public school, and because my teachers stifled my creativity." She studies algebra, English, biology, history, and other subjects using textbooks, but also focuses heavily on ballet; she takes classes *and* teaches classes at the YMCA. She has put together a youth group for teenagers within her local home-educators' group, and attends a church youth group. She plans to go to college and also hopes to get into a ballet company.

Hanna Lee, thirteen, of New York, rides her horse a lot and skates every Tuesday at an arena. She plans to go to Skidmore College to become a horse trainer.

Jason Lescalleet, fourteen, of Ohio, researches whatever seems interesting, programs his computer, reads a lot, and also uses textbooks and works problems. (For science, he uses the same texts his mother teaches with at Ohio State University.) He draws and reads "spacey, futuristic, high-tech things." He plays the violin, and advises beginning unschoolers, "If the school sends you a curriculum guide, ignore it." He plans to attend college and says, "I will definitely get into computers, maybe write video games that will make Nintendo turn as green as a John Deere Tractor."

Jessin Lui, thirteen, of Maryland, enjoys working closely with her mother in her studies of science, history, social studies, math, literature, and composition. Although she has never been to school, she is aware that without it, she has "extra time on [her] hands" for not only being with friends but also involving herself in interests like drama, singing, piano, ice and roller skating, and swimming. She plans to go to a university, and enjoys trips to the symphony, museums, and many different plays. Also, she says, "Sometimes we travel for long periods during the school year. We're usually not in a rush to come back."

Rebecca McGuire, fourteen, of Alaska, enjoys picking berries, making jam, gardening, cooking, sewing, biking, and boating. She appreciates the extra time no school gives her for being outdoors.

Rosemary McGuire, thirteen, also of Alaska, says that she is able to learn things like cooking, violin, piano, painting, and embroidery since "I have so much more spare time because I do not have to do any useless, boring, repetitive worksheets." She helps in the barn, garden, and house. Also, she enjoys drawing, swimming in the ocean, bird and animal watching, biking, skiing, canoeing, and hiking. She plans to go to college and to write.

Amanda McPherson, sixteen, of California, practices piano, cares for her rose bushes, reads her Bible, and arranges flowers. Her academic work includes all the "usual" plus music theory, and German and computer literacy at a junior college. (Last year she took algebra and biology through the junior college.)

Jesse McPherson, fourteen, of California, spends most of his time riding his bike, for which he belongs to a racing club/team. Also, he plays violin at least one hour every day, backpacks frequently in the Sierra, works part time, attends church, does chores, swims, and plays pool and basketball with his friends. (Part of his academic work includes Spanish and algebra at a junior college.)

Joel Maurer, thirteen, California, studies only math in a formal sense. Aside from that, he says, to learn, "first you have to be interested in something. The rest is easy. If you really like something you just track it down and soak it in like a sponge." In contrast, he recalls that in school he once "had a teacher that ran a classroom like a jail. Eventually I gave up and stopped turning in work." Skateboarding claims a big chunk of his time, and he insists emphatically that "homeschoolers have a better sense of humor than 'schooled' people."

Patrick Meehan, fourteen, of Florida, is thoroughly enthusiastic about this past year—his first out of school. Designated "profoundly gifted" by the school system, Patrick had desperately wanted to quit school since the fourth grade, and finally had a chance to do so this year. "I was frustrated," he writes, "by the poor attitude of the students toward learning/school, the low caliber of most of the teachers, the cruelty of the students toward each other, and intolerance of differences. Many teachers seemed to dislike students who asked questions." He reports that the greatest advantage of unschooling is "Time, time, time. I have my life back for my own use." What does he do with all that time? "I read a great deal," he says, "I draw, I create graphic art on my computer, I take time to *think*. This is the MOST important: thinking! We go to museums, art shows, travel... We watch a lot of documentaries... I help in the yard and sometimes in the house. I am learning to cook. I do sculpture. I take music lessons and practice."

Several months after I heard from Patrick, his mother Gwen sent an update:

> The projects he has undertaken have been very real, professional quality undertakings. He has just completed an amazing portfolio of his work which was mailed out to a video game company for consideration . . .
>
> The portfolio took great planning, hours and hours of drawing (there are over 63 individual drawings of varying complexity which took anywhere from an hour to three or more hours to design and execute). He then wrote all the descriptions of the games and the characters, a cover letter and the copyright paperwork. It took several months to complete and he worked so hard.

Gwen reports that Patrick, who began his first music lessons less than a year ago, is also learning to compose music, taking a class and using a keyboard synthesizer: "Pat puts in hours and hours a week practicing and composing. He could never have made such strides trying to fit lessons and back-up and creating into the few moments at his disposal were he being crushed under the traditional school burden! A whole, new level of accomplishment for him."[1]

Rebecca Merrion, thirteen, of Indiana, has never been to school. She says one of the greatest advantages of unschooling is the opportunity to travel "whenever you want;" she looks forward to a trip to Haiti during this "school" year. She does "academics" through reading and talking, and also works on her garden, takes two ballet lessons each week, and swims. She wants to become a photographer and travel to the outback of Australia.

Cathy Moellers, seventeen, of Iowa, has been taking gymnastics for eight years. She sews, hand-quilts, plays the piano, and works with cattle on her family's farm. She has been president of her 4-H club for the past two years and belongs to wildlife and gun safety clubs. Her goals for her adult life include living on a farm, having a sewing business, and raising a family.

Ariel Mortensen, fifteen, of Washington, has been out of school for four and a

---

[1] See Pat's essay in *Real Lives*, in which he discusses his further progress toward his goal of designing video games. At age seventeen, Pat went on to become SEGA's first intern, working on the game Sonic Spinball. Still seventeen, he was hired by a TV producer to work on an animated children's program, and did all the character development, background design, and animation for the program. His next endeavor was to enroll in an innovative new school for game designers in Vancouver, British Columbia, from which he recently graduated. In *GWS* #99, his mother Gwen comments, "I think that so much of what has materialized for Patrick is the direct result of his absolutely single-minded concentration and his conviction that he *is* a video game designer who knows how to design a successful game, and that he can convince employers of this. At no point has he thought of himself as *becoming* a game designer; he has always *been* one."

half years. After academics, she pursues a wide range of artistic interests. She "draws a lot," takes two two-hour ballet classes each week, and two piano lessons each month. A major focus of her life is costume design—she sews and designs costumes on her own and for a local theater. She plans to go to an art college in Seattle.

Tabitha Mountjoy, fourteen, of Missouri, writes,

> I have three horses, two that I am training. I also like to play hackeysack, swim and ballroom dance. I was on our town's swim team last summer and plan to be a lifeguard this coming summer. With hackeysack and ballroom dance I go through the Communiversity. It is mainly for older people but they are usually very open minded toward young people.

Helen Payne, thirteen, Virginia, uses six textbooks and spends quite a bit of time on academics. She appreciates the extra time she has for taking six different dance classes, playing on a soccer team, babysitting, and reading. She feels that learning outside of school is more effective because she is not pressured to learn.

Janet Petsche, thirteen, Minnesota, also follows an extensive academic program overseen by her mother. With her extra time (after chores) she enjoys reading, embroidery, fishing, and canoeing.

Aurelia Rector, twelve, Arizona, learns math, English, science, geography, and history "by example, by reading, paying attention, wanting to learn, being curious, working, and just living!" No textbooks, thank you. Very involved in the arts, she takes two ballet classes weekly, sings all over the country with a performing group called Kids Alive, and acts in a community theater. She considers her academic knowledge and skills higher than that of people in school, and admits to having a reputation of "being smart."

Kacey Reynolds, sixteen, of North Carolina, spent seventh through ninth grades out of school. She went back to public school for tenth grade to see if she was "keeping up," and was placed in several advanced classes and invited into the National Honor Society. She finished the year with a straight-A average and says, "I account this to my homeschool experience." Being out of school gave her time to focus on her main academic interest—history—and on her love of acting. She's taken several acting courses at a local theater, and has been in two plays and a promotional commercial for a TV station. She hopes to go to college for a BFA in Theater Arts, and also plays the violin.

Jean Rezac, thirteen, of Massachusetts, is one of the free spirits who informed me that she doesn't "study," although she considers her academic skills and knowledge as well rounded and otherwise equal to that of her schooled peers. She says she learns "by whatever I do during the course of the day." She is very interested in horses and works on a horse farm.

Jeff Richardson, fourteen, Oklahoma, draws and skateboards, with the goal of becoming a pro skater.

Debra Roberts, fifteen, of Oklahoma, takes pride in the variety of household skills she is comfortable with that "most schoolgoers do not learn until on their own." "I can sew and do household work," she says, "I know how to change a baby's diaper and rinse it out, and I know how to handle a houseful of kids." Also, her responsibilities include washing lots of dishes, and caring for a hundred chickens, two turkeys, and nine goats. Her scores on the Iowa Achievement Test recently showed that she was working academically at the eleventh grade level overall. She often goes to work with her father, where she is training to become an electrician. Some possibilities for college—if she decides to go—include library science, sign language, and veterinary science.

Erin Roberts, fourteen, Maryland, is focused in several directions. She uses textbooks some months and other months "just pick[s] up something here and there." She plans to go to college and despite her loose academic schedule, she figures she's a bit ahead of her schooled peers academically in everything except possibly math. An avid reader, she consumes mysteries, science fiction, animal stories, sports stories, classics, novels, "just plain anything." She lives on a farm and keeps busy with the animals.

Jennifer Ryan, thirteen, Minnesota, uses texts for math, computer, and history, and learns science, piano, and writing "by doing them." She loves to read and write, bake, play sports, act, sew and do crafts, and garden.

Michael Scott, twelve, of Georgia, supplements his academic program by using and programming a computer, "building things," and biking. He says that his freedom to explore robotics and computers has led him to become greatly interested in these fields, enough that he wants to become an engineer or programmer. He is lucky to enjoy a variety of equipment at home, including tools, a computer, a lab quality microscope, a sewing machine, and lots of books.

Kevin Sellstrom, fourteen, California, volunteers at a school for the mentally impaired and takes piano lessons. His academic work includes math, history, English, and science. As a Boy Scout, he works as a den chief, assisting a group of first- through fourth-graders. In his own troop, he is a Senior Patrol Leader responsible for planning activities. Mechanically inclined, he rides and repairs bikes. He writes:

> I am relatively experienced in repairing gasoline engines on cars, as well as bicycles, tractors, and other mechanical equipment. I learned these skills by watching my dad and other people when they repaired machinery. I like to build power supplies and other electronic and electrical devices that may or may not have particular uses.
>
> In earning my amateur radio license, I had to learn to send and receive Morse Code as well as electronic theory and on-the-air operating techniques. As an amateur, I participate in radio nets as well as talk to other amateurs in person. My dad earned his amateur radio license in the 1950's and still has it and has taught me much of the electrical and electronic theory that I know. He earned his license when he was fifteen and I earned mine at the age of thirteen.

Christin Severini, thirteen, of North Carolina, says,

> I dance at a ballet school nearby. I am also in the company. I care for and help animals by not eating them or wearing them; being friendly, kind, and helpful to the animals I come across; and also by being a member of People for the Ethical Treatment of Animals. I also make a lot of different crafts at home. Some of them are: dolls, clothes for myself, friendship bracelets, baskets, and cards for special occasions—birthdays, holidays, anniversaries, etc. etc.

Michael Severini, fifteen, also of North Carolina, enjoys karate, woodworking, airplane flying, and ham radio. "I go to a karate school nearby six days a week," he writes, "and I sometimes compete in tournaments. I take flying lessons at a nearby airport and I do Ham Radio at home." Michael plans to earn a black belt and to become a commercial airline pilot.

Mae Rose Shell, thirteen, of Vermont, has never been to school and seems to be a particularly relaxed, healthy person with a wise outlook on life. She spends a great deal of time outdoors—swimming, biking, gardening, cross country skiing, ice skating. She loves to read because "it opens a whole world" to her. From books, parents, friends, and everyday situations, she learns math, geography, history, and spelling. Her "learning" is not structured; she is free to do as she likes all the time. "I ask questions," she says, "I read books." About her future, she says she'll probably take college courses in the event that there's a specific subject she wants to learn more about. She wants to be a mother and a writer, and considers herself very "in tune with nature."

Matt Snead, twelve, of Georgia, plays on basketball, tennis, baseball, and soccer teams. Also, he plays the piano and sings in choirs. He wants to attend college and become a pediatrician.

Anthony Stabile-Knowles, thirteen, of California, learns by completely choosing his activities, books, and interests. "No coercion, rewards, or force are used, no set 'school' schedule." He has never used textbooks or "courses," but reads a lot, especially in the areas that interest him most: geography, U.S. history, science, astronomy, art. He also likes aircraft, watching the news, discussing current affairs, drawing, and designing games. "I read a lot and study a little."

Colleen Stevens, fifteen, of California, was out of school from fifth to eighth grades, although she is now in school. She worked as a volunteer both at a "living history" historical site and at an animal museum.

Patricia Young wrote to *GWS* #25 after fourteen years of homeschooling her children,

> Our youngest is now in college in an honors program having received a scholarship from Interlochen Arts Academy for her last year of high school, graduating with honors. Three are currently doing honors work in college. Older ones have become: a lawyer, nurse, legal assistant, computer company executive, medical secretary. None had the least difficulty going on to the school of their choice. Our oldest daughter now teaches her four children at home.

And an anonymous teenager from California wrote in *GWS* #20,

> Almost four months ago, I took the California High School Proficiency test which is equivalent to being a high school graduate. I am now a fifteen-year-old high school graduate. I am going to Los Angeles Valley Junior College—I couldn't afford to go to a university. I go at night and work part-time in the mornings as a tutor for retarded teenagers . . . In the afternoon, I tutor first and second graders at the local elementary school. Each job pays $300 a month . . . I'm still living at home and probably will for a while . . . I'm still doing some writing, The Santa Monica *Evening Outlook* printed a short story I wrote, and another will be in my college's pamphlet on how to write, for which I am being paid $50.

What you can do with all the examples in this chapter

1. Be inspired and emboldened, but not limited. Pursue *your* dreams; don't try to duplicate someone else's life. If there's something you've dreamed of doing in "the future," dream of doing it now.

2. Don't you dare be intimidated.

Do some of the people I just described sound more mature than you? If they are, it's not programmed in their genes; it's just a side-effect of unschooling. It will happen to you too.

Do the people I just described sound more "gifted" than you?

One thing that unschooled teenagers and their parents have continually emphasized to me is that they do *not* consider themselves gifted or otherwise inherently different from other people. And they're not, except in one important sense—they're gifted with time and trust. If you are quitting school, these gifts can be yours too. With them, anyone can develop expertise and a wide range of happy interests. (Many unschoolers spent disastrous, unpromising years in school before they bloomed outside of school.) Of all the points I want to make in this book, this is one of the most important. Let me quote a few people on the subject:

Bonnie Sellstrom, whose son Kevin is described above, wrote me, "I should emphasize that our boys are not gifted. They simply have a curiosity about life and living that we have not tried to squelch. When a question is asked we try to find an answer to meet their needs."

Chapter 26 admires Ishmael and Vita Wallace, talented young musicians. Their mother Nancy wrote a wonderful book called *Better Than School*. In a review, John Holt said:

Many school people [say] that home schooling parents like the Wallaces, taking their talented children out of the schools, leave them [the schools] to struggle along with the less talented . . . The answer, as I said in the introduction to the book, is that it is as sure as anything can be that neither Ishmael nor Vita would have been stars in school. Not only would they have done very badly in most school subjects, but they would almost certainly have had all kinds of damaging psychological labels stuck on them—Learning Disabled, Psychologically Disturbed, the whole disgusting package. The school would have seen them not as assets, only as problems, and would probably have convinced them that they were nothing but problems.

Indeed, Nancy reports in *Better Than School* that before she took Ishmael out of school, his first grade teacher had this to say:

Ishmael does seem to have a problem with listening skills . . . I've been playing a record that gives the children instructions on how to follow specific directions, and Ishmael invariably gets lost. His hearing appears to be normal, so I'm just not sure what to do. He also has a problem grasping "whole concepts." For example, if I read the class a paragraph, he can't tell me the main idea. He gets too involved with all the little details. I'm thinking that maybe we should have Ishmael tested, just in case we discover some kind of developmental problem. Then we can send him to the resource room for, say, ten minutes a day, so they can help him.

Maria Holt tells in *GWS* #35 about the time the education department officials came to visit her family's homeschooling operation. They were impressed, and Maria reports, "One of them said to me as they took their leave of us, 'You have unusual children.' I returned, 'That is where you make your worst mistake.' And I meant it. Our children are 'average.' There is not a genius among them."

"What amazes me," writes Penny Barker in *GWS* about her kids,

Is that these are not "gifted" children—they spend most of their time doing what they want to do (after chores, that is). In the winter we do structured studies for a couple of hours each morning but that's about it. Most of their learning is completely spontaneous. As I write, Maggie and Britt stopped by the orchard (where I'm typing) to tell me they are going off to the woods to look for a doe Britt spotted this morning and to spot birds and record their calls on paper . . . I could go on and on about my average kids and their wonderful growth. It seems they have simply more time to grow and develop than other children I know who have probably more potential but so much less time to realize it because they are always stuck away in a school building.

3. On the other hand, don't underestimate.

Don't dismiss this list of multifaceted teenagers by saying, "Yeah, well, I take dance classes too, and I go to school." Naturally, just because you go to school doesn't mean you can't also do other things. But the question of time and energy is a big question. People who both go to school *and* want to focus on outside interests essentially have several choices:

1) Skimp on homework time, turning in work which does not reflect their full abilities. End up feeling guilty and humiliated.

2) Treat their personal interests as secondary, devoting only a few hours each week to them, or pushing them into weekends and vacations.

3) Sacrifice time they'd like to spend with friends.

4) Sacrifice time spent with their families.

5) Sacrifice sleep or relaxation time. Get stressed.

6) Take "easy" school classes which do not require homework (and which may be boring, and which will not impress admissions officers of selective colleges).

7) Be born genetically engineered to calculate differential equations in seconds and to carry on a meaningful conversation while rewriting a sonnet.

In other words: if you already live an amazing life with school, you can live an even more amazing and far more relaxed life without it.

Joshua, our last heroic guinea pig in this chapter

Joshua Smith, now busy in college, wrote me a most delightful letter about his experience with quitting school. It made me smile all day. If only I'd read it when I was twelve! In part, it says:

It started about two and a half years ago . . . at the time I was attending what is known as a "magnet" school—a school designed for "advanced" students. During a period in late fall of my junior year, with upcoming exams I found myself stressed out beyond belief. It was not because of the subject content but because of the bulk amount of work assigned. There was essentially no time left for regular life outside of school. I would come home from school worn out and disgusted. Like any other student I would always look forward to Fridays as if they were a blessing from some divine being.

One particularly disgusting week essentially became the catalyst for the dramatic change over in educational methods. Arriving home one Friday I flopped down on the couch and after a few minutes announced my intentions to my mom. She had just recently pulled my sister, now ten, out of school . . . and so was supportive. It wasn't until she had removed my sister from school that I realized that there was an alternative.

Always being one not afraid to challenge the system I marched into school the following Monday and resigned. And oh did that cause a stink with the officials. My guidance counselor insisted that if I dropped out I essentially was through with my education. (School is not the only place we learn things; there is that small thing known as life.) No matter how much I explained the situation there was no recognition from her or from my ex principal. Oh well, no real big surprises there. The big surprise came when I explained it to my teachers—they were supportive of the idea. And my classmates? Most of them did not know what was happening until it was over for I literally breezed through school that day. The ones I call my friends all exhibited either acceptance, admiration, or envy . . .

I left school early that day and walked into the record of becoming the first official "drop out" of Hume Fogg Academic High School. That is a day I shan't forget in a long,

long time.

Over the next week I got an offer from the school board of Nashville to return to the school system but to a different school (rather than the one that I went to and rather than the one I was zoned for, where violence [and teen pregnancy were] common). I was offered a school all the way across town with transportation. They were willing to break zoning restrictions just to keep me in the school system.

Needless to say I thumbed my nose at them and never regretted the decision. Hume Fogg had marked the eighth school I had been in and I was ready for a change.

Over the next year and a half I worked, studied, traveled. I went back to my home country, Canada, to visit a friend, went to Florida, East Tennessee, and Wisconsin. Over this time I developed an intense interest in photography and psychology. And something else, something more important. I discovered myself . . . I [had] never fit the mold they made for me at school completely. Oh sure, I got along okay with the teachers, but I got away with whatever I wanted to in school. For instance, I didn't like gym particularly so I showed up for roll count and then slipped out walking right past the principal in doing so. I assume they couldn't assume that I was quietly rebelling. So I smiled and stabbed them in the back. Leaving school gave me no one to rebel against so I had more time to self reflect and change subtly, to become someone I felt comfortable with.

To go to college I had to take two tests, the GED (for lack of a HS diploma) and the SAT. I have always done well on standardized tests no matter what I think of them, and these were no exception. The SAT scores put me in the [running for the] "highly competitive" range or colleges. But I chose to apply to two colleges that both had attendance of around six hundred and where there was not an exceptional atmosphere of competitiveness. I had already had my fill of that scene and wanted no more. I was accepted to both colleges and am now pursuing two degrees in Psychology and conflict resolution. I go to Northland College which is in upper Wisconsin away from most major cities. I like it there; the weather suits me better... and there is a large percentage of foreign students, which provides a good way to get a multi-cultural experience . . .

Right now I exist as a quiet but highly influential individual in college. I helped found a chapter of the Green Political Party, worked on implementing environmentally and socially sound measures, such as increased recycling, G.E. boycott and stopping a low level radioactive waste dump in upper Michigan. When I work on campus it is as a photographer and as such my photos have gone around the world when they were included in the college directory which goes to several countries such as Japan, India, China, Canada, Korea, and many others.

Not bad for a drop out, eh? ☺

your allies among the Rich and Famous

I SUPPOSE IT shouldn't have surprised me, but it did. I'd heard of a few famous people who hadn't gone to school, so I went to the library to check up on them. I steered into the reference section and sat down with a stack of *Current Biography Yearbook*s. I started by looking up the names on my list, but pretty soon I was just turning pages and laughing. Why?

1. On the average, one out of every five or six people featured had dropped out of school or else not attended much formal school. (The *Current Biography Yearbook* is published every year. It contains hundreds of short biographies on people who are currently prominent in some field—worldwide government leaders, entertainers, scientists, writers, artists.)

2. In almost all of the biographies, it was clear that the forces which had shaped these brilliant lives had little or nothing to do with school. Instead, other experiences had inspired and nurtured them.

For instance, Luc Montagnier, French virologist famous for his research on the AIDS virus, was inspired to become a scientist mainly because his father, a CPA, kept a laboratory in the garage; he was allowed to have his own laboratory in the basement; and at age fifteen, he watched his grandfather die of cancer.[1]

Also for instance, Steven Spielberg learned filmmaking by experimenting with his father's 8mm camera. In high school, he spent a lot of time making films in order to escape studying algebra and French. Later, he sneaked onto movie sets to watch (his high school grades were too low to get him into film school).[2]

3. Lots of famous people had to go to school—they'd probably never heard of "unschooling"—but made nasty comments about it. Examples at the end of this chapter.

I am not bringing up the subject of rich famous people to suggest that it is

---

[1] Information from *Current Biography Yearbook 1988.*

[2] Information from *Current Biography Yearbook 1978.*

necessarily fulfilling to be rich and famous. However, information like this is a good kick in the pants for all the unimaginative, illogical people who believe quitting school generates "failure." Keep your ears open, and compile your own list of admirable independent learners. On the Internet, see Karl Bunday's list.[3] Here is part of mine:

Some people who dropped out of high school or otherwise escaped much or all of the usual teenage schooling: Ansel Adams, Joan of Arc, Roseanne Barr, Irving Berlin, Rosamond Bernier, Claude Berri, William Blake, Art Blakey, John Boorman, Pearl Buck, Liz Claiborne, Samuel Clemens (Mark Twain), Buffalo Bill Cody, Noel Coward, Charles Dickens, Bo Diddley, Thomas Edison, Benjamin Franklin, Henry Ford, George Gershwin, Whoopi Goldberg, Samuel Gompers, Maxim Gorki, Robin Graham, Patrick Henry, Eric Hoffer, John Houston, John Paul Jones, Cyndi Lauper, William Lear, Abraham Lincoln, Jack London, Beryl Markham, Liza Minnelli, Wolfgang Amadeus Mozart, Sean O'Casey, Florence Nightingale, Beatrix Potter, David Puttnam, Keith Richards, Clement W. Stone, Randy Travis, Frank Lloyd Wright, Orville and Wilbur Wright, Brigham Young. [4]

Also: one third of the men who signed the Declaration of Independence, the Articles of Confederation, and the Constitution of the United States had no more than a few months of schooling up their sleeves. Historian Harry G. Good describes several of them:

Stephen Hopkins of Rhode Island, a farm boy, became a practical surveyor and learned politics as moderator of town meetings. Roger Sherman of Connecticut was apprenticed to a shoemaker and became successively a writer, publisher, and lawyer . . . Others read medical books and helped a doctor in his practice.[5]

And of course, since blacks and other people of color were not allowed to attend school (or, of course, to have governesses and private tutors) during much of U.S. history, many black (and other) leaders during the past few hundred years were autodidacts. For example, John Jones—a leading nineteenth-century abolitionist and activist—taught himself to read and write, became a successful businessman, and lectured throughout Illinois on the rights of blacks. Other prominent nineteenth-century black autodidacts included Harriet Tubman and Sojourner Truth.

Ironically, most biographers share the mainstream prejudice against unschooling. Therefore, if their subject has had little or no schooling, instead of pointing out this very cool fact and showing how that person took the initiative to educate himself, they downplay it or just leave out all mention of "education."

Wanna-be unschoolers

Brilliant people often got that way not because of school, but despite it.

Woody Allen said, "I loathed every day and regret every day I spent in school. I like to be taught to read and write and add and then be left alone."[6] *Winston*

---

[3] "U.S. Founders Learned Without Public School" and "Nobel Prize Winners Hate School" at Karl's "School is Dead/Learn in Freedom" Web site.

[4] Sources: *Current Biography, Famous Homeschoolers,* by Malcolm and Nancy Plent, *Dove,* by Robin Graham, various other biographies, *The Norton Anthology of English Literature, volume 2, School Days of the Famous,* by Gerhard Prause.

[5] Harry G. Good, *A History of American Education,* p.84.

[6] *Current Biography Yearbook,* 1979.

Churchill said, "I was happy as a child with my toys in my nursery. I have been happier every year since I became a man. But this interlude of school makes a somber grey patch upon the chart of my journey. It was an unending spell of worries that did not then seem petty, and of toil uncheered by fruition; a time of discomfort, restriction and purposeless monotony." [7] German novelist *Franz Kafka* said, "As far as I have seen, at school . . . they aimed at blotting out one's individuality." According to Gerhard Prause, Kafka

> not only hated the system and the increasing anxiety before examinations, but he was also convinced that school offered too little in relation to the amount of time he spent there. Above all he felt it did not offer enough that was practical and relevant. His greatest criticism was aimed at the fact that education in general attempted to make everyone equal and therefore ignored an individual's talents and abilities.[8]

Melina Mercouri, a Greek Minister of Culture, former member of parliament, and an actress, hated school. "The one great affliction of Miss Mercouri's childhood," reads *Current Biography* 1988, "was formal schooling, which bored her to tears, but since she grew up in a household frequented by politicians, scholars, writers, and artists, she nonetheless received a good liberal education." *Claude Monet*, French impressionist painter, "grew up a lad of unembarrassed daring, rebellious and self-willed," says Charles Merrill Mount's biography *Monet*. According to this biography, Monet said:

> I was undisciplined by birth; never would I bend, even in my most tender youth, to a rule. It was at home I learned the little I knew. Schools always appeared to me like a prison, and never could I make up my mind to stay there, not even for four hours a day, when the sunshine was inviting, the sea smooth, and when it was a joy to run about the cliffs in the free air, or to paddle in the water.

Monet was especially rebellious in his art classes, where he made parodies and caricatures instead of the realistic drawings he was asked to do. Although his drawing teacher considered him untalented, by the time he turned fifteen he was in demand as a professional caricaturist. Pulitzer-prize winning historian *Edmund Morris* hated high school, and *Current Biography* 1989 says he "entertained himself by writing novels 'behind cover of an atlas at the rearmost possible desk of every class.'" And *Charles Trenet*, French singer, songwriter, and writer, went to a Catholic School—the "Free School of the Trinity," about which he said, "The school might have been free, but I was shut up inside."[9] ☀

---

[7] Sir Winston Churchill, *Great Destiny*

[8] Gerhard Prause, *School Days of the Famous*, translated by Susan Hecker Ray, p. 38.

[9] *Current Biography Yearbook* 1989

the life freestyle: Seth Raymond

A NEWSPAPER CLIPPING on the refrigerator catches my eye—a photo of a boy balancing on the handlebars of his bike, a few words underneath. It's cleverly written, but contains one small mistake.

> Seth Raymond, a fourteen-year-old Port Townsend High School student, spent part of last Friday studying physics, geometry, physical education, and possibly philosophy as well. The teacher was his bicycle; the classroom a slab of concrete near the beach at Fort Worden State Park. Raymond said he's getting ready for the February 4 Northwest Freestyle Association competition in Seattle. He's been studying his course only seven months, but by the looks of his twirls, hops, and balancing act, seems ready to graduate with honors.

Exactly. Except: Seth Raymond is not a Port Townsend High School student.

Instead, he is—as the clipping points out—a student of his bike, and also of a math textbook, some good novels, the marine science center on the beach, his parents, the Olympic mountains, and his Pentax camera. Seth Raymond is an unschooled student of life.

He is fifteen now, in October 1990, and I am visiting. I am welcomed not only by Seth, but also by his sisters Vallie, eleven, and Lydia, four, and by his parents, Kath and Dan. They live in an elegant, simple, spacious wooden frame house. The honest beauty of wooden beams, ceilings, floors, and door frames mixes with the warmth of worn oriental carpets and pumpkins heaped in the windows. Right off, the Raymonds strike me as being a lot like their house: in their company, there is no pretense, nothing doctored up or faked. No wonder—it turns out they built this house themselves, together, over a span of three years.

Seth has never been to school, thanks to his parents' courage and independence. Kath recalls the decision. A cousin had begun teaching school and given up in disillusionment. "I'd never put my kids in public school," she had warned Kath and Dan. Hoping to hear some good advice about other choices—Montessori, maybe, or alternative schools—they'd gone to hear John Holt speak in St. Paul. But he didn't talk about Montessori; he talked about unschooling. Kath reminded me of my own first reaction to Holt's books when she said, "I'd never even heard of unschooling before, but as soon as he started talking, I felt like I'd always believed in it."

Over the years, sometimes they have been legal, sometimes perhaps not. As far as they are concerned, it doesn't much matter. If they should ever have to fight for their right to stay out of school, they'll fight. All the same, they are thankful they've never been harassed.

As Seth grew, the family lived in different areas. Wherever he was, Seth took advantage of local opportunities and followed his own changing interests. At eight and nine, for instance, he took ballet classes from a "tough guy" teacher at the Minnesota Dance Theater in Minneapolis. The high point was performing in *The Nutcracker*—six times on stage and once for the half-time of a Vikings football game.

One of Seth's largest memories is his work on the house. He recalls clearing and burning brush, cutting down trees, watching the excavation and laying of the foundation, helping with beams, pouring cement, running errands, nailing up sheet rock, helping install insulation under the house, sanding and gluing pipes, putting in windows, cutting siding, mudding, taping, painting, paneling. "It was a lot of fun," he says, "I learned a lot. It will be a lot easier if I ever decide to build a house myself."

Last year, he worked about eighteen hours a week at The Shanghai, a Chinese restaurant where no one else spoke much English. He bussed tables and brought food out to customers. After a year, he wanted more time for other interests, so he quit.

Academics

The Raymonds belong to a homeschool group with the local school district's stamp of approval; the district pays a part time teacher, Marcie, who helps homeschoolers document their academic work, gives them credits for this work, and organizes a weekly educational activity, which takes two hours every Wednesday afternoon. In return, the school district gets to officially "enroll" the homeschoolers, which gives them more money.

Seth and Kath explain their mixed feelings about the program. "It isn't the best part of homeschooling," says Seth, "But it's only two hours a week. It's not like six hours a day, every day. And Marcie helps a lot with finding textbooks when we need them." He recalls one time the group set a goal for how many books they'd read in a month. "That was fun," he remembers, "because I did read more than usual." Furthermore, in exchange for the minor bother of keeping logbooks and going to the weekly activity, Seth and Vallie are unquestionably legal, legitimate, and even working toward high school diplomas—though none of this matters a whole lot to them.

Clearly, the Raymonds do not feel the least bit dependent on the program. If it wasn't there, they'd homeschool anyway. If homeschooling was illegal, they'd homeschool anyway—and they wouldn't hide it. In Minnesota they knew homeschoolers who lived in fear and hiding; every time their doorbell rang the kids ran and hid under a bed. The Raymonds don't want to live like that.

Seth enjoys the other teenagers in the group, who have their own "specialties" in dance, writing, and sports. His best friends, though, happen to go to school; they are his friends because they share his interests in biking and backpacking.

I flip through Seth's log book. Some days there are entries for science, history, Spanish. Sometimes it's just math, reading, and biking. There are brief notes under each category: "watched and identified birds," "bike comp, placed 4th," "edited music tapes for biking," "edited video for bike sponsor," "made poster for room," "bought used bike frame and started sanding it," "marine center," "read 'Berniece Bobs Her Hair.'"

In the back of the logbook are some pockets full of academic paraphernalia and things Seth has written. There are a handful of bulletins ("teacher's guides") to accompany the PBS series *Scientific American Frontiers*, with instructions for labs and notes. "Explain to students," says one of them, "That ordinarily, water freezes and ice melts at 0° Celsius."

*

I ask Seth about his work in various subjects.

Writing is not his favorite thing to do, although he sometimes likes creative writing. One of his stories won an honorable mention at Centralia College's writing contest (mostly school kids entered) last year. Also, he keeps a journal. No one else reads it.

Last year he worked through most of the Harcourt Brace Jovanovich textbook *Biology*, doing the labs and reading—although he was also involved with the local marine science center. He started in the middle of the textbook, with the chapters that interested him most, and later went back to the beginning. He wrote away for more information on ectobiology, because the idea of life on other planets especially intrigued him. Also, he enjoyed a "science champions" day in Seattle, a sort of science fair populated mainly by public school students.

History? "I've always liked history," he says, "but never used a textbook for it." Aside from reading books on specific historical events, Seth explores history in the field. With his backpacking friend Reg, Seth figures he's investigated every one of the thirty World War I bunkers at Fort Worden State Park.

Math, reading, Spanish, and physical education? I get to see these in action. While I am at the Raymonds, this is what happens after I get up on Monday morning:

Right off, I notice a conspicuous absence of the early morning frenzy that dominated when my siblings and I used to rush to get ready for school. People make their own pancakes, talk a bit, and at nine Seth and Vallie sit down at the dining room table to work math problems, with Kath occasionally answering questions. Seth uses the book *Math: A Human Endeavor*, which he likes much better than some previous math texts that "try to trick you." Math is okay, he says, but not his favorite thing to do. The clock ticks. Kath reads in the family room. I am overwhelmed by the calm, by the feeling of life *happening* instead of waiting to happen.

Vallie gets up a few minutes before ten and shuts her book. "How'd you do?" asks Kath. "Fine," says Vallie, "I got one wrong because I divided instead of multiplied." She gets a Shel Silverstein book off the shelf and curls up on the sofa.

At ten, Kath says to Seth, "Do you want to watch that star show?"

"It's been on a long time, hasn't it?"

"No, you just missed one."

"Okay."

But no one watches the star show. By the time it comes on at 10:30, Seth is upstairs on his bed, engrossed in his reading, *The Count of Monte Cristo*. It is his third novel since September. The others were *Of Mice and Men* and *To Kill a Mockingbird*. Since September, he has also read short stories by John Updike, Richard Wright, Ernest Hemingway, Willa Cather, and F. Scott Fitzgerald. He picks out his own novels, from the family's shelves, from booklists. He uses the public library heavily. "What if you started a book and didn't like it?" I ask. "I'd read something else," he says matter-of-factly, but points out that rarely happens. He loves to read, although he didn't start until he was about eight.

While he reads, Kath is next door at the neighbors'. Charming Lydia sings downstairs, "One of these things is not like the other," shaking the rattle she made last night out of two bowls and some beans. Dan is away doing construction work. Vallie works intently on a zigzagged friendship bracelet—today's mail brought instructions from DMC.

I look around in the quiet. C.S. Lewis and John Holt dominate the bookshelves. I also notice *Drawing on the Right Side of the Brain*, a jar of Play-doh, Steinbeck, Kipling, encyclopedias, A.A. Milne, Gibran's *The Prophet*, Bibles, *Black Elk Speaks*, *Othello*, *How to Stay Alive in the Woods*, *The Anatomy of an Illness*, a pile of *National Geographics*, *Pond Life*, *St. Francis of Assisi*, *Robert Frost's Poems*, *A Whale for the Killing*, *The Craftsman Builder*, *Woodstock Handmade Houses*. A globe sits on top of the shelves. Clearly, this is not one of those houses where they have a complete set of The Great Classics in order to appear intellectual in the upper-class way. Each book at the Raymonds' house makes sense, and each is worn and a bit creased.

On the walls in the family room, I find a map of the world and a glass encased poster commemorating Seth's dance debut. It has words: "Twentieth Anniversary Loyce Houlton's Nutcracker Fantasy, Minnesota Dance Theater."

I visit Seth again. In his closet hangs a sleeping bag and a wetsuit. From behind a stack of sweatshirts on the dresser, I catch the golden glint of three trophies from freestyling bike competitions. A stack of bike magazines—*Go*, *BMX Plus*—covers the desk. Seth sits on his bed, leaning comfortably against the wood paneling that he put up by himself. From a framed photograph across the room, a Seth original, the wide soft eyes of a deer gaze at him. In the window above his head sits his old Petri camera, gazing at *me*.

At noon Seth and I take sandwiches and sit down in the family room to watch *España Viva*, a Spanish instruction program on PBS. He has the accompanying workbooks, ordered through the mail, and completes one lesson a week to go along with the TV program.

After lunch, academics are sort of officially over, though Seth spends some more time with *The Count*. The rest of his day is dominated by biking, with a lot of conversation and a VCR movie on the side.

At dinner, we all hold hands and sing grace, and then Seth cuts a pineapple for dessert, far more elegantly than I ever could. Trained by The Shanghai.

*

With his calm schedule, Seth has had plenty of energy to pour into his major interests. At the moment, these are marine biology, biking, and photography.

The Marine Science Center
Last year, Seth's homeschool group organized a weekly "class" at the local Marine Science Center. Seth particularly enjoyed the center, discovering his love for marine biology, and he is now quite involved there, although the homeschool group has moved on to other activities. In the beginning, Seth recalls that they spent a lot of

time just looking at the tanks full of starfish, crabs, anemones, fish, and octopi, and listening to the director. The director, Frank D'Amore, talked about the names of animals, the food chain—"who eats who," and the care of different species. The homeschoolers also used the Center's gauges to keep charts graphing the weather, precipitation, cloud patterns, and water temperature.

Although Seth has enjoyed all his time at the center, he did notice a sort of "teacher-class" feel in the beginning, "like they were the adults and we were the kids." Later, this feeling eased as the homeschoolers took responsibility for chopping meat, feeding animals, cleaning tanks, helping to collect plankton, using microscopes, and answering the questions of school kids on field trips. As time went by, Seth spent extra time there on his own, anywhere from two to four hours a week, and came to feel more involved on a serious level.

Last summer, Frank offered Seth a job at the center, but various other things got in the way. This year, however, Seth looks forward to continued working and learning at the center on an informal, individual basis. Last week, he helped during a fourth grade field trip, answering questions and setting up the microscope. Frank has talked about involving him in helping to set up a research project monitoring the ocean's temperature, collecting and studying plankton, or investigating the fragility of eelgrass. Next summer, Seth thinks he'll make working there a priority.

How will Seth's work at the center affect his future? He's not sure. He is grateful that it has awakened him to his love of marine biology. He'd like to combine this love someday with diving and snorkeling, preferably somewhere warmer than the Puget Sound. He does some skin diving now, but he explains that the Sound has low visibility, since algae grows thickly in cold climates.

Biking

Three things go whoosh. One is the crash of waves on the beach. Two is a seagull's wings. Three is Seth's bike making circles in the air. Not the whole bike, actually—one wheel stays on the ground. It's hard to describe where Seth is. Sometimes he's standing on a small lever at the hub of the front wheel. Sometimes he's kicking his legs over the crossbar as it pivots around. Always, his eyes are intent. This weekend, he will travel to Lewiston, Idaho, for a freestyle bike competition.

Seth has been freestyling for a year now. When his friend Mike gets out of school, they head down to Fort Worden State Park and practice for two or three hours. When the weather's good, Seth starts earlier.

A local shop, Aurora Cycle, sponsors Seth and Mike, meaning that it donates brake cables and "stuff like that." Mike's been biking for three years. Other local teenagers have been involved off and on, but Seth and Mike are the hardcores. Their practice is quiet, focused work, hushed except for the whooshing and an occasional comment. The sky is a bit damp. Soft coastal scrub surrounds their concrete arena. After a few hours, they take turns photographing each other.

Then they go to the Raymonds' house to look at a bike frame Seth is working on. After that, they go to Mike's and invent a strange unicycle with handlebars and a wheel but no pedals. To ride it, they stand on the fender or on the levers by the hubs of the wheel. For two hours they ride it up and down the street, experimenting with a rope tied onto the handlebars like reins. The rope provides tension, a bit more control. Neighbor kids come out to watch. When Dan gets home, he and Lydia come out too.

Though he enjoys his day to day biking experience more than competition, Seth competes well. At North American Freestyle Association competitions in Eugene, Vancouver, and Portland, he placed third in the novice category. In Spokane and at the regional finals in Kelso, Washington, he took first. (A few months after my visit, I learned that at the 1990 finals in Bremerton, Washington, Seth took first in his division, and also came in first in total points for the year.)

How serious is Seth about biking? "I don't think of it as a possible career or anything," he says, "but right now I like it a lot. Sometimes I think it could be fun to design bikes."

Kath tells me that the homeschool group invited Seth to teach a class on biking, for pay. He refused. "If anyone wants to learn," he told them, "they can come along and do it with us, anytime."

Photography
Seth smiles when I mention that Ansel Adams quit school at the age of twelve, because Adams' photographs have inspired a lot of Seth's own work. I can tell, as I admire the black and white print that took the "Best of Show" prize (including a $20 bill) at the 1990 Jefferson County Fair. A strangely angled view of a Victorian building, its hundred shades of grey give an almost 3-D quality.

Seth works with a Pentax he bought last year. Before that, he'd taken photos for two years with an old Petri he bought at a garage sale. It had no light meter, which forced Seth to think especially hard about what he was doing. He reads books on photography and experiments a lot. His interest in camping and the outdoors has intensified along with his photographic skills, and he sometimes dreams of a future in photojournalism. "I'm interested in outdoor work," he tells me, "Not in studio photography."

So far, Seth has put all of his focus into the first part of the photographic process—composing a picture, exposing the film. Now, he feels ready to get involved in developing his own prints, and is looking for access to a darkroom. There is talk in his homeschool group of setting up a darkroom this year. "That would be just great," says Seth, with a faraway look in his eyes.

One evening, we all nestle into Seth's bedroom. He shows slides taken during two Washington backpacking trips—one with his family in Neah Bay, the other with teenaged friends in the Olympics.

During the presentation, I gasp a lot. I find Seth's slides even more stunning than his black and white prints, dramatized by color as well as pattern and shape. One, taken at the Point of Arches in Neah Bay, depicts a soft grey landscape of mist, beach, and water, punctuated by sharp triangles of huge rocks in the water. Another vividly presents three boys' bare wet sun-tanned backs in front of a blue-white waterfall with a red flower in the corner.

Seth races through the slides, as if they don't deserve long appreciation. I plead with him to go slower. He obliges. We pause at a portrait of a spiraling plant. "What is it?" asks Dan. "Skunk cabbage," says Seth, "an alpine form."

There are a bunch of close shots of bald eagles. They had been eating a dead

Photography class... Seth's shot of Lydia and Kath won the youth photography award at a 1991 contest sponsored by the Jefferson County Museum for National Library Week.

dog, so intent on their feast that they ignored Seth's artistic intrusion.

"For our national bird," comments Dan, "They sure are scavengers."

I pay special attention to a candid picture of Lydia minding her business about camp. "Seth doesn't usually do people pictures," laughs Kath, "If we want people pictures of our backpacking trips, we have to do that ourselves."

"I like taking pictures of Lydia," he tells me later, "She doesn't *pose*. But I don't like to line people up in front of things. It looks so fake."

*

No doubt, Seth's unschooling works largely because his parents believe in it. There's not the least bit of "school" feeling in the house, even in the mornings when the math books are out.

Kath and Dan sparkle when they talk about unschooling. "Sometimes people use the Real World argument," says Dan, "You know—how are your kids going to survive in the real world if they don't go to school and learn how to live with adversity? John Holt said that was like putting your head in a vise since you know you're going to have a headache anyway. Also, part of the idea is that maybe instead of adjusting to the world as it is, you can help create a better one."

"And maybe," adds Kath, "people who watch homeschoolers will finally start to see that happy kids turn into happy adults."

We talk about the issue of unschooling with two-career families. With four-year-old Lydia, Kath feels some conflict over the idea of going to work, but she readily admits that Seth and Vallie would be fine without her. If they ran into problems with academics, they could ask her or Dan in the evenings, just like other kids ask their parents for help with homework.

"Yes," agrees Dan, "By the time kids are teenagers, parents don't need to be heavily involved anyway."

Kath points out that even though she's at home during the day now, she's not responsible for Seth's education. "I don't feel that I can, or should, keep up with everything he does," she says.

Kath went to college for one quarter. Dan never went. "We were schooled out," they tell me. "We probably went to the wrong end—we should have skipped all the early stuff and gone to college." They want Seth to be able to go to college, if he wants to. He does want to, unless a better idea turns up.

One of the biggest unschooling challenges for Kath and Dan has been a sense of inadequacy. For one thing, Seth was a late reader. He'd listen attentively to very long stories from the age of five, but didn't start reading until around eight. Kath read a lot of stories in *GWS* which told about kids reading at four and five. At times, she panicked, certain they must be doing something wrong. Fortunately, she restrained her impulses to push reading on Seth, and when he was ready, it happened.

For another thing, as they have heard about the glamorous activities of other unschoolers, they have sometimes felt lacking. "We'd read about homeschoolers in a big city, with museums and concerts and all, and we'd think, 'That's where we should be, in a city!' Then we'd hear about homeschoolers on a farm, raising goats and gardening, and we'd think, 'That's where we should be—on a farm! We'd hear about families who took long exotic trips, and we'd think, 'That's what we should be doing—traveling!'"

"But we couldn't travel, because we were busy building a house," laughs Kath,

"And of course in our moments of sanity we realized that if any of those city, farm, or traveling people heard about us, maybe they'd say 'That's what we should be doing—building a house!'"

I point out to them that Seth, with his expertise in biking and photography and his growing involvement in marine biology, is just as impressive as any other homeschooler. Then Dan speaks the truth: "And yet that's *not* the point, is it? Homeschooling isn't about competition. It's about living a meaningful life." ☀

Soon after I wrote this profile, Seth put together an inexpensive darkroom in part of the laundry room, began restoring a kayak, and performed with Mike for an elementary school. After the first edition of this book was published, Seth started working for the Pygmy Boat Company in Port Townsend, which makes boat and kayak kits—he did everything from building prototypes to answering the phone. During that time, Seth also took several long trips: to the East Coast with biking friends; a solo trip to Costa Rica, Nicaragua, and Panama; and a driving trip around the U.S. with a side excursion to Jamaica. He took up the guitar and played in two bands, Pin Fish and Civil to Strangers. Oh, and somewhere along the way, Port Townsend's high school opened an alternative branch, which translated Seth's past life into credits and gave him a diploma. At 22, Seth lives in Portland, Oregon, works in a French restaurant, and takes classes at the Northwest Film Center.

bike class...Seth (left) and friend Mike Nash prepare for a competition.

The journal, etc., of Ms. Kim Kopel, Autodidact

*K*IM *K*OPEL *IS sixteen. She's never been to school. She lives in St. Louis, Missouri, she gives Irish dance lessons to two young girls, she's teaching herself to play a tin whistle, she weaves, writes, plays piano, and has from time to time been interested in physics, motors and machines. I am delighted to share with you a few bits of her journal, her explanation of the way she learns, and some of her thoughts on the future of her education and lifestyle.*

Kim was fourteen years old when she wrote this section.

Tuesday, September sixth, 1988 10:00 A.M.

Today is the first day of a new school year. So why am I sitting at home at the typewriter, instead of at a desk in a classroom? Because I'm self-educated. What I mean by that is that I'm in charge of my own education, of living my own life. For a long time I've called myself a "homeschooler," but I don't like to anymore because I don't think it's accurate in my case. I think of homeschooling as being just that— school at home.

For myself, I wouldn't choose any form of "school" as we know it—not in a building designated as a "school," not at home, not on my neighbor's front yard. I don't want to have a teacher pour knowledge into my brain—knowledge that someone else decided I should have. I don't want someone telling me what to think, when to think, when to read on what page out of what book, when to eat lunch, etc. I don't want to be "schooled" at all, and since I'm not, I don't want to *say* I'm "schooled." I've decided that "home-educated" isn't really any better than "homeschooled," because it sounds like I only learn things in one place—at home. That's such a foreign concept to me that it seems ridiculous.

So I've come up with the term "self-educated," even though people usually have no idea what I mean. I imagine it sounds like I teach myself everything, which isn't much more accurate than saying I'm "homeschooled." When I say I'm self-educated, what I mean is that I can decide what I want to do, when, where and how I want to do it, and who, if anyone, I want to help me. I can decide what kind of help I want, and find someone who will give me that help, and won't start giving me help I haven't asked for.

Since I'm in charge of my education/life (I have the freedom to decide how I spend my time), people often tend to assume that I just do whatever I want; whatever feels good at the moment. That's not true. I'd rather not sweep floors, wash dishes, do laundry, fix meals, mow lawns, but they're all things that have to be done, and so even though they're not things I really like or want to spend time on, I still do them. (For the obvious reasons that if I didn't, I wouldn't have any clean clothes or dishes, and I wouldn't eat!) Besides those things, there are also all the other requirements of daily life here—maybe we need to go shopping, or Mom needs me to watch my younger sisters while she drops books off at the library, or we're having company, or one of my siblings wants me to help them with something, etc. I'm not just off in my own little world, floating around totally oblivious to what's going on around me.

I don't think there's anything wrong with doing what I want—I don't see any sense in spending my time doing things I hate! I guess it's just that people think that if you don't have someone making you do things, you'll never do anything that's hard for you, or take on any challenges, and that you'll probably just sit around and watch TV, hang out with your friends, party all the time—in short, "vegetate." In talking with people about self-education, I've found that most of them find it very hard to believe that anyone would actually do meaningful or hard or challenging things without being forced to.

I guess that's because people look at the kids they know, and see that a lot of them don't like school (which people translate as meaning that they don't care about getting a "good" education, and are therefore irresponsible), have to be reminded to do homework, won't do much around the house without being made to, and would rather just sit and watch TV, etc. And so they think, "Look; kids will hardly do anything worthwhile now, imagine what would happen if they weren't being forced to do things!" If they imagine that if kids were let out of school for good they'd probably just vegetate, I'd say they guessed right. It seems to me that after you've spent a good part of your life with someone else doing all the thinking and decision making for you, you're going to need some time to get used to thinking for yourself, to being responsible for your own life. There's a period of adjustment that kids go through after they've been taken out of school, in which they have to recover from whatever effects school is responsible for having caused—low self esteem and self confidence, etc. etc.—before they can start focusing on what they want to do in their lives.

But I've never been to school, so I haven't had to go through that process of undoing what school does. I've grown up thinking for myself, making decisions, being responsible for my life, so I'm at the point right now where I'm finding out what I want to do, and finding ways to do those things. Watching TV, hanging out, etc., are very empty and unsatisfying pursuits to me. I know that there's more to my life than that. I don't want to spend (waste) my time on those things; there are too many other important things to do (like watching the grass grow, for instance. That's how low those other things are on my list).

If I were saying this to someone in a conversation, I'm sure they'd want to know—as it seems everyone does—"Well, then, what *do* you do?"

I hope this journal will answer that question, and many others that I've been asked. I'm writing this journal for that reason, and also to try to create a picture of what my life is like, and to express my thoughts about a lot of things.

I'll tell you a bit about myself. I'm fourteen years old. I love to write—stories, letters, music, in my diary, and now in this journal. This is really the first non-fiction I've written—besides letters and my diary, of course.

I have a four harness, six treadle floor loom here at home which I weave on. I've liked weaving for a long time and had used a lap loom, but what I really wanted to do was learn to weave real things on a floor loom. In the fall of 1986, I went to an open house at a restored historic home where there was a weaving shop that gave lessons, so I signed up and took lessons for about a year, which I loved. And now I have my own loom. I'm trying right now to come up with a pattern for a Scotch tartan—the plaid the Scotch weave their kilts out of. I want to make a kilt or something out of the MacGallum tartan for myself, and Grandpa (Mom's dad) wants me to make some placemats or centerpieces out of it for him and some of our relatives (we have some Scotch ancestors on Grandpa's side of the family who we think were MacGallums).

I love music, too—I've taught myself, with some help from Mom (when I asked for it), to play the piano and keyboard (synthesizer), and I can play the guitar a little. I love to sing—when I play the keyboard, or any other instruments, when someone else is playing, when I'm listening to tapes or the radio, and any other time when I feel like it—which is pretty much all of the time! Even when I'm not singing or playing an instrument or listening to music, I think there's always a song running through my head!

I also like dancing. I've taken ballet lessons over the years, but I never seemed to get anywhere—I guess I got tired of all the barre work and of never really dancing. So now I'm going to start taking Irish step dancing lessons—I'm going to learn to do, among other dances, the Irish jig, which you've probably heard of. Sara [Kim's sister] and I are going to take lessons from Mary Mayer . . . at the Mary Mayer School of Irish Dance; our first lesson is September 16th. I can't wait; I've seen the dancing, and it looks really neat—and I like Mary Mayer, so I think it's going to be fun.

Those are my main interests right now, although there are many other things I like to do.

Now I'm going to write down all the questions I'm asked most frequently about my education, and answer them as I wish I had when someone actually asked me! I don't know why it is that I can always think of a million better explanations after the conversation is over!

Q. What do you do?
A. That's the number one question I'm asked—unfortunately, because I hate answering it. It makes it seem as if the important thing is what I do, and not who I am, which is entirely backwards. I do lots of things, and I *could* do a lot of things that I don't. If I said I liked to draw, I don't think anyone could decide from hearing that whether they liked me or not. Now, I don't ask people what they do so I can decide whether they're weird or not; I ask them because I'm genuinely interested in hearing about the things that are important to them. I could be friends with someone who liked to do totally different things from me; just because they're not exactly like me doesn't mean they're weird or mentally ill. But I get the feeling that people ask me this question not because they're interested in hearing about what I like to do and in learning more about me, but because they want to know if I'm really getting an education "like everyone else." Well, I'm not! If I was, I might as well just go to school! Another reason why I dislike this question is that it makes me feel like I'm under investigation. From how strangely I get treated sometimes, when people ask

me what I do, I feel like I should say, "Oh, I eat, drink, breathe, sleep, just like other humans!"

Q. How do you make friends?

A. By going places and doing things, like anyone else—just by being alive. I think people ask this question because they have the false notion that school is the only place where you can meet people and make friends. (Well, if it is, you'd better make some lifelong friends there, or else your social life will be nonexistent after you graduate!) I think you're very limited if you think that—who you have for friends is left totally up to what kids happen to be in your grade or classes at the particular school you go to. And that's another thing about school—you don't get to have many friends older or younger than yourself, because you spend most of your day with people your age, give or take a year.

I have met most of my friends while pursuing my interests—for example, I count the teachers I had at weaving lessons as my good friends.

[In a later part of her journal, Kim commented, "I don't think it's how many friends you have that matters, but how good a friend each one is."]

Q. Do you have homework?

A. That sounds like I'm being asked if I have to do work around the house—like sweeping or dusting! But I guess what people really mean by "homework" is extra "schoolwork." Since I don't do *any* schoolwork, I definitely don't do "extra" schoolwork! But even if I did do "schoolwork" (working out of workbooks, textbooks, doing assignments, etc.), the question is still irrelevant, because I would be doing all my schoolwork at home, so it would all be "homework!" I wonder sometimes exactly what people expect me to answer—"No, Mom gives us assignments after our homeschool is out for the day, and we go to school to do them"?!

Q. How do you learn things your parents don't know about?

A. I don't think of Mom and Dad as being the ones responsible for educating me and living my life, so it has never occurred to me that I should only learn things they know about or that they deem important. I'm perfectly capable of and have always liked doing things and finding things out for myself; I don't need someone to tell me what I need to know or do and how to go about finding out and doing those things. When I decide I'd like someone to help me and ask them for help, I'm not asking them to step in and take over; I'm simply asking them to help me with a specific thing. Mom and Dad are just two of the many people I know who are willing to help me when I ask. If I don't already know anyone who can teach me something I want to know, then I find someone who can. I can either enlist other people's help in doing that, or I can do it myself—usually, I use a combination of both. A good example of this is when I became interested in Irish dancing and wanted to take lessons. I decided to ask Mom to help me get information on the different Irish dance schools in St. Louis, so I could decide which one I wanted to go to. Even though she couldn't teach me Irish dancing herself, Mom was able to help me find someone who could. The most helpful thing anyone can do for me is to listen and respond when I ask them to help me find ways to do the things I want to do.

Q. Is your mom a teacher?

A. No, although she had a minimal amount of teacher's training in college—and that training was part of what turned her off to schooling! (Her own school education also contributed to her decision to quit training to be a teacher, and to allow her children to educate themselves.) . . .

Q. How can your mom teach you if she's not a teacher?

A. Well, I'm not a "teacher" (in the sense that I don't teach at a school), and yet I'm perfectly capable of showing my four year old sister Katie how to make the letters of the alphabet. My brother Burt isn't a "teacher," but I've learned a lot of things from him by talking to him, about things he's read or heard about, and what he thinks about them. Besides, it would seem logical to assume that if a person understands something and/or can do it themselves, they ought to be able to explain it at least a little to someone else. (I've found that I learn a lot more about something I already know if I teach it to someone else—maybe because I notice things in teaching it to them that I hadn't before, or from a question they asked.)

And since Mom went to school, most people would assume that she learned there, and should therefore be able to pass what she learned onto us. How could anyone dispute that? By saying that you really need to be trained to teach, and not just know the subject you're teaching? Well, most of teachers' training (and actual work in school) is classroom management, and since Mom only has four (going on five) of us, she doesn't need to know how to manage a classroom of fifty. (I won't even get into the fact that many teachers in private schools aren't certified to teach.) Mom's qualified to be a parent, and she doesn't need to be anything else. Mom doesn't "teach" me anything—in the sense that she doesn't say, "OK, Kim, I'm going to teach you trigonometry now." I've learned many things from her, just by observing what she does, how she lives, and from talking with her. She always helps me if I ask her to—but she only gives me the specific help I ask for, no more, no less. If she can't give me the help I need or want, I'll find someone else who can—and often times I'll ask Mom to help me find someone who can.

Reading, writing, and arithmetic

From a longer essay about the way Kim has learned "the basics":

I have had very little formal "school" instruction; Mom has never planned out a curriculum for me, and has never instructed me in English, history, etc. I have learned things in my own way, my own time, at my own pace, while pursuing interests of my own choosing.

I learned to write when I was between the ages of three and four; I wanted to be able to write, so I asked people (Mom and Dad and other relatives and friends) how to make the letters of the alphabet. As soon as I could form the letters, I began writing letters to people; I would decide what I wanted to say, and then ask people how to spell the words. In this way, I learned correct spelling and grammar, and gained a knowledge of letters and words that later made it possible for me to learn to read. When I was about ten I began keeping a diary, which I'm still writing in now, and at the same time I also began writing stories.

I learned to read pretty much the same way I learned to write, a few years later. I remember being read to a lot, which I really enjoyed, and wanting to be able to read. I learned to read from being read to, being answered when I asked, "What's that say?" (which was quite frequently), and writing, which helped me to recognize words. Most of all, I learned to read (and write—and do everything I know how to do) because I wanted to be able to. I never used any workbooks, flashcards, etc., when I was learning to read or write.

I learned math by using it—math is logical; you really don't need to have someone explain it all to you, because you learn it naturally while trying to count and figure things out. I learned to add, subtract, multiply and divide simply because I needed to do those things. I may not have always seen the fastest way to figure something out right away, but I knew what I was trying to find out, and what I needed to do in order to get the answer . . .

Unfortunately, when I was around thirteen I took the CAT (my first test) and discovered I was below grade level in math—mainly because I didn't know the different processes by which they expected you to come up with the answers (although I was perfectly capable of finding them my own way). And being timed made me nervous, besides the fact that finding answers as quickly as possible had not been the focus of the math I had used before. Accuracy was the most important thing; speed comes from using math many times, and I really didn't need to do a whole lot of figuring at that time in my life. If I had had some real reason for being able to do math that fast, I know I would have been able to. But being able to figure quickly just so I could pass a test wasn't a good reason for learning something to me.

And yet, even after I'd finished the test, I felt nervous about not being at my grade level in math; I got it into my head that I needed to study math to "catch up"— merely for the reason of being at a certain place that some person who didn't know me at all had decided that I should be at simply because I was a certain age. So I got our workbooks and textbooks, and asked Mom to work with me on math, which she did.

That turned out to be a disaster—I ended up with a math block, because I'd worked myself into such a state over the test and trying to catch up that there was no way I could learn anything. I decided that math was stupid, because that was better than deciding that *I* was stupid because I couldn't understand it.

Also, I was unconsciously rebelling against doing something that had no real meaning or importance to me in my life. So I was making it impossible to learn math, because underneath, I really didn't want to learn it; I was just doing it because I felt I should. Finally I wore myself out with it so that I had a block toward it and was saying I hated it.

It's taken me nearly three years to get to the place where I can think about math again without panicking or feeling inferior—and I'm still not completely over the block. I'm trying now to regain the practical, applicable understanding of math that I once had.

Facing the future with integrity
In this later piece, Kim reflects on issues that have confronted her in her late teens.

About two years ago I began to feel dissatisfied with my life the way it was. I was bored and restless; I wanted to be doing more things, but I didn't know what. I had a sense of standing on the threshold of a whole new world, of coming to a turning point in my life. I started asking myself a lot of questions about what purpose my life had, where I belonged, what I wanted to do; struggling to find myself.

In the midst of this, people began to question me more frequently about what plans I had for my life, and the tone with which they asked was noticeably more serious and intense than it had been a few years before. After all, I was high school age, and, "it was high time I knew what I was going to do with my life," they seemed to be saying. Needless to say, I started to feel pretty stupid for not knowing what I wanted to do with my life. I no longer felt comfortable saying, "I don't know," when people asked me if I was going to college, because, inevitably, they would be shocked, and start impressing upon me how impossible it is to get a "good job" (whatever *that* is) without a college degree, that one would never be able to live happily and be accepted by society if one did not attend college and pursue a career for the rest of one's natural life. So I couldn't *seriously* be considering anything but the "traditional" route of college and a career; that would be dangerous and immature. So I was told.

That made me angry—if I felt like ruining my life, it was no one's business but my own! And being expected to do something, anything, really irritated me—so much that at times I felt like going out and doing the exact opposite of what people said I was "supposed" to do.

I also resented having college, careers, decisions, etc., shoved in my face, because dealing with them distracted me from my search for a meaningful life. It was very frustrating to feel that I needed to be resolving the conflict and turmoil in my life, but not be able to because I had to deal with the confusions other people injected.

By continually pushing and pressuring me to go to college and do this and do that, people implied a complete lack of respect for and trust in me. I felt that they were saying, in effect, that I was incapable of taking care of myself, and would never "turn out all right" if they didn't hold my hand and steer me in the "right" direction. All in all, I was infuriated over the whole matter.

But at the same time, I was also scared. Suppose what they said was true? What if it really was impossible to get a job and support myself without a college degree? Hundreds—no, thousands—of nagging doubts, worries, and "what-ifs" crowded into my mind, and I began to feel that I should seriously consider attending college. I sent for information on several colleges and carefully read through it, feeling all the while that I was trying to wear a shoe that didn't fit. I spent a lot of time trying to decide where I wanted to go to college, what I wanted to major in, and what single thing I wanted to spend the rest of my life earning a living at. I bounced back and forth for a while—one minute I was definitely going to college, and the next wild horses couldn't drag me there.

I finally decided it was time to face all the pressures and fears, and find out if they were truly valid. I started to question the beliefs that had been presented to me as truths and facts. Like the idea that people should pick one thing to do (as a career) and then spend the rest of their lives doing it. How can you know and decide today what you'll be interested in doing ten or five or even two years down the road? Furthermore, should you be expected to know? And why isn't it considered normal to grow and change your priorities—what's wrong with moving onto something else when you've outgrown where you are right now?

I began to see that so much of this pressure to go to college, get a "good job," be successful, and so on, was based mainly on fear. "Do this, or this will happen to you." "Go to college, or you'll never be able to get a 'good job' and support yourself." And so forth. No one expected me to go to college because I thought I'd find a life worth living there, or that it'd be a place where I would mature as a person. They expected me to go because I'd end up a social reject and starve to death on the street if I didn't.

Something inside of me snapped at this realization. "That's it," I said to myself. "I'm not going to run my life on fear; what point is there in a life in which you do things because you're afraid of what will happen to you if you don't? How can you ever be happy if you live on fear—there will always be something else you have to do to keep something terrible from happening to you. I'd rather starve to death and be rejected than be afraid forever and never have a moment's peace!"

With that pressure off my shoulders, I was determined to get to the bottom of all the myths and fears. As I looked closer, I discovered a fear that was greater than all the others put together—the fear of not "measuring up" to society's standards, and therefore being unacceptable and rejected. You must go to college, because that's what every respectable person intent on "making something" of themselves is doing so they can get a "good job—one they can make a lot of money at, and that has prestige.

It became clear to me that schools exist for the purpose of instilling the "moral" that acceptance is the most important thing in life. I also realized that this "moral" is instilled so people can be controlled—if people believe that happiness is being accepted, they'll do whatever they're told they "have" to in order to be accepted, because they want to be happy.

After this revelation, I was able to see all the pressures and worries for what they really were—basically a lot of false fears and insecurities. It was sort of like turning on the light and finding that what had looked to be a terrible monster was just a shadow.

Now I had the time and space to focus on resolving the personal conflict and dissatisfaction with my life that I was feeling. I began to look closely at my life, and question many things about it. I asked myself, why had I always followed my interests day by day, letting them lead me? Why had I never planned my life out? Once I'd become interested in writing, why hadn't I immediately begun looking for places to have my writing published, or for people to read and criticize it? Why hadn't I said, "I'll write short stories for six months, then experiment with the essay format for two months, then delve into poetry for three months, try my hand at journalism for a month, revise my short stories and work on publishing them for the next six months after that," etc.? Why had I been content to live each day open to any new ideas for articles, or stories, or something entirely different to write; unafraid of the uncertainty that tomorrow held—actually, welcoming that very uncertainty as a possible exciting opportunity? And was there anything wrong with living that way? Did I need to abandon it, after it had served and suited me perfectly for so many years, because I felt the need for a change in my life?

After a lot of searching and questioning, I've come to the conclusion that I don't have to find one thing to do now and for the rest of my life. The whole world has opened up to me in a new sense since I've come to this revelation, and many important opportunities are becoming available to me now.

For example, last year I read an article about a children's choir here in St. Louis that sounded neat to me because I've always loved singing. Although I'd never had voice lessons, or been in a choir before, I decided to audition for the choir. I was accepted, and now, six months later, I've moved up into the highest levels of the choir, have ten two-hour rehearsals per month, and am planning to go on the choir tour to Atlanta this summer. Choir has become a very big part of my life.

As a result of being in the choir, another opportunity became available to me just recently. About a month ago I became interested in taking voice lessons, so I asked one of my choir directors if he knew any voice teachers he'd recommend. He told me that he wanted to start giving voice lessons, and asked if I'd like to take lessons from him. Because he's a really terrific person, and we get along very well, I told him I'd rather take lessons from him than anyone else. So I've been taking voice lessons from him for the past month, and I love it! And who knows what other opportunities will become available because I'm taking voice lessons—maybe chances to perform solo, etc.

Along with choir and voice lessons, writing is also very important to me. I've always loved to write—letters, stories, in my private diary, a journal of my education, and most recently, articles about homeschooling and related subjects. While I was trying to deal with the pressures and fears surrounding college, careers, etc., I spent a lot of time writing, in order to straighten my thoughts out. When I write, things that have been blurry become clear to me, and I see more and more of the picture, instead of just a tangled, confusing mess. Even when I'm not trying to describe and analyze beliefs, fears, philosophies, etc., it helps to write what I feel *without* trying to figure out why I feel the way I do. It's like I have to get it all off my chest first, and then I can start trying to work things out.

I'm almost always working on some article—whether it's one I've been asked to write, or one I've thought of myself. Even when I'm not working on anything specific (which is rare), I'm still writing; in my diary, and letters to people. I like to write a lot about learning, homeschooling, educational philosophies, and that kind of thing, because those issues are important to me. Right now I'm in the revising stages of an article about how I learned to read, write, etc., which I wrote not too long ago. I'm planning to submit it to a magazine, or several, once I'm finished with it. And I've got lots of ideas in the back of my mind for more articles I want to write.

My biggest project at this time is revising the journal of my education that I kept from September 1988 to 1989, and I'm hoping to have it published. The journal is full of descriptions and accounts of everything I did and read, people I met, etc., during that year. I poured out my thoughts, feelings and ideas about so many things into the journal as well; trying to understand myself and the rest of the world, trying to find out where I stood, and why. It's essentially my self portrait. I have so much material that revising it is a long, hard process. But it's worth all the time and work.

During the past four years or so I've established a writing apprenticeship with Susannah Sheffer, editor of *Growing Without Schooling*. Susannah always has helpful suggestions and comments on whatever I send her—for example, she'll say, "This part isn't very clear; is this what you mean?" "What you said here makes me curious to know more about such and such; maybe you'd want to expand on it," or, "You could change this sentence around like this to make it clearer," etc. Those kinds of suggestions really help me when I'm revising, because a lot of times I know that I've left something out somewhere, or that a paragraph needs to be rewritten, but I can't put my finger on exactly what's wrong, or how to fix it. I think that being able to have Susannah read and critique my writing is making me a better critic of my own work, because she makes me more aware of how my writing is going to sound to someone else.

Working on writing with Susannah has led to several trips to Boston to visit her, and the chance to volunteer in the Holt Associates office, to meet a lot of neat people, including one of my closest friends. Not to mention that Susannah has become one of my best friends as well.

I don't have all the answers to my questions yet, but as I continue to try to resolve and find the answers, things are falling into place and becoming clear to me. I've realized that it's okay to not have all the answers. I know now that all through my life I'll be growing, and that going through these periods of confusion and frustration is just part of the lifelong process of growing up. Instead of dreading these processes, I should welcome them, because each time I go through another one of them it means I'm moving onto the next stage of my life

After the first edition of The Teenage Liberation Handbook *was published, Kim kept at her journal, and during the next few years she chronicled her further adventures. One of the things she did was to set up an internship, with the help and encouragement of her friend and mentor Susannah Sheffer, at a living history farm in New Hampshire called Strawbery Banke. She spent over a year there— demonstrating spinning, working on event planning with the director, and undertaking other challenges. You can read a lot of her Strawbery Banke journal in GWS #99. Here is a bit, which conveys some of the things interns do at living history farms and other sites:*

August 6, 1992

I met Kathleen in her office and she took me down to the visitor center so I could watch the brief orientation video and then take a short guided tour of the museum. Afterwards we went to the museum's Nutter House and Thomas Bailey Aldrich memorial; I'll be working in the latter as an interpreter from 1:00 to 3:00 every Tuesday and Thursday . . .

Kathleen and I made up a tentative schedule for me to follow until my spinning wheel gets here. Two days a week I'll be doing research for two projects of Kathleen's. The first one is to find out what kinds of spinning were done here at Strawbery Banke, what kinds of fibers were used (wool, flax, etc.), where they got them from (were the sheep here?), what kinds of materials were made from the yarn. She wants me to write a paper about what I find out, if I collect enough to write about.

The second project came up because Kathleen wanted me to help her plan this year's Fall and Halloween festivals. She asked me if I would do some research and find out what was going on at Strawbery Banke during the Salem witch trials, if there were any reports of witches or witchcraft here, and read up on witchcraft, superstitions, the origin of Halloween, and so on.

I'm also doing some reading on Thomas Bailey Aldrich so I'll know enough about him to answer questions visitors have when I interpret at the TBA memorial. TBA was an author, famous at the time he lived, I guess. Aldrich's book is sitting on my desk, along with a stack of about ten other books, all on spinning and weaving, which I plan to read.

After she'd been on her own for a while (and moved on into more adventures, like becoming a massage therapist and getting married), Kim wrote, "One thing I've always believed, and that being on my own has reinforced, is that it's impossible for me to think in terms of forever. I have to look at what I want to do now, and find a way to do that; when I'm ready to move on, I'll know." ❖

appendix A

the unschooler's bookshelf

I PUT ONLY a few books and other items in this resource list, with excerpts, so you'd notice each of them. There are now many good books on unschooling; you can find others on your own at the library. The resources here are the cream of the crop *and* the most relevant choices for teenagers. They deal with unschooling or learning in a general sense. Numerous resources for particular subjects are, of course, recommended throughout this book. Resources and organizations to help you contact other unschoolers are listed in Appendix D.

Books by John Holt

John Holt, *Escape From Childhood.* This book goes beyond the issue of school, covering many other ways that "minors" are prevented from living fully. It argues that children of all ages should have access to the same rights as adults: to work, vote, own property, travel, choose a guardian, control their own learning, etc.

> For a long time it never occurred to me to question this institution [of childhood]. Only in recent years did I begin to wonder whether there might be other or better ways for young people to live. By now I have come to feel that the fact of being a "child," of being wholly subservient and dependent, of being seen by older people as a mixture of expensive nuisance, slave, and super-pet, does most young people more harm than good. I propose instead that the rights, privileges, duties, responsibilities of adult citizens be made *available* to any young person, of whatever age, who wants to make use of them.

John Holt, *Freedom and Beyond.* In this book, Holt started questioning whether we need schools. He investigates the nature of freedom, choice, authority, discipline, and the relationship between schools and poverty.

> Not understanding freedom, we do not understand authority. We think in terms of organization charts, pecking orders, stars on the collar and stripes on the sleeve. If someone is above us on the chart, then . . . he has a right to tell us to do what he wants, and we have a duty to do whatever he tells us, however absurd, destructive, or cruel. Naturally enough, some people, seeing around them the dreadful works of this kind of authority, reject it altogether. But with it they too often reject, naturally but unwisely, all notions of competence, inspiration, leadership. They cannot imagine that of their own free will they might ask someone else what he thought, or agree to do what he asked, because he clearly know or perhaps cared much more about what he was doing than they did. The only alternative they seem to see to coercive authority is none at all. I have therefore tried to explore a little further the nature of freedom, so that we may better understand how people of varying ages and skills may live together and be useful to each other without some of them always pushing the others around.

John Holt, *Instead of Education: Ways to Help People Do Things Better*. This book gives many ideas for ways to improve and change communities so people have more opportunities to learn outside of school. It also develops the idea that learning and doing are the same thing, and explains the difference between healthy teaching and school situations and unhealthy situations.

> This is a book in favor of *doing*—self-directed, purposeful, meaningful life and work— and *against* "education"—learning cut off from active life and done under pressure of bribe or threat, greed and fear.

John Holt, *Teach Your Own*. This is the first and still the best overall introduction for families who want to get out of school. Despite the title, Holt does not advocate that parents teach in the usual sense; rather, it encourages them to support their kids' learning, largely by staying out of their way. Some of the information won't apply to you, as it concentrates mostly on younger children and talks a lot about the way people learn basic math, reading, and writing skills. However, it also has solid thought and information on good work situations for unschoolers, on the philosophy of unschooling, and other topics. This is an especially good book to have your parents read; a chapter called "Common Objections to Home Schooling" will help them clarify their own thoughts.

> Even in supposedly "free" or "alternative" schools, too many people still do what conventional schools have always done. They take children out of and away from the great richness and variety of the world, and in its place give them school subjects, the curriculum. They may jazz it up with chicken bones, Cuisenaire rods, and all sorts of other goodies. But the fact remains that instead of letting children have contact with more and more people, places, tools, and experiences, the schools are busily cutting the work up into little bits and giving it to the children according to some expert's theory about what they need or can stand.
>
> What children need is not new and better curricula but *access* to more and more of the real world; plenty of time and space to think over their experiences, and to use fantasy and play to make meaning out of them; and advice, road maps, guidebooks, to make it easier for them to get where they want to go (not where we think they ought to go), and to find out what they want to find out. Finding ways to do all this is not easy. The modern world is dangerous, confusing, not meant for children, not generally kind or welcoming to them. We have much to learn about how to make the world more accessible to them, and how to give them more freedom and competence in exploring it. But this is a very different thing from designing nice little curricula.

Books by or about unschooled teenagers

(Also see autobiographies or biographies of any of the people mentioned in Chapter 40.)

Tania Aebi, *Maiden Voyage*. When Tania was eighteen and living in New York City, her father worried that her life was going nowhere. Instead of pushing her into college, he gave her a sailboat, with the stipulation that she circumnavigate the globe—alone. She did so, becoming the first American woman to sail the world solo. Her resulting book is many wonderful things: a dramatic story of adventure, a romance, and an inspiring narrative of intense spiritual and emotional growth.

> There have always been people who called my father crazy. We never thought so. Why walk when you can run? he'd say. Why be inside when you could be out? Why stay home balancing your checkbook when you could be off riding a camel in Timbuktu, or climbing

Mont Blanc, or driving a Land Rover across Africa? His dreams for himself and for us were all we wanted to hear when we were growing up. The world through his eyes was full of excitement and promise, of taking risks and landing on your feet, always with another great story to tell.

David and Micki Colfax, *Homeschooling for Excellence.* After three homeschooled Colfax boys went to Harvard, their parents wrote this book and explained. It tells some of the books and other resources they used, points out that the boys' main "curricula" were their activities around their homestead, and answers the usual questions about socialization, etc.

Later that year Grant interviewed at nearly a dozen colleges and applied to two. We submitted a letter to each, describing his course work and evaluating his strengths and weaknesses as objectively as possible. In lieu of teacher and counselor recommendations, Grant provided letters from a half dozen people who could variously attest to his work in the community health center, his character and intellectual potential. He wrote a long essay that described his years on the ranch, his homeschooling experiences, and his hopes for the future. He was admitted to Yale and Harvard and entered the latter that fall.

Robin Lee Graham, *Dove.* In 1965, sixteen-year-old Robin quit school and sailed a 24-foot sloop around the world in an extraordinary, romantic five-year-long adventure. Here, at eighteen, he has just met his future wife Patti:

We were children as we sailed the islands of the Yasawa group, kids reveling in sun and surf, knowing a glorious sense of freedom and timelessness. When the sun had risen high enough to warm our bodies and light the caverns and ledges in the coral reefs, we dived for shells and poured our treasure into *Dove's* cockpit. We found violet conchs, zigzag and spotted cowries, grinning tuns (*Malea ringens*), quaint delphinia snails, pagoda periwinkles, murex, tiny moon snails, fashioned with a jeweler's skill, delicate striped bonnets, tritons, augers and olives. The cowries we loved best—some as large as a fist, skins silken smooth, dappled in warm browns. We swam together, Patti graceful as a dolphin.

Kendall Hailey, *The Day I Became an Autodidact.* Fed up with formal education, Kendall arranged to graduate early from her ritzy prep school, and at age sixteen took complete control of her own education. While her classmates graduated on schedule and went to college, Kendall wrote (a play, a novel, a mystery), read (Dostoevsky, Dickens, James), and acted (in her own play, *The Bar off Melrose*). In this book, she also describes falling in love, relating to her family, and feeling frustrated with the lives of her college-bound friends. Her book is an especially great companion for anyone with a literary bent. Kendall is warm, honest, funny, and insightful. In this passage, she hasn't yet graduated from high school:

A little time left for education before school starts, and I just read the sentence "I am writing for myself and strangers" from *The Making of Americans* by Gertrude Stein.

That is the way I have always felt, but I never knew how to say it. Little did I know Gertrude Stein had said it for me.

I can't wait to say to any teacher who makes a snide remark about one of my papers, "Well, I only wrote it for myself and strangers."

However, I have still not got the courage to write on a quiz, as Gertrude Stein once did, "I do not feel like taking a quiz today."

I wonder if Miss Stein would have had the courage had she not had a great teacher. He wrote on her empty quiz paper, "I know just how you feel—A+."

Grace Llewellyn, editor, *Freedom Challenge: African American*

Homeschooolers. Fifteen essays by parents, teenagers, and younger children. Sunshine apprentices at an herb nursery and learns about architecture, Spanish, and astronomy from family friends. Khahil and Latif collect bugs and read physics books. Tunu wins piano competitions and joins with other black homeschoolers to learn robotics from an engineer. At six, Maya taught herself to read; at seven, she decided to learn to row a boat... The writers discuss self-directed learning, socialization, how single parent families homeschool, and they examine issues particular to African American homeschoolers.

> Un-/homeschooling certainly is not for everyone. But if you think that school is long and boring, I'd consider it. Talk about it with your parents, because (although it may not seem like it) they generally know what's best. At first people (even your friends) may be a little skeptical of the idea. But hold on, they'll get used to it. (And if they don't, who needs 'em anyway?) Some people might call you a dropout. In this case just remember, there is a distinction. Dropping out means that you left school, got a bum job, and aren't doing anything educationally worthwhile. Un-/homeschooling means you left school, got a bum job, but are still pursuing learning, instead of just giving up.
>
> Every time I look at the lives of schooled kids I see what I don't want to become. I don't want to be "normal." I want to be me. Some kids have been in school all their lives. Some kids have been homeschooled all their lives. I've done both. I've even gone to school part-time while still unschooling. I wouldn't call my experience incredible or unique, it's just the way I live. It's normal to me. –Fahiym Basiyr Acuay, fourteen

Grace Llewellyn, editor, *Real Lives: eleven teenagers who don't go to school*. These writers tell, in-depth, what it's like to be responsible for their own educations. Their adventures include: publishing a newsletter on peace issues, volunteering at a marine science center, writing to over fifty pen-pals worldwide, biking alone through Colombia and Ecuador, performing with a violin quintet, working at a shelter for homeless people, raising honeybees, compiling portfolios of writing and artwork to prepare for a career in video game design, talking with people all over the world on ham radio, building houses with Habitat for Humanity, working through the mail with a writing mentor, playing banjo in bluegrass jam sessions, answering the phone at a crisis line, and helping midwives at births. They also discuss issues such as socialization and finding work, and answer the question, "Do you have to be a genius to unschool?" From an essay by Ayanna Williams:

> I have a pen-pal in South Africa in his forties who teaches people about my age. He writes long interesting letters and illustrates them. I have another pen-pal who is a native of Ghana, went to school for a year in Cuba, and now works in Libya. In Nigeria I have many pen-pals, one of whom is an eighteen-year-old Igbo:
>
> *The Christmas celebration was very dull this year in Enugu state. The reason was that many people moved out of the state since the creation of new states recently. During Christmas day everywhere was so dull that it looked like a ghost town. The masquerades that usually chase people around were nowhere to be seen. I went out that afternoon with my brother in our car. We drove to some of the places that are usually congested with people and masquerades, but no one was seen. Only a few people loitering around. Back home we celebrated happily with our family. After prayers, we dined on rice cooked with coconut juice, stew with chicken, and goat meat and some drinks.*

Nancy Wallace, *Child's Work: Taking Children's Choices Seriously*. Nancy watched with sensitivity, insight, and trust while her homeschooled kids grew up. Both her son and daughter focused their lives around music, so this book will be especially (but not only) interesting to musicians.

Vita and Ishmael now spend most of each working day playing and composing music. Aside from the sheer glory of doing my own work to the melodic strains of Chopin ballades, Beethoven sonatas, and Bach preludes and fugues, living with Vita and Ishmael's music and being as involved as I am in their musical work has meant that of everything they do, it is the way they approach music that I understand and know most intimately. Often, I find myself using this understanding as a base or guidepost for looking at how they work on everything else in life. Watching the way Vita explores a new piece on the violin or piano, for example, teaches me about how she explores spelling or numerical relationships or art.

Unschooling magazines

Growing Without Schooling magazine, bimonthly, currently $25/year from Growing Without Schooling, 2269 Massachusetts Avenue, Cambridge, MA 02140, 617-864-3100. This is the most ultimate, important resource for unschoolers, written mainly by teenagers, children, and adults who are busy doing what the title says. I don't like to tell people they *need* anything in particular in order to unschool, but I *do* think you need a subscription to the superb *GWS*. Also consider getting the whole set of available back issues, or selected back issues related to your concerns and interests. (The *GWS* staff will choose back issues for you; you specify the topics.)

Home Education Magazine, bimonthly, currently $24/year from Home Education Magazine, P.O. Box 1083, Tonasket, WA 98855, (509) 486-1351. *HEM* offers long articles and superb regular columns by people like Cafi Cohen, who wrote *And What About College?* and the delightful and insightful Earl Stevens, an unschooling father. Legal information, lots of stuff about learning resources for younger kids, news and ideas on teenagers too.

Drop Out, c/o The Hindenburg, 1114 21st Street, Sacramento, CA 95814, (916) 441-5526, dropout@emrl.com. Send $1 for the current issue or $5 for a stack of twenty. Write or phone for subscription information. This is a newspaper-format zine with an anarchist edge, largely inspired by John Holt and unschooling philosophy, but oriented towards self-identified "drop outs" rather than "unschoolers." (The language and straightforwardness may offend some people.) Wonderful articles by dropouts, many of whom are now adults. Letters and submissions are always welcome, too. (And, for people living in or traveling through Sacramento, there's a *drop out* resource center too.)

Zines: there are several delightful zines produced by teenaged unschoolers, but they often last just a few years, until the publishers want to do something else with their energy. They are mentioned and advertised in *GWS* from time to time, so you can find out about them there.

College admissions and credentialism

John Bear and Mariah Bear, *Bear's Guide To Earning College Degrees Nontraditionally*. This is the best strategy book for getting a degree, if you need one, without sacrificing some of the best years of your life and your parents' life savings. Discusses credit for life experience, correspondence and on-line coursework, unusual programs (earn while you hike), and scams to avoid. Well written, overtly opinionated. In addition to the discussion sections, over 1,600 schools are listed and described briefly.

Whether pursuing a degree for the learning, the diploma, or both, the alternative student seems far more likely:

- to be motivated to complete his or her program;
- to select courses and programs that are appropriate and relevant to his or her needs;
- to avoid cluttering up campuses and dormitories (which, in the words of former Columbia University president William McGill, are in danger of becoming "storage houses for bored young people");
- to save years over the time of traditional programs (or, alternatively, to pursue educational objectives without giving up job or family), and, perhaps most importantly for most people, to save a tremendous amount of time and money, compared with the demands and costs of a traditional degree program.

Cafi Cohen, *And What About College? How homeschooling leads to admissions to the best colleges and universities.* This is a decent *overall* guide to homeschooling as a teenager, but it focuses on preparing for and then getting into college. Cafi's son went on to the U.S. Air Force Academy (after also being accepted at many other institutions, and offered numerous scholarships). Her daughter entered a selective liberal arts college with a substantial scholarship. Cafi tells what their homeschooling was like (*not* "school-at-home"), how they kept records, and how they conveyed it all to college admissions people. And she offers well-researched information for other college-bound homeschoolers in a variety of situations. The appendices include copies of the Cohens' homemade transcripts, cover letters, application essays, and course descriptions.

> University of Denver has also good experience with homeschoolers. Our son, Jeff, applied to one of their high school summer programs called "The Making Of An Engineer." According to the admissions officer, they had 180 applicants for 60 spaces. The admissions officer told me he filled the first 30 slots with students who had sky-high standardized test scores. Jeff did not fit into this category. That left 150 applicants for the remaining 30 slots. The admissions officer told us that Jeff got one of those 30 places *because* he was a homeschooler. Their experience told them that—all other things being equal—homeschooled students would do a better job.

Other very important resources for life and learning

Thomas Armstrong, *Seven Kinds of Smart: Identifying and Developing Your Many Intelligences.* Based on the Harvard research which "proves" the radical notion that there is more to intelligence than linguistic and mathematical aptitude. Armstrong points out the importance of each intelligence—"word smart," "picture smart," "music smart," etc., and gives fascinating examples. (Heart-surgeons operate on body-smart, William Shakespeare and Jane Addams were people-smart.) He also offers self-tests to discover your own hidden strengths, and numerous strategies—some quick, some intensive—for developing each intelligence in your own life. I really love this book—it's packed with useful ideas, and easy and inspiring to read.

> Spatial thinkers should also consider working with their ideas in three dimensions. James Watson and Francis Crick stunned the world and won a Nobel Prize in 1962 when they discovered the double-helix structure of the DNA molecule by using a large three-dimensional model as a thinking tool. Designers at General Motors and NASA regularly create elaborate cardboard mock-ups of cars and space modules that save them millions of dollars in development costs. You can create your own visual thinking lab at home with inexpensive materials such as Styrofoam or Foamcore (a laminated paper-and-Styrofoam sandwich) for mock-ups and miniature models; soda straws and paper clips or

commercially made sticks and connectors for geometrical shapes; and a box of miscellaneous odds and ends (string, tape, blocks, toothpicks, clay, wire, wood scraps, rubber bands, tinfoil, paper scraps, and so forth). In addition, consider the power of modern technology in aiding visual thought. The computer industry has opened up a wide range of options for visual thinkers through CAD (Computer Aided Design) programs, "paint and draw" software, interactive video, and other emerging technologies.

Clifton Fadiman, *The New Lifetime Reading Plan.* This book introduces you to 130 of the best writings that have come out of Western civilization—not just novels and poetry but also history, politics, philosophy, psychology, biography, and autobiography.

The *Iliad* is probably the most magnificent story ever told about man's prime idiocy: warfare. The human center is Achilles. The main line of the narrative traces his anger, his sulkies, his savagery, and the final assertion of his better nature. He is the first hero in Western literature; and ever since, when we talk of heroic qualities, Achilles is somewhere in the back of our minds, even though we may think we have never heard of him.

Richard Fobes, *The Creative Problem Solver's Toolbox: A Complete Course in the Art of Creating Solutions to Problems of Any Kind.* Unlike most books on thinking skills, this one deals with solving real-life problems, rather than made-up brain teasers. Strategies you can use on all kinds of problems—the hunger of homeless people in your city, a friend's offensive jokes, the challenge of finding a great summer job.

A very useful way to create new ideas is to create new combinations of existing ideas. A simple form of combining ideas consists of combining existing objects to create a useful new object. For example, the clock radio was invented by combining a radio with an alarm clock. Notice that the resulting combination offers an advantage—namely the clock can turn on the radio—that isn't available if a radio and alarm clock are simply placed side-by-side.

John Taylor Gatto, *Dumbing Us Down.* If your parents, relatives, or friends have any doubts as to what school does to minds and souls, let Gatto wake them up! Gatto taught for 26 years, winning titles like New York State Teacher of the Year. Powerful and uncompromising, this book lays down the truth.

It is absurd and anti-life to be part of a system that compels you to listen to a stranger reading poetry when you want to learn to construct buildings, or to sit with a stranger discussing the construction of buildings when you want to read poetry.

Ronald Gross, *The Independent Scholar's Handbook.* Proof that unschooling doesn't have to stop when academically inclined people reach college and grad school level. This excellent, detailed book will help you become an expert in any subject without giving up control to a university or other institution. Charles Darwin, Albert Einstein, and Betty Friedan are among the many independent scholars who have used the approach Gross describes.

Major intellectual journeys quite often begin with browsing. As a teenager, Joel Cohen was browsing at his local bookstore . . . leafing through the pages of *Elements of Physical Biology* by Alfred J. Lotka. "Here's a guy who thinks the way I do," he recalls exclaiming to himself. "Mathematics might be a useful way to make some sense of life." Cohen had been amazed to learn that the degree to which an earthworm turns its head in the direction of light is directly proportional to the logarithm of the intensity of the light. "I had just learned about logarithms in school. This simple organism was behaving in a mathematically lawful way, and it knew logarithms without school! It seemed to me I had better learn some math." Another book, Abraham Moles's *Information Theory and Esthetic Perception*, so captivated the youngster that he wrote the author in France, asking permission to translate the book into English and enclosing his version of the first chapter as a sample. Moles granted the request and Cohen then wrote to the University of Illinois Press, which subsequently published the translation Neither author nor publisher knew that their translator was sixteen years old. Twenty-five years later, Cohen conducted his research in "biology by the numbers" as head of the laboratory of populations at The Rockefeller University.

Herbert Kohl, *From Archetype to Zeitgeist: Powerful Ideas for Powerful Thinking*. A wonderful guide to the language of ideas. Thorough definitions of several hundred intriguing and important terms (like *postmodernism, paradigm, synergy, semiotics, pluralism, colonialism, gaia hypothesis, stream of consciousness,* and *anarchy*). Organized by topic: arts, literature, religion, psychology, economics, political science. Definitions (with historical anecdotes) range from a couple paragraphs to a couple pages.

> Pedant: 'ped-nt, n [from Greek *paidagogos*, from *pais*, boy + agogos, leader]. The word pedant is derived from the Latin *pedagogus*, which means teacher. This meaning has been extended to refer to a teacher who adheres to strict and formal rules in teaching, and is dry and uninteresting. More generally a pedant is a person who is unduly concerned with book learning and formal rules and regulations without an understanding or experience of practical affairs. A pedantic argument is one that is full of quotes and references to books and authors but lacking in intelligence or wisdom.

Howard Rheingold, editor, *The Millennium Whole Earth Catalog*. This giant book opens up more options than you ever knew existed, by describing and quoting from the best books (and other resources) in every imaginable category, from Exploring Space to Storytelling. It is also a graphic masterpiece, full of fascinating drawings and photographs charmingly splayed across the pages. Also see the earlier (still very useful) versions: *The Essential Whole Earth Catalog, The Whole Earth Catalog, The Last Whole Earth Catalog, The Next Whole Earth Catalog*. Look for all in libraries and used book stores.

Barbara Sher, *Wishcraft: How to Get What You Really Want*. The best book I know of to help you first set delicious goals you really care about, and then make those dreams come true. Helpful, too, for people who feel unmotivated and not thoroughly excited about anything. And excellent for adults who wish they'd unschooled—it's not too late! Here, Sher introduces a concept she calls the "Buddy System":

> The Buddy System is a way of creating your "ideal family" in miniature. It's the most compact and efficient way I know to give yourself the kind of support system I've been describing throughout this book. Its principle is simple: you and a friend make it your shared goal to meet both your individual goals. It works because it's about a thousand times easier to have faith, courage, and good ideas for someone else than it is for yourself—and easier for someone else to have them for you. So you team up and trade those positive resources: your buddy provides them for you and you provide them for her or him.
>
> How do you pick a buddy? She or he can be a close friend or roommate, but doesn't have to be. A new acquaintance or a neighbor can be just as good. This is an action-oriented arrangement first and an intimate friendship only if you want it to be. Your buddy will be giving you emotional and moral support, yes, but for a purpose: to keep you in motion. In fact, if you are close friends, you're going to have to keep the long, rambling heart-to-heart talks out of the business part of your relationship and save them for after hours. ⊛

appendix B

afterword to the second edition

WHEN I FINISHED the first edition of this book and cast it to the wind in 1991, I had no idea what to expect. I didn't know if the first thousand copies would sell or just dent my bedroom floor. I wasn't confident that even one person would read my wild words and be convinced to leave school and get a bigger life, but I felt that if even that one person did so, my efforts would be worthwhile.

Seven years and 20,000 copies later, *The Teenage Liberation Handbook* is still underground, obscure, nowhere near the bottom rungs of anybody's bestseller list. Yet, through letters, phone calls, articles and letters in homeschooling newsletters, e-mail, reliable gossip, and face-to-face meetings, I've heard from and about *hundreds* of teenagers who have read this book and unschooled themselves (so I figure there may be many more I haven't heard about) ....and hundreds more who were already homeschooling but have started living more proactively. Teachers, parents, college students, and other adults also write to me. They tell me how they are unschooling themselves, recovering trust in their own brains and desires, and how they are trying to respect and support the young people they teach, or their own children.

So, I live in a state of continual ecstatic shock. Hardly a day goes by that I don't feel grateful and stunned that I happened to be at the right place and the right time, that *I* was the person who got to rephrase the wisdom of the unschooling movement for teenagers. To be sure, it took a lot of work to write this book (and again, to revise it) and I am pleased with myself for doing that work as well as I could, but I'm also immensely thankful that my life offered the opportunity to do so. Most of this book is communal wisdom; I just absorbed it, digested it, and re-directed it—like a passive solar wall.

Where the unschooling movement has gone since the first edition of this book
It's gotten bigger and bolder and although the term *unschooling* still mystifies Jane Average on the street, everybody at least in the U.S. has heard of *homeschooling* by now and thinks they know what it is. Urban unschooling is growing rapidly—people used to think of homeschooling as exclusively a rural trend and if that ever was the case, it isn't now.

Recently, the media has discovered the term *unschooling*. (It's annoying, though, when they call it a new subcategory of homeschooling, as if John Holt didn't launch it in the 1970's.) In general, homeschooling laws are better now, and in most states it's quite simple to get out of school.

Partly because of this book, many young people have themselves initiated the process of unschooling, rather than waiting for their parents to think of it. For that reason, and also because the homeschooling movement in general is growing rapidly, and also because homeschooling toddlers get older every day, there are now way more unschooling teenagers than there were in 1991. Go, team. And, I see again and again that our movement evolves not only because unschooling makes sense, but also because unschoolers consider themselves a community and are heartbreakingly generous with each other.

Unschoolers keep leapfrogging over the backs of other unschoolers, and thereby getting better and better at living and learning. As always, many choose activities that are deeply fulfilling for them but that are not particularly "newsworthy"—lots of reading, neighborhood volunteering, questioning everything, watching birds, intimate friendships. Others choose spectacular adventures or large projects—undertakings which do often happen to be newsworthy, but that's not the point: bicycling alone through Columbia and Ecuador. Writing and editing books. Designing and building a recumbent bike. Opening and operating a retail store. Publishing a serious unschooling zine for several years. Building a yurt, a straw bale house, a solar oven of one's own design. Bicycling alone across the U.S., becoming the youngest American woman to do so. (Of course, the people who accomplish these feats also spend long quieter periods at home reading, watching birds, questioning everything....)

How this revision is different from the original edition

I added: A section on international homeschooling laws and practices. E-mail addresses and Web sites. More resources (books, suppliers, camps, etc.). More anecdotal examples and quotes from people inventing unschooling—including new excerpts from *GWS*, whose cutting-edge articles continue to knock my socks off. An armload of my own new comments and suggestions. An appendix packed with favorite letters from readers.

I deleted: about three cuss words, to make my mother happy and have a better chance of infiltrating a broader range of households. Recommendations for resources which are no longer available, or which are not as good as newer stuff. (I did *not* delete mentions of important out-of-print books, since books go out of print lickety-split and are still findable at libraries and used book stores.) The long list of U.S. homeschooling organizations, since they change quickly and it's best for you to get current information, such as the annual directory published by *GWS*.

I changed: not much. I de-Americanized some passages where the original text was confusing to the rest of the English-speaking world. And since I blasted through the first edition in less than one intense year—I urgently wanted to get this message *out*—I've taken the liberty, this second time around, to do a bit of re-organizing and polishing. But, although I'm a different person now than I was seven years ago, and I now choose and string words together differently, it didn't make sense to rewrite a lot. This book has become its own entity, with a life quite separate from my own, and I don't feel I have the right (not to mention the energy!) to overhaul it much.

Where the author has been

Well, I fell in love, got married, rolled past my thirtieth birthday, started gardening, got better at dancing, spent seven years being the secretary to the person who wrote the *Teenage Liberation Handbook*... and tried a whole bunch of projects related to unschooling: edited and self-published two more books; started about five more books (now lurking unfinished in my ominous filing cabinet); published a newsletter, *Unschooling Ourselves*; worked on a video about unschooling (also not finished, yet); opened a resource center; chattered on a lot of radio shows and a few TV shows and to a gazillion journalists; gave a bunch of talks at homeschooling conferences and other events; gave a few consultations; started Not Back to School Camp; started a support group for unschoolers; started a support group for dropouts; started a mail-order book business. And I answered hundreds—maybe thousands, I lose track—of letters. (Sometimes I am overwhelmed with guilt that I cannot keep up with all my mail, and that I can't be a personal friend or consultant to the many teenagers who reach out to me, looking for support as they begin to take responsibility for their own lives, often with confused or skeptical parents.)

The biggest lesson I learned by doing all those things is that *doing too much is a sick way to live*, and it's wasteful and ungrateful to live too fast to breathe. I also had a lot of good moments and was able to help a number of people—but not, I feel, as well as I would have had I carefully chosen fewer projects and given each more focused, clear attention. I no longer publish a newsletter, run a resource center, speak at homeschooling events, talk much to media people, give consultations, or run support groups. With the help of my charming husband Skip, I do still—with great joy and excitement—run Not Back to School Camp, operate Genius Tribe (our mail-order book business), answer some of my mail, continue to write, and consider finishing old projects or taking on new ones... selectively.

People often ask how my own views about education have changed in the past seven years. Mostly, my feelings have simply intensified. I'm now *less* tolerant of the kind of homeschooling in which the parents set up school at home and follow a packaged curriculum. (This very morning, I was the reluctant guest on a conservative radio show in Colorado. One irate caller said, "I'm *shocked*. Self-directed learning? That's why I pulled my kids out of *school*.")

But I'm even more excited now about the kind of homeschooling in which people take charge of their own learning. I wrote the first edition of this book on the strength of my convictions about my own adolescence, John Holt's work, and the examples of a bunch of teenagers who were already directing their educations. My understanding runs deeper now, and I've added new material and updated old information on the power of my mailbox and new friendships. I'm fortunate to count among my close friends several grown up unschoolers who remind me again and again of what's important in life, of how *I* want to live. And the letters that have filled my heart and my file cabinets show me, over and over, that unschooling saves lives, that this message is even more important than I realized the first time around.

Eugene, Oregon
Friday the 13th, February 1998

appendix C

the Power and
Magic in my mailbox

I GET THE most stunning letters from readers of all ages, in school and out, teenagers, parents, teachers, college students, other adults. They come from all over the U.S. and Canada, and occasionally from other places. Usually they're exuberant, sometimes frustrated, often both. Their insights floor me; their announcements put a spring in my step. I want to share with you excerpts from a handful, along with a few of my responses. Each letter, of course, is a unique reflection of a unique individual, though I've labeled them by categories here.

Teachers
I hear from teachers who feel the same conflicts I did when I taught school. Sometimes they're thinking about leaving, sometimes they plan to stay in but are struggling hard to be authentic and harmless, sometimes they have recently quit and display the same kind of amazed delight that many new unschoolers do.

Grace,

I recently read your books *Real Lives* and *The Teenage Liberation Handbook* and was completely blown away . . . After twelve years as a "successful" student in the public schools of Memphis, Tennessee, I graduated at the top of my class in 1984 and enrolled at the University of Tennessee. I had always felt a certain desire to teach and in fact felt that I probably would become a teacher, most likely a high school math teacher, at some point. But, having been subtly discouraged from that career path by teachers (it would be a "waste of my talents") as well as parents (not lucrative enough), I decided that teaching would at least wait until I had earned some money and so I instead majored in engineering. In 1988 I graduated from UT with a degree in Electrical Engineering and immediately accepted a job as a computer programmer with IBM in Research Triangle Park, North Carolina.

Well, after a few years of corporate America I began to feel a little dissatisfied and began once again to consider teaching. I found a program at Wake Forest University which would allow me to earn a graduate degree in education as well as a teaching certificate and, much to the shock of friends and family, I sold my house, quit my job at IBM, and enrolled. By this time I had become fairly well-read in the area of "education," and was particularly enamored with Jonathan Kozol, whose passion about teaching and public schools very closely matched my own. I had also decided that one of the biggest problems with schools was grading and that if grading were eliminated then all sorts of wonderful things would happen in schools.

(I was considered pretty radical at Wake Forest.) My thesis was a study of a pilot program of an "Essential School," a school modeled on principles of Ted Sizer's *Coalition of Essential Schools*. I came to believe that the solution to the woes of public education included not only the abolition of grading but also other Coalition principles such as lower student/teacher ratios, fewer subjects taught, etc. In short, I believed essentially what all school reformers believe, that if we could just correct these few (though non-trivial) problems, then our schools would be wonderful. I finished my degree at WFU in the summer of 1993 and accepted a job at a "troubled" inner-city high school in Durham, North Carolina. I was nervous but confident; after all, these were the kids who were most in need of idealistic, dedicated, young teachers, and I was certainly all of those things.

It was a disaster from the first day of school. The school itself was hopelessly bogged down in political wrangling, the brand-new principal tried to cover up his lack of experience and competence with authoritarianism and blame-placing, the students, of course, had problems of their own, and I was left feeling overwhelmed and unsupported. In between my bouts of depression, anxiety, fear, worry, and frustration, I began to see for the first time that although some of the difficulties I was experiencing were due to my own inexperience, many others were in fact built-in absurdities of the school system itself. Many of my students were either pregnant or already parents (at fifteen years old), most lived in public housing complexes, and all of them had no reason whatsoever to be interested in learning about right triangles or linear equations. If I were in their position, I soon realized, I would feel exactly the same way.

It didn't take long for Durham High to wear me down. After only a few months I realized that not only did I not believe in what I was doing, but also that if I stayed I would continue to jeopardize my marriage, my health, and my sanity. So, after one grueling semester, I quit. I took a part-time job at an after-school program at a nearby private middle school and, still angry and confused, set about trying to piece together what I believed about teaching, learning, and education. Maybe private schools were the answer; maybe "school choice," which I had always condemned as being a sort of elitist smokescreen for the real problems of public education, was the answer; maybe homeschooling was the answer; maybe there wasn't an answer.

(Praise and adulation starts here.) Then, as I was browsing through the education section one day in the public library, I happened upon your book *Real Lives*, and knew that I had come across something different. My big concerns about homeschooling were rooted in the image of a parent sitting with a child at the kitchen table for six hours a day, and your book blew that idea right out of the water (Kyla's story about her bike trip through South America was particularly fascinating). For the first time in my life I found myself seriously considering the possibility that maybe math, science, English, and social studies were not in fact the most important things in the world; maybe building houses, riding horses, and biking through South America were just as important. In fact, after finishing *Real Lives*, I went through a period of several weeks feeling rather angry about the fact that I had wasted so much of *my* life in classrooms and that, at 28 years old, I still hadn't learned how to decide for myself what things I was interested in and what things I wanted to devote my time to. I was living confirmation of the damage done by traditional schooling.

After that I began to explore the ideas of "unschooling" and self-directed learning in earnest. I read *The Teenage Liberation Handbook, Dumbing us Down* by John Taylor Gatto, and everything I could find by John Holt. Gatto's writings, in particular, spoke eloquently to me about the struggles of a man who "succeeded" dramatically in the public school system before deciding that he wanted "a job where I don't have to hurt kids to make a living." I now understood exactly what he was talking about.

I should wrap this up. I left out of my autobiography the part about my wife's similar struggle with her life and her decision to enter the ministry. We now live on Ocracoke island off the coast of North Carolina where she is the pastor of the United Methodist church. We are also expecting our first child in February and I am looking forward to being a full-time father. I also have begun to "unschool myself," a difficult and thrilling process in itself, but one which I have enjoyed immensely so far.

Lance Bledsoe, Ocracoke, North Carolina

College students
I was happy and surprised to discover that lots of college students use this book too. Some of them are assigned to read it in education courses and other courses! Of course, many of them find it merely "interesting" or downright ridiculous. Others decide to apply it to their lives. For some of them that means leaving college, for others it means changing their major, taking time off, or simply(?) changing their perspective and their priorities.

Dear Grace,

I am sitting here in my little apartment kitchen, at 1:30 A.M., writing in my journal and rereading your first book for what is probably the twentieth time. I came upon your last sentence in the first chapter. Something like, hope that you soar, and tell me where you land.... Well, I've landed south of the equator in Buenos Aires. I don't know if you remember but I wrote you about eight months ago from Swarthmore college, in the cold winds of November, agonizing over whether I should continue teaching Hebrew school because I felt so many conflicts just occupying the "teacher" role. I was also having doubts about my college process, although I'm not sure if I wrote that in my letter. (And yes, your response was very helpful; I was also pleased that you'd taken time to answer me.)

The second semester brought me here, to Buenos Aires, where I'd planned to study abroad the year before. But something happened. I'd been so depressed that past fall, when I wrote you, I thought a few months away would cure all. But towards the end of the semester I realized something. I wasn't ready to go back. I was enjoying my life of renting an apartment, working, studying, speaking Spanish, basically just living. And I wanted to stay, to develop these "skills." At first, I was terrified. This was a huge leap, a giant change in the program, which would mean a change in the college process. I would no longer be allowed the "legitimacy" of a *semester abroad*, I would just be Aviva, living in sin (sin, because I wasn't in college—not, unfortunately, the other sense) in South America, teaching English, traveling, studying, free, at the university with no immediate guarantee of credit upon return.

But you know something? I've never felt more free; I feel like I have so many opportunities. So many things to learn. Perhaps I will return to the same college in the spring, perhaps not. I don't have to decide now. But the beautiful feeling is I know I will accomplish what I want to, and this is the first time I don't feel trapped. I am realizing that it's not too late to take advantage of all you offer in your book. I keep thinking of that one girl in *Real Lives* who rode her bike through parts of South America at sixteen. If she can do that, I should have no fear of staying a bit longer in Argentina.

So why did I share this with you? . . . Because you contributed to my decision to stay. Don't worry, my mother is not going to call you up, and say "why have you brainwashed my daughter?" Your words just reinforced what I've known in my heart for a while, but was too scared to admit. That, right now, the college lifestyle, that system just isn't what I want. That focused inward approach is not how I want my life to be right now. And my choice, whatever that is, is definitely valid and worthwhile, because it is, and always should have been, mine to make. Every once in a while, when I can't sleep at fourish in the morning, I skim through your book, always finding some inspirational quote, so I can say, "Yes, that's it exactly." And then I can return to sleep, dreaming of all the delicious experiences the world has to offer me. I used to feel sad that I hadn't taken advantage of all the possibilities the high school years had to offer (in terms of time), but now I get excited because I can say, "Hey, this is fun, and I'm only twenty. I have so much more I can do." So for all that—inspiration, education, and support, I thank you.

Aviva Kushner, Argentina via Swarthmore college

Parents

I get lots of letters from parents, and they blow my mind. I love being reminded how brave some people are.

Dear Ms. Llewellyn,

I finally allowed my son to start "homeschooling" in December of 1995. He had been begging me to homeschool him for years. As a matter of fact, he had come home early in the first grade and informed me that as soon as he got his prize from the school's magazine sale he was dropping out. When I finally let him out of school he was in the seventh grade. I knew school made him miserable, and I sympathized since school made me miserable too—but I didn't think we had a choice. You see, I'm a single parent and I thought I would need to be home all day to homeschool my children.

In December I decided that Kevin had already learned enough in school to teach himself anything else he would need to know. (He's an excellent reader and completed math all the way to basic algebra.) I agreed to let him *try* to homeschool, but I still assigned school work to him.

A few weeks ago the children's librarian gave me *The Teenage Liberation Handbook* for Kevin and my daughter Jessica to read. (Jessica joined Kevin as a homeschooler in late January.) The kids weren't too excited about your book, so I started reading it! I love it! By the third chapter I had informed the children that I would no longer be assigning school work. Jessica (who will be thirteen in August) asked me, "So if I don't learn anything for a whole year you won't say anything?"

I told her I didn't think she could go for a whole year without learning something—she's too curious for that—but she was welcome to try. She decided to read your book. I didn't even get to finish it!

I wish I had been given this information when I was a kid. Or even before I spent four irritating years at the community college I just finished at! I *hated* school—Kevin *hated* school—Jessica tolerated school. I'm so glad that the kids can be free now (I also wish I had set them free years ago) and also that I now have alternatives to my own higher education.

Since I have removed the pressure to perform from Kevin, the depression and anger which have been increasing by the year have disappeared. Jessica has been making plans to intern with any vet who will take her. (By the way, both still participate in their school bands.)

Finally, here are a few of Jessica's reactions to what she's read so far . . . "Mom, I don't think this is an *authorized* book, because she's saying what I've been thinking but I thought I was only thinking it."

Rebecca Mae Loos, Spokane, Washington

People already unschooling

I was surprised, in the beginning, that my advice was useful for people who were already unschooling. I didn't expect that—my intent was just to tell schoolers what unschoolers were doing, so they could decide whether they wanted to try it for themselves. It turns out that this book has helped many longtime unschoolers realize just how much is open to them, more of the breadth of the possibilities for education and life. That makes me outrageously happy—I've learned so much from unschoolers, so it thrills me that my work is useful to some of them also.

Dear Grace Llewellyn,

I'm fifteen (soon sixteen), and I hail from Madison, Wisconsin. . . . I'm writing to you about your book, and how much it helped me get a real life. I have been meaning to write you a letter for a long time. Just last year I read your book....At the time I was a little unhappy with the way homeschooling was working out for me, and was contemplating returning to school. Your book totally turned me around! I really figured out a lot about my life....I have heard many success stories from people who have read your book, but first, let me tell you mine.

I am a heretic of society. I am constantly challenging the traditional beliefs and rules of *everything*. So when school came along and sucked me up, my soul cried out for freedom. I was dying every day of my life. You know the rest...

At the end of my fifth-grade school year, my parents and I talked about the possibility of homeschooling. I had my doubts; what if people think I'm a drop-out, how will I learn anything without a teacher, how will I make friends, etc. We talked about these issues with some homeschooling/unschooling families we know. (I'm sure they thought we were totally American and standard, but they were very understanding and gentle to us altogether.) I was still very nervous... but on the first day of sixth grade, I didn't go. I didn't go the next day, or the day after that, or the day after that. I didn't go ever! (Good thing, too!) The only problem was, "What do I do with all this free time?" It was such a change to have aeons of time on my hands, to do whatever I wanted with. With no one there to tell me what to do every nano-second, well, I didn't do anything. And not doing anything made me feel guilty and incompetent and shitty and tired, etc.

Then an interesting thing happened. An interesting chain of events, actually. All my life, I have always loved movement. I have taken dance classes in ballet for seven years now. A year and a half ago I was starting to get bored with it, so I decided to take a modern class. I took one class in Graham, and immediately was obsessed. I couldn't stay away! I signed up for one class per week (only because one was all I could afford). I never dreamed how a body could be moved in so many different ways! In ballet, I was always trying so hard to get it right all the time, so of course I never got anything right. And then I took one little Graham class. It sealed my fate. I became enamored of the contraction and release, the spiral and the high lift, the third position of the back, the pulses, the deep stretches, and especially the pretzel!

At about the same time, I began to read your book. I realized that the world *is* an orchard, as you put it, and that I was wallowing in bounty. You can't be a dancer and go to school. Twenty-five hours of practice per week is impossible....And just as I realized this, I suddenly noticed what fruit had been right above me all along. So I reached up, and took it:

One day in Graham class, we were breaking down movement on the floor. (Graham does a lot of work on the floor at the beginning of each class.) Lisa, the instructor, was giving us praises, comments, and corrections. Lisa was impressed with how quickly everyone in the class was understanding the movement (and so were we!) and she exclaimed that she wished we could all come and take classes at Kanopy, the school where she teaches and directs. She also added that me and one other girl in the class, since we had been taking dance lessons longer, could come and get a shot at being in Kanopy Dance Company, with the professional dancers. I was so excited I nearly jumped out of my leotard! "Really?" I asked. "You bet. I think you guys are strong enough dancers for at least an apprentice position," Lisa replied, "The only problem is" (you guessed it) "We rehearse during the day, so I guess you couldn't come during the week because of school." I zoomed in for the kill: "I don't go to school."

Now I have a full scholarship to the Kanopy Dance Company, and the Kanopy Youth Ensemble, and I love every moment of it!

I'm also an avid fan of the Bard. Every summer, my sister Nora (who is eleven), and I take part in the Young Shakespeare Players, a young people's acting program that presents full-length, unabridged, un-bullshitted Shakespeare. Naturally, the program attracts homeschoolers and unschoolers like a magnet, as well as kids who know they deserve better than the high school acting programs and so called "Children's Theaters," many of which, in reality, only put kids down. The Young Shakespeare Players (or YSP) hands kids the opportunity to discover what they can do, and doesn't rub in their face what they can't. This past summer we did "Othello." It was sublime, exciting, disturbing, everything Othello should be. And I played a part I will probably never play again. I was Iago. Malevolent, cold, sneaky, cynical, satanic, and well liked by everyone, he was the ultimate acting challenge. He had to seem completely good and well-meaning and nice to the characters, while plainly showing his true intentions to the audience. He is also the third largest part in Shakespeare's works. With over a thousand lines, he is only exceeded by Richard III and Hamlet. And speaking of *Hamlet*, that's the play YSP is doing this summer. Because I don't go to school, I have been studying the play since October. All my friends at school who read *Hamlet* say they wish they had as much time to read it as I had. No comment.

A few other things I can finally sink my teeth into are Mythology, Astrology and Astronomy, Earth Sciences (by volunteering at the arboretum), Algebra (I was scared to death of it before), Computers, Philosophy, the Library, "Alternative" and Ancient Medicines, Science (another thing I was scared of before), Theater (I have established a working/learning relationship with the Stage Manager at a local community theater, and she teaches me the ins and outs of lighting, set design and construction, fiber-optics, pyrotechnics, and sound boards), good Literature and Movies...Physiology, Anatomy, Greek Plays, Elizabethan Costume Construction, Anthropology, Anthropology, *Anthropology!* (*Everything* and *everyone*, from Hamlet to Jesus to Rush Limbaugh (gag!) to my mother, are my teachers in this area!) the Great Lakes, Chemical Pollutants, Early theories on why Nuclear Energy will never work, my own non-performing Artistic Ability (recently I realized that yes, I can draw every bone and muscle in the human body without a teacher) and Reprehensible Institutions and Why They Don't Work . . .

Kristen Emily Kehl,
Anthropologist, Autodidact, and Free-as-a-Bird Adolescent!
Madison, Wisconsin

About a year and a half later, I heard from Kristen again:
Since my last letter, I have lent your book to so many people. I've managed to get four out of ten to quit school...I've been accepted to the National Shakespeare Conservatory, up in the Catskill Mountains in New York state. It's my first "professional" training in acting. The Conservatory's summer program takes fifty people from the nation each summer. There's a two-year program you can take as well. It's so far been incredible. There are a handful of other seventeen-year-olds here as well, but mostly I'm in the same stew pot with grad students and professionals. It's a wonderful part of the journey, and I love it! There is so much here of which I can learn and partake. I can test my wings, and fly . . .

Just to keep you up to date, I'm not dancing in the dance company any more . . . Last year I focused less on dance and acting, and more on music. I joined the mixed voice choir of the Madison Children's Choir, an incredible experience of music and beauty. I started writing music for piano as well. In the fall I'll be singing in two choirs, having managed to worm my way into the awesome concert choir at Madison West high school. My opportunities that spring from this are awesome as well. Tomorrow never knows...

Soon-to-be unschoolers

Paul Donnelly wrote me this letter a few months before he actually went ahead and quit school:

Dear Ms. Llewellyn,
Thank you for giving young people *The Teenage Liberation Handbook*. I was already planning on quitting school before my mother gave your book to me. Both she and I see school as constricting. I am unsure of my father's opinion, but I suspect that he feels the same way. (I haven't asked him yet.) The way she put it was

"You're being given four years with which to do whatever you please. You don't have to pay any bills yet, and you're probably never going to get another opportunity like this. Therefore, I suggest that you do not waste these years." I agree with her.

I'm thirteen years of age and in the eighth grade. I am schooled at a private Christian institution beginning at grade three and continuing through grade eight in Ypsilanti, Michigan. I am satisfied with the school, as schools go. It is a relatively acceptable place to learn. There is a total of about 220 students, 48 of whom are in my grade. We are very close-knit, but the teachers do not know much about our lives outside of school, in contrast to your experience. Its method of teaching is not "experiential education," but it is not conventional, either. It mixes in literature, philosophy, and theology with the usual line-up of courses and electives. This is one of the reasons I've stayed for so long, aside from the relatively positive atmosphere. (I consider it to be a very good school atmosphere, as schools go, despite its shortcomings.) I'm more interested in philosophy than anything else we're learning.

For the first half of this past year, my social studies teacher had us extensively outline a small section of the textbook every night, in preparation for our daily quiz.... On each quiz, he'd ask us ten questions to test our memorization and reading skills. The questions, such as "How many men did George Washington lead into such-and-such a battle on this date?" were petty and irrelevant to history, and the quizzes were a waste of time. They taught us nothing that was worth knowing, and succeeded not in teaching us to effectively absorb information, but to quickly commit to our memory useless facts, dates, names, etc. We would become excessively nervous in anticipation of the quiz, and promptly forget everything we'd learned soon afterwards. We accomplished nothing. I told my teacher this, and he realized that it was true. Since then, he has changed his style of instruction. He now assigns reading to us and gives the test questions to us in advance. The questions, which we answer in essay form, are based on broad generalizations and concepts of history. A recent questions was "What were the underlying political philosophies behind President Johnson's and the Radical Republicans' policies on Reconstruction, what were those policies, and how were those policies implemented?" . . . I find the new method much more challenging (you actually have to think), more effective in teaching us about our nation's cultural, political, social, and economic background, and more worthwhile. However, the answers aren't useful to us as of now, so his method is not completely satisfactory. Because of my dissatisfaction with school, I'm quitting.

I am tired of being unable to enjoy my family, my friends and myself for lack of time. This is another of the reasons that I have decided to unschool next year, until college. I won't have to stay home when I am invited to go out to a play or a movie with my friends because I have a big test hanging over my head, and I won't have to wake up tired at six A.M., and I won't have to worry about my parents' reaction to a less-than-perfect report card, and I won't have to shape my life around school. I will get my life back.

I am planning on apprenticing myself to several friends of my parents, just observing them and helping them at work for a couple of days every week. I'll learn skills more easily and effectively than I would reading about them. I also plan on taking drawing and/or guitar and/or piano lessons, pursuing only what interests me. I love listening to and making music, dancing, singing, reading, learning. Since I was very little, I've loved to read. School has quenched this healthy thirst for intellectual stimulation. I have become disinterested in most books, and even those that I am interested in, I have no time to read. I'm looking forward to unschooling next year, because I'll be able to renew my love of books. I believe that voluntary reading teaches you more than forced reading ever could. With the exception of plastic *Sweet Valley High*-type books, I think books are some of the most valuable learning tools available to us. (Shakespeare can say in two lines what Jessica Wakefield and her twin sister Elizabeth can say in 150 pages.)

As I mentioned, I'm also interested in philosophy. In my school, we sometimes hold brief (one class-period, at most) discussions of philosophy, mostly by discussing spatial, theological, and/or psychological relationships. However, some of my classmates get bored, don't understand philosophical concepts, or just don't bother to participate. Sometimes, not participating is okay, if you just want to absorb and process the information you're hearing, and mentally debate your opinion. To refrain from participating because you don't want to think, however, is immature and lazy. They waste class time with their absurdly silly, off-the-point jokes and remarks, which they make in a miserably vain attempt to appear as if they know what they're talking about. I know I sound snooty, and maybe they do have a point which I just can't comprehend, but they make the stupidest comments, and they're not employing the intelligence that I know they have. I'd much rather visit a college philosophy class, because these discussions always leave me wanting more after the bell rings. (Minus the above mentioned jokes/remarks, of course.) One thing that I've noticed while visiting my sisters' college classes is that a lot more people actually want to be there . . . Today my teacher told us that in order to be Christian, upstanding citizens who are responsible for their actions "when we grow up," we have to think in a certain way, which he explained to us. We are not supposed to see history as a series of linear equations, with specific and solitary causes and effects. I agree that history is a network of causes and effects, but it's bullshit that he tells us how we have to think. What does your view of history have to do with your status as a citizen, anyway?

Teachers are now dictators, telling us what to think and how to think it, save most of my teachers. They are taking complete control over our lives, abusing their "authority," and generally treating us as if we were their incompetent, anemic pets. Forgive me for saying so, but I sincerely believe that my intelligence and independence exceeds that of my next-door neighbor's dog. I'm more than capable of thinking for myself.

He also cracked a vacuous joke, and became very offended when we did not laugh. His insensitive remark in response to our silence was "You people just have no sense of humor. I mean, you laugh at all the corny jokes, but the more sophisticated ones just fly right over your head." Can teachers now blatantly insult the intelligence of their students without reprimand, or has it always been that way? His inane flummery is further proof of his mindlessness. Should I speak up? This is not the way schools should be.

I think it's useful to know how to be obedient, but not to the point of complete dependence and abandonment of freedom. You shouldn't be blindly shuffling through life, missing the best opportunities that come your way. We who are schooled are taught to do exactly that. We are told that it's okay to compromise our time in exchange for an education. "Compromise" used to mean mutual concession. It has come to mean forsaking free will and individuality. Time, the relentless passage of existence, is more valuable to me than a mediocre education in preparation for "the real world."

Paul Donnelly, Ypsilanti, Michigan

Trials and tribulations

Lots of writers tell me of their anger and frustration with the school system— whether they're still in it, or escaped.

Grace—

Please excuse the quality of this letter. But somehow I don't think you'll mind too much. When I was one my parents got divorced. And as a single mother my mom didn't have much choice except to get me into school as soon as possible. And so starts my eleven years of wasted time. She enrolled me at a Montessori kindergarten and preschool. When it was time for first grade she enrolled me in a Nova Program. We had to take a test to get in. I had one of the top ten scores.

As I write this I am currently a freshman in my second semester, only (precisely) 42 days left. For a long time (since fifth and fourth grade) my grades have been "less than exemplary."

After reading a chapter of your book I burst into tears of anger, sorrow, and frustration. Everything is right on target. My elementary/junior high school was one of the most oppressive. And quite confidently I can say, I have learned nothing except oppression. Whatever I have learned in my short life has been in spite of them not because of them.

I want my freedom back, my childhood, those lost years. What saddens me the most is I can only take my freedom. A good adult friend of mine once said, "After a moment goes by you can never go back and take it." And being realistic, I realize that the most I will be able to do is take back my future. And I hope that's enough.

For three years (and plus more than even I'm willing to admit) I've been struck with bouts of depression. That tore very deep in me. I want my freedom! I want my untroubled sleep. I want to be able to stand up for what I believe in. I just now realize I have woken up from a fourteen year dream . . . Most sincerely from my heart, thanks for helping me take back my life.

Hannah B., Minnesota.

The undecided

Often people write to me before they have decided whether they want to quit school, and talked with their parents about it. They're still immersed in the system and sometimes they feel confused about their choices. Here's some of my exchange with one person.

Dear Ms. Llewellyn,

I am writing to express my anger with your writing. Perhaps if I had never come upon your book while working at my after-school job as a library page, the idea of freedom would never have come into my mind. If you had not written such inspirational books, I could have settled into my life in my new prestigious boys' school without a hitch, allowed my creativity to be beaten into submission without a fight, and moved on through college, a job, a mortgage, and then died without ever realizing I had another option. But you have written these books. And now I am lost.

My name is Andrew B____. I am sixteen years old, and a junior at University School. As I mentioned above, I have been reading *The Teenage Liberation Handbook* and *Real Lives*. Not all the way through of course. I haven't had the time or energy to get all the way through a book of my own choice since I began high school. But everything I have read in the Handbook seems right on-target for me. Last year, I realized that I wasn't learning anything in school, and I feared not getting into a "good" college. So I begged my father to allow me to attend a private school. I now attend school in one of the richest suburbs of Cleveland, where I am forced to pray, sing the national anthem, remove my facial piercings, and generally recreate a military dictatorship. My education? The same as at my culturally diverse public high school, only more homework.

My name is Andrew B____. I am a writer, a would-be traveler, an aspiring film-maker, and an activist. I love life so much that the idea of suicide seems appalling to me, yet I can understand those intense feelings for a need to escape. I have wanderlust. I want to explore, both geographically and personally. I want to make beautiful films . . . I am brilliant. I am a visionary.

As I write this letter, I am preparing for another school day, and watching my two personas duke it out. "Stay in school!" says the former. "You've been given a great opportunity! From University School you could go to NYU, or even Harvard!"

"Who cares?" says the latter. "We're unhappy, lethargic, miserable. We have great ideas but no time to follow through with them. Why, right now, there's six hours of great footage from our first short film that's been sitting idle for two months, and who knows when we'll get to edit it."

I want to go to film school at the Academy of Art in San Francisco. I know I could get in with my GED. But, the school board won't let me take the damn test unless I've already been withdrawn from school, and I'm afraid to drop out (drop in?) unless I have something for sure to go to next. I'm so afraid to talk to my father. I *begged* for this school. How can I tell him that I want to quit altogether?

I guess I'd better sign off. I have to get up at six in the morning to drive to school. Please, I beg of you, write me back. So few people are supporting me, but I can't convince myself that you are wrong . . .

Andrew B., Cleveland Heights, Ohio

Dear Andrew,

It's hard for me to know how to respond to a letter as anguished as yours. All I can really say is, "I heard you. I'm on your side. Thank God/dess you're alive enough to know you're in trouble. Go, team!" Everything you said makes sense to me, as it would to most of the people I associate with, and to the ninety unschooled teenagers who spent the last week of August with me in Oregon. (I mention this just because you probably feel very alone in your convictions at present.)

Because you have nearly two years left in your school career it seems to me that you stand to lose a lot by staying in, and to gain a lot by getting out. I do suggest that you read Kyla's essay in *Real Lives* if you haven't already, because she quit in the spring of her junior year and never looked back. She's still on a roll—she was one of the counselors at August's Not Back to School Camp so I got to catch up on her life some. Sometimes people write me and say "Your book stabs my heart but I only have six months/a year/three years/five weeks left so shouldn't I just stick it out?" The reason I think they (and you) should perhaps *not* stick it out is that sticking one thing out often leads to sticking the next thing out (college, hateful job, etc.) plus, why waste another moment?

You're fortunate in that you already have a focus and passion and thus some fuel for your discussion with your father. Sounds to me like you should 1) talk with your dad, 2) talk to him again (and again) if necessary, 3) quit school, 4) get your GED[1], 5) apply to film school at the Academy of Art in San Francisco. Also like you should begin, at your earliest convenience, to make friends and acquaintances who prove by example that it's better to be doing what you truly want to be doing than to be wasting away your precious breath where you don't want to be.

Oh—and when you talk to your father perhaps you will sound more convincing if you present the idea that you wanted to develop and be challenged, and you thought you'd get that at University School, but that turned out not to be possible and after much thought you'd like to try another (much much less expensive!) option *with the same goal in mind.* So that the overall theme is "I'm still seeking the same thing, but I've learned a lot more about where to find it" rather than the apparent confusion of "Last year I wanted to go to prep school and now I've done a 180 and I want to drop out."

You have my sincere best wishes. Now take courage and have that talk with your dad. And please do let me know what happens.

Yours,

Grace Llewellyn

Andrew sent me a note about three months later: "My dad is letting me quit!!"

People whose parents won't let them leave school
The hardest letters for me to read (besides the rare nasty, hateful ones) come from people who want badly to leave school and have tried some or all of the tactics I laid out in Chapter 10, "The Perhaps Delicate Parental Issue," but their parents nevertheless refuse to let them out. Undoubtedly there are a lot of teenagers in this position, and I am furious that young people don't have more legal control over their own lives. I am often amazed by the strength and creativity these writers show, in their determination to stay sane and grow despite having to stay in school. Here's some of my correspondence with one such young woman.

Dear Miss Llewellyn,

Sorry, first of all, for this informal, quickly scrawled letter. I hope you can read it. But my hands are shaking so hard I can barely do this right now. I s'pose it'd have been better for me to type this to you but I have to stay upstairs right now, cuz I'm expecting company... and my computer is downstairs. Gosh, I love it when weather closes school down.

But poppa came home from lunch about an hour ago, and he sat me down for a

---

[1] I suggested the GED, rather unimaginatively, only because Andrew suggested it was necessary to get into film school. I should have said, "Talk with the Academy of Art about their admissions requirements, and get your GED if necessary."

little heart-to-heart or something. This was a surprise. Poppa doesn't speak to me very much. He's a pretty uncommunicative type of guy. Sullen. (I don't think he used to be.) Anyway, he told me straight out that my chances of becoming homeschooled were completely "impossible," said our "family standards" would never allow my wish, my current greatest wish, to be fulfilled.

Oh, I don't know how to express everything that has led up to this so far.... I've been debating it out with my parents for the past month now, armed with your *Teen Lib Handbook*, a November 22nd front page *Kalamazoo Gazette* clipping of a homeschooled seventeen-year-old's entrance into the University of Michigan as a junior, three of my homeschooled friends' testimonies, John Gatto's speech, one single issue of *Growing Without Schooling*, the Colfax book, and most importantly, my emotions. But the last is getting so much wear. I'm not sure how long I can keep this up on my own.

I admit I still have to finish reading *Teen Lib* yet. I'm at the guinea pig chapter right now, despite that it's been my only reading book (even over textbooks at times, I admit) for the past four weeks. But it's been very important to me. Very. I've felt frustrations with school for well over two or three years now. I... hmmm... I don't know if you know much about Oriental families, but a commonly recurring theme is "education *first*." I've lived with gold stars and A+'s all my life. I know they don't make me happy. What I essentially feel now is that my many breakdowns over the last three years were so unnecessary, so unneeded, for I could have known about homeschooling back then. I could have. But I'm a fifteen-year-old sophomore now and it's "too late" for me to start—so say my parents. But I still want it so badly.

I'm sorry. I jump all over the place. Mainly I don't know where to begin my thoughts and where to continue them... they're so dysfunctional, and overwhelming...

Hmmm... perhaps I'll give you some facts... so maybe you think you will therefore know a little more about me and what I do . . .

I'm a student at Portage Central High School, the Kalamazoo area math and science center (an institution for the "gifted"), and Portage Northern where I am in the Portage High School Orchestra playing as fourth (out of eleven) chair cellist. I've also played piano for nine years, and am currently working on a Chopin polonaise, Bach impromptu, and Beethoven "pathetique" sonata. I also play an er-hu, a Chinese two-stringed, lap held folk instrument. I remain fairly dedicated to my cultural roots, speaking mandarin Chinese at home, and participating in the Chinese folk dancing troupe, which is led by my momma. The teen and preteen division is led by me. My hobbies include bikeriding all across town in spring and summer, exploring downtown Kalamazoo on foot, modeming, and writing. I've been very actively involved in the online community for the past four years now, and am recognized as one of the original members of the online "scene." I have staff access on the golden Unicorn, Kalamazoo area's most popular bulletin board system, and also run a public message forum on there. I also publish a self-produced zine called *Sidetracked*, which basically contains my personal thoughts, opinions, writings, art sometimes, and whatever I choose to put in. Last year, I passed out over three hundred copies of five issues that I've put out. I also am a co-editor of the minizine "quirt" . . .

[Cindy goes on to explain how she co-edits an art-literary zine, writes fifty to eighty letters per month, played second cello in a production of The Music Man, *works at Joy Fong Chinese restaurant, tutors an eighth grader in math, goes to*

numerous camps, and reads widely.]
    I'll put all this to a close. The point of this letter was... well... to ask your help in finding resources? Complain about how, despite what a clear-cut and simple process you gave, things are still difficult in convincing my parents? Prove I'm not crazy? Beg for a kind word? . . .
Cindy H., Kalamazoo, Michigan

Dear Cindy,
There was an urgency in your letter that made me want to respond right away. Sometimes I'm frustrated since answering my mail feels like the most important thing I do in my work . . . but it's often hard to find the time to get to all of it . . .
    Of course, I don't really know what to say, assuming your basic situation has not changed. I have ideas, but none of them really seem like ideal solutions, and particularly since I don't know your family, I don't know what would work. I do sometimes get letters from kids whose parents refuse to let them out of school, but in turn the kid basically refuses to *go* to school and the parents realize that when it comes down to it, they can't really force the kid to go to school, unless they want to involve police, the legal system, brute force, and/or other really drastic measures like kicking the kid out of the house, etc. And apparently there are at least some parents who would rather back off than really push the issue via any of these means.
    Naturally the cost of such extreme situations is high, and in many families probably not worth it for the kid as well as for the parents. One of the cases that haunts me most is a girl who wrote me when she was seventeen, full of fire and passion because she'd left school—despite her parents' wishes to the contrary. She was full of dreams and plans—which all sounded viable and exciting to me. About a year later she contacted me again, deflated, and told me that she'd been "wrong" to leave school and make things so difficult for her family. She felt guilty and personally responsible for all the trauma her parents had gone through. And with the weight of that guilt, she hadn't been able to channel any energy into the dreams and plans she'd originally been so excited about. That news was hard for me to hear— why did she have to see it as her fault, her mistake, rather than as a tragic narrow-mindedness on their part? I certainly couldn't share her sense that she was guilty, and I couldn't help but feel angry at her parents who, in their ignorance, had helped crush her dreams. But at any rate, her story did drive home the point that it can cost too much, in some families, for kids to "disobey" their parents.
    On the other hand, I also get letters that say something like, "I played hooky for a week, and when my mom found out she realized how serious I was and that she couldn't make me go to school, and things have been great ever since."
    It's especially frustrating to read your letter because your life is so full; your projects and activities both numerous and significant; you would obviously soar if you were free from the time constraints and mental static that school inflicts on you. I often get letters from parents that say, "If only my kid was interested in anything, I'd be glad to let them leave school." I've seen many situations where previously unmotivated/uninterested kids fall in love with the world once they're out of school. But it's so much easier when someone is in love and full of desire *before* they leave.
    By now it may be clear to you that I can't really "help." I can't push a magic button that will convince your parents to let you out. I assume you've thought of

things like suggesting a trial run, or making some kind of compromise (perhaps just at first) like registering to take Advanced Placement tests or such. When these sorts of strategies don't work, I just don't know. I don't know what to say.

It occurs to me that it might help to communicate with other Asian homeschooling families? I'm aware of that "education first" paradigm that most Asian American families share . . . and it's not often that I meet Asian homeschoolers. I did meet a teenage girl last year here in Oregon, and she was one of the most "schooled-at-home" homeschoolers I've ever seen. But I know there are Asian American *un*schoolers out there. Since you're so wired, you probably have a much better idea than I of how you might connect with them on the Internet. There are a lot of homeschooling and unschooling discussions going on in cyberspace, that I know. I don't participate; my life is too complex already.

You might want to write to Donna Nichols-White, who publishes *The Drinking Gourd*, which is a sort of multi-cultural homeschooling magazine. She herself is African American, but she's gregarious and travels a lot, and I suspect she knows of Asian American unschoolers and could put you in touch with them.

I guess in a broader sense (I'm sure you've already thought of this) you might want to forget trying to make your parents understand how important it is to *you* to unschool—it sounds like that isn't going to convince them. Instead, you might focus more on showing them how respectable and seriously intellectual unschooling can be (which I realize you've already put a lot of energy into, but perhaps there's more to be done). To this end, I'm thinking of a new book [*And What About College?*]... on college admissions (. . . I've heard the author speak, and she's fabulous)—not that I think you should necessarily go to college, of course, but for your parents' benefit the info might be helpful. In the presentation I heard, the author (Cafi Cohen) talked about how exceptionally well prepared her *un*schooled (not schooled-at-home) son was for the Air Force Academy, which is not only an extremely selective institution, but *military*... I'm also thinking of the Colfaxes (whose kids went to Harvard) and their books *Homeschooling for Excellence* (especially) and *Hard Times in Paradise*. I'm thinking of Ronald Gross's *The Independent Scholar's Handbook*, which could help you formulate some sort of serious plan (if you're willing) to help sway your parents. I'll enclose one of my mail-order catalogs, which has *The Independent Scholar's Handbook* and some other good resources.

I'm sad that you have such a difficult (though probably not rare) situation and I wish I could tell you what to do to make it go away. Perhaps some of the ideas above will help. If they don't, let me just say (I know this may sound patronizing or irrelevant) that at least you only have two more years of school to go, and maybe you can find ways to manipulate the system, while you're stuck there, to use *it* rather than let it use you. I hope, above all else, that if you have to stay in school long enough to graduate, that you manage to hold onto the vision, passion, and determination that obviously fuels you now. You certainly have my very best wishes. And, in the short term, there's summer vacation to escape to. May yours be long, sunny, bright, and peaceful.

Sincerely,

Grace Llewellyn

Dear Grace,

I've tried starting a couple letters to you over the course of this past year... but somehow I'd always end up going overboard and explaining more than I meant to and the whole letter would cease to be relevant and so I wouldn't send it.

Well, I'm still in school, but I have reached the conclusion... determination... that it won't kill me because I won't let it. Cuz despite how much I still hate school and so much of what it represents... I have learned to cope with it. For one, my schedules are crazy so the most I ever spend at any school at once is two hours. I go to four different schools a week... one of them being the community college.

Basically now I'm compromising myself for the sake of my parents. A bit of crazy stuff happened in the midst of our arguments... I got to the point where Momma was starting to *really* question *her* roles in life too... her past education, her job... and then even her marriage. It was exciting and frustrating at the same time to watch her through this . . . Knowing I was a key factor in her new "enlightenment" or whatever.

We're all suppressing parts of ourselves now for the sake of the stability of our family. I don't know if that is wise... but it's part of a game. For me, my academic game . . . I don't know how I can uproot so many years of tradition and classic Chinese values now just to get what I want... but I will find ways to win at this academic game without homeschooling . . . But I am not allowing myself to forget... especially since I want to become a teacher—and I know this is risky because so many teachers can get jaded, and I've read essays discussing why even teachers with good intentions end up killing youth spirit anyways... but it's something I have passion for. And something I want to at least try to do well for as long as my conscience will let me... smirk.

I'm working on a compilation zine right now as a branch off from my regular zine, *Sidetracked*. It's just coming to a close . . . about bullshit punishments and rules that that kids have been made to endure... from dress code violations to one-sided arguments with administration to major trouble for innocent mistakes... whatever. Only one set of real-life examples why school makes no sense sometimes.

Cindy H., Kalamazoo, Michigan

People who read this book and quit school! Three cheers!

The sweetest treats in my mailbox come from people who have acted on my advice, i.e. quit school. One of the first I heard from was Kyla Wetherell, now one of my favorite friends and greatest heroines. I remember finding her letter at the post office, sitting outside on the steps reading it, and shaking with tears and happiness in plain view of everybody and their poodle.

After leaving school and her position as the editor of the high school newspaper, Kyla (among many other things) biked alone through Columbia and Ecuador, and wrote an essay for my second book Real Lives: eleven teenagers who don't go to school, *after which her example sparked many other people. (So please, take a cue from her and write me about* your *unschooled adventures, and give me permission to publish your letter, so more people can be sparked and the fire can spread. Or write to GWS or Ann Landers or the editor of a newspaper or use your Web site to tell about your unschooling adventures or produce a zine or write your own book.)*

As I write, Kyla is 22 and has done a superb job of finding situations where she learns what she wants to know—about organic farming, seed saving, alternative building methods, oven design, solar technology, and much more; she has recently formed a non-profit organization whose purpose includes teaching girls and women to build ecologically sane, inexpensive houses. And, she's one of the people who helps me run Not Back to School Camp each summer.

Dear Grace,

About a month ago my newspaper advisor said to me, "I have a book that you're going to want to steal away from me, but you can't borrow it until I'm finished." It was your book, *The Teenage Liberation Handbook*, and he was right: I took it from him for a day, then gave it back and immediately got my own copy.

That was a Monday. The following Friday was my last day of school. I can't thank you enough. My last few months in school were a nightmare. I had so many plans, so many dreams, and school felt like such a waste of time. I wanted my life to start right then, but there was still some orthodox voice ringing in my ears telling me that people like me just don't drop out of school. It insisted that quitting is bad and that I would be "burning my own bridges" and "ruining my life." Your book convinced me that any doors that might have closed due to a decision to leave school weren't worth going through in the first place . . .

I would never have guessed that there are so many opportunities for people who don't spend their days in school because I was too blinded by the expectation that I had to finish high school, get perfect grades, win a full scholarship to a well respected college, receive degrees, etc. Thank you . . . for helping my mom understand. It took only one long conversation with her and an evening of reading select passages from your book to convince her that leaving school was an excellent decision for me! . . .

Kyla Wetherell, Corvallis, Oregon

Sometimes I get letters from people who quit school the day they wrote to me. The bursting, joyous energy of their letters feeds my soul and I walk around with a huge, devilish grin.

Dear Grace,

I love you! . . . I am fifteen years old, and today, I liberated myself. As far as I know, today was my last official day of compulsory school. I am so happy, I'm ecstatic! I'll just tell you the story before I keep going on about my feelings:

Well, I had already talked to my parents about homeschooling, they were skeptical but willing to let me unschool starting next school year (about eight and a half months away) and I was waiting for info about it from a friend of mine who lives in New York and unschools. (With Clonlara, where I am now enrolled, yay!) Anyway, today was the day I was about to crack... I already knew all about having my life controlled—I went to public school for *eleven* years (K-10) yet I didn't know how to verbalize my torture of being in the school systems for so long. The only words I could use to express my unrest were and still sort of are: "*Fuck that!*" My friend and I (she is not able to unschool; her mother, *a teacher*, does not believe that she has enough intelligence at seventeen to know what she wants and needs—that makes me very ANGRY) anyway—our favorite words are "fuck that!" because (mostly) we are not allowed to say them in school and they're just about the only words that give our pain any justice at all. Well, I know I've gotten way off of the point, so I'll get back on—In addition to being awfully depressed about having no control over my life, I was also reading your book, and I knew in my heart every word was true, I knew all those terrible things were true, *and* they did those things to *me*, for eleven years!

I wanted to cry, I wanted to scream, I wanted to bite and kick and do that to all of them (it already has been done to them, how else could they commit that act on any other living being?).

[*Marie explains how one day in school she felt terribly sick, but the school nurse wouldn't take her seriously since she didn't have a fever, and made her go back to class, and how that was the last straw on the camel's back.*]

So, when I got home, I spoke reasonably to my mother about it. I told her that there was no possible way I could make it through the rest of the year, let alone the rest of the week at that school. And I said, I have all the info I need for now, I want to call Clonlara to quit regular school.

She said, "OK."

To my surprise, she said that she remembers school, and how terrible it was.

I called Clonlara and got the help I needed, wrote my letter to my school (my letter of *resignation!*) and I'm going to school tomorrow to *QUIT!*

I am going to keep on taking the art class there that I have been enjoying, which is basically independent study. I am going to finish up my CPR course there because I want to, and that's all. I am also going to take Driver's Ed next semester there. They can't control me! I'm so happy! I'm free! Thank you for providing one of the big tools I've used to be liberated!

Marie L., Illinois

P.S. Guess what? I'm a night person, but for eleven years I had to go to bed too early and wake up too early. I'm staying up as late as I like tonight!

And sometimes I hear from people who have been out for a while longer, so their freedom is beginning to bear fruit.

Dear Ms. Llewellyn,

I just began reading *The Teenage Liberation Handbook* for the second time. I love it, adore it, cherish it, and I want to thank you for it! I've been unschooling with Clonlara school for over a year now and it's the best "high school" experience I've ever had. Before this I had gone to both my local evil public high school and what I thought would be my magic answer to my hatred of school and stupid school kids but love of learning: the Illinois Mathematics and Science Academy. IMSA theoretically is one of the best high schools in the nation and accepts only the "top" one percent of students in the state. When people learn that I was accepted into and went to that prestigious evil hell hole they are shocked and appalled that I am now "homeschooling." The people who don't know *me* and my great interest in the world assume I've become a lazy apathetic drug addicted delinquent and "dropped out" of school. The adults who know me have wonderful conversations with me not only about my plans and thoughts on schooling, but also on philosophy, religion, art, society (ours and others), and world affairs.

Those who don't know me think I rise at 3:00 P.M. daily and watch TV until my enslaved friends get out of school, then I corrupt them for a while before retreating to my dark lair to take drugs and sleep. Little do they know, I'm becoming well versed in religion, culture, literature, and ecofeminist, lesbian philosophies! I read up on social and political issues. Study forms of government. Go to protests nearly every week. Know more about vegan nutrition than they ever dreamed existed.

I feel so delightfully deceitful when people ask what school I go to and I reply "I homeschool"!

I just finished a four-month stay in New York. Three of those months I was in an internship with a national animal rights group and shelter for abused "farm" animals (i.e. *all* farm animals!) called Farm Sanctuary. I learned an incredible amount of things there, including how to care for genetically engineered, hormone pumped, factory-farmed-but-now-rescued animals, how to investigate stockyards, farms, slaughterhouses, how to rescue animals from those places and how to rehabilitate them. I also learned more on veganism, the current status and processes of farming animals, communication with animal exploiters, legal systems, and not-for-profits. Most importantly, I learned that I do not want to work in an animal rights organization. Before my internship, that was all I wanted to do as a job or career later in life but now there's no way I'd ever do that! Unless I were working for Feminists for Animal Rights . . .

The last month I was in New York, I lived in my friend and former boss's trailer and took care of her cats while she was gone. I'd never lived in a trailer, by myself, in a rural area before, and it was quite the experience. I'm *so* glad I can get out and have these *experiences* instead of sitting in tiled rooms with fluorescent lights, being frustrated, bored, and depressed 33 hours a week. I'm so happy I'm getting to interact with real people (and non-humans, too!) and not just dull, non-thinking, conformist, jingoist, sexist, heterosexist, speciesist clods from the public school. They've got no spirit and no thoughts. Public schools are little status quo machines designed to strip all individual thought, identity, culture and make people into proud, faithful minions of the State, or, for those who don't fit in, wretches with no self-esteem who think they are wrong somehow but never bother to think that perhaps *society* is wrong about them and everything else.

Getting out of traditional school was the most wonderful thing I've ever done for all aspects of my life (well, it might share a space with veganism)—my depression went away, I realized I'm gay, I shaved my head, I get to pee whenever I want to, and I'm learning so much and reclaiming my lost teenagehood! I really am enjoying myself *and* unschooling has made me a lot more open about discovering who I am and what I want to do instead of being clueless and just following the expected societal plan for a Smart Kid Like Me (finish high school, go to a college with a good name immediately, get a good career, stay in one spot, think within the dominant paradigm . . .). And your book started it all! Thank you ever so much! I've lent it to a couple friends since I received it from a family friend—one of them began unschooling with me this October. The other friend is having a torturous time in public school and wants (and NEEDS) out, but her evil status quo mum works in the public school system and won't allow my poor pal to liberate herself because, as we know, public school is the Only Way and homeschoolers are really just lazy, irresponsible, apathetic menaces to society who never learn and never get anywhere and become Homeless Drug Addicts (i.e. really Bad people). It hurts me to see so

many of my friends suffering and trying to maintain their thoughts, integrity, and identity in traditional schooling. I keep wondering what sick, domineering, person-hating asshole designed that whole system. And then who was the interior decorator?
T.L., Chicago, Illinois

Dear Grace,
I haven't written you a real letter for almost two years. The reason I haven't written is because so many awesome and exciting things have happened in my life—writing and telling you about them would take forever! So instead, I just want to, once again, say thank you so much for . . . opening my eyes to the world of unschooling, for giving me the ticket to freedom. I know that no matter what I do in my life, quitting school will always be my number ONE "best decision I ever made." . . . All the wonderful opportunities I've had and will have, and all the experiences I've had and will have, all would not have happened if I'd stayed in school. I would never have gone on all the amazing trips I've been on (cross country skiing in Vermont, 5½ weeks of travel in Eastern and Southern Africa, five weeks of camping across the country, three weeks on the Colorado River through the Grand Canyon, etc.). I would never have had the time to pursue the various interests I've had (whitewater kayaking, geography, the Beatles, learning French, HIV and AIDS . . . etc.)

My life is so much happier without school. Life moves at a slower pace, but I get to spend genuine time on things that really mean something to me. I'm sure my self-confidence is better than most girls in school, and I know that I seem much more mature—people constantly assume I'm in college (oh, I'm not in school"... "oh! so you've already graduated..."), and I have lots of adult friends.

My perspective on the world is much broader than my friends (partly because of my traveling). In general, they have small, confined views of the world and life, consisting mostly of going to school, studying for exams, cruising for hot guys, drinking and smoking. They've already been too brainwashed by the school system—they all complain that they hate school, it's boring, a waste of time, and they don't learn anything. Yet none of them make any move to get out of it! It's like they assume the situation can't be changed, that that's the way it is.
Adrian Deal, sixteen, Greensboro, North Carolina ☀

appendix D

international unschooling resources and organizations

For Everyone
- *Growing Without Schooling* magazine—Important and inspiring for unschoolers in the U.S. and around the world. Growing Without Schooling, 2380 Massachusetts Ave. Suite 104, Cambridge, MA 02140, 617-864-3100, info@HoltGWS.com.
- Directory issue of *Growing Without Schooling*. Even if you can't subscribe to *GWS*, you can get a copy of the annual directory issue, which is published each January but available year round. It provides addresses for hundreds of homeschooling organizations in all fifty states and around the world. It also lists related organizations, including umbrella schools, correspondence schools and other private schools that help homeschoolers. Better yet, this directory includes thousands of homeschooling families, organized by state and country—most are in the U.S. but there are hundreds of others also, representing 32 countries in all. If you can't find an organization listed for your country, you can usually get information from one of the families listed in this extensive directory. $6.00 (plus postage if you're outside the U.S.—surface $1, airmail $3) from Holt Associates, 2269 Massachusetts Ave., Cambridge, MA 02140.
- Clonlara's Home Based Education Program. Serves unschoolers in all fifty states and around the world—helps with record keeping and legal negotiations, grants diplomas. The Home Based Education Program, Clonlara School, 1289 Jewel, Ann Arbor, MI 48104, www.clonlara.org, (313) 769-4515, info@clonlara.org.
- Genius Tribe, Grace's mail order book catalog for unschoolers, $1 U.S. or one International Reply Coupon, from Genius Tribe, Box 1014, Eugene, OR 97440.
- Not Back To School Camp, an annual week-long gathering of international unschoolers aged thirteen to eighteen. Sessions in Oregon and, by the time you read this, near the East Coast also. Complete information $2.00 U.S. or two international reply coupons, from NBTSC, Box 1014, Eugene, OR 97440, www.nbtsc.org.

Great unschooling Web sites

- Jon Shemitz's "Jon's Homeschool Resource Page," www.midnightbeach.com/hs/
- Karl M. Bunday's "School is Dead/Learn in Freedom" Page, http://learninfreedom.org/.
- The Home Education Press page, www.home-ed-magazine.com.
- The Homeschooling Zone, www.homeschoolzone.com.

Specific Countries (If your country isn't listed, contact Clonlara, above.)

American military families

- Consult DoD Manual 1342.6-M and UR 10-12.
- Contact Valerie Bonham Moon at HQs USAREUR, CMR 420, Box 606, APO AE 09063, starrmoon@hotmail.com.

Australia

- Homeschoolers Australia Pty Ltd, Box 420, Kellyville NSW 2153, (02) 6293727
- Eleanor Sparks' wonderful, funny Australian Home Schooling Resource Page, http://homeschool.3dproductions.com.au/content.html.

Canada

- The Canadian Homeschool Resource Page (outstanding and comprehensive), www.flora.org/homeschool-ca/
- The Canadian Alliance of Home Schoolers, 272 Hwy #5, RR 1, St. George, ON N0E 1N0., (519) 448-4001.
- Virtual High and the WonderTree Education Society, P.O. Box 3803, Vancouver, BC, V5Z 4L9, (604) 739-5941, www.wondertree.org (These are outstanding "independent schools" that truly serve unschoolers—a great choice for British Columbians.)
- The Calgary Montessori Home Education Program, Community Connections, 101 Point Drive, NW, Calgary, AB T3B 5C8. (For Albertans. This program is affiliated with a school district and fulfills legal registration requirements, but the director, Barbara J. Smith, is a longtime unschooling mom.)

England

- Education Otherwise, P.O. Box 7420, London N9 9SG, phone 01926 886828 or 01926 886828, www.educate.co.uk/edother.htm
- Education Now, 113 Arundel Drive, Bramcote Hills, Nottingham NG9 3FQ, phone 0115 925 7261
- Home Education Advisory Service, P.O. Box 98, Welwyn Garden City, Herts AL8 6AN, www.heas.org.uk

France

- Les Enfants d'Abord, c/o Shosha, 4, rue de League, F-34800 Brignac, phone (+33) 4 67 96 90 44 (alternate address: c/o Grde Rue, Valence 26000).
- Homeschooling Bulletin, c/o Sophie Haesen, 7 rue de la Montagne, F-68480 Vieux Ferrette

Germany

- Valerie Bonham Moon (the mother of an American military family), HQs USAREUR, CMR 420, Box 620, APO AE 09063, starrmoon@hotmail.com.

New Zealand

- Homeschooling Federation of New Zealand, Box 41 226, St. Lukes, Auckland

- New Zealand Home Schoolers' Association (NZHSA), P.O. Box 41-226 St Lukes, Auckland, phone/fax (09) 849-4780

Ireland
- Sa Baile, c/o Theresa Murphy, Clahane, Ballard, Tralee, Co Kerry
- or c/o Marguerite Egan, Cillmhicadomhnaigh, Ventry, Co Kerry

Japan
- Otherwise Japan, P.O. Box Kugayama, Suginami-ku, Tokyo, owj@comax.net

The Netherlands
- Netherlands Homeschoolers, Raadhuislaan 31, 2131 Hoofddoorp
- The Alternative Learning Exchange, www.alternative-learning.org/ale.

South Africa
- National Coalition of Home Schoolers, P.O. Box 14, DUNDEE, 3000, South Africa, phone 0341-23712.

Spain
- Crecer Sin Escuela, c/o Norberg-Szil, Apdo 45, E-03580 l'Alfàs del Pi, (Alicante), Spain.

Sweden
- Natverk for HemSkola, c/o Ywonne and Gunnar Jarl, Bjorksater, 640 34 SPARREHOLM, Sweden. Phone +46 (157) 214 35.
- MATS, c/o Bris Svanberg, Rydnasvagen 33, 570 60 OSTERBYMO, Sweden, phone +46 (381) 501 88.

Switzerland
- Homeschooling mother Marie Heitzmann is willing to be contacted at Au Village 12, 1277 Borex. She also suggests contacting the French organization, Les Enfants D'Abord, at Relations Internationales, Claudia Gringmann, impasse Jean Pierre, 66130 Trevillach, France, or at the address listed under "France." If enough Swiss are interested, Marie says she will consider forming a Swiss organization, though her traveling schedule may prevent her from doing so right away.

The United States
- Holt Associates, 2269 Massachusetts Avenue, Cambridge, MA 02140, 617-864-3100, 76202.3703@compuserve.com.
- The American Homeschool Association, which is affiliated with Home Education Magazine, publishes a free monthly online newsletter, with legal updates and information on conferences, pen-pals, resources, and news of other online opportunities. Free on request from AHAonline@aol.com.
- Jon Shemitz's "Jon's Homeschool Resource Page," www.midnightbeach.com/hs/
- Karl M. Bunday's "School is Dead/Learn in Freedom" Page, http://learninfreedom.org/.
- The Home Education Magazine page (includes information on laws in all 50 states), www.home-ed-magazine.com.β

appendix E

addresses, Web sites, phone numbers...

Here's HOW TO get in touch with most of the people, organizations, Web sites, and magazines recommended throughout this book. (See Appendix D for international homeschooling organizations.) If you request information from any of these people, consider enclosing a SASE or international reply coupon. All addresses are U.S. unless otherwise noted.

ACT—*see American College Testing.*
Alder, Reanna: http://hojpoj.independence.net/nbtsc/
American College Testing, P.O. Box 168, Iowa City, Iowa 52243, (319) 337-1000.
American Friends Service Committee, 1501 Cherry Street, Philadelphia, PA 19102-1479, (215) 241-7000.
American Hiking Society, 1422 Fenwick Lane, Silver Spring, MD 20910, (301) 565-6704, www.americanhiking.org.
American Map Corporation, 46-35 54th Road, Maspeth, NY 11378, (718) 784-0055.
American Science and Surplus, www.sciplus.com.
American Youth Hostels, 733 15th Street NW, Suite 840, Washington, DC 20005, (800) 444-6111.
Amnesty International USA, 322 8th Avenue, New York, NY 10001-4808, (212) 807-8400.
Aprovecho Research Center, 80574 Hazelton Road, Cottage Grove, OR 97424, (541) 942-8198, www.efn.org/~apro/index.html.
Archaeology magazine, Subscription Service, P.O. Box 420425, Palm Coast, FL 32142-9808, (800) 829-5122.
Arcosanti Workshops, HC 74 Box 4136, Mayer, AZ 86333, (520) 632-7135 or 254-5309.
Atlapedia Online, http://www.atlapedia.com.
Audio-Forum, 96 Broad St., Guilford, CT 06437, 74537.550@Compuserve.com. (800) 243-1234.
Augusta Heritage Center, Davis and Elkins College, Elkins, WV 26241, (304) 637-1209, augusta@DnE.wvnet.edu.
AWOL c/o CCCO, 655 Sutter #514, San Francisco, CA 94102.
Bolchazy-Carducci Publishers, 1000 Brown St., Wauconda, IL 60084, (847) 526-4344, orders@bolchazy.com, www.bolchazy-com.
Budget Text Home Education, 1936 N Shiloh Drive, Fayetteville, Arkansas 72704, (800) 643-3432.
Bunday, Karl M., "U.S. Founders Learned Without Public School," and "Nobel Prize Winners Hate School," at http://learninfreedom.org/.

California Homeschool Network, Box 44, Vineburg, CA 95487, (800) 327-5339, CHN Mail@aol.com.

Carolina Biological Supply Co., 2700 York Road, Burlington, NC 27215-3398, (910) 584-0381, www.carolina.com.

Center for Global Education, 2211 Riverside, Minneapolis, MN 55454, (612) 330-1159, (800) 299-8889, www.augsburg.edu/global/

Center for Interim Programs, P.O. Box 2347, Cambridge, MA 02238, (617) 547-0980, InterimCIP@aol.com. Western States Branch, 45640 Highway 72, Ward, CO 80481, (303) 459-3522, SamuelBull@aol.com, www.interimprograms.com.

CHSPE, Box 23490, Oakland, CA 94623, (510) 596-5656.

Clearing, 12171 Garrett Bay Road, P.O. Box 65, Ellison Bay, WI 54210-0065, (414) 854-4088. www.theclearing.org

Clonlara Home Based Education Program, 1289 Jewett, Ann Arbor, MI 48104, (313) 769-4515, www.clonlara.org, info@clonlara.org.

College Board, 45 Columbus Avenue, New York, NY 10023-6992, (212) 713-8000, www.collegeboard.com.

Concord Review, P.O. Box 661, Concord, MA 01742, (617) 828-8450, fitzhugh@tcr.org, www.tcr.org.

Council on International Educational Exchange (CIEE), http://www.ciee.org/, CIEE, 205 East 42nd Street, New York, NY 10017, (212) 661-1414.

Country Dance and Song Society, 132 Main Street (Route 9), P.O. Box 338, Haydenville, MA 01039-0338, (413) 268-7426.

Country School, 5221 township road 123, Millersburg, OH 44654.

Cultural Survival, 215 Prospect St., Cambridge, MA 02139, (617) 441-5400, CSINC@CS.ORG.

Drinking Gourd Multicultural Home-Education Magazine, P.O. Box 2557, Redmond, WA 98073.

Dover Publications, Inc., 31 East 2nd Street, Mineola, NY 11501.

drop out resource center, phone for hours. 1114 21st street, Sacramento, CA, 95814, (916) 441-5526.

Earth Magazine, 21027 Crossroads Circle, Box 1612, Waukesha, WI 53187, (414) 796-8776.

Earthwatch Institute, 680 Mount Auburn Street, Box 9104, Watertown, MA 02272-9104.

Edmund Scientific Company, 101 E. Gloucester Pike Barrington, NJ 08007, (609) 573-6250.

Educational Testing Service, Rosedale Road, Princeton, NJ 08541, (609) 921-9000.

Equality Now, P.O. Box 20646, Columbus Circle Station, New York, NY 10023.

Esperanto League of North America, P.O. Box 1129, El Cerrito, CA 94530-1129. SASE required.

Experimental Musical Instruments, Box 784, Nicasio, CA 94946, (415) 662-2182.

Exploratorium Store, 3601 Lyon Street, San Francisco, CA 94123, (415) 561-0393, http://www.exploratorium.edu/.

4-H Central Office, 7100 Connecticut Avenue, Chevy Chase, MD 20815.

Foxfire Project, P.O. Box 541, Mountain City, GA 30562, (706) 746-5828.

Franklin Institute's hotlists: http://sln.fi.edu/tfi/hotlists/hotlists.html.

Gateway Apprenticeship Program, 1545 Upland Avenue, Boulder, CO 80304.

GED testing service, www.acenet.edu/calec/ged, GED Testing Service of the American Council on Education, One Dupont Circle, Washington, DC 20036.

Green Center, 237 Hatchville Road, East Falmouth, MA 02356.

Greenpeace USA, 1436 "U" Street NW, Washington, DC 20009, (202) 462-1177.

Groundworks, P.O. Box 381, Murphy, Oregon 97533.

Hardenbergh, Nicky. Box 1514, Manchester, MA 01944. Send $5 for an information packet on working for legislation that allows homeschoolers to participate in school sports.

Heartwood, Johnson Hill Road, Washington, MA 01235, (413) 623-6677.

Holt Associates/John Holt's Bookstore: 2269 Massachusetts Ave., Cambridge, MA 02140, (617) 864-3100, info@holtgws.com, www.holtgws.com.

Home Education Magazine, P.O. Box 1587, Palmer, AK, 99645, (907) 746-1336, www.home-ed-magazine.com.

Home Education Press, P.O. Box 1587, Palmer, AK, 99645, (907) 746-1336, www.home-ed-magazine.com, HomeEdMag@aol.com.

Homefires, 180 El Camino Real, Suite 10, Millbrae, CA 94030, (415) 365-9425, homefires@aol.com.

Homeschoolers for Peace and Justice, P.O. Box 74, Midpines, CA 95345.

Hulbert Center, RR 1, Box 91A, Fairlee, VT 05045, (802) 333-3405.

Inkwell, c/o Dori Griffin, 920 Kennington Hills Drive, Hixson, TN 37343.

Inner City Outings (Sierra Club): www.sierraclub.org/ico

International Human Powered Vehicle Association, Box 727, Elgin, IL 60121-0727, ihpva.org.

International Music Camp, 1725-11th Street SW, Minot, ND 58701, (701) 838-8472.

International Re-Evaluation Counseling Communities, 719 Second Avenue North, Seattle, WA 98109, (206) 284-0311, ircc@rc.org.

International Youth Service, PB 125, FIN-20101 Turku, Finland.

Ithaca Money, Box 6731; Ithaca, NY 14851, (607) 272-4330, paglo@lightlink.com.

Jon's Homeschool Resource Page, http://www.midnightbeach.com/hs/.

Learning Things, Inc., 68A Broadway, P.O. Box 436, Arlington, MA 02174.

Listening Project of the Rural Southern Voice for Peace, 1898 Hannah Branch Road, Burnsville, NC 28714

Living History Re-enactor Network, http://www.reenactor.net/.

Lonely Planet, 155 Filbert Street, Suite 251, Oakland, CA 94607, info@lonelyplanet.com. http://www.lonelyplanet.com/whoweare.htm

Luno (Learning Unlimited Network of Oregon), 31960 SE Chin Street, Boring, OR 97009.

Merlyn's Pen, www.merlynspen.com/, 98 Main St., East Greenwich, RI 02818, (800) 247-2027.

Middle Eastern Music and Dance Camp, 3244 Overland Ave. Unit 1, Los Angeles, CA 90034, (310) 838-5471.

Moon, Valerie Bonham, HQs USAREUR, CMR 420, Box 606, APO AE 09063, starrmoon@hotmail.com.

Nasco Science Catalog, 901 Janesville Ave., Fort Atkinson, WI 53538-0901, (414) 563-2446.

National Audubon Society Expedition Institute Program, P.O. Box 365, 243 High Street, Belfast, ME 04915, (207) 338-5859.

National Center for Fair and Open Testing, 342 Broadway, Cambridge, MA 02139, (617) 864-4810, FairTest@aol.com. SASE required.

National Child Rights Alliance, www.ncra-youthrights.org, Box 61125, Durham, NC 27705, (919) 479-7130.

National Geography Bee, National Geographic Society, 1145 17th St. NW, Washington DC 20036.

National Home Education Research Institute, P.O. Box 13939, Salem, OR 97309, (503) 364-1490, bray@nheri.org, www.nheri.org.

National Muzzle Loading Rifle Association, Box 67, Friendship, IN 47021, (812) 667-5131.

National Outdoor Leadership School, www.nols.edu, free catalog from NOLS, 288 Main Street, Lander, Wyoming 82520, (307) 332-6973 admissions@nols.edu.

National Park Service Office of Chief Archaeologist, Division of Archaeology and Anthropology, National Park Service, Archaeology and Ethnography Program, P.O. Box 37127, Washington, DC 20013-7127.

National Storytelling Association, P.O. Box 309, Jonesborough, TN 37659 (800) 525-4514.

National Teaching Aids, Inc., 1845 Highland Avenue, New Hyde Park, NY 11040.

Natural Life, RR1, St. George, ONT, N0E 1N0, Canada.

Nichols-White, Donna, see Drinking Gourd Multicultural Home-Education Magazine.

Outward Bound, www.outwardbound.org, for a free catalog: Route 9D, R2 Box 280, Garrison, NY 10524-9757, (800) 243-8520 or (914) 424-4000.

Oxfam America 26 West Street, Boston, MA 02111, (617) 482-1211.

Parabola, 656 Broadway, New York, NY 10012-2317, (800) 560-MYTH.

Pathfinder Learning Center, 256 N Pleasant St., Box 804, Amherst, MA 01004, (413) 253-9412.

Peace Links, 729 8th St. SE, Suite 300, Washington, DC 20003, (202) 544-0805.

PETA, P.O. Box 42516, Washington, D.C., 20015 and 501 Front Street, Norfolk, VA 23510, (757) 622-PETA.

Pinewood School, 112 Road D, Pine, CO 80470.

Planet Drum Foundation, P.O. Box 31251, San Francisco, CA 94131, (415) 285-6556, planetdrum@igc.org.

Rainforest Action Network, 450 Sansome Street #700, San Francisco, CA 94111-3306, www.ran.org.

Resource Center for Homeschooling, RR2 Box 289-C, St. Albans, VT 05478.

Riggs, Jim: 72501 Hwy 82, Wallowa, OR 97885.

Saxon Publishers, 1320 W. Lindsey, Norman, OK 73069, (800) 284-7019, www.saxonpub.com/

School is Dead/Learn in Freedom, http://learninfreedom.org/.

Science News, 231 West Center Street. P.O. Box 1925, Marion, OH 43305, (800) 669-1002.

Second City, www.secondcity.com.

Seed Savers Exchange, 3076 North Winn Road, Decorah, IA 52101, (319) 382-5872.

Shelter Institute, 38 Center Street, Bath, ME 04530, 207-442-7938, www.shelterinstitute.com.

Shemitz, Jon: http://www.midnightbeach.com/hs/.

Sierra Club, 85 Second Street, 2nd Floor, San Francisco, CA 94105-3441, (415) 977-5500, http//www.sierraclub.org, information@sierraclub.org.

Society for Creative Anachronism, The Office of the Registry, Box 360789, Milpitas, CA 95036, (800) 789-7486.

Society of Primitive Technology, Box 905, Rexburg, ID 83440, (208) 359-2400, dwescot@aol.com.

South American Explorers Club, www.saexplorers.org, 126 Indian Creek Road, Ithaca, New York, 14850, (607) 277-0488 explorer@samexplo.org

Stone Age Living Skills School, Box 19693, Boulder, CO 80308.

Sudbury Schools, www.sudval.org, 508-877-3030

Time Dollar Network, P.O. Box 42160, Washington, DC 20015, www.cfg.com/timedollar.

Time Out, 3030 Bridgeway, Sausalito, CA 94965, (415) 332-1831.

Transitions Abroad, Box 3000, Denville, NJ 07834, trabroad@aol.com.

Traveler's Earth Repair Network, c/o Friends of the Trees Society, P.O. Box 1064, Tonasket, WA 98855, (509) 485-2705.

Utne Reader, P.O. Box 7460, Red Oak, IA 51591-0460, (800) 736-8863.

Volunteers for Peace, 43 Tiffany Road, Belmont, Vermont 05730, (802) 259-2759, vfp@vfp.org, www.vfp.org.

War Eagle Seminar, 11036 High Sky Inn Road, Hindsville, AR 72738, (501) 789-5398.

War Resisters League, 339 Lafayette St., New York, NY 10012, (212) 228-0450.

Willing Workers on Organic Farms, Donald Pynches, 19 Bradford Road, Lewes, Sussex BN7 1RB England.

World Game Institute, University City Science Center, 3215 Race St., Philadelphia, PA 19104, www.worldgame.org.

YES! 706 Frederick Street, Santa Cruz, CA 95062, (408) 459-9344, yes@cruzio.com.

appendix F: selected bibliography

Abrams, M.H. *A Glossary of Literary Terms.* Rev. ed. Holt, Rhinehart, and Winston, 1998.
Adams, Ansel, and Mary S. Alinder. *Ansel Adams.* New York Graphic Society Books, 1990.
Adams, Ansel. *Examples: The Making of Forty Photographs.* Bulfinch, 1989.
Aebi, Tania. *Maiden Voyage.* Ballantine, 1989.
Alexander, Christopher, et al. *A Pattern Language.* Oxford University Press, 1977.
Alexander, Christopher, et al. *The Timeless Way of Building.* Oxford University Press, 1979.
American Hiking Society. *Helping Out in the Outdoors.* American Hiking Society, 1997.
Anderson, Jay. *Living History Sourcebook.* American Assoc. State and Local History, 1985.
Andruss, Van, et al. *Home! A Bioregional Reader.* New Society Publishers, 1990.
Anno, Mitsumasa. *Anno's Math Games (Volumes I, II, and III).* Putnam, 1997.
Armstrong, Thomas. *In Their Own Way.* Tarcher, 1988.
Armstrong, Thomas. *Seven Kinds of Smart.* Penguin, 1993.
Asimov, Isaac. *Asimov on Chemistry.* Doubleday, 1974.
Auden, W.H. *A Certain World: A Commonplace Book.* Viking, 1970.
Baldwin, J. ed. *Whole Earth Ecolog.* Harmony, 1990.
Bangs, Richard, and Christian Kallen. *Rivergods.* Sierra Club Books, 1986.
Barba, Eugenio. *A Dictionary of Theatre Anthropology.* Routledge, 1991.
Barker, Britt. *Letters Home.* Home Education Press, 1990.
Barraclough, Geoffrey. *The Times Atlas of World History.* Rev. ed. Hammond, 1995.
Bateson, Gregory. *Steps Toward an Ecology of Mind.* Ballantine, 1990.
Bauermeister, Erica, et al. *Five Hundred Great Books by Women.* Penguin, 1994.
Beach, Mark. *Editing Your Newsletter.* Writer's Digest, 1988.
Bear, John. *Bear's Guide to Non-Traditional College Degrees.* Rev. ed. Ten Speed, 1997.
Bell, Ruth, ed. *Changing Bodies, Changing Lives.* Random, 1988.
Benedict, Ruth. *The Patterns of Culture.* Houghton Mifflin, 1989.
Berkman, Robert. *Find it Fast, 4th edition.* HarperCollins, 1997.
Berry, Wendell. *Home Economics.* North Point Press, 1987.
————. *Standing By Words.* North Point Press, 1983.
Beveridge, W.I.B. *The Art of Scientific Investigation.* Random, 1960.
Blackenship, Bart and Robin. *Earth Knack.* Available from The Stone Age Living Skills School.
Blake, Jeanne. *Risky Times: How to be AIDS-Smart and Stay Healthy.* Workman, 1990.
Boston Women's Health Book Collective. *The New Our Bodies, Ourselves.* Simon & Schuster, 1984.
Brandt, Barbara. *Whole Life Economics: Revaluing Daily Life.* New Society, 1995.
Braudel, Fernand. *Structures of Everyday Life.* University of California, 1992.
Britz, Richard. *Edible City Resource Manual.* William Kaufmann, 1981.
Brooks, John, ed. *South American Handbook.* Passport, revised annually.
Brown, Dee. *Bury my Heart at Wounded Knee.* Holt, 1970.
Brown, Rita Mae. *Starting From Scratch: A Different Kind of Writer's Manual.* Bantam, 1988.
Brown, Vinson. *The Amateur Naturalist's Handbook.* Prentice-Hall, 1993.
Bunnin, Brad and Peter Beren. *Author Law and Strategies.* Nolo, 1983.
Burns, Marilyn. *The I Hate Mathematics! Book.* Little Brown, 1976.
Campbell, Joseph, with Bill Moyers. *The Power of Myth.* Doubleday, 1988.
Carey, John, ed. *Eyewitness to History.* Avon, 1987.
Churchill, Sir Winston. *Great Destiny.* Putnam, 1965.
Cohen, Cafi, *And What About College?* Holt Associates, 1997.
Coles, Robert, M.D. *Children of Crisis (five volumes).* Little Brown, 1973-1980.
Colfax, David and Micki Colfax. *Homeschooling for Excellence.* Warner, 1988.
Collins, Nancy. *Professional Women and Their Mentors.* Prentice Hall, 1983.

Cook, James G. *The Thomas Edison Book of Easy and Incredible Experiments*. Wiley, 1988.
Council on International Educational Exchange. *The High-School Student's Guide to Study, Travel, and Adventure Abroad*. St. Martin's Press, revised frequently.
Cremin, Lawrence A. *American Education: The National Experience 1783-1876*. Harper, 1980.
Current Biography Yearbook. H.W. Wilson and Co., annual.
Davidson, Robyn, and Rick Smolan. *From Alice to Ocean*. Against All Odds, 1992.
Davidson, Robyn. *Tracks*. Vintage, 1995.
DiGeronimo, Theresa. *A Student's Guide to Volunteering*. Career Press, 1995.
Dumouchel, Robert. *Government Assistance Almanac*. Omnigraphics, revised frequently.
Durrell, Gerald. *The Amateur Naturalist*. Knopf, 1983.
Earth Works Group, *Fifty Simple Things You Can Do To Save the Earth*. Earthworks, 1989.
Ebenstein, William, ed. *Great Political Thinkers*. Holt, Rhinehart and Winston, 1969.
Edwards, Betty. *Drawing on the Right Side of the Brain*. Tarcher, 1979.
Electronic University: A Guide to Distance Learning Programs. Peterson's, 1994.
Erickson, Judith B. *Directory of American Youth Organizations*. Rev. ed. Free Spirit, 1998.
Essential Whole Earth Catalog. Doubleday, 1986.
Fadiman, Clifton, and John S. Major. *The New Lifetime Reading Plan*. HarperCollins, 1997.
Farber, Barry. *How to Learn any Language*. Citadel, 1991.
Fernández-Armesto, Felipe. *Millennium: A History of the Last 1000 Years*. Simon & Schuster, 1995.
Feynman, Richard P. *'Surely You're Joking, Mr. Feynman!'*. Norton, 1997.
Feynman, Richard P., *Six Easy Pieces: Essentials of Physics*. Addison-Wesley, 1996.
Fire, John (Lame Deer) and Richard Erdoes. *Lame Deer, Seeker of Visions*. Washington Square, 1972.
Fobes, Richard. *The Creative Problem Solver's Toolbox*. Solutions Through Innovation, 1993.
Foster, Steven. *The Book of the Vision Quest*. Rev. ed. Simon & Schuster, 1992.
Fuller, Graham E. *How to Learn a Foreign Language*. Storm King, 1987.
Gatto, John Taylor. *Dumbing Us Down*. New Society Publishers, 1992.
Geertz, Clifford. *The Interpretation of Cultures: Selected Essays*. Basic, 1973.
Geisel, Theodor (Dr. Seuss). *I Can Lick Thirty Tigers Today....* Random, 1969.
Gilbert, Sara. *Lend a Hand: The How, Where, and Why of Volunteering*. Morrow, 1991.
Goldberg, Natalie. *Wild Mind*. Bantam, 1990.
————. *Writing Down the Bones*. Shambhala, 1986.
————. *Writing the Landscape of Your Mind*. Writer's Audio, 1993. Audiocassette.
Goldstein, Richard, ed. *Mine Eyes Have Seen*. Avon, 1997.
Good, Harry G. *A History of American Education*. Macmillan, 1962.
Good, Kenneth. *Into the Heart*. Simon and Schuster, 1991.
Goodall, Jane. *My Life With the Chimpanzees*. Pocket Books, 1985.
Graham, Robin. *Dove*. New York: HarperCollins, 1972.
Grand, Gail. *Student Science Opportunities*. Wiley, 1994.
Great Speeches of the Twentieth Century. Rhino, 1991. Compact Disks and Audiocassettes.
Griffin, Susan. *Woman and Nature*. Harper and Row, 1978.
Griffith, Susan. *Work Your Way Around the World*. Peterson's, revised frequently.
Grisham, Roy, ed. *Encyclopedia of U.S. Government Benefits*. Government Data Pub., 1985.
Gross, Ronald. *The Independent Scholar's Handbook*. Ten Speed, 1993.
Haeckel, Ernst. *Art Forms in Nature*. Dover Publications, 1974.
Hailey, Kendall. *The Day I Became An Autodidact*. Dell, 1989.
Hakim, Joy. *A History of US*, Ten Volumes. Oxford University Press, 1993-1995.
Hamilton, Edith. *Mythology*. New American Library, 1991.
Harrington, John. *Dance of the Continents: Adventures with Rocks and Time*. Tarcher, 1983.
Hart, Michael. *The 100: A Ranking of the Most Influential Persons in History*. Carol, 1992.
Hart, Mickey. *Drumming at the Edge of Magic*. Harper, 1990.
Hass, Robert, and Stephen Mitchell. *Into the Garden*. HarperCollins, 1993.
Hawken, Paul. *Growing a Business*. Simon and Schuster, 1987.
————. *The Next Economy*. Holt, Rinehart, and Winston, 1983.

Hawking, Stephen W. *A Brief History of Time*. Bantam, 1990.
Hayes, Charles, *Proving You're Qualified*. Autodidactic Press, 1995.
Hazlitt, Henry, *Economics in One Lesson*. Arlington House Publishers, 1979.
Healthy Harvest Global Directory of Sustainable Agriculture and Horticulture Organizations. Agaccess, 1992.
Hein, Hilde S. *The Exploratorium: The Museum as Laboratory*. Smithsonian Institution, 1990.
Henderson, Bill, ed. *Minutes of the Lead Pencil Club*. Pushcart, 1996.
Henderson, Kathy. *Market Guide for Young Writers*. F&W Publications, revised frequently.
Hewitt, Paul G., *Conceptual Physics*. Addison Wesley, revised frequently.
Highwater, Jamake. *Words in the Blood*. New American Library, 1984.
Holdt, Jacob. *American Pictures*. American Pictures Foundation, 1985.
Holt, John, *Escape From Childhood*. Holt Associates, 1995.
———. *Freedom and Beyond*. Heinemann, 1995.
———. *Instead of Education*. Holt Associates, 1976.
———. *Never Too Late: My Musical Life Story*. Addison-Wesley, 1978.
———. *Teach Your Own*. Rev. ed. Holt Associates, 1997.
Hopkins, Bart. *Making Simple Musical Instruments*. Sterling, 1995.
Howes, Barbara. *Eye of the Heart*. Avon, 1990.
Huser, Verne. *River Camping: Touring by Canoe, Raft, Kayak, and Dory*. Dial Press, 1981.
Independent Study Catalog. Peterson's, revised frequently.
Insight Travel Guides. APA Productions.
Institute for Advanced Study of Human Sexuality. *The Complete Guide to Safer Sex*. Barricade Books, 1992.
Isaacs, Alan, ed. *Concise Science Dictionary*, 3rd Edition. Oxford, 1996.
Ives, Edward. *The Tape Recorded Interview*. University of Tennessee Press, 1995.
Jacobs, Harold R. *Mathematics: A Human Endeavor*. W.H. Freeman, 1982.
Jacobsohn, Rachel. *Reading Group Handbook*. Rev. ed. Hyperion, 1998.
Joudry, Patricia. *And the Children Played*. Tundra, 1975.
Kahn, Lloyd. *Shelter*. Shelter Publications/Ten Speed Press, 1990.
Kamoroff, Bernard, C.P.A. *Small Time Operator*. And Books, revised frequently.
Kapit, Wynn, and Lawrence Elson. *Anatomy Coloring Book*. Rev. ed. Addison-Wesley, 1993.
Kenschaft, Patricia Clark. *Math Power*. Addison-Wesley, 1997.
Klauser, Henriette Anne. *Put Your Heart on Paper*. Bantam, 1995.
Knowles, Dr. J. Gary. "Now we are adults: Attitudes, beliefs, and status of adults who were home-educated as children." Paper presented at the Annual Meeting of the American Educational Research Association, Chicago, IL. April, 1991.
Kogelman, Stanley and Joseph Warren. *Mind Over Math*. McGraw, 1978.
Kogelman, Stanley, and Barbara Heller. *The Only Math Book You'll Ever Need*. Rev. ed. HarperCollins, 1994.
Kohl, Herbert. *From Archetype to Zeitgeist*. Little Brown, 1992.
———. *The Question is College*. Heinemann, 1998.
Kotin, Lawrence, and William F. Aikman. *Legal Foundations of Compulsory School Attendance*. Kennikat Press, Port Washington, NY, 1980.
Krich, John. *Music in every Room: Around the World in a Bad Mood*. Atlantic Monthly, 1988.
Kroeber, Theodora. *Ishi in Two Worlds*. University of California Press, 1962.
Lane, Margaret. *The Tale of Beatrix Potter*. Penguin, 1986.
Lanes, Selma G. *The Art of Maurice Sendak*. Abrams, 1980.
Leach, Maria, ed. *Funk and Wagnall's Standard Dictionary of Folklore, Mythology, and Legend*. HarperCollins, 1984.
Lembeck, Ruth. *Teenage Jobs*. David McKay Co., 1971.
Leslie, Clare Walker. *Nature Drawing: A Tool for Learning*. Rev. ed. Kendall Hunt, 1995.
Levi-Strauss, Claude. *The Savage Mind*. University of Chicago, 1966.
Lewis, Barbara. *Kids' Guide to Service Projects*. Free Spirit, 1995.

————. *The Kid's Guide to Social Action*. Rev. ed. Free Spirit, 1998.
Linderholm, Carl E. *Mathematics Made Difficult*. World Publications, 1972.
Lines, Patricia M. *Homeschooling*. ERIC 96-5033. Pamphlet, 1996.
Llewellyn, Grace, ed. *Freedom Challenge*. Lowry House, 1996.
————. *Real Lives: Eleven Teenagers Who Don't Go to School*. Lowry House, 1993.
Loewen, James. *Lies my Teacher Told Me*. Simon and Schuster, 1995.
Lopez, Barry. *Of Wolves and Men*. Scribner, 1982.
Louden, Jennifer. *The Woman's Comfort Book*. Harper, 1992.
Lowenthal, Phil, ed. *Alternatives to the Peace Corps*. Food First, revised frequently.
MacArthur, Brian, ed. *Penguin Book of Twentieth-Century Speeches*. Penguin, 1992.
Macaulay, David. *The Way Things Work*. Houghton Mifflin, 1988.
MacEwan, Grant. *Tatanga Mani, Walking Buffalo of the Stonies*. M.J. Hurtig, Ltd., 1969.
Madaras, Lynda. *The What's Happening to My Body? Book for Boys*. Newmarket Press, 1987.
Massie, Suzanne. *The Land of the Firebird*. Simon and Schuster, 1983.
Maybury, Richard. *Whatever Happened to Penny Candy?* Bluestocking, 1992.
McLuhan, T.C., ed. *Touch the Earth*. Simon and Schuster, 1971.
McMillon, Bill. *Volunteer Vacations*. Chicago Review Press, 1997.
Mernissi, Fatima. *Dreams of Trespass: Tales of a Harem Girlhood*. Addison-Wesley, 1994.
Mintz, Jerry. *Almanac of Education Choices*. Solomon, 1995.
Moody, Anne. *Coming of Age in Mississippi*. Laureleaf, 1997.
Mount, Charles Merrill. *Monet*. Simon and Schuster, 1966.
Myers, Dr. Norman, ed. *Gaia: An Atlas of Planet Management*. Rev. ed. Anchor, 1993.
National Homeschoolers' Travel Directory. Available for $5.00 from Meg and John
        McClorey, P.O. Box 275, Somerset, KY 42501.
Neal, Arminta. *Exhibits for the Small Museum: A Handbook*. Rev. ed. Altamira, 1996.
Nelson, Richard. *Make Prayers to the Raven*. University of Chicago, 1986.
Netter, Frank. *Atlas of Human Anatomy*. Ciba-Geigy, 1989.
Newby, Eric. *A Book of Travellers' Tales*. Penguin, 1987.
Nilsen, Richard, ed. *Helping Nature Heal*. Ten Speed, 1991.
Northrup, Christiane, M.D. *Creating Health*. Sounds True, 1997. Audiocassette.
————. *Women's Bodies, Women's Wisdom*. Rev. ed. Bantam, 1998.
Papert, Seymour. *Mindstorms: Children, Computers, and Powerful Ideas*. Basic, 1993.
Pappas, Theoni. *Joy of Mathematics: Discovering Mathematics All Around You*. Tetra, 1989.
Penny, Representative Timothy J., and Major Garrett. *Common Cents*. Avon, 1995.
Peters, Ed, ed. *Mountaineering: The Freedom of the Hills*. Rev. ed. The Mountaineers, 1997.
Peterson, Ivars. *The Mathematical Tourist*. Freeman, 1988.
Peterson's Internships. Peterson's, revised frequently.
Peterson's Summer Opportunities for Kids and Teenagers. Peterson's, revised annually.
Phillips, Michael. *The Seven Laws of Money*. Shambhala, 1997.
Plent, Malcolm and Nancy Plent. *Famous Homeschoolers*. Farmingdale, NJ: Unschoolers Network.
Polking, Kirk. *Writing Family Histories and Memoirs*. F & W Publications, 1995.
Prause, Gerhard. *School Days of the Famous*. Trans. Susan Hecker Ray. Springer, 1978.
Prescott, Orville. *The Undying Past*. Doubleday, 1961.
Press, Frank, and Raymond Siever. *Understanding Earth*, Rev. ed. W.H. Freeman, 1997.
Quang Nhuong. *The Land I Lost: Adventures of a Boy in Vietnam*. Harper, 1982.
Rainer, Tristine. *The New Diary*. Putnam, 1978.
Rapaport, Diane Sward. *How to Make and Sell Your Own Recording*. Prentice-Hall, 1992.
Rapp, Doris. *Is This Your Child's World?* Bantam, 1996.
Rappaport, Roy A. *Pigs For the Ancestors*. Yale Universtiy, 1984.
Ray, Dr. Brian. *Marching to the Beat of their Own Drum*. Home School Legal Defense Assoc., 1992.
Rheingold, Howard, ed. *Millennium Whole Earth Catalog*. HarperCollins, 1995.
Richman, Howard. *The Story of a Bill*. Pennsylvania Homeschoolers, 1989.
Rico, Gabrielle. *Writing the Natural Way*. Tarcher, 1983.

Riehm, Sarah L. *The Teenage Entrepreneur's Guide.* Surrey Books, 1990.
Robinson, Adam, and John Katzman. *Cracking the System.* Random, 1998.
Roth, Gabrielle. *The Wave.* Raven Recording, 1993. Videocassette.
Rothenberg, Jerome, ed. *Shaking the Pumpkin.* University of New Mexico, 1991.
———. *Technicians of the Sacred.* University of California, 1985.
Rucker, Rudy. *Mind Tools: The Five Levels of Mathematical Reality.* Houghton Mifflin, 1988.
San Diego Chapter of the Sierra Club. *Wilderness Basics.* Rev. ed. Mountaineers, 1993.
Sanders, Mike. *Backcountry Bikecamping.* Stackpole Books, 1982.
Sauer, Carl O. *Man in Nature.* Turtle Island Foundation, 1975.
Savage, Barbara. *Miles From Nowhere.* Mountaineers, 1983.
Saxon, John. *Physics.* Saxon, 1993.
Schwartz, Brian M. *A World of Villages.* Crown, 1986.
Schwartz, Elaine. *Econ 101½.* Avon, 1995.
Scurlock, William, ed. *The Book of Buckskinning.* Scurlock, 1983.
Seiter, Charles. *Everyday Math for Dummies: A Reference for the Rest of Us.* IDG, 1995.
Sheffer, Susannah. *Everyone is Able.* Holt Associates.
———. *A Sense of Self: Listening to Homeschooled Adolescent Girls.* Heinemann, 1995.
———. *Writing Because We Love To: Homeschoolers at Work.* Heinemann, 1992.
Sher, Barbara. *Wishcraft.* Viking, 1979.
Shields, Katrina. *In the Tiger's Mouth.* New Society, 1991.
Sibley, Mulford Q. *The Quiet Battle.* Quadrangle Books, 1963.
Simer, Peter, and John Sullivan. *The National Outdoor Leadership School's Wilderness Guide.* Simon & Schuster, 1983.
Slavin, Steve. *All the Math You'll Ever Need: A Self-Teaching Guide.* Wiley, 1989.
Smith, George O. *Mathematics: The Language of Science.* Putnam, 1961.
Stanek, Lou Willett. *Writing Your Life: Putting Your Past on Paper.* Avon, 1996.
Stanislavski, Constantin. *An Actor Prepares.* Theatre Arts, 1989.
Stein, Sara. *The Body Book.* Workman, 1992.
Steinhaus, H. *Mathematical Snapshots.* Oxford University Press, 1969.
Strunk, William, and E.B. White. *The Elements of Style,* Rev. ed. Allyn and Bacon, 1995.
Taylor, Dr. John Wesley. "Self-concept in home-schooling children" in *Home School Researcher.*
Terkel, Studs. *Hard Times: An Oral History of the Great Depression.* Pantheon, 1986.
———. *The Good War: an Oral History of World War Two.* New Press, 1997.
———. *Working.* New Press, 1997.
Tobias, Sheila. *Overcoming Math Anxiety.* Rev. ed. Norton, 1994.
Transitions Abroad Alternative Travel Directory. Transitions Abroad, revised annually.
Turner, Frederick. *The Portable North American Indian Reader.* Viking, 1977.
Unsworth, Walt, ed. *Classic Walks of the World.* Oxford University, 1985.
Videohound's Independent Film Guide. Visible Ink, revised frequently.
Wallace, Nancy. *Better Than School.* Larson Publications, 1983.
———. *Child's Work.* Holt Associates, 1990.
Warriner, John E. *English Composition and Grammar*—6 volumes. Harcourt, 1988.
Watson, James D. *The Double Helix.* New American Library, 1991.
Watters, Ron. *Ski Camping.* Great Rift, 1989.
Whitmeyer, Claude and Salli Rasberry. *Running a One-Person Business.* Ten Speed, 1994.
Wigginton, Eliot, ed. *Foxfire, Vol. 1—10.* Doubleday, 1972-1993.
Wittgenstein, Ludwig. *Remarks on the Foundations of Mathematics.* MIT Press, 1983.
Wolfe, Joan. *Making Things Happen: How to Be an Effective Volunteer.* Island Press, 1991.
Wright, Frank Lloyd. *Frank Lloyd Wright: An Autobiography.* Duell, Sloan and Pearce, 1943.
YES. *Student Action Guide,* available from YES!
Zinn, Howard. *A People's History of the United States.* Rev. ed. HarperCollins, 1995.
Zinsser, William. *On Writing Well.* Rev. ed. HarperCollins, 1998.
———. *Writing to Learn.* HarperCollins, 1988. ❀

index

ABOUT THE AUTHOR

Grace Llewellyn taught school for three years before unschooling herself and writing the first edition of *The Teenage Liberation Handbook* in 1991. She has since edited *Real Lives: eleven teenagers who don't go to school tell their own stories* and *Freedom Challenge: African American Homeschoolers,* and, with Amy Silver, co-authored *Guerrilla Learning: How to Give Your Kids a Real Education With or Without School.* In 1996 she founded Not Back to School Camp, a gathering for unschooled teenagers which she continues to direct each summer. A passionate student, performer, and teacher of bellydance, and an obsessive beginning student of Argentine tango, she lives in Eugene, Oregon.

While Grace loves to hear from readers, she regrets that she cannot answer all of her mail or email. Her website includes current information on her projects; ways you can be involved; links to interviews with her and articles about her work; and links to helpful consultants and resources for unschoolers: www.GraceLlewellyn.com.

Not Back to School Camp

for unschoolers ages 13-18

Meet 100 people as free and brilliant as you. Frolic in the sun and rain. Share your talents and learn from others. Talk until the sun comes up. Gather strength. Play soccer or tag. Teach a workshop. Walk in the forest. Sing around the campfire. Swim. Drum. Encourage each other to new heights. Take risks. Learn kung fu. Laugh. Prepare for a year of joyful, creative, meaningful, challenging, and excellent work.

NBTSC takes place in Oregon and Vermont, late summer and early fall. For complete information, see WWW.NBTSC.ORG (or send $3 to NBTSC, Box 1014, Eugene OR 97440).

Campers say

- *"This camp totally changed my life. I feel confident and proud to walk the path I chose."*
- *"The atmosphere surrounding a big group of unschoolers like this is the most life-giving energy I have ever experienced, and I've become addicted to it! Ever since camp, which I left with the determination to incorporate this energy into everything I do, I've been enjoying life much more. I've felt more free, more passionate, and happier with life!"*
- *"See, it's like this...you go to camp, your life changes. Drastically. It's that simple."*
- *"NBTSC is the only place where I have met so many totally inspiring, giving, caring people in one week—let alone people my one age. As soon as I got off the bus, all these people came up and hugged me—that's completely the spirit of NBTSC. Another thing that deeply impressed and delighted me was the fact that I didn't hear a single negative remark or put-down about another person the entire week! Instead everyone was constantly building each other up and helping one another out. I'm just sad I didn't find out about camp sooner."*

Parents say

- *"My son returned from your camp with renewed enthusiasm for life and learning! Thank you so much for having this get-together of, apparently, some of the most gifted and interesting people on earth!"*

- *"[Our daughter] returned to us full of self assurance, excitement, and positive loving energy. The revelation that there are other teenagers out there with her unschooler ideas was a delightful awakening for her."*

Grace Llewellyn's books

~are available through booksellers &
www.LowryHousePublishers.com.

REAL LIVES

eleven teenagers
who don't go to school
tell their own stories

*11-year-anniversary edition
with updates by all the writers*

Erin's favorite teacher is her horse,
who's blind in one eye. Kyla rode
her bike through Colombia and
Ecuador—alone. Jeremiah and
Serena publish a peace newsletter.
Ayanna keeps pace with 50 pen-
pals—mostly in Africa—while Kevin talks with people worldwide through ham radio...

"Buy this book! ...It may stun some teens—more likely their parents and their teachers—but it is a mind-expanding experience... These autodidacts' days embrace a challenging freedom unimagined by those of us bound by the limits and assumptions of the classroom....a consciousness-raising journey of a special kind."—Kliatt Young Adult Paperback Book Guide

---

FREEDOM CHALLENGE
African American Homeschoolers

Sunshine apprentices at an herb nursery and learns about architecture, Spanish, and astronomy from family friends. Khahil and Latif collect bugs and read physics books. Indira challenges herself far more than school ever did. Tunu wins piano competitions and joins with other Black homeschoolers to learn robotics from an engineer. At 6, Maya taught herself to read; at 7, she decided to learn to row a boat...

"Strong stuff...Revelations about the power of learning and love."—Bloomsbury Review

---

GUERRILLA LEARNING
How to Give Your Kids a Real Education With or Without School
By Grace Llewellyn and Amy Silver

"One of the most important books yet written on education and our current school-child crisis." –Joseph Chilton Pearce, author of *Magical Child.*

"A big-hearted book of important ideas. Be prepared to have your eyes opened to secrets the classroom hasn't learned!" –John Taylor Gatto

Unschooling T Shirts

Definition and design by Grace Llewellyn,
printed on 100% cotton sweatshop-free shirts.

"unschooler \un-skül-er\ *n* : one who learns from life and love and great books and late morning conversations and BIG PROJECTS and eccentric uncles and eyes-wide-open and mountains and mistakes and volunteering and starry nights. *Synonyms*: HOMESCHOOLER, SELF-SCHOOLER, AUTODIDACT, RISE-OUT."

"I have become a walking billboard with my unschooling shirt! It's wonderful! Makes me feel well read! But most importantly, it tends to put people in the frame of mind that is excited and curious about what one would do if not spending all their time at school. I end up having more enthusiastic philosophical conversations, rather than upsetting, one-sided, floods of invasive, accusatory questions."

"The unschooler T-shirt was fabulous!
It has started many interesting conversations!"

"My 13-year-old son loves his unschooling
T-shirt and always wears it to his once-a-week public school class."

Four styles available at www.LowryHousePublishers.com